A History of the Maghrib

A History of the Maghrib

JAMIL M. ABUN-NASR

Associate Professor of History, University of Ibadan

CAMBRIDGE at the University Press, 1971

Published by the Syndics of the Cambridge University Press
Bentley House, 200 Euston Road, London N.W.1
American Branch: 32 East 57th Street, New York, N.Y.10022

© Cambridge University Press 1971

Library of Congress Catalogue Card Number: 73-128635

ISBN: 0 521 07981 0

Printed in Great Britain
at the University Printing House, Cambridge
(Brooke Crutchley, University Printer)

Contents

[v]

Maps

Preface

I have attempted in this volume to present a history of the Maghrib sufficiently detailed to meet the needs of university students without encumbering it with technical jargon and numerous footnotes that usually put off the general reader. In preparing it I have had to lean, sometimes heavily, on the work of other historians of the Maghrib, especially in Arabic and French. Nevertheless, in many places I have found it necessary to go back to the original sources to verify points of detail or interpretation, and sometimes to reconstruct the general picture as well. The bibliography, while listing books useful to the reader, also indicates those I have found especially helpful.

In the field of Maghriban history the problem of spelling place and personal names is especially difficult. Many place names have undergone several mutations as a result of peculiarities in the different languages used by the indigenous inhabitants of the Maghrib and various settlers and conquerors. In some cases no single universally recognized form exists, or if it does exist it is in an Arabic form which has been transcribed in various ways in European languages. I have tried, at the expense of consistency, to avoid unduly confusing the reader. I have chosen for each place name a spelling that would be readily recognizable to a reader familiar with any of its other variants. In some cases the place names have taken a definitive form in English, such as Fez, Tangier, and Algiers. These I have kept unchanged. Other names I have changed slightly to remove the non-English orthography while avoiding a mere transcription of the Arabic form. Hence Laghwat, Tlemsen, and Bizerta, for Laghouat, Tlemcen, and Bizerte (French) and al-Aghwat, Talamsān, and Bin Zirt (Arabic). In other names the Arabic form has been transliterated systematically either because they are not so well known or transliterating them would not lead to any confusion, such as Fazzan (for Fezzan), Banghazi (Benghazi), and Marrakish (Merrakech). Arabic personal names or Arabized ones I have transliterated systematically when they are not internationally known in a specific form or when consistent transliteration does not lead to much confusion. However, such names as Bourguiba I left untouched for fear that ' Bu Ruqaiba ' would not be recognized as the name of Tunisia's president.

In transliteration I have followed a simplified system. Of the usual diacritical marks I have used only ' for the Arabic *hamza* and the ' for the Arabic guttural *'ain*. The ‾ over a vowel to indicate that it is long I have used only when its omission would make it difficult even for the Arabic-speaking person to recognize the name, as in Sālim to distinguish it from Salīm.

I have received help and encouragement from the following disting-uished scholars: Professor Ernest Gellner of the London School of Economics and Political Science, Professor L. A. Thompson of the Department of Classics, University of Ibadan, and Professor J. O. Hunwick of the Department of Histoɪy, University of Ghana, Legon. Professor Thompson has read my chapters on the Roman and Carthagi-nian periods and made valuable suggestions which enabled me to avoid specialized controversies I am not qualified to enter. To all of them I wish to express my gratitude. I am also indebted to the editorial staff of the Cambridge University Press for the meticulous care with which they carried out the work of editing my typescript and generally preparing it for press. The greatest help I have received from my wife, Marlies Abun-Nasr, who read the whole manuscript, contributing in various ways to making it more readable, and took up the task of typing the final copy at a crucial stage.

JAMIL M. ABUN-NASR

University of Ibadan, Nigeria
March 1971

1

Introduction

The Maghrib: land and people

The choice of "Maghrib" as a collective name for the four countries whose history the present book purports to outline requires some explanation. This name has been preferred to "North Africa" which includes Egypt, because Egyptian history falls outside the scope of this introductory volume. The French have made this last name additionally misleading by using its French equivalent "Afrique du Nord" to refer to their former possessions on the southern shores of the Mediterranean, thus excluding Egypt and Libya from its connotation. Other names which have been used to refer to the area are equally misleading. They are linked with either its original people or prominent features of its topography, such as "Barbary" and the "Lands of the Atlas".

The Arabs called the area to the west of Egypt the Maghrib (the land of sunset) from the time when their warriors began its conquest about the middle of the seventh century. The present state of Libya, with its eastern part (Cyrenaica) often falling under the influence of Egypt and its western part (Tripolitania) under the domination of the other Maghriban states, gradually ceased to be included in the area covered by the connotation of the name. The "Maghrib" thus gradually became synonymous with the French "Afrique du Nord". For convenience, and in recognition of the dominant religious and cultural influence of Islam, the name "Maghrib" will be used throughout in its original connotation, comprising the entire area from the western borders of Egypt to the Atlantic. In the north this area is bounded by the Mediterranean, and in the south less definitely by the Great Sahara.

The Maghrib, as defined above, extends over a coastal strip of about 4,200 km along the southern shores of the Mediterranean. Its location along the Mediterranean coast has exposed it to the climatic and cultural influences of this great lake. As one proceeds southwards the impact of the Sahara is felt at varying distances from the coast. The known history of the Maghrib can, in fact, be viewed as the product of the interplay of climatic and cultural influences reaching it from the Mediterranean region and from the south. The numerous conquerors of the Maghrib came from the Mediterranean area, and all left their imprint on the character and outlook of its people. The cultural influence of the Sahara is not as evident, and possibly as great, though also important. One has only to keep in mind such important political movements which emerged from the Sahara as the Almoravid, the dissident religious movements which found refuge on the fringes of the desert and later spread their influence northwards, as well as the trans-Saharan trade, to realize that the cultural influence of the desert and countries beyond it was also real.

The greater part of the Maghrib is elevated land. The average altitude in Algeria is about 900 metres, in Morocco about 800, and in Tunisia 300. Climatically, one can recognize in it three parallel east–west regions: the northern Mediterranean region, a Saharan one in the south, and an intermediate transitional zone which varies in size from one place to the other, completely disappearing in parts of Libya. The Atlas systems of mountains in Morocco, and their extensions into Algeria and western Tunisia, mark the limits between the three regions. The climatic conditions which prevail in them have shaped the occupation of man who inhabited them over the centuries. In their turn the climatic conditions are to a considerable extent the product of the relief, and of air-masses from the Atlantic (especially in Morocco), the Mediterranean, and the desert.

The vegetation of the Maghrib diminishes progressively from north to south as the rainfall diminishes. The Mediterranean zone represents about one-fifth of the total area of Morocco, Algeria, and Tunisia. This includes the Rif mountainous region of northern Morocco, the Atlantic-facing slopes of the Middle Atlas, the Tall Atlas in Algeria, and the High Tall and Dorsale (Fr. "backbone") in Tunisia. In Libya, which is predominantly a desert country, Mediterranean climatic conditions exist only in a narrow strip on the Mediterranean separated into two strips by the Gulf of Sirta (Syrte) which bulges south into desert land. These are Jabal Nafusa in the west and Jabal al-Akhdar (the Green Mountain) in the north of Cyrenaica. A coastal fringe on either side of Tripoli receives more rain than Jabal Nafusa; but the Jaffara around the Jabal receives insufficient rain for sedentary life, and is thus predominantly semi-nomadic. In Cyrenaica most of the settlements are near the coastal slopes of Jabal al-Akhdar, where plains are confined to the neighbourhood of Banghazi and Ajadabia. The lee-side of Jabal al-Akhdar, namely the region of Marmarica which extends between Darna and the Egyptian frontier, is more arid.

In other parts of the Maghrib an intermediate zone of steppe land separates the Mediterranean from the desert. The mountainous Mediterranean zone receives sufficient rainfall occurring mostly in the winter: in some localities over 1,000 mm. In the steppe region to its south rainfall is considerably less, occurring mostly in the spring and autumn, and its unreliability makes cultivation without irrigation hazardous. The main areas falling in this intermediate zone are the High Plateaux in Algeria and eastern Morocco, and the High Steppe in Tunisia. The first extends over a distance of about 700 km from the backside of the Middle Atlas in the west to the Auras mountains in the east. With an average altitude of about 900 metres, this region consists nevertheless of semi-arid alluvial plains. Jujube trees and dwarf palms grow along the sides of the water-courses, but elsewhere the low rainfall is sufficient to support only steppe vegetation. The High Steppe in Tunisia lying to the south of the Dorsale also has a meagre rainfall. The water-courses descending into it from the Dorsale mostly evaporate before reaching the sea. An important product of both the High Plateaux and the High Steppe, one which forms an important item in the exports of both Algeria and Tunisia, is the esparto grass used for making fine paper.

The Atlas mountains are an important factor in shaping the climatic conditions of the first two of the three regions mentioned above. In Morocco they are broken into three ranges which, together with the Rif mountains in the north, determine the amount of rainfall received in various parts of the country. The High Atlas is a giant mountain: rising suddenly above the synclinal depressions of Sus, it extends east-north-east over a distance of about 750 km until it flattens in the direction of the high plains of eastern Morocco. It has an average altitude of over 2,000 metres, and its highest peak, the Tubkal, is 4,150 metres. To the north of the central parts of the High Atlas extends the Middle Atlas, whose relief becomes high and broad only to the north of the Higher Mulawiyya (Moulouya). There it forms a strong massif which extends to the Taza pass. Some of the chains of the Middle Atlas are above 2,500 metres, and two of its summits, Bu Iblan and Bin Nasir, reach 3,157 and 3,354 metres respectively. Both the High and Middle Atlas chains act as water-sheds, with their seaside slopes enjoying an abundant supply of water, and their eastern and south-eastern sides being near-Saharan in character. The western part of the High Plateaux region, falling in the rain shadow of the Middle Atlas, is drier than the eastern part. The regions of Morocco which are best suited for cultivation, and where consequently the major part of the population lives, are located to the north and west of these two ranges. These are the Sibu (Sebou) plain, the southern foothills of the Rif, the Meseta plateau on the Atlantic, and the western slopes of the High Atlas. The Sus plain, which extends between the High and Anti-Atlas ranges over a distance of about eighty miles from Agadir, has a near-Saharan climate due to its closed character and its southerly location.

The Sahara is separated from the rest of Algeria by the Saharan Atlas mountains. These rise to the east of the High Atlas, where the last parts of this chain disperse just before the Algerian border. This range extends in

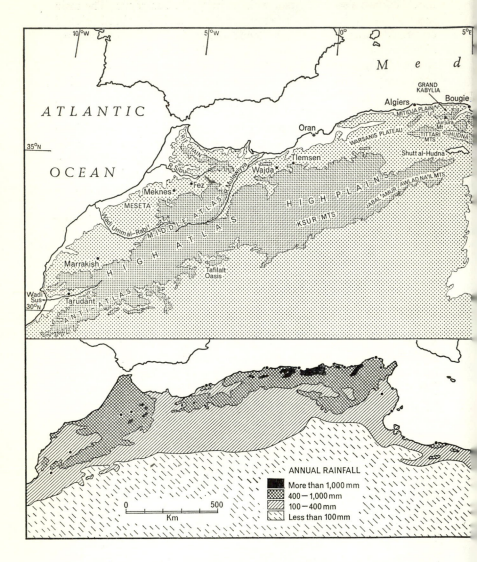

1   The Maghrib: relief and rainfall

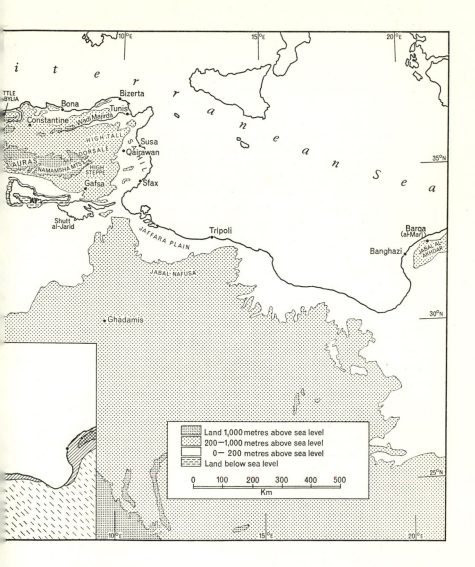

a south-west/north-easterly direction over a distance of about 700 km, and includes the Ksur mountains, the Jabal 'Amur (Djebel Amour), the Awlad Na'il, and the Ziban (or Zib) mountains. At the eastern side of the Awlad Na'il mountains the relief emerges in a plateau that rises over the Shutt al-Hudna basin, with easy communications between al-Hudna plains and the oases to the south remaining possible across the basin of al-Wataya (el-Outaya). The Shutts of al-Hudna and those to the south of Biskra are all below sea-level. Immediately above them towers the heavy Auras massif from which rises the highest mountain in Algeria, Jabal Shalia, which is 2,329 metres. From the Auras to Tunisia the relief gradually becomes lower. The Tunisian Dorsale is an extension of the Algerian relief, formed principally by the convergence of the Saharan and the Tall Atlas chains.

The Tall Atlas chain which rises in the north-east of Morocco is separated from the Rif by plateaux. Its western part, which reaches the neighbourhood of Algiers, is a variegated ensemble of mountains, depressions, and longitudinal plains. This coastal chain, which on the whole enjoys a Mediterranean climate, is separated from the High Plateaux, which do not, by the Warsanis (Ouarsenis) mountain barrier and by the Matmata, culminating in the Warsanis Peak, which reaches about 2,000 metres. The eastern part of the Tall Atlas, rising from the massifs of Miliana and Midia, is more rugged than in the west. In this chain are to be found the Grand and Little Kabylia and the gigantic Jurjura reaching 2,308 metres. The only important plains in the region of the Tall Atlas are those of Oran and the Mitidja around Algiers. To the east of the Warsanis, however, extend the internal plains of Tafna, Makarra, and Mascara. Extending on the edge of the tabular relief of the western part of the High Plateaux, these plains are in fact an extension of the internal plain of Wajda.

Tunisia has no geographical boundaries to separate it from Algeria, and its principal river, the Majirda, rises in the upland mass of eastern Algeria. The climatic conditions in northern Tunisia are similar to those on the coast of Algeria. Like Algeria, Tunisia has a steppe area to the south of the Dorsale, but unlike Algeria, it is blessed with fertile coastal plains called collectively the Sahil (Arabic: the littoral). Although the Sahil is only the coastal extension of the steppes, it contrasts with the latter by its sandy soil and the existence of subsoil waters. It has a mild and regular climate, and a rainfall which ranges from about 500 mm in its northern parts to about 200 in the south. Extending from Hammamat near Tunis to Sfax it is in places about 40 km deep. This region is renowned for its olive trees, especially in the stretch from Susa (Sousse) to Sfax. The Sahil is the most populated part of Tunisia, and most of the ancient towns existed in it.

When the Maghrib first came into the light of history as a result of the arrival of the Phoenicians on its coast in the first millennium B.C., it was inhabited by the Berbers. The name "Berber" derives from the Latin *barbari*, an appellation equivalent to the English "barbarian", which the Romans used to call peoples who spoke neither Latin nor Greek. The early Greek writers used "Libyan" (derived from Libou) as a generic name to refer to the indigenous population of the Maghrib as distinct from such colonizers as the Phoenicians and the Greeks. By the third century B.C. the Greeks had come to use the name "Libyan" to refer specifically to the non-Phoenicians living within the Carthaginian state, while speaking of the other Berbers as the Numidians, the "Nomads", a name which reflected the fact that most of them were pastoralists.

The Berber people emerged as a result of the admixture of an eastern people, the Libou, who migrated into the Maghrib during the third or the second millennium B.C., with its prehistoric inhabitants. Ethnological and archaeological research in the area, mainly since the beginning of the present century, has shown that it was inhabited by man earlier than the fifteenth millennium B.C. Prior to the arrival of the Libou migrations the Stone Age of the Maghrib had known two cultures which overlapped in places, but remained distinct in basic traits. The earlier of these, the Oranian, flourished in the coastal hinterland, and seems to have produced the first blade industry in the Maghrib. An industry similar to that practised by the Oranians was found as far east as Cyrenaica, and appears to have belonged to the same culture. The origins of this culture are not easy to determine, although the human type associated with it, the Mechta el-Arbi (named after the site in north-western Algeria where its remains were found), indicates that it was of western origin, possibly from southern Spain. The earliest Oranian culture, C.B.M. McBurney suggests, could have started as early as 15000 B.C., and its spread eastwards, which occurred in the tenth millennium, could have gone beyond Cyrenaica to reach Upper Egypt.

The other Stone Age culture in the Maghrib, the Capsian (called after the ancient name of Gafsa), appeared between 9000 and 5000 B.C. Its main area comprised the eastern Algerian parts of the Atlas mountains and their Tunisian slopes, but it also spread northwards to influence the Oranian culture on the coast. The human type connected with it is Levantine, but the absence of traces marking the passage of the Capsians through Egypt and Cyrenaica makes it difficult definitely to accept that this culture originated in the east. The Neolithic Capsian culture survived even after the Libou displaced the people who practised it.

The Berbers are thus a composite race, formed of dissimilar ethnological elements within which the Mediterranean type dominates. The process of interbreeding in prehistoric times largely accounts for the existence today of marked physical distinctions amongst the Berbers. Their language, the Berber or Libyan, is Hamitic. It is now spoken, either singly or together with another language (often Arabic), in restricted areas spread from the Siwa oasis in Egypt to the Atlantic Ocean, and even south of the Niger river in the Hombori cliffs. A Berber dialect called Guanche was also spoken by the aboriginal inhabitants of the Canary Islands. The spread of the Arabic language in the Maghrib since the seventh century, and especially after the arrival of the nomadic Arabian tribes of Banu Hilal and Banu Sulaim during the eleventh, left the Berber language widely spoken only in those regions which were not of easy access to the invaders. The main points of concentration of the Berber-speaking peoples today are either in mountainous regions or on the fringes of the desert: in the southern part of the Jabal Nafusa in Tripolitania; in the Khrumir region in north-western Tunisia; in the Kabylia and Auras mountainous districts of eastern Algeria, as well as in the Hoggar; and in Morocco, mostly in the valleys of Sus (Sous) and Dra'a, in the High and Middle Atlas, and in the Rif.

The Berber language is broken into several dialects which are mutually incomprehensible. It is possible that a common Berber usage existed in ancient times in the form of ancient Libyan, and later in the usage of the Numidians and Mauritanians of the Carthaginian and Roman periods. But the lack of a usable alphabet, and consequently of a common literature, did not favour the preservation of a common linguistic bond. The Berber alphabet, called Tafinagh, existed since ancient times and is still used by the Tuaregs. Inscriptions in it have been found in Numidia (north-eastern Algeria) which date from the second century B.C., and others from the third or fourth centuries A.D. But this alphabet consists of geometric characters – points, squares, lines, crosses, and circles – and is as inconvenient to write as it is to read. Consequently, the Berbers adopted the languages of their various conquerors – Carthaginian, Roman, Arab, and French – for literary and government purposes. After their conversion to Islam and the spread of the knowledge of Arabic among them, at least one attempt was made to use a Berber dialect in place of Arabic as the language of religious instruction and government. The founder of the Almohad movement, Ibn Tumart, used the Masmuda dialect for the purpose of teaching his doctrines to his followers in Tinmal; but as soon as the Almohads expanded beyond the limits of the High Atlas they had to use Arabic in their government and religious instruction.

The social organization of the Berbers has been tribal from the earliest known periods of their history. Their final allegiance was to a tribe, or to a real or imagined ethnic bond uniting the individual to a part of the race, but almost never to the whole. Thus a Berber national consciousness has never existed. The Maghriban Arab historian and sociologist of the fourteenth century, Ibn Khaldun, distinguished three major groups amongst the Berbers: Zanata, Sanhaja, and Masmuda. These divisions do not seem to coincide entirely either with ethnic groupings or distinctions of dialect.

Ibn Khaldun was at pains to create for them different genealogies, but what in fact his divisions seem to record was the existence of bonds of loyalties which were manifested in the course of Maghriban history. Berber states were formed on a tribal basis, and were sustained by the support of other tribes belonging to the larger group to which they were attached.

The Zanata Berbers, whose original home was in Tripolitania and southern Tunisia, were predominantly nomadic during the first centuries after the Arab conquest of the Maghrib. They cooperated with the Arab invaders more than the other major Berber groups, and consequently they have become more Arabized. Their close association with the Arabian tribes that invaded the Maghrib in the eleventh century, especially in the conflict for power at the end of the Almohad period, made some of the Zanata tribes claim Arabian descent. The dialect of the Zanata, Znatiyya, is now spoken on the eastern fringes of the desert, in small islands in the central Maghrib, in the Rif, and in the northern parts of the Middle Atlas. The Sanhaja are as widely dispersed in the Maghrib as are the Zanata. They are split into two main branches: the Kabylia Berbers, who are sedentary, and the nomadic Zanaga (the name being a corruption of "Sanhaja"), whose traditional home has been the western Sahara from Senegal to the southern parts of the Anti-Atlas. The Masmuda are the sedentary Berbers of Morocco, whose original home is in the western part of the High Atlas. They are now also spread over the area from the surroundings of Rabat to Azru (Azrew) and Khanifra.

Centrifugal and centripetal forces in Maghriban history

If there is a geographical unity in the Maghrib, it is one which consists of a "repetitive pattern of mountains, plains, steppes and desert, and a related pattern of economic activity..."[1] In the valleys and the coastal plains from Cyrenaica to the Atlantic the important urban settlements have appeared. The steppes have been the domain of semi-nomadism, whereas the desert lands to the south and the high mountains have been reservoirs of men from which warriors poured out into the plains to pillage or graze their flocks, and in the process sometimes were able to found states. The urban and the rural communities have been complementary to one another in the supply of goods and services: the towns provided the processed goods, and the countryside the agricultural produce and the raw materials. In the urban centres, particularly since the introduction of Islam, the scholars who taught the children and instructed the rural communities in their religion would normally have studied under a teacher in the town; the tribesmen of the countryside often provided the fighting forces that

[1] A. B. Mountjoy and C. Embleton, *Africa, a geographical study* (London, 1965), p. 158.

defended the towns and generally served the rulers based in the urban settlements.

In spite of this interdependence the history of the Maghrib was shaped by another pattern of relationship between the rural tribal communities and the urban society, between the plains on the one hand and the high-lands and the desert on the other. Until the eleventh century the founda-tion of urban centres was associated with the intrusion of foreign elements: the Carthaginians and Greeks founded settlements on or near the coast, the Romans created urban centres for the troops and citizen class of farmers both inland and on the coast, then the Arabs founded new urban centres inland, such as Qairawan and Fez, and developed those left them by their predecessors. These centres appeared in the midst or on the edge of a territory inhabited by a predominantly pastoralist community of Berber tribes. They grew and survived only to the extent that the tribes could be prevented from encroachment on them or were led to understand that they could obtain greater advantages from serving as soldiers in the urban centres than by looting them. The Carthaginians, always short of manpower, enlisted Berber tribesmen in their army. The Romans, not so much in need of manpower, could build their urban centres and develop agriculture by clearing the area of the Maghrib they occupied of its forests, wild animals, and nomadic tribes. The Romans battled against all three: the pastoralists were driven behind the lines of fortifications called *limes* or were persuaded to work on the farms or serve in auxiliary units of the army, the forests were hewed down, and the lions and elephants which the Maghrib had in large numbers during the Carthaginian period were taken to Rome or destroyed. The Arab conquerors did not have at their disposal the disciplined militia which the Romans and the Byzantines could employ to push out the tribes from the areas where they settled. But they had another advantage in the form of a religion which offered the Berber tribes association with the new rulers and an opportunity of taking part with them in profitable wars of expansion. This was an advantage whose usefulness could only be temporary. Consequently, as soon as the period of conquest in North Africa and Spain came to an end at the beginning of the eighth century, and the racist policies of the Umayyad administration took effect, even those Berbers who had cooperated with the Arabs (mostly Zanatas) turned against them. In the limited region which the Arab administration could thereafter control, the area of present-day Tunisia and parts of eastern Algeria, urban life flourished. Outside it, with the exception of the small urban enclaves of Fez and Tahirt, the centres of the Idrisid and Rustamid principalities respectively, the Maghrib remained the domain of tribes obeying no central political authority outside themselves and contributing little towards the developments of settled urban life.

Until the eleventh century the dichotomy between urban and rural remained one between foreigner and native. Henceforth, the Almoravid and later Berber states shifted the centres of political authority away from the coast and thereby aided the growth of important urban centres in the interior. Furthermore, by championing the cause of political unity in the name of Islam, the Almoravids accustomed the other Berbers to the notion that a centralized political authority could evolve out of the Berber society itself. The conduct of the Banu Hilal and Banu Sulaim nomads, who appeared in the Maghrib about the same time as the Almoravids, confirmed the latter in their role as the custodians of legitimate Muslim rule and the defenders of stability and order. The Arabian nomads swarmed into the lowlands of Cyrenaica, the Tunisian Sahil, and the plains of eastern Algeria. Their destruction was great. In Cyrenaica, where the early Greek colonists could farm through an elaborate system of irrigation, their presence caused lands which had been cultivated to revert to semi-desert conditions. In Tunisia the inland urban settlements dwindled and even the population of Qairawan, the first Islamic centre in the Maghrib, had to migrate to the coastal towns. In eastern Algeria they forced the Banu Hammad rulers to move their capital to Bougie on the coast.

Thus from the eleventh century centralized government and the defence of the urban and settled communities became the responsibility not of the foreign conquering peoples but of the local Berber dynasties. The structure of governments remained tribal, since political authority was built on and sustained through the bond of solidarity uniting members of the tribal ruling group. But government had also to go beyond tribalism and justify itself in terms of upholding, or appearing to uphold, the authority of the Muslim law. This in itself was an indication that a political consciousness connected with the Islamic belief of the ultimate unity of all believers had come to exist side by side with the sense of belonging to a tribal unit.

Tribal government in the end created the means of its own destruction. The rulers of the states that succeeded the Almohads were conscious of their illegitimacy in an Islamic sense. These rulers, Hafsids, Zayanids, and Marinids, were not Arab, and consequently could not establish a caliphial authority which the majority of Muslim thinkers still reserved to the Arabs. The Zayanids and the Marinids also could not claim to be heirs of the Almohads, whose authority as caliphs had gained some legitimacy on account of its identification with a reformist Islamic doctrine. To the tribal rulers of the Maghrib the patronage of the men of religion and religious scholarship became a means of legitimizing their authority. In this way the Islamic consciousness was heightened, a consciousness which politically was incompatible with the tribal system of government. Thus it was under the Marinids that the cult of *sharifs* (descendants of the Prophet) became an important one. The Turkish occupation of Algeria, Tunisia, and Tripolitania prevented the sharifian rulers of Morocco since the sixteenth century from expanding their rule over the rest of the Maghrib. But their appeal outside Morocco as the custodians of political legitimacy is illustrated by Tlemsen's turning to them whenever the city felt that Turkish rule was becoming unbearable.

Another way in which the tribal governments created the means of their destruction lay in the fact that the political stability which they could provide resulted in the growth of urbanization and the expansion of agriculture. The two processes are connected. The cultivated regions were the fertile well-irrigated plains in whose midst the towns were usually built and where the troops stationed in the towns could be effective in checking the havoc of the unsettled tribesmen. All the important internal towns of the Maghrib were either built or expanded considerably since the eleventh century. The most notable of these are Marrakish, Fez, Meknes, Tlemsen, and Constantine. The coastal towns also became important as centres of administration and sometimes of external commerce too. Amongst these were Tunis, Tripoli, Oran, Tatuan, Tangier, and Rabat. In addition a number of oasis-towns grew up as a result of the trans-Saharan trade, such as Sijilmasa and Tarudant in Morocco, Mzab in Algeria, and Murzuq in Libya. The growth of large urban communities, which were dependent on internal and external trade for their prosperity and on the flow of agricultural produce from the rural areas around them, was an important factor in undermining the tribal political structure. The tribal system not only excluded the urban leadership from exercising political authority, but also plunged the society in periodic conflicts which were particularly harmful to the economic welfare of the towns and settled rural communities. In Morocco the sharifian cult had a strong association either with such towns as Fez or with the agriculturists of the south, and it was through the support of the urban and agricultural communities that the two sharifian dynasties that ruled Morocco since the sixteenth century could be built. The drive towards creating non-tribal political authority reflecting the interests of the urban communities also explains the survival of the Husainids in Tunisia and Qaramanlis of Tripoli, although both dynasties had to battle against the tribes and the Turkish troops. From the nineteenth century the modalities of the problem of political authority are changed by the European penetration.

The conceptual framework outlined above is inspired by Ibn Khaldun's ideas on the rise and fall of states and the role of religious doctrines as instruments of political cohesion. It assumes the dependence of urbanization on political centralization. It also implies that the only two concepts of political legitimacy the Maghriban society knew before the cultural impact of Europe became important were the tribal and the Islamic. Two further assumptions implied, generally accepted by Islamists, are that Islam is an urban religion and one that encourages political centralization.

2

The mercantile empire of Carthage

Carthage until the wars with Rome

Some time in the course of the third or second millennium B.C. Aegeans probably established the first foreign posts on the Algerian littoral. The Cretans might have landed in the Maghrib before the Phoenicians and established "factories" in the north of Tunisia between Baja (Beja) and Tabarqa which served as centres of Minoan civilization. Nevertheless the Berbers began to take a part in the history of the Mediterranean world only after, and as a result of, the establishment of Phoenician colonies on the Maghriban coast.

Trade with the Iberian peninsula was the original motive in the penetration of the western Mediterranean by the Phoenicians. They traded at first mostly with the city of Tartessus (Tarshish, at the mouth of Guadalquivir), where they bartered their wares with silver, copper, lead, and tin. About the year 1100 they founded, with the consent of the Tartessians, their earliest settlement in Spain at Gades (Cadiz). The exigencies of ancient navigation forced the Phoenicians to follow the North African coastline, rather than cross the open sea, on their westward journey, and to put in for shelter and fresh supplies on convenient points on it. Thus the first Phoenician establishments on the coast of the Maghrib were intended as landing-places for the ships on their way to Spain. Gradually commercial relations with the Berbers were established. The Phoenicians bartered with them manufactured goods for victuals and items suitable for resale, such as hides and the ivory of the elephants. The earliest Phoenician settlement was perhaps Lixus, near present-day Larashe on the Atlantic coast of Morocco, which was founded about the same time as Gades. Other settlements were later created further east, also on the coast: Rusaddir (Malila), Sharshal (Cherchel), Hippo Regius (Bona, Bône), Utica, Hadrumetum (Susa), Sabratha, Oea (Tripoli), and Leptis (or Lepcis).

Carthage was founded at the end of the ninth century B.C. (tradition puts the date at 814) by emigrants from Tyre. The traditional story about the cause of this emigration is that Elissa, sister of King Pygmalion (who is a historical figure), left Tyre when her royal brother killed her husband and confiscated his property. In the course of retelling, the name "Dido",

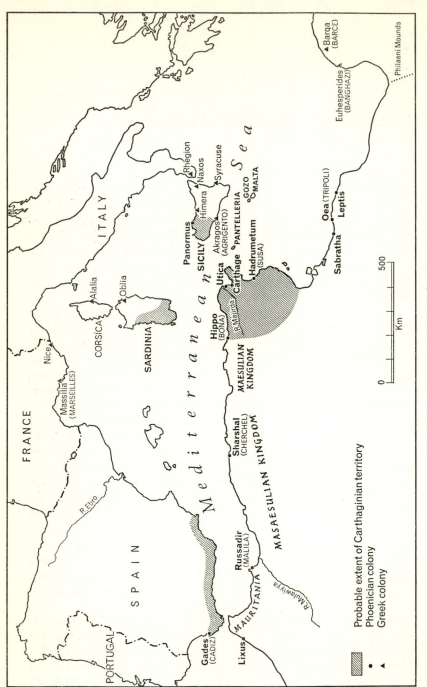

2   The Carthaginian empire in the sixth century B.C.

which is Greek rather than Phoenician, came to be given to Elissa, and it became famous through Virgil's *Aeneid*. Thus conflict in Tyre, which might have been of a political nature, was responsible for the emigration to what became called Qart Hadasht (the new town) from which the name "Carthage" derived. Assyrian pressure might also have contributed to cause this unprecedented mass migration from Phoenicia. As early as 876 Tyre had to pay tribute to the Assyrian king Ashornazirpal; and to escape from further Assyrian exactions Carthage was built as "an autonomous centre where the wealth of the West could grow".[1]

Very little is known about the history of Carthage from the time of its foundation to the fifth century B.C. when it emerges as a prosperous city and the capital of a vast empire. The "new town" must have received more emigrants from the east, as Tyre suffered from later Assyrian and Chaldean attacks. About the middle of the sixth century B.C. the Persians overran the Phoenician coast, and under their rule Sidon took the position of supremacy from Tyre. The Phoenicians became the seamen of the empire, and the prince of Sidon, not of Tyre, became its admiral. The misfortunes of Tyre helped Carthage in still another respect, for as the metropolis became weak the Libyphoenicians (western Phoenicians as distinct from the eastern or Syrophoenicians) looked to Carthage for leadership. Carthage was fitted to lead the other colonies, which were all tiny trading settlements, because of her superior power and geographical position. But the other colonies might not have submitted to her hegemony except for the aggressive Greek expansion into Sicily, Italy, Provence, the islands of the Tyrrhenian sea, as well as Cyrenaica. It is possible to assume that they sought a confederate alliance with Carthage for defensive purposes and she, as the dominant partner, compelled them to surrender their independence. The colonies must have preserved a high measure of autonomy in internal affairs: it is known that some of them had their own ruling councils and elected magistrates (*suffetes*), as was the practice in Carthage herself. What Carthage demanded in return for her protection was the control of the other colonies' foreign trade, and the contribution of contingents, money, and provisions when she was engaged in war. The Carthaginian empire which thus emerged in the sixth century included the colonies founded by Phoenicians along the coast of the Maghrib from Lixus to Leptis and along the Iberian coast from Gades to the site where Cartagena was later built; the Phoenician cities in the west of Sicily and in the south and west of Sardinia; the islands of Malta and Gozo; and Pantelleria near the Tunisian coast.

Greek colonization in the south of Italy and eastern Sicily began about the middle of the eighth century B.C. Kyme, the oldest Greek colony in Sicily and Italy, was founded on the western coast of Italy in about 750.

[1] Gilbert Charles-Picard, *Carthage* (London, 1964), p. 32.

Its foundation was intended to facilitate trade, especially in copper ore, with the neighbouring territory and with the Etruscans. In Sicily, Syracuse and Naxos were founded some twenty years later. The founders of Naxos were Ionians coming mostly from the island of Naxos, whereas Syracuse was a Corinthian city. Cyrenaica was colonized by Dorian Greeks from the barren island of Thera soon after the middle of the seventh century. Unlike the Greek colonists in Sicily, Italy, and Egypt, the Therans came as farmers attracted by the fertility of the Cyrenaican seaboard. They settled at first on the island of Platea off the coast, then moved shortly afterwards to the mainland and installed themselves at Aziris. In about 630 they occupied the site of Cyrene. They founded Barqa (Barce) about the middle of the sixth century; and Euhesperides (Banghazi) to its west came into being sometime later and was politically dependent on it.

The Greek colonies in Cyrenaica lived from the yield of agriculture and exported corn, horses, and an indigenous plant, the Silphium, which was eaten as a vegetable and used as a herb for medicine and seasoning. Relations between the Greek colonies in Cyrenaica and the Libyan tribes during the first half-century were good: the tribes are said to have guided the Theran farmers to the fertile site of Cyrene, and the latter took Libyan wives. By the sixth century, however, the Libyans were asking Egyptian help against the Greeks. An Egyptian expedition was sent to Cyrenaica in 570, but was repulsed. As a result of the Persian conquest of Egypt in the sixth century B.C. the Greek colonies in Cyrenaica lost their independence. In 535 Cyrene (Barqa) and Euhesperides fell under Persian rule, and this annexation to Egypt lasted until after the Macedonian conquest and the foundation of the Ptolemaic kingdom. In 324, one year after Ptolemy founded his dynasty in Egypt, he appointed Ophellas, a former member of Alexander's bodyguard, as governor of Cyrenaica. The three colonies of Sabratha, Oea, and Leptis remained the only Phoenician ones in the territory of present-day Libya. Relations between them and the Greeks in Cyrenaica seem to have been very limited, but not altogether hostile. Sometime about the middle of the fourth century the boundary between the Carthaginian territory in Tripolitania and that of the Greeks in Cyrenaica was fixed by an agreement reached between Carthaginian and Cyrenean envoys. This boundary was marked by what was called the mounds of the Philaeni, some 350 kilometres east of Sirta. It was not until Ophellas was appointed to govern them that the Greek colonies in Cyrenaica were drawn into the conflicts of the other Greeks with Carthage.

Phoenician colonists came to Sicily from Africa in the seventh century and, finding eastern Sicily already occupied by the Greeks, they established their settlements in the west. Relations between the two mercantile peoples in the western Mediterranean remained peaceful until the Greek expansion in the sixth century, which resulted in the foundation of

Antibes, Nice, and Massilia (Marseilles), threatened the interests of the Phoenicians as well as the Etruscans. The Phoenicians were especially concerned about Greek expansion in Spain and Sicily. The conquest of Sicily would have been the prerequisite for permanent Greek colonization in the Iberian peninsula, and would have endangered the Phoenician colonies in Sardinia. The Etruscans were by about the middle of the seventh century in possession of rich mineral deposits on continental Italy and the island of Elba, and of the fertile Campanian plains round Capua. The flood of Greek refugees from Asia Minor following the Persian conquest, which was responsible for the foundation of the colonies on the coast of Provence, also resulted by about the middle of the sixth century in the foundation of Alalia in eastern Corsica and possibly also Olbia in northern Sardinia. The outcome of this was that the Etruscans were hemmed in by the Greeks from the south, north, and west. Although they resented Phoenician presence in Sardinia, they recognized the advantages of an alliance with Carthage against their common enemy. A commercial agreement is known to have been concluded between Carthage and the Etruscans in the last years of the sixth century which enabled the latter to trade with Tripolitania, the Phoenician colonies in Sicily and Sardinia, and Carthage herself. In return for this privilege they had to undertake not to make any contacts to the west of the Gulf of Carthage.

The upsurge of Greek colonization in the sixth century ushered in a protracted scramble with the Libyphoenicians for the mastery of Sicily which lasted until Rome contested with Carthage the domination of the central and western Mediterranean. Syracuse was the mainstay of Greek power on the island. The Graeco-Carthaginian conflict reached a high pitch in the 480s when the Greek mainland was occupied with repulsing the Persian invasion. Gelon, upon becoming the tyrant of Syracuse in 485, entered into an alliance with Theron, tyrant of Akragas (Agrigento), for a decisive war against the Carthaginians. But the two tyrants could not draw the other Sicilian Greeks into the alliance; rather the increasing power of Gelon alarmed Anaxilas, the tyrant of Rhegion and Gelon's opponent, to such an extent that he threw in his lot with Carthage. The visible act of this alignment was Anaxilas' marriage to the daughter of Terillos, the ruler of the Greek city of Himera and the ally of the Carthaginians. Terillos' expulsion from Himera caused the dispatch of a major Carthaginian expedition to the island. Both Greeks and Carthaginians had anticipated conflict over Sicily: Gelon and his allies had been making preparations for it since 485, and the Carthaginians had been for three years past building ships and assembling men and equipment for the expedition which they sent to the island in 480. The Carthaginian army was led by Hamilcar the Magonid[1] and consisted according to a tradition

[1] See below, p. 22.

recorded by Herodotus of 300,000 men carried, according to another tradition, by 200 ships of war and 3,000 transports. It was an ill-fated expedition from the start, since the transports carrying the cavalry and the chariots were lost before the army landed at the Panormus harbour. The main Carthaginian force which marched to Himera was attacked outside the town, and Hamilcar was taken by surprise and killed while offering sacrifice. His ships were set fire to before they could take part in the battle, and the main Carthaginian camp was attacked and captured.

According to Greek tradition the destruction of the Carthaginian expedition at Himera occurred on the same day as the battle of Salamis. This coincidence, which according to ancient authorities including Herodotus and Aristotle was fortuitous, might have been the result of an understanding between the Carthaginians and the Persians. It is known that an embassy was sent in 481 to Gelon from the Greek mainland which urged him to join the Greek alliance against the Persians. It seems probable, in the face of a possible grand Greek alliance, that the Carthaginians and Persians might have come to an understanding about facing it, although that could have amounted to nothing more than "that the two powers which had long been preparing to invade Greek lands chose to do it in the same season. This prevented either western or mainland Greeks from helping the other, if they had been so minded, and [the simultaneity of the Carthaginian and Persian invasions] may have been no accident."[1]

Another bout of fighting occurred in Sicily in the wake of the Athenian expedition of 415–13 against Syracuse which awakened the Carthaginians to the danger of outside intervention affecting the balance of power in the island. The Carthaginians won initial victories which they consolidated in 405 by a treaty with Dionysius, the new tyrant of Syracuse. During his long reign Dionysius (405–367) could offset the military advantage which the initial victories of Carthage had given her, so that afterwards the two parties faced each other helplessly for about a century. The stalemate came to an end when a rebellion against the aristocratic party in Syracuse brought a new tyrant, Agathokles, to power in 316, and he began to extend his authority over the other Greek cities in Sicily. War seemed inevitable in 311 when Agathokles attacked Akragas, and it was saved only by Carthaginian naval help. In 310 a Carthaginian army was brought into Sicily with which Hamilcar, son of Gisco, defeated Agathokles at the mouth of the river Himera. Greek cities fell to Hamilcar one after another in the course of the year, until Agathokles was left with only Syracuse, which his fleet could not defend for long against the superior Carthaginian naval power.

At this stage Agathokles decided to gamble by attacking Carthage herself. With a force of 14,000 men carried on sixty ships he set sail on

[1] T. J. Dunbabin, *The western Greeks* (Oxford, 1948), p. 423.

14 August, 310; and having successfully eluded the Carthaginian fleet, he landed on the coast of Cape Bon. The success of the manoeuvre depended on his gaining victory sufficiently quickly to force Hamilcar to lift the blockade of Syracuse. Agathokles' army was reinforced in Africa by the Libyan tribes; and Ophellas, the Macedonian governor of Cyrenaica, was persuaded by the promise of the government of the entire Carthaginian territory in Africa to march against Carthage. Accompanied by some 10,000 soldiers and a large number of civilians, Ophellas crossed Tripolitania in the summer of 309 or 308, apparently prepared to settle in the territory which he was to conquer. He was treacherously murdered near Carthage by Agathokles when the ambitions of the two rulers proved irreconcilable. Carthaginian territory in Africa, never having been attacked before, was not fortified, and within a few months of his arrival in Africa Agathokles overran most of eastern Tunisia. In a pitched battle he also defeated the Carthaginian army between Tunis and Carthage; but Carthage herself remained impregnable. In Sicily Hamilcar was taken captive early in 309 in a surprise attack from the Syracusan army and was killed. This weakened the Carthaginian position in Sicily; and the news of Agathokles' victories made the surrender of Syracuse much remoter than it had been a few months earlier. In the winter of 308–7 Agathokles built a fleet to blockade Carthage from the sea. Before he could do this, he had to return to Syracuse with 2,000 of his men to drive back a joint attack from other Greek cities led by Akragas. In his absence his army was defeated and his son Archagethus was blockaded in Tunis. Agathokles returned to Africa in the same year (307), but he found his troops disheartened and their chiefs negotiating with Carthage over the surrender of the positions they held. Under these circumstances Agathokles had to make peace with Carthage, especially since Syracuse was again under pressure from his Greek enemies. Most of the soldiers he brought with him to Africa in 310 enlisted in the Carthaginian army, and those who refused were enslaved. Carthage thus survived, but Agathokles set the path which the Romans were to follow when faced with a similar deadlock.

Graeco-Phoenician relations in Sicily saw long spells of peace during which the two peoples traded with each other and even intermarried. Through contacts, peaceful or otherwise, the Carthaginians became better acquainted with Greek armament and other products. It is a serious reflection on the creativity and intellectual interests of the Carthaginians that after centuries of association with the Greeks they failed to develop an industry comparable in quality with theirs, or to take any interest in their philosophic achievements. Carthage had imported Greek artifacts, such as statuettes, masks, jewels, etc. as early as the seventh century. The products manufactured in Carthage were such crude imitations of Greek goods that they could be sold only to the barbaric tribes. From about the middle of the fourth century, however, there is evidence of a gradual but persistent Hellenization of Carthage in other respects. This process was the outcome of commercial relations with the Ptolemaic monarchy which comprised the eastern Phoenician lands, besides Egypt and Cyrenaica. Trade with the eastern Mediterranean compensated Carthage for her losses in the west, and as a result Greek goods flowed into Carthage in large amounts during the third and second centuries, and an increasing number of Greeks settled in it. To fit into this Greek-dominated world coins were minted in Carthage to the Syrophoenician standard current in Alexandria. A true art, mainly in the form of engravings on metal or stone, also made its appearance in Carthage under Hellenistic influence; and the Carthaginians learnt to build houses after Greek models, especially the towered house.[1] Even in religion, as will be discussed further below, Carthaginian conservatism gave way to Hellenization. Only to their language the Libyphoenicians held tenaciously, so that the Punic language was used in the Maghrib even after the destruction of Carthage.

The inland territory which Carthage directly controlled in the Maghrib remained limited to northern Tunisia and the north-east of modern Algeria as far as Bona, Mudawra (Mudaure), and Tabassa. Outside this area Carthage was satisfied to cultivate friendly relations with the Berber chiefs, which included intermarriage between them and the Punic aristocracy. In the area to the west and south of the Carthaginian territory, three Berber kingdoms had emerged by about the third century B.C. The boundaries of these kingdoms fluctuated and cannot be delineated for the entire Carthaginian period. To the west of Carthage were the two Numidian kingdoms, the Maesulian and the Masaeslian. The area to the west of the Mulawiyya, corresponding approximately to present-day Morocco, constituted the kingdom of Mauritania. The majority of the populations of these states led a primitive pastoralist life until the end of the Carthaginian period. A few cities of the Punic type existed in Numidia during the reign of Masinissa (d. 149 B.C.), but most of his people remained shepherds in spite of his policy of encouraging agriculture. The Berbers outside the Carthaginian territory lived in skin tents or primitive huts, and they used iron weapons and tools, for "There seems to have been no Copper or Bronze Age in Northwest Africa."[1] The Carthaginians cultivated the friendship of the Berber chiefs for the purposes of trade and recruiting mercenaries from among their tribesmen. The Numidian cavalry, carrying several javelins, a dagger, and a small round shield, who were instrumental in the final defeat of Carthage in 146 when they fought on the side of Rome, served the Carthaginians in many a battle.

[1] Cf. Charles-Picard, *Carthage*, pp. 107–8.
[1] F. R. Wulsin, *The prehistoric archaeology of north-west Africa* (Cambridge, Mass., 1941), p. 102.

In the fifth century trade with the negroes of western Africa by means of caravans starting mostly in Tripolitania became an important part of Carthaginian commercial activities. About the middle of the century two naval expeditions were undertaken by the state to explore the eastern shores of the Atlantic. One of these followed the western coast of Europe and reached the markets of tin in the British Isles, but returned without founding commercial posts. The other, led by Hanno the Magonid, sailed along the West African coast, reached as far south possibly as the Gulf of Guinea, and established colonies in southern Morocco and Rio de Oro. It is believed that the purpose of founding these colonies was to promote commerce with those parts of western Africa not accessible to the trans-Saharan caravans. It is not known that this purpose was ever achieved.

Although during the fifth century northern Tunisia and the Sahil were planted with fruit trees, olives, and cereals, agriculture remained of secondary importance to Carthage until the last century of her existence. The main occupation and source of revenue of the Carthaginians was commerce, and they traded most of the time in articles which they neither produced nor even consumed. Money they carried with them only rarely: in the "barbaric" countries they bartered their goods with the raw materials provided by these countries; and in the other markets they immediately bought new goods with the money which they obtained from the sale of their wares. This explains why the Carthaginians did not mint their own coins until late in their history: they first struck coins in Sicily about the end of the fifth century, and in Carthage herself as late as the fourth century. The most important items in Carthaginian trade until the third century were the precious metals, especially gold, silver, and tin, which they obtained from backward tribes. Manufactured goods were imported from Egypt, Greece, and Campania to Carthage, and from there they were sent to Spain, Sardinia, and to the Berber tribes. From the fourth century Carthaginian traders also profited from the exportation of victuals to the countries of the eastern Mediterranean. In the last fifty years of the existence of Carthage, deprived by defeat of her source of metals in Spain, the exportation of foodstuffs became the major source of her income.

The political structure of Carthage, which emerged during the first half of the fifth century, survived without material alteration until she was conquered and destroyed by Rome. As was fitting for a mercantile state, the government was an oligarchy of the rich. Public life was controlled by a senate, whose members were drawn from the patrician families and held office for life, and vacancies in it were filled by cooption. In the third century we know of the existence of a senatorial committee of thirty members which ran the day-to-day state affairs. An earlier institution, one which existed at the end of the sixth century, was a panel of 100 judges elected by the senate which acted as supreme court and committee of control. This court served the additional purpose of ensuring the preponderance of the aristocracy and preventing the usurpation of power by one man. It seems that prior to the fifth century the title *malik* (king) was assumed by the chief magistrate of Carthage. One such king ruled in Carthage until the middle of the sixth century when the Magonid dynasty succeeded to power.[1] The founder of this dynasty, Mago, was the organizer of the Carthaginian mercenary army. Other members of the family became prominent as generals, and sometimes as chief magistrates of the state. Mago and his sons Hasdrubal and Hamilcar distinguished themselves in the wars against the Greeks, and the last – as has been mentioned above – lost his life at Himera in 480. After this defeat the remaining chiefs of the family, Hanno and Gisco, were exiled. About this time the title *suffete* became used to refer to the chief magistrate of the realm, and the change might be connected with the downfall of the Magonids. The chief magistracy as it emerged in the fifth century was more akin to the institution of the Roman consulship than to kingship. Two *suffetes* were elected by the citizen body to hold power simultaneously for a year; and, possibly to safeguard against military dictatorship, a *suffete* was forbidden to hold the office of commander of the armed forces.

Besides their reputation as merchants, the Carthaginians were known in the ancient world for their superstition and intense religiosity. They imagined themselves living in a world inhabited by supernatural powers which were mostly malevolent. For protection they carried amulets of various origins and had them buried with them when they died. These included the cowry of the Negroes, representations of Egyptian gods, and symbols of the evil eye. Masks of Greek origin were also buried with the dead. Until the fifth century Baal Hammon was venerated as the supreme god and the protector of Carthage. In the fifth century, when Carthage was developing her agriculture, Tanit, the goddess of fertility, was elevated in popular belief to a position which outranked that of Baal. The Carthaginians had an organized priesthood, which was in all likelihood celibate, and they developed a vague notion of life after death which led them to entomb with their dead, besides amulets to guard against evil spirits, statuettes of Tanit and articles intended for use in the second life. What especially attracted the attention of outsiders, such as the Greeks and Romans, was the Carthaginian practice of human sacrifice for the appeasement of the gods. Sacrifice of animals was also practised, but the sacrifice of humans was considered a higher duty incumbent upon the leading families who were expected to offer their male children. Among the significant aspects of the Hellenization of Carthage in the third and second

[1] Charles-Picard, *Carthage*, p. 59.

centuries was the introduction of the cult of the Greek goddess Demeter. A Greek colony existed in Carthage as early as 396 B.C., and the priests of Demeter who catered for their spiritual needs enjoyed official status. At a later date Demeter came to be worshipped side by side with Tanit. The austere religious beliefs of the Carthaginians were further undermined by the introduction of Hellenic mysticism in the form of the cult of Dionysius.

During the third and second centuries, when the intransigent religious outlook of the Carthaginians was being undermined by the more humane Hellenistic outlook, Carthage was becoming a more cosmopolitan town, and a plebeian class of artisans, sailors, mercenaries, and all kinds of adventurers appeared in it. Charles-Picard maintains that, as a result of this social development, the aristocratic regime of Carthage was no longer able to impose the same strict discipline which had ensured her survival in the face of grave dangers in the past. Carthage could no longer have absolute control either over her mercenary troops or over the commanders. The Mercenaries' War[1] showed that the Berber tribes were ready to support the predominantly Berber soldiers against the aristocracy of Carthage, and the Barcid family in Spain could act independently of the wishes of the senate. Like the kings of Macedonia, the Barcids used their military authority to possess political power. The army which they organized was modelled on that of the Greeks, and their imperialism in Spain was akin to that of Alexander. Hannibal's invasion of Italy also was inspired by Alexander's method of warfare, which consisted of "the concentration of all available forces in a shock troop of limited size, and then the rational determination of the breaking points where the action of this human battering-ram would bring about the enemy's collapse".[2]

The collapse of Carthage

The conflict between Carthage and the youthful Roman state, which lasted over two centuries and resulted in the extermination of Carthage, was preceded by an even longer period of friendly relations and alliance. The love of Dido and Aeneas in Virgil's *Aeneid* is possibly an echo of the entente between the two Mediterranean powers. In a commercial treaty signed in 508/7 between the Roman republic and Carthage, the Romans were given the right to trade in Sicily, Sardinia, and Africa including Carthage. In return they agreed not to establish commercial relations in the west of the Mediterranean. The Carthaginians undertook not to build fortresses in Latium or to attack Latin towns under Roman control; they also gave recognition to Rome's claims to other parts of Italy by promising to hand over to her any towns in it which they might conquer. In a second treaty signed in 348 Rome's commercial sphere was curtailed by the adding

---

[1] See below, pp. 24–5.   [2] Charles-Picard, *Carthage*, p. 139.

of Sardinia, Africa outside Carthage, and Spain south of Cartagena to the area closed to her merchants.

In the 270s B.C. Carthaginians and Romans found themselves in alliance against the ambitious King Pyrrhus of Epirus who in 278 landed an expedition in Sicily and was acclaimed by the Sicilian Greeks as king. The concerted action of the two nations frustrated Pyrrhus' schemes in Sicily and southern Italy: in 276 the Carthaginians sunk seventy of his ships as he crossed to the Italian mainland; and in 275, failing to gain a decisive advantage over the Romans in Italy, he returned to Epirus. Soon after the Pyrrhian threat receded, Carthaginians and Romans began their own conflict over the control of Siciliy. After Pyrrhus retreated to Epirus, the Carthaginians were able to improve their position in the island by installing a garrison in Messina. The Romans felt that this move might lead to a Carthaginian conquest of Syracuse, which would amount to a complete Carthaginian control of Sicily. As Carthage was already the master of Sardinia, the Romans feared that the developments in Sicily might threaten the security of the Italian mainland. An expedition commanded by the consul Appius sent in 264 to drive the Carthaginians from Messina started the First Romano-Carthaginian War.

The Roman expedition to free Messina from Carthaginian control failed to win a decisive victory in spite of the support of Hiero, the tyrant of Syracuse. Since 261 the Romans had started to build a fleet, and the deadlock in Sicily led Rome to use it in a direct attack on Carthage. The expedition against Carthage was a costly undertaking, for between 256 and 241, when the Roman army was in Africa, the Romans suffered heavy losses in the land battles in which the Carthaginians could put their elephants to effective use and from sea disasters caused by their lack of nautical skill. But Roman manpower was immense, and Rome could put new recruits into the field. In 243/2 the Romans, learning from their disastrous experiences, built a new fleet after the more manoeuvrable Carthaginian quinquereme model. In 241, in a decisive battle against the Carthaginian fleet commanded by Hanno, they scored a major victory and brought Carthage to seek peace. Rome obtained under the terms of the peace treaty her main objective in starting the war, namely the whole of Sicily, in addition to a war indemnity. Carthage was defeated but not crushed; as for the Romans, they won the war at a very great cost, their losses amounting to about 500 warships and 1,000 transports sunk, and over 100,000 men drowned.

Soon after the end of the First Romano-Carthaginian War in 241 Rome found in the rebellion of the Carthaginian mercenaries the occasion to capture Sardinia. The rebellion began when the mercenaries who had served in Sicily, more than half of whom were Libyan, were not paid by the Carthaginian government the sums which their commander in Sicily,

Hamilcar Barca, had promised them. At the head of the government in Carthage was Hanno, who was unpopular with the Libyans for his extortionist collection of taxes during the war. It was difficult to bring down the insurrection, even when payment was made to the troops, because they, especially the Libyans amongst them, feared future Carthaginian reprisals. The rebels elected two of their members, Matho, a Libyan, and Spendius, an Oscan slave, as generals; and with some 20,000 Libyan volunteers they overran Carthaginian territory. Thus the rebellion of discontented troops developed into a civil war which has gained the name of the Mercenaries' War. The war lasted for four years, in the course of which Hamilcar Barca was brought to Carthage to share the supreme command with Hanno. The Mercenaries' War is important as a manifestation of the forces of disintegration in the Carthaginian state. In the context of the war with Rome it was important because it brought to power Hamilcar Barca, the man who was to enlarge Carthaginian possessions in Spain, and because Rome used Carthage's preoccupation with the war to capture Sardinia. The seizure of Sardinia, and the additional indemnity which Rome extracted from Carthage when it became known that she was making preparations to recover the island, stood in the way of a Carthaginian reconciliation to the humiliation of defeat, and aroused in the new generations of Carthage the desire for revenge.

The loss of Sicily and Sardinia made the Carthaginians concentrate their attention on strengthening their position in Spain. The loss of the two islands increased the economic dependence of Carthage on Spain; it also made the Phoenician colonies in the Iberian peninsula more vulnerable. The architects of the Carthaginian restoration in Spain were Hamilcar Barca, his son-in-law Hasdrubal, and Hamilcar's son Hannibal. The Carthaginian army there was strengthened, friendly relations were cultivated with the tribes, and a new capital Cartagena (or Carthago Nova as the Romans called it) was founded on the eastern coast of Spain.

The Romans resented the activities of the Barcids in Spain and feared Carthaginian expansion northwards. Rome had established friendly relations with Massilia. To guarantee her security Hasdrubal, who in 229 became commander of the Carthaginian army in Spain upon Hamilcar's death, was made in 226/5 to sign a treaty with Rome undertaking that the Carthaginian army would not cross the Ebro river. Nevertheless conflict over the northern boundary of the Carthaginian territory in Spain started the Second Romano-Carthaginian War.

In the winter of 220/19, when Hannibal was in Carthage, a Roman embassy arrived there with a message that Saguntum, a small town on the coast of Spain to the south of the Ebro, was under Roman protection and in consequence Hannibal was warned against interfering in her affairs. Hannibal viewed the Roman claim as a breach of the treaty with Hasdrubal which, by implication, set the Ebro as the northern boundary of Carthaginian territory in Spain; and as the authorities in Carthage, with the exception of Hanno, together with popular sentiment were in favour of a revenge, Hannibal took the initiative in starting it. In 219 he laid siege to Saguntum, and early in 218 he crossed the Ebro river in a forced march to Italy.

Hannibal's decision to march on Rome resulted from a number of considerations, the most important being that Rome had come to hold unquestioned mastery over the waters of the Mediterranean, and thus possessed a mobility which would have enabled her to move the threatre of hostilities to either Africa or Spain. By attacking Rome on home territory, Hannibal hoped to deprive her of this advantage. He seems also to have calculated that his presence in Italy would break the Italian confederacy, and thereby deprive Rome of another major advantage which she possessed over Carthage, namely her vast resources of manpower.

When Hannibal crossed the Pyrenees in the spring of 218 he had with him about 40,000 men; when he passed the Alps he had lost about half his men and all his elephants in the cold, but he could draw fresh recruits from the Gallic tribes in northern Italy. The warriors of these tribes distinguished themselves in the two major battles which Hannibal fought in the following two years: in 217 at Lake Trasemene and in 216 at Cannae. Hannibal's brilliant military victories and the surrender of Capua, the second important city in Italy, which took place in the wake of the battle of Cannae, did not enable him to capture Rome. His position was becoming difficult after 216 because he was unable to get any reinforcements from Spain, where members of the Scipio family were in command of the Roman army from 218 to 206 and were expanding Roman influence in the peninsula. During this period he entered into a military alliance with King Philip V of Macedonia. But as the Romans kept Philip V occupied with fighting anti-Macedonian Greek states, whose hostility towards him was sustained by the threat of the Roman fleet, he could send no succour to his Carthaginian ally. Thus Hannibal, though occupying the south of Italy, found himself unable to score a decisive victory against Rome.

After 210 the Carthaginian position in Spain was considerably weakened by the arrival there of the twenty-five-year-old P. Cornelius Scipio (later to be surnamed Africanus) as commander of the Roman forces. In the four years during which he remained in Spain he captured Cartagena and defeated two Carthaginian armies, one commanded by Hannibal's brother Hasdrubal and the other by Mago, the governor of Gades. Both commanders subsequently left for Italy with the remnants of their armies to reinforce Hannibal. The destruction of Hasdrubal's force, and his death in 207 on the Metaurus river, shattered Hannibal's one remaining hope of receiving help from outside.

Since Scipio's return to Italy in 206, and his election as consul in the same year, he advocated the dispatch of another Roman expedition to attack Carthage in Africa. In 204 the army was sent to Africa with Scipio himself in command. As expected, Hannibal was forced to leave Italy in order to defend Carthage. However, before his arrival in Africa at the end of 203, Scipio had already won a decisive victory against the Carthaginian army. The Carthaginian senate had also agreed to a humiliating peace treaty in which it consented to evacuate Italy and Gaul, surrender Spain and all the islands between Italy and Africa under her control, hand over the greater part of her ships, and pay a heavy indemnity of war.

While in Spain Scipio had tried to win to the side of the Romans two Berber chiefs who were fighting there with their men on the Carthaginian side: Syphax (*c.* 250–200 B.C.), king of the greater part of Numidia who had his capital in Cirta (Constantine), and Masinissa, chief of the Massyli Berbers and master of the area between Cirta and the western boundary of the Carthaginian state. Upon Scipio's arrival in Africa Syphax, whose loyalty to Carthage had been rewarded by his being given Sophoniba, a beautiful aristocratic Carthaginian woman, as wife, rallied to the side of Carthage. Scipio dealt with him with great expedition: he defeated him at Camp Magni and took him to Italy where he died in prison. Masinissa, seeing the scales turned in favour of the Romans, threw in his lot with them. He had married Sophoniba when her husband was defeated and she came seeking his protection; but after he decided to fight on the side of Rome, he gave her poison. His cavalrymen, who had distinguished themselves in Spain between 212 and 206 B.C. on the Carthaginian side, reinforced Scipio's army in the decisive battle with Hannibal.

Upon Hannibal's arrival with the remaining 15,000 men under his command, the Carthaginians repudiated the peace treaty with Rome and decided to resume the war. Hannibal and Scipio Africanus met in a decisive battle in the Majirda valley in the autumn of 202. The Romans, reinforced by the warriors of Masinissa, put into the field about 40,000 men, nearly as many soldiers as Hannibal could muster, but their army was superior to the Carthaginian in cavalry. This battle, fought on the site of present-day Saqiat Sidi Yusuf and commonly known as the battle of Zama, resulted in a crushing defeat for the Carthaginians. After it Hannibal saw that further resistance was futile and counselled his country-men to accept a still more stringent peace treaty than that of 203. Carthage under the terms of this treaty was left with only the north-east of Tunisia under her control; she had to surrender all but ten of her ships, and for fifty years had to pay an annual indemnity of 200 talents. By this treaty the right of Carthage to declare war was restricted to Africa, and even there she could do so only after obtaining the consent of an altogether hostile Roman senate. This stipulation was to prove especially harassing in view of Masinissa's ambitions. The services of this prince had been rewarded by the annexation of western Numidia to the territory which he had ruled, thus forming a united kingdom extending from the Mulawiyya river to the new Carthaginian boundary.

After his defeat Hannibal remained in Carthage until 196 B.C. In this year the aristocratic government which ruled Carthage, tired of his championing the cause of the poor inhabitants who were made to pay the greater part of the indemnity, denounced him to the Roman senate as plotting war. He was thus forced to leave Carthage. After stopping for a while in Tyre, Hannibal took refuge with King Antiochus of Syria and tried, without success, to make him send an expedition to Italy. Hannibal was forced to escape to Bithynia when Antiochus could no longer resist Roman pressure for surrendering him. In Bithynia he took poison when he learnt that King Prusias had agreed to hand him over to his enemies.

In spite of the loss of all her territory outside Africa and her confinement to a small area in present-day Tunisia, the Carthaginian state preserved a measure of her former prosperity after 202 mainly through her profitable trade in corn with the countries of the eastern Mediterranean. She was able to pay the indemnity to Rome regularly, and ten years after the peace treaty she offered to pay in advance for the remaining forty years. But Rome, wanting to keep Carthage in a state of dependence, would not accept this offer.

The major concern of Carthage after 202 arose from Masinissa's policy of territorial aggrandizement at her expense. This ambitious and energetic prince aspired to the inclusion in his state of the whole of the Maghriban coast inhabited by Berbers as far as Egypt. Relying on the fact that Carthage could not declare war without the consent of his Roman allies, he succeeded through raids on Carthaginian territory in capturing the southern parts of what remained under the control of Carthage. By 160 his domains extended as far as Cyrenaica. When in this year the Carthaginians raided the territory which he had usurped, a wave of discontentment swept over the Roman senate. Prominent Romans like the octogenarian Porcius Cato, who had fought in the Second Romano-Carthaginian War, warned against the revival of Carthage and advocated her destruction. Carthage paid the last instalment of the indemnity in 151 when she was engaged in a military conflict with Masinissa which Rome used as the occasion for her final annihilation. The defeat of the Carthaginian army by Masinissa was followed by the demand of the Roman consuls as soon as they arrived in Africa that Carthage must surrender all the weapons she possessed. This order was complied with; but when the Carthaginians were ordered to evacuate their town and settle anywhere at a distance of ten miles from the sea, they decided on resistance. New arms were made for the 20,000 men who defended the town which until then had remained impregnable. As

Carthage could obtain provisions by the sea, she was able to resist for three years. When in 146 the town surrendered, fire raged in it for five days, after which it was pillaged and razed to the ground. What remained after the destruction of this the most important of the Libyphoenician cities was the impact of her civilization, which spread widely among the Berbers during Masinissa's reign, and the Punic language. Masinissa, having died in the course of the siege, was not alive to see Carthage demolished. He was also spared seeing the new policies of his Roman allies causing the failure of his ambition to create a united Berber state.

3

Roman Africa under the Caesars, Vandals, and Byzantines

The Roman provinces

The decision of the Roman senate to wipe Carthage out of existence sprang from the fear of her revival, not from the desire to acquire dominions in Africa. For a century after 146, Rome ruled the territory which had comprised the Carthaginian state after 202 without any plans for further expansion in Africa. This Roman province was governed by a praetor who resided at Utica; and as no attempt was made to develop the land during this century, the number of officials and emigrants to it from Italy remained limited.

Outside their province, the Romans established a protectorate over Numidia, thus enabling Italian merchants to trade with the Berbers without assuming the burdens of its military occupation. Scipio Aemilianus, the destroyer of Carthage, divided Numidia between Masinissa's three legitimate sons, and placed the eldest, Micipsa, in control of Cirta, the former capital. The death of Masinissa's two other sons left Micipsa as the sole ruler, who then unified Numidia and absorbed into it the western part which had been given to the descendants of Syphax. Upon Micipsa's death in 118, this kingdom was once more divided among three heirs: two sons and Micipsa's nephew Jugurtha whom he had adopted as son. Hardly was the division undertaken before Jugurtha (*c.* 150–104 B.C.) reunified Numidia, having assassinated one of Micipsa's sons, Hiempsal, and forced the other, Adherbal to take refuge in the Roman province. Ambitious and able, Jugurtha cherished Masinissa's aspiration of unifying the Maghrib into one Berber kingdom; but in the endeavour to realize it he clashed with Roman interests. In 113 he besieged Cirta, whither Adherbal had escaped. When he captured the town, he not only put his cousin to death but also persecuted the Italian merchants who took part in defending it. In the conflict between Rome and Jugurtha which ensued, Roman generals found themselves fighting an exasperating war against an elusive enemy, and in the midst of a population hostile to them. The war ended when King Bocchus I of Mauritania, Jugurtha's father-in-law, handed him over to his enemies. Jugurtha was taken to Rome, where he died of cold and hunger in the prison of the Capitol; whereas Bocchus was rewarded by the addition of western Numidia to his kingdom.

In spite of the war with Jugurtha, Rome did not embark upon a policy of territorial expansion in Africa until another Numidian king, Juba I, fought against the victorious party of Julius Caesar in the civil war between the latter and Pompey. Juba I helped the Pompeians to gain control of the province of Africa. In 46 B.C. Caesar went to Africa and defeated both the Pompeians and the Numidians at Thapsus. Before he returned to Italy, he annexed to the province of Africa the area between Thabraca (Tabarqa) and the mouth of the Ampsaga river (Wadi al-Kabir), to which he gave the name Africa Nova, though in current parlance it continued to be called Numidia, since it corresponded to the territory which had constituted this kingdom. The area to the west of Wadi al-Kabir formed the kingdom of Mauritania. After the annexation of Numidia, the independence of the Mauritanian kings became purely nominal, and their country was treated as a Roman protectorate. When King Bocchus II of Mauritania died in 33 B.C. his country was administered by Roman prefects until in 25 B.C. Augustus installed as king in it Juba II, a Romanized prince both in education and citizenship. It remained for Caligula to arrange in 40 A.D. for the assassination of Ptolemy, Juba's son who dared to wear purple (the colour of the Roman emperors), and to annex Mauritania to Roman possessions. Thus in this year the Maghrib as far as the eastern limits of Tripolitania became ruled from Rome, and remained so until 430 when it was captured by the Vandals.

In the early period of the empire the area under actual Roman rule in the Maghrib was limited, except in Tunisia, to the coastal line and the immediate hinterland. In Tunisia the southern boundary of Roman territory started in Tacapae (Gabis), went westwards as far as the boundaries of Shutt al-Jarid, and then in a north-westerly direction passing by Capsa (Gafsa), Firiana, and Theveste (Tabassa). Beyond Tunisia's borders, the boundary of Roman territory remained to the north of the Auras and al-Hudna mountains and went in a north-westerly direction until it reached the sea at the mouth of the Mulawiyya river. Further west, the Romans held a series of ports between Tingi (Tangier) and Sala (Salé), but did not penetrate inland until after the annexation of Mauritania.

This territory was divided in the first three centuries of the empire into four provinces without any central authority in Africa ruling over them. The most important of these provinces was Proconsular Africa, which included Tripolitania, the greater part of Tunisia, and north-east Algeria as far as Hippo Regius (Bona), Calama (Gulma), and Suq-Ahras. In this province Roman colonization was more extensive than in the three others. In 27 B.C., when Octavian received the title of Augustus from the senate,

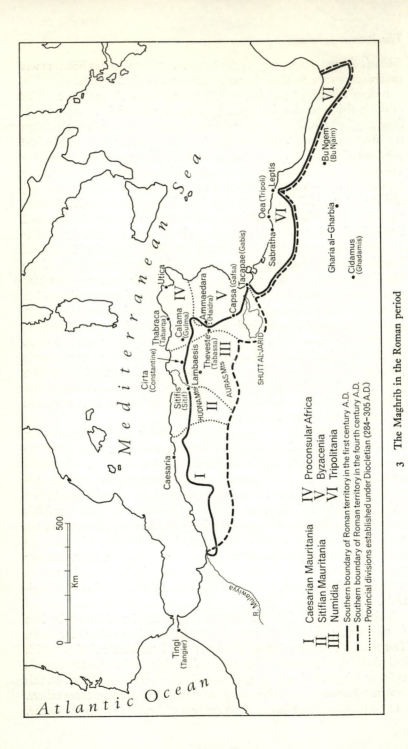

3 The Maghrib in the Roman period

I   Caesarian Mauritania   IV   Proconsular Africa
II   Sitifian Mauritania   V   Byzacenia
III Numidia   VI   Tripolitania

—————— Southern boundary of Roman territory in the first century A.D.
━ ━ ━ ━ Southern boundary of Roman territory in the fourth century A.D.
········· Provincial divisions established under Diocletian (284–305 A.D.)

Atlantic Ocean

Mediterranean Sea

Tingi (Tangier)

Caesaria

Cirta (Constantine)
Thabraca (Tabarqa)
Calama (Guîma)
Utica

Sitifis (Sitif)
HUDNA Mts
Lambaesis
AURAS Mts
Theveste (Tabassa)
Ammaedara (Haidra)
Capsa (Gafsa)
Tacapae (Gabis)

SHUTT AL-JARID

R. Mujarwwya

Sabratha
Oea (Tripoli)
Leptis
Bu Ngem (Bu Njaim)
Gharia al-Gharbia
Cidamus (Ghadamis)

he divided the Roman empire for administrative purposes into two parts: one under the direct control of the senate, consisting of the peaceful and intensely Romanized provinces, and the other controlled by the emperor who, in his capacity as commander-in-chief of the army, exercised the authority of supreme military governor over the newly acquired territories. In the Maghrib only the Proconsular province, with its capital at Carthage (which had been rebuilt by Caesar and Augustus), was under the control of the senate, which appointed to govern it a proconsul normally elected for a year, although in some cases this period was extended to two or even three years. The proconsul was the chief judge of the province, and responsible for its financial and economic life, especially ensuring the delivery of supplies to Rome. That the division of the empire into senatorial and imperial provinces was more theoretical than real is seen from the fact that in Proconsular Africa the representatives of the emperor often rivalled the proconsul in power. The most important of these imperial officials were the procurator in charge of the financial interests of the emperor in the province, and the legate in charge of a regiment from the Third Augusta legion, which was stationed in Carthage as a bodyguard to the proconsul.

Until the beginning of the third century Numidia was theoretically a part of Proconsular Africa. In fact, however, it was governed before as well as after it became an independent province by the commander of the Third Augusta – the only legionary force in Africa – who resided in the main quarters of the legion, first in Ammaedara (Haidra), then in Theveste, and from the beginning of the second century A.D. in Lambaesis. To the west of Numidia between Wadi al-Kabir and Mulawiyya extended Caesarian Mauritania, which took its name from its capital Caesarea (Sharshal); and further to the west existed Mauritania Tingitana, named after its capital Tingi (Tangier). Both these provinces were governed by imperial agents who wielded the civil as well as military authority in them.

Administrative changes in Roman Africa under Diocletian (284–305) resulted in the creation of three new provinces: eastern Caesarian Mauritania, which was more settled than the western part, was made a separate province called Sitifian Mauritania after its capital Sitifis (Sitif); a distinct province was made of Byzacenia, the southern part of Proconsular Africa, and the latter was given in return a part of Numidia including the important city of Theveste; and Tripolitania was taken away from Proconsular Africa and made an independent province. Numidia was divided into two provinces in about 305, but was reunified in 315.

In the east, Roman territory extended as far as the Sirta desert. Tripolitania had been occupied and pacified before the end of the first century A.D., and its three emporia – Sabratha, Oea (Tripoli), and Leptis – prospered from the caravan trade with the interior of Africa. The increasing wealth of these three cities won them recognition as Roman colonies: Leptis under Trajan (98–117) and the two others before the end of the second century. Leptis was the birthplace of Emperor Septimius Severus (193–211). During his reign many of the monumental public buildings of the town were constructed, together with the two large water reservoirs in Wadi Labda outside it. To the east of Leptis, the Roman presence was reduced to a few coastal agglomerations. In the interior, advanced posts were founded with permanent garrisons in the oases of Bu Njaim, Gharia al-Gharbia, and Ghadamis; and Roman merchants are known to have reached Fazzan.

From the beginning Rome wanted a definite frontier separating the territory which belonged to herself from that which did not. Scipio Africanus began the digging of *fossa regia* (royal ditch) in Africa, but from about the beginning of the second century the fortifications which had been used in other parts of the empire since the previous century, the *limes*, were constructed in the Maghrib. The *limes* consisted of forts, signal towers, and camps which, together with the natural barriers where they were usually situated, served the purpose of withholding attacks until the forces behind them could be alerted. In some parts of the Maghrib the Romans also constructed *fossata*, which consisted of ditches flanked by walls, to take the place of the natural barriers which in most of the frontier territory were lacking. Parts of *fossata* have been found near present-day Fez, marking the frontier of Mauritania Tingitana, and to the south and west of the Auras. These defences, *limes* and *fossata*, were also constructed in the interior of the provinces, mostly in order to check the inroads of unsubdued tribes. *Fossata* or *limes*, and sometimes both together, have been found to the north and south of the Jurjura mountain and in the Bu Talib mountainous area. As the line of *limes* became too extended for the regular forces to defend, it was entrusted in some parts, such as in Tripolitania, to *limitanei* (borderers). At first the *limitanei* were veteran soldiers who were settled on lands near the frontier with the sole obligation of defending it; but as their children were permitted to keep the land if they could defend the frontier, the tradition of recruiting the *limitanei* from retired soldiers was dropped.

Security within Roman Africa was provided by the Third Augusta legion, which was stationed in Numidia and had an effective force of 5,500 men, as well as by auxiliary corps stationed in the Mauritanias and in whose ranks about 15,000 men enlisted. The legionaries were Roman citizens, and in Africa some were of Berber extraction. The auxiliaries in Africa were recruited from amongst the Berbers and other non-Roman peoples like Spaniards, Thracians, etc. But the number of non-Africans who served in these corps diminished gradually so that by the middle of the second century A.D. "it was the Africans who ensured order in Africa on behalf of Rome".[1] In addition to the legionary force and the auxiliaries, the town of Carthage had a police force of about one thousand men.

Economically Roman Africa depended on agriculture. Until the end of the first century A.D. the production of wheat was encouraged and the emperors prescribed its cultivation on the vast imperial domains. The preference in Italy for home-produced olive oil and wine made the Romans neglect the culture of olives and vines in Africa during the first century-and-a-half of their rule. From the second century, as the central government left more initiative in economic matters to the provinces and as the decadence of Italian agriculture made it necessary for Italy to import olive oil and wine, the production of these in the Maghrib progressed. Consequently, olive oil, wine, and wheat came to be of equal importance in the exports of Roman Africa to Italy. The areas where olives came to be grown most intensively were the province of Byzacenia, the northern slopes of the Auras mountains starting in Theveste, and the area between the Auras and al-Hudna. Before the foundation of Constantinople, the burden of supplying food to Italy was shared between the Maghrib and Egypt. Later on, as the provisions from Egypt were needed to supply Constantinople, Rome had to depend on Africa alone. Other supplies sent from Africa to Italy during the Roman period were marble (especially Numidian marble), wood (mostly Thuja), and mules.

Large agricultural estates appeared in the Maghrib during the Roman period. Public lands, which had been such before the Roman period or became so as a result of confiscation from Carthaginian or Numidian aristocracy, were either turned into imperial estates, or used for the creation of colonies in which Italian colonists were settled, or were purchased by the Roman aristocracy who converted them into private estates. Most of the colonists were ex-soldiers, and thus the greater part of the land on which they were settled was in Numidia where the legion was stationed. The private owners of the large estates, living mostly in Rome, left their cultivation and administration to contractors who sublet them to tenant-farmers. The largest landowner in Roman Africa, and thus the biggest absentee landlord, was the emperor himself. The social position of the tenants who worked on these estates deteriorated in the course of the first three centuries of the Roman period until "in places it came to resemble that form of tenancy known to the European Middle Ages as serfdom".[2] The attempt on the part of the authorities in the fourth century to tie the tenants to the estates in which they worked gave rise to the riots of the Circumcellions, the allies of the schismatic Donatist Church[3].

The greater part of the taxes in the Maghrib during the Roman period

---

[1] Eugene Albertini, *L'Afrique romaine* (Algiers, 1949), p. 47.
[2] B. H. Warmington, *The North African provinces from Diocletian to the Vandal conquest* (Cambridge, 1954), p. 66.   [3] See below, p. 41.

were collected in kind. The produce so collected, the *annona*, was used to feed the army both within and outside Africa and to supply Roman officials in it with provisions. What remained of the *annona* was shipped to Rome for free distribution by the state or sale at reduced prices. Wholesale merchants handled the part of the Maghriban crops which was not taken by the state and destined for sale in Italy.

Although the Maghriban society during the Roman period was agricultural, many towns appeared, and life in the cities was considered the cornerstone of civilized life. Carthage during the Roman period had a population of about 100,000, ten other towns had more than 20,000, but other centres of urban life did not exceed 5,000. Roman cities in the Maghrib had forums adorned with honorific monuments, such as statues of emperors, patrons of the town, and distinguished citizens. The rich Romans in Africa built luxurious villas in the countryside to which they occasionally retired, but had their regular residences in adjacent towns in order to participate in the social and political life centred around the forum.

The Berbers, not bound by a strong nationalist sentiment or nostalgia for a glorious past like other peoples under Roman rule (such as the Greeks and the Jews), showed great readiness to accept the civilization and political institutions of Rome. What made the Berbers accept the Roman way of life all the more readily was that the Romans, though a colonizing people who captured their lands by the might of their arms, did not display any racial exclusiveness and were remarkably tolerant of the Berber religious cults, be they indigenous or borrowed from the Carthaginians. However, the Roman territory in Africa was unevenly penetrated by Roman culture. Pockets of non-Romanized Berbers continued to exist throughout the Roman period, even in such areas as eastern Tunisia and Numidia. In the two Mauritanias the area which resisted to the end the implantation of Roman civilization was larger than that in which it was firmly established. These non-Romanized areas, inhabited by hostile tribes, coincided in most of the cases with the mountainous regions and with the outskirts of the desert. The construction of *fossata* and *limes* in the interior, especially on the slopes of mountainous regions, shows that they were inhabited by unsubdued tribes. This is further proven by the state of insecurity on the highways and the existence of brigandage since the middle of the second century even in the vicinity of Carthage.

After the destruction of Carthage in 146 B.C. the intermingling of the descendants of the Carthaginians with the Berbers gave rise to a corrupt form of Punic, references to which found in the writings of St Augustine[1]

---

[1] The author does not accept the view that "Augustine merely used 'punic' as the undifferentiated, Latin term for *any* native language in Africa..." expressed by P. Brown in "Christianity and local culture in late Roman Africa", *The Journal of Roman Studies*, LVIII, 1968, parts 1 and 2, p. 85.

suggest that it was in use in the countryside at the end of the Roman period. But Latin, which naturally was the official language, spread widely amongst the Berbers especially in the urban centres. It was also the language of the cultured and the clerics, even of the Donatists who rejected the supremacy of the Roman church. Several individuals of native background distinguished themselves as authors in Latin, not only of religious literature but also of secular letters. The best known of the Latin writers of the second century in Africa was Fronton, who was born in Cirta and was the teacher of the Emperor Marcus Aurelius.

Christianity in Roman Africa

As has been mentioned above, the Roman period was marked in religious matters by the toleration of the beliefs of the indigenous people. The native Berber cults and the Semitic gods introduced by the Carthaginians were worshipped side by side with the gods of the Capitol. Like the inhabitants of the Maghrib after the thirteenth century in their veneration of several Muslim saints simultaneously, the Berbers in the Roman period considered it advantageous to worship as many divinities as possible in order to secure the greatest degree of protection. The Roman state did not attempt to curb this tendency as long as the Berbers participated in the cult of the emperor, the mark of political loyalty and the symbol of belonging to the community of interests and sentiments constituted by the Roman empire.

The first significant instance of Roman religious intolerance in the Maghrib occurred when Christianity first came to the attention of the authorities in 180 A.D. Before this date, the preaching of the gospels in the Maghrib had taken place unobtrusively. It seems likely that they were first preached to the Jewish community, and reached the rest of the population only about the end of the second century. In spite of their toleration of foreign pagan cults, the Romans saw in Christianity a serious threat and strove to stem its tide through persecution. This attitude towards Christianity was due to the fact that the Roman political system was based upon a conception of man and the universe which could assimilate the foreign pagan cults, but not the Christian ideology. The Christian outlook proved incompatible with that of classical Rome, and it cut off the Christians from the Roman political frame, thereby rendering them suspect.

Evangelization in Roman Africa before 180 was conducted predominantly in the countryside: this is attested for both by the unawareness of the authorities of its occurrence and by the intellectual crudeness of the first martyrs. The persecutions of 180, and those which occurred under Septimius Severus between 203 and 213, proved ineffective in checking the progress of Christianity. A church council held in Carthage under the presidency of Bishop Agrippinus some time before 200 A.D. was attended by as many as seventy bishops. Following the Severian persecutions, the African Church saw a period of peace which lasted until the persecutions of the Emperor Decius (249–51) began in 250. In these thirty-seven years Christianity made progress in the cities. About a hundred bishops ruled over the Christians from Tripolitania to Numidia during this period, with the greatest density in the region of Carthage. Mauritania remained little influenced by Christianity. The number of bishoprics, and the appearance of distinguished churchmen in the first half of the third century, made the African Church occupy an important place in the general Christian movement.

The best known of the African leaders of the Church from this period was Tertullian, the first Christian theologian to write in Latin. The son of a Roman centurion, Tertullian was born in about 160. After receiving a classical eduation in rhetoric, he was converted to Christianity in 195 or 196 under unknown circumstances. By the beginning of the third century reverence for the martyrs of Roman persecution was becoming valued in Roman Africa as an essential part of the Christian faith; to many it was greater than submission to church discipline, and "second only to God".[1] At the beginning of the Severian persecution Tertullian became a convert to Montanism,[2] and from this date the Christian dissenters in the Maghrib found in him an intellectual leader who defended their beliefs and led them in their defiance of the ecclesiastical authority of their bishops. Henceforth he spoke of the Church as a brotherhood and as a community of saints. This brotherhood was to be presided over by elders, and every Christian belonging to it could administer the sacraments. A Christian who sins, Tertullian believed, lapses from the faith and can attain salvation only through martyrdom, the baptism of blood. Furthermore, the Church must cultivate the renunciation of the world, and the property of its members must be shared in common.[3] Like St Cyprian after him, Tertullian's reverence for the see of Rome was based on its being the original see, but he refused to recognize the Pope's right of jurisdiction over the entire Church.[4] Tertullian's doctrines gained special importance in the later history of African Christianity from the fact that they formed the basis of the Donatist schism.

In spite of Tertullian's teachings and the appearance of dissenters who

---

[1] W. H. C. Frend, *The Donatist Church, a movement of protest in Roman North Africa* (Oxford, 1952), p. 116.

[2] Montanism was started in the second half of the second century by Montanus of Phrygia. It was an ascetic movement, which built its position on the revival of the tradition of prophecy in the Church, and belief in the imminence of the second coming of Christ.

[3] Frend, *The Donatist Church*, p. 119.

[4] *Ibid.* pp. 122–3.

rebelled against the authority of the bishops, the period of peace from 213 to 250 was on the whole one of moderation. The majority of the African Christians accepted ecclesiastical authority, and the bishops' sovereignty was becoming so widely recognized that many of them, such as Cyprian of Carthage, had emerged as autocrats by the time persecution was resumed.

The promulgation in 250 of the Decian edict requiring the Christians to appear individually before the local commissions, abjure their faith, and sacrifice to the emperor, made many Christians apostatize for fear of torture and sometimes certain death. Cyprian left Carthage at the beginning of the persecution, and remained in hiding until the spring of 251 when its rigour waned. When he reappeared the African Christians were facing the intricate theological problem of defining the position in the Church of those who lapsed during the period of persecution, amongst whom were some bishops. Cyprian's ability to combine the puritan moral creed with his episcopal office enabled him to resist the rigorists among the African Christians, especially Bishop Novatian and his followers, who insisted on refusing to readmit the apostates into the community of the faithful. In the church council summoned by Cyprian, which met in Carthage at Easter 251, terms were laid down under which the lapsed could be readmitted into the Church. This implied, as Frend points out,[1] that the visible Church could include the sinners as well as the righteous, and that it was left to God to distinguish between them. But the more important consequence of this measure was the preservation of the unity of the African Church. The reputation which Cyprian left behind him, after he was tried by the proconsul and executed on 14 September 258, was that of a moderate who succeeded in preventing the Church from giving way either to the Novatianists or the lapsed. His writings show that he considered the Church as a spiritual body and a brotherhood of the righteous, but also an institution. Thus there was a place in its ranks for the martyrs as well as the bishops. It was this middle course which led to Cyprian's veneration by the Donatists as well as by their redoubtable opponent, St Augustine.

In the fifty years between Cyprian's execution and the Great Persecution of the years 303–5 initiated by Emperor Diocletian (284–305), the Carthaginian clergy was won over to the standpoint of the Roman Church in the matter of dispensing with rebaptizing the lapsed. The gulf between the puritans and the leaders of the Church at Carthage was also widened as the latter proved more pliant towards the secular authorities. The election in 312 of Caecilian, the candidate of the citizen body of Carthage, as bishop of Carthage started a conflict between the puritanically minded and the state-favoured primate which led to the appearance of the Donatist schism.

[1] *Ibid.* pp. 133–4.

Opposition to Caecilian came from two directions: from the Carthaginian lower classes, and from the Church of Numidia which had always had a rigorist tradition. The problem of the great number of Christians who surrendered their scriptures and sacrificed to the emperor during the Diocletianic Persecution was dividing the Church; and Caecilian, in addition to being accused of subservience to the Roman authorities, was said to have denied food to the imprisoned Christians of Abitina. In the autumn of 312 a council held in Carthage under the leadership of Bishop Secundus of Tigisis, which was attended by over seventy bishops, condemned Caecilian on the grounds that he had betrayed fellow Christians under persecution and, furthermore, his consecration as bishop was not valid. The Council then elected Majorinus as bishop of Carthage in place of Caecilian; and when Majorinus died in the summer of 313, Donatus of Casae Nigrae, after whom the schism was called, was elected to replace him.

The beginning of the Donatist schism coincided with Emperor Constantine's Edict of Milan of 312, which promulgated universal religious toleration in the empire. While in Milan, the emperor was informed of the conflict in Africa and decided, without hearing the views of the Donatists, that Caecilian was the rightful bishop of Carthage. In the winter of 312–13 he also ordered his agents in Africa to give material help to Caecilian, and later in 313 he exempted the clergy in communion with Caecilian from municipal levies. A church council (the Lateran Council) summoned by orders of the emperor, meeting in Rome on 2 October 313 and dominated by Italian bishops, pronounced against Donatus. Constantine's intervention in support of the Caecilianists, and the decision of the Lateran Council, mark the beginning of a close alliance between the Catholic Church and the Roman state in the Maghrib, which was to last until the Vandal invasion. The Caecilian party henceforth depended on state support. The Donatist schismatic church, bringing together the rigorist Numidian clergy and the Carthaginian lower classes, came to represent the party of opposition.

For the following three centuries southern Numidia was to be the important centre of Donatism, whereas in Proconsular Africa Roman Catholicism was predominant. The Donatist Church spread its influence in Roman Africa very quickly: in 336 it could bring together 270 bishops in a council in Carthage, and by the end of the fourth century the number of Donatist bishops had risen to 400. The Donatists contended that theirs was the only true church in Africa, founded to protect the community from *traditors* ("surrenderers", i.e. those who surrendered their scriptures to the authorities). They honoured the martyrs of the Great Persecution and considered as martyrs those who fell in clashes with the authorities, thus earning to their church the epithet of the "Church of Martyrs". The sacraments administered by Catholic priests were considered by the Donatists invalid, because their givers were not in a state of grace. Nevertheless in 330 a Donatist council meeting in Carthage decided to admit Catholics to their ranks without a second baptism, a decision which enabled the Donatist Church to gain many new adherents.

Whereas the Caecilianist party received the full support of the Roman authorities in Africa, in 316 Donatist basilicas and other property were confiscated. The leaders of the Donatist Church replied to repression by acts of violence, which were committed on their behalf by the Circumcellions. This group drew its members from agricultural labourers, fugitive slaves, tenant-farmers, and Berber tribesmen. From about the middle of the fourth century the Circumcellions committed numerous outrages especially against the rich; and by the end of the century they had come to constitute a serious menace to peace and order. The attitude of the Donatist bishops towards the Circumcellions was an ambivalent one: they encouraged their acts of violence against the rich and the Catholics but were sometimes so much disturbed by their deeds that they betrayed them to the magistrates. Nevertheless when a member of the group was killed, the Donatist Church considered him a martyr. At the same time the Donatists did not lack intellectual leaders to defend their doctrines. Bishops Donatus and Tyconnis were learned classical scholars, and the versatility and erudition of Petilianus were praised even by St Augustine, with whom he debated Donatist doctrines.

In 347 the authorities attempted for the first time to suppress Donatism by force. The Circumcellions were accused of armed action against the state, and the Donatist clergy of being their accomplices. Corporal punishment was administered to the lower orders, whereas the leaders, including Donatus, were exiled. As a result of these measures the Donatist movement went into abeyance, but it revived during the reign of Emperor Valentinian I (364–75), who granted freedom of worship to all Christians.

In the latter part of the fourth century, the alliance between the Berber chief Gildo and Optatus, the influential Donatist bishop of Thamugadi in southern Numidia, enabled the Donatist Church for the first time in its history to win a tacit recognition from the Roman authorities as the dominant African church. Gildo's father, Nubel, was chief of the Juabaleni Berber clan living near Mitidja; and his brother Firmus had rebelled against the Roman state between 372 and 375 and was proclaimed king with Donatist support. Gildo was appointed in 386 commander of the troops of Africa by Theodosius, the son of the general of the same name who had defeated Firmus in 375. Theodosius the son was placed in charge of Africa by Gratian and was instrumental in securing the loyalty of the African province to Valentinian II, emperor of the East, in his conflict with Maximus. In 387 Maximus occupied Africa; but in the following year he was defeated and killed by Theodosius and Africa returned to its loyalty to Valentinian. In the period of struggle between Maximus and Theodosius Gildo maintained good relations with Maximus; but as he also ensured the shipment of grain to Italy, he avoided incurring the hostility of Theodosius and Valentinian. The elevation of Theodosius in 392 to the imperial throne upon Valentinian II's assassination improved Gildo's standing in Africa; and when Theodosius died on 19 January 395, Gildo – now the virtual ruler of Africa in his capacity as commander of the armed forces – gradually waived his loyalty to the emperor.

During the ten years which ended with Theodosius' death in 395 the Donatist Church was beset by internal strife between the group of extremists dominated by Optatus, and the moderate and conservative Donatist bishops of Byzacenia and Tripolitania, strife from which the party of Optatus emerged triumphant. During this period, Optatus led a religio-social revolution which aimed at dispossessing the Romanized landowners and suppressing Catholicism in Numidia. Seconded by inroads of Circumcellion terrorists, his efforts succeeded in making Donatism a stronger social force in the western provinces than the Catholic Church; and the events of 393 and 394 show that his influence was also great outside Numidia. On 24 June 393 a Donatist church council held in Cebarsussa in Byzacenia replaced Primian, the primate of Carthage, by Maximian, who enjoyed the support of the bishops of Byzacenia and Tripolitania. As the Numidian and Mauritanian Donatist bishops contested Maximian's election, another council dominated by these bishops, which was held on 24 April 394 in Bagai in southern Numidia, pronounced Maximian a schismatic and reinstated Primian. The conflict was similar to the one which started the Donatist movement. The difference between the attitude of the secular authorities towards this ecclesiastical quarrel and their attitude when Caecilian was elected, reflects the importance of Donatism in this period and the great standing of the bishops of the western provinces in this church. Rather than support the candidate of the conservative bishops of Tripolitania and Byzacenia, the proconsul and the city magistrates assisted Primian in suppressing his opponents.

In 397 when Primian, backed by the Proconsul Seranus, completed his victory by bringing to obedience the last recalcitrant bishops in Byzacenia, Gildo started his rebellion by withholding the shipment of wheat to Rome. During the short period when Gildo could defy the Roman state, the Catholics were visited with systematic persecution. By preventing the supply of wheat to Rome, and thus threatening it with famine, Gildo gambled on the power he had held before 397. The Roman senate acted fast, and an expedition was sent against him in the same year commanded by his own brother Mascazel, who had taken refuge in Italy after Gildo had quarrelled with him and killed his two children. Gildo was defeated in the spring of 398 near Theveste, was taken captive in Thabraca from where he was trying to escape, and died either by his own hands or by strangulation. Optatus was executed at about the same time, and the period of the ascendancy of Donatism thus came to an end. The following thirty years witnessed the eclipse of Donatism, though not its complete disappearance, as St Augustine, relying on the support of the Roman state, took up the cudgel against it.

In the same year (395) that Theodosius died and Gildo began to prepare for his rebellion, St Augustine was consecrated bishop of Hippo. Allied with Aurelius, the Catholic bishop of Carthage, he started to work towards bringing the Donatists under the authority of the Roman Church by holding debates with their leaders. As Gildo's defeat enabled St Augustine to rely on state support in the suppression of Donatism, he came gradually to accept coercion as an instrument for leading Donatists into the Catholic faith. In June 399 the Donatists were officially brought under existing legal sanctions against religious dissenters. However, legal proscription was not sufficient to break the tenacity of a movement which viewed martyrdom as a way to Paradise. On the other hand, St Augustine's theological arguments against the movement were rebutted by learned Donatist bishops who entered into a battle of tracts with him, especially Petilianus, the bishop of Constantine. In their replies to St Augustine the Donatists condemned the Catholics for their alliance with the secular powers and stressed their belief that persecution was, to the true Church, a means of purification. Contending that the efficacy of a sacrament depended on the conscience of its giver, Petilianus also publicized the fact that St Augustine had been a Manichee, claiming that he remained one at heart, and drew attention to his self-admitted past sinfulness in order to shed doubt on the validity of the sacraments which he, and the priests under his influence, administered.

The official ban against Donatism was strengthened in 405, when Emperor Honorius issued an edict and several decrees proscribing the movement. Donatism was pronounced a heresy, the meetings of its followers were banned, and its church property was ordered to be turned over to the Catholic Church. Inheritance from a deceased Donatist was also restricted to those of his children who were converted to Catholicism. The result of the persecution which followed was that the leaders of Donatism went into exile and the Catholics increased their strength, but the schismatic church was not crushed. St Augustine soon realized that whereas persecution won back to the Catholic Church the weak at heart, it confirmed the staunch Donatists in their beliefs. His next step, therefore, was to bring together the Donatist and Catholic bishops in a church council and endeavour to have Donatist doctrines formally condemned, so that the Donatists would no longer rest in the assurance that theirs was the true Church and that death at the hands of her enemies was martyrdom. Emperor Honorius was at the time concerned with Atalic's threat and, therefore, anxious to end the religious conflict in Africa and re-establish peace. Thus in response to the appeal of a Catholic delegation that waited upon him in Ravenna in 410, he ordered Heraclian in Africa to convene a church council of Catholic and Donatist bishops to debate their doctrinal differences. He also sent to Africa a high court official and a close friend of St Augustine's, Marcellinus, to preside over the conference.

The idea of the conference was Augustine's master plan; for should the Donatists refuse the summonses, which were sent to them in January 411, they would have appeared as misguided dissenters who were unable to defend their doctrines in a public debate; and should they attend the conference, Augustine was certain that the pronouncement of Marcellinus, as president and arbiter, would condemn them. The Donatists decided to attend, seeing that to do so would be less harmful to their cause, and hoping to be able to bring the conference to deadlock so that no verdict would be given. The conference, which was assembled in June 411, was attended by 286 Catholic bishops as against 284 Donatist. From the beginning it was clear that the Catholics were favoured by the president of the conference; and the emperor's edict, which was read in the opening session, stated that the purpose of the conference was "to confirm the Catholic faith".[1] When at the conclusion of the proceedings Marcellinus declared the Catholic Church the only true church, orders were issued banning Donatist assemblies and for completing the confiscation of Donatist property. An appeal by the Donatists to the emperor was to no avail, and on 30 January 412 Honorius issued an edict confirming Marcellinus' report.

The cause of Catholicism in Africa suffered a momentary setback when Marcellinus and his brother were beheaded in September 413, in the purge of Heraclian's friends which occurred in the wake of the latter's futile rebellion earlier in that year. But in the summer of 414 the proscription of Donatism was once more confirmed by imperial edicts. Consequently hardly anything was recorded about Donatism in the last years before the Vandal conquest, although it survived in Numidia and, to a lesser extent, in Mauritania. In the last years of his life St Augustine turned his attention to combating other heresies, and his death in 430 coincided with the Vandal invasion which brought the Arian heresy into ascendancy in Africa. In the latter part of the sixth century Donatism once more emerged as an organized movement, especially in Numidia; and there is evidence that it survived until the Arab conquest in the second half of the seventh century.

[1] Frend, *The Donatist Church*, p. 280.

The Vandals

The civilized life which the Romans developed in the Maghrib during four centuries suffered an unmistakable setback in one century of Vandal rule. Recently it has been shown[1] that the acts of wanton destruction attributed to the Vandals by writers of the fifth and sixth centuries, which went by the name "Vandalism", were much exaggerated. Yet, as the Vandal rulers exercised direct control only over the eastern Maghrib, the two Mauritanias and the greater part of Numidia were ruled by the Berber chiefs under customary law and thus reverted to primitive tribal life.

The Vandals were induced by the attacks of the Visigoths to leave their home in Spain, where they had lived since 409; they went to North Africa in the expectation of finding in it both security and abundant food. The occasion for the migration was provided by the rebellion of Boniface, the Roman military governor in Africa since 423, against Empress Placidia and her young son Valentian III. According to Procopius, Boniface offered to cede to the Vandal king Gunderic two-thirds the land ruled by Rome in Africa, in return for his support in resisting imperial authority. After two Roman expeditions were sent against Boniface in 427 and 428, he was reconciled with Placidia through the good offices of St Augustine, but the Vandals came nevertheless.

King Gaiseric (428–77), who led the Vandals to Africa in 429, was the illegitimate child of King Godagesil. He was born in 389, and thus was forty years old when he succeeded his brother Gunderic to the throne. A convert from Catholicism to Arianism, he cherished a strong hatred for the faith which he had relinquished. Though decisive and ambitious, his tastes were simple, and the limit of his aspirations was to lead his people to the land of corn in Africa. That he had come to North Africa to stay is evident from his bringing with him the whole of his people, who numbered about 80,000 persons. Crossing the straits in May 429, most probably to Tangier, he proceeded westwards to the wheat-producing lands *par excellence* of Proconsular Africa and Byzacenia. He travelled from his landing-place on the Moroccan coast in all probability by land, and was not met by any organized opposition until he reached the boundaries of the Proconsular province. Near its boundaries Boniface gave him battle, and when the latter was defeated and escaped to Hippo Regius, Gaiseric besieged this town for fourteen months beginning in June 430 until he captured it. After the surrender of Hippo, Boniface received reinforcements of imperial troops led by the Patrician Aspar; but he was once more defeated and escaped to Italy. Aspar escaped to the east, and thus Gaiseric was left as the sole master of Roman Africa. Only Carthage remained for a

[1] The author owes the greater part of his information on the Vandals in Africa to Christian Courtois's *Les Vandales et l'Afrique* (Paris, 1955).

while outside his control, and he seems to have abstained from attacking it immediately because of its strong fortifications and in order not to provoke both Rome and Constantinople to send armies against him.

There was general confusion in Roman Africa as a result of the Vandal conquest. The Catholic clerics, whose first impulse was to flee the land *en masse*, were prevailed upon by St Augustine to stay. St Augustine died on 28 August 430 during the siege of Hippo Regius, leaving as legacy to the new rulers a hostile and relatively strong Catholic Church with which they had to wrestle to the end. The Vandals committed atrocities during the period of conquest, but these do not seem to have exceeded what was common at the time. The exaggerated accounts of these atrocities owe their origins to the tendentious writings of contemporary Roman Catholic clerics. These were the sworn enemies of the Arian Vandals, and some of them, such as the author of *Vita Augustini*, Possidius bishop of Calama (Gulma), escaped from their parishes upon the approach of the Vandals and sought by their exaggerated accounts of Vandal cruelty to justify their dereliction of duty. The only wilful destruction that the Vandals under Gaiseric seem to have committed was the demolition of the walls of the fortified cities which they captured, and this was done in order to make it difficult for the recalcitrant inhabitants to rebel against them.

A treaty signed at Hippo Regius on 11 February 435 between Gaiseric and the imperial delegate Trigetius secured to the Vandal king recognition of his authority over the area in Numidia between Sitif in the west and Calama in the east. By so doing, the Romans sought to contain the Vandals by treating them as *foederati* who, like the other Barbarians in the empire, were placed in command of Roman territory without ceding sovereignty to them. This implication of the treaty does not seem to have been heeded by Gaiseric, who acted in the capacity of sovereign when he established a capital for his state in Hippo and in 437 sent the Catholic bishops into exile. On 19 October 439, having consolidated his power in Numidia, he also captured Carthage. This event had great moral significance to both Vandals and Romans. The Vandals considered it the beginning of their reign in Africa. Taking 19 October as the beginning of their year, they relinquished the Roman custom of reckoning according to the consular years and dated their regnal years from 439. To the Romans Carthage was the symbol of imperial authority and the dominance of the Catholic faith in Africa. When Gaiseric occupied it he did so while expecting Roman reprisal, and he anticipated it by fitting his fleet to defend the town. A Byzantine army intended for Africa arrived in Sicily in 441; but it never reached its destination and was withdrawn in 442 when a second treaty was concluded with the Vandals.

Unlike the one of 435, the treaty of 442 ceded to Gaiseric the part of the empire which he occupied. When it was signed, Gaiseric had already consolidated his power in the Proconsular province and Byzacenia, these being the parts of Roman Africa which he especially coveted. The treaty of 442 recognized his sovereignty over these two provinces, besides eastern Numidia. In the second half of the fifth century Gaiseric's authority came also to extend over the Tripolitanian coast. Rusicade (Philippeville) and Chullu (Collo), both on the coast, as well as Cirta inland, became once more imperial possessions. Thus as a result of the treaty of 442, the western parts of the Maghrib reverted to Roman rule; but this restitution of Roman authority was merely nominal. By 455 Roman authority disappeared completely from Caesarian and Sitifian Mauritania, and it was never to return; in Numidia it was reimposed effectively only during the Byzantine period. To fill the vacuum in the west of the Maghrib there appeared strong and stable confederacies of Berber tribes, whose chiefs sometimes used the title *rex* (king) and sought an official investiture in this capacity from the Roman state.

The territory under Vandal rule in the Maghrib remained unchanged until the Byzantine conquest. Outside Africa, the Vandals annexed the Balearic Isles sometime at the end of Gaiseric's reign or the beginning of that of his successor, Huneric. They also exercised some measure of control over Corsica and Sardinia, in both of which the church became attached to the see of Carthage. Sicily was the principal object of attraction to the Vandals soon after their establishment in Africa. They raided and pillaged it since 440, but were not able to occupy it until 468. In 476 the island was leased to Odovacar, the Ostrogoth king of Italy, who held it as a feudal lord, paying tribute to the Vandal king; but in 491 these feudal ties were broken, and the king of Italy assumed full sovereignty over Sicily. Thus in 500 King Theodoric of Italy could give the region of Lilybaeum (Marsala) in Sicily as dowry to his sister Amalafrida on the occasion of her marriage to the Vandal king Thrasamund.

Marauding expeditions seem to have played an important part, at least in the early period, in providing the Vandal kings with the means of meeting the expenses of the state. In addition to their repeated attacks on Sicily before its occupation, they raided Spain; and in 455 Gaiseric attacked Rome. In March 455 Valentinian III was massacred and his widow Eudoxia was made to marry Maximus, his murderer and the usurper of his throne. Gaiseric used the occasion to sail to Italy with a formidable fleet. As he was approaching Rome, the populace rose against Maximus and put him to death. Thus Gaiseric entered the capital of the empire on 2 June unopposed, and plundered it for fourteen days. When he returned to Africa he took with him Empress Eudoxia and her two daughters, Placidia and Eudoxia, besides other booty.

Avitus, who became emperor in Rome in July 455, tried to induce Marcian, emperor of the East, to send a joint expedition against Gaiseric.

Marcian's unwillingness to take part in such an enterprise led to inactivity on the part of Avitus. In 460 Avitus' successor, Majorian, mustered a large army in Spain with which he wanted to cross to Africa; but in 461 he made peace with Gaiseric after the Vandals had seized a number of the ships assembled in Cartagena, to carry the Roman army. Majorian was subsequently deposed in August 461, partly because of his failure to invade North Africa. Pressure on Gaiseric both by the new west Roman emperor Libius Severus, and the Byzantine emperor Leo, made him release Empress Eudoxia and her younger daughter Placidia, both of whom then went to Constantinople. The other daughter Eudoxia had been married to Gaiseric's son Huneric and therefore remained in Carthage until 472, when she escaped to Jerusalem.

In 465 the Byzantines drove the Vandals out from Sicily and some time later from Sardinia. When Gaiseric refused to accede to the imperial demands, made through the legate Phylarchos who was sent to Carthage in 467, for the conclusion of peace on the basis of the accomplished fact, Emperor Marcian decided to dispatch an expedition to Africa. Though commanded by the emperor's brother-in-law Basiliscus and costing the empire immense sums, this expedition turned out to be a complete failure. After landing on the western coast of Cape Bon in 468, Basiliscus was persuaded by Gaiseric to allow him five days, ostensibly so that he could consider whether to submit to the emperor's commands. Gaiseric in fact needed time until the wind turned north-west; and when a favourable wind came, the Vandal fire ships scudded into the midst of the Byzantine fleet. The ravage caused by the fire was completed by Gaiseric's men. Basiliscus could escape to Italy, but most of his men perished, together with some 340 ships. In 470 Emperor Leo sent another expedition against the Vandals, which landed at Oea and from there marched on Carthage. However, internal difficulties at home forced the emperor to withdraw it; and Zeno, who in 474 succeeded Leo, concluded a peace treaty with Gaiseric under whose terms the Vandal king promised to guarantee to the Catholics freedom of worship. This peace lasted until the expedition commanded by Belisarius landed in Africa sixty years later.

Internally the Vandal state was beset with difficulties which it did not have the means to surmount. The Vandals had neither an advanced civilization, nor great numbers with which to dominate the area they ruled. The Berbers (or Mauri, as they were called since the third century) were satisfied to be left alone by their new masters and caused them much less trouble than they later did the Byzantines; but the urban communities, which constituted the larger part of the population in Proconsular Africa and Byzacenia, maintained to the end an attitude of antipathy towards the Vandals. The vigour with which some of the Vandal kings tried to convert the Roman population to Arianism, like the efforts of the Romans before them to suppress the heresies, had the political objective of creating loyal subjects. But the Vandal attempts at conversion failed to make Arians out of the Romans, and only succeeded in widening the gulf between the two communities. This gulf was rendered the more difficult to bridge by the Vandal system of government, under which the Romans and Vandals were kept apart. The Vandals were kept under the jurisdiction of their customary law and the control of the "leaders of thousands" (the *millenarii*), who were each responsible for the affairs of a thousand heads of families in administrative, fiscal, and judicial matters. Although the Vandals occupied some of the estates seized from the Romans, they paid no taxes, whereas the Romans did. The property which remained in the hands of Roman individuals was not taken away, nor were the taxes levied on them exorbitant. But the Vandal kings took no interest in the day-to-day affairs of their Roman subjects, and made a fusion between them and the Vandals nearly impossible by prohibiting intermarriage with them.

The government of the Vandal state was centred in the person of the king. Gaiseric was chosen king by the will of the people, but he gradually became an absolute ruler. The tanistry order of succession he laid down, prescribing that the throne must go to the eldest male member of the royal family, left no say in the matter to the Vandal chiefs. In 442 he executed several Vandal nobles who rose against him, accusing him of overstepping his powers as king. The rest of the nobility was constrained to take an oath of fealty to him; and when the need arose, they were assigned government functions and sent on missions to foreign countries. The two organized offices in the state were those of the *praepositus regni*, the *major domo* of the state occupying a position similar to that of prime minister, and the head of the chancellery, who drafted the written royal edicts and was entrusted with important political missions. Some Roman ideas of government were preserved, such as centering both administrative and judicial functions in the hands of the provincial governors; and Roman titles were also used, such as "proconsul", which the chief judge of Carthage held. Also Latin was the language of legislation and diplomatic intercourse in the Vandal state.

Conflict between the Catholic and Arian churches began during Gaiseric's reign. The Arian Church, which had an organized hierarchy whose supreme head in Africa was the Patriarch of Carthage, considered itself the only true Church. During the period of conquest Gaiseric confiscated the property of the Catholic Church. However, upon the request of Valentinian III he permitted in 452 the consecration of a Catholic bishop for Carthage; but when this bishop, Deogratias, died some two years later, Gaiseric pursued a rigorous anti-Catholic policy. He did not permit the consecration of a successor and confiscated all the Catholic churches but one.

During Gaiseric's long reign, ending with his death in January 477, the changes which took place in the outlook of the Vandal people had begun to alter the character of their government. The generation of Vandals which grew up in Africa was less warlike than the invaders of 429; and none of the Vandal kings after Gaiseric, with the exception of the last (Gelimer), was distinguished as a soldier. Gaiseric's son Huneric, who succeeded him when he was about fifty, was thoroughly Romanized as a result of his sojourn in Rome as hostage in accordance with the treaty of 442 and his marriage to a Roman princess. The Vandal army, which consisted predominantly of cavalry, gradually lost its importance as a fighting force, so that the Vandal kings had to rely on Berber contingents. The Berbers first made their appearance in the Vandal army in the sack of Rome; afterwards, Gaiseric also chose Berber troops to garrison Sardinia. The ease with which Belisarius could conquer the Vandals in 533, though not the Berber tribes, shows that of Vandal martial valour there remained by then only the name.

Though Romanized, Huneric was no nearer to Catholicism by sentiment than his father; but when he found himself in difficulty with his own people over changing the order of succession, he did not hesitate to try and make a deal with the Catholic Church. In 481 he began the liquidation of the family of his younger brother Theuderic, the next after him in the tanistry[1] order of succession, thus preparing the way for the succession of his son Hilderic and adopting the primogenitary order so as to keep the throne in his own direct line. Theuderic's wife disappeared first, then his elder son; and when Theuderic went into hiding, his daughter and other son, who was only an infant, were also killed. When Huneric sensed the hostility of the Vandal nobility to the modification of the order of succession and to his ruthless methods of achieving this, he sought to win the support of the Catholic Church by making concessions to it. He permitted the celebration of Catholic rites in Proconsular Africa and authorized the election of a new bishop of Carthage. Soon he realized, however, that the Catholics were as opposed to his son's succession as were the Vandal nobility, and so he resorted to suppression. He employed against the Catholics the same methods that had been used by the Romans to combat Donatism. The Catholics who refused to accept Arianism were deprived of their property and banished to Sicily or Sardinia. He confiscated the property of the bishops when they died and levied an imposition on new bishops before allowing them to be consecrated. He also exiled into the al-Hudna mountains some 500 Catholic priests who refused to recant. There the Berber tribesmen reduced some of them to slavery.

[1] Under this system the oldest of the deceased king's kinsmen would have been entitled to succession, as opposed to the primogenitary system which reserved this right to his eldest child.

Huneric copied St Augustine's methods when in May 483 he issued a decree summoning the Arian and Catholic bishops to a conference, which was to convene on 1 February 484, in order to debate their doctrines. Byzantine representations and the protestation of Eugene, the Catholic bishop of Carthage, that the bishops of Africa could not themselves alter the doctrines of the Universal Church, did not deter him. The conference opened on the date set to it with greater confusion than attended the Catholic-Donatist conference of 411. After a week of disorderly discussion Huneric brought its proceedings to an end. Although no official verdict against Catholicism was adopted by the conference, Huneric issued on 7 February a decree ordaining the confiscation of the Catholic churches and ecclesiastical property and transferring them to the Arian Church. Another decree of 25 February required the Catholics to renounce their religion before June of the same year and threatened them with fines, confiscation of property, flagellation, and exile. At the same time, Huneric tried to cajole the Catholic priests into taking an oath of loyalty to his son as successor. Their refusal to yield made him send more of them into exile in al-Hudna or Corsica, where they were employed in cutting wood for the royal fleet. General persecution was also undertaken: children and adults were made to accept rebaptism by threats, death or exile being the two penalties inflicted on those who refused to obey.

Huneric's efforts to crush the Catholic Church failed. After his death in December 484 it remained sufficiently strong for his two immediate successors, Gunthamund (484–96) and Thrasamund (496–523), to consider it in the interest of stability to tone down the persecution of Catholics. But the Vandal nobility could not accept extending to the Catholics more than toleration. In a world dominated by Roman civilization, the Arian faith remained their only mark of distinction as a ruling class. The citadel of Arianism remained intact until Thrasamund's death. This king reinforced it by an alliance with Theodoric, the Arian king of the Ostrogothic state in Italy. But when he died Hilderic (523–30), the effeminate son of Huneric and Eudoxia, made a breach in its walls. The consequences for the Vandal state were serious indeed.

The influence of his mother and his long sojourn in Constantinople inclined Hilderic towards Catholicism. As soon as he acceded to the throne he allowed the Catholics freedom of worship, re-established them in their churches, and permitted the return of their exiled bishops. The Catholic Church could consequently reorganize and expand its influence, as is evident from the fact that 220 Catholic bishops were present at a council held in Carthage four years after Hilderic's death. Hilderic further offended the Vandal nobility when he replaced the alliance with the Ostrogothic kingdom by dependence on the Byzantine empire, to the extent of striking coins bearing the effigy of Justin I. While flouting the sentiments of his people in his religious and external policies, Hilderic did not have any great abilities as a ruler or military commander with which to appeal to them. Injury was added to insult when he proved incapable of checking the menace of the Berber tribes.

The Berber confederacies, which had emerged mostly in the second half of the fifth century on the periphery of the Vandal state, had become at the beginning of the sixth century strong and organized. One of them occupied the area around present-day Oran, and an inscription dated 508 shows that it was ruled by King Masuna. A second Berber confederacy ruled the Auras; a third occupied al-Hudna, and was ruled until 496 by a king called Masties. The Berber confederacy which caused the greatest disturbance to the Vandals was one whose king during the reign of Hilderic was called Antalas. This confederacy was founded around 510 by Guenfan, Antalas' father and chief of the Frexes Berbers who inhabited the district of Thala. The tribes forming it had been active in southern Tunisia since the reign of Gunthamund; but during Hilderic's reign they made more frequent inroads into the plains, seizing herds and produce which they took to their strongholds in the central Dorsale. The defeat of a force sent by Hilderic against Antalas somewhere on the slopes of the Dorsale had the result of making Antalas the undisputed master of the region.

Hilderic's shattered prestige, and the continuous threat to the Vandal state from the Berbers living in it, led to his deposition. Gelimer, Hilderic's cousin who wielded much of the power of the state since Thrasamund's death, had the Vandal nobility elect him to the throne on 15 June 530. Gelimer was Hilderic's legitimate successor under the tanistry order, and he justified his premature seizure of the throne by claiming that his cousin had conspired to deprive him of it by turning the Vandal lands over to the Byzantines. Justinian's subsequent use of Hilderic's deposition as the excuse for invading the Vandal state made this last charge seem plausible.

The Vandal period, which was brought to an end by the Byzantine conquest, was one of relative stability. In spite of the persistent hostility of the Roman population and the numerical inferiority of the Vandals, no organized rebellion against them took place on the scale of the uprisings of the first twenty years of Byzantine rule. The only known revolts occurred in the last decade of the Vandal period, and one of them at least, that of Pudentius of Oea in 523, was instigated by the Byzantines. The Vandal period in the Maghrib was not one of great construction, but it was one of prosperity. Commercial activities flourished in the towns, the crafts known in the Roman period continued, and agriculture provided the country with its needs of food. When the Byzantine conquerors arrived in Tunisia in 533 the country was not desolate; rather it was one in which agriculture, especially horticulture, flourished. Africa no longer supplied Italy with wheat, but it maintained commercial relations with the countries of the eastern Mediterranean. The Vandals sold mostly slaves and bought predominantly clothes. Byzantine coins from the Vandal period which were found in great numbers in Africa show, as Courtois points out,[1] that the balance of trade in these relations was in favour of the Vandals. The relative prosperity of the Maghrib explains why Vandal rule, in spite of its basic weaknesses, lasted as long as it did.

The Byzantines

The conquest of the Maghrib by the Byzantines in 533 was part of Emperor Justinian's scheme of restoring the unity of the Roman empire. Though Roman territory in Europe and the Maghrib had by the fifth century fallen into the hands of the German tribes, the concept of the unity and universality of Roman rule persisted in the thinking of both Romans and Barbarians. As we have seen above, the Vandals wrung a *de jure* recognition of their sovereignty over the part of Africa which they occupied; nevertheless the Roman population under their rule continued to view their government as merely transitory. The territory ruled by the other Barbarians continued in theory to be Roman.

The occasion for the Byzantine conquest of the Maghrib was provided by Gelimer's usurpation of the Vandal throne and the imprisonment of Hilderic. Justinian's first move after this occurred was to demand that Hilderic be reinstated, or at least released and permitted to travel to Constantinople. Had the latter request been granted, Justinian would have had in his custody the rightful king of the Vandal state in whose name he could invade Africa.

In 532 Justinian concluded peace with the Persians in order to direct the military effort of the empire against the Vandals; but the African expedition was slow in starting because the emperor's enthusiasm for invading Africa was not shared by the prominent members of his advisory council, the Consistorium. The great losses in life and treasure incurred in the expedition of Basiliscus were recalled to the emperor's attention, as well as the fact that the soldiers were weary of the Persian wars and apprehensive of undertaking an expedition that might involve them in naval warfare to which they were not accustomed. These objections were counterbalanced by the representations of the African Roman nobility, whom Gelimer deprived of the property which Hilderic had returned to them. A decisive influence on the emperor, and the one which in the end provided him with a moral incentive to undertake the expedition, was that of the orthodox religious circles. It is said that an orthodox bishop, having learnt of the emperor's hesitation to undertake the campaign against the

[1] Courtois, *Les Vandales*, p. 323.

Vandals, assured him on the basis of a vision he had seen that the "Lord will march before him in his battles, and make him sovereign of Africa ".[1]

The expeditionary force, which was led by Justinian's famous commander Belisarius and set out from Constantinople on 22 June 533, was small compared with that of 468. It consisted of 5,000 cavalry and 10,000 foot soldiers, carried on 500 ships. But Vandal military power had declined since the days of Gaiseric, and the Vandal state lost its alliance with the Ostrogothic state in Italy during Hilderic's reign. Byzantine diplomacy could win the goodwill of Amalasuntha, the queen-regent of Italy, who permitted the Byzantine army to buy provisions when it stopped in Sicily. A timely rebellion in Sardinia against the Vandals also deprived Gelimer of the cream of his troops, who were dispatched there under the command of his brother Tzazo to put down the rising.

Initial difficulties which the expeditionary force encountered on the way, arising from the unruliness of the Hunnish confederates and the spread of intestinal infection caused by the decay of the imperfectly baked biscuits provided for the army, were overcome by Belisarius' unswerving firmness and severity. The historian Procopius, who went on the expedition as Belisarius' secretary, obtained in Sicily the information that Gelimer was unaware of the approach of the Byzantine army. This intelligence, which proved to be true, induced Belisarius to hasten his departure for Africa. The army disembarked early in September 533 in Caput Vada (Ras Kapudia), some 150 miles to the south of Carthage. Belisarius chose this place for landing against the advice of his officers, for fear that the soldiers would desert if a naval battle was forced upon them by the Vandal fleet near Carthage.

Having established a foothold in Africa, Belisarius tried to win over the population by good treatment. He punished his troops severely when they looted private property, and permitted them to raid only the domains of the Vandal king. He also had letters from Justinian read which represented the purpose of the expedition as being the reinstatement of the lawful Vandal king. When Gelimer had his brother Ammatas in Carthage put Hilderic to death, Belisarius dropped this claim and stressed the fact that he came to Africa to bring the former Roman provinces back into the empire.

From Caput Vada Belisarius marched northwards towards Carthage and had the fleet follow the movements of the army without allowing it to go out of sight. Although the arrival of the Byzantine expedition took Gelimer by surprise, he prepared to intercept its advance. He instructed his brother Ammatas to meet the Byzantine vanguard in a narrow pass at Decimum (Sidi Fathalla, about 15 kilometres to the south of Carthage); Gelimer's nephew Gibamund, also coming from Carthage, was to attack the Byzan-

[1] Lord Mahon, *The Life of Belisarius* (London, 1848), p. 77.

tine left wing, whilst he himself was to fall on their back. It was a well-planned strategy, which could have won the day for the Vandals had Ammatas not acted rashly by attacking the Byzantine vanguard with only a small party of his men on 14 September 533, while instructing the rest of his soldiers to follow. Ammatas showed much courage in the encounter, but he was killed and his men escaped towards the capital. This wrecked Gelimer's plan, since Gibamund's attack on the left wing was in consequence easily repulsed. Gelimer's charge on the Byzantine rear at first proved successful; but instead of following up his success, the Vandal king, consumed with grief over his brother's death, gave Belisarius the time to organize his ranks for a counter-attack. Gelimer was routed. Rather than make for Carthage, whose population's loyalty to him he could not trust, he fled to Numidia. Belisarius then entered Carthage, the gates of which were laid open before him by the Roman population. The battle of Decimum took place on 15 September, the eve of St Cyprian's festival. Belisarius made his entry into the capital on the day of the festival, and in place of the Arian priests it was the Catholic priests who celebrated it.

Meanwhile the Vandal king was reorganizing his army. In addition to the soldiers which his brother Tzazo brought back from Sardinia after defeating and killing the rebel leader Godas, his troops were reinforced with Berber warriors. Gelimer could assemble a force of about 100,000 men in the plains of Bulla Regia (Hammam Daraji) near the Numidian boundary. At the same time he tried to buy the loyalty of the Hunnish confederates in the Byzantine army. These troops, whose allegiance Belisarius could not trust, were kept loyal only by the promise of being taken back home after Gelimer's defeat. Belisarius marched against Gelimer three months after his entry into Carthage. The two armies met at the village of Tricamarum in mid-December 533. After two unsuccessful attacks on the Vandal centre, the Byzantines succeeded in breaking through and killing Tzazo. Gelimer's escape soon afterwards won the day for the Byzantines. Belisarius captured at this battle the greater part of the Vandal treasury; the rest he took when he entered Hippo Regius, whither the Vandal king had taken it for it to be sent to Spain. The Byzantine army, which had so far maintained its discipline, could not be restrained after this victory from looting the vanquished Vandals and from debauchery.

The battle of Tricamarum spelled the final defeat of the Vandal king, who subsequently escaped and took refuge with the Berbers in the small town of Medenus on the Papua mountain. Sending a detachment of the army to blockade Gelimer there, Belisarius returned to Carthage. From there he sent troops to occupy Oea and the fortress of Septem (Ceuta), and other forces to conquer Sardinia and Corsica. Gelimer surrendered to his enemies three months after his escape to Medenus, preferring captivity to the rugged life he had to lead in his retreat. In the meantime Justinian's

suspicions that Belisarius might create for himself an independent kingdom in Africa resulted in the latter's recall in the middle of 534, and his
replacement by Solomon, an Armenian, who was Belisarius' chief lieutenant during the campaign.

The area which the Byzantines ruled for about a century-and-a-half
started by being more or less that which the Vandals occupied. It included
the Proconsular province, Byzacenia, and Tripolitania; and in Numidia
they occupied at first only as far as the environs of Constantine. On
paper the three Roman Mauritanias were included within the structure
of Byzantine administration, although they were yet unconquered. The
Byzantine fleet occupied some fortified places on their coast, and
Septem was made an important military post; but these remained
isolated from the mainland and had communications with the eastern
Maghrib only by sea. In Tripolitania, Byzantine domination was
limited to the strategic highway linking Gabis with Cyrenaica, and to
exercising influence of a diplomatic and religious nature on the neighbouring Berber tribes. In 539, having completed the conquest of the
Auras, Solomon consolidated Byzantine positions in Numidia and conquered Sitifian Mauritania. In spite of Justinian's grandiose ambition
of bringing all the former Roman territory under his rule, only a part
of Caesarian Mauritania was later brought under Byzantine government, whereas into the interior of Tingitana the Byzantines could not
penetrate at all. Septem remained under Byzantine rule until the Arab
conquest.

Having restored the greater part of Roman Africa to the Roman empire,
Justinian tried to reorganize it along the lines of the era before the Vandal
conquest, while effecting only those changes which were necessary to
make it an integral part of the Byzantine administration. In his ordinance
to Belisarius of April 534 the African provinces, together with Corsica and
Sardinia, were combined in a single prefecture. This vast administrative
unit was to be governed by a praetorian prefect, who wielded the chief
civil authority and was to be responsible for the finances and the administration of justice. The prefecture was divided into seven provinces, each
governed by a consul or a praeses (praesides). These provinces have been
identified[1] as Proconsular Africa, Byzacenia, Tripolitania, Numidia,
Mauritania Prima (Sitifian), Mauritania Secunda (Caesarian and Tingitana), and Sardinia. During the reign of Emperor Maurice (582–602),
Tripolitania was annexed administratively to Egypt; Sitifian Mauritania
was combined with newly acquired positions in Caesarian Mauritania to
form Mauritania Prima; whilst Septem and the Byzantine possessions in
Spain and the Balearic Isles formed Mauritania Secunda, an arrangement
which implied the relinquishment of Mauritania Tingitana. Sicily was

[1] By Charles Diehl, *L'Afrique byzantine* (Paris, 1896), I, 107–10.

placed under the government of a praetor, and was administratively independent of the African prefecture.

Acting on the principle of the separation of military and civil authorities, the emperor divided the African provinces into four military districts: Tripolitania, Byzacenia, Numidia, and the Mauritanias; a fifth military district was later created for Sardinia. At the head of each of these units was a *dux* (duke) who was assigned an official place of residence: in Leptis for Tripolitania, Capsa (Gafsa) and Theveste for Byzacenia, Cirta for Numidia, and Caesarea for the Mauritanias. An officer of an inferior rank, who was under the command of the *dux* of the Mauritanias, was in charge of Septem. The functions of the *dux* were principally the defence of the *limes* and keeping the tribes under control. In the matter of frontier defences the Byzantines revived the *limes* established during the Roman period, rebuilt the fortifications which the Vandals had destroyed, and constructed new ones. When peace was fully established in Africa, they also revived the practice of relying for the protection of the *limes* on the provincial peasant soldiers, the *limitanei*. The commander-in-chief of the army of Africa, the *magister militum*, was in theory independent of the prefect; but in Solomon's two terms as governor (534–6 and 539–44) he exercised the powers of prefect and commander-in-chief. This arrangement, which was considered an exceptional one reserved for periods when external attacks were expected, became the rule during the reign of Emperor Maurice. The civil and military governor was given the rank of exarch, which was superior to that of prefect in that its holder was the personal representative of the emperor. The position of prefect was retained in Africa, but its holder was an administrative officer receiving his orders from the exarch.

The Vandals almost completely disappeared from the Maghrib after 536. Of the members of the royal family none remained in Africa; Hilderic's children, as well as Gelimer and the immediate members of his family, were all taken to Constantinople. The Vandal nobility had been purged by Gelimer himself; and after their defeat, the warriors were either killed or taken to Constantinople, where they formed a special cavalry regiment which served in the cities of the east and took part in the wars with the Persians. Lacking leadership, the small part of the Vandal people that survived and was not taken into slavery was soon absorbed into the indigenous population.

Resistance to the Byzantines in the Maghrib after the recall of Belisarius in 534 came from the Berber tribes. The references to these tribes in the works of Byzantine historians enable us to know more about their social and political life in the first years of Byzantine rule than in any earlier period. In the mountainous areas and the plains they were sedentary, but on the fringes of the desert and in the steppes they were nomadic. In

Tripolitania they used the camel as a beast of burden and for combat; in other parts of the Maghrib the horse and the mule were more widely used. Although Christianity had spread among them, many – especially in Tripolitania – still worshipped pagan gods. Polygamy was widely practised and women had a humble social status, caring for the animals besides doing all domestic work, so that the men could devote themselves fully to the business of fighting. The men were excellent riders, and in war they knew how to use to great advantage the tactics of surprise and ambush. The Berber tribes resented the rule of the Byzantines because the latter aimed at bringing under their authority territories which the Vandals had left completely under Berber control. Byzantine policy towards these tribes was aimed at pacifying and then making them allies of the administration. The tribes which agreed to cooperate, like the confederacy ruled by Antalas in Byzacenia, were bound by a formal written convention and described in official language as "Mauri pacifici". These conventions usually provided for the payment of an annual stipend to the tribal chief, in return for which he was required to render certain services, such as preserving peace and order and placing under the command of the *dux* of his district a contingent of warriors. This policy only began to be effective around 550, when the major tribes had been reduced to submission.

When Solomon took over the command from Justinian in 534, the Byzantines in the Maghrib were especially disturbed by the attacks of Berber warriors in Byzacenia and the Auras. In Byzacenia Antalas remained on good terms with the new rulers between 535 and 544; but a group of nomadic camel-driving Berbers, coming most probably from Tripolitania, harassed the Byzantine troops. At the beginning of the Byzantine period the Auras was controlled by King Iaudas (Iabdas), whose authority also extended over the fertile plains which bordered it in the north. The warriors of this king made regular raids into the plains, and some time after 535 attacked and destroyed the towns of Thamugad (Timgad) and Bagai. Solomon dealt first with the nomadic Tripolitanians. He scored two important victories against them: one at Mamma (between Sbiba and Qairawan) at the end of 534, and the other at Mount Burgaon in the south-west of Byzacenia in the first months of 535. He killed large numbers of these nomads; the rest, led by Coutzina, escaped to Numidia and placed themselves under the protection of Iaudas. Coutzina was the son of a Berber chief and a Roman woman, and had wavered before the battle of Mamma between allying himself with the Byzantines or rebelling. He had at first accepted the title of *magister militum* from the emperor, but when the opportunity for pillage came, he did not scruple in attacking the Byzantine forces. However, when Solomon defeated Iaudas in 539, Coutzina submitted to Byzantine authority. Solomon invaded Iaudas' territory in the latter part of 535, approaching the Auras from the east;

but as Iaudas had made effective defensive preparations, a decisive victory could not be achieved quickly. The disaffection of his troops for reasons which shall be explained presently, coupled with bad weather, forced Solomon to retreat after a few months of campaigning. He hoped to make another attempt in the spring of 536; but an insurrection in the ranks of his army invalidated his plan.

In spite of his great ability as soldier, Solomon was not popular with the troops because of the rigorous discipline he imposed on them. Discontentment developed into rebellion when Solomon attempted to put into effect two imperial decrees which affected their material interests. In the first Justinian prescribed that the payment of the troops and the expenses of the administration should be defrayed from taxes collected in Africa. This caused a delay in paying the troops when they were about to leave on the expedition to the Auras. In the second he decreed that former Vandal lands were to become state property. The enforcement of this decree was resented by the troops who clamoured for a share of the lands they conquered, especially since many of them had married Vandal women and felt entitled to the property of their former husbands.

In March 536 the troops in Carthage rose in rebellion. Solomon, fearing for his life, sailed on the same day to Sicily where Belisarius was preparing for war against the Goths of Italy. In Africa the rebels looted Carthage, then marched to the plains of Bulla Regia. They were joined there by 400 Vandal captives who had overpowered their captors while on their way to Constantinople and forced the captain of their ship to steer back to Africa. Altogether about 8,000 men consisting of Byzantine soldiers, Vandals, and Berber warriors from Numidia joined forces under the command of a Byzantine soldier called Stozas in rebellion against Byzantine authority. Upon hearing Solomon's news, Belisarius immediately sailed from Sicily with only 100 men carried on board one ship. He entered Carthage without resistance; and having organized the ranks of the Byzantine forces that remained loyal, he defeated Stozas at Membressa (Majaz al-Bab) in April 536. After returning to Carthage he removed Solomon from his command, and appointed two men to replace him. He then sailed back to Sicily, and was never to return to Africa.

To deal with the grave situation in Africa, Justinian appointed his nephew Germanos as its prefect with the additional powers of *magister militum*. Germanos remained in Africa until 539, when the emperor reappointed Solomon as governor. Before Solomon's return a large number of the dissident troops had been won back through a general pardon and the payment of the arrears of their salaries. Germanos also defeated Stozas in 537, who then fled to Mauritania where he settled and married the daughter of a local chief.

With the insurrection of the troops brought to an end, Solomon's first task upon returning to Africa with the combined functions of prefect and *magister militum* was to combat the rebellious Berber tribes. Thanks to the work of Germanos, the military situation had improved since 536; and the arrival of reinforcements in 539 enabled Solomon once more to take the offensive against King Iaudas. King Iaudas was defeated, and he subsequently fled to Mauritania. His defeat was a great help in bringing the other rebellious tribes into submission, since they could see that Byzantine forces would next be marching against them. In 540 the tribes of Tripolitania – the Lawata, Ifuraces, and Mecales – accepted Byzantine sovereignty, and in Numidia Coutzina allied himself with the Byzantines.

The period of quiet, brought about by Germanos' and Solomon's victories, came to an end in 544. As a result of some disorder in the district under Antalas' control, Solomon suspended the latter's pension and put his brother Buarizila to death. Later in the same year another bloody deed was perpetrated in Leptis against the Lawata Berbers by the governor of Tripolitania, Solomon's nephew Sergius. Eighty Lawata chiefs, having secured a solemn promise of their safety taken on the Bible, were treacherously massacred by Sergius' guards when they called on him in order to complain against the devastation caused to their property by his troops. Roused by this outrage, the Lawata tribesmen attacked Leptis. Having failed to enter the town, they went to Byzacenia and placed themselves under Antalas' command. The result of these two cruel and impolitic deeds was that the Lawata and Antalas' men joined forces in numerous acts of destruction in Byzacenia. About the end of 544 they forced battle on Solomon, after he had tried in vain to reconcile them, and succeeded in defeating and killing him south of Theveste. Stozas reappeared in Byzacenia in 545. With the help of the other rebels he defeated the *dux* of Byzacenia, Himerius, near Hadrumetum, capital of this province, which consequently fell into the hands of the rebels. Byzantine troops defected to join Stozas in large numbers, and those troops that remained loyal sought their safety in Carthage, so that Byzantine control over Byzacenia completely collapsed.

In the meantime the emperor, wanting to honour Solomon's memory, appointed his nephew Sergius to replace him. Realizing, however, the impetuosity of this young patrician, after the fall of Hadrumetum he appointed an older man, the senator Areobindus, to govern Roman Africa conjointly with him. The rivalry between the two men defeated the emperor's purpose in appointing them together and added to the confusion of an already grave situation. The disorder in Tunisia in 544 and 545 was such that a section of its inhabitants deserted their homes and sought safety in various islands in the Mediterranean. In the latter part of 545 Stozas was active with his now considerable forces in the environs of

Sicca-Veneria (al-Kaf, Le Kef). At the end of the year Areobindus led against him the forces at his disposal, commanded by one of his best officers by the name of John. Stozas, as well as the Byzantine commanding officer, died in the engagement which ensued. The Byzantine losses were great; and Sergius, who failed to appear with his forces on the battlefield as had been agreed, was held responsible for the indecisive result of the battle. The emperor consequently withdrew Sergius in 546, leaving Areobindus to govern alone.

This measure, intended to eliminate the ill-effects of rivalry at the highest level in the African provinces, failed to improve Byzantine authority because of Areobindus' incompetence. The Berber revolt was universal; and Guntharith, the *dux* of Numidia to whom Areobindus gave the general command of the troops, betrayed him. Guntharith entered into alliance with the rebel Berber chiefs Iaudas, Antalas, and Coutzina, and seems to have aspired to establishing with their help an independent kingdom. He was successful to the extent of having Areobindus assassinated in March 546 and assuming the supreme command in his place. Byzantine sovereignty over Roman Africa was never more threatened, and the work of Belisarius and Solomon seemed lost. However, Guntharith soon fell out with Antalas over the division of the land; and the party in the army which remained loyal to the emperor brought his rebellion to an end by killing him thirty-six days after he had murdered Areobindus.

For the task of pacifying the African provinces Justinian chose John Troglita, an able soldier who had distinguished himself in the wars in Mesopotamia and served under Belisarius in Africa. The conclusion of the Persian wars made the dispatch of reinforcements to Africa possible; and Troglita's diplomatic skills won over to the side of the Byzantines no less an enemy than Iaudas. In a decisive battle in 547 near Hadrumetum the combined forces of Antalas and the Lawata were defeated; but when immediately after the battle Troglita sent reinforcements to Belisarius in Italy, the Tripolitanian tribes again became active in Numidia. In May 547 they scored a victory against Byzantine forces near Gabis. But in Numidia Coutzina and Iaudas remained loyal, and gave Troglita military assistance in the pacification of Byzacenia during 548. Henceforth peace reigned in the Maghriban provinces, and the acceptance of Byzantine rule by the tribes made it possible for the civil authorities to take over the task of administration from the military. Although the Berber tribes accepted Byzantine sovereignty, they remained strong and ready to rebel if provoked. When in 563 the governor John Rogathinos had Coutzina assassinated, the tribes in Numidia rose in rebellion; an expedition commanded by Marcian, the emperor's nephew (later his successor), had to be sent from Constantinople to put this uprising down. The Berber confederacies survived until the Arab conquest in the second half of the seventh century and when Byzantine rule collapsed in the face of the Arab invasion, it was they who took up resistance to the new invaders.

Byzantine government brought with it the reinstatement of the Catholic Church. Arianism and all other heresies, and even Judaism, were banned in the African prefecture. An imperial edict issued in 534 required the secular authorities in Africa to return to the Catholic Church all the landed property, church buildings, and religious articles of which it had been despoiled by the Vandals. Justinian also ordered the tax officials to restore the system of contribution to the Church, so that the population was subjected to a double system of taxation, one to the state and another to the Church, both of which having official sanction. But the authorities in Africa, religious and secular, forbore to enforce the imperial ban against the heresies too rigorously in order, it seems, to avoid internal dissension. The Arian priests who had been converted to Catholicism were allowed to resume their office, and the Donatists, who reappeared in Numidia in the second half of the sixth century, were tacitly tolerated. In the last decade of the century, however, Pope Gregory's persistent pressure on the secular authorities and the Catholic bishops in Africa resulted in the enforcement of the ban against Donatism, so that it lost any effective force it still had in Numidia.

Though indebted to Justinian for reinstatement, the African Church refused to toe the imperial line in its teachings. When in the 540s Justinian favoured the Monophysite doctrine, which had been pronounced heretical by the fourth Ecumenical Council of Chalcedon in 451, western Christendom was outraged. In Africa a vehement campaign against the emperor's religious policy was conducted by the deacon of Carthage, Fulgentius Ferrandus, and Bishop Victor of Tennuna. This campaign culminated in the excommunication of Pope Virgilius for his acquiescence in the emperor's deviation from the dogma of Chalcedon; his excommunication was passed by a synod held in Carthage, presided over by the bishop of Carthage, Repartus.

At the beginning of the seventh century a rebellion in the Maghrib prevented the disintegration of the empire at a time when there was a serious threat of this. In 602 Phocas usurped the imperial throne with the help of the army and executed Emperor Maurice. The Persian Emperor Chosroes II, who owed his throne to the support which he had received from Maurice, came forward to avenge him and in 603 declared war on the empire. There was also an internal threat from the rebellion of the commander Narses in Edessa. Chosroes scored important victories against the Byzantine forces in 604 and 605, and in 607 he overran Syria and Palestine. To the loss of prestige caused by these military defeats the emperor added the reputation of bad faith when Narses surrendered in 605 on the promise of safety, but was nevertheless buried alive. Rebellions in various parts of the empire broke out against Phocas, which he suppressed when he could with the greatest cruelty. The rebellion of the exarch of Africa, Heraclius, in 608 saved the situation. Aided by the Byzantine forces in Tripoli and the Pentapolis of Cyrenaica, he could send a naval expedition to Constantinople. As he himself was old, his son, also called Heraclius, commanded the army, which reached Constantinople on 3 October 610 after putting in at various islands on the way. Treachery on the part of Phocas' ministers made the task of young Heraclius easy. Phocas was dragged before him and executed on 5 October, and in the same day Heraclius was crowned by the patriarch.

Heraclius' reign (610–41) was one of quiet and prosperity in the African provinces. Byzantine authority was respected and Catholicism expanded its influence to include the Jarid in Tunisia, the Auras, and the Zab. During this period the Zanata bedouin in Caesarian Mauritania, as well as the strong Auruba confederacy in the Auras, were converted to Catholicism. The prefecture of Africa could also contribute valuable help to the empire at a time of grave danger. The Persians, who had already captured Jerusalem, invaded Asia Minor and threatened even Constantinople, also conquered Egypt in the spring of 619. At a moment of desperation Emperor Heraclius considered sailing to Carthage so as to start a war of reconquest from there. However, he was prevailed upon not to leave his capital. So he used the help which the Maghriban provinces could give in men and treasure in his war against the Persians.

During Heraclius' reign Monotheletism was adopted by Sergius, the Patriarch of Constantinople, and by Cyrus who succeeded him in 631. This doctrine, which stated that the divine and human natures of Christ had one active force or energy, was promulgated in the hope that it would serve as a basis for reconciliation between the Monophysites and the adherents to the dogma of Chalcedon. In 438 an edict from the emperor pronounced this doctrine the official dogma of the state. The hostility of the Monophysites in the Near East to this doctrine facilitated the conquest by the Arabs of Syria and Palestine in 638 and of Egypt two years later. Opposition to the new doctrine from the orthodox circles in the Carthaginian province and Byzacenia led to a rebellion against imperial authority after the death of Heraclius in 641, which also served to weaken the position of the Byzantines in the face of the Arab invasion.

Following the invasion of Egypt by the Arabs in 640, Christian refugees coming from Syria and Egypt arrived in Carthage and Byzacenia and preached the Monophysite doctrine with a vigour which caused much consternation in religious circles and nearly led to riots. In the midst of these disturbances Heraclius died; his son Constantine III reigned until the end of May 641, when he too died. Under Heracleonas, the Empress-Dowager Martina worked zealously to have Monotheletism adopted by the Christians of the empire. About the end of 641 George, the prefect in charge of the civil administration of the Carthaginian province, received imperial orders from Constantinople to abandon the prosecution of those Christians against whom charges of unorthodoxy had been preferred. Instead of complying, the prefect tried to quieten the agitation in his province by announcing that the letters containing the orders were apocryphal, and that the empress herself was free of all heresy. His recall to Constantinople soon afterwards only increased the agitation.

Opposition to Monotheletism in Africa was organized and led by a remarkable religious personality, St Maximus the Confessor (*c.* 580–662), who had held an important position in the court of Heraclius. It is not known when he arrived in Carthage, but by 640 he had already achieved an important standing there. When at the end of September 641 Heracleonas and his mother were overthrown and Constans II (641–68) ascended the throne, Pyrrhus, the Patriarch of Constantinople, was forced to resign his office and go into exile. In 645 he was in Carthage, and Maximus the Confessor used his presence there to advance the cause of orthodoxy by debating publicly with him the Monothelete doctrine. The disputation occurred in a conference convened in July 645, attended by the exarch Gregory and the leading personalities of the province. At the end of the conference Pyrrhus declared his abandonment of Monotheletism. It is probable that his recantation was intended to win him the help of the exarch in regaining his position; nevertheless it had a great impact on the Christians of Africa. In 646 Maximus summoned, with the, encouragement of the exarch, three provincial synods in Numidia, Byzacenia, and Mauritania in which the bishops affirmed their attachment to the orthodox doctrines. In letters which the African bishops, more than a hundred in number, subsequently wrote to the Patriarch of Constantinople and the emperor, they invited the former to renounce Monotheletism and informed the latter of their submission in matters of doctrine to the Apostolic See. During the time when the synods were being held, a new bishop of Carthage was elected; and when he announced his election to the Pope, he declared his wish to be united closely with the see of Rome and to defend the true faith.

The outcome of this doctrinal conflict was further to separate the African prefecture from the rest of the empire. Constans II, being only a boy of about fifteen at the time, did not contribute towards the prestige of imperial authority. Moreover, the empire was receiving one blow after another: Syria, Palestine, and Egypt had fallen into the hands of the Arabs; in 642 a rebellion broke out in Rome which was suppressed only with difficulty by the exarch Isaac; and in 644 a pretender to the throne appeared in the east. Under these circumstances the temptation was great for the powerful exarch Gregory to break his links with the empire. By championing the cause of orthodoxy, he enjoyed the support of the influential African Church; and Pope Theodorus evinced sympathy towards him. In 646, when the African bishops were condemning Monotheletism, Constans II was making his attachment to this doctrine known; in the same year Gregory declared himself independent, assuming the title of emperor. In this he was supported by the Roman population and the Church in Africa; it was also said in Byzacenia at the time that the Pope was party to Gregory's decision to rebel against Constantinople.[1] Gregory's rebellion constituted a serious threat to the central government; but before the dangers inherent in it were felt in Constantinople, he met his death at the hands of the Arabs in 647. After this date, the Byzantines continued to hold a limited area in Tunisia and some of the coastal towns for half a century, but they ceased to exercise effective authority in the interior.

If the Vandals left no traces behind them in the Maghrib, the numerous fortified places which the Byzantines left spoke eloquently of the insecurity and unsettlement of their period. Compared with the Vandal period, the Byzantine was one of extensive building both for defensive and religious purposes. The canals and barrages the Romans had built were repaired so as to revive agriculture; and trade with the countries of the eastern Mediterranean, which had existed under the Vandals, increased in the sixth century. Nevertheless the Byzantine period in the Maghrib was not one of great prosperity. To the destruction of the Vandal-Byzantine war, and the conflict between the Byzantine forces and the Berber tribes, were added the heavy impositions by which the inhabitants paid for the army occupying their lands and the works of construction.

During the first Roman period in the Maghrib the Berbers showed themselves ready to adopt Roman civilization and the Latin language. Christianity also spread widely among them and, as we have seen, the African provinces not only produced an important religious schismatic movement in Donatism, but also became a main centre of orthodoxy. The institutions, customs, and language which the Romans had brought with them began gradually to disappear in the districts which remained outside the reach of government during the Byzantine period. The Arab invasion completed the destruction of the Roman heritage in the Maghrib; and as the Arabs brought with them a new language of culture closely linked to a dynamic faith, and customs which were nearer than the Roman to those of the non-Romanized Berbers, no cultural traces from the Roman period apart from monuments have survived in the Maghrib. Christianity almost completely disappeared after the Arab conquest. In the sixth and seventh centuries Volubilis in Morocco was the place of refuge for Christians fleeing from Algeria and eastern Morocco. This typically Roman town seems to have been ruled in the early Arab period by a council of Christian chiefs

---

[1] Diehl, *L'Afrique byzantine*, II, 556.

and remained for a time outside the hold of the Muslim rulers. Another centre of Christianity which remained in existence for some time after the Arab conquest was Tangier. In the early part of the eighth century Tangier is known to have had an episcopate, but by 883 it had disappeared from the episcopal list which Pope Leo drew up. Whether any pockets of Christians survived beyond this date in other parts of the Maghrib is not known. However, by the twelfth century no indigenous Christians remained in the area, and when Christianity began to reappear in the Maghrib during this century, it was as a foreign religion introduced by Europeans.

4

The call of the minaret in the "West": the establishment of Arab rule in the Maghrib and Spain

Arab conquest and Berber resistance

The Arab army under 'Amr b. al-'As started the penetration into the Maghrib as soon as the conquest of Egypt was completed with the fall of Alexandria in September 642. This expansion was undertaken upon the initiative of 'Amr himself who saw in it a means of gaining greater military prestige and booty for his warriors. These motives, combined with the religious zeal for extending the domain of Islam, had been important in practically all the Arab wars of expansion so far. In the Maghrib, however, permanent conquest was slower than in other parts because of two main obstacles. The first was the struggle for power in the Muslim state following the accession of 'Uthman to the caliphate in 644, which did not end until the assassination of 'Ali, the fourth caliph, in 661. Penetration into the Maghrib remained in the period of conflict a means by which the Muslim authorities in Egypt satisfied their ambitions for booty and military prestige, and consequently it took the form of raids rather than systematic conquest. Some of these raids were long, such as the one carried out by the forces under 'Abdulla b. Sarh in 647–8. Ibn Sarh reached Tunisia, and although he defeated Exarch Gregory at the head of the Byzantine army near the town of Sbaitla, he did not attempt to establish a permanent base west of Egypt.

The Umayyads, having firmly established their control of the Muslim state since 661, started to take interest in the Maghrib in the mid-660s. In January 664 Caliph Mu'awiya removed the responsibility for the conquest of the Maghrib from the jurisdiction of the governor of Egypt. Henceforth expansion into the Maghrib was viewed within the context of the religio-imperial confrontation of the Umayyad state with the Byzantines. The conflict between the Umayyads and the Byzantines in the east was long-drawn. The Umayyad armies entered Asia Minor in 667, and by 670 had reached Constantinople which they then besieged. Simultaneously with the penetration of Asia Minor a systematic war of conquest in the Maghrib was initiated. However, when the Arab armies entered the

Maghrib for the first time to stay, the second main obstacle to their conquest came to light. This was the resistance of the strong Berber tribes. Between 643 and 667 the Arab forces which raided the Maghrib avoided the Byzantine positions. Tripoli, which 'Amr b. al-'As had taken in 643, was re-occupied by the Byzantines. 'Uqba b. Nafi', who led an Arab army into the Maghrib in 666, avoided the coast. He went to Fazzan, where he gained a booty of black slaves, and reached Gafsa in Tunisia, without attempting to engage the Byzantines. But in the context of the Umayyads' strategy, attacking the Byzantine positions was of paramount importance. The army they sent in 667 under 'Umar b. Hudaij's command penetrated deep into Tunisia, reaching as far northwards as Bizerta. It engaged the Byzantine forces at the fortress Jalula' which it captured, but for unknown reasons Ibn Hudaij retreated to Egypt in 668. The veteran 'Uqba was appointed in the following year to command the army in the Maghrib. The moment was propitious for a frontal attack on the Byzantines since Emperor Constantine IV (Pogonot, 668–88) had just withdrawn a large part of the Byzantine troops in Africa in order to fight a pretender to the imperial throne in Sicily. 'Uqba could thus occupy Byzacenia in 670 without encountering any resistance, and started the foundation of Qairawan, which he intended to use as a military base for further conquest and a centre for spreading Islam among the Berbers. Far-sighted as 'Uqba's policy was, its advantages were not appreciated in Damascus, since he did not take any Byzantine positions at a time when the war with the Byzantine empire was at its height in the east. His enemies could consequently prevail upon Caliph Mu'awiya to dismiss him.

The African Christians, feeling threatened by the Muslim invasions, were more ready to cooperate with the imperial authorities, especially since Constantine IV did not try to impose heretical doctrines on them. However, as no important reinforcements could be sent to the garrisons in Tunisia from Constantinople, which was from 674 to 679 subjected to Umayyad attacks from land and sea, Byzantine ability to resist the Muslim invaders during this period was not materially improved. The Berber tribes had therefore to fend for themselves. The Arab forces commanded by Abul-Muhajir Dinar were pushing after 'Uqba's departure into eastern Algeria. In this region they were encountered by the forces of a Berber chief called Kusaila. The records of the wars between the Arabs and Kusaila have a legendary character. They suggest however that Kusaila led sedentary tribes of Christianized Berbers from the Auras region, the Arabs defeated his forces some time in the late 670s, and he was taken captive.

Dinar retained his position in Africa until 682 when he was replaced by 'Uqba. Reinstated, 'Uqba was bent on achieving the military glory which had so far eluded him. Having reinhabited Qairawan, which had been deserted by Dinar, he set out westwards without a clear plan of conquest. He defeated a combination of Byzantine and Berber forces near Tahirt, and reached Tangier by way of the Zab. After a short stay in Tangier, where he was well received by its governor Julian (the Yulian of the Arab historians about whose position accounts are vague and contradictory), he travelled south-westwards until he reached the Atlantic Ocean at an unknown place. Before 'Uqba reached Tangier Kusaila had escaped from his camp; and having mustered a force of tribal warriors, he attacked 'Uqba while on his way back to Qairawan near the Roman fortress of Tahuda in the neighbourhood of Biskra. 'Uqba was killed with most of his men and was buried near Biskra, where his tomb-mosque, the oldest monument of Islamic architecture in this part of the Maghrib, remains to this day. Since 'Uqba's deputy in Qairawan, Zuhair b. Qais, evacuated it upon his leader's death, Kusaila could enter it without fighting. The retreat of the Arab army enabled Kusaila to found a Berber kingdom which survived until Zuhair b. Qais defeated him in about 686. As the Arab siege of Constantinople had ended some four years before 'Uqba's death, the Byzantines could send reinforcements to their fortified places and hold effectively the coastline from Susa to Bona, leaving to Kusaila the control of the interior.

The dates of Ibn Qais' reconquest of the province of Byzacenia are not certain, and it is not known whether he led any expedition to it after 683 other than the one in which he put an end to Kusaila's state. Upon the approach of the Arab army, which was reinforced by Zanata Berber warriors from Tripolitania and Cyrenaica, Kusaila withdrew from Qairawan and gave battle to the Arabs near the town of Mems in the Auras. The Byzantines left the Berbers and Arabs to fight each other without themselves interfering in the conflict. In this battle Kusaila was killed and his army routed; and after it Ibn Qais penetrated into the Auras in pursuit of Kusaila's fugitive warriors. Before returning to Qairawan he captured the Byzantine fortress of al-Kaf, but the Byzantine strongholds on the coast he did not approach. Ibn Qais died in 690 in an attack on Barqa, which Byzantine forces reoccupied during his stay in Tunisia and from it threatened to intercept the Arab army's line of communications with Egypt.

Ibn Qais' death brought home to Caliph 'Abdul-Malik (685–705) that permanent conquest of the Maghrib and its incorporation in the Arab state could not be achieved while the Byzantines held important footholds on its coast. The next Arab campaign, therefore, was intended to capture the Byzantine positions. An Arab army of about forty thousand men was assembled in Egypt soon after Ibn Qais' death, but it was kept immobile until 695 for fear it would be needed in the conflict in Iraq with the rebel 'Abdulla b. al-Zubair. The Byzantine garrisons were reinforced by

Emperor Justinian II (685–95) before the Arab army, commanded by Hassan b. al-Nu'man, appeared. When it came they did not give battle to the Arabs in the open. Thus the Arab army marched across Cyrenaica and Tripolitania without encountering any opposition. Upon entering Tunisia it attacked and captured Carthage; and even then Byzantine forces preferred to hold aloof in their remaining posts. However, Ibn al-Nu'man encountered resistance from the Jarawa Jewish tribe living in the eastern Auras. Led by a queen to whom Arab historians give the name al-Kahina (the priestess), whose capital was at Bagai, the Jarawa warriors defeated the Arab army on the river Nini. Ibn al-Nu'man escaped to Cyrenaica after this defeat, and the Byzantines reoccupied Carthage in 697.

Unlike Kusaila, al-Kahina did not follow upon her victory, nor did she seem interested in founding a larger state than the one over which she already reigned. Acting on the belief that the Arabs were only after booty, she wrought havoc in the Tunisian countryside so that the Arabs would not have an incentive to come back. At the same time she did not molest the Muslims in Qairawan, possibly in order not to provoke a war of revenge. Hassan b. al-Nu'man remained in Cyrenaica, in the place called Qusur Hassan (Hassan's palaces), until Caliph 'Abdul-Malik sent him reinforcements in 698. When he made his second campaign into Tunisia, al-Kahina seemed so uncertain of the outcome of the war that she ordered her two sons to go over to the Arab side, but she herself fought to save her kingdom and repulse the invaders. Her second encounter with Ibn al-Nu'man took place near Gabis. She was defeated, pursued by Arab warriors, and eventually killed at a place in the Auras which came to be called Bir al-Kahina (al-Kahina's well).

With al-Kahina's death the last serious Berber attempt to resist the Arabs during the period of conquest came to an end. Before Ibn al-Nu'man left Tunisia in 705 he recaptured Carthage and founded the town of Tunis near it which he intended to become the base of the Arab fleet in the Maghrib. In order to cut the isthmus which connected the lake of Tunis with the Mediterranean, he had Coptic artisans brought from Egypt, whom he also employed in founding workshops for building ships. The Arab naval supremacy in the Mediterranean at the time forced the Byzantines to evacuate their remaining possessions on the Maghriban coast, taking their Christian inhabitants to the islands of the Mediterranean. Between 704 and 711 Ibn al-Nu'man's successor Musa b. Nusair overran the western parts of the Maghrib. He followed the route which 'Uqba had taken to reach Tangier; and having occupied this town, he appointed as its governor the Berber Tariq b. Ziyad who was later to distinguish himself in the conquest of Spain. Count Julian this time resisted the Arabs, but we find him now holding Ceuta. Whether Musa b. Nusair attacked Ceuta or not is not known. From Tangier he marched southwards reaching Wadi Dra'a and Tafilalt. He seems to have been contented to accept from the Berber chiefs through whose territory he passed a token submission and conversion to Islam in return for confirming them in their chieftaincies.

Kharijite-Berber reaction to Arab domination

The Islamization of the Berbers went further than their Arabization, and in many ways the latter process was the product of the former. 'Uqba's heroic martyrdom impressed the Berbers and might have caused some of them to adopt Islam. A greater inducement to Islamization was enlistment in the Arab army and being treated (at least during the period of conquest) on an equal footing with the Arabs in the distribution of booty. The Arab conquest of Spain in the eighth century especially contributed towards the Islamization of the Berbers, since it opened to their warriors a new field for fighting and gain. It also introduced into their midst warriors from Arabia who possessed a good knowledge of Islam and an unadulterated mastery of the Arabic language. The Berbers who were the more readily willing to accept Islam were those who belonged to what French historians call ' l'Afrique oubliée ' (the forgotten Africa), consisting of the nomadic tribes of Tripolitania, Cyrenaica, southern Tunisia, and the greater part of present-day Morocco. Nomadic, and having acquired no real attachment to the Christian faith or Latin civilization, the price which these tribes paid in a nominal conversion to Islam was trivial by comparison with the advantages they gained from enlisting in the armies of the new conquerors.

Although 'Uqba founded Qairawan partly in order to spread Islam amongst the Berbers, it does not appear that any systematic effort was made in this direction until after the conquest of Spain. Since Islam did not develop an institution similar to the Christian Church, conversion to this religion depended on the initiative of the rulers or, as was to happen after the thirteenth century, on the work of voluntary preachers such as the *shaikhs* of the Sufi (mystical) orders. Consequently, in the newly acquired territories a profound knowledge of Islamic doctrines could become widespread only after the consolidation of Muslim rule; in the period of conquest a nominal conversion was considered sufficient. During the reign of the pious Caliph 'Umar b. 'Abdul-'Aziz (717–20) the first serious attempt at preaching Islam systematically to the Berbers was made. In 718 the Caliph appointed Isma'il b. 'Abdulla governor of the Maghrib, and sent with him ten learned theologians to instruct the Berbers in the precepts of the Muslim faith. Although the Berbers' knowledge of Islamic doctrines remained superficial during the first century of Arab rule, it seems that attachment to the new religion was widespread and its political tenets were taken seriously by them. Their acceptance of the stringent Kharijite doctrine, and the fact that they fought their Arab rulers under its banner in the middle of the eighth century, point to this fact.

Kharijism was a religious and political movement which harassed the Umayyad dynasty nearly throughout the period when it was in power from 660 to 750. The movement had its origins in the conflict over the caliphate between the fourth caliph 'Ali and Mu'awiya, the head of the Qarashite house of Banu Umayya and the governor of Syria, which followed the assassination of the third caliph 'Uthman in 655. At the battle of Siffin near the Euphrates in 657 a section of 'Ali's followers, numbering about 12,000, rejected his leadership when he agreed to submit to arbitration his right to the caliphate. The name of this group "Khawarij" (sing. "Khariji", "outgoer") was given to them when they withdrew from the fighting and went to settle in Karura', a village two miles from Kufa. The Kharijites were later attacked by 'Ali and many of them were massacred; in 661 he was assassinated by one of them.

The Kharijites developed into a doctrinally narrow and uncompromising movement. Unlike the majority of other Muslims they believed that the mere profession of the faith did not entitle one to be treated in times of war and in taxation as a Muslim, and considered as infidels all professing Muslims who did not perform the rites of Islam. Politically they differed from both the Sunnite Muslims and the Shi'ites[1] over the question of eligibility for the caliphate: the Sunnites believed that the caliphate was the preserve of Qarashite Arabs, whereas the Shi'ites restricted it to the descendants of 'Ali. The Kharijites began by rejecting government altogether, but later realized that it was necessary. Believing that authority came only from God, who alone was the lawgiver, they made the legitimacy of the caliphate dependent on the strict application of the religious law. They believed the caliph should be elected by the community, and that any Muslim of good faith was eligible for this position regardless of whether he was an Arab or not. The Kharijites also put forward the view that Muslims have the right to rebel against an unjust caliph. Accordingly they led several rebellions against the Umayyads in Iraq and Persia in the course of the first half of the eighth century. The severity with which their rebellions were put down, and their own uncompromising doctrinal position, caused many of them to emigrate to distant lands conquered by the Muslims, and a group of them found refuge in the Maghrib.

Kharijite beliefs appealed to the Berbers, especially the doctrine that non-Arabs could become caliphs and Muslims had the right to depose an

---

[1] Shi'ism is the cult of the fourth caliph 'Ali. Shi'ites believe that only 'Ali and his descendants were entitled to be the Prophet's successors; thus to them the first three caliphs, as well as the Umayyads and 'Abbasids, were usurpers.

unjust *imam*.[1] But they also had economic grievances against the Arab administration. In 720 Yazid b. Abu Muslim was appointed governor of the Maghrib, and in order to increase the revenues he levied on the Berbers the *jizya* (poll-tax) in addition to the *kharaj* (land-tax).[2] Ibn Abu Muslim also had the Berber warriors tattoo their names on the right arm and on the left the words ' The Guard of Yazid '. This humiliated the Berber warriors in the army so much that they ended by murdering him. After this outrage the Berbers remained quiet until the appointment in 734 of 'Ubaid-Allah b. Habbab as governor of the Maghrib. He too followed a policy of extortion, and during his governorship the Maghrib was made to supply slaves to the eastern parts of the Muslim empire, captured mostly from Berbers in Sus in southern Morocco. His deputy in Tangier, 'Umar al-Muradi, who rigorously applied this rapacious policy, was assassinated in 740. A general Berber rebellion in that district immediately followed.

The rebellion in the district of Tangier was at first led by Maisara, the chief of the Kharijite Masghara tribe. Maisara occupied Tangier, but shortly afterwards he was killed by his own men. Led by Khalid al-Zanati the Berber tribes in northern Morocco subsequently advanced towards the Shaliff where they were met by an army composed of Arabs of pure race. In the ensuing battle, called the Battle of the Nobles, the Arab army was routed. In 741 another Arab army sent from Syria with reinforcements from Egypt and Tripolitania, was defeated by the Kharijite Berbers near the Sibu river; but in the following year a new governor of the Maghrib, Hanzala b. Safwan, arrived in Qairawan and could check the Berber rebellion. Having assembled their forces in the Zab, the Berber rebels advanced on Qairawan in two groups, one led by the chief of the Huwwara Berbers and the other by 'Ukasha al-Fazzari, an Arab who had led the vanguard of the Syrian army in the battle of Sibu, but defected afterwards and adopted Kharijite doctrines. In 742 Ibn Safwan defeated both armies: al-Fazzari's at al-Qarn near Qairawan, and the other at al-Asnam, about five kilometres from Qairawan. These two battles came to be hailed by Arab chroniclers as being among the most decisive in the history of Islam, equal in importance to the battle of Badr in which the Prophet defeated his Meccan opponents.

During the governorship of Ibn Safwan's successor, 'Abdul-Rahman b. Habib (745–55), the 'Abbasids took over the command of the Muslim

[1] Originally meaning the leader in prayer, "imam" came also to mean the political and religious head of the Muslim community.

[2] The *jizya* was a tax which Christians, Jews, and followers of other tolerated religions paid as a sign of their subjection to, and in return for protection by, the head of the Muslim community. Converts to Islam were usually exempted from it. The *kharaj*, on the other hand, was generally collected in the first century A.H. from new converts to Islam who were left in possession of their lands.

community without any particular repercussions in the Maghrib. When this governor was assassinated by his two brothers in December 755, the Berbers resumed their rebellion. One of Ibn Habib's brothers took refuge with the Warfajuma tribe in southern Tunisia, and with their help he captured Qairawan in 657-8. The Warfajuma Berbers, who belonged to the Sufrite branch of Kharijism, outraged other Muslims, even other Kharijites, by the atrocities which they committed and their desecration of the Grand Mosque of Qairawan where they kept their mounts. They were driven out from this city in 758 by Berbers from Tripolitania belonging to the Ibadite branch of Kharijism, but the latter in their turn were forced by Muhammad b. al-Ash'ath, the governor of Egypt, to evacuate the town. After capturing Qairawan, Ibn al-Ash'ath led systematic attacks on the Berbers in Tunisia by which he brought them back to submission. Kharijism lost more ground in Tunisia during the governorship of Yazid b. al-Muhallab (772-5), but it remained strong in the extreme south of the country.

To the west of Tunisia the rebellious tribes remained in full control. Since 765 the Banu Yifrin and Maghila tribes, both of which were Kharijites, held Tlemsen. The governor al-Aghlab b. Sālim (765-8) led two unsuccessful campaigns against them. When he was killed as a result of a riot in his army, his successor 'Umar b. Hafs (768-72) could achieve a *modus vivendi* with these tribes by means of a bribe of 40,000 dirhams to the leader of the rebels, Abu Qurra al-Yifrindi. Besides Tlemsen two main centres of Kharijism appeared about the middle of the eighth century. In about 757 a Sufrite Kharijite from Meknes, 'Isa b. Yazid, arrived as a refugee in the oasis of Tafilalt. Having found there about four thousand Sufrites willing to accept him as leader, he set out to establish the town of Sijilmasa (present-day Rissani) as a Kharijite settlement. In 806 or 807 (A.H. 191) control of Sijilmasa fell into the hands of Sam'un b. Yazlan, nicknamed Midrar, also a Sufrite Zanata coming from Meknes. The dynasty he founded ruled Sijilmasa until it was captured in 976-7 (A.H. 366) by a Maghrawa Berber called Mas'ud b. Fulful. Kharijism was the accepted doctrine during the greater part of the Midrar dynasty's rule, and only the last ruler, Abu Muhammad al-Mu'izz-Billah, rejected it. In 960 the Fatimid commander Jawhar conquered Sijilmasa, but the Fatimids held it only until 963 when it reverted to the rule of the Midrar dynasty. It is not known whether Kharijism survived in Sijilmasa after 976, but it had a centre near the town. Al-Bakri, writing in the eleventh century, mentions the existence of a Sufrite Kharijite settlement to its north on the route to Fez at a place called Maghilat b. Tijaman.[1]

The second important centre of Kharijism which appeared about the

---

[1] 'Abdulla b. 'Abdul-'Aziz al-Bakri, *Kitab al-Mughrib fi dhikr bilad Ifriqya wa 'l-Maghrib* (Paris, 1965), p. 147.

middle of the eighth century was at Tahirt, capital of the Rustamid state. The founder of this state, 'Abdul-Rahman b. Rustam, was a Persian by origin who adopted the Kharijite doctrine before he came to the Maghrib. He was governor of Qairawan between 758 and 761 when the Ibadites controlled it. In 761 he occupied Tiaret, an old Roman establishment about 300 km south-west of Algiers, with the help of Zanata Berbers, especially the Huwwara of Tripolitania, and founded about ten km to the west of Tiaret his own capital Tahirt (present-day Tagdempt). This town soon became the "metropolis of Kharijism as Qairawan was for Orthodoxy".[1] The Arab governors of Tunisia, realizing their inability to defeat the Rustamids, recognized the accomplished fact and maintained friendly relations with them. In 811 the Rustamids attacked Tripoli at the head of Huwwara warriors. The Aghlabids, who had by then become the masters of Tunisia, had to buy peace from them by recognizing their rule over the territory in the Maghrib outside the parts of Tunisia and Algeria which they governed, and the parts of Morocco held by the Idrisids. Occasionally Zanata tribesmen rebelled against the Rustamids, but the state was stable and it survived until its invasion by the Fatimids in 909.

The Rustamid state was a theocratic one. Ibn Rustam assumed the title of *imam* in 776, and after his death in 784 all his successors did the same. In theory Kharijite *imams* were elected by the elders of the community, but in fact the imamate of Tahirt was hereditary in the founder's line. Some of the Rustamid *imams*, like the fifth Abul-Yaqzan (d. 894), assumed a pontificate over the rest of the Kharijites in the Maghrib, and the Sufrites of Sijilmasa paid him tithes. The *imams* were well instructed, and they cultivated, in addition to religious studies, knowledge of such secular subjects as the art of government, mathematics, astronomy, and astrology. The Muslim law was strictly applied within the domains of the state: the adulterers were stoned, the hands of thieves were cut off, and in war pillage and massacring of non-warriors were not permitted.

Tahirt was a flourishing town, well provided with water and rich in fruit gardens. It was also economically prosperous since goods coming across the Sahara and products from the north were exchanged in it. The prosperity of Tahirt, and the fact that it was ruled by Muslims of Persian descent, attracted to it many Arabized Persians from Iraq. Christians also settled in it, since the Rustamids accorded them the protection for which the Muslim law provided; and it is related that the *iman* Abu al-Hatim, Abul-Yaqzan's son, consulted them in state affairs.

The Rustamid state controlled the area to the east of Tahirt as far as Tripoli, including the island of Jirba. Thus it controlled the line of communication by land between Tunisia and Egypt. It was over the request of

---

[1] Georges Marçais, *La Berbérie musulmane et l'Orient au Moyen Age* (Paris, 1946), p. 104.

the Aghlabid ruler Ibrahim (895–6) to be given the right of passage along the seacoast of Tripoli that conflict between the Aghlabids and the Rustamids started, resulting in the latters' defeat. This military setback made it easy for the Fatimids to conquer the Rustamids a few years later. The Umayyad rulers in Spain entered into relations with the Rustamids, whom they viewed as their natural allies against the Aghlabids, the agents of the 'Abbasids. When two of 'Abdul-Rahman b. Rustam's sons visited Cordova in 822 the Umayyad Caliph 'Abdul-Rahman II spent a million dinars on buying them gifts.

When Tahirt was captured by the Fatimids in 909, the Rustamids were massacred, and those who could escape took refuge with the Sadrata bedouin, who were Kharijites of the Ibadite branch, in the oasis of Wargala. The town of Sadrata (or Isdertain) became during the tenth century the most important centre of Ibadite Kharijism around which the Mzab settlement grew. What has survived of the Rustamid state today is the Ibadites living in Mzab and a smaller group in the island of Jirba. The Ibadites in Mzab have undergone considerable transformation since the destruction of the Rustamid state: they have become an exclusive community, organized along tribal lines and governed by elders who endorse a rigorously strict moral code. In Mzab, as previously in Tahirt and Sijil-masa, the Kharijites were active in the trans-Saharan trade. The merchants of Wargala traded in Negro slaves until modern times when the demand for slaves in the north gradually disappeared. Nowadays the Mzab settlement is a self-sufficient and prosperous theocratic community, many of whose members are money lenders.

The Aghlabids

At the end of the eighth century Spain and the western part of the Maghrib had shaken off 'Abbasid rule. Only Tunisia remained loyal, but even there the authority of Baghdad became nominal at the turn of the century when the garrison of Tunis rebelled against the governor Ibn Muqatil. Ibrahim b. Aghlab, governor of the Zab, helped in suppressing the rebellion. But instead of restoring Ibn Muqatil, he usurped his position. The caliph recognized Ibn Aghlab as governor of Tunisia in 800. He had little choice in so doing, but Ibn Aghlab made it easier for his suzerain to accept the accomplished fact by foregoing the subsidy which Tunisia had been receiving from Egypt and undertaking to pay tribute to Baghdad.

After Ibrahim b. Aghlab the government of Tunisia became hereditary in his line. Assuming the title of "amir", the eleven Aghlabids who ruled Tunisia until 909 preserved their autonomy in relation to the central government of the caliphate, although they paid the tribute regularly and had the prayer said in the name of the 'Abbasid caliphs. It was only during the time when Aghlabid territory was falling into the hands of the Fatimids at the beginning of the tenth century that the 'Abbasid caliphs could exercise their sovereign rights in Tunisia. In 902 the Aghlabid amir Ibrahim III, having become unpopular on account of his tyranny, abdicated in favour of his son 'Abdulla II upon the command of the caliph. Before this time the interference of the 'Abbasid caliphs in the affairs of the Aghlabid state was limited to sending aid, as happened in 859 when Tunisia was struck by an earthquake, and to the symbolic command of al-Mu'tasim in 864 that a new wing should be added to the Zaituna mosque in Tunis.

Aghlabid territory comprised the greater part of Tunisia (the southern parts being under the control of the Rustamid state) and eastern Algeria to the Zab. Internally the state was beset by the rebellions of the regular Arab army (the *jund*) stationed in Tunis, who were extortionist to the population and generally hostile to their rulers. The insubordination of the troops was encouraged by the unpopularity of the Aghlabid rulers with the religious circles of the country, especially of Qairawan. By the ninth century this town had become an important centre of religious learning. The study of Muslim law, especially the Malikite rite, flourished in Qairawan, and the major theological controversies of the Muslim east echoed loudly there. In this zealous religious atmosphere the personal conduct of the Aghlabid amirs, most of whom led a life of pleasure and drank wine, was held amiss. They were also condemned on account of contravening the Muslim law with respect to taxation, especially the imposition under the second amir, 'Abdulla b. Ibrahim (812–17), of a fixed cash levy on the crops instead of the authorized tithe collected in kind.

To mitigate the hostility of the religious dignitaries, the Aghlabid princes were lavish in their construction of religious buildings: among others the great mosques of Qairawan and Tunis (the Zaituna mosque) were completely rebuilt. For the protection of the country they constructed fortresses on the Tunisian coastline, which were mostly built on Byzantine foundations; and after two rebellions of the *jund* in 802 and 809, Ibrahim b. Aghlab built a fortified palace at Raqqada near Qairawan where the ruling amir henceforth resided. Of special significance was the construction of the *ribat* of Susa in 821 by Ziyadat Allah I (817–38). The institution of the *ribat*, as a fortified monastery where warriors were trained for the holy war, was to become important in the defences of the Maghrib against Christian attacks in the sixteenth century. Under the Aghlabids it seems to have been designed to inculcate the spirit of holy war in the Arab army, and to prepare them for the conquest of Sicily.

Before the Aghlabid period the Arabs had attacked Sicily on several occasions without succeeding in establishing Arab rule there. Ziyadat

Allah I undertook the conquest of this island after the suppression of the rebellion of the *jund* led by Mansur al-Tunbudhi in the fort of Tunbudh near Tunis from 824 to 826. The rebellion was put down with the help of Berber warriors from the Jarid. A year later the amir organized the former rebels in the expedition which was sent to Sicily in 827. By appointing the *qadi* (religious judge) Asad b. Furat to command the expedition against Sicily, Ziyadat Allah channelled the zeal of the pious, as well as the energies of the troops, in a direction which brought profit to the state. The expedition was successful, and the main towns of Sicily were captured in rapid succession: Palermo, which became the capital of the Arabs in Sicily, was taken in 831, Messina in 843, and Castrogiovanni in 859. Finding themselves face to face with Christian Europe, the Aghlabids attempted to extend their rule over the Italian mainland. Raids across the straits of Messina were made annually. In one of them (846) Rome was attacked and the Basilica of St Peter sacked. Several attempts by the Italian principalities and the Carolingians to drive the Aghlabids out of Sicily all failed. Instead Syracuse was captured in 878 and Taormina in 902. Thus by the time the Fatimids conquered Tunisia from the Aghlabids, the whole of Sicily had fallen into Arab hands.

The attention which the Aghlabid rulers gave to the development of agriculture, especially the building of hydraulic works on Roman foundations, together with the conquest of Sicily made their period a prosperous one. Culturally Tunisia was transformed into a Muslim and predominantly Arabic-speaking country. The other parts of the Maghrib were to await the Arab tribal invasions of the mid-eleventh century for their greater Arabization, and the religious zeal of the Almoravids and the Almohads for the development of better knowledge of Islamic doctrines.

The Idrisids

Although the Idrisids posed in the ninth century as the champions of orthodoxy in Morocco and attempted the suppression of Kharijism, their state might not have been founded without the separation of Morocco from the centre of 'Abbasid authority in Tunisia by the Kharijite rebellion and the appearance of the Kharijite state in Tahirt. The founder of the Idrisid state, Idris b. 'Adbulla, was a 'Alawite *sharif*[1] who escaped from Arabia after the battle of Fakh near Mecca in 786 between the partisans of 'Ali, led by his great-grandson Husain, and the 'Abbasids. The persecution of the 'Alawites in Arabia and Iraq forced Idris b. 'Abdulla to go to Egypt, accompanied by his liberated slave Rāshid. From there they travelled in disguise to the extreme west of the Maghrib where they knew they would

[1] A 'Alawite is a descendant of 'Ali, the fourth caliph. The 'Alawites are *sharifs*, i.e. descendants of the Prophet, since 'Ali was married to the Prophet's daughter, Fatima.

be outside the reach of 'Abbasid authority. By the end of 788 they were already safely settled in the town of Walili (ancient Volubilis and present-day Qasr Far'un) on mount Zarhun under the protection of Auruba Berbers.

Idris b. 'Abdulla was recognized in February 789 as religious and political leader (*imam*) of the Auruba. Shortly afterwards other Berber tribes living between Fez and Meknes accepted his leadership. Both his noble descent and profound knowledge of Islamic doctrines contributed to his prestige with these zealous, but generally ignorant, Muslim tribes. With their help he extended his authority by force of arms over Tadla, inhabited mostly by Berbers who were still either Jewish or Christian. In 790 he conquered Tlemsen, which was under the control of the Banu Yifrin and Maghrawa tribes, and had then a Maghrawa chief by the name of Muhammad b. Khazar. Before he died in July 793, he brought under his control northern Morocco outside the coastal strip and to the south as far as the Bu Ragrag river.

Idris b. 'Abdulla died poisoned by an agent of the 'Abbasid caliph Harun al-Rashid or of the Aghlabids. He had no male heir to succeed him, but his loyal freedman Rāshid could prevail upon the tribes which supported his master to postpone choosing another *imam* until after the confinement of Idris' concubine who was pregnant. The boy born on 15 October 793 was named Idris after his father. Rāshid, who brought him up, exercised authority in his name until he (Rāshid) was murdered by an agent of the Aghlabids in 802. Two years later when only eleven years old, the young Idris was recognized *imam*.

About Idris II's reign somewhat more is known than of his father's. The Idrisid state took a concrete shape during his reign as a result of the building of the capital Fez, on which work was started in 808. Its site had already been chosen by his father, who possibly also began its actual construction but died before getting very far with it. The arrival of Arab refugees from Spain after a rebellion which took place in Cordova in 818, and from Tunisia in the wake of the rebellion of 824–6, gave the state an Arab character which it did not have before. Idris II took an Arab bodyguard to himself and an Arab minister by the name of 'Umair b. Mus'ab, commonly known as al-Maljum. The Arab refugees settled mostly in the capital whose two main quarters came to be called after them: 'Adwat al-Andalus (the Andalusian Bank) was called after the refugees from Spain and 'Adwat al-Qarawiyin (the Qairawanian Bank) after those who came from Tunisia. Idris II led several attacks against Kharijite conglomerations in which he is said to have been successful. When he died in August 828 his state included the area between the Shaliff river in Algeria and Sus in southern Morocco. The Arabization of Morocco begins with Idris II's reign, and by the time of his death the district of Fez was becoming predominantly Arabic-speaking.

Upon Idris II's death the Idrisid state was broken up into nine small principalities ruled by nine of his thirteen sons. Muhammad, the eldest, ruled Fez and exercised only nominal control over the others. Under him and his successors Fez was transformed from a primitive town into a flourishing capital, and after the foundation of the Qarawiyin mosque in 859 and the Andalus mosque three years later, it began to emerge as an important centre of religious learning. Shortly before its conquest by the Fatimids in 917 the state of Fez was weakened by conflict with the Kharijites. In about 900 a Kharijite of Andalusian origin called 'Abdul-Razzaq al-Fihri rebelled in the Madyuna mountains near Fez. After taking Safru he advanced to the capital and occupied 'Adwat al-Andalus. The Kharijites were driven out from Fez by the Idrisid *imam* Yahya b. Idris (d. 904), but Kharijism was not extinguished. It seems that the resurgence of Kharijism in the domains of the Idrisid state in its latter years was a consequence of this state's Arabization. To the Berber tribes which had supported Idris b. 'Abdulla against the 'Abbasids, the profession of Kharijism became an expression of their resentment at the increasing domination of this state by the Arabs, and the enshrinement in it of the concept of the legitimacy of Arab rule very much as was the case in the territories under 'Abbasid government.

The Fatimids

At the end of the ninth century A.D. the Isma'ilis too, persecuted in the east, sought to create a centre for their activities in the Maghrib. The Isma'ilis were an extremist religious group which split off from the main body of the Shi'ites over succession to the leadership upon the death of the sixth *imam* in 765. They recognized his eldest son Isma'il as the seventh *imam*, although other Shi'ites considered him, on moral grounds, to be unworthy of the imamate. They unwaveringly opposed the 'Abbasids, whom they considered usurpers of the caliphate, and attempted to gain ascendancy in the Muslim community by clandestine dissemination of their doctrines. From about the end of the ninth century the centre of the Isma'ilis was in Salamiyya, a small town between Hums and Hama in present-day Syria. From there they sent *da'is* (religious propagandists) to various parts of the 'Abbasid empire, especially Iraq, Persia, and Yemen, to establish contacts with religious groups and to win Muslims to their cause. One of these missionaries, al-Hasan b. Zakaria, commonly called Abu 'Abdulla al-Shi'i, was assigned the task of making contact with the Kutama Berber tribe living in Little Kabylia.[1]

Abu 'Abdulla, a Yemeni from San'a', made his first contacts with the tribe through some of its notables when in Mecca on pilgrimage in 893–4.

[1] The area between Sitif (Setif) and the Mediterranean in present-day Algeria.

The meeting was not fortuitous, for two Isma'ili *da'is* had been sent to that tribe, which was well known for its past opposition to both the Umayyad and the 'Abbasid caliphs under the banner of Kharijism. Following up these contacts, Abu 'Abdulla travelled to the Kutama homeland, arriving there in 901. He established his base in Ikjan (the Tzajian of the Romans) where he preached Isma'ili doctrines and recruited warriors. The Kutama Berbers accepted his leadership because he could instruct them in the tenets of the faith and administered the Muslim law among them, and also because the doctrines which he preached, like the Kharijite doctrines which they had previously adopted, represented a cause incompatible with the authority of the caliphs in the east.

For two years after his arrival in Kabylia Abu 'Abdulla remained on the defensive *vis-à-vis* the attacks of the Aghlabids from Tunisia. In 903 he felt sufficiently strong to take the offensive against them. He conquered the Tunisian towns one after the other until in 909 he captured Qairawan and destroyed the last vestige of 'Abbasid authority in the Maghrib. His success in winning over the Kutama tribe induced the chief of the Isma'ilis in Salamiyya, 'Ubaidalla Sa'id, to travel to the Maghrib to lead in person the Isma'ili movement there. Unable to join Abu 'Abdulla in the north he travelled in the south to Sijilmasa, where he was imprisoned by its Kharijite ruler al-Yasa' (883–910). He remained a prisoner in Sijilmasa until Abu 'Abdulla, having completed the conquest of Tunisia and Tahirt, attacked Sijilmasa in August 910, killed al-Yasa', and liberated 'Ubaidalla.

After his release 'Ubaidalla Sa'id assumed the leadership of the Isma'ili state, called himself the Mahdi,[1] and had the prayer said in his own name. When Abu 'Abdulla showed signs of disaffection, because of his loss of power and possibly also because he questioned 'Ubaidalla's claim to be the expected Mahdi, he was assassinated together with his brother in February 911. Subsequently 'Ubaidalla consolidated Abu 'Abdulla's conquests and founded in 915–16 a new capital on the eastern coast of Tunisia which he called Mahdiyya. The state which he founded was out-and-out Shi'ite: he assumed the title of *imam* and claimed, with what measure of accuracy it is not possible to ascertain, that he was a descendant of Fatima, the Prophet's daughter. Hence the name of the dynasty, which has also been known in history as 'Ubaidiyya.

In Abu 'Abdulla's lifetime his *da'is* attempted to penetrate among the inhabitants of Tunisia and win them over to Shi'ism. Before his death these efforts had achieved some measure of success even in Qairawan, the centre of orthodox Islam in the country. Unlike his predecessor, the Mahdi lacked the patience to convert his subjects to Shi'ism through methodical preaching; he also showed disrespect in public to the memory of the

---

[1] "The divinely guided one" who appears to give victory to the faith, and to reign over all Muslims in justice. To the Shi'ites the Mahdi was the hidden imam revealed.

Prophet's companions and attempted to suppress the characteristically orthodox forms of worship. An example of his severity in punishing the upholders of orthodox Islam in Tunisia was the treatment of the jurist Muhammad al-Hudhaili, whom he had flogged naked in the Grand Mosque of Qairawan because he pronounced a *fatwa* (an opinion on a point of Muslim law) according to the Malikite rite, notwithstanding that most of the Muslims in Tunisia belonged to this rite.

The Mahdi seems to have viewed the state which he founded in Tunisia merely as a stepping-stone to the conquest of Egypt, and eventually the destruction of the 'Abbasid caliphate. In the winter of 913–14, before he founded his capital, he led a campaign against Egypt and occupied Alexandria. However, he was soon driven out by a 'Abbasid army sent against him by al-Muqtadir (908–32). After this setback he settled down to the task of political organization in Tunisia and the conquest of the rest of the Maghrib.

For forty years the Fatimids attempted to establish their hegemony over Morocco without achieving any permanent success. In this endeavour they faced two major obstacles: the hostile Zanata Berbers and the influence of the newly resuscitated Umayyad state in Spain under its illustrious monarch 'Abdul-Rahman III. In 917 the Fatimid armies attacked Nuqur[1] on the Mediterranean coast of Morocco and killed its ruler Sa'id b. Salih b. Mansur. The state over which Sa'id b. Salih had ruled dated back to 710. It was orthodox and had been able hitherto to hold its own against the Kharijites and Idrisids. 'Abdul-Rahman III had established friendly relations with this state as part of his policy of resisting Fatimid expansion northwards, and when the Fatimids conquered Nuqur in 917, Sa'id b. Salih's three sons escaped to Spain. A few months later they returned to Morocco and reoccupied Nuqur. The youngest, Salih, who became its ruler, proclaimed 'Abdul-Rahman's suzerainty over the territory under his rule.

The Miknasa Berber tribe, under the leadership of its chief Masala b. Habus, acted as agents of the Fatimids and conquered northern Morocco in their name. In 917 Masala besieged Fez and forced its Idrisid ruler Yahya b. Idris to recognize the suzerainty of the Fatimid Mahdi, and then deposed him in 921. Masala's successor in the leadership of the Miknasa, his cousin Musa b. Abul-'Afiya, conquered Tlemsen in 931. Shortly afterwards he recognized the suzerainty of the Umayyads in Spain in an attempt to liberate himself from Fatimid control. This rebellion was the beginning of a conflict within the Miknasa tribe between the faction led by Abul-'Afiya, and another led by Masala's nephew Hamīd, who governed Tahirt for the Fatimids. In 933 Abul-'Afiya was forced by the arrival of Hamīd's forces to evacuate Fez; but in the following year, when the Mahdi died, a rebellion in Fez once more shook off the control of the Fatimids.

---

[1] This town has been destroyed, but its ruins are extant.

Although in 935 the Fatimid commander Maisur recovered Fez from its usurper Ahmad b. Bakr al-Judhami and defeated Abul-'Afiya, forcing him to go into hiding in the basin of the Mulawiyya, Fatimid control over Morocco remained precarious. The Umayyads established garrisons in Malila and Ceuta, the two important ports in northern Morocco, in order to direct resistance to the Fatimids more effectively and to hinder any attempt on their part to invade the Spanish mainland. Consequently the suzerainty of the Umayyads came to be recognized in most of the central and western Maghrib, even in the vicinity of Oran and Algiers. In 947 an expedition led by the Fatimid commander Ziri was able to re-establish Fatimid authority over the central Maghrib. Subsequently, Ziri was placed in charge of Morocco and Tahirt, but could exercise little authority until a major expedition in 958–9, led by the Fatimid general Jawhar, established Fatimid rule over Morocco for the first time.

Abu 'Abdulla's victory over the Aghlabids occasioned an uprising in Sicily in favour of the Fatimids, and the inhabitants of the island chose a Shi'ite named Abu al-Fawaris to be their ruler. But the Mahdi could not rest while Sicily was ruled by a non-Isma'ili, though a Shi'ite, and so he sent a Berber from Kutama called Hasan b. Ahmad to replace Abu al-Fawaris. The Arabs in Sicily, who found it difficult to say prayers in the name of the Mahdi, could not accept as governor a Berber who discriminated against them. Consequently, in 912–13 they rose in open rebellion, and elected as ruler one of themselves, Ahmad b. Qarhab, who professed submission to the 'Abbasids, hoping thereby to receive help from Baghdad. Ibn Qarhab's regime lasted a very short period, and the Fatimid governor Abu Sa'id brought the island to submission. Subsequently it became a base for the Fatimid fleet and a source of minerals and fruits.

The onslaught upon orthodox Islam in Tunisia which was initiated by the Mahdi was carried further by his son Abul-Qasim (934–46). Several Muslim theologians were assassinated during his reign, but persecution increased the resistance of Tunisian Muslims to the Isma'ili doctrines and to Fatimid rule. The victims of this persecution came to be looked upon by Tunisian Muslims as martyrs, and their memory was kept alive by tales which exaggerated their numbers and piety. Religious oppression was accompanied by economic extortion. Besides what was required for the administration, the Fatimids needed money to finance their numerous campaigns in the west and east, and for the fleet which defended their coasts. Consequently, in addition to the taxes authorized by the *shari'a* (Muslim law) they introduced a system of indirect taxation. They collected a tax on the right of pasturage by the nomads and on the sale of manufactured goods, tolls from travellers on certain roads, and fees on government concessions. To this was added the nefarious system of selling government offices.

Armed resistance to the Fatimids in the eastern Maghrib was organized by the Kharijites. The leader was a man from the oasis of Tuzar in southern Tunisia called Abu Yazid, popularly nicknamed Abu Himara (the man with the ass). Since the days of the Mahdi he had been noted by the Fatimids as a dangerous agitator, for he was known to have travelled in the Algerian part of the Fatimid state and tried to rouse the Berbers against their rulers. During Abul-Qasim's reign he raised an army of Berbers from Algeria, conquered the northern parts of Tunisia, and in 944 laid siege to the Fatimid capital of Mahidyya. The siege lasted until the following year when the zeal of Abu Yazid's followers abated. Hoping to receive support from the inhabitants of Qairawan against its garrison he laid siege to that town. During the siege Abul-Qasim died, and his son and successor Isma'il al-Mansur took up the fight against the Kharijites with fresh impetus. Abu Yazid was defeated near Qairawan on 15 August 946 and was forced to escape. A year later he died from wounds he received in battle, and with his death the movement he had led collapsed.

Al-Mansur's successor al-Mu'izz (953–75), whose reign marks the zenith of Fatimid domination in the Maghrib, was able to realize the plan which the dynasty had cherished since its foundation, namely the conquest of Egypt. Egypt was ruled from 935 to 969 by the Turkish dynasty of the Ikshids, under nominal 'Abbasid suzerainty. Muhammad Ikshid, the founder of the dynasty, died in 946, and his two sons who ruled after him in succession were only the nominal rulers of the country, as real authority was held by an Abyssinian eunuch called Abul-Misk Kafur. The state of chaos existing in Egypt under the last of the Ikshids made the conquest of the country by the Fatimid army commanded by Jawhar an easy task. In July 969 Jawhar completed the conquest of Egypt and entered Fustat, its capital. Immediately afterwards he started to build a new capital which he at first called al-Mansuriyya, but it was renamed al-Qahira al-Mu'iziyya after the Fatimid caliph al-Mu'izz made his entry into it: hence the Arabic name al-Qahira (Cairo). Jawhar also laid the foundations of the Azhar mosque.

The Fatimids ruled in Egypt until their state was destroyed by Saladin in 1171. In the Maghrib they left to rule in their name the Berber chief Bologuin, whose father Ziri had served them loyally in Morocco. The Zirids, as the dynasty came to be called, proved to be competent rulers, and succeeded in making a stable state of an area which included the whole of present-day Tunisia and eastern Algeria. For the first thirty years they governed this territory in the name of the Fatimids either from Qairawan or from 'Ashir, a capital which they built on a strategic site on the southern slopes of mount Tittari. Satisfied with the Zirids' ability and loyalty, the Fatimids in 978 bestowed upon Bologuin the government of Tripolitania as well. The imprudence of this step became evident when Bologuin's son, al-Mansur (984–96), started his reign by declaring himself independent of the Fatimids. The Fatimids responded by sending propagandists who incited the Kutama tribe to rise against the Zirids. The tribe rebelled twice between 986 and 989, but on both occasions they were suppressed. Al-Mansur's grandson al-Mu'izz (1016–62) eventually recognized the suzerainty of the 'Abbasids in 1051.

About the time when the Zirids broke off their allegiance to the Fatimids their state was already in decline. They were no longer able to control the Zanatas in Morocco, and during the reign of Badis (996–1016), the latter's uncle Hammad carved out for himself an independent state in Algeria. Having built in 1007 a fortified town, Qal'at Banu Hammad in Little Kabylia, Hammad waived his allegiance to his nephew and created a state which vied with that of the Zirids. The Banu Hammad were able to resist two attempts by the Zirids to destroy their state; and when al-Mu'izz broke off his links with the Fatimids, they followed an independent policy in sending emissaries to Cairo offering their obedience.

The invasion of the Maghrib by the Arabrian nomads was connected with the Zirid rebellion against the Fatimids. The Fatimid caliph al-Mustansir (1036–94), acting upon the advice of his vizier al-Yazuri, induced by the promise of rich booty two tribes which had recently settled in the Egyptian Delta, the Banu Hilal and Banu Sulaim, to invade the Maghrib in order to punish the Zirids. These tribesmen were a threat to peace and order in the country, so that encouraging them to invade the Maghrib served the additional purpose of ridding the Fatimids of their lawlessness.

When the Banu Hilal and Banu Sulaim invaded the Maghrib in 1052, their number was estimated at about 50,000 warriors, in addition to women and children. This was a mass migration, and like the Vandal invasion of the fifth century its main purpose was the attainment of a more secure life, both economically and politically. Like the Vandals, too, the Arabian tribes set their sights on the fertile plains of Tunisia. The Zirids could neither drive them out nor induce their warriors to enlist in their army. For the first five years after entering Tunisia the Arabian tribesmen invested Qairawan, besieging it during the warm months and migrating to the south in the winter. Weary of this life of siege, al-Mu'izz left the town in 1057 and settled in Mahdiyya, which was better fortified than Qairawan. The tribes then entered Qairawan and looted it. The Zirid state survived in Mahdiyya, but it was powerless in the face of the Arabian tribes, and its rulers helplessly witnessed the disintegration of their territory. Similarly, the Banu Hammad in Algeria were unable to resist the Banu Hilal and Banu Sulaim for very long: starting off by allying themselves with these tribesmen against the Zirids, they gradually became puppets in their hands. Eventually they abandoned Qal'at Banu Hammad in 1090 for fear of a treacherous raid, and moved the centre of their government to Bougie which they had founded eighteen years earlier. They survived there in as helpless a situation as the Zirids until the Almohad conquest took place.

The result of the bedouin domination in the greater part of the Maghrib was a state of anarchy; and as happened in Spain after the disintegration of the Umayyad state, small city states appeared to fill the political gap. Even the towns of the prosperous eastern Tunisian coast had been reduced to extreme poverty by about the end of the thirteenth century as a result of the domination of the tribes. One permanent effect which this invasion had on the Maghrib was that of spreading knowledge of the Arabic language in the countryside instead of it remaining limited to the towns. Prior to this invasion the Berber dialects formed the means of communication in the Maghriban countryside, but as groups of these Arabic-speaking nomads came from Egypt, Arabic gradually replaced the Berber dialects.

Spain under the Arabs

Spain was conquered on the initiative of the governor of the Maghrib, Musa b. Nusair, and during the first thirty-five years remained administratively attached to the Maghrib. The wealth of Spain and its political weakness directed the attention of the Arab rulers of the Maghrib to it. In 710 Ibn Nusair sent a reconnaissance party which enabled him to form an idea about the weakness of the Visigothic state in Spain; and in the following year he sent his freedman Tariq b. Ziyad at the head of a small expedition consisting of 7,000 warriors who, like their chief, were mostly Berbers. The Visigothic rulers were hated by their subjects, both Christian and Jewish: most of the Christian inhabitants had been reduced by them to the level of serfs; and the Jews, who constituted about one-third of the population, had been required since 612 to baptize their children under threat of the confiscation of their property. Shortly before Tariq b. Ziyad's expedition took place, an abortive Jewish revolt resulted in the reduction of the whole Jewish community to a state of slavery; amongst other forms of persecution during this time, Jewish children were taken away and forced to become Christian, and Jews were prohibited from intermarrying among themselves. It is not surprising, therefore, that the Jews in Spain viewed the Muslim invaders as deliverers from Visigothic tyranny, and that the bishop of Seville openly sided with the Muslims. What further weakened the Visigothic state was the conflict over succession which followed the death of King Witizia in 710. In accordance with custom the aristocracy elected a new king, Roderic. Witizia's son Akhila, who had been prepared by his father for succession, defied his authority and retained control of his north-eastern province Tarraconensis. Thus only a section of the Visigothic warriors fought with Roderic when on 19 July 711 he faced Tariq at the river Barbate. His defeat at this battle meant the collapse of Visigothic government.

Musa b. Nusair joined Tariq in Spain in the summer of 712. In July he captured Seville, and before his departure in 713 he appointed his son 'Abdul-Aziz as governor in Spain. Thus the fruits of the conquest of Spain by a Berber army were usurped by the Arab ruling hierarchy. Musa brought with him a larger number of Arab warriors; and after the Battle of the Nobles mentioned above,[1] the remnants of the Arab army sent to subdue the Kharijite rebellion made for Spain and settled there. The troubled political situation in the eastern parts of the Muslim empire also induced many Arabs to emigrate to Spain, where they found refuge and became prosperous. Although the Arabs in Andalus were never more than a minority, and although they despised work on the land, they retained for themselves the best lands in the peninsula. The Berbers, most of whom came from northern Morocco, were left with the mountainous parts.

The period from the conquest of Spain to the foundation of the Umayyad amirate forty-five years later was beset with conflicts within the Arab community, and with general political unrest resulting from a rapid succession of governors. 'Abdul-Aziz b. Musa (713–16) was assassinated by the agents of the Umayyad caliph Sulaiman b. 'Abdul-Malik (715–17) who had maltreated his father Musa, and accused the son of Christian leanings and of planning to found for himself an independent kingdom. The struggle for power among the Arabs in Spain, organized under the banners of the old Arabian tribal rivalries between the Qaisids (North Arabians) and the Yemenites (South Arabians), added to the problems of governing the country. The majority of the Arabs who settled in the peninsula were Yemenites; and as long as the provincial governors, appointed by the governors of the Maghrib who were mostly Yemenites, belonged to the same group, the Arab community remained orderly. The appointment in 729 of a Qaisid, al-Haitham, to govern Spain, an appointment made by the Qaisid governor of the Maghrib, 'Ubaida, initiated a period of political disturbance which lasted until 746, when the Qaisid Yusuf al-Fihri seized power. His appointment came as a result of the agreement between the Qaisids and Yemenites in Spain that they should govern Spain alternately, each ruling for a period of one year. Having secured his appointment and received the confirmation of the Umayyad caliph, al-Fihri refused to stand down on the expiration of his term of office and held power until he was ousted by the Umayyad prince 'Abdul-Rahman in 756.

The founder of the Umayyad state in Spain was a fugitive from the

[1] P. 73.

'Abbasid persecution which followed the collapse of the Umayyad caliphate in Damascus in 750. 'Abdul-Rahman, the grandson of the tenth Umayyad caliph Hisham, fled for his life from Baghdad during a raid on the partisans of the Umayyads. He travelled incognito to Palestine with his freedman Badr, then across Egypt and the Maghrib until he arrived in Ceuta. There he was well received and gained the support of his maternal uncles, the Nafza Berber tribesmen living in the vicinity; and in the safety of their protection he made contact with the large Umayyad group which had by then settled in Spain. Since 746 Spain had been administratively independent of Qairawan, and the Kharijite rebellions consumed the energies of the governors of the Maghrib and prevented them from exercising any authority in Morocco, so that 'Abdul-Rahman was safe from their molestation. His emissaries had succeeded in raising a small army which met him when he landed in Almuñecar in August 755. Yusuf al-Fihri had grown unpopular during his ten years as dictator; and the readiness with which the Spanish towns opened their gates to 'Abdul-Rahman can be explained mostly in terms of their hatred towards al-Fihri. Gradually 'Abdul-Rahman advanced northwards until on 14 May 756 he defeated al-Fihri in a decisive battle on the Guadalquivir, and then entered Cordova.

Resistance to the Umayyads was not quelled overnight: al-Fihri held out in Toledo until he was defeated in 758 and killed in the following year, but the Fihrid faction in this town continued to resist the Umayyads for a long time afterwards. A Berber rebellion led by a man named Saqya in the Santaver district, beginning in 769, harassed 'Abdul-Rahman for ten years. In 777 four rebellious Muslim chiefs from eastern Spain joined forces against him and sought help from Charlemagne. The Frankish king was ready to seize this opportunity of extending his power into Spain, but was prevented by a Saxon rebellion directed against himself. In spite of these and other threats to his rule, 'Abdul-Rahman was able to consolidate his power, thanks to the professional army which he created and to a policy of brutal and summary punishment of all opponents. During his reign of thirty-three years he was able to lay the foundations of a state which lasted until 1031.

Until the reign of 'Abdul-Rahman III (912–61) the heads of the Umayyad state in Spain ruled simply as amirs. In 929 'Abdul-Rahman III took the title of caliph and the honorific appellation "al-Nasir li din Allah". Although since 773 the prayers in Spain had no longer been said in the name of the 'Abbasids, they were said in the name of the Umayyad rulers in Spain only from 'Abdul-Rahman III's reign. 'Abdul-Rahman III's principal achievement was the suppression of the rebellion of the Muwallads (neo-Muslims) who between 852 and 912 held sway in most of the countryside, leaving the Umayyads only Cordova and its environs to rule. Three clans of Muwallads became especially influential: the Banu Qasi, who controlled the northern marshes; the Banu Marwan, who ruled in the west; and the Banu Hafsun in the south. Of the three the Banu Hafsun were the most dangerous to the Umayyads. 'Umar b. Hafsun, the leader of this clan, was the descendant of a Spanish count. In 880 he took to brigandry; after a brief period of service in the Umayyad army he rebelled in 884. His base was the castle of Bobastro in the south, and with an army consisting of Spanish Christians and new converts to Islam, by 886 he had succeeded in making himself the virtual master of almost the whole of the Andalus. About 890 he negotiated with the Aghlabids to obtain military support and to have the 'Abbasid caliph recognize him as amir of Spain, and about 910 he made contact with the Fatimids in order to secure their help against their common enemies, the Umayyads. Military setbacks at the hand of the Umayyad amir 'Abdulla (888–912), especially in 891, weakened Ibn Hafsun, and his profession of Christianity in 899 alienated most of his Muslim followers. Before he died in 917 he lost much of his power, but his sons held Bobastro and kept up the rebellion. 'Abdul-Rahman defeated and killed Ibn Hafsun's son Sulaiman in 926, and forced his brother Hafs to capitulate in 927. Bobastro was captured in 928, and gradually 'Abdul-Rahman regained control of the Spanish towns which had been held by the rebels.

During 'Abdul-Rahman III's reign the Umayyad state in Spain faced external dangers from two directions: the Fatimids, and the Christian kingdoms in the north. The connections he established with the Maghrib in order to control the Fatimids have been mentioned above. It is worth noting here that his assumption of the caliphial title in 929 was designed to induce the Maghriban Muslims to recognize his authority. This measure, therefore, was directed more against the Fatimids than against the 'Abbasids, whose authority they both challenged. In 914, two years after 'Abdul-Rahman II acceded to the Umayyad throne, King Ordono II of Leon commenced hostilities by attacking the district of Merida. Two expeditions against Leon in 916 and 917 ended in the rout of the Umayyad army. The threat of the Fatimids, especially after their conquest of Nuqur in 917, forced 'Abdul-Rahman to discontinue his war against Leon. But after the Fatimids were ousted from Nuqur, he once more turned to face his Christian enemies. In September 920 he defeated Sancho, king of Navarre, and in 924 conducted another successful campaign against him. These victories, and the conflict between Ordono's sons Alfonso and Sancho over the throne of Leon following Ordono's death, gave 'Abdul-Rahman a respite during which he completed the suppression of the Banu Hafsun rebellion in the south. During the reign of Romiro II of Leon (932–50) 'Abdul-Rahman's influence in the north was diminished through his army's defeat at Simancas in 939. But after 950 he benefited from the internal conflicts of the Christian kingdoms by extending his hegemony over them. Leon, Navarre, Castile, and Barcelona came to pay him annual tribute.

'Abdul-Rahman III was driven by the ambition of fusing into one nation the various ethnic groups which lived in the Andalus. After 929 he was no longer content with the payment of tribute as a sign of submission to his authority, but demanded that the semi-independent chiefly families surrender their castles and towns. In 930 Badojoz was surrendered by the Ibn al-Jilliqi family, Toledo passed under his direct control two years later, and Saragossa was fully incorporated in the Umayyad state by about 940 after it had accepted Leon's suzerainty in 937. During the Umayyad amirate and caliphate in Spain the accent was more on the Arab than on the Muslim character of the state. The Arabs were the rulers and, though they formed only a small part of the inhabitants of Muslim Spain, they were the wealthiest group since they possessed the best lands. Consequently their cultural influence was great, evidenced in the widespread knowledge of the Arabic language and interest in its poetry and philology at this time. Literary and religious ideas were flowing into Spain from the east throughout the Umayyad period, but during the reigns of 'Abdul-Rahman III and his son al-Hakam II a conscious attempt was made to promote the cultural connections with Baghdad, although political ties with it were broken.

'Abdul-Rahman III's reign was the golden age of the Umayyad state in Spain, and with his death in 961 it started to decline. The Andalus during his reign enjoyed a prosperity unmatched in the Islamic period; it was said at the time that he and the Hamdanids of Mesopotamia were the wealthiest rulers in the world. Agriculture, industry, commerce, the arts, and the Islamic sciences flourished during his time; and through a well-organized police system security and order prevailed. Cordova, the former Roman establishment which became the capital of Muslim Spain in 722, reached the apogee of luxury and comfort during his reign, boasting half-a-million inhabitants, 13,000 houses, 300 bathing places, and a large number of mosques.

During the reign of 'Abdul-Rahman III's son, al-Hakam II (961–76), the prestige of the caliphate was preserved. Al-Hakam continued the war against the Christian north, and in 966 he forced Sancho of Leon to sign a peace treaty. He also continued the war against the Fatimids although, having once more turned their attention towards Egypt in 969, they were no longer in a position to threaten Spain. Between 972 and 974 the Umayyad army brought Tangier and its environs under the control of Cordova, and took as captive to Spain its governor Ibn Gannun, who had wavered between loyalty to the Umayyads and to the Zirids. In spite of these wars, al-Hakam is best remembered for his interest in scholarship and learning. His clerks are known to have travelled to Egypt, Syria, and Iraq to copy and buy manuscripts.

When al-Hakam II died in 976 his son and successor Hisham was only ten years old. The affairs of the state fell into the hands of Ibn Abi 'Amir, who had acted as chief judge during al-Hakam's reign. Having won the favours of Hisham's mother, the Basque Aurora or Subh, Ibn Abi 'Amir ruled first in Hisham's name, then, after 981 when he moved the admini-stration to his palace called al-Madina al-Zāhira and assumed the title of al-Mansur, he ruled on his own. Until he died in 1002 he ruled as a dictator, while the caliph's position was reduced to a purely religious one, as was the case at the time in Baghdad. He made the king of Leon pay him tribute, and in his conquests he reached as far as the Galician shrine of Santiago of Compostella in the north-west of the peninsula.

Upon al-Mansur's death his son 'Abdul-Malik held his position for six years, during which he preserved the Muslim position of ascendancy *vis-à-vis* the Christian states in the north. But upon 'Abdul-Malik's death in 1008 the Andalus fell into a state of civil war. Hisham II was deposed in 1009 but reinstated in 1010. The caliphate of Cordova lasted in name until 1031. Its shadowy authority was held after Hisham II by six Umayyad princes and three members of the Hamudid family. When in 1031 the caliphate was formally abolished a council of state was constituted in its place, but it was only able to hold Cordova. The particularist tendencies which existed in the Andalus, which 'Abdul-Rahman III and al-Mansur had been able to curb, reasserted themselves as the central authority weakened. Small feuding principalities appeared whose inability to resist the Christian Reconquista led to the Almoravid intervention discussed below.[1]

[1] Pp. 97–8.

5

Puritans and unitarians: the Almoravid and Almohad empires

The Almoravids

About the middle of the eleventh century, when the Arabian Banu Hilal and Banu Sulaim bedouin were invading the eastern Maghrib and causing the destruction of its main urban centres, another nomadic invasion of the Maghrib was laying the foundations of the Almoravid empire. The power vacuum following the collapse of Fatimid rule in the Maghrib made both invasions possible; otherwise they were two disconnected events. The Sanhaja Berbers who founded the Almoravid state, like the Arabian invaders, were displaced nomadic tribes. They sought in the plains of Morocco a more secure life than the uncertain one to which they had been reduced in the western Sahara by the eleventh century. The difference in the character of the two invasions can be explained mainly in terms of the religious discipline to which the Sanhaja, unlike the Arabian, tribes were subjected by their leaders.

The nomadic Sanhajas had for centuries inhabited the Sahara from Mauritania to Hoggar, and to the south as far as the Sudan. The Arabs called these Berbers the *mulaththamun* (the muffled), because their men wore a *litham* (face-muffler). The use of the camel enabled them to trade with the peoples of the Sudan, exchanging for gold the salt which they dug out in their desert land. In the ninth century the leading Sanhaja tribes in the western Sahara, the Lamtuna, Massufa, and Guddala were joined loosely in a confederacy. The Lamtuna tribe seems to have had the ascendancy over the others since they controlled Awdaghast (modern Tedgadawast), the important trading centre on the western Saharan caravan route connecting southern Morocco with the Sudan. The eleventh-century Arab writer al-Bakri describes Awdaghast as a big town with a large mosque and several small ones, and as having plenty of sweet water and vegetable gardens. Its market-places were rife with activity, and its buildings large and elegant. Al-Bakri also mentions that its Sanhaja ruler in the 960s, Tin Yarutan, had more than twenty Negro chiefs from the Sudan as tributaries.[1]

---

[1] Al-Bakri, *Kitab al-Mughrib*, pp. 158-9.

[92]

By the eleventh century the fortunes of the Sanhaja in the western Sahara had foundered. Sijilmasa which, as mentioned above, was founded about the middle of the eighth century by Kharijite Zanata Berbers, and had been controlled since the end of the tenth century by Zanatas belonging to the Maghrawa tribe, contributed towards the domination of the western Saharan trade route by the Zanatas. Al-Bakri describes the inhabitants of Awdaghast as Negroes and Berbers belonging to the Nafusa and Lawata tribes, both being Zanatas originally from the eastern Maghrib, besides other Zanata Berbers. But more important than the activities of the Zanatas in Sijilmasa in undermining the fortunes of the Sanhaja was the expansion of the Soninke state of Ghana at their expense. In 990 Awdaghast fell under the control of Ghana and remained so until it was conquered by the Almoravids in 1054. Thus at the very time when the Almoravid movement appeared amongst the Sanhaja, their political domination of the western Sahara and their major source of livelihood were in jeopardy. By providing them with effective leadership and a religious basis of solidarity, the Almoravid movement gave them the means of offsetting their political and economic losses.

Islam had spread amongst the Sanhaja of the western Sudan since the ninth century, but their knowledge of this religion remained rudimentary and they continued such un-Islamic practices as drinking wine and marrying more than four women. The impulse for religious reform came when Yahya b. Ibrahim, a chief from the Guddala tribe, went on the pilgrimage to Mecca in 1035. Like many African Muslim reformers after him, Ibn Ibrahim received decisive inspiration from the religious scholars he met while on his way to and from the Muslim holy places. When he returned to his people he brought with him a man of learning from Nafis named 'Abdulla b. Yasin, to instruct his people in the tenets of Islam. The two men found, however, that the Sanhaja were not prepared to shed their traditional customs in order to conform to the teachings of a religion which had not yet taken deep roots in their lives. Consequently, Ibn Ibrahim and Ibn Yasin decided to seek their own salvation in a life of pious seclusion, and retired to a place whose exact location is unknown. Most Arab historians say that it was on an island which could have been in the Senegal river or off the Atlantic coast. The austere religious life which the two reformers with a few devoted followers led in what they called *ribat*[1]

---

[1] Much discussion has been going on in the circles of African Islamists as to what should be understood by Ibn Yasin's *ribat*. The *ribat* as a place, usually fortified and located so as to intercept an enemy dreaded by Muslims, and where warriors for the faith live, is an old institution in the Maghrib. The conscientious practice of religion is an essential part of life in a *ribat*, because in it a Muslim prepares himself for religious duty, namely the holy war. Much of the discussion centres on whether Ibn Yasin established a fortified monastery like the *ribat* founded in Susa by the Aghlabids in the ninth century, and the *ribats* which appeared on the Maghriban coast in the fourteenth and fifteenth

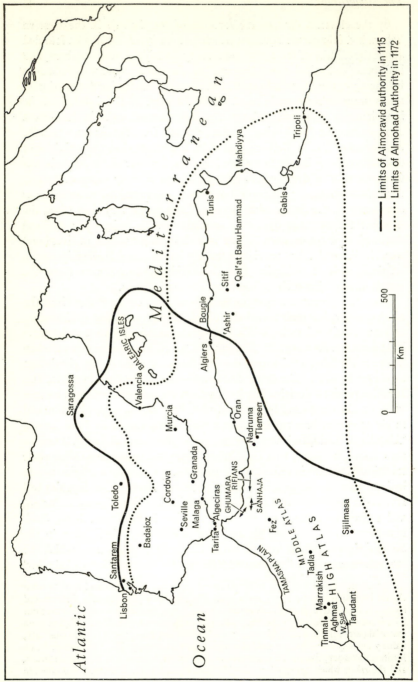

4　The Almoravid and Almohad empires

proved to be a greater inducement to the Sanhaja to lead a pious Muslim life than Ibn Yasin's religious admonitions. In their retirement they were joined by other Sanhajas seeking salvation, who came to be called *al-murabitun*,[1] hence the name of the movement and the state it was to found. Ibn Yasin imposed upon his followers a strict religious discipline, and prepared them for war against fellow Sanhajas whom he tended to consider as apostates,[2] so that a staunchly zealous and warlike religious community developed in his *ribat*. In 1042, when Ibn Yasin is said to have had under his command about 3,000 warriors, he began what he called a *jihad* (holy war) against the Sanhaja tribes.

In the first decade of the active history of the Almoravid movement (1042–53) its aims seem to have remained predominantly religious in the wider Islamic sense of the term, namely to establish a political community in which the ethical and juridical principles of Islam were strictly applied. The Sanhaja tribesmen outside the community were summoned to recant their error and to submit to Ibn Yasin; when they refused, the zealous and disciplined warriors under his command fought them. As Ibn Yasin forbade his men to commit pillage and rape, which victors in tribal warfare considered their customary right, the vanquished Sanhajas accepted membership in the Almoravid community without many misgivings. Yahya b. Ibrahim's tribe, the Guddala, was the first to be so subjugated, followed by the Lamtuna, then the other tribes. Ibn Ibrahim died a little before 1053, and Ibn Yasin chose a man from Lamtuna, called Yahya b. 'Umar, to replace him as military chief.

The political ambitions which the Almoravids cherished in the middle of the eleventh century seem to have been limited to the restoration of Sanhaja domination in the western Sahara. In 1053 they attacked and occupied Sijilmasa, and in the following year Ibn Yasin turned south and captured Awdaghast. It is possible that Ibn Yasin's ambitions would have remained limited to the western Sahara, after he had beaten back the Zanata and the Soninke whose two advance outposts he conquered, had not the people of Sijilmasa rebelled and put their Almoravid governor to

centuries, as a defensive measure against Christian attacks, or merely established a religious confraternity. The author, who prefers to take a *ribat* to mean a place where Muslims prayed and prepared to fight a dreaded enemy of the community of the faithful, because this seems to him the only meaning which the word can carry, feels, however, that this discussion is irrelevant in determining the character of the Almoravid movement, which is well known to us.

[1] "Almoravid" is a Spanish corruption of the Arabic *al-murabit* (pl. *al-murabitun*), meaning the inmate of a *ribat*.

[2] The author is tempted to see a connection between Ibn Yasin's reforming zeal and the Kharijite movement mentioned above. None of the known sources says that he was a Kharijite, but his theological position, especially his readiness to anathematize sinning Muslims and his considering war against them a *jihad*, is very close to the Kharijite position.

death in 1054. The chiefs of Sijilmasa tried to justify their insubordination to Ibn Yasin in terms of the threat to them from the Zanatas. That Ibn Yasin considered his real enemies on the northern fringes of the Sahara to be the Zanatas is clear from al-Bakri who says that Ibn Yasin "urged the Almoravids to attack the Zanatas once more, but they refused, and the Guddala tribe broke off with him and went to the sea shore".[1] While 'Abdulla b. Yasin led a small Almoravid force against Sijilmasa, Yahya b. 'Umar was engaged in fighting the Guddala and he died in this conflict in 1056. The war in which Ibn Yasin became engaged in the north, the initial purpose of which seems to have been defensive – to beat back the Zanatas – gradually developed into an offensive one whose aim was the conquest of the plains of Morocco. As military chief in the north 'Abdulla b. Yasin appointed Abu Bakr b. 'Umar, Yahya's brother, before the latter's death. In 1056 Abu Bakr captured Tarudant in Sus, and shortly afterwards the Almoravids reoccupied Sijilmasa.

In 1059 Ibn Yasin died in an attack on the Barghawata nomads living in the Tamasna plain between Rabat and Casablanca, who followed a prophet of their own and were considered infidels by the Almoravids. Thus at a decisive moment in the history of the movement, which was the beginning of the conquest of Morocco, a change of leadership occurred which proved a fortunate one. Ibn Yasin was replaced as spiritual leader by Sulaiman b. Haddu, but he too died soon afterwards in the conflict with the Barghawata. After his death no single person was appointed to take charge of the spiritual leadership of the Almoravids; instead this function was henceforth performed by the collective body of the religious scholars. That the conquest of Morocco had become by now the main objective of the Almoravids is seen from the fact that Abu Bakr led a campaign in 1060 as far north as Meknes. But at the same time the Almoravids were not prepared to relinquish permanently their control over the Sanhaja tribes in the south. Shortly after Abu Bakr's campaign in the north he led another one southwards to chastise the insubordinate Guddala and their allies. When Abu Bakr went southwards, he left his cousin Yusuf b. Tashfin as commander of the forces in southern Morocco. Abu Bakr returned unexpectedly a year later; but his cousin, who had become popular with the troops, refused to surrender the command to him, and forced him by subtle threats to go south where he remained with the Lamtuna until his death in 1087. The year 1061, when Abu Bakr returned to the western Sahara, marks the formal beginning of the rule of Ibn Tashfin, the real founder of the Almoravid state.

The occupation of southern Morocco by the Almoravids seems to have been accomplished without difficulty, such that in 1062 Ibn Tashfin could begin to establish his capital Marrakish at the foot of the passes in the

---

[1] Al-Bakri, *Kitab al-Mughrib*, p. 167.

High Atlas which he traversed with his men. But as they advanced north-wards the Almoravids were met with relentless hostility from the Zanatas. In 1063 they conquered Fez, then marched northwards as far as Tangier, which was ruled in the name of the Banu Hammud amir of Malaga by Suqut al-Barghwati. Ibn Tashfin did not attack the place, and returned to Fazzaz (Qal'at al-Mahdi) which a detachment of his forces had been left to besiege. When he was engaged in the siege of Fazzaz, the Zanatas struck on Fez. Led by Mu'ansar al-Maghrawi (of the Maghrawa tribe), they cap-tured it and killed its Almoravid governor. Another group of theMaghrawa and other Zanata Berbers intercepted the march of the ruler of Meknes, Mahdi b. Yusuf al-Qazna'i, who had submitted to Almoravid authority and was trying to join forces with Ibn Tashfin. Mahdi was killed and his forces were dispersed. Ibn Tashfin had to put off the conquest of Fazzaz in order to deal with the Zanatas. Leaving a detachment of his men before Fazzaz, he moved to the vicinity of Fez, and without attempting to capture it he subdued the whole of the area around it. Fez he attacked and re-captured only in 1069, when the Zanatas of northern Morocco had been reduced to submission. By the year 1082 his rule extended as far as Algiers.

The collapse of the Umayyad caliphate of Cordova in 1031 made the consolidation of Almoravid rule in Morocco possible, since the Sanhaja conquerors were not hampered by Umayyad interference as the Fatimids had been a century earlier. Its collapse also meant that no central authority remained to unite the Muslims in Spain, and the Andalus was consequently split into small city-states ruled by Muslim princes of various origins. These states existed before the collapse of the caliphate, and most of them were only theoretically under its authority. Its disappearance removed from the Spanish Muslim scene the only authority with any influence to check the unruly whims of the rulers of these states and to mitigate the ill-effects of their mutual rivalry. Some twenty-six such states existed in the eleventh century, whose rulers Arab historians have called "the party kings" (*muluk al-tawa'if*). The name comes from the fact that in every region a party was dominant and the ruling prince represented its interests. Though politically and militarily weak, these princes led a life of luxury and pleasure, and were generous patrons of scholars, craftsmen, and musicians. The situation which existed at this time in Spain was similar to that of the principalities of Italy in the sixteenth century, where an urban and sophisticated literary culture flourished in a period of political decay. In this cultural flowering the religious sciences occupied only a secondary importance. On the other hand, profane letters had much popularity, especially amorous poetry which reflected the relaxation of moral standards and the political insecurity of the times. It was the culture of a society which sought to forget the anxieties of the moment through the enjoyment of the arts and depraved festivities.

Since 1082 the Muslim kings of Seville, Granada, and Badajoz had been trying to induce Ibn Tashfin to send an army into Spain to aid them against the rising power of the Christians. During the reign of Ferdinand I (1035–65) the Muslim princes started to pay tribute to Castile. Originally intended as a temporary arrangement to secure Ferdinand's goodwill, by the end of his reign the tribute had become an integral part of the state revenue which his successors viewed as a part of their inheritance. The refusal of al-Mu'tamid of Seville to pay the tribute brought about the invasion of Muslim territory by the armies of Castile under Alfonso VI. The Almoravid ruler was wary of going to the aid of corrupt Muslims who were to him not much better than infidels, and when in 1086 he sent his army to Spain, he acted as master of its Muslim rulers rather than an ally. The Muslim princes who had welcomed the Almoravid intervention soon regretted it, and al-Mu'tamid of Seville sought Castilian military help in 1091 when trying to prevent the Almoravid troops from occupying his town. He was later taken to Morocco, and died in prison in Sus. By 1106, when Ibn Tashfin died, the only Muslim state in the Iberian peninsula which had not been brought under the direct rule of the Almoravids was Saragossa, but it too was taken by them in 1110.

Yusuf b. Tashfin was a puritanical and austere Muslim under whose guidance the Malikite rite in its legal and devotional facets was observed with rigour. Though ambitious, his strict orthodoxy set a limit to his aspirations. Even when at the zenith of his power, he viewed the state which he founded as an integral part of the universal and theoretically indivisible Muslim community headed by the caliph, and abstained from taking to himself the caliphial title of *amir al-mu'minin* (prince of the faithful). After his first major victory against the Castilians at Zalaqa in 1086 he sought investiture as ruler of the Maghrib from the 'Abbasid caliph, and when this was granted he assumed the title of *amir al-muslimin* (prince of the Muslims). The influential position occupied by the *fuqaha*, the custodians and interpreters of the Muslim law, in the Almoravid state during Ibn Tashfin's reign is further evidence of his strict religious orthodoxy. After the death of Sulaiman b. Haddu, Ibn Yasin's successor as spiritual director, the Almoravids followed the customary Muslim practice of relying on the collective body of the *fuqaha* for spiritual and legal advice. This was to a great extent due to the transformation of Ibn Yasin's reformist religious movement into a state in which the head could not at the same time dispense the functions of chief executive, commander-in-chief, and interpreter of the religious law. The elaboration of positive laws based on the *shari'a*, and their application in everyday problems, required the delegation of this function to those who had the qualifications to perform it. Ibn Tashfin allocated stipends to the *fuqaha*, had them sit in his executive council, took them with him when he went on military campaigns, and sought *fatwas* from them before undertaking important action. The *fuqaha* were also influential in the government of the provinces, especially in the administration of justice. But the position of the *fuqaha* remained subordinate to the ruling prince who was at the same time spiritual and secular head of the state, besides being the commander-in-chief.

Ibn Tashfin's son 'Ali (1106–43) who succeeded him, having been brought up in Ceuta and lived in Spain, was less of the bedouin than his father and more cultured. However, he had an ascetic and withdrawn nature which began to tell on the fortunes of the dynasty, especially when Ibn Tumart, the founder of the Almohad movement, began his rebellion against the Almoravids in 1125. This date, which falls in the middle of 'Ali's long reign of thirty-seven years, divides it into two periods during which the prestige and the prosperity of the dynasty were contrasted radically: the first was the golden age of the dynasty; the second was one of continuous conflict with the Almohads which sapped the resources of the state and prepared the way for its collapse a few years after 'Ali's death. In the first half of his reign 'Ali consolidated his father's conquests and he assumed the style of a grand prince. His authority extended over the whole of present-day Morocco, the greater part of Algeria, as well as the Andalus to which in 1115 were added the Balearic Isles. In this state the *fuqaha* continued to hold a position of ascendancy and to apply the religious law strictly, though unimaginatively. The historian 'Abdul-Wahid al-Marrakishi, who lived during the Almohad period, says that the only religious studies sanctioned during 'Ali's reign were those directly connected with the Malikite rite of jurisprudence. The jurists no longer sought inspiration from the Qur'an and the Prophetic traditions, and Muslim scholasticism (*'ilm al-kalam*) was condemned as an innovation which might lead to the undermining of the faith.[1] This narrow and uncompromising legalism was carried to such an extent that al-Ghazzali's writings were condemned, although he had supported Yusuf b. Tashfin's conquest of the Muslim states in Spain, because he stressed the efficacy of the mystical (Sufi) calling as a guide to religious truth, an attitude which implied that the mere application of the law was insufficient as a means of salvation.

'Ali's reign witnessed a second flowering in Morocco of those aspects of Andalusian culture which were not considered reprehensible by the jurists. The impact of the Andalus began to tell on the Almoravids soon after their occupation of Morocco. The buildings which Ibn Tashfin constructed in Fez bore the mark of Andalusian decorative art, and Andalusian secretaries found their way into the Almoravid administration and helped in organizing it. During 'Ali's reign the influence of the

[1] 'Abdul-Wahid al-Marrakishi, *Al-Mu'jib fi talkhis akhbar al-Maghrib* (Cairo, 1949), p. 172.

Andalus became more pronounced. The art of letters flourished as a result of his engaging the great prose writers of the Andalus in his chancellery. His secretaries were nearly all renowned men of Arabic letters recruited from Spain: one of them, Abu Bakr b. al-Qasira, had served al-Mu'tamid of Seville before he was deposed by the Almoravids. But the Andalusian influence is most noticeable in the public buildings erected during 'Ali's reign. The Grand Mosque of Tlemsen, completed in 1136, was modelled on the Grand Mosque of Cordova, and the extensions introduced into the Qarawiyin mosque in Fez during 'Ali's reign received the full impact of Andalusian workmanship. But in Spain itself the influence of the Andalusian civilization on the Almoravids was not altogether wholesome. The single-minded pursuit of the moral creed of the early Almoravids began to falter as the commanders and officers in the Andalus learned to appreciate the refined life with which they were surrounded, and sought to acquire the means to cultivate it. The loss of the sense of purpose among the Almoravid administrators led to rivalries whose ill-effects were aggravated by the intrigues of the dispossessed aristocratic families.

The Almoravids pursued the war against the Christian states in Spain with a sense of religious duty, but they failed to check Christian expansion permanently because they could not destroy its main bases. In 1109 'Ali led the Almoravids in person against Toledo. He took a number of fortified places in Castile including Madrid, but Toledo itself he failed to capture. Another expedition against Toledo in 1113 also failed. Although the Almoravids were more successful in Portugal, where Sīr b. Abu Bakr captured Lisbon and a number of smaller towns in 1110, in the overall confrontation between Christians and Muslims in the peninsula the initiative remained with the former. Even before the Almoravids became preoccupied with the conflict with the Almohads, Alfonso I of Aragon captured Saragossa in 1118. Of special importance to the situation in the Andalus upon the collapse of the Almoravid state was the appointment in about 1126 of Yahya b. Ghanya as governor of Valencia and Murcia, and his brother Muhammad to govern the Balearic Isles. The two brothers were the sons of 'Ali b. Yusuf, a chief of the Massufa tribe who was married to a relative of Yusuf b. Tashfin called Ghanya, after whom the dynasty which Muhammad founded in the Balearic Isles came to be known. Yahya, who at a later date became the sole Almoravid governor of Spain, distinguished himself in the war against the Christians. When the rebellion which brought Almoravid rule in Spain to an end took place in 1143, he valiantly fought the Muslim rebels as well as the Christians until his surrender to the Almohads in 1148.

In the continuous warfare of the Almoravids against the Christian states the position of the Arabized Spanish Christians (the Mozarabes) became critical. Suspected of fifth column activities, many of them were deported to Morocco. The desire of the Almoravids to follow the injunctions of the Muslim law with regard to taxation contributed towards alienating the Jews as well. Having decided to collect from the Muslims only those taxes which the *shari'a* sanctioned, 'Ali b. Yusuf found himself in need of new sources of revenue to defray the increasing expenses of the state. The *fuqaha* reminded him of his right under the Muslim law to levy a poll-tax on non-Muslims. The collection of this tax soon developed into extortion to which the wealthy Jews were specially subjected. The lot of the Jews worsened when they were accused of giving help to Alfonso I of Aragon when in 1125 he led a campaign into the south, attacked Granada (which had by then become the capital of the Almoravid administration in Spain) but failed to capture it, and then routed the Almoravid army at Arnisol near the Jewish town of Lucena. After this battle the influential Malikite *qadi* Ibn Rushd, the grandfather of the famous philosopher of the same name known to Europe as Averroes, advocated the deportation of the Jews from Spain. Many of them were taken to Morocco and settled in Sala and Meknes.

Although in Spain the Christians and the Jews during 'Ali's reign found themselves under suspicion with the Almoravid rulers, in Morocco 'Ali employed Christian mercenary cavalry troops, a practice which the *muluk al-tawa'if* had followed in Spain before the Almoravid conquest. These troops were stationed in fortified places near Marrakish, and permitted the free exercise of their religion and to build churches. Commanded during 'Ali's reign by the Catalonian Reverter, they distinguished themselves in the conflict with the Almohads. The Almohads made the employment by the Almoravids of Christian soldiers against fellow Muslims an important issue in their religious propaganda, although they too were to use Christian mercenaries. In a political system built on the hegemony of one tribal group in a tribally divided society, foreign mercenaries are indispensable. Apart from the new military skills which they bring with them, they spare the rulers the need to rely heavily on the services of tribes which are potential rivals. The logic of the tribal state requires that when the rulers sense the military insufficiency of their own group, they should seek reinforcement from elements with no tribal ties in their territory. This remained an axiom of tribal government in the Maghrib until the sixteenth century.

Under the tribal system of government military service is a privilege, not a duty. This is so in particular because there is no distinction between the military and administrative functions. The Lamtuna tribe, who were given the special name of "al-Murabitun", was the mainstay of the Almoravid state. It formed the social aristocracy, and its warriors constituted the core of the army. There are references to the existence of Zanata warriors in the army, but these do not seem to have played any part in the administration. Because the command of the troops went to the Lamtuna chiefs, most of the posts in the provincial administration were occupied by them. The Christian troops seem to have taken part in the collection of the taxes. The few dispersed references made to the central administration under the Almoravids suggests that it was simple and undifferentiated. The amir was the supreme ruler wielding all powers in his capacity of political and religious head of the community. The only executive officers the state had were the army chiefs and the clerks of the chancellery. The Almoravid chiefs formed with the *fuqaha* a group of advisors, and the stability of the state depended to a great extent on their readiness to cooperate with and aid the amir.

When the Almohads began their rebellion in 1125, the Almoravid state showed no signs of decline. The strictness with which the Muslim law was applied led to stability, especially in the Almoravid territory in the Maghrib. In an area which had been the scene of tribal conflicts for centuries, stability did not fail to produce prosperity. The rapid decline of the Almoravid state after 1125 can be attributed, therefore, to Ibn Tumart's remarkable ability as leader of men and to 'Ali b. Yusuf's marked in-decision in combating him. 'Ali is said to have resisted, on religious grounds, the pressure of his counsellors to kill, or at least imprison, Ibn Tumart when he expounded in Marrakish itself his religious doctrines whose incompatibility with the Almoravid position and prestige was clear to the *fuqaha*. The origin of the Almohads and the history of their conflict with the Almoravids are discussed below. Suffice it to mention here that 'Ali b. Yusuf spent the second part of his reign defending his state against them. More Christian cavalry soldiers were brought to Morocco, and fortifications were raised on the north-western slopes of the High Atlas to contain the Almohads. The capital Marrakish, which Yusuf b. Tashfin did not think it necessary to wall, was fortified during his son's reign after the first attack by Ibn Tumart's warriors in 1129.

When 'Ali b. Tashfin died in 1143 his eldest son Tashfin was leading the Almoravid forces against the Almohads. He was recognized as *amir al-muslimin* without any dissension; but as he was engaged in the war away from the capital, his brother Ishaq, who was only a boy, was appoin-ted his deputy in Marrakish. Tashfin spent the entire period from his recognition as *amir al-muslimin* until his death near Oran in March 1145 fighting the Almohads. His short reign marks the beginning of the end for the Almoravid dynasty for Marrakish was captured from his son Ishaq about two years after his death, and a rebellion against the Almoravids in the Andalus facilitated its conquest by the Almohads.

The achievements of the Almoravids during their century of power have been less appreciated than they deserve, partly because their greatness was overshadowed by the lustre of the Almohads. Their legalistic religious standpoint also contributed towards their unpopularity in the world of Islam. Muslims had come by the twelfth century to relish the lively spirituality of the Sufis and the intellectual sophistication of scholastic theology, aspects of Islamic culture which the Almoravids condemned. Nor did they endear themselves to Muslims and others who appreciated the artistic flowering in Muslim Spain before the Almoravid intervention. However, when the Almoravid period is viewed from the standpoint of Morocco as a state and as a Muslim country, their achievements look formidable. When they entered Morocco it was split into petty tribal chieftaincies, with the forces of disunity and disintegration triumphant in it; by the time they lost power to the Almohads, it had emerged as a unified country. Since then the legal concept of the Moroccan state has never disappeared, though at times Morocco's rulers have not possessed the means to make their authority felt in the entire country. The Almoravids did not contribute to the development of Andalusian culture, and in Spain they suppressed its most pleasing aspects; nevertheless they provided a home in Morocco for those versed in its more durable arts, the men of letters and the decorative artists. On the religious level, through them orthodox Islam of the Malikite rite became established in Morocco; in Spain they revived religious zeal after a period of indifference.

The Almohads

Like the Almoravid movement, the Almohad began as one of religious reform. Its upholders were also Berbers, but unlike the nomadic Almoravids they were settled Masmuda Berbers from the Atlas. Abu 'Abdulla Muhammad Ibn Tumart, the founder of the movement, belonged to the Hargha, one of the Masmuda tribes. He was born some time between the years 1076 and 1080 in the village of Igilliz, probably on the northern slopes of the Anti-Atlas. Hardly anything is known of his early life, and only after he performed the pilgrimage to Mecca and returned to the Maghrib do we know something about his activities. It was said during the Almohad period that when Ibn Tumart went on the pilgrimage he met al-Ghazzali, whose writings the Almoravids condemned; also that the eastern theologian predicted the collapse of the Almoravid state at his hands. Although, as Goldziher has shown, this meeting could not have taken place,[1] al-Ghazzali's theology exercised a lasting influence on Ibn Tumart's religious outlook.

When in the east, Ibn Tumart visited Baghdad, Jerusalem, and Cairo in addition to Mecca. He seems to have dedicated himself to studying the

[1] Cf. I. Goldziher, "Muhammad Ibn Toumert et la théologie de l'Islam dans le Maghreb au XIᵉ siecle": the introduction to *Le Livre de Mohammed Ibn Toumert*, ed. Luciani (Algiers, 1903), pp. 8–12.

main schools of Islamic thought current in these centres of learning, returning to the Maghrib an erudite and zealous reformer. The first important occasion on which he propagated his theological views, which later came to form the Almohad doctrine, was a confrontation with Almoravid theologians in the presence of the *amir al-muslimin* 'Ali b.Yusuf, which occurred when Ibn Tumart arrived in Marrakish, probably in 1121. He is said to have got the better of all the Almoravid theologians, except one from Spain called Malik b. Wuhaib who proved to be his match. Ibn Wuhaib counselled the amir to put Ibn Tumart to death; but 'Ali b. Yusuf's piety forbade him to commit this outrage against a zealous Muslim, although Ibn Tumart had had the audacity of throwing the amir's sister off her horse when he saw her in the street unveiled. Banished from Marrakish, Ibn Tumart stopped in Aghmat where he had another disputation with Almoravid theologians. From Aghmat he had to flee to the mountains where Almoravid authority did not extend, for 'Ali b. Yusuf, disturbed by the agitation he caused, had issued an order to arrest him.

As an intellectual disciple of al-Ghazzali, Ibn Tumart could not be satisfied with being a good Muslim himself while leaving other Muslims to act much as they wanted. Al-Ghazzali had taught that it was the duty of Muslims to try to change what the faith condemned. Ibn Tumart attacked some of the Almoravid social customs, such as their permitting the aristocratic Lamtuna women to go unveiled, and tolerating the use of musical instruments and other marks of pleasure-loving. On the theological level he condemned the legalism of the Almoravid *fuqaha*. In their excessive zeal to achieve mastery of the secondary books (*kutub al-furu'*) of the Malikite rite, and for the application of the prescriptions of these books in specific situations, Ibn Tumart thought that the *fuqaha* tended to ignore the Prophetic traditions. While condemning reliance on the secondary legal texts, he was anxious to discourage irresponsible adaptations and rational deductions in the religious law. He stressed that reason had no place in religion, and excluded personal and subjective opinion (*zann*) which he believed played a dangerously large part in the formulation of the law by the recognized Muslim jurists. Thus only the objective material sources of the Qur'an, the traditions of the Prophet, and the concord of the Prophet's companions should be accepted as valid norms for Muslims. This explains why Ibn Tumart refused to follow any of the four recognized schools of jurisprudence.

Leaning towards Ash'arite theology, which formed the foundations of al-Ghazzali's religious outlook and was becoming the dominant Muslim theology in the east, Ibn Tumart also condemned the anthropomorphism of the Almoravid theologians. The Almoravids still adhered to the literal interpretation of those Qur'anic passages which spoke of God's physical qualities. The ninth century Mu'tazilite theologians, and after them the Ash'arites and al-Ghazzali, considered that the literal interpretation of these passages, which led to the assumption that the Divine Being had human physical characteristics, constituted a rejection of the belief in His immateriality and unity. Following the Ash'arites, Ibn Tumart stressed the need for interpreting these passages allegorically so that the belief in the unity and the oneness of God, so important to Muslims, would not be undermined. He called his adherents *al-muwahhidun* (the unitarians),[1] hence the name of the state which his successor 'Abdul-Mu'min founded.

After his escape from Aghmat, Ibn Tumart settled with his people, the Harghas, and from the moment of his arrival he enjoyed the support of an influential chief of the Hintata tribal confederacy, Abu Hafs 'Umar. Secure in this support he carried on as a religious reformer, although his teachings soon took a political turn when he attacked the abuses of the Almoravid system. With the growth of his following his ambitions grew too: he created a genealogy showing that he was a descendant of the Prophet, and had himself recognized as the expected Mahdi after having paved the way for this claim by describing the characteristics of this expected revivor of the faith. After about four years of preaching in Igilliz Ibn Tumart moved in 1124 (or 1125) to the village of Tinmal, which henceforth became the base of the Almohad movement. Tinmal in the valley of Nafis in the High Atlas was then an inaccessible retreat. The account of Baidaq, a devoted companion of Ibn Tumart after his return from the pilgrimage, shows that he contemplated rebellion against Almoravid rule shortly after he came back from Mecca. However, before moving to Tinmal Ibn Tumart was only a religious reformer; in Tinmal he became the head of a religio-political movement.

The Mahdi Ibn Tumart viewed himself as a spiritual heir of the Prophet, and modelled his religious career on the Prophet's as much as was practicable. He spoke of his retreat to Tinmal as a *hijra* (migration) similar to the Prophet's *hijra* to Medina, and divided his followers, as the Prophet had done, into *muhajirin* (emigrants), meaning those who came with him to Tinmal, and *ansar* (supporters), meaning those from the High Atlas who joined the community. The *hijra* of the Prophet to Medina enabled him to organize his community politically; Ibn Tumart's migration served the same purpose. But he could not carry the parallel much further, since the political community which he founded was a Berber tribal confederacy in its organization. The tribes remained under the control of their chiefs, and every member of the community had to belong to a tribe. 'Abdul-Mu'min, who was a foreigner to the Masmuda, was adopted into the Hargha.

As political and religious chief of this community Ibn Tumart was

[1] Almohad is a Spanish corruption of the word.

assisted by a council of ten consisting of confidants like 'Abdul-Mu'min
and Abu Hafs 'Umar. These ten, with forty representatives of the tribes,
formed the grand assembly of the community to which, under Ibn Tumart
and his successors, matters of great moment were referred for discussion.
In the community of Tinmal, Ibn Tumart was the custodian of the faith,
the arbiter of moral questions, and the chief judge. The chiefs of the tribes
were his assistants in supervising the application of the religious law, and
all negligence was severely punished. In a purge lasting forty days which
Ibn Tumart carried out in 1128, dissident elements in the community were
killed together with their families. This bloody deed seems to have stamped
out dissension from within. The Mahdi had also to deal with neighbouring
tribes who refused to accept his hegemony. From 1126 until his death in
1130 he sent out regular expeditions into various parts of the High Atlas.
The struggle with the Almoravids was not yet begun, and Ibn Tumart
seems to have put it off until he became certain of his position amongst his
own tribal community.

    Besides taking measures designed to stamp out opposition in the Tinmal
community, the Mahdi systematically carried out the work of religious
instruction. The Masmuda Berbers' ignorance of Arabic was a handicap,
especially in teaching them the Qur'an; but Ibn Tumart was not put off.
He taught them the Holy Book in an ingenious if untraditional way:
bringing a group together in a circle, he would give each of them a name
consisting of a word from a Qur'anic verse; then organizing them in the
order in which the words occurred in the verse, he would have them call
out their "names" in turn until the verse was memorized. Theological
questions he expounded in the Masmuda Berber dialect, and we are told
that he even composed treatises in this dialect containing his doctrines.[1]

    The conflict with the Almoravids began in earnest only in the last year
of the Mahdi's life. When he was still in Igilliz several attacks by the
Almoravid governor of Sus were repulsed; in Tinmal the Mahdi expected
Almoravid attacks at any moment and built fortifications around the
settlement. The first expedition against Marrakish, led by 'Abdul-Mu'min
and an old and trusted companion of the Mahdi called Bashir, was sent in
1129. The Almohads invested Marrakish for forty days; they were routed
near it at a place called Buhaira, and Bashir was killed. This defeat was a
serious setback; but 'Abdul-Mu'min's survival made it less disastrous to
the movement than it might have been. Upon Ibn Tumart's death in the
following year, 'Abdul-Mu'min assumed the command of the Almohads
and led them to victory. The Mahdi's death is said to have been kept secret
within a small circle of his confidants for three years until 'Abdul-Mu'min

---

[1] Ibn Tumart's theological treatises have been preserved only in an Arabic version.
They have been edited by Luciani and published under the title *Le livre de Mohammed
Ibn Toumert*, cited above, p. 103, n.1.

became certain that his assumption of supreme authority over the Masmuda community, to which he was a foreigner, would not be opposed.
Be that as it may, the fact that he became the uncontested master of this
community points to the sense of religious solidarity which the Mahdi
was able to create in it.

'Abdul-Mu'min b. 'Ali, the Mahdi's successor, was a Berber from the
Zanata tribe of Kumia which lived in Nadruma to the north-east of
Tlemsen. He met Ibn Tumart in the village of Mallala near Bougie when
'Abdul-Mu'min was on his way to the east in search of learning, and the
future Mahdi was returning from the pilgrimage. Legend has it that Ibn
Tumart predicted in Mallala the coming of 'Abdul-Mu'min, and when the
two met 'Abdul-Mu'min gave up the journey eastwards to attach himself
to Ibn Tumart as his first disciple. 'Abdul-Mu'min became Ibn Tumart's
trusted lieutenant, and in Tinmal was looked upon as the Mahdi's deputy.
When Ibn Tumart died, 'Abdul-Mu'min was thirty-six years old. His
reign of thirty-three years witnessed the defeat of the Almoravids in the
Maghrib and Spain, and the unification of the whole of the Maghrib under
Almohad rule.

The defeat of 1129 taught 'Abdul-Mu'min the inadvisability of launching another premature attack on the fortified Almoravid capital. For
twenty-five years after taking over the Almohad leadership he limited his
campaigns to the fringes of Almoravid territory in Morocco and western
Algeria. From 1133 he led the Almohad forces to the north and, while
avoiding engaging the Almoravid army in the plains, he had brought under
his authority by 1141 the entire High and Middle Atlas ranges. Between
1141 and 1145 'Abdul-Mu'min was active further north. After conquering
the coastline to the east of Tatuan he reached the district of Nadruma
where his own tribe lived. From this region he advanced towards the
Almoravid base at Tlemsen. Tashfin b. 'Ali, who had just become the
head of the Almoravid state, had hurried together with the Christian
regiment to intercept his progress. Reverter was killed in an engagement in
1144. The movement at this stage among the Sanhaja Berbers of Kabylia
in support of the Almoravids was rendered ineffective by the attack of the
forces of Banu Hammad on them. 'Abdul-Mu'min approached Oran
when Tashfin b. 'Ali, deserted by most of his troops, was there awaiting
the arrival of his fleet to sail to Spain. He was killed in March 1145, and a
few days later Oran was captured. Tlemsen was taken next. It remained
for 'Abdul-Mu'min to capture the main Almoravid towns in Morocco. Fez,
governed by an Almoravid chief called al-Sahrawi, resisted 'Abdul-
Mu'min for nine months but was eventually taken. Marrakish was
captured in 1147 after resisting for eleven months, and henceforth this
became the Almohad capital. A general massacre of the Lamtuna Berbers
was carried out, and the Almoravid sanctuaries and palace were destroyed.

'Abdul-Mu'min had the Kutubiyya mosque constructed on the foundations of the palace.

In the Iberian peninsula a Muslim rebellion against the Almoravids was
precipitated by 'Abdul-Mu'min's victories in Morocco, and this paved the
way for an Almohad take-over. In 1143 a Muslim chief called Ahmad b.
Qasi captured Mertola in Portugal and declared himself independent of the
Almoravids. Two years later rebellion spread eastwards: Ibn Hamdin of
Cordova, Abul-Hākim b. Hassun of Malaga, and the governors of minor
towns gave up their submission to the Almoravids. Yahya b. Ghanya,
then the sole commander of Almoravid forces in the peninsula, captured
Cordova from Ibn Hamdin at the beginning of 1146 and pursued him to
Andujar in the east. At this juncture Alfonso VII of Castile, whose help
Ibn Hamdin solicited, joined the conflict and forced Ibn Ghanya to
escape to Cordova. It was occupied shortly afterwards by the Castilians,
but Ibn Ghanya held out in the citadel. The Almohad army arrived in
Spain shortly after the Castilians occupied Cordova. Its arrival had the
effect of making Alfonso stop short of crushing Ibn Ghanya completely.
In return for the payment of tribute, he left him Cordova to rule so as to
enable him better to resist the Almohads. Alfonso's subsequent insistence
that Ibn Ghanya should increase the tribute he paid, or surrender Cordova,
drove the Almoravid chief to submit to the Almohads. In the middle of
1148 Ibn Ghanya sought a meeting with the Almohad commander Barraz
b. Muhammad al-Massufi, and surrendered Cordova and Carmona to him.
By 1148 the Almohads thus became the masters of the south-western part
of the Andalus, but their suzerainty was not recognized in eastern Spain.
A Muslim soldier of Christian origin, Muhammad b. Sa'd, commonly
known as Ibn Mardanish, brought Valencia, Murcia, and the rest of
eastern Spain under his control upon the death of the ruler of this area,
Muhammad b. 'Iyad, in 1146 or 1147 (A.H.541). He was on good terms
with the Christian states in the north, and with their help he resisted the
Almohads until his death in Murcia in 1172. Since to 'Abdul-Mu'min
Spain was a diversion from the consolidation of Almohad rule in the
Maghrib, he was content to hold on to the position his commanders had
reached by 1148. He died in 1163 in Sala where a major expedition he was
to lead to Spain was being assembled.

Until the conquest of Marrakish the wars of the Masmuda under
'Abdul-Mu'min can still be understood within Ibn Khaldun's theory of
the rise of the tribal state. Ambition for power, with the concomitant
attraction of descending into the prosperous lowlands, was an important
sustaining drive, and the Almohad dogma gave the tribal rebellion a
religious legitimacy. The intrusion into western Algeria was a military
necessity in the conflict with the Almoravids. But the expansion further
east is difficult to explain either in terms of tribal ambitions, which had

been satisfied with the conquest of Morocco, or of any clear economic objectives. The Almohads gave a religious explanation for this expansion, and this may not have been altogether unconnected with their motives. In the Maghrib they were the only remaining rulers with a religious basis for their authority. The unification of the Muslim community was their responsibility and the means of creating a caliphial structure. Furthermore, in the eastern Maghrib the weakness of the Muslim rulers enabled the Christians to establish a foothold on its coast. The weakness of the Zirids had enabled the Normans of Sicily to take possession of important towns along the east Maghriban coast. In the fifty years beginning in 1134 they occupied Tripoli, the island of Jirba, Gabis, Sfax, and Susa. Although these places were used by the Normans only for commercial purposes, their occupation by the Christians was strongly resented. In 1151 preparations were made for an Almohad expedition which was generally believed to be destined for Spain, but was sent eastwards instead. After capturing Algiers the Almohad army marched on Bougie, the Banu Hammad capital. The last of this dynasty's princes, Yahya b. 'Abdul-'Aziz (1122–52) was defeated near his capital. In an important engagement near Sitif in 1152 the Almohad forces dealt a crushing defeat to the Arabian tribes who attempted to reconquer Bougie. After this battle 'Abdul-Mu'min induced large numbers of these bedouin to go to Morocco, where they were settled in the Atlantic plains, mostly between Rabat and Casablanca. The good treatment which the chiefs of the Arabian bedouin received from 'Abdul-Mu'min suggests that he looked upon them as a counterbalance to the Masmuda, from whom he expected opposition to his son's succession to the Almohad throne. Their occupation of the western part of Morocco further contributed towards its Arabization.

Instead of following up the conquest of Bougie in 1152 by attacking the Zirids in Tunisia, 'Abdul-Mu'min spent the next seven years organizing his state internally with a view to establishing the government of the Almohad state in his family. He was growing old, and, short of establishing a hereditary monarchy in his line, Ibn Tumart's former protector Abu Hafs 'Umar would have been his natural successor. In 1154 'Abdul-Mu'min, then in Sala, formally appointed his son Muhammad as heir-apparent; others of his sons he sent to the principal towns as governors. To each one of his sons he appointed as governor, he attached a leading Almohad *shaikh* as counsellor, thus identifying the interests of the religious leaders of the community with the dominance of his family. Open opposition to the appropriation of the Almohad state by 'Abdul-Mu'min's family, especially from Ibn Tumart's relatives, was not lacking. Shortly after 'Abdul-Mu'min announced the appointment of his son Muhammad as successor, Ibn Tumart's two brothers, 'Abdul-'Aziz and 'Isa, then in Fez, marched with some of their partisans to Marrakish with the intention

of capturing power. As they advanced 'Abdul-Mu'min followed them with
the army without attempting to overtake them. He gave them time to enter
Marrakish and add to the ill-fame they achieved in Spain in 1146 by
killing its governor. He then interfered, and seizing 'Abdul-'Aziz and
'Isa, he put them to death, together with a number of Hargha chiefs of
whom he expected further opposition.

During the time when 'Abdul-Mu'min was engaged in the internal
organization of the state (1152–9) he was also preparing for war with the
Normans in Tunisia. Fighting the Normans made naval warfare necessary,
and so a fleet of seventy ships was built in Morocco, which followed the
movements of the Almohad land forces of about 200,000 men which in
1159 marched to Tunisia. While a detachment besieged Tunis, then ruled
by the Sanhaja chief Ahmad b. Khurasan under Norman protection,
'Abdul-Mu'min led the main part of his army against the well-fortified
town of Mahdiyya which the Normans had taken only three years earlier.
The siege of Mahdiyya lasted seven months, ending in January 1160 with
an agreement under which the Normans evacuated the town in return for
a safe passage to Sicily. During these seven months Tunis was captured
and the Almohads subjugated the interior of Tunisia. Immediately afterwards Tripoli, which had two years earlier rebelled against the Normans,
recognized the authority of the Almohads. Thus, according to the Almohad
historian al-Marrakishi, "through him ['Abdul-Mu'min] God stamped out
disbelief in Ifriqya [Tunisia]...Religion revived there after decline, and
the star of faith shone bright after its eclipse."[1] This was the first time that
the Maghrib became united under one local political authority.

In the state which 'Abdul-Mu'min founded the supremacy of the
tribes which had constituted the Tinmal community was preserved. The
original tribes formed the aristocracy of the empire, and during the whole
of the Almohad period, and afterwards in the Hafsid state, the name
"Almohad" (al-Muwwahidun) was used to refer specifically to them. The
Almohads were the only group entitled to discuss and elaborate the
Mahdi's doctrine, to the extent that under 'Abdul-Mu'min the religious
scholars (*talaba*) were divided into two classes, Almohads and town
scholars. As the Almohads were also given preferential treatment in
taxation, they were a distinct and exclusive class of conquerors, much as
the Vandals had been in their own state. The Masmuda tribes' jealousy of
their favoured position was such that 'Abdul-Mu'min was unable to bring
his own tribe, the Kumia, into their community until as late as 1162, and
then only through a subterfuge. The Kumia cavalry arrived before
Marrakish without being expected by the population, so that their appearance caused concern as to their intentions. 'Abdul-Mu'min sent a delegation headed by the venerable Almohad chief Abu Hafs 'Umar to inquire

---

[1] Al-Marrakishi, *Al-Mu'jib*, p. 230.

their purpose. They had come to pay their respects to the caliph, the delegation reported; whereupon 'Abdul-Mu'min welcomed them and settled them in Marrakish. From this date the Kumia warriors formed 'Abdul-Mu'min's and his successors' bodyguard.

'Abdul-Mu'min retained the council of fifty in which the founding tribes were represented, and it remained a constant feature of Almohad government to the end. In this way the heads of the founding tribes continued to have a recognized position in the administration of the empire. Within this ruling class members of 'Abdul-Mu'min's family, who were called by the honorific title of *sayyids*, formed the elite. 'Abdul-Mu'min himself was called the *khalifa* (caliph). Although in the context of the Almohad state this meant that he was the Mahdi's successor, to whom the Almohads referred as the *imam*, 'Abdul-Mu'min also assumed the proper caliphial title of *amir al-mu'minin*. He was the first non-Arab to be so called. 'Abdul-Mu'min kept Abu Hafs 'Umar as a personal advisor, and the deference with which he and his family were treated seems to have reconciled him to the designation of Muhammad b. 'Abdul-Mu'min as his father's successor. Abu Hafs served as the first vizier of the state, and when a proper government machinery was organized he was replaced in this function by men of inferior position, while retaining 'Abdul-Mu'min's friendship. His sons were appointed to positions of command in the army, and some served as viziers under 'Abdul-Mu'min's successors, so that Abu Hafs too was the founder of a dynasty, which occupied a position in the state second only to the *sayyids*.

'Abdul-Mu'min tried to create a unified Muslim community in the Maghrib on the basis of Ibn Tumart's teachings. He considered – as Ibn Tumart had done – only the Qur'an, the Prophetic traditions, and the concord of the Prophet's companions as valid bases of legislation. But although reliance on the manuals of the Muslim jurists was formally banned, the practical needs of justice led to the tacit toleration of the Malikite system. This rite was suppressed only during the reign of 'Abdul-Mu'min's grandson, Abu Yusuf Ya'qub. And in order to ensure the dominance of the Mahdi's religious doctrines and their enforcement, 'Abdul-Mu'min organized special training for the provincial administrators. Relying on intelligent young men from the Masmuda tribes in the administration, he had them trained under his personal supervision. They were made to learn the writings of the Mahdi, hence their name, the *huffaz*;[1] but they were also trained in horsemanship, shooting with bow and arrow, swimming, and other athletics. 'Abdul-Mu'min gave his own sons this education before appointing them as governors.

Upon 'Abdul-Mu'min's death in 1163 his son Muhammad succeeded him, but he ruled for only forty-five days. There was general agreement

---

[1] Plural of *hafiz* from the verb *hafaza*, to retain or memorize.

amongst the Almohad chiefs, including 'Abdul-Mu'min's other sons, that Muhammad was ill-suited to be caliph. His brother Abu Ya'qub Yusuf was chosen to replace him. The removal from the throne of the son whom 'Abdul-Mu'min had chosen to succeed him was the occasion for dissidence from two other sons. Since at this time a tribal rebellion was beginning in northern Morocco, and the tribal warriors assembled in Sala for the war in Spain were becoming restless, Abu Ya'qub disbanded the tribal warriors and used the regular forces for combating the rebels.

Abu Ya'qub spent most of his reign suppressing rebellions or fighting the Christians. The tribal rebellion in the north of Morocco was started by the Ghumara, but it spread to the Sanhaja living near them. After three campaigns, one led by Abu Ya'qub in person, the rebels were subdued in 1166. His two refractory brothers, who were the governors of Bougie and Cordova, were placated and confirmed in their positions. In Spain the long-drawn conflict between the Almohads and Muhammad b. Mardanish was indecisive, and in this situation Abu Ya'qub's statesmanlike qualities proved more effective than war in gaining control of the eastern Andalus. Although Ibn Mardanish himself was bent on resisting the Almohads, many members of his family favoured submitting to them. In 1170 his commander Ibn Hamushku rallied to the Almohads. Ibn Mardanish still held Murcia, but as he feared that his Muslim troops might betray him to the Almohads he came to rely after 1170 on Christian mercenary soldiers. In 1171 or 1172 (A.H. 567) Abu Ya'qub arrived in Spain with the long-expected expedition. He besieged Ibn Mardanish in Murcia, but directed greater attention to his Christian foes in the north and west. In 1172 Ibn Mardanish died of natural causes, and his brothers and sons – assured of Abu Ya'qub's good treatment – surrendered to him. The caliph made a second crossing to Spain with his army in 1183 to relieve the towns of Cordova, Malaga, and Granada, attacked by Castile acting in conjunction with Portugal. He died there on 22 July 1184 as a result of wounds sustained in the siege of Santarem defended by the Portuguese.

In summing up the career of Abu Ya'qub Yusuf, al-Marrakishi says, "none of 'Abdul-Mu'min's offspring...was a true king except Abu Ya'qub".[1] This was written in the 1220s, when the Almohad state was already declining, and it specifically refers to Abu Ya'qub's magnanimity, his interest in learning, and his patronage of scholars, as well as to the material prosperity of his reign. In spite of the fact that during almost the whole of Abu Ya'qub's reign the state was at war, either against the Christian states in Spain or against defiant leaders within his domains, the greater part of the Almohad lands enjoyed the fruits of order and stability. The centres of resistance were limited to the fringes of the empire: Spain, northern Morocco and Algeria, and southern Tunisia. In the interior,

[1] Al-Marrakishi, *Al-Mu'jib*, p. 243.

agriculture and the crafts flourished; and as an organized system of tax-collection was enforced during Abu Ya'qub's reign, the revenues of the state were abundant. His reign is best remembered, however, for the association with it of the two most distinguished figures in the history of Islamic philosophy in the west, the Andalusians Abu Bakr Ibn Tufail (Abubacer to medieval Christian scholastics) and Ibn Rushd (Averroes).

From the reign of Abu Ya'qub the Almohad state began to face a social crisis. The only expression of this that is known to us was religious and intellectual. While living at the caliph's court from 1169 onwards Ibn Rushd worked on his commentaries on Aristotle which were to make him famous in Europe. He also wrote a treatise in which he tried to prove that the study of Greek philosophy was permitted by Muslim law. Abu Ya'qub himself was interested in philosophy and encouraged Ibn Rushd in its study. Ibn Rushd's defence of this subject was intended to counter general popular opposition to it. He argues in it that there are two means of arriving at truth: one is the way of philosophy which should be reserved to the elite, and the other is that of revelation more suitable for the masses. This intellectual dichotomy between the masses and the elite reflected a social one, for philosophy and intellectual pursuits in general were the preserve of the leisured classes. On the popular level the mystery cults were becoming important. To the masses Ibn Tumart was becoming a saintly personality, who possessed occult sciences and mysterious powers. The cult of the Sufis was also becoming important.

The tension between the simple beliefs of the Muslim populace and the sophisticated and tolerant ideas of the elite became acute during the reign of Abu Ya'qub's successor, his son Abu Yusuf Ya'qub (1184–99). A staunch Muslim, Abu Yusuf tried to put into effect the religious policy outlined in the writings of the Mahdi Ibn Tumart, which had been followed only partially by his two predecessors. He tried to suppress Malikism without allowing it to be replaced by any of the other three rites. He had the legal manuals of these rites burnt, and directed his religious scholars to prepare compilations of the Prophetic traditions and classify them according to subject so as to make them readily available for consultation. The traditionists consequently gained a prominent position during his reign. But Abu Yusuf's religious reforms were obstructed by the beliefs of the populace. Sufism was starting to have wide popularity among the uncultured. As an easy way to salvation, it appealed to the masses more than either the Malikite rite or the more enlightened though no less intellectually demanding reliance on the original sources of the law. The belief in Ibn Tumart as the impeccable Mahdi offended the pious sentiments of the caliph. He reprimanded the scholars who gave more prominence in their studies to Ibn Tumart's teachings than to the Prophetic traditions and rejected the doctrine that Ibn Tumart was the Mahdi and impeccable. But as this dogma formed a basis for the belief of the Almohads in their own superiority, and as its open rejection would have caused much popular commotion, he expressed his objections to it only to his confidants. In his attitude towards philosophy he also avoided flouting popular religious sentiments. Ibn Rushd was denounced to him as having included in his commentaries statements not reconcilable with Islam. Consequently he banished him from his court, and when Ibn Rushd went to Spain he ordered the burning of his books, together with other philosophical works, sparing from the bonfire only those containing useful information on medicine and astronomy. However, in the privacy of his court in Marrakish he applied himself to the study of philosophy, and when popular indignation against Ibn Rushd subsided, he returned him to favour, so that the aged philosopher died peacefully in the capital.

The dichotomy in the Almohad society between the popular level of belief and that of the rulers remained important to the end of Almohad rule. The caliph al-Ma'mun (1229–30) ended by renouncing the doctrines of Ibn Tumart, and ordered the omission of his name from the Friday prayers and a return to the Malikite rite in juridical matters. Acceptance of Ibn Tumart's doctrines had been an expression of the unity of the Masmuda ruling class. The religious conflicts which were partly centred on these doctrines reflect the fragmentation of the tribal group which had constituted the mainstay of Almohad authority. Since Abu Yusuf's death in 1199 the Haskura tribe, one of the original Masmuda group, had allied itself with Arabian tribesmen and sought gain in brigandage. The Almohad chiefs in the capital exploited their privileged positions in order to advance their interests through intrigues and political manipulations. Their influence became detrimental to the stability of the state though earlier they had been the guardians of its interests. They assassinated two caliphs in 1224 and 1227 when promised rewards by pretenders. Caliph al-Ma'mun, who abolished Ibn Tumart's cult, was able to attain the throne only with the help of Ferdinand III of Castile.

The second major problem in Almohad history since the reign of Abu Yusuf was the control of the eastern Maghrib. This problem can be understood best in the context of the attempt by the Banu Ghaniya, the last Almoravid governors in Spain and the Balearic Isles, to establish a state for themselves in Tunisia and eastern Algeria. After losing their position in Spain in 1148, the Banu Ghaniya continued to rule in the Balearics and gave refuge there to Almoravid fugitives. For thirty years after the fall of Marrakish to the Almohads, they were able to hold their own, although the Almohads sent their fleet several times to attack the islands. In 1183 Abu Ya'qub sent an emissary to Ishaq, the son of Muhammad b. Ghaniya the founder of the dynasty, urging him to submit to the Almohads. Ishaq temporized; and while continuing to recognize the sovereignty of the 'Abbasids in Baghdad, he avoided conflict with the Almohads by giving costly presents to their caliph. Ishaq died about the same time as Abu Ya'qub (1184), and the former's son Muhammad, recognizing that he had little chance of defending the islands against the Christians and the Almohads, sent notice of his submission to the court of Marrakish. Consequently, an Almohad force under the command of Ibn Reberter, a Christian renegade, was sent to Majorca. Before it arrived, Muhammad b. Ghaniya was deposed by the Almoravid chiefs and replaced by his brother 'Ali who was known to oppose the recognition of Almohad sovereignty. Thus when the Almohad force arrived the Banu Ghaniya drove it back, after taking its commander captive. This, the Banu Ghaniya knew, meant war; and rather than wait until the islands were blockaded by the Almohad fleet, 'Ali decided to take the offensive by invading the eastern Maghrib while the new caliph Abu Yusuf was still occupied with consolidating his position.

The Banu Ghaniya seem to have been well informed about the situation in the eastern Maghrib; they made contact with the Arabian tribes known for their hostility to Almohad rule, and expected them and other malcontents to come to their support against the Almohads. 'Ali b. Ghaniya and the veteran Almoravid troops attacked Bougie in November 1184, when its governor was in Marrakish, and captured it without difficulty. Soon after installing himself in the town he received new recruits from former supporters of the Banu Hammad, the Sanhaja Berbers of Kabylia, and from the Jusham, Riyah, and Athbaj clans of the Banu Hilal Arabian tribe. After a short period of reorganization 'Ali set off westwards, capturing Algiers and Miliana. He reversed his direction soon afterwards, possibly because he realized the dangers involved in penetrating deeper into territory completely pacified by the Almohads. Henceforth he limited his activities to the east of Bougie, where Almohad control was uncertain and the tribes could be relied upon to support any successful rebel. In May 1185 the Almohad army recaptured Bougie; 'Ali b. Ghaniya, who was then besieging Constantine, fled southwards, conquering Tuzar and Gafsa on the way. He also went to Tripoli and entered into an alliance with its ruler Qaraqush. The two rebels were in full control of the Tunisian Jarid during the years 1185–6; Qaraqush even moved his headquarters from Tripoli to Gabis.

In the meantime important changes occurred in the Balearic Isles. In 1185, when 'Ali b. Ghaniya was driven to the south by the Almohad army, a rebellion was organized by Ibn Reberter from his prison, with the support of the Christian population of the islands, which restored to power 'Ali's brother Muhammad, who had submitted to the Almohads. When in the same year Muhammad learned of the mobilization of the Almohad fleet to occupy the islands, which he suspected would lead to his deposition, he tried to get help from the Christians of Barcelona. This move caused his Muslim troops to depose him and to choose his brother Tashfin as ruler. Tashfin ruled under Almohad suzerainty until 1187 when 'Ali b. Ghaniya, now the master of the greater part of Tunisia, sent an expedition led by another brother called 'Abdulla. Tashfin was deposed, and 'Abdulla ruled the Balearics in the name of 'Ali until 1203, when the Almohads at last conquered these islands.

In Tunisia 'Ali had by 1187 conquered almost the entire country from the Almohads, who retained control of only the capital Tunis and Mahdiyya. He recognized the suzerainty of the 'Abbasid caliph al-Mustadi', and was formally invested by him as heir of the Almoravids in the Maghrib. In 1187 the Almohad caliph Abu Yusuf arrived with an expedition of 20,000 cavalry to relieve Tunis, then invested by Ibn Ghaniya. The latter resorted to tactics which he and his son Yahya after him were to use again and again, namely to retire when hard-pressed by the Almohads to the Jarid, where the tribes were cooperative, and from which he could easily escape to the desert in case of defeat. During 1187 and 1188 Abu Yusuf reconquered Tunisia, and had the Arabian tribes that cooperated with 'Ali b. Ghaniya leave the country and settle in Morocco. He himself returned to Morocco soon afterwards, where his brother 'Umar and his uncle Sulaiman were trying to use his absence to have him deposed. Although the disaffection caused by the two relatives was soon quelled, and they were put to death, Abu Yusuf did not think it safe to leave Morocco and return with the army to Tunisia; the Banu Ghaniya, therefore, were able to resume their activities. 'Ali b. Ghaniya died about the end of 1188, but the rebellion was continued by his brother Yahya.

At the moment of Abu Yusuf's death in 1199, the Almohad hold over Tunisia was weaker than it had ever been; shortly afterwards it became almost non-existent. Yahya b. Ghaniya, who then held southern Tunisia and Tripoli, was not easy to dislodge. In Mahdiyya, which had remained in Almohad hands since it was taken from the Normans, Muhammad b. 'Abdul-Karim al-Ragrag, while professing loyalty to the Almohad caliph, in June 1199 rebelled against the governor of Tunis. In the following year the town was captured from him by Yahya b. Ghaniya, who in December 1203 also conquered Tunis. 'Ali b. Ghaniya's ambitious aim of reestablishing Almoravid rule in the Maghrib seemed on the way to realization. However, in the year that Yahya captured Tunis, the new Almohad caliph al-Nasir (1199–1213) led an expedition against the Balearic Isles in person, and after he captured Majorca the other islands surrendered to him. The conquest of the Balearics determined the outcome of the conflict in Tunisia between the Almohads and Yahya b. Ghaniya, since at the critical moment of the war the succour from the Balearics that might have saved Yahya was not forthcoming.

In 1204 or 1205 (A.H. 601) al-Nasir set out with his army from Marrakish marching towards Tunis, and the fleet moved at the same time from Ceuta. Although the master of Tunis and the other principal towns in Tunisia, Yahya b. Ghaniya was not certain of the loyalty of the population who favoured the Almohads, in the hope that they might be able to restore the order and stability which he was unable to establish. As he did not have the military strength to halt the progress of the Almohad army, and could not remain in Tunis without a fleet to protect it from the sea, he moved his treasure to Mahdiyya when the Almohads reached Bougie and then went to the Jarid to organize tribal resistance. Tunis surrendered as soon as the Almohad fleet arrived, so that al-Nasir could go southwards immediately. In the meantime Tripoli revolted against Ibn Ghaniya. He attacked it, and having entered and looted it went into hiding in Jabal Dummar. Al-Nasir pursued Ibn Ghaniya, conquering on the way the main centres of resistance in Tunisia. Ibn Ghaniya was defeated near the mountain of Tajura' in the vicinity of Gabis. Mahdiyya was still in the hands of the Banu Ghaniya, but after this battle it surrendered in January 1206.

Before leaving Tunisia in May 1207 al-Nasir appointed as governor Muhammad b. Abu Hafs, a descendant of Abu Hafs 'Umar, Ibn Tumart's close companion. The appointment proved important both for Tunisia and in the career of Ibn Ghaniya: for Tunisia it was the first step towards the foundation of the Hafsid dynasty, which was to rule the country until the Turkish conquest in the sixteenth century; to Ibn Ghaniya this meant that Tunisia was no longer an easy prey for him and, except for a short period following Muhammad b. Abu Hafs' death, he had to content himself with raiding its periphery. Muhammad b. Abu Hafs was appointed, upon his own insistence, on a temporary basis with the promise that he would be relieved within three years. In order to induce him to accept the appointment the caliph gave him full powers with regard to the choice of subordinates and the organization of the army. What was intended as a temporary appointment became permanent, because the caliph always found a suitable excuse for postponing the sending of a replacement.

Yahya b. Ghaniya died thirty years after the appointment of Muhammad b. Abu Hafs as governor of Tunisia. He conquered Waddan in 1212–13 and settled there until the death of Muhammad b. Abu Hafs in February 1221. Some time after this date he moved with his men to southern Tunisia and remained there until another Hafsid, Abu Muhammad 'Abdulla, arrived in November 1226 to take charge of its government. Yahya then moved north-westwards, and in 1227 conquered Algiers but could not retain it. This marks the end of Yahya's career as a political rebel. In the following ten years he led the life of a brigand, until he died in 1237 or 1238 (A.H. 635) near Miliana.

The Banu Ghaniya rebellion and the important part played by the Hafsids in suppressing it paved the way for the appearance of the Hafsid state in Tunisia which was to claim to be the heir of Almohad authority. But the destruction of the Almohad state was the work of the nomadic Zanatas whom the rulers of Marrakish could not prevent from leaving their desert lands and expanding into the fertile plains of Morocco and western Algeria. The construction of a rival centre of authority in Tunis and the beginning of the Zanata migrations coincided with the worst periods of civil strife in Marrakish following the elevation to the caliphial throne in 1213 of a minor, Abu Ya'qub Yusuf al-Mustansir. What prevented the state from total collapse before the Zanata invaders until 1269 was not so much its own resources as the fact that the intruders had to contend with other tribes before they could establish themselves in Morocco and deal the decrepit state its *coup de grâce*.

6

The successors of the Almohads

The collapse of the Almohad state brought the political unity of the Maghrib to an end. It also marked the close of an epoch in which leading the Muslim good life was the professed aim of politics. The Kharijite Berbers introduced this reformist religious strain into the politics of the Maghrib when they rebelled against their Arab rulers, and the Almoravids and the Almohads developed it. The three states which succeeded the dynasty of 'Abdul-Mu'min in ruling the Maghrib were all Muslim states, but none of them started as a religious movement; and when their rulers championed Islam, for example against the Christians in Spain, they did so from political rather than religious motives. The historian Ibn Khaldun, who served these three states at one time or another in his chequered political career, could see that possession of power for its own sake had become the undisguised aim of rulers. His experiences in the Maghrib in the fourteenth century inspired his cyclical theory of the rise and fall of states. In urging that only through the application of the Muslim law could the cyclical course of history be broken, he implied that this law no longer constituted the ultimate moral and juridical norm of the Maghriban society as he knew it.

During the period beginning in the middle of the thirteenth century, when the political unity of the Muslim community in the Maghrib was broken, and the injunctions of the Muslim law ceased to constitute the justifications of political action, the Sufi (mystical) orders spread their influence widely in the area. The Sufis considered themselves orthodox Muslim, and they claimed that they obeyed the Muslim law. Nevertheless, the spiritual gifts which the *shaikhs* of the orders promised their followers were sought as a means of salvation, and rendered the adept less concerned about his own and other people's transgression of the law. By joining these orders Muslims also participated in a communal life that was especially rewarding at a time when the general Muslim community to which they belonged was split into warring states. In the lodges of the Sufi orders the Muslims gradually came to find a home, both spiritually and physically; and in the spiritual authority of the *shaikhs* they had a substitute for the religio-political authority which the Almoravid and Almohad rulers possessed in the zenith of their power, but which their successors could rarely command.

During the eleventh and twelfth centuries the Maghrib was ruled by two of the three main branches of the Berbers mentioned above.[1] Of the three states which appeared in the Maghrib in the thirteenth century, two – the Marinid in Fez and the Zayanid (or Banu 'Abdul-Wad) in Tlemsen – were founded by tribes which belonged to the third branch, the Zanata. The third state, the Hafsid in Tunisia and eastern Algeria, represented a continuation of Almohad rule.

The Marinids

Like most Zanata Berbers, the Banu Marin, the founders of the Marinid state, led a nomadic pastoral life until they became involved in political conflict with the Almohads. Until the end of the twelfth century this tribe roamed the area between Figuig and Sijilmasa, moving northwards into the basin of the Mulawiyya during the spring and summer seasons in search of pastures, and returning to the south for the winter. While the Almohads under 'Abdul-Mu'min were engaged in fighting the Almoravid army in the neighbourhood of Oran and Tlemsen in the 1140s, several Zanata tribes, such as the Banu 'Abdul-Wad, fought on the side of the Almohads. The Banu Marin did not do so, and so the Almohad victories pushed them to the south where they lived in political oblivion. In 1195, however, they participated with the victorious Almohad army in the battle of Alarcos in Spain. Whether they took part in it out of religious zeal or the expectation of booty, or both, is not easy to say. Their chief Muhyu died from wounds received in this battle. His son 'Abdul-Haqq was later to lead the Banu Marin into Morocco.

The Banu Marin made their entry *en masse* into Morocco a few years after the Almohad caliph al-Nasir, disheartened by his defeat in Spain, died in 1213. The little we know about them at the beginning of the thirteenth century suggests that they were lured into Morocco by the prospect of good pasturage and booty. Until they entered Morocco they were crude pastoralists, and unlike the Almoravids and the Almohads, they did not champion any peculiar religious doctrine which would have inspired them to rise above the limited aspirations of the nomads. Their political ambitions seem to have developed only about the middle of the century as a result of their conflict with the Almohads.

Led into Morocco by 'Abdul-Haqq, the Banu Marin first occupied the north-eastern area between the rivers Za and Mulawiyya. In 1216 the Almohads sent an army to drive them out, but it was defeated in Wadi Nuqur in the Rif. The Banu Marin followed up this victory in the spring

[1] Chapter 1, p. 8.

of 1217 by occupying Taza. Later in 1217 an Almohad force, reinforced by Banu Riyah Arab warriors and a dissident Marinid clan, defeated the Marinids on the Sibu river near Fez. 'Abdul-Haqq and his eldest son Idris were killed in this battle. The Marinids still had enough men, who were commanded by 'Abdul-Haqq's son 'Uthman, and they routed the allies of the Almohads. A series of raids between 1217 and 'Uthman's death in 1239 established the hegemony of the Marinids over the tribes of eastern Morocco. Fez and Qsar al-Kabir, besides Taza, submitted to the Marinids during this period. The Almohad caliph Sa'id decisively defeated the Marinids in 1244 at a place near Fez called Abu Bayash. They fled to the Ghiyatha mountain near Taza, and from there to their home in the south. But by now they had savoured political power, and were not content with nomadic life on the fringes of the desert. Under the able leadership of another of 'Abdul-Haqq's sons, called Abu Yahya, they returned to Morocco.

On their second entry to Morocco in 1245 the Marinids consciously aimed at capturing power from the Almohads. Abu Yahya made this clear when he divided Morocco into fiefs which he assigned to his military chiefs before starting the invasion by attacking Meknes. This town submitted to him without fighting in 1245 or 1246 (A.H. 643). Abu Yahya was content to have its people say prayers in the name of the Hafsids of Tunisia, while keeping the tribute for himself. During the following thirty years the Marinids maintained the practice of having the places they conquered, and in fact controlled, acknowledge the Hafsids' nominal suzerainty. Loyalty to the Mahdi Ibn Tumart was deeply ingrained in Morocco, and the Hafsids had claimed since 1229 to be the heirs of his authority and had the Friday prayer said in his name. By paying homage to them, the Marinids compensated for not having a religious appeal of their own, and for taking up arms against the family which founded the Almohad state. As the Hafsids were at the same time geographically distant, accepting their suzerainty in no way reduced the control of the Marinids over the lands they conquered.

Abu Yahya's realism also led him to make a nominal submission to the Almohad caliph Sa'id when he found himself without the means of defeating him. In 1248 Sa'id left Marrakish at the head of a large army with the aim of recovering Meknes from the Marinids and Tlemsen from the Zayanids, who also had accepted Hafsid suzerainty six years earlier. Before he reached Meknes Abu Yahya sent a token force of 500 men to serve in the Almohad army, while himself retiring to the Tazuta fortress in the Rif. Before Sa'id reached Tlemsen, its ruler Yaghmurasan sent him his submission; but in June the Zayanids ambushed the caliph and killed him as he was exploring the approaches to the castle of Tamzardakt to the south of Wajda, which his army was blockading.

The confusion occasioned by the death of the Almohad caliph was exploited to great advantage by Abu Yahya. His warriors intercepted the Almohad army as it retreated in disorder from Wajda; soon afterwards we find the Christian mercenary troops who had served the Almohads serving in the Marinid army. Within two months following Sa'id's death, Abu Yahya reoccupied Meknes and captured Fez. The Christian militia, having been left in Fez to defend it, rebelled in January 1250 and killed its Marinid governor, so that Abu Yahya had to return from Fazzaz, which he was besieging, in order to recapture Fez. The new Almohad caliph Murtada, alarmed at the Marinid victories, made common cause with his other enemies, the Zayanids. When Abu Yahya returned to Fez to besiege the rebels in it, Yaghmurasan advanced in the direction of Morocco. Abu Yahya lifted the siege, met Yaghmurasan in the plain of Isly near Wajda, and defeated him. In September 1250 the Marinids reoccupied Fez, and before Abu Yahya died of illness in July 1258 he had captured Fazzaz, Sala, and Rabat.

Abu Yusuf Ya'qub, Abu Yahya's brother and successor, faced in 1260 two incursions from outside which occurred more or less simultaneously: one was another invasion from Tlemsen, the other from Spain. In September, when Abu Yusuf was in Taza preparing to check the advance of the Zayanids, Sala was occupied by a Spanish Christian force. The origin of this force in Spain is not certain, although in all likelihood it was Castilian. Its arrival coincided with the rebellion in Sala of Abu Yusuf's nephew Ya'qub b. 'Abdulla. When the Christians landed, the rebel withdrew to Rabat, leaving Sala unprotected. Abu Yusuf arrived from Taza by forced marches in one day, and compelled the Christian invaders to evacuate Sala after fourteen days of siege; his nephew had in the meantime escaped to the Ghumara mountains. Yaghmurasan, who had committed diverse acts of destruction during Abu Yusuf's absence in the west, was later forced to retreat to Tlemsen.

The Christian attack on Sala, though militarily a minor episode, had great significance for the Marinids. From the beginning of their conflict with the Almohads they considered the war against the Christians necessary for their prestige in Morocco. While constituting a moral challenge, the attack on Sala also aroused fears that Morocco itself might become a theatre of the conflict between the Marinids and the Christians. Henceforth, Abu Yusuf found it necessary to make at least a token participation in the conflict in Spain until he could take part in it in person. He executed this duty, and won religious prestige for the dynasty by channelling into it the youthful energies of his numerous and restless nephews. His nephew Ya'qub b. 'Abdulla, after fleeing to the Ghumara, was joined by other discontented relatives. Abu Yusuf used much tact in dealing with this mass defection of his relatives: he went in person to meet them, cajoled and made them promises, and when he succeeded in appeasing their leaders, he persuaded them to go to Spain and fight against the Castilians. One of them, 'Amir b. Idris, was made commander of the expeditionary force which crossed to Spain in 1262, in which most of Abu Yusuf's nephews took part. These scions of 'Abdul-Haqq enlisted under the command of the king of Granada, and seem to have distinguished themselves as warriors.

With this family riot brought to an end, Abu Yusuf was free to pursue the conquest of Marrakish. This he was able to achieve seven years later in September 1269 after a long period of siege. During this period the Marinids had to face another incursion from the Zayanids of Tlemsen whom they defeated on the Mulawiyya in February 1268. Even after capturing Marrakish, Abu Yusuf continued to pay homage to the Hafsids and took the title of *amir al-muslimin* instead of the caliphial appellation *amir al-mu'minin*, by which the Hafsid rulers wished to be known. This obsequiousness on Abu Yusuf's part was due to the strength of the Hafsids, then at the zenith of their power, and to the still unsettled political situation in Morocco. The Almohad caliph Murtada, who escaped in 1263 to Azammur, had been killed in January 1267 by order of his cousin Abu Dabbus who usurped his throne. But in Tinmal several descendants of 'Abdul-Mu'min survived, and in 1267 they elected Murtada's brother Ishaq as their "caliph". With Yaghmurasan in Tlemsen ever ready to attack Morocco, and the question of who was to succeed Abu Yusuf unsettled, the open rejection of Hafsid nominal authority would have played into the hands of Abu Yusuf's enemies without adding to his power. In 1271, while on his way from Marrakish to Fez, he stopped in Sala and there appointed his son 'Abdul-Wahid as heir. This caused some of his nephews to rebel and go to the Ghumara; but once more they were defeated, forgiven, and sent to Spain.

Of the many military tasks which claimed Abu Yusuf's attention after 1269, war against the Zayanids was the most pressing. Though defeated twice by the Marinids, Yaghmurasan was not ready to tone down his hostility. During the final conflict between the Marinids and Abu Dabbus, he strengthened himself by an alliance with the Manbat bedouin, a branch of the Banu Ma'qil tribe, and with their help captured Sijilmasa in 1264 from the Almohads. Although control of this town was in the 1260s the major bone of contention between the Marinids and Zayanids, it was only one facet of the general conflict between these two leading Zanata tribes. Sijilmasa was the western gateway of the Sahara; to the Marinids control of it was also important for the political stability of southern Morocco. But to concentrate the military strength of the Marinids against it would have left northern Morocco exposed to attacks from Yaghmurasan, who had proved himself mobile and elusive. Consequently Abu Yusuf invaded

Tlemsen itself. His son 'Abdul-Wahid recruited from Marrakish an army of Arabian, Masmuda, and Sanhaja warriors, in addition to the remnants of the Christian Almohad militia. This army was joined on the Mulawiyya in September 1271 by the northern contingents which had accompanied Abu Yusuf from Fez. The Marinids inflicted another defeat on Yaghmurasan at Isly in February 1272, and then destroyed Wajda, his advanced post. They besieged Tlemsen until June but failed to take it. Nevertheless they captured Sijilmasa two years later.

Some time before 1257, a local chief from Ceuta, Abul-Qasim al-'Azfi, usurped power in it. Tangier too rebelled against the Almohads at about the same time and submitted to the rule of a local chief, Yusuf al-Hamadani. With the latter Abu Yusuf arrived at a *modus vivendi* shortly after 1258, under which the ruler of Tangier agreed to pay tribute in return for his autonomy. When in 1266 or 1267 (A.H. 665) Marinid partisans in Tangier assassinated al-Hamadani, a popular uprising in favour of his son prevented a Marinid take-over. Five months later al-'Azfi attacked Tangier by land and sea and annexed it to Ceuta. In 1273 Abu Yusuf conquered Tangier, but the conquest of Ceuta was more difficult because it was better fortified, and al-'Azfi's fleet was able to keep him well provisioned. Abu Yusuf turned for help to the king of Aragon, Jack the Conqueror, who for about twenty years had maintained friendly commercial relations with the Hafsids.[1] In February 1269 Jack the Conqueror had concluded a commercial treaty with al-'Azfi, but he did not allow his commitments to this minor ruler, nor the objections of a fugitive Almohad prince living in Barcelona, to thwart his plans for extending his influence into Morocco. On 18 November 1274 he came to terms with Abu Yusuf's emissaries, agreeing to supply 500 cavalry troops and 50 naval pieces to besiege Ceuta, in return for Abu Yusuf's undertaking to pay a sum of money immediately and thereafter the sum of 500,000 besants annually. The sea blockade forced al-'Azfi in 1275 to accept Marinid suzerainty, and he was consequently confirmed governor of Ceuta. Christian Europe hailed this as a victory for Christian arms, and the king of Aragon was gratified to see his fleet augmenting its prestige.

After completing the conquest of Morocco, the Marinid sultan Abu Yusuf evinced no signs of aspiring to build a Maghriban empire. Yaghmurasan's repeated attacks on Morocco, and his alliance against the Marinids – with the Almohads in the 1260s and with the Nasrids of Spain in 1279 – stemmed from his fear that the Marinids would follow their predecessors in the government of Morocco and attempt to conquer the rest of the Maghrib. On two occasions, before the Battle of Isly of February 1272 and before the Battle of Tlemsen in 1281, Abu Yusuf tried to persuade Yaghmurasan to resolve the conflict through peaceful negotia-

---

[1] See below, pp. 139–43.

tions. This conciliatory policy seems to have sprung from the insecurity which the Marinids felt on account of the increasing power of Castile. As long as the Muslims in Spain were weak and Morocco was exposed to the dangers of a Castilian attack, the Marinid sultan could not allow himself to become involved in extensive warfare in the east. His wars with the Zayanids had, therefore, the purpose of merely checking their encroachment.

In the Iberian peninsula the positions still held by the Muslims had been considerably reduced by the time the Marinids completed the conquest of Morocco. Many of the important towns of the Andalus, including Seville, Jerez, and Murcia, had been conquered by Castile. In Granada a Muslim dynasty came to power in 1235 called the Nasrid which in the 1270s ruled an enclave comprising the area between Tarifa and Vera along the coast, and inland extending just beyond Ronda. This small but prosperous state survived for about two-and-a-half-centuries through the astuteness of its rulers and the fact that both the Castilians and the Marinids considered it a useful buffer. When Abu Yusuf first crossed with his army to Spain in 1275 his aim seems to have been neither to impose his rule over the Andalusian Muslims, nor to launch a holy war against the Christians. That he asked the help of Aragon in the conquest of Ceuta showed that to him the religious motive was subordinate to political considerations. His campaigns in the Iberian Peninsula seem to have been aimed only at maintaining a Christian-Muslim balance of power that would safeguard Morocco from further attacks.

Abu Yusuf crossed to Spain at the head of his army four times. He occupied positions which the army were able to use as landing places in the south or as advanced posts from which to conduct raids on Castilian territory, but he did not attempt to establish a Marinid administration. These positions had been ceded by the Nasrids, upon whose request the first Marinid expedition was sent in 1275. Since the second Marinid campaign in the peninsula between June and November 1277, the Nasrids had come to fear that Marinid intervention might lead to the annexation of their territory; consequently they turned to Castile for help. When in 1279 a large Marinid expedition was being prepared for the war in Spain, the Nasrid king Muhammad II was so alarmed that he offered his help to Castile in the occupation of Algeciras where the main Marinid force in Spain was stationed. He also persuaded Yaghmurasan of Tlemsen to attack Marinid positions in Morocco. Nevertheless, as he witnessed the inability of the Castilians to capture Algeciras, he changed sides and sent his warships to take part on the side of the Marinid fleet in a major sea battle in which the Castilians were defeated off the coast of Gibraltar on 22 July 1279. The Nasrids continued to act in this vacillating fashion until the mid-fourteenth century when the Marinids were no longer able to intervene in the peninsula: they called on the Marinids for help whenever they were threatened by the Castilians, and turned to the Christians whenever their Muslim allies seemed strong enough to threaten them. The Marinids, however, continued to view the aim of the war in Spain as being that of maintaining the *status quo*. In July 1282 Abu Yusuf even crossed to Spain to give aid to Alfonso V of Castile against his rebellious son Don Sancho. When in April 1285 Don Sancho acceded to the throne of Castile Abu Yusuf once more led an expedition into Spain. After raiding the neighbourhood of Jerez and Seville, and after the Marinid fleet had forced the Castilians to withdraw their warships from the neighbourhood of Algeciras, Abu Yusuf agreed to a meeting with Don Sancho on 22 October 1285 at which occasion a peace treaty was signed and gifts were exchanged. Abu Yusuf died in January 1286 in Algeciras and his successor Abu Ya'qub Yusuf followed his policy of intervening in Spain in order to restrain Castile but not to occupy territory.

For Castile this *modus vivendi* with her Muslim neighbours was useful as long as she felt threatened by Aragon. In 1291 her long period of rivalry and a three-year war with Aragon ended, and the two Christian states reached an agreement over their respective ambitions in the Maghrib. In the Treaty of Monteagudo of December 1291 it was agreed that the Zayanid and Hafsid states, with whom Aragon had enjoyed diplomatic and commerical relations since 1250, were the latter's preserve, whereas Castile was considered to have special rights in Morocco because of her long tradition of fighting this country's rulers since the Almoravid intervention in Spain. Aragon lost nothing by recognizing Morocco as Castile's sphere of influence, since her attempts to establish relations with the Marinids had so far failed. Abu Yusuf had declared void his agreement of 1274 with Jack the Conqueror as soon as Ceuta was brought under his control in 1275, and in 1276 he refused to negotiate a treaty of peace and commerce proposed by the king of Aragon. In 1286, on the eve of Aragon's war with Castile, Alfonso III sought to conclude with Abu Yusuf a military alliance directed against Castile. This attempt also failed, and in the war between Castile and Aragon both the Marinids and the Nasrids preserved an attitude of neutrality.

The end of the Aragon-Castile war renewed the fears of the Marinids of Christian attacks on Morocco. Consequently, Abu Ya'qub considered it necessary to undertake a demonstration of military strength at the end of 1291 when he attacked Jerez and Seville. After this the alliance of the two Christian states aggravated the Marinids' long-standing fears of Christian expansion into Morocco, especially after Castile occupied Tarifa in 1292.

From the end of the thirteenth to the middle of the fourteenth century the establishment of a Maghriban empire seems to have been viewed by the Marinids as a means to withstand the combined power of Castile and

Aragon. It was also a means of extirpating the influence which Aragon had developed in the Zayanid and the Hafsid states. In 1290 Abu Ya'qub led his army against Tlemsen, and although he pillaged and destroyed the town's surroundings, he was unable to enter the town itself. In 1295 he once more turned to the Zayanids and spent the remaining twelve years of his life in war against them. After occupying Tawrirt, Wajda, Nadruma, and Tawint, all in Zayanid territory, he proceeded in May 1299 to besiege Tlemsen. To ensure that no provisions reached it, he had a wall built around its fortifications and skirted it with a deep moat. For his residence and that of his officials and troops he built a residential village near Tlemsen which he called Mansura (Victorious). During the long siege, which lasted eight years, he conquered the important Zayanid towns in western Algeria: Oran, Talmut, Hunain, Tamzardakt, Mustaghanim, Sharshal, and Wanshiris. The Maghrawa tribe submitted to him, the ruler of Algiers Ibn 'Allan recognized his suzerainty, and the two branches of the Hafsids in Tunis and Bougie vied with each other to win his favour. While near Tlemsen he also established relations with the Mamluk sultan of Egypt, Muhammad Qalawun, and a delegation from Mecca offered the recognition of his religious authority by its *sharifs*. But the siege dragged on, and the Zayanids refused to surrender even when 'Uthman, the Zayanid sultan, died in 1304. His son Muhammad took over the command and continued the resistance in spite of the hardships which the population of Tlemsen endured. About 120,000 of the people of Tlemsen perished in the course of the siege, which came to an end only when Abu Ya'qub was assassinated by one of his eunuchs on 11 May 1307.

The project of building a Marinid Maghriban empire was revived by Sultan Abul-Hassan (1331–51). This occurred in the wake of increased Christian belligerency in which not only Castile but also Aragon took a part. Aragon, which since 1250 had pursued a policy of peaceful penetration of the central and eastern Maghrib and had banned Christian piracy in the western Mediterranean, became in 1314 the official patron of privateering. In this year Jack II authorized the city of Barcelona to collect special taxes for the purpose of building ships intended for a war against the Muslims, and founded a religious militant confraternity to combat Muslim pirates and other adherents of the Muslim faith. In the spring of 1319 the admiral of Aragon, Francesc Carroz, was appointed to command the fleet furnished by Barcelona and Valencia to attack the Maghriban states. The Hafsids and the Zayanids suffered as much as the Marinids from the revival of Christian piracy in the Mediterranean, but, unlike them, the Marinids had not learnt to live with the changing moods of European politics and to preserve commercial and diplomatic relations with Europe even when their towns were destroyed and looted. The Marinids were also more vulnerable, since they were the object of the ambitions of both Aragon and Castile. Thus it appears that the new expansion eastwards was intended to create a strong state, large and strong enough to face the new wave of the Christian threat. Abul-Hasan was able to exploit his connections with the Hafsids in his attempt to build a state that would inherit Hafsid authority together with its associations with Almohad religious legitimacy. He was married to the sister of the Hafsid ruler Abu Bakr, and the importance he attached to this relationship can be gauged from the fact that when his first Hafsid wife was killed in Spain in 1340 he arranged in 1346 to marry Abu Bakr's daughter.

That there was a connection between the expansion eastwards and the fear of Christian expansion is suggested by the fact that Abul-Hasan started to re-establish the Marinid military presence in Spain at the time when preparations for the conquest of Tlemsen were under way. In 1333 he sent an army to recover Gibraltar from Castile; and as soon as he began the invasion of Zayanid territory in 1335 he ordered the construction of *ribats* for the purpose of defending the Maghriban coast against Christian attacks. When in April 1337 Tlemsen surrendered to the Marinids, they had already conquered most of Algeria's towns including Algiers and brought the other important Zanata tribes, the Maghrawa of the Shaliff and the Banu Tujin of the Midia plain, to submission. When at the zenith of his power Abul-Hasan once more turned to Spain, sending his son Abu Malik in 1339. But this ardent youth got himself killed in a rash attack on Jerez. Another expedition led by the sultan in person in 1340 resulted in a disastrous defeat by the Castilians on the river Saldo. The fall of Algerciras[1] in March 1344 to the Castilian army reinforced by the elite of the cavalry of England, France, and Italy, after a twenty months' siege, meant that the offensive across the straits was once and for all in Christian hands. It was then that Abul-Hasan proceeded to complete the creation of a Maghriban empire.

The Hafsids' fear of Abul-Hasan's ambitions started with his conquest of Tlemsen. It is said that the Hafsid sultan Abu-Bakr consented to give his daughter in marriage to Abul-Hasan in 1346 only after much hesitation, fearing that this would enable his son-in-law to claim his throne after his death. Abu Bakr died on 19 October 1346, when Abul-Hasan's new bride was on her way from Tunis. The heir, Abul-'Abbas, was then living in Gafsa as viceroy of southern Tunisia; when he arrived in Tunis he was killed by his brother 'Umar who had himself recognized as sultan in the capital. Early in 1347 Abul-Hasan received in Tlemsen Abu Bakr's former chamberlain, Abu Muhammad 'Abdulla b. Tafrajin, a descendant of one of the old Almohad families of Tinmal, who came urging him to invade

---

[1] The impression this conflict between Christianity and Islam left on the imagination of Europe is recorded by Chaucer, who makes the knight in the *Canterbury Tales* fight in this battle.

Tunisia. With Abul-'Abbas killed, and the support of the head of the Almohad notables secured, no serious obstacles remained in the way of Marinid conquest. In May 1347 Abul-Hasan advanced eastwards with his army, and before reaching Tunis the governors of the Zab, the Tunisian Jarid, Gabis, and Tripoli recognized his authority. Abu Bakr's son Muhammad, until then governor of Bougie, was given the governorship of Nadruma, a Zayanid town, but he was made to accompany Abul-Hasan to Tunis. Soon after entering the capital Abul-Hasan went southwards, stopping in Qairawan, Susa, and Mahdiyya, and appointed governors over the towns and also over the rural districts which had so far been left under the control of the Arabian tribal chiefs. At the close of 1347 the Maghrib, from Misurata to the Atlantic, was once more united under the rule of a Berber dynasty.

Of the Arabian nomads who invaded the Maghrib in the eleventh century, most of those still in Tunisia at the time of the Marinid invasion were members of the Banu Sulaim tribe; most of the Banu Hilal had by then settled in Morocco, although a small fraction remained in Tunisia. By substituting direct government for the system of tribal overlordship, Abul-Hasan robbed the Arabian chiefs of the feudal privileges they had come to consider their customary right. By the end of 1347 they were already restive, and they approached 'Abdul-Wahid al-Lihiani[1] to lead them in battle against the Marinids, but he betrayed them to Abul-Hasan. In January 1348 Abul-Hasan imprisoned several of their chiefs who, not aware of al-Lihiani's treachery, came to him to carry out the customary rite of congratulating him on the occasion of 'Id al-Fitr. The Arabian tribesmen thereon broke out in open rebellion, choosing as their figurehead a descendant of the last Almohad sultan Abu Dabbus, Ahmad b. 'Uthman, who worked as a tailor in Tuzar. Abul-Hasan attacked the rebels, near Qairawan on 8 April 1348, but the tribal warriors under his command, especially the Zanatas who joined him after the conquest of Tlemsen, deserted him in the battle. Defeated, he retreated to Qairawan, leaving his camp to the pillage of the Arabian tribesmen. While Abul-Hasan was blockaded in Qairawan, a popular uprising in Tunis forced Yahya b. Sulaiman, his deputy there, to flee for his safety with other Marinid officials to the citadel (the Qasba). The wily 'Abdulla b. Tafrajin, having accompanied Abul-Hasan in his former capacity as chamberlain, deserted to the rebels when his new master sent him to negotiate terms of peace with them. Abul-Hasan later escaped to Susa with the help of the Banu Muhalhal Arabian clan; whereupon 'Abdulla b. Tafrajin fled to Egypt, and in Tunis the populace lost heart, so that by the time Abul-Hasan arrived in the capital in June 1348 Yahya b. Sulaiman had regained its control. In the following few months Abul-Hasan was able once more

[1] See below, pp. 145 ff.

to make his authority felt in the Tunisian countryside, but by this time two serious rebellions had occurred in the west.

In eastern Algeria most of the important towns declared themselves independent of the Marinids when Abul-Hasan was defeated near Qairawan. Abu Bakr's son Fadl, whom Abul-Hasan had appointed governor of Bona, repudiated his allegiance to him; Bougie followed suit and renounced its loyalty to the Marinids. Constantine also rebelled a short time after two delegations from Castile and ancient Mali arrived there with gifts for Abul-Hasan. The secession of these towns was accompanied by the uprising of Algerian Zanata tribes – the Banu 'Abdul-Wad, Banu Tujin, and Maghrawa – who submitted to Abul-Hasan's rule when he was strong and able to tempt them with booty and official preferment, and deserted him as soon as his fortunes foundered.

Of more importance to Abul-Hasan's fate was the rebellion of his son Abu 'Inan, whom he left in Tlemsen as governor of the central Maghrib when he began the invasion of the east. The expectation that his father would not survive the conflict in Tunisia, and the fear that if he did not act with promptitude his nephew Mansur, the governor of Fez, would seize the opportunity to become sultan, led Abu 'Inan to declare himself sultan in June (or July) 1348. He was recognized in Tlemsen without difficulty, and the fugitives from his father's army enlisted under his banners. In July he defeated Mansur near Taza, and the whole of Morocco passed under his control without much resistance; only the governor of Ceuta withheld submission until Abul-Hasan's fate became clear.

Within a year of his rejection of Marinid hegemony in the spring of 1348, Fadl b. Abu Bakr, with help from the Abul-Lail Arabian clan, succeeded in making the greater part of Tunisia accept him as ruler. He also tried twice, unsuccessfully, to capture Tunis. Eventually, as his companions became weary of the life of siege in the hostile country, Abul-Hasan left by sea in December 1349 for northern Morocco. Most of his ships were wrecked near Bougie, but he reached Algiers, where he was joined by his son Nasir who was governor of Biskra. With the small army the two were able to muster, they marched on Tlemsen which had reverted to the Zayanids after Abu 'Inan left the town for Fez. Defeated by the Zayanids near Tlemsen, where his son Nasir was also killed, Abul-Hasan escaped southwards to Sijilmasa. Chased from this town by Abu 'Inan early in 1350, he went to Marrakish, where he was well received by its people, but in May he was defeated near Marrakish by Abu 'Inan. Again he fled, this time to take refuge with the Hintata tribe in the High Atlas. He died there a year later on 25 May 1351, but not before Abu 'Inan's blockade had forced him to abdicate in his favour.

The match of his father in ambition and energy, Abu 'Inan made the third Marinid attempt to build a Maghriban empire. He too failed, though with less disastrous results. In 1352, a year after his father's death, he invaded Zayanid territory and defeated an alliance of Zayanids and Arabian tribesmen in the plain of Angad north of Wajda. The Zayanid sultan Abu Sa'id 'Uthman was taken captive and killed, and the Marinids reoccupied Tlemsen. Oran and Algiers had remained in Marinid hands since Abul-Hasan's invasion. Bougie was taken in 1353 in spite of the resistance of the Sanhaja there, and in 1356 Constantine was conquered. In August 1357 Abu 'Inan entered Tunis after a feeble show of resistance, and the Hafsid sultan Abu Ishaq fled with the army to Mahdiyya. But Abu 'Inan was soon forced by his own troops to evacuate Tunisia. Fearing to be caught in the hostile country, they insisted, with the encouragement of Abu 'Inan's vizier Faris b. Maimun, on returning to Morocco. Abu 'Inan paid no attention to their clamour, but they started to leave Tunisia all the same, thus forcing him to evacuate it. Constantine, Algiers, and Oran remained, however, in the hands of the Marinids; and the tribes in the areas of the Zab and Biskra accepted Abu 'Inan's authority, so that his state included the greater part of present-day Algeria.

The Nasrids of Granada, ever anxious to maintain a balance of power between their Christian neighbours in the north and their co-religionists in the south, became concerned around the middle of the fourteenth century about the growing strength of the Marinids. Their natural allies in the Maghrib, the Zayanids, were crushed by Abul-Hasan's and Abu 'Inan's invasions. Concerned lest Abu 'Inan should turn to them after completing the conquest of Tunisia, they incited internal rebellions in Morocco to keep him occupied, at a time when Castilian pressure on them was at an ebb. For this purpose they used the Marinid princes to whom they gave asylum in Granada. In 1353 the Nasrid king Abul-Hajjaj Yusuf secured a Castilian ship which transported Abul-Fadl, Abu 'Inan's brother, to Sus, where he joined forces with the Saksawa tribe and rebelled against his brother. This rebellion was easily crushed, and Abul-Fadl was killed. Muhammad V, who succeeded Abul-Hajjaj in 1354, tried to appease the Marinid sultan and induce him to send an army against the Castilians. In 1354 he sent the veteran minister Lisan al-Din Ibn al-Khatib, famous as a man of letters and historian, at the head of a goodwill delegation. The poets who accompanied Ibn al-Khatib sang Abu 'Inan's praises, and the religious scholars pleaded with him in the name of Muhammad V to send help to the Muslims of Spain. Although in 1355 Abu 'Inan sent a force across the straits to chastise the insubordinate Marinid governor of Gibraltar, he did not send any army to fight the Castilians.

In November 1357 Abu 'Inan fell ill, and the courtiers expected him to die. The vizier Hasan b. 'Umar al-Fududi hastened to nominate the sultan's son Abu Bakr Sa'id as successor, so that the heir-apparent Abu Zayan Muhammad, with whom the minister had had a dispute, should not attain the throne. But December passed and Abu 'Inan was still alive. Fearing his revenge for his precipitous nomination of a man of his own choice to succeed, al-Fududi strangled his ailing master on 10 January 1358. Abu 'Inan was thirty-one years old when he died, and Abu Bakr only a boy. His reign formed the start of a period which was to last until the end of Marinid rule in 1465, in which the sultans were largely figure-heads, placed on the throne by ministers who exercised power in their name. Abu Bakr himself was under al-Fududi's control, a fact which was resented by Abu 'Inan's other sons, and caused the rebellion of one of them, al-Mu'tamid, the governor of Marrakish. Al-Mu'tamid was able to rebel only with the help of the Hintata chief Abu Thabit 'Amir. This alliance between the governor of Marrakish and the Hintata chief is significant because it marks the beginning of the dominance of the High Atlas chieftaincies over the politics of Marrakish.

During the period following Abu 'Inan's death in 1358 a tradition of cruelty in Moroccan politics set in which survived until the twentieth century. Viziers achieved and retained power through guile, transient alliances, and using the right opportunity to liquidate those who hampered their ambitions. Failure in the struggle for power meant death, generally preceded by torture designed to force the victim to disclose his hidden fortunes, a part of which he would have acquired from those he had displaced. Fear of such a fate gave added strength to any pretender to the throne capable of marching on Fez with a few hundred warriors. The viziers, rather than risk all they possessed, including life itself, shifted their loyalty to the pretender for fear he should succeed. The extent of the confusion in Morocco caused by these fears and ambitions when two claimants to the throne appeared at the same time, as happened in 1359, can only be imagined.

Some stability was achieved in Moroccan politics during the reign of Abu Faris 'Abdul-'Aziz (1366–72) through his ability to curtail the influence of the ministers. Abu Faris owed his throne to the vizier 'Umar b. 'Abdulla al-Yabani, who had killed Sultan Abu Zayan in 1366 when he tried to remove him from office; but as soon as he consolidated his position, he had the vizier assassinated. The Marinid sultanate revived temporarily, as is indicated by the submission of Marrakish to Fez, and the ability of the latter to resist the Nasrid interference. In Marrakish the minister al-Yabani had installed the Marinid prince Abu Fadl as governor during Abu Zayan's reign. Abu Fadl became independent of Fez, but was controlled by the Hintata chief Abu Thabit 'Amir, al-Yabani's ally. When Abu Faris had al-Yabani killed, Abu Fadl sought to rid himself of his own powerful mentor. The Hintata chief sensed this and retired to his castle in Mount Darin. From there he sent word to the sultan urging him to capture Marrakish. Early in 1368 the army of Fez entered Marrakish, then it attacked the Hintatas in their stronghold. In April 1370 their castle was taken, and Abu Thabit was captured in a cave nearby where he waited for the melting of the snow before travelling to Sus.

Although Abu Faris's successors were to become tools in the hands of Muhammad V, king of Granada, Abu Faris defied him successfully. Muhammad V was helped by the Marinid sultan Abu Sālim (1351–62) when in adversity. In 1359 he was deposed, and Abu Sālim, who had been the Nasrid king's guest when exiled to Spain by his brother Abu 'Inan, prevailed upon the usurper of his throne, his brother Isma'il, to allow him to travel to Morocco together with his minister Ibn al-Khatib. The fugitive king remained in Fez as the guest of Abu Sālim and his successor until he regained his throne. During Abu Faris' reign, relations between Muhammad V and his veteran minister worsened. In defiance of the Nasrid king's wishes, Ibn al-Khatib was offered asylum in Morocco, and in 1371 Abu Faris facilitated his escape through the Marinid garrison in Gibraltar. Ibn al-Khatib's presence in Fez, and the deference with which he was treated, became a sore point in relations between the Nasrids and the Marinids.

After the death of Abu Faris in 1372, Muhammad V, benefiting from a temporary lull in the Castilian attacks, was able to extend his influence over Morocco. In 1374 he captured Gibraltar from the Marinids, and demanded that the young sultan Abu Zayan should cede Ceuta to him and extradite Ibn al-Khatib. As Abu Zayan rejected both demands, Muhammad V sent to Morocco two Marinid princes, first 'Abdul-Rahman b. Yaflusin, then Abul-'Abbas Ahmad b. Abu Sālim, both of whom he had held in custody in Granada. With his help they overran northern Morocco and laid siege to Fez, thus inducing the vizier Abu Bakr b. al-Kas to depose Abu Zayan. Abul-'Abbas became sultan in Fez, taking as his vizier a man chosen by Muhammad V. The other pretender, 'Abdul-Rahman b. Taflusin, became governor of Marrakish, which he ruled independently of Fez, with Wadi Umm al-Rabi' forming the boundary between his 'kingdom' and that of Fez. The new sultan of Fez complied with Muhammad V's wishes: he had Ibn al-Khatib executed on flimsy charges of religious blasphemy, and surrendered Ceuta to the Nasrids. Muhammad V at the same time altered the status of the Marinid princes in his domains. So far they occupied an honoured position as commanders of the warriors stationed on the frontiers between the kingdom of Granada and Castile; in 1374 they were removed from this position and held as prisoners. During the reign of the last but one Marinid sultan, Abu Sa'id 'Uthman (1398–1420), the danger of Christian expansion into Morocco became a reality when Ceuta was occupied by the Portuguese in 1415. This was but the beginning of a drive for colonization which was to result later in the century in the occupation of several Moroccan towns by the Portuguese and the Spaniards. In the context of Marinid–Nasrid relations the occupation of Ceuta meant that both felt threatened, and in 1419 they cooperated in a futile attack on Ceuta. The presence of the Christians between Fez and Granada brought to an end the influence which the Marinids and Nasrids had exercised on each other's political destiny.

Sultan Abu Sa'id met his death at the hand of an assassin. His death and the low prestige of the dynasty was exploited by one of the Wattasid cousins of the Banu Marin called Abu Zakariyya Yahya, who was able to seize power as regent in the name of Abu Sa'id's son 'Abdul-Haqq, who was one year old. The Wattasids had settled in the Rif where they had controlled the fortress of Tazuta since the last days of the Almohads, and although related to the Marinids their loyalty was suspect to the early Marinid leaders. But in time several Wattasid chiefs came to hold important posts in the Marinid administration. Abu Zakariyya Yahya was governor of Sala when Abu Sa'id was assassinated. His intervention saved the dynasty from overthrow, but only temporarily. The inability of the sultanate of Fez to parry the Portuguese attacks on northern Morocco was a source of general discontentment and, as will be discussed in greater detail in connection with the rise of the Sa'dians to power, the Jazuliyya Sufi order organized opposition to the Marinids. The Arabian tribes were agitating, and two pretenders to the throne appeared on the death of Abu Sa'id, one supported by Tlemsen and the other by Granada. Abu Zakariyya was able to defeat the pretenders and assert the authority of the sultan in whose name he ruled. He was also successful in the war with Portugal. In 1437 a poorly equipped Portuguese expedition attacked Tangier, and Abu Zakariyya's forces defeated it and took all the survivors as captives on 16 October. Among the captives was the infante of Portugal, Fernando, who was made to agree in the name of his brother, King Duarte, to evacuate Ceuta. Fernando was to be held hostage until this was accomplished; but since his brother refused to honour the agreement, he remained in prison until his death in 1443. Abu Zakariyya's success against the Portuguese contributed much to his political standing so that, although 'Abdul-Haqq came of age in 1437, the vizier still remained the most powerful man in the state.

Wattasid control over the kingdom of Fez lasted until 1457. Abu Zakariyya himself was killed by bedouin from Angad in 1448. He was replaced by another Wattasid, 'Ali b. Yusuf, who held the vizierate until his death in June 1457, and was succeeded by Abu Zakariyya's son Yahya. This last Wattasid chief remained in power for only seventy days. His overbearing methods, and his removal of the *qadi* of Fez from his office, won him the hostility of influential people in the capital. 'Abdul-Haqq exploited this hostility to rid himself of Wattasid control. Yahya and the other influential Wattasids in Fez were killed by the sultan's orders. This marked the beginning of the end for the Marinid sultanate. In 1458 the Portuguese occupied Qsar al-Kabir, between Ceuta and Tangier, and Tangier itself was continually threatened. The Muslim masses, always ready to disown a ruler who could not defend them against Christian invasion, seethed with discontentment; and the reliance of the sultan on Jewish officials in the execution of unpopular financial policies led to the rebellion which ended 'Abdul-Haqq's reign and the Marinid dynasty.

It was known that the sultan borrowed money from the rich Jews of Fez. When he wanted to introduce financial reforms, he entrusted them to a Jew called Harun, the sultan's supervisor of the finances. Since under Harun's directions the *sharifs* and the *shaikhs* of the Sufi orders were for the first time made to pay taxes, they could represent the reforms as a Jewish plot directed against themselves. The *sharifs* had become especially important in the religious life of Fez after the tomb of Mawlay Idris, the founder of the Idrisid state from whom most of them claimed descent, was discovered in 1437 and became a popular shrine. In 1465 they rebelled when the sultan was absent from Fez, rousing the masses by a claim, whose truth is difficult to ascertain, that one of the tax-collectors had maltreated a woman of *sharifian* descent. The *shaikh* of the Qarawiyyin mosque called the faithful to rebellion, and in the process the *sharifs* took control of the town and proclaimed their head, the Idrisid *sharif* Muhammad al-Juti, as ruler. 'Abdul-Haqq was brought to Fez in May 1465 and was beheaded, and al-Juti retained control until the Wattasid Muhammad al-Shaikh captured Fez in 1472.

The Marinid *makhzan* (government) continued the traditions of the tribal state, insofar as, apart from the central administration located in Fez, no civil administrative structure was developed in the provinces. The army chiefs exercised administrative functions outside the capital. But since the army consisted predominantly of contingents provided by those tribes associated with the ruling dynasty, the rule of the Marinids implied the domination of the favoured tribes over those that were not. The tribal contingents were drawn predominantly from the Banu Marin and Zanata tribes living in Algeria, such as the Banu Tujin. Some of the Arabian tribes in Morocco were employed in the army, particularly the Banu Zughba and al-Athbaj, but the Masmuda and Sanhaja Berbers associated with the two preceding dynasties were excluded. The Marinids also inherited the practice of employing Christian mercenary troops, who were mainly cavalry and formed the bodyguard of the sultan. The more distinguished of the army chiefs often held the more important offices in the central administration, and the chief executive officer under the sultan was a vizier. A vizier attained his authority through the sultan's favour and his family's power. As the fortunes of the vizier's clan depended on his success or failure, a change of vizier was often the occasion for conflicts between contending clans. The situation became especially disastrous for the country when the authority of the sultans weakened after Abu Inan's death in 1358 and sultans became the appointees, and therefore the partisans, of rival vizieral families.

In a society where the political appeal of rulers depended to an important extent on their religious standing, the Marinids laboured under a disadvantage in being the heirs of the Almohads. The founder members of the dynasty, Abu Yahya and Abu Yusuf, tried to offset the fact that their authority lacked a religious foundation by their homage to the Hafsids of Tunisia. Their successors tried to achieve the same end by posing as patrons of religious learning. They encouraged higher education in the *madrasas* which they founded in Fez, and as a result this city became in the Marinid period the intellectual capital of the Maghrib. The *madrasas* were attached to the three main mosques of the capital: the Qarawiyyin, the Andalusian mosque, and the Grand Mosque of New Fez. Lodges for the students were founded in which gifted young men from outside Fez resided. Abu Saʿid, Abul-Hasan, and Abu ʿInan were all interested in religious learning; the last two began the practice of convening the religious scholars regularly in the court to discuss various aspects of learning, especially points of Muslim law with direct bearing on state action. Poetry and history also received the attention of the Marinid sultans, but because of their attachment to religious orthodoxy they avoided the controversial subject of philosophy.

Fez benefited from being the capital of Morocco in another way, in becoming the leading centre of economic activity in the country. Handicrafts had formed a prominent part of the life of Fez since the period of the Almoravids, when the influence of the Andalus on the artisans' work began to become noticeable. R. Le Tourneau[1] estimates that about 150 corporations of artisans existed in Fez during the reigns of Abul-Hasan and Abu ʿInan. The most important industry was that of the weavers, employing about 20,000 persons. The councils of the corporations were links between the government and the artisans, and were active in securing aid through appeals to the public for members who fell on bad times. Some of the corporations of artisans had patron saints, in whose honour they organized annual festivals. Most of the raw materials used in the industries of Fez came from the city or its neighbourhood. However, gold for the jewellers, who were predominantly Jews, was brought from the western Sudan. Most of the products were bought locally, though some were sold in other Maghriban towns, especially the towns of Morocco. The annual pilgrimage caravan was the occasion for selling the goods of Fez in the eastern countries through which the pilgrims passed; these goods also reached the Niger bend by way of the caravan route starting in Sijilmasa.

[1] In *Fez in the age of the Marinides* (Norman, Okla., 1961).

But there was something parochial about Fez during the Marinid period, and this parochialism seems to have been due to the limited outlook and authority of some of its rulers. Whereas religious learning in Fez received the patronage of the Marinid sultans, it was neglected in the provinces. As the Marinids made no attempt to create an organized army, and neglected to organize and control the government of the provinces, Fez led its administrative, religious, and, to a lesser extent, economic life independently of the rest of Marinid territories. In the religious sphere the parochialism of Fez is especially apparent. As its religious scholars and administrators failed to influence the provinces, the Sufi orders occupied the gap by providing religious instruction, spiritual guidance, and even political leadership. A situation consequently developed, such as existed also in other parts of the Maghrib, whereby the large towns – Fez, Tlemsen, Tunis, etc. – became the centres of "orthodox" religious scholarship, whilst in rural areas the Sufi calling predominated. This is not to say that Sufism did not take root in the towns. Indeed it did, but in the countryside it dominated the religious outlook of the Muslims, whereas in the towns it was not to do so until some centuries later.

The Hafsids

The idea of Maghriban unity associated with the Almohads survived the destruction of their state, although strong tribal loyalties continued to divide the Maghriban society into feuding communities. It was basically a religious idea, closely linked with the Muslim doctrine of the *umma* as an indivisible community, to which the Almohads were the first to give a concrete historical existence in the Maghrib. The Hafsids exploited this idea and claimed to be the legitimate heirs of the Almohads in building their state. The Almohads, i.e. the descendants of the founding tribes of the Tinmal community, occupied a privileged political position in the Hafsid state, and the Hafsids continued to say the Friday prayer in the name of Ibn Tumart until 1311. But important as their claim to being the heirs of the Almohads was, the ability of the first Hafsid rulers in Tunisia was the decisive factor in the construction of a viable state.

During the fourteen years when Muhammad b. Abu Hafs was the viceroy of Tunisia,[1] from 1207 until his death in 1221, he ruled independently of the Almohad government in Marrakish. The Almohad caliphs trusted the Hafsids to remain loyal to their family; and seeing Abu Muhammad's ability to defeat Yahya b. Ghaniya and to keep Tunisia under control, they left him to govern the country much as he wished. They kept him well provided with money, so that he was able to create a disciplined army without making heavy impositions on the people. When he died a

[1] See above, p. 117.

state council in Tunis proceeded to elect his son Abu Zaid 'Abdul-Rahman to succeed him without waiting for instructions from Marrakish. But the caliph al-Mustansir still had the power to prevent the Hafsids from becoming Tunisia's reigning dynasty, and in 1221 he placed the vice-royalty of this country in the hands of an aged Almohad prince of the family of 'Abdul-Mu'min. The confusion in the centre of the caliphate, and the turbulence of Tunisia under the new regime, eventually combined to bring back the Hafsids to Tunisia.

The prince appointed by the caliph al-Mustansir to govern Tunisia was Abul-'Ala' Idris, whose brother 'Abdul-Wahid was to hold the caliphate for a short period in 1224. Being old, Abul-'Ala' brought his son Abu Zaid to assist him in his functions, and this prince occupied himself with campaigns against Yahya b. Ghaniya who had again become active in Tunisia. At the beginning of 1224 he defeated Ibn Ghaniya at Majdul. His father had by then died, and he acted as his natural successor. Notwithstanding this, a new governor was appointed by Abu Zaid's uncle 'Abdul-Wahid; but before he arrived the caliph was deposed on 10 September 1224, and his successor al-'Adil left Abu Zaid in charge of Tunisia. Abu Zaid retained office for two years, during which he was the object of general execration because of his unruly whims. His conduct only increased the esteem which the Hafsids had in the country, so that al-'Adil was left with little choice but to appoint another Hafsid, Abu Muhammad 'Abdulla, as viceroy of Tunisia. Abu Muhammad arrived in Tunis in November 1226. Abu Zakariyya, his brother, had gone to Tunisia before him and pacified the tribes in eastern Algeria, and when Abu Muhammad arrived Abu Zakariyya was appointed governor of Gabis. The rebellion of the pretender al-Ma'mun in Spain against the caliph al-'Adil in October 1227 caused much confusion in Tunisia, especially since Abu Muhammad refused to submit to al-Ma'mun. His brother, however, did submit and in 1228 he was appointed by al-Ma'mun to replace Abu Muhammad.

Abu Zakariyya was twenty-six years old when he assumed the vice-royalty of Tunisia. Favourable circumstances enabled him to establish an independent state which was relatively stable internally and received recognition as the leading Maghriban kingdom from the European states interested in Africa. In 1229 the caliph al-Ma'mun massacred the Almohad chiefs in Marrakish and rejected the doctrines of the Mahdi Ibn Tumart. This gave Abu Zakariyya justification for discarding his authority, without at first renouncing the authority of 'Abdul-Mu'min's family altogether. He recognized the suzerainty of a rebel Almohad prince called Yahya b. al-Nasir, who rose against the caliph in Haskura; and when this prince proved unable to capture the throne from al-Ma'mun, Abu Zakariyya later in the year discarded his authority too. He had the Friday prayer said in the name of the Mahdi Ibn Tumart, and his own name was mentioned after the Mahdi's, with the title of amir. After this discreet declaration of independence the Hafsids posed as the true heirs of the Mahdi's authority, thereby implying that the rulers in Marrakish, by rejecting his authority, renounced their title as caliphs. A few years later, in 1236 or 1237, Abu Zakariyya assumed the full dignity of an independent sovereign and took to himself the caliphial title of *amir al-mu'minin*.

As a result of the power vacuum in eastern Algeria, the Hafsids were able to incorporate this area into their state between 1230 and 1233 without much difficulty. Tripolitania had submitted to Abu Zakariyya's authority in 1228. After suppressing a rebellion against him by the governor of Tripoli in 1241, Abu Zakariyya even sought to extend his rule over the western Maghrib, and to substantiate his claim to be the only legitimate heir of the Almohads. The two powerful Zanata chiefs of western Algeria, 'Abdul-Qawi of the Banu Tujin and al-'Abbas b. Mandil of the Maghrawa, offered their cooperation in conquering Tlemsen from the Zayanids. In 1242 the Hafsid army, reinforced by the warriors of these chiefs, occupied Tlemsen. But Yaghmurasan was able to escape southwards, and no Zanata chief would agree to take up the governorship of Tlemsen while he was at large. Abu Zakariyya was therefore compelled to come to terms with Yaghmurasan and, having obtained from him the promise of submission, he reinstated him in Tlemsen. In 1242 Sijilmasa and Ceuta also recognized Abu Zakariyya's authority. Sijilmasa, however, was again brought under the authority of Marrakish later in the same year, but the governor of Ceuta, Ibn Khalas, continued to govern the town in Abu Zakariyya's name.

As heirs of the Almohads, the Hafsids were regarded by the Muslim towns in Spain directly threatened by the Christian expansion as their natural protectors. Valencia, threatened by Aragon's expansion, submitted to Abu Zakariyya's suzerainty and appealed to him for help. Eighteen Hafsid ships were sent in 1238 to take part in defending the town against the Aragonese, but it surrendered in the autumn of the same year. Seville, Jerez, Tarifa, and even Granada also accepted Hafsid suzerainty in the hope of receiving military help from Tunis, but Abu Zakariyya abstained from further participation in the war in Spain. It appears that he tried to help Valencia remain independent because it was an important source of the wood which the Hafsids needed for their fleet. As the Reconquista did not threaten the Hafsids directly, Abu Zakariyya avoided further involvement in the Christian-Muslim confrontation in the peninsula. Instead, about a decade later he responded favourably to Aragon's overtures towards establishing commercial relations with Tunis.

More involved in Mediterranean politics than Castile, and less animated by the spirit of the crusade, Aragon under Jack the Conqueror (1213–76) wavered until 1250 in augmenting its political and commercial interests between sustaining the war against the Muslim states in the Maghrib and embarking upon a policy of peaceful penetration. In the 1230s the Catalonian corsairs, receiving Aragonese official and religious sanction, attacked Muslim ships in the Mediterranean. Nevertheless in 1235 Jack the Conqueror sent a legation to Tunis which sought to establish commercial relations with the Hafsids similar to those Venice had had with them since 1231 and Pisa since 1234. The legation failed, because the Hafsids could not establish relations with Aragon without damage to their religious standing because Aragon had occupied Majorca in 1232, and was at the time expanding in Spain at the expense of Muslim states. After the fall of Valencia Abu Zakariyya became more tractable. Commercial relations between Tunis and some of the dependencies of the king of Aragon began in 1239 without a formal agreement, and one of his subjects in business in Tunis, Ferrer de Nina, was active in starting the negotiations which were carried on between the two states in either 1240 or 1241. But Abu Zakariyya still avoided a direct formal agreement with Aragon. The treaty of peace and commerce which resulted from these negotiations was concluded between Abu Zakariyya and the infante Peter of Portugal who ruled Majorca in the name of Jack the Conqueror, though its provisions were viewed by the Hafsids as applying to all the domains of Aragon. Ampurias, the first Aragonese ambassador in Tunis, arrived only five years later. From this time onwards Aragonese diplomacy was aimed at convincing Pope Innocent IV that Tunisia should not become the object of an attack by the crusade which was then being considered. The Catholic Church was already entertaining the naive hope, based on Abu Zakariyya's readiness to establish peaceful relations with Christian states, of converting him to Christianity. Nevertheless the Pope rejected Aragon's representations which were obviously designed to improve her commercial relations with the Hafsid state. In the interest of these relations Jack the Conqueror in 1250 banned the Catalonian corsairs from attacking Muslim ships in the Mediterranean.

Abu Zakariyya's son al-Mustansir, who succeeded him in 1249, also considered himself the caliph and heir of Almohad authority, and was recognized as such by the Marinids. The Nasrids of Granada ceased to accept Hafsid suzerainty on Abu Zakariyya's death, and the Zayanids, without rejecting it, cooperated with the Almohad caliphs in Marrakish in their conflict with the Marinids. But rather than trying to resuscitate the Almohad empire, al-Mustansir was content merely to consolidate his hold over the territories which his father had ruled. He did not interfere in the affairs of the Zayanids, and he also let Ceuta pass under the nominal suzerainty of the Almohad caliphs in Marrakish without further ado. He used the military strength of the state in maintaining law and order, and in putting down the numerous uprisings which occurred during his reign.

The relative stability of the Hafsid state during al-Mustansir's reign, at a time when the Marinids had not yet consolidated their authority in Morocco and the Muslim Near East was passing through the cataclysmic upheaval caused by the Mongol conquest of Baghdad in 1258, made al-Mustansir the leading Muslim monarch. The Marinid Abu Yusuf Ya'qub sent a delegation to Tunis confirming his recognition of Hafsid suzerainty in 1258, upon his accession to the leadership of the Marinid movement; and in 1259 the *sharif*-governor of Mecca, Abu Numaiy (1254–1301), sent al-Mustansir a letter recognizing him as the caliph. In 1257 the king of Kanem-Bornu had sent a delegation with a gift to al-Mustansir; and in 1260 the infante of Castile, Don Henri, having rebelled against his brother Alfonso X and been defeated, came to Tunis and placed himself under Hafsid protection. At the same time the commercial relations which the Hafsid state enjoyed with Europe and the Sudan gave it a high degree of prosperity. Ibn Khaldun informs us that prosperity and stability were accompanied by an increase in Tunisia's population, and fostered the development of a sophisticated urban life. He adds that in the pursuit of gracious living al-Mustansir himself set the pace: he furnished his palace with great splendour, and founded near Tunis the magnificent Abu Fihr park to which he channelled water from Zaghwan in an ancient aqueduct. Near Bizerta he enclosed a vast terrain and transformed it into a hunting park, the equal of which, Ibn Khaldun says, did not exist in the world.

Aragon's influence in Tunisia increased after 1250. Since 1253 subjects of Aragon had had a *fondouk*, consisting of a compound in which they lived and had their shops, a tavern, and their consulate. A similar Aragonese *fondouk* was founded in Bougie in 1259. A company of Catalonian militia also entered the service of the Hafsids in either the last years of Abu Zakariyya's reign or the early ones of al-Mustansir's. Non-Catalonian Christians joined it later, but the king of Aragon had the right of appointing its commander, the *alcayt* (*al-qa'id*), who was required to remit to the treasury of Aragon a fixed proportion of the salaries he and the militiamen received from the Hafsid sultan. Al-Mustansir allowed the Christians living in Tunisia to practise their religion freely to the extent that the Dominican and Franciscan friars were permitted to preach Christianity to the Muslims. In 1250 the Dominicans founded in Tunis what they discreetly called "Studium Arabicum", an institution in which the missionaries of the order studied Muslim beliefs in order to be able to refute them effectively. The famous Catalonian missionary Raymond Martin (Ramon Marti) worked in this institute from 1250 to 1269.

In spite of al-Mustansir's tolerant attitude towards Christianity, Tunisia was invaded by the crusaders during his reign. The motives of the saintly king of France, Louis IX, in directing the eighth crusade to Tunisia are not easy to explain, although some of the important influences exercised on him are known. Fr Raymond Martin, who was in Louis IX's entourage immediately after his departure from Tunis in 1269, is said to have led him to believe that al-Mustansir would become a Christian if his country was invaded. Ibn Khaldun provides a financial explanation of Louis IX's decision. Some time before the eighth crusade sailed for Tunisia, al-Mustansir's tax-collector, Abul-'Abbas al-Luliani, was put to death on a charge of corruption. According to Ibn Khaldun, al-Luliani had borrowed large sums from French merchants living in Tunisia, and after his execution al-Mustansir refused to pay these debts. The representations of these merchants, Ibn Khaldun believes, were decisive in diverting the crusade to Tunisia. It seems, however, that St Louis' brother Charles of Anjou, king of Sicily since 1266, exercised the decisive influence over him. Since 1266 al-Mustansir had refused to pay Charles of Anjou the tribute he had previously paid to the Hohenstaufens, the former rulers of Sicily, and had given asylum to the king's political opponents. In 1267 the Napolitanian Conrad Capece and the infante Frederick of Castile used Tunis as a base for an attack on Sicily. Frederick later returned to Tunisia and remained with al-Mustansir throughout the time the army of the crusade was in the country. Charles of Anjou might also have seen the conquest of Tunisia as a preface to the realization of his grand oriental scheme of restoring the Latin empire of Constantinople and the Latin kingdom of Jerusalem, since he could not undertake an expedition to the east without first securing the safety of Sicily from attacks by his Christian adversaries, many of whom were under al-Mustansir's protection.

Once he was told of the progress of the crusade, al-Mustansir made whatever preparations he could before St Louis disembarked his troops at Carthage on 18 July 1270. He declared a holy war against the invaders, called upon the tribes to defend the country, and had the fortifications of Tunis repaired and provisions stocked in it and in other coastal towns in expectation of a siege. For over a month Tunis sustained the attacks of St Louis' army. Al-Mustansir was already preparing to move his head-quarters inland to Qairawan when relief came unexpectedly. St Louis fell ill and died on 25 August. His brother, arriving in Tunisia on the same day and finding al-Mustansir ready to come to terms with him, agreed to withdraw the army. Besides a general truce for fifteen years, al-Mustansir concluded with Charles of Anjou a special treaty which provided for Charles' particular requirements: the payment of an indemnity of war and an annual tribute double that al-Mustansir had paid to the Hohenstaufens, the extradition of the Sicilian political refugees from his realms, and the safeguarding of the commercial interests of the subjects of the kings of France, Sicily, and Navarre.

Relations between the Hafsids and Aragon improved rather than suffered as a result of the eighth crusade. Jack the Conqueror's efforts in 1246 to convince the Pope that Tunisia should be spared the attacks of the crusaders were remembered in Tunis. In 1270 he refused to compromise his relations with Tunisia by taking a part in the crusade, especially since he feared that its success would advance the commercial interests of rivals such as Marseilles. Shortly after the departure of the crusaders al-Mustansir signed on 14 February 1271 a new treaty with Aragon, which affirmed previous agreements between the two countries concerning the security of Catalonian merchants and the freedom of worship in Tunisia.

When al-Mustansir died on 16 May 1277, the Hafsid state was at the zenith of its prosperity, and apparently stable. How ephemeral stability was in a society dominated by tribal rivalries became clear in the following seven years, during which five different sultans acceded to the Hafsid throne, ending with the division of the state into two parts, one ruled from Tunis and the other from Bougie. Al-Mustansir's successor Yahya al-Wathiq began his reign well with a general amnesty which included all political prisoners. But soon his Andalusian minister, Abul-Hasan al-Ghafiqi, seized complete control and exercised a repression which alienated the Almohad notables. As vizier al-Ghafiqi replaced a highly respected Almohad chief called Sa'id b. Husain. The Almohad chiefs especially resented this encroachment on their position because al-Ghafiqi imprisoned his predecessor, confiscated his property, and had him tortured so as to obtain information about his hidden treasures. Al-Ghafiqi was soon accused of amassing large fortunes illegally through the help of a renegade he appointed as supervisor of revenues in Tunisia. His brother, whom he placed in charge of the revenues of Bougie, offended the governor of Bougie and its notables by his overbearing attitude to such an extent that they assassinated him in 1278.

Relations between Tunis and Aragon had in the meantime worsened since Jack the Conqueror's death. Peter III demanded tribute from al-Wathiq, claiming that the payments which al-Mustansir had made intermittently to his father were in fact tribute and a sign of his acceptance of Aragonese suzerainty. Al-Wathiq rejected these demands, thus prompting Peter III to try to replace him with Abu Ishaq, al-Mustansir's brother, whom al-Mustansir had banished to Spain. After arriving in Africa Abu Ishaq settled under Yaghmurasan's protection in Tlemsen. He was there when al-Ghafiqi's brother was killed in Bougie. The people of this town, fearing al-Ghafiqi's vengeance, invited Abu Ishaq to become their ruler. An army sent from Tunis in the summer of 1279 to drive him out deserted to him, and at the same time an Aragonese force commanded by Conrad Lancia occupied Gabis and advanced towards Tunis. In July al-Wathiq recognized the futility of resistance and abdicated in Abu Ishaq's favour.

Having ascended the throne, Abu Ishaq was no more willing than his predecessor to accept Aragonese suzerainty or to pay tribute. As Peter III was at the time planning the conquest of Sicily, he could not easily give up the attempt to instal a subservient ruler in Tunisia, and he turned to the powerful governor of Constantine, Abu Bakr b. al-Wazir, and encouraged him to rebel against Abu Ishaq. Assured of Aragon's support, Ibn al-Wazir rebelled in April 1282. But before Peter III arrived with his fleet at Collo on 28 June, Constantine had already been captured by Abu Ishaq's son Abu Faris and Ibn al-Wazir had been killed. The Aragonese army developed a crusading spirit before its departure, under the influence of Raymond Martin's religious exuberance. But its size and movements after arrival in Collo suggest that installing Ibn al-Wazir on the throne of Tunis was only the first stage in Peter III's enterprise. Aragon's expeditionary army remained in Collo for two months without attempting any conquest, although the troops made excursions into the countryside to plunder. This army left for Sicily as soon as a delegation from the rebels against Charles of Anjou came requesting Peter III's intervention. On 4 September the king of Aragon entered Palermo in triumph.

When the army of Aragon was in Collo, or shortly after it left for Sicily, a rebellion against Abu Ishaq began in 1282 in Tripolitania, and it is possible to see Peter III's hand in this too. The timing of the rebellion is significant as well as the fact that its chief Ahmad b. Abu 'Umara, who claimed to be al-Wathiq's son al-Fadl, was supported by Murghim b. 'Askar, chief of the Dabbab Tripolitanian tribe who had taken part in Lancia's expedition of 1279 against al-Wathiq. After a futile attack on Tripoli the pretender marched into southern Tunisia, entered into an alliance with the governor of Gabis, and immediately afterwards occupied the island of Jirba, al-Hamma, and then Tuzar. It appears that Ibn Abu 'Umara's claim to be al-Wathiq's son was believed. The Almohads deserted to him in October when Abu Ishaq led the army to intercept his progress near Qairawan, an action which forced Abu Ishaq to escape to Bougie and enabled Ibn Abu 'Umara to enter Tunis in February 1283. In Bougie Abu Ishaq's son forced him to abdicate in his favour; but he in turn was defeated and killed by Ibn Abu 'Umara as he was advancing towards Tunis.

Ibn Abu 'Umara ruled the Hafsid state until June 1284. Uncertain of the loyalty of the chiefs who joined him during his conquest of Tunisia, he resorted to suppression. His increasing unpopularity made the capture of power from him by Abu Hafs, a brother of Abu Ishaq and al-Mustansir, an easy matter. Abu Hafs styled himself caliph and took the title of al-Mustansir II, but his power was limited to Tunisia. At the end of 1284 Abu Ishaq's son Abu Zakariyya, until then a refugee in Tlemsen, occupied Constantine. He captured Bougie in the following year, and taking this town as capital, he set up an independent state which included the whole of eastern Algeria. Even in Tunisia the caliphial authority under Abu Hafs was a shadowy one. The strength and turbulence of the tribes increased, especially of the Banu Sulaim bedouin, to whom Abu Hafs was indebted for their help in the capture of Tunis. During his reign the Banu Sulaim chiefs became the feudal masters of the area between the Jarid and Sfax, and this resulted in the further deterioration of urban life and agriculture in the area. The Tunisian traveller al-Tijani, who visited this area in 1306 in the company of his employer al-Lihiani, found that the olive groves of Sfax had disappeared. The uncertainty of the military support which Abu Hafs received from these tribes prevented him from attempting the conquest of Bougie. But at the same time his rival Abu Zakariyya was restrained from invading Tunisia by the threat of Zayanid attacks on his domains.

Internal weakness and the mounting pressure of Aragon led Abu Hafs to capitulate to Peter III. Peter III's vassal, Roger de Lauria, the ruler of Sicily and its dependencies, occupied the island of Jirba in 1284 and Qarqanna (Kerkenneh) in 1286. Immediately after the occupation of Jirba, Abu Hafs came to terms with Aragon. In a treaty signed at Panissar in the Pyrenees in 1285 he agreed to pay tribute to the king of Aragon in his capacity as king of Sicily, with effect from 1282 when Sicily had been annexed to Aragon. Previous agreements concerning freedom of worship and the appointment of the commander of the Christian militia were confirmed, and Abu Hafs further agreed to appoint a Catalonian as supervisor of customs in his state. The treaty made possible the resumption of commercial relations between the two states, interrupted since 1277; but of more importance to Peter III was Aragon's political ascendancy in Tunisia, and the fact that by concluding this treaty Abu Hafs recognized the *de facto* Catalonian occupation of Jirba and Qarqanna.

The grand illusions of the 1260s of winning Tunisia back to Christianity revived after 1311, and were nurtured by the usurper al-Lihiani. This wily Almohad chief was the vizier of Abu Hafs' successor Abu 'Asida (1295–1309), and was instrumental in arranging an agreement in 1306 between his master and the sultan of Bougie Abul-Baqa' to bring about the reunification of the Hafsid state. The agreement specified that whichever of the two Hafsid sovereigns survived the other would rule both kingdoms. Al-Lihiani must have expected conflict to arise over the implementation of this family concord, and in order to make preparations against future developments he left the country in December 1306. After a short stay in the east, where he established contacts with the Mamluks in Egypt, he settled in Tripoli where he was when Abu 'Asida died in September 1309. As vizier al-Lihiani had negotiated with Aragon a treaty signed on 21 November 1301 which gave Aragon half the customs revenues received by the Hafsids from Catalonian merchants in Tunisia. He made further contacts with Aragon in 1304 when he went to Barcelona, ostensibly to protest against the raids of Catalonian pirates. While in Tripoli he seems also to have established relations with both Sicily and Aragon in his attempt to secure help in attaining the Hafsid throne. Al-Lihiani began his invasion of Tunisia in 1311. By this time Abul-Baqa' had united the states of Tunis and Bougie, but his brother Abu Bakr had already rebelled against him in eastern Algeria. Al-Lihiani had a small army recruited from Tripolitanian tribesmen, but more decisive in his victory were the ships sent from Sicily to give him support, and the desertion of the Christian militia to him when he approached Tunis in October 1311.

As sultan, al-Lihiani was very uncertain of his position. General political unrest in Tunisia and tribal fickleness made the success of any sultan dependent on his ability to play off the tribes and the leaders of the Almohad community against one another. Furthermore, in Bougie Abu Bakr consolidated his control over eastern Algeria, in spite of the repeated attacks on his domains from the Zayanids, and refused to accept al-Lihiani as caliph. In Aragon an important change was taking place: Jack II, unable to stem the crusading tide which gave rise to acts of Christian piracy in the Mediterranean, placed himself at the head of the crusaders in 1314. Needing Catalonian support for his survival, al-Lihiani made use of the fact that his mother was a Christian slave in order to give the impression that he was about to become a Christian. He told Moncada, the commander of the Christian militia, that he was a Christian at heart, and wanted to be baptized and to die a Christian, but that some prudence was called for in making this public. Jack II pressed on with inducing al-Lihiani to profess Christianity, since he considered his conversion the first step towards his own seizure of power in Tunisia. In July 1314 an ambassador (Oulomar) was sent from Aragon with a priest (Galvany de Verdaguer) to pursue the matter on the spot. Ramon Llull, a famous Franciscan missionary who knew Arabic and had visited Tunis in 1292, saw in this the great opportunity of his life and went to Tunis. For two years he engaged Muslim scholars in religious discussions, and wrote some thirty theological tracts, some in Arabic, for the benefit of the Muslim scholars he encountered. He returned to Majorca in 1315 where he soon died; but the hope of regaining Tunisia back to Christianity was kept alive by political interests. In 1316 Jack II sent Oulomar to Pope John XXII, trying in vain to interest him in sending a crusade to Tunisia, and he staged a Catalonian naval demonstration before Tunis as a means of creating the atmosphere for al-Lihiani's conversion. But before any action was taken al-Lihiani was deposed. In the spring of 1317 he went to southern Tunisia to inspect the provinces and collect the taxes, leaving his son Muhammad Abu Darba, whom he had brought up to be his eventual successor, as viceroy. In his absence Tunis was invaded by land and sea by Abu Bakr, the king of Bougie. Abu Darba fought valiantly with the Christian militia to defend Tunis, but in 1318 he was forced to evacuate the town.

Southern Tunisia and Tripoli remained independent of Tunis for about twenty years after 1318. This was due to the existence of relatively strong local authorities and to the Zayanid pressure on the eastern boundaries of the unified Hafsid state. The tribes controlled the countryside in the south, and the main towns were ruled by their leading families: Gabis by the Makki family, Gafsa by the Banu Rind, Tuzar by the Banu Yamlul, and Nafta by the Banu Khalaf. Ibn Abu 'Umran, the governor of Tripoli appointed by al-Lihiani, remained in control, and in 1321 he made an unsuccessful attempt to conquer Tunis. Two years later the Zayanids and Abu Darba's warriors jointly invaded eastern Algeria, but were defeated by the Hafsid army at Raghis, between Bona and Constantine. This Hafsid victory seems to have inspired the rebellion against Ibn Abu 'Umran in Tripoli in the following year, which forced him to evacuate the town and lead the tribal warriors he commanded to enlist in the service of the Zayanids. He accompanied the Zayanid army which invaded Tunisia in 1329, defeated Abu Bakr's army, and occupied Tunis in December. Ibn Abu 'Umran became the nominal ruler of Tunis under Zayanid control until May 1230, when Abu Bakr recovered his capital.

The difficult months of December 1329 to May 1330 saw the alliance of Abu Bakr with the Marinids. Abul-Hasan's pressure on the Zayanids from the west enabled the Hafsid sultan to capture Zayanid positions near Bougie and to strengthen his position in southern Tunisia. Between 1334 and Abu Bakr's death on 19 October 1346 his son Abul-'Abbas brought Gafsa, Gabis, Tuzar, and the island of Jirba again under the control of Tunis. The Arabian tribes also paid tribute after their chief Hamza b. 'Umar was induced in 1337 by the Marinid sultan Abul-Hasan to submit to Abu Bakr.

The conflict for power following Abu Bakr's death and the two Marinid invasions mentioned above[1] led to the Hafsid state again splitting into two. In southern Tunisia autonomous principalities reappeared in the main towns, and the Arabian tribes regained ascendancy in the countryside. The tribal leader 'Umar b. Hamza (son of Hamza b. 'Umar who had been assassinated in 1341) took an active part in July 1350 in removing from the throne Abu Bakr's son Fadl, and replacing him by his brother Abu Ishaq. This prince, who had hardly reached the age of puberty, was the choice of his father's aged chamberlain, Abu Muhammad 'Abdulla b. Tafrajin. Allied with 'Umar b. Hamza, Ibn Tafrajin ruled until his death in 1365 in Abu Ishaq's name. The Arabian tribes, whose hostility to the Marinids had forced Abu 'Inan to evacuate Tunisia in 1357, were able to obstruct Abu Hafs' efforts to bring the south of the country under his control when Ibn Tafrajin died. Their insubordination also weakened his position *vis-à-vis* his nephew Abul-'Abbas, who in 1359 captured Constantine with Marinid

[1] Pp. 127–31.

help and used it as a base for conquering the territory formerly ruled from Bougie.

The ebbing of Marinid power after Abu 'Inan's death in 1358, and internal conflicts in the Zayanid state and repeated Marinid incursions into its territory in the 1360s and 1370s, gave the Hafsid state of Bougie a respite which was used by Abul-'Abbas to conquer Tunis and restore the unity of Hafsid territory. In 1370 Abul-'Abbas captured Tunis from Abu Ishaq's son. He was the first of a line of three illustrious princes under whom the Hafsid state enjoyed a final flowering that lasted until about the end of the fifteenth century. The power of the central government of Tunis, which can be measured by its ability to keep eastern Algeria and southern Tunisia under control, revived under Abul-'Abbas (1370–94). The feudal privileges of the tribal chiefs living in southern Tunisia were suppressed, and the principal towns submitted to his authority, albeit only nominally. A new development in Tunisia's relations with Europe emerged as a result of the revival of Hafsid power. Tunisian Muslim privateering appeared in the first two decades of the fourteenth century as a reaction to the revival of Christian piracy. Under Abul-'Abas the privateers, whose two main bases in Hafsid territory were Bougie and Mahiyya, became organized and enjoyed state protection. In 1390 joint forces from Genoa, Sicily, France, and Aragon formed an expedition against Mahdiyya and besieged the town for six months, but failed to capture it.

The fifteenth century thus opens with the external standing of the Hafsid state improved, and its authority consolidated internally. During the reign of Abul-'Abbas' son Abu Faris (1394-1434), the autonomous principalities – Tripoli, Tuzar, Gafsa, Biskra, and Algiers – disappeared. Embassies and gifts were sent to Tunis from Granada, Fez, Cairo, and the Muslim holy places in recognition of the Hafsids as a leading Muslim power. And in spite of the activities of Christian and Muslim pirates in the Mediterranean, commercial relations with the European states revived during the reigns of Abu Faris and his successors. Aragon, Milan, Genoa, and Venice were the principal European states involved in this trade. Florence, after its recent victories against Pisa and the acquisition of Leghorn, concluded a commercial treaty with the Hafsids in 1423; in 1461 a similar treaty was signed between the Hafsids and the Grand Master of Rhodes.

During the reign of Abu 'Amr 'Uthman (1435–88) Bougie and Constantine were ruled independently for seven years by Abu 'Amr's uncle Abul-Hasan. When in 1452 Bougie and Constantine were recovered, the Hafsids were able to extend their domination westwards. Two expeditions against Tlemsen by Abu 'Amr in 1462 and 1466 restored the Zayanids to the position of vassals. Even the founder of the Wattasid state in Morocco, Muhammad al-Shaikh, accepted Abu 'Amr's suzerainty in 1472. This was, however, but the last drop of glory. Internal strife sapped the authority of the Hafsid state during the last century of its existence, and the Spanish occupation of important coastal positions in Hafsid territory, including Tripoli, in the first decade of the sixteenth century heralded the end of Hafsid rule.

The survival of the Hafsid state for so long, in spite of the grave upheavals through which it passed, can partly be attributed to the group of original Almohads who constituted its aristocracy throughout. From this group the sultan's consultative council of ten was drawn, and in the case of a young or inept sultan, an Almohad chief usually exercised power in his name as minister. During periods of turmoil the Almohads secured the accession to the throne of a Hafsid prince, or one – such as Ibn Abu 'Umara – who could make a convincing claim to be one. Andalusian emigrants sometimes attained high positions of state, but the Almohads usually closed in their ranks in opposition to such intruders. The exclusiveness of the Almohads as an aristocratic class contributed towards encouraging large numbers of the Andalusian emigrants to settle in Zayanid rather than Hafsid territory.

In the foregoing account of Hafsid history reference has occasionally been made to the part which the Arabian tribesmen played during periods of political upheaval. When the Hafsid government was strong it was capable of checking their power; but tribalism and nomadic threat to urban life and agriculture remained a part of the social life of Tunisia, as well as Algeria and Morocco, well into modern times. To the evidence of al-Tijani about the destructiveness of the Arabian nomads in the thirteenth and fourteenth centuries, Leo Africanus adds instances of the havoc they wrought in the fifteenth and the beginning of the sixteenth century. The inhabitants of Mahdiyya, he relates, were unable to cultivate their lands because of the animosity of the Arabian nomads. He found Qairawan, which had been devastated by the Arabs, beginning to become repopulated when he visited it around 1515, but the lustre of its life had gone; and in Gabis the marauding raids of the nomads forced the inhabitants to flee. The role of these nomads remained on the whole the antithesis of organized government and urban and settled life. Because of their domination in the interior, urban life flourished only in the coastal towns. The nomads were not disposed towards life on the coast, and the presence of European merchants, organized in *fondouks* and representing the military power of their states, kept them in check.

Under the Hafsids, Tunis became the uncontested capital of the country and an important centre of Mediterranean commerce. Christians of various nationalities lived in the town, but amongst them the Italians and Catalonians predominated. At the same time traditional Islamic learning was assiduously cultivated there. The Zaituna mosque, built in the eighth century and enlarged by the Aghlabids, became during the Hafsid period one of the foremost centres of learning in the Maghrib. The famous historian of the period 'Abdul-Rahman b. Khaldun studied in the Zaituna. In spite of the Hafsids' reverence for the traditions of the Mahdi Ibn Tumart, the Malikite rite revived in their lands, and in the Zaituna it was taught and developed. The great Malikite theologian of the fourteenth century, Muhammad b. 'Arafa (1316–1401), came from Tunis, and besides his juridical functions he served in the capacity of superintendent to the Zaituna library, which is said to have contained about 60,000 volumes.

The Zayanids

In his classification of the Zanata tribes according to numbers, Ibn Khaldun placed the Banu Marin in the first rank, together with the Banu 'Abdul-Wad, the mainstay of the Zayanid state; the Banu Tujin and the Maghrawa tribes he placed second. The history of the Zayanid state is to a great extent the record of the relationship between these four Zanata tribes. The Banu 'Abdul-Wad, led by the Zayanid clan, maintained a precarious predominance over the central Maghrib for three centuries in spite of the Marinid ambition since the fourteenth century to establish a Maghriban empire, and the continuous attempts by the Maghrawa and the Banu Tujin to seek their political fortunes independently of the Banu 'Abdul-Wad or in defiance of their authority.

In the first half of the thirteenth century the Banu 'Abdul-Wad were better placed than the Banu Marin to benefit from the decline of the Almohad state. Having cooperated with the victorious Almohad forces in the twelfth century they were settled by 'Abdul-Mu'min in the area between Oran and Tlemsen, thus permanently relinquishing their erstwhile home between Mzab and Figuig. In 1230, when the Almohads were no longer able to control the central Maghrib effectively, the chief of the Banu 'Abdul-Wad, Jabir b. Yusuf, was appointed governor of Tlemsen. He set out to reconquer the dependencies of this provincial capital of the central Maghrib, but his career was cut short by his death in 1232 in an attack on Nadruma. His authority as governor and tribal chief was inherited by his son, then by his brother. In 1234, when the latter was deposed by his people, the chieftaincy of the tribe went to the Banu Zayan clan. It was first held by Zaidan b. Zayan who was killed in 1236, and then by his brother Yaghmurasan, the founder of the Zayanid state.

The political vacuum in the central Maghrib made the foundation of the Zayanid state possible; its consolidation owes much to Yaghmurasan's remarkable ability as a warrior and his skill as a tribal leader. Expansion in any direction involved the Banu 'Abdul-Wad in conflict with other Zanata tribes: the Maghrawa tribe controlled the area between the Shaliff river and the Mediterranean in the north, and the Banu Tujin were the masters of the area south of the Shaliff as far as Midia in the east. The only locality of interest to the Zayanids in the south was Sijilmasa, the western gateway of the Saharan trade, by this time controlled by Zanatas. To the west the Marinids were gaining the upper hand over the Almohads; and when Yaghmurasan penetrated into Morocco, he found himself in the paradoxical position of harassing the enemies of the rulers against whom he had rebelled. Thus, although Almohad control of Tlemsen ceased in 1236, Yaghmurasan's territory remained for over a decade limited to this town and its immediate environs. Arabian tribesmen, such as the Banu Zughba living near Tlemsen, obeyed him; but as the Arabian tribes in north-western Algeria were not strong, their support did not add much to his military strength.

In the 1230s and 1240s Yaghmurasan's ambitions perforce remained limited to retaining control of Tlemsen. His territory was invaded by the Hafsids in 1242 and the Almohads in 1248; however, his position was improved rather than weakened as a result of these invasions. The first invasion demonstrated that the Zayanid state could not defend itself against the organized army of the Hafsids, reinforced by the Maghrawa and Banu Tujin tribesmen; but it also showed that Yaghmurasan was the strongest Zanata chief in western Algeria. Tlemsen was conquered, but the Hafsid caliph Abu Zakariyya handed it back to him in return for nominal submission. The Almohad invasion ended with Caliph Sa'id's death near the castle of Tamzardakt. Nevertheless Yaghmurasan avoided a complete rupture with the Almohads, whose continued existence as rulers he came to value, if only as a force which would prevent the Marinids from taking complete possession of Morocco and threatening his state. He enriched himself by looting the caliph's camp, seizing, among other things, a copy of the Qur'an made during the caliphate of 'Uthman (d. 656); but he treated the caliph's sister and wives with great deference and facilitated their return to Marrakish.

The territory of the Zayanids fluctuated to such a great extent according to the strength of their neighbours that it would be impossible to give a precise delineation of the limits of their authority. Following the retreat of the Almohad army in 1248 they used the prestige they gained from this victory to bring the Banu Tujin to their side as subordinate allies. In 1250 the Banu Tujin warriors fought on the side of the Zayanids against the Marinids in Morocco, but the death of the chief of Banu Tujin, 'Abdul-Qawi, shortly afterwards brought this alliance to an end. His son Muhammad was not disposed to accept Zayanid hegemony, and several raids by Yaghmurasan's warriors failed to bring about his submission. The promise of profitable commercial relations with Aragon after 1250 led

Yaghmurasan to turn towards subjugating the Maghrawa. Henceforth, Zayanid territorial expansion under Yaghmurasan and his son 'Uthman (1283–1304) aimed, besides founding a strong and viable state, at controlling Sijilmasa and the hinterland of western Algeria for the purpose of preserving and strengthening the commercial relations which they had established with various European states, especially Aragon.

The circumstances under which Yaghmurasan captured Sijilmasa in 1264 have been described above.[1] During the ten years when he retained control of this town – it was conquered by the Marinids in 1274 – he was occupied in establishing his ascendancy over the Maghrawa. He took possession of some of the northern towns by timely interventions in the conflicts between the members of the Maghrawa chiefly family, the Banu Mandil. In 1270 he received Miliana from 'Umar b. Mandil in return for helping him against his brother; in 1273 he forced Thabit b. Mandil to cede Tenes. Between 1283 and 1287 his son 'Uthman incorporated the rest of Maghrawa territory in the Zayanid state by conquest. In the following three years 'Uthman subjugated the Banu Tujin, defeating them in 1288 in their stronghold in the Wanshiris mountains and taking Midia in 1289. Thus by 1290 most of the central Maghrib submitted to the Zayanids, and their state extended over the entire coastal line of Algeria from the Mulawiyya river to the Summam (Wadi al-Kabir), just short of Bougie. Leo Africanus, writing at the beginning of the sixteenth century, i.e. shortly before the conquest of Tlemsen by the Turks, found the Zayanid state to have about the same boundaries as at the end of the thirteenth century. It is remarkable that they survived as a ruling dynasty for so long, and by the sixteenth century had recovered the territories they had in 1290, although in the meantime Tlemsen itself was several times taken away from them. It seems that the same factors which made it possible for them to found a state in the thirteenth century remained operative throughout the period of their history: in the unsettled tribal society of the central Maghrib the Banu 'Abdul-Wad tribe prevailed in the absence of outside intervention because it was more numerous than, and politically and militarily as mobile as, any other tribe inhabiting the area.

It would be wrong, however, to assume that because the society in which the Zayanids ruled was tribal, urban and civilized life did not develop in their realm. The Zayanid state, like the Marinid and to a lesser extent the Hafsid, profited from the administrative and artistic skills of Andalusian refugees in creating the rudiments of an administration and embellishing the capital with mosques and *madrasas*. All the great monuments of Tlemsen date from the Zayanid period, though two of the less important ones were founded by the Marinids during their occupation of the town

---

[1] P. 123.

from 1337 to 1349.[1] During the Zayanid period Tlemsen became for the first and only time the capital of an independent state, receiving ambassadors from Muslim and Christian rulers, Muslim religious scholars, poets, men of letters, as well as foreign merchants. The frequent periods of siege were times of stress for the people of Tlemsen (possibly about 100,000 during the Zayanid period); but Tlemsen, the "pearl of the Maghrib", also knew periods of felicity in the intervals between wars. At a height of about 800 metres in the interior, its air is dry and cool, and its position was favourable to commercial activity.

The western coastal towns of Algeria, especially Oran, were frequented by the merchants of Genoa, Pisa, Marseilles, and Barcelona, before the foundation of the Zayanid state. But after 1250 Aragon came gradually to control the commercial relations which the Zayanids had with Europe. By contrast with the Hafsid state, the Zayanid state occupied a position of no significance to Aragon's political ambitions in the Mediterranean; but it controlled the most direct route from the north to Sijilmasa, the gateway of the trans-Saharan caravan trade in gold and slaves. Relations between Aragon and the Zayanids began on a purely commercial basis, and although in the 1280s they came to have a political dimension, this remained their less important side. The success of Catalonian businessmen in the Zayanid state, as in the Hafsid, was due largely to Jack the Conqueror's and his immediate successors' direct interest in their activities. But there were other factors. As Aragon had a large number of Muslim subjects seeking to move to Muslim lands, she could use these as a means of exerting pressure on the Zayanids for the purpose of obtaining concessions. More important in the actual development of trade was the fact that many of Barcelona's mercantile families were Jewish, and colonies of Jews were engaged in commerce both in the central Maghrib and further south along the caravan route to the western Sudan. The importance attached in Barcelona to the cooperation of the African Jews in developing commercial relations with the Zayanids is seen in the official protection extended in 1247 by Jack the Conqueror to two Jewish families living in Sijilmasa.

Direct contact between the Zayanids and Aragon existed as early as 1250, when Yaghmurasan sent an ambassador to Barcelona to start wholesale trade between the two countries. By this time Catalonians had already entered the service of the Zayanids as mercenaries. Among the Christian troops that the Almohad caliph Sa'id took with him to invade Tlemsen in 1248 there were some Catalonians, though the majority were Castilian. After the death of the caliph a part of this Christian militia defected to the Zayanids, and the rest served with the Marinids. In 1254 one of Yaghmurasan's sons was killed in an uprising of the Christian

[1] These are the minaret of Agadir and the small Sidi Ba 'l-Hasan mosque, now a museum.

troops in Tlemsen, whose chief was possibly Castilian. As a result of this fracas the Castilian mercenaries were dispersed and replaced by Catalonians. The commander of the militia (the *alcayt*) was also replaced by a Catalonian, and was recognized from 1255 as the chief of all the European communities in the Zayanid state. In this capacity the *alcayt* performed the functions of consul and commander, and was well placed to advance the commercial interests of the Catalonians at the expense of other European merchants. The Aragonese ambassador Bernat Porter, who had failed to persuade the Marinid sultan Abu Yusuf Ya'qub to enter into negotiations towards a commercial treaty with Aragon, was more successful in Tlemsen. An agreement made in 1276 was formally adopted in 1277 during a visit of the Zayanid envoy Ibn Baridi to Barcelona. The exact terms of this agreement are not known, but it appears from later events that it provided for the payment of tribute by the Zayanids to Aragon. Some time before 1286 the Zayanids also agreed to refund to the king of Aragon part of the customs levied on goods in which Catalonians dealt.

A treaty signed in 1286 between the Zayanids and Aragon marks the culmination of Catalonian influence in the kingdom of Tlemsen. The *alcayt* was confirmed in his authority over all Europeans residing in or passing through Zayanid lands, and mention was made of a chaplain for the Christian militia whose salary was paid by the sultan. The Zayanids were spared the humiliation of paying tribute, but they agreed to pay 5,000 golden dinars, this presumably being the arrears of the tribute agreed upon in 1277. The Zayanids compensated the throne of Aragon for the loss of the tribute by giving Aragon the right to receive fifty per cent of the customs levied on the trade of all Europeans in Zayanid territory. An Aragonese agent resident in Oran, the official port of trade between the two countries where a Catalonian *fondouk* existed, was empowered to collect these revenues directly on behalf of his monarch. This diplomatic triumph, unequalled in Aragon's dealing with other Maghriban states, became complete when the Zayanids agreed to place under Alfonso III's command, whenever requested, a contingent of cavalry for which they were to provide the equipment, salaries, and transport. This agreement took place shortly before Aragon's war with Castile, in anticipation of which the king of Aragon tried unsuccessfully to conclude a similar military alliance with the Marinids. The assurance of outside military help was also useful in Alfonso III's dealing with Barcelona's hostile nobility.

The heyday of Aragonese-Zayanid trade lasted until the first two decades of the fourteenth century. The Zayanid state exported gold, slaves, woollen articles, and livestock. Besides advancing the commercial interests of his subjects the king of Aragon drew a substantial income from his share of the customs revenues accruing to the Zayanids and of the salaries of the *alcayt* and the members of the Christian militia. The revival of piracy in the Mediterranean during the second decade of the four-teenth century under Aragon's official sponsorship wrought havoc in this mutually profitable relationship, and the resurgence of Maghriban hopes for unity and strength in the 1330s under the leadership of the Marinid sultan Abul-Hasan further contributed towards the interruption of commerce between Europe and the Zayanid and Hafsid states. The confidence gained by Maghriban Muslims as a result of the Marinid conquest of Gibraltar in 1333, and the Hafsid recovery of the islands of Qarqanna and Jirba from the Catalonians in 1335, made them less willing to accept the part of subordinate partners in their dealings with Aragon. The Marinids had constantly opposed Aragon's attempts to establish amicable relations with them, and, as suggested above,[1] Abul-Hasan's expansion eastwards in the 1330s and 1340s was connected with a sense of insecurity engendered by Marinid defeats in Spain. His occupation of Tlemsen between 1337 and 1349, and his invasion of Tunisia in 1347 had an adverse effect on Aragon's position in the Hafsid and Zayanid states.

Abu 'Inan's conquest of the central and eastern Maghrib had a more permanent effect on trade with Europe, since between 1353 and 1359 Tlemsen and its dependencies, including the coastal towns, remained in Marinid hands. The result of the Marinid invasions was that ties forged during more than fifty years of diplomacy between Aragon on the one hand, and the Hafsids and the Zayanids on the other, were broken, and the militant religiosity of Muslims and Christians on either side of the Mediterranean was not conducive towards their restoration. The position of European merchants in the Maghrib and their journeys by sea became hazardous, but trade did not entirely cease. When in 1387 the Zayanid sultan Abu Hamuw II was dethroned by his son Abu Tashfin, he was sent on a Catalonian merchant ship sailing from Oran to Alexandria and calling at Tunis. Leo Africanus observed that before the Spanish occupation of Oran in 1509 Aragonese and Genoese merchants still traded in the town, although the mercantile Muslim oligarchy there equipped a number of brigantines which attacked the Catalonian coast and the Balearic Isles, capturing Christians who were sold in Oran as slaves. Nevertheless since the middle of the fourteenth century and possibly some twenty years earlier, Catalonian ascendancy in the foreign commercial dealings of the Hafsids and Zayanids had been at an end.

The Zayanid state emerged from the first Marinid siege of Tlemsen (1299–1307) strong and also independent of the Hafsids. 'Uthman b. Yaghmurasan had tried until the siege began to preserve good connections with the Hafsid ruler of Bougie, his brother-in-law Abu Zakariyya, while recognizing the suzerainty of the caliph in Tunis. But because the Hafsid caliph Abu 'Asida had entered into an alliance with the Marinid sultan

[1] Pp. 126–8.

Abu Ya'qub during the siege, 'Uthman could no longer accept Hafsid suzerainty. Before 'Uthman died in 1304 the Friday prayer in Tlemsen was no longer said in the name of the Hafsids. It remained for his son Abu Hamuw Musa, who succeeded his brother Abu Zayan Muhammad in 1308, one year after the termination of the siege, to introduce the ceremonials and protocol of royalty. With the help of the Andalusian family of Banu Mallah who served him as chamberlains, he organized a court fitting for an independent monarch. As the Marinid sultans who immediately succeeded Abu Ya'qub were preoccupied with Morocco's internal problems and the Hafsids engaged in their internecine political conflicts, Abu Hamuw was able to reconquer Zayanid territory without harassment from either. As a result of his campaigns in 1310–11 against the Banu Tujin they agreed to pay him tribute, and their chiefs, placed in charge of their respective districts, became functionaries in the Zayanid administration. In about 1313 Algiers was also annexed to the Zayanid state, and its former ruler Ibn 'Allan spent the rest of his life in honourable captivity in Tlemsen. Between 1320 and 1331 the Zayanids advanced into Hafsid territory seeking to conquer Bougie. They attacked the town several times and built three fortresses nearby which they used as bases for their forces. But as a result of his alliance with the Marinids, the Hafsid caliph Abu Bakr was able to drive the Zayanids back.

After the second wave of Marinid invasions under Abul-Hasan and Abu 'Inan the affairs of the Zayanid state became inextricably entangled with Hafsid and Marinid politics. Internally, the Zayanids were no longer able to coerce into submission the tribal population living in their domains, since Abul-Hasan had reduced the Banu 'Abdul-Wad politically to the level of the other Zanata confederates who joined him in the conquest of Tunisia in 1347. After the battle of Qairawan, when the Zanatas of the central Maghrib deserted Abul-Hasan, the Maghrawa and the Banu 'Abdul-Wad emerged as allies against the Marinids, but also as equals. In the interval between Abul-Hasan's and Abu 'Inan's invasions (1348–52) the Maghrawa tribe had its own "king", 'Ali b. Mandil, and was independent of Tlemsen, then ruled by the Zayanid 'Uthman b. 'Abdul-Rhaman.

After Abu 'Inan's invasion Tlemsen was recovered from the Marinids in February 1359 by Abu Hamuw II, through help from the Dawudiyya and Awlad Sa'id Arabian tribes. The reign of this king (1359–89) was one of continuous tribal conflicts interspersed with Marinid attacks which forced him to flee his capital four times, in 1359, 1360, 1370, and 1383. Furthermore, his attack on Bougie in 1366 unleashed against him another powerful enemy. The Hafsid ruler of Bougie and Constantine, Abul-'Abbas (later the sultan of Tunis), released Abu Zayan, Abu Hamuw's cousin, from custody in Constantine when the Zayanid ruler was before

Bougie. Receiving initial help from Abul-'Abbas, Abu Zayan engaged his cousin in a protracted tribal war which ended only in 1378 when Abu Hamuw captured Algiers, where Abu Zayan had recently been proclaimed sultan. This conflict was interrupted briefly by the Marinid invasion of 1370 which forced both Zayanid princes to escape southwards into the desert. Some three years after the Marinid occupation of Tlemsen in 1383 Abu Hamuw decided to move his capital to Algiers, where he would be less vulnerable to Marinid attacks. In 1386 he sent his treasures to his son al-Muntasir in Algiers, planning to join him at a later date. But the jealousies of his eldest son Abu Tashfin obstructed this plan. Abu Tashfin had feared that his father might favour al-Muntasir's succession; and having learnt in advance of the dispatch of the treasures of the state to Algiers, he intercepted them. Letters which he seized from his father's messengers confirmed his fears. Consequently, in January 1387 he carried out what might be called a court rebellion, by arresting his father in his palace and sending him as a prisoner to Oran.

The conflict between Abu Hamuw and his son led to the imposition of Marinid control over Tlemsen. Abu Hamuw escaped from the Catalonian ship on which, by order of his son, he was being transported to Alexandria, when it called at Tunis. When in July 1388 he recovered Tlemsen his son placed himself under Marinid protection, and returned from Fez with an army which occupied Tlemsen. Abu Hamuw was later pursued to Gharian by the Marinid troops and killed. Abu Tashfin became the ruler of Tlemsen, but had to recognize Marinid suzerainty and to pay an annual tribute. To ensure Abu Tashfin's and his successors' submission the Marinids kept in their court a Zayanid prince ready to rebel with their support against his reigning kinsman. In 1424 the Zayanids changed masters by accepting the suzerainty of the Hafsid sultan Abu Faris when he attacked Tlemsen. The subordination of Tlemsen to Tunis lasted until the end of the century, when the authority of the Hafsids, as well as the Zayanids, was weakened by the Spanish expansion along the Maghriban coast.

The significance of the Castilian conquest of Granada in 1492 to the Christian-Muslim balance in the Mediterranean will be discussed in the next chapter. In the context of Maghriban history proper this event had far-reaching consequences both socially and politically. The influx of Andalusian Muslims (the Moriscos or Moors) into the Maghrib, which began in the twelfth century, reached its culmination in 1492 and continued until the seventeenth century when their final expulsion took place. Before 1492 the Andalusians left their impact on the architecture of the Maghrib and the government service. After 1492 they came to constitute a sizable minority vociferous in its disillusionment, and exclusive in its attempt to achieve a status in the Maghriban society. In the seventeenth century the Andalusians in Tunisia were organized as a distinct community under a leader of their own, entitled "shaikh al-Andalus". In this country and other parts of the Maghrib the skills which they brought with them rendered them a useful accretion to the society, but as they came to monopolize certain industries, this served to distinguish them further from the rest of the population. Throughout the Maghrib they held a monopoly in the *shashiyya* (headcloth) industry, in Algiers they monopolized the manufacture of silk, and in Morocco they found employment as soldiers.

As mentioned before, to the Marinids the kingdom of Granada became from the thirteenth century a buffer state between themselves and Christian Spain. Its fall, and the Portuguese and Spanish expansion on the Maghriban coast, placed the Muslim society of the Maghrib face to face with the military strength of Christian Europe. Until the end of the sixteenth century the Muslims of the Maghrib were on the defensive *vis-à-vis* a Europe that was advancing under the banner of Christianity, and this situation infused into Maghriban theology an uncompromising strain comparable to the strictness of the Kharijite doctrine. The best known Maghriban theologians at the turn of the sixteenth century, Muhammad b. 'Abdul-Karim al-Maghili of Tlemsen (d. A.H. 909/A.D. 1503-4) and Ahmad al-Wanshirisi of Fez (d. 1508), represent this trend. Al-Maghili sanctioned the persecution of the Jews of Tuat on doubtful theological grounds and concurred with the attitude of Askia Muhammad (1492-1528), the king of Songhay in the western Sudan, of condemning as infidels all professing Muslims who combined pagan practices with Muslim rites. Al-Wanshirisi went to the extent of pronouncing infidels the Andalusians who were of the opinion that life in Spain was preferable to what they experienced in the Maghrib, on the grounds that a true Muslim should always prefer to live under a Muslim prince. These standpoints would have been condemned by Muslim theologians during periods of strength and prosperity; indeed, al-Maghili's attitude towards the Jews of Tuat was widely criticized by Muslim theologians in the Maghrib even during his lifetime. As will be shown in a later chapter, a more enlightened Islamic revival was to play an important part in the twentieth century in the opposition to French political and cultural domination in the Maghrib. In the sixteenth, seventeenth, and eighteenth centuries the Maghriban Muslims – so far as one can generalize about them – adopted a more bellicose and less informed attitude towards the Christian world. European attacks on the Maghrib were responsible for the emergence of this standpoint, the wars of the privateers in the Mediterranean sustained it, and Turkish domination over the central and eastern Maghrib made it durable by linking it to Ottoman championing of the cause of Islam.

7

Ottoman rule in the Central and Eastern Maghrib

Spanish expansion and Ottoman intervention

The conquest of the kingdom of Granada was the product of the crusading fervour of the Castilian aristocracy and peasantry; Spanish expansion along the Maghriban coastline was the result of the religious ardour of the Castilians being harnessed to Aragon's long-standing occupation with Mediterranean politics. The idea of the crusade was deeply ingrained in Castile, and the nobility had grown to look upon fighting the Muslims as a fitting means of enrichment and proving their aristocratic qualities. After the fall of Constantinople to the Turks in 1453 the Pope took a special interest in exciting the crusading spirit of the Castilian aristocracy, so that when in 1479 Isabella ascended the throne of Castile she and her husband Ferdinand of Aragon found the idea of the crusade ready at hand to be used for rallying their people behind them. From 1482 the war against Granada was pursued methodically, and the conquest of Granada ten years later was achieved mostly through exploiting the internecine conflicts of its ruling dynasty.

When the war was resumed the king of Granada Abul-Hasan was at loggerheads with his brother al-Zaghal, the ruler of Malaga. In the same year or early in 1483 al-Zaghal replaced his brother, who had become blind; but Abul-Hasan's son Abu 'Abdulla (Boabdil), who had rebelled against his father in Guadix, resented his uncle's assumption of the throne and installed himself in Granada when al-Zaghal was away in one of the battles with Castile. Al-Zaghal retained Malaga and from there continued the war against Castile. Abu 'Abdulla too fought the Christians, but was captured in 1483 at Lucena. As the two parts of the Nasrid state were immediately reunited under al-Zaghal, Castile saw its interest to lie in entering into a secret alliance with Abu 'Abdulla, by which he accepted vassalage to Castile in return for liberation. Abu 'Abdulla regained Granada shortly afterwards and ruled it until 1492. Although he was to prove a vacillating ally, his withdrawal from the war considerably weakened Muslim resistance. In 1487 Malaga was captured from al-Zaghal, and two years later Abu 'Abdulla publicly submitted to the authority of Castile. However, as this weakened his position *vis-à-vis* his subjects, he later decided on resistance; but the Castilian campaigns against Granada in

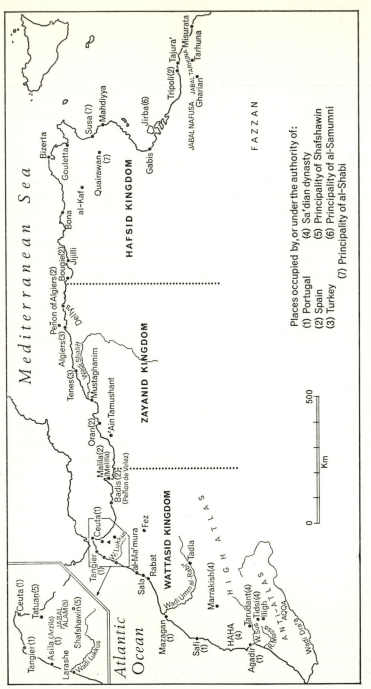

5   Political centres in the Maghrib in 1529

1490 and 1491 caused its population so much hardship that they decided to seek an honourable surrender. Negotiations which began in October 1491 ended in an agreement on 2 January 1492 as a result of which the Castilians entered Granada without fighting. The terms of the surrender were liberal, permitting the Muslims to retain their property, practise their religion, and remain under the jurisdiction of the Muslim law. They were, however, encouraged to emigrate, and in 1493 Abu 'Abdulla, who had remained in an estate at Alpujarras, left for the Maghrib with some 6,000 other Muslims. Christianity was henceforth systematically preached to the Muslims, but as preaching proved ineffective in making them give up their religion, a policy of forcible conversion was adopted in 1499 under the direction of Archbishop Cisneros of Toledo. All this did was to make them nominal Christians while in fact they held tenaciously to their rites and customs.

The project of carrying the crusade against the Muslims to the other side of the Mediterranean was upheld from 1492 by many interested parties connected with the court of the Catholic Monarchs. In 1493 and 1494 two Castilian captains, Lezcano and Lorenzo Zafra, visited several parts of the central Maghriban coast. They reported that such places as Tawint (Taount), Malila, and Hunain were held by *qa'ids* who could readily be persuaded to surrender their commands to the Spaniards because their garrisons were small, ill-paid, and badly provided with ammunition. The fact that rather than command the tribes in the neighbourhood the *qa'ids* were often their prisoners, was also believed to be an important factor in favour of an early capitulation. Fernando Zafra, the secretary of the Catholic Monarchs' council entrusted with supervising the passage of the Muslims to Africa, urged as a first step in the conquest the occupation of Malila, after which the peninsula on which it stood could be taken without difficulty. No action, however, was undertaken because by the terms of the treaty of Alcacovas of 4 September 1479 with Portugal, this peninsula fell within the recognized Portuguese zone of influence. The prospect of a Spanish occupation of Malila was referred to Portuguese and Spanish plenipotentiaries who met in June 1494 at Tordesillas. Although it was agreed that the boundary between the kingdoms of Fez and Tlemsen, which marked the line of demarcation between the Portuguese and Spanish preserves fell to the east of Malila, John II of Portugal waived his rights over it. Papal consecration put the seal on this arrangement, and by a bull dated 12 November 1494 Pope Alexander VI required the faithful to help the Catholic Monarchs with their persons and property in their African crusade. Nevertheless conflict with France over Naples prevented Spain from undertaking any conquest in the Maghrib for three years. Malila was occupied in September 1497 at a time when it was empty of troops and its fortifications destroyed because of internal conflicts. The Wattasid king of Morocco Muhammad al-Shaikh sent a detachment of cavalry to prevent the installation of the Spaniards in Malila, but it was kept at a distance by the guns of the Spanish ships.

After 1499 Archbishop Cisneros vociferously urged the permanent occupation of the central Maghrib and the foundation of a Spanish empire. But since Isabella, who was motivated by the same religious zeal, died in 1504 and Ferdinand's ideas prevailed with regard to expansion in the Mediterranean, the project of the conquest of the Maghrib was sacrificed to Aragon's ambition of building an empire in Italy. Henceforth, the Spanish objective in the Maghrib became the establishment of garrison posts (*presidios*) on strategic points on the coast, while leaving the interior to be held by indigenous rulers. During the first decade of the sixteenth century the Spaniards occupied most of the posts they coveted on the Maghriban coast. In 1505 Qasasa was taken as well as Marsa al-Kabir, the port of Oran. Pedro Navarro conquered the Peñon de Velez (Badis in the eastern coastline of the Rif) in 1508, then Oran in 1509. In 1510 he conquered Bougie and Tripoli, after which Tenes, Dellys, Sharshal, and Mustaghanim paid him tribute. Algiers sent a delegation headed by the tribal chief Sālim al-Tha'alibi, who controlled its oligarchic government, to negotiate a truce with the Spaniards in Bougie. The Algerines agreed to pay a tribute in return for peace, and surrendered one of the four rocky islands opposite the town on which the Spaniards built their fortified Peñon.

The Spanish *presidios* in the Maghrib were well fortified, but the territory they controlled remained limited, in most cases not including the lands immediately behind them. For this reason they were dependent on Spain for munitions as well as food supplies, and the garrisons were often demoralized by the irregularity with which these and their pay reached them. Oran alone was fortunate in that it could obtain some of its basic provisions through tribal allies in the neighbourhood. As the sections of the coast held by the Spaniards were small, the Muslim corsairs had long stretches of the coast from which to operate. The establishment of Ottoman rule in the Maghrib was the result of the corsairs' activities and the increasing religious fervour amongst the Muslims caused by the Spanish presence. As has been indicated in the last chapter, the religious mood of the Muslims in the Maghrib at the turn of the sixteenth century was one of intolerance towards non-Muslims; and as their own rulers could not protect them against the Christians, they welcomed outside Muslim help. By exploiting the religious sentiments of the Maghriban Muslims, the Barbarossa brothers were able to establish a foothold in the Maghrib from which they gradually extended into the interior their own control, as well as the authority of the Ottoman sultan which they came to accept. But it would be wrong to assume that the Turks were readily or voluntarily accepted as rulers in any of the countries of the eastern and central Maghrib which they came to control.

The architects of Ottoman rule in the Maghrib, 'Aruj and his younger brother Khair al-Din Barbarossa, were foreigners to the region. They came from the Greek island of Mytilene (ancient Lesbos), their father having been either a member of the Turkish garrison there or a Greek converted to Islam. In any case the two brothers were born Muslim. From 1504, when they first come into the light of history, they were already launched on the career of sea-rovers using Gouletta in Tunisia as a base. They operated from Gouletta with the authority of the Hafsid sultan Muhammad b. al-Hasan (1493–1526) who received a share of their prizes. In 1510 they were also authorized to establish a second base in the island of Jirba, and 'Aruj might have helped its local authorities in repulsing the Spanish attack on the island in that year. So far the two brothers worked in harmony with the Hafsids, so much so that in 1512 'Aruj used the twelve ships he then had to blockade the Spaniards in Bougie by sea while the Hafsid governor of Bougie, who had been expelled from the town, attacked it by land. The attack failed and in its course 'Aruj lost an arm. Two years later he again attacked Bougie in cooperation with a Hafsid land force but again failed to take it. Either shortly before this attack or immediately afterwards he installed himself in Jijilli (Djidjelli) on the eastern promonotory of the Gulf of Bougie and started to found an independent piratical principality. While there he established relations with the tribes of Kabylia, providing them with wheat when they were struck with famine and recruiting warriors from their midst.

As 'Aruj thus began to use the resources and prestige with which his career as a chief pirate had provided him for political leadership, the Hafsids came to view his activities with apprehension and hostility. His attempts to expand his authority into the interior with the help of his local allies led the Hafsid prince Ahmad, the governor of Bona, to place himself under Spanish protection. From Jijilli 'Aruj moved his base to Algiers in 1516. The town had a large Andalusian community, but the political leadership was exercised by Sālim al-Tha'alibi, chief of the Tha'aliba tribe which had occupied the town shortly before Pedro Navarro's campaign of 1510. The Spanish presence lay heavily on the Algerines, who not only paid tribute but were also continually threatened by the cannons of the Peñon. 'Aruj's help was sought to dislodge the Spaniards from their commanding position, and although it was popular clamour which led to his intervention, al-Tha'alibi concurred in it. But 'Aruji did not possess the means to recover the Peñon immediately, and as his presence tended to rob al-Tha'alibi of his power, the latter sought Spanish help to drive him out. 'Aruj used force to bring the Algerine leaders to accept his authority, and al-Tha'alibi was killed.

In 1517 'Aruj occupied Tlemsen. The ease with which this was accomplished indicates the extent of the cooperation he received from Tlemsen's zealous population. He removed from the throne Abu Zayan Ahmad who accepted Spanish suzerainty and, having installed in his place another Zayanid prince, he entered into negotiations with the Wattasids for the purpose of bringing them actively into the war against the Spaniards. But 'Aruj's victory was short-lived. A Spanish force from Oran, reinforced by local tribal warriors, cut his lines of communication with Algiers and proceeded to besiege him in Tlemsen. After defending the own for six months 'Aruj fled, but he was pursued and killed with his escort in 1518. Although Khair al-Din immediately replaced 'Aruj as military ruler of Algiers, the expansion into the interior stopped and Tlemsen, under yet another Zayanid sultan, Abu Hamuw III, renewed its submission to the Spaniards. While in Algiers Khair al-Din repulsed an attack on one town by a Spanish squadron commanded by Hugo de Moncada in 1519, but was forced to evacuate the town in the same year. The little that is known suggests that the treachery of his Kabylia warriors enabled the Hafsids to seize Algiers from him. From then until 1525, when he recovered control of Algiers, he was in Jijilli engaged in piracy and expanding his authority into the interior. During this period he conquered Bona and Constantine.

At what moment in his career Khair al-Din entered the service of the Ottoman government is uncertain. The Porte had looked with favour on the two brothers since they were in Jirba, and when 'Aruj went to Algiers in 1516 he had Turkish soldiers with him. It is likely that Khair al-Din asked for Ottoman help on a large scale shortly after his brother's death, but he seems to have received it only when he was in Jijilli. After his return to Algiers he acted as an Ottoman official. He was given a contingent of 2,000 Janissary troops to serve under him, and was granted leave to recruit others in Turkey. During the eight years he held the government of Algiers he transformed the town from an unimposing anchorage place into an important naval base. In 1529 he captured the Peñon, after which he constructed an earth platform to connect the town with the four rocky isles facing it. A formidable fleet was built in the port, a fleet which the Ottoman government regarded as the official western division of its naval forces. The fleet was, however, used mostly for piracy against Spaniards and other Christians not on a friendly footing with the Porte, an activity at once a part of the Muslim-Christian military confrontation in the Mediterranean and a means by which the government of Algiers obtained its basic revenues. As Oran and Bougie were in the hands of the Spaniards, Algiers was able to monopolize Muslim privateering along the Algerian coast.

Khair al-Din's success in the Christian-Muslim warfare in the western

Mediterranean led to his being entrusted with the supreme command of the Ottoman fleet in 1533. In this year he was invited to Istanbul, and amidst tokens of welcome and appreciation for his services to the empire was appointed kapudan-pasha (captain-pasha); because of this he could not return to Algiers. Nevertheless the role he played in maritime Mediterranean politics until his death in 1546 is of direct relevance to Ottoman position in the Maghrib. Under his supervision a fleet of eighty-four vessels was fitted out in the winter of 1533–4, which he used in 1534 to occupy Tunis. Four years earlier Charles V had granted Malta and Tripoli to the Knights of St John,[1] a measure intended to be as much a thorn in the side of the French as of the Turks, since from their new positions the knights could hamper the dispatch of Turkish reinforcements to the French across the Sicilian straits. Khair al-Din's occupation of Tunis was expected to offset the Spanish advantages resulting from the activities of the crusading knights, and to give backing to the Ottoman regency in Algiers. However, as the French were also alarmed by it, Francis I felt compelled to intimate to his enemy Charles V that should he attack Tunis, the French would preserve a neutral position. Consequently, a Spanish expedition sailed for Tunisia, captured Gouletta in July 1535, and six days later took Tunis. Not wanting to become entangled in local administration, the Spaniards retained authority in the hands of the Hafsid sultan al-Hasan b. Muhammad.

The fluid military situation in the Mediterranean took an important turn in 1536 as a result of the treaty concluded between Francis I and the Ottoman sultan, a treaty which was denounced by the Pope. In its secret clauses the treaty provided for military cooperation between the two Mediterranean powers against Spain, their common enemy. In spite of papal denunciation of the French military alliance with the Muslims, Charles V made attempts towards a secret alliance with Khair al-Din, the real holder of Ottoman naval power in the Mediterranean, in order to destroy the effects of the treaty between Francis I and the sultan. The exact terms offered by Charles V are not known, but they seem to have included the recognition of Khair al-Din as king of Algiers, Bona, Bougie, Bizerta, Tunis, and Tripoli under Spanish suzerainty in return for his bringing over with him the fleet under his command, and helping to crush France and Venice. Protracted negotiations which began in 1538 achieved no result, partly because of the lack of confidence on both sides. The conclusion in 1544 of the Treaty of Crespy between Charles V and Francis I brought to an end both the Franco-Ottoman alliance and the project of winning Khair al-Din over to the Spanish side.

Before Khair al-Din's death in 1546 Jirba became the headquarters of a new group of Muslim pirates commanded by Dragut. Enslaved for four

[1] See below, pp. 192–3.

years by Giannetino Doria, a Genoese naval captain who in 1528 defected to the Spaniards, Dragut had been ransomed by Khair al-Din in 1544 and after this launched his attacks on Christian ships with all the bitterness to which his enslavement had contributed. In 1550 he occupied Mahdiyya, but in 1551 it was conquered from him by Doria, and he himself was nearly captured. Following Khair al-Din's example when in adversity, Dragut immediately placed himself at the disposal of the Ottoman sultan. In 1551 he went to Istanbul and returned a commander in the Ottoman fleet led by the kapudan-pasha Sinan. This fleet captured in the same year both the island of Gozo and Tripoli from the Knights of St John.

The regency of Algiers

From 1525 Algiers became the principal centre of Ottoman authority in the Maghrib and the main base from which the Turks carried out their war against the Spaniards in the western Mediterranean, expanded their control into the interior of Algeria, and invaded Morocco. Khair al-Din laid the foundations of the military organization of the regency. Until 1587 the ruler of Algiers and its dependencies was an officer carrying the title of *beylerbey* and appointed by the sultan. Besides governing the parts of Algeria which the Turks gradually came to possess, the *beylerbey* exercised the authority of suzerain in the name of the Ottoman sultan over the pashas of Tunis and Tripoli. As such he was the supreme Ottoman authority in the western Mediterranean, and responsible for conducting the war against the Christian enemies of the empire in this area, especially Spain.

Adventurers and renegades played an important part in the political and military life of the regency from the start. These men were usually from the poorer parts of the Mediterranean area, often Sicily and Corsica; sometimes they came to Algiers as captives of the Algerine corsairs and gained admittance to the *ta'ifa* (society) of seamen through conversion and by virtue of their knowledge of the ports which the corsairs were to raid. The prosperity and prestige of the regency depended to a great extent on the exploits of the corsairs. For this reason, although the majority were non-Turkish Ottomans, they came to wield considerable power which the *beylerbeys* often used to counter the unruliness of the Turkish infantry corps. The infantry, almost entirely recruited from Anatolia, were organized along the lines of the famous Ottoman Janissary corps. They possessed a high sense of group solidarity and egalitarian spirit in the ranks, and elected their commander-in-chief, the *agha*, and a *diwan* which protected their group interests. Being Turkish, they enjoyed a privileged position in the state: they were not subject to the regular system of justice in the regency, and were entitled to rations of bread, meat, and oil, to a regular salary, and to a proportion of the yields of piracy. Competition between the seamen and the Janissaries existed, but in times of war, especially against the Spaniards in Algeria, their cooperation and high discipline as soldiers and seamen won the regency important military victories. It appears that renegades also formed infantry contingents in the early history of the regency: information obtained by spies for the Spanish authorities in Oran in 1540 indicated that the fighting force in Algiers consisted of 800 Janissary troops and 1,400 renegades, besides a much larger number of tribal auxiliary warriors. The Algerian tribes, primarily concerned with preserving their own independence, joined the Turks, Spaniards, or Zayanids in transient alliances but did not accept the authority of any party in any real way. It appears that some of the *beylerbeys* tried to recruit Kabylia warriors on a regular basis, and a contingent of these warriors, usually cavalry, was often available to take part with the Turks in their wars.

Under Turkish rule Algiers was transformed from a small and relatively unimportant port into a capital town. Its motley population of Turks, Andalusians, Jews, Christian renegades, and local Arabs and Berbers was estimated[1] at 60,000 people in the period of the *beylerbeys*. The renegades may have been the most numerous single group living in the town in the early period; but the official language was Turkish, though Arabic was also widely spoken. Life in Algiers was judged pleasant by Europeans who visited it about the middle of the sixteenth century. It is described as having beautiful houses and numerous public baths, and food was rarely lacking. Though piracy was the most important revenue, local industries such as dyeing also existed. In the early period at least, Algerines were not interested in commerce. Trading was mostly done by those Europeans, such as the French, who were allowed to conduct business in it. The French opened a consulate in Algiers in 1564, by which time several trading establishments belonging to merchants from Marseilles had already been in existence for several years.

Turkish expansion from Algiers into the interior was hampered by the limited resources of the regency, the tribal nature of the society, and the presence of the Spaniards in Oran. At the beginning of the sixteenth century the authority of the Zayanids of Tlemsen did not extend much beyond the limits of their capital and their survival as rulers for another half-century was mainly due to the balance of power between Turks and Spaniards which prevented either party from permanently annexing Tlemsen. For the greater part of the first half of the sixteenth century the interests of the Spaniards coincided with those of the Banu 'Amir, a clan of the Banu Zughba Arabian tribe which had cooperated with the Zayanids during the earliest period of the Zayanid state. Previously

[1] Cf. Charles-André Julien, *Histoire de l'Afrique du Nord* (Paris, 1956), II, 264.

inhabiting the plateaux to the south of Tlemsen, the Banu 'Amir had extended their control northwards by the beginning of the sixteenth century as far as 'Ain Tamushant (Temouchent). The other important tribe in the vicinity of Tlemsen, the Banu Rashid, pursued its interests through alliance with the sultan of Tlemsen until Turkish domination over him since 1543 led them to align themselves with the Spaniards. Neither the Spaniards nor the Turks could rely on the continuous loyalty of their tribal allies, but the Turks, as Muslims, enjoyed the goodwill of the urban communities. Along the western coast of Algeria they used Mustaghanim as an advanced post, which was occupied by 'Aruj in 1516 and fortified by Khair al-Din. In Tenes, halfway between Mustaghanim and Algiers, a new authority emerged in 1516 when a Zayanid prince called Hamida 'Awda declared himself independent of Tlemsen. 'Aruj deposed 'Awda in 1517, but Khair al-Din reinstated him, and he henceforth remained loyal to the Turks. His loyalty was militarily important since it meant that the Turks could bring their artillery by sea to Tenes whenever they were engaged in fighting in the west.

The alliance of the Zayanids with the Spaniards, dating from 1518, continued until the Spaniards received their first major setback after their installation in the Maghrib, in the capture of the Peñon of Algiers from them in 1529. Abu Hamuw III accepted Spanish tutelage and paid an annual tribute of 12,000 ducats until his death in 1528. His successor Abu Muhammad 'Abdulla was pressed by the religious circles of Tlemsen to abandon the Spanish alliance, and the Turkish victory of 1529 encouraged him to yield. Upon his death in 1533 the Turks were able to secure the throne for his son Muhammad, who two years earlier had taken refuge with them upon rebelling against his father. With Turkish backing and popular support Muhammad was able to retain his throne for almost twenty years, although on two occasions he was driven out from Tlemsen.

In 1534 a Spanish nobleman, Count Alcaudete, whose family had a long history of fighting the Muslims in Spain, was appointed captain-general of Oran. Unlike his predecesssors, who had had to seek the approval of Spain on all important issues, he was given plenary powers with regard to the government of Oran and dealings with the tribes, whom he was expected to organize against the Turks. When he arrived the Banu 'Amir chief 'Abdul-Rahman b. Radwan had already prepared a project for the replacement of Sultan Muhammad of Tlemsen by his young brother 'Abdulla. This young Zayanid prince was Ibn Radwan's protégé and agreed to become a tributary of Spain. With the impetuosity which characterized nearly all his undertakings in the Maghrib, Alcaudete supported the project and had 600 of his men join Ibn Radwan's warriors in attacking Tlemsen in 1535. Sultan Muhammad does not seem to have had any Turkish soldiers to fight for him, but the Banu Rashid tribe, whose chief Mansur Bu-Ghani was his *mazwar* (chief vizier), helped to repulse the invasion. In spite of initial successes, the bulk of the Spanish force was trapped at the Tibda fortress and, except for seventy soldiers taken prisoner and a few that escaped, the army was completely destroyed.

In respect of the Spanish standing in the Maghrib the effects of this setback were offset by the Spanish conquest of Tunis from Khair al-Din in the same year. The conquest of Tunis might have been the reason for Sultan Muhammad's conciliatory conduct after his victory. He sent delegates to Oran offering to sign a defensive alliance with the Spaniards, and in September 1535 gave his initial consent to a treaty which placed him under Spanish suzerainty. In return for Spain's promise to provide him with 500 soldiers when needed (presumably to defend himself against the Turks), he agreed to channel all merchandise coming to Tlemsen through Oran, and to pay an annual tribute. It appears that Alcaudete had no intention of asking Charles V to ratify this treaty, which would have alienated his allies the Banu 'Amir, and that he negotiated it in the hope that before it came to ratification the Spanish captives would be set free. But Muhammad regarded the captives as hostages ensuring the safety of Tlemsen, and insisted on ratification before their release. By mid-1536 it became clear that Alcaudete was only playing for time before he again attempted to depose Sultan Muhammad, and in consequence the latter sought to improve his relations with Algiers.

Further Spanish attempts to conquer Tlemsen required the dispatch of reinforcements from Spain. The wars of Charles V with France precluded this, and after 1538 he hoped to gain ascendancy in the Maghrib through an agreement which he tried to reach with Khair al-Din Barbarossa.[1] During the period of Charles' negotiations with Khair al-Din (1538–40), Alcaudete made overtures to Hasan Agha (who governed Algiers as Khair al-Din's deputy from 1536 to 1543), trying to secure his defection too. The failure of the negotiations with Khair al-Din forms the background for Charles V's attack on Algiers in 1541. The Spanish expedition, commanded by the emperor in person, was a mammoth one by the standards of the time. It consisted of about 500 ships, carrying a land force of 24,000 soldiers and about 12,000 marines. Distinguished generals like Cortez, the conqueror of Mexico, took part, and Alcaudete joined it with a part of the Oran garrison. The Spaniards chose to attack in the autumn, calculating that bad weather in this season would prevent the Ottoman fleet from coming to the rescue of Algiers. But the stormy weather in which the fleet was caught near Algiers, coupled with the determined resistance of the garrison, led to the invaders' defeat. Having lost about one-third of his fleet and himself having narrowly escaped captivity, Charles V ordered the retreat of the expedition three days after the beginning of the attack on

[1] See above, p. 165.

23 October. Spanish prestige in the Maghrib was at its lowest ebb after this failure, and in July 1542 Hasan Agha felt confident enough to attack Marsa al-Kabir, the port of Oran.

Alcaudete used forces newly recruited from Spain to invade Tlemsen and replace Sultan Muhammad with his brother 'Abdulla in 1543. But as Alcaudete could not spare any men to protect 'Abdulla, the latter was able to retain the throne for only a few months. The chief of the Banu Rashid, Bu-Ghani, finding his position in Tlemsen threatened by increasing Turkish influence, threw in his lot at this juncture with the Spaniards. In June 1545 he invaded Tlemsen with Spanish help, and installed on the throne another of Muhammad's brothers called Ahmad; but in the same month Muhammad was restored by a Turkish force commanded by Hasan Agha, and a Turkish garrison was stationed in Tlemsen to protect its sultan. What can be gleaned about the conduct of Sultan Muhammad after 1535 suggests that he tried to remain independent of both Spaniards and Turks. In this respect he received the support of the population of Tlemsen, whose help seems to have been decisive in his restoration in 1543, if not in 1545 as well. But when the Zayanids became totally dependent on the Turks in 1545, the inhabitants of Tlemsen seem to have preferred the Sa'dians of Morocco as rulers.

Simultaneously with Alcaudete's endeavours to place a Spanish protégé on the throne of Tlemsen, he attempted to capture Mustaghanim from the Turks. He attacked it in 1543 and 1547. On both occasions his army was repulsed and pursued by tribal warriors and Turkish soldiers, harassing it all along the way to Oran. The defeat of 1547 was so demoralizing that Alcaudete retired to Spain to recover from it, leaving his son Don Martin in command of Oran. He returned briefly to Oran in 1549, then was absent again until 1554. During the seven years ending in 1554 the Spaniards lived in a state of siege in Oran, and were unable to take any initiative in the affairs of the rest of Algeria. This was the time when the Turks made their first serious bid to penetrate Morocco.

About the time that the Turkish control of Tlemsen became a reality in 1545, the Sa'dian *sharifs* of southern Morocco defeated Ahmad, the Wattasid sultan of Fez, and took him prisoner.[1] The elder Wattasid statesman and prince 'Ali Abu Hassun was able, however, to keep the sultanate in the hands of the Wattasids, and ruled on behalf of Ahmad's young son Nasir al-Qasiri. In the name of his young protégé he also sought Turkish help to check the advance of the Sa'dians. It appears that the Turks did not respond to this appeal immediately. This was the time when the chief of Banu Rashid, Mansur Bu-Ghani, was engaged in recruiting a force in Spain to drive the Turks out from Tlemsen, and it is likely that the Turkish authorities in Algiers felt unable to interfere in

---

[1] For the background, see below, p. 208.

Morocco when a renewal of Spanish attacks threatened. In 1547, just before the Spanish defeat at Mustaghanim, the Turks felt unable to prevent Bu-Ghani from replacing Sultan Muhammad by his brother Ahmad; after the defeat they restored Muhammad. In July 1548 an ambassador arrived in Marrakish carrying a letter from the Ottoman sultan bidding the Sa'dian leader Muhammad al-Shaikh release the Wattasid sultan and make amends to him, and indicating that the Turks did not recognize al-Shaikh's claim to the rule of Morocco since he was addressed in the letter as *shaikh* of the Arabs. The threat of Turkish intervention only spurred the Sa'dians to act immediately against the Wattasids. Muhammad al-Shaikh began to prepare for attacking Fez in the second half of 1548, and occupied it in 1549. Soon afterwards he also started his preparations for the invasion of Tlemsen.

As indicated above,[1] Tlemsen became in the fifteenth century a dependency of the Marinids in Fez. Cultural and religious ties between these two Muslim towns were henceforth fostered, and some of Tlemsen's distinguished men of learning – such as Ahmad al-Wanshirisi and Muhammad b. al-Khatib b. Marzuq – found a home for themselves in Fez and enjoyed the favours of its sultans. Because of these links the inhabitants of Tlemsen tended to look to Fez in times of adversity, and the Sa'dians after their occupation of Fez were inclined to look upon Tlemsen as their proper sphere of influence. But when Muhammad al-Shaikh sent his son al-Harran at the head of an army of about 30,000 men to occupy Tlemsen in 1551 he no doubt intended to use it as an advanced post to check Turkish expansion westwards. Sultan Muhammad had died some time before. As the Turkish garrison installed in 1545 had been withdrawn in 1547, his successor Hasan was able to establish amicable relations with Oran which aroused the hostility of his people. When al-Harran arrived before Tlemsen in 1551, its gates were thrown open to him with such alacrity as to suggest that some contact had been made in advance with its people. After taking the town al-Harran penetrated into the Shaliff valley and reached Mustaghanim. The Spaniards in Oran held aloof, but their allies the Banu 'Amir, for some thirty years the enemies of the Turks, joined forces with the latter to drive out the Sa'dians. Al-Harran is said to have exceeded his father's instructions by overrunning the Shaliff at a time when the latter was occupied with rebellions in Sus and the High Atlas and could not send him substantial reinforcements. The Turkish Janissaries, led by their *agha* Hasan Qusru, and supported by the Banu 'Amir and other tribes threatened by the Sa'dian invasion, drove al-Harran's army from the Shaliff. Al-Harran himself died of illness in Tlemsen as the Turks were approaching it, and cavalry reinforcements sent from Fez in haste were dispersed by the Turks before reaching the town. Sultan Hasan

[1] P. 157.

fled to Oran, and from there went to Spain where he died in obscurity a few years later. Hasan Qusru installed a garrison in Tlemsen, and appointed a governor, granted an amnesty to those of its inhabitants who recognized Sultan Sulaiman's authority, and confiscated the property of those who refused to submit.

The Turks used their ascendant power after 1552 to capture Bougie from the Spaniards in 1555. Both the Sa'dians and the Spaniards in Oran, already alarmed, tried to achieve a military alliance against the increasingly powerful state of Algiers. Contacts between Fez and Oran occurred shortly after the return of Count Alcaudete to his post at the end of 1554. A preliminary agreement reached between Alcaudete and Muhammad al-Shaikh in the first months of 1555 provided for the participation of 10,000 Spanish harquebusiers and a thousand cavalry in an expedition which Muhammad al-Shaikh intended to launch against Algiers. The Sa'dian ruler expressed readiness to pay the expenses of the Spanish expedition in advance, and in order to assure him that the troops would be sent Alcaudete offered to hand over his son as hostage. But in Spain the authorities were suspicious of a military deal of this magnitude with a Muslim ruler, and in 1555 they refused to endorse it. They changed their mind after the Turks attacked Oran in 1556. The attack, though it failed, alarmed the Spaniards. Hardly had the siege begun in August 1556 when the forty Ottoman galleys taking part in it were withdrawn for service in the east. The *beylerbey* Hasan Ra'is had died in May, and the old hand Hasan Qusru who assumed *de facto* authority had to lift the siege. Immediately afterwards Alcaudete went to Spain to recruit men to use against the Turks, and his ambassador was sent to Fez to sustain the Sa'dian interest in the alliance along the lines previously accepted. In Spain Alcaudete was authorized to enlist 8,000 men. He recruited 11,000, but before the army embarked at Cartagena in July 1558 he received the news that Muhammad al-Shaikh had been assassinated (October 1557) by a Turk. Nevertheless Alcaudete embarked his troops and, instead of leading them against Algiers, he attacked Mustaghanim.

The invasion of Mustaghanim by a Spanish army consisting mostly of raw recruits brought Alcaudete's chequered career to a disastrous conclusion, and ended his grandiose scheme of creating a Spanish protectorate in western Algeria. As a result of numerous mistakes in planning the expedition and failure to seize favourable moments for action the Spaniards found themselves before Mustaghanim without provisions, with a determined garrison within, Hasan Qusru's Algerine army approaching from the east, and tribal warriors attacking them from all sides. The battered and hungry army of 11,000 men was ordered to retreat from Mustaghanim on 25 August 1558. It was surrounded by Turkish soldiers who had landed on the coast and Hasan Qusru's troops and the tribal warriors attacking from the other sides as it arrived at nearby Mazargan on the 26th. Alcau-dete was killed with about half his men, The rest, including his son Don Martin, were taken captives to Algiers. At this moment Oran could have been taken by the Turks if they had attacked it, but Hasan Qusru preferred to return to Algiers with his victory unblemished by a possible setback which the uncertainty of tribal support might cause. Oran remained in the hands of the Spaniards until they ceded it to the deys of Algiers by treaty in September 1791. In the rest of Algeria Turkish authority was recognized, although the tribes retained a measure of autonomy in their respective areas.

Thus the period of the *beylerbeys* witnessed the creation of Turkish Algeria. The Janissaries, who distinguished themselves in the battles against the Sa'dians and the Spaniards, did not always bend before the authority of Istanbul's representatives. Upon the death of Salah Ra'is in 1556 they prevented his successor Tekelerli from entering Algiers; and when the *ta'ifa* of seamen helped him disembark he was assassinated. Hasan Pasha, Khair al-Din's son who had served as *beylerbey* between 1544 and 1552, was again dispatched from Istanbul to discipline the unruly Janissaries. He was able to quieten the situation, but in 1561 was sent in chains to Istanbul by the Janissaries who were infuriated by his levying of troops in Kabylia. Hasan Pasha was able to return to Algiers in the follow-ing year, but not before a special Ottoman envoy undertook a campaign to suppress the malcontents. In the riot of 1556 the Janissaries, aiming at ensuring their political predominance, tried to have their popular *agha*, Hasan Qusru, appointed *beylerbey*. Their opposition to the levying of troops in Kabylia by Hasan Pasha seems to have sprung from the same motive. The Janissaries of Tunisia made several attempts in the course of the seventeenth century to wield power, but the representatives of the sultan in Tunisia were able to draw enough local support to check their ambitions permanently, and in the process they created a reigning dynasty. In Algeria the independent spirit of the tribes precluded such sustained co-operation with the pashas.

Under the last of the *beylerbeys* 'Ulj 'Ali (commonly known in European literature as Ochiali), the links between Istanbul and Algeria were streng-thened. 'Ulj 'Ali was appointed in March 1568 and was given the task, besides ruling the regency, of conquering Tunisia from the Hafsids. He accomplished this task in 1569. In 1573 Don John of Austria recaptured Tunisia. 'Ulj 'Ali, who had by then become the kapudan-pasha of the Ottoman fleet, accompanied the expedition commanded by Sinan Pasha which reconquered Tunisia in 1574. 'Ulj 'Ali retained the position of *beylerbey* of Algiers while commanding the Ottoman fleet. He visited the regency occasionally, but his duties in it were performed by deputies. As a result of his holding the two positions simultaneously, the regency was drawn closer into the administration of the Ottoman government. His death as a very old man in 1587 was the occasion for the introduction by the Ottoman government of changes in the administration of the regency.

From 1587 Algeria was ruled by the so-called "Triennial Bashaws", pashas appointed by Istanbul to rule the regency for terms of three years. But as they received no material help from Istanbul, they had to rely for their authority on the prestige of their office and their personal abilities. The sultan's authority was accepted, but it was distant and consequently that of his representative tended to be a shadowy one in a state where the chiefs of the seamen (the *ra'is*) were continuously in the limelight because of their attacks on European ships and ports. One of the most famous of the *ra'is* called Murad became something of a national hero. He took part in the Ottoman siege of Malta in 1565, in 1585 attacked Lanzarote, one of the Canary Islands, and in 1589, after a successful attack on *La Serena*, a Maltese galley, was honoured by being mounted on the pasha's horse and escorted to the palace by the Janissaries. Murad's reputation was great in Turkey too, where he was regarded as "a 'miracle' and a 'saint', without whom nothing at sea could be accomplished".[1]

During the time of 'Ulj 'Ali the fleets of Algiers, Tripoli, and Tunisia were controlled by the Ottoman kapudan-pasha. By the beginning of the seventeenth century, however, we find the captains of the sea of these three regencies again acting independently of him. In the case of Algeria this meant that the captain of the sea came to have full control over the affairs of the marines, whereas internally the *diwan* of the Janissaries exercised real authority, with the pasha remaining as the nominal head of the administration. In 1626 a change in the government of Algeria was effected with the sanction of the Porte, by which the *diwan* came officially to exercise all powers and control all branches of the administration, as well as appointments, promotions, and the management of the estates. The captain of the sea's position after this change became more precisely defined, as he came to be appointed by the *diwan* for life and was assigned a fixed salary. The *agha* of the Janissaries, who was the governor of the city of Algiers, was at the same time the president of the *diwan*. The *diwan* met daily except on Friday, and it met in the official residence of the pasha once a week, on which occasion he communicated to it the commands of the sultan. The chancellery was controlled by four secretaries of state who were at first attached to the pasha and later to the *diwan*. The administration of Algeria during this period was well organized, and records were kept of the sultan's commands, the texts of treaties, the prizes gained by the corsairs, and the income accruing to the state from the sale of slaves and he collection of taxes.

[1] Godfrey Fisher, *Barbary Legend* (Oxford, 1957), p. 89.

Another development which occurred in 1659 placed all the powers in the hands of the *agha* of the Janissaries. The excuse for the change was that the pasha's corruption hampered the relations of the regency with European countries. The government of the regency underwent another change in 1671 when the destruction of seven of the best Algerine ships by a British squadron commanded by Sir Edward Spragg occasioned a rebellion of the *ra'is* and the assassination of Agha 'Ali (1664–71), the last of four Janissary chiefs to rule the country since 1659, all of whom were massacred. In place of the *agha* of the Janissaries the *ra'is* chose as ruler of the regency an officer to whom the title of "dey"[1] was given, the same title as used by the rulers of Tunisia after 1591. Although by 1689 the dey came to be elected by the militia, the change meant that its *agha* was no longer *ex officio* the ruler of the country. The pasha sent from Istanbul retained the ceremonial duties as the sultan's representative, and conveyed the orders of Istanbul, but he exercised no real authority in the regency. In 1710 the title of pasha was taken by the dey, who subsequently became the nominal as well as the real head of the Algerian state.

The government of Algeria which developed since 1671 and lasted until 1830 was a military oligarchic government. It rested upon the existence of a foreign army, relatively well trained and armed, in whose interest the country was ruled, under the nominal suzerainty of the Ottoman sultan and with the concurrence of indigenous notables. The Ujaq, as the collective body of the Turkish military colony was called, never exceeded 15,000 men, and remained to the end a distinct class of foreign rulers. The soldiers were allowed to marry women from the country, but their offspring (the *kouloughli*) were rarely admitted into the militia. The taxes that were collected were almost entirely spent on paying the salaries of the militia, with the result that public works and education were totally neglected by the state.

The administration of the country was a military one, whose main purposes were to preserve peace, administer justice, and collect the taxes. The dey was assisted in his functions by a *diwan* consisting of his confidants, and including five ministers of state. Besides the headship of the entire government, the dey was directly responsible for the administration of Algiers, its suburbs, and the Mitijda plain around it. The rest of the country was divided into three provinces (*beyliks*) governed by beys directly responsible to the dey: the eastern province whose capital was Constantine, the central province or *beylik* of Tittari had its capital at Midia, and the western province had its capital at Oran after 1792, when this town was evacuated by the Spaniards. The beys were given contingents from the Ujaq, but could also recruit auxiliary soldiers from privileged tribes (the *makhzan* tribes), which were usually exempt from

[1] Literally "dey" means maternal uncle.

taxation. In their provinces the beys could act much as they liked provided that the taxes were collected and remitted to Algiers at the appointed times in the autumn and spring.

Under this kind of government it was to be expected that urban life should decline. With the exception of Algiers, and possibly Constantine, the main cities of Algeria lost their importance; Tlemsen in the interior lost its position as a centre of commerce and culture under the control of a group of *kouloughlis* who were given charge of its affairs. Julien estimates that between five and six per cent of the population of Algeria were urban when the French conquered the country.[1] Non-Turkish Muslims constituted the majority of the inhabitants of Algiers. Jews also came to live there in considerable numbers, since Khair al-Din Barbarossa encouraged them to settle in the regency. Rich Jewish families gradually came to become influential in the commerce of Algiers, amongst whom Jews from Leghorn became prominent about the end of the eighteenth century. Among these, the Bakris and Bushnaqs became the best known because of their connection with the commercial dealings with France that precipitated the crisis of 1827 which was used in 1830 as the pretext for the French conquest of Algiers.

The countryside was little affected by the Turkish administration. Tribalism continued to be the most important feature of social organization, and the Turks contributed towards its entrenchment by using tribal chiefs for keeping their respective areas under control. Whereas in the cities the Hanafite rite of the Muslim law was administered in cases involving the Turks, and the Malikite rite with respect to the rest of the Muslim population, the tribes practised customary justice which, without being fully Islamic, incorporated some precepts of Islamic law. In the areas outside the direct control of the government, and therefore of the Muslim jurists, the Sufi cult made great progress during the Turkish period. This was true of all four countries of the Maghrib, but it gained perhaps its greatest ascendancy in Algeria. The functions which the Sufi orders performed explain their popularity in a country where the government provided little security outside the immediate vicinity of the towns, and hardly any public services. The members of the orders were united in a spiritual bond by veneration and complete obedience to their *shaikhs* through whom they received divine blessing. The *zawiyas* (lodges) of the orders, located in distant parts of the country and outside it, gave shelter to the wayfarer, their superintendents provided a rudimentary kind of justice, and sometimes the children learnt to read and write in them. Through the donations which the *zawiyas* received they could perform these services and dispense charity to the poor. It is not surprising, therefore, that when the French conquered Algeria in the nineteenth century,

[1] Charles-André Julien, *Histoire de l'Algérie contemporaine* (Paris, 1964), p. 10.

they found the Sufi orders an important political force in the countryside and even in the cities, and felt compelled to work with and through
them.

Tunisia under the deys and the Husainids, 1574–1837

At the beginning of the sixteenth century the Hafsid rulers of Tunisia had
relapsed into such a degree of weakness that in the conflict between the
Ottomans and the Spaniards they were able to be little more than helpless
spectators. During the reign of Muhammad b. al-Hasan (1493–1526) the
south of the country once more defied the authority of Tunis. It was this
sultan who is said to have permitted 'Aruj to establish a base for his
operations first in Gouletta and then in Jirba. The Hafsid sultan's allowing 'Aruj to use Jirba as a base could hardly have been more than a
formality, since the island had its ruling dynasty, al-Samumni. In 1510 the
Jirbians led by Yahya al-Samumni took part in repulsing the Spaniards,
and as late as 1560 a member of the family, Mansur al-Samumni, led the
inhabitants of the island against them. During the reign of Muhammad's
son al-Hasan, which began in 1526, another chiefly family emerged in
southern Tunisia. This was the al-Shabi family which from a base in Susa
came also to control Qairawan. As in 1525 Khair al-Din Barbarossa
regained control of Algiers, after he had acquired control of Bona and
Constantine, Sultan al-Hasan ruled only the northern part of Tunisia, and
even there his authority was uncertain.

Sultan al-Hasan's weakness in the face of such redoubtable enemies as
the Turks of Algiers led him to seek Spanish protection. When in 1534
Khair al-Din conquered Tunis, al-Hasan went to Spain seeking help. He
was reinstated as a result of the Spanish conquest of Tunis in 1535.
Henceforth he was a Spanish protégé, whose authority in the north could
be maintained only through the presence of a Spanish garrison at Gouletta.
At some unknown date his son Ahmad used the hostility which his
dependence on the Spaniards engendered in the people to depose him
while he was in Spain trying to have reinforcements sent to Tunis for
conquering the south. Ahmad himself was forced to fall upon the mercy of
the Spaniards when 'Ulj 'Ali conquered Tunis in 1569. Chased out by the
Turks he went to Spain, returning in 1573 with a force which reinstated
him on terms of tutelage similar to those under which his father had ruled.
But as he proved less pliant than his father, he was taken soon afterwards
into exile in Sicily and his brother Muhammad was placed on the throne.
When Sinan Pasha conquered Tunis in 1574 Muhammad was taken to
Istanbul, and with his removal the Hafsid dynasty came to an end.

Sinan left in Tunis a regiment of 4,000 Janissary troops divided into
units of 100, each commanded by an officer called the dey. The head of the

Ottoman administration in Tunisia was at first the pasha appointed by the Porte, assisted by an officer called the bey who supervised the internal administration and the collection of the taxes. As in Algeria, there was also a government council called the *diwan*, which between 1574 and 1591 consisted of the senior army officers (*buluk-bashis*) and notables from Tunis. The troops nipped this collective system of governement in the bud when they rebelled in 1591, massacred several members of the *diwan*, and forced the pasha to entrust to one of their junior officers (deys) the charge of law and order in the capital and the affairs of the military. This development meant that the chief dey, elected by the other deys, became the virtual ruler of the country.

Through the administrative abilities and statesmanlike qualities of 'Uthman Dey (1598–1610) and Yusuf Dey (1610–37), the prestige and dignity of the deys were established in the country. These two deys were able to check the turbulence of the troops and direct their energies towards combating insubordinate tribes. Peace and order were thus established, and parts of the country that had for nearly a century defied the orders of Tunis were brought under control. As at the same time the regency was not required to send tribute to Istanbul, and these two deys were not fond of luxury, money was available for organizing the administration and for works of construction. In Yusuf's period a mosque in the capital, a fortress in Bizerta, and barracks for the army were built, and aqueducts in various parts of Tunisia were repaired. As a sign of the strength of the Tunisian administration the island of Jirba, under Tripoli's control since 1558, was in 1604 once more brought under the control of Tunis. During Yusuf Dey's rule privateering became an important source of revenue to the state, and the Tunisian fleet is said to have consisted at this time of seventeen ships and several brigantines.

By undermining the authority of the *diwan* and the practice of collective government, the deys paved the way for the appearance of dynastic rule in Tunisia. This trend started in Yusuf Dey's time with the bestowal of the title of pasha on the bey Murad. Murad was a Corsican who had gone to Tunis as a boy and had been brought up by an officer called Ramadan who distinguished himself as bey under 'Uthman and Yusuf Deys. He succeeded his benefactor as bey, and gained repute for suppressing rebellious tribes. The appointment of the bey as pasha, who in the power hierarchy of Tunisia was the dey's subordinate, was an admission on the part of the Ottoman government that its representative in Tunisia had lost the position of supremacy in the country. The deys, viewing these two civilian positions with indifference, allowed them to be inherited in the family of Murad. By doing so they short-sightedly permitted the development of a centre of power that could rival theirs. Among the Muslim population of the country the pasha enjoyed a special position on account of being the representative of the sultan-caliph. As he was also bey, and as such supervised the administration and toured the countryside, he was able to establish relations with the local Muslims which proved useful in the future conflicts with the military.

When Murad died in 1631 the notables of Tunisia joined forces to ensure the succession of his son Hammuda to Murad's two positions. It is significant that when Hammuda sought investiture from the sultan in 1657 he did so upon the behest of Tunisia's notables. This suggests that Tunisia's local leaders sought to invest their chosen ruler with the dignity of being the sultan's representative as a counterbalance to the authority of the military. A dynasty of pasha-beys thus gradually emerged, which restored authority to the sultan's representative through local support. The nineteenth century historian Ibn Abi al-Diaf, who as secretary to the beys of Tunisia had access to records belonging to this early period, starts listing the deys serving under the Muradists since Hammuda in the way one lists governments that held power during the reign of a monarch.[1] From the time of Hammuda the collaboration between the Muradists and the Tunisian notables enabled the *diwan* to regain the authority which it exercised briefly after 1574. As Hammuda's successor Murad Bey (1666–75) gave support to the *diwan* in its dealings with the deys, this body was able to remove from his office Hajj Muhammad Ughlu Dey (1666–70) on the charge of insanity. Ughlu's successor Sha'ban Dey (1670–2) began by being subservient to the wishes of Marad Bey and when he showed signs of insubordination Murad had the *diwan* replace him by Muhammad Mantashali. The Janissary troops could now see which way the wind was blowing, and attempted to regain a predominant position by rebelling against Mantashali. Using the occasion of Murad's absence in the spring of 1673 to collect the taxes, they replaced Mantashali by 'Ali Laz, one of their deys who was known for defending the privileged position of the Turkish troops. Members of the *diwan* who were outspoken in favour of Murad Bey were massacred before the uprising collapsed. Although the Mathalith and Awlad Sa'id tribes, who had suffered from Murad's attacks, gave their support to the rebellious troops, Murad Bey was able to carry the rest of the country with him. Later in 1673 he regained control of the capital and re-established his authority over the military. The Muradists continued to hold the position of bey until the last of them, Murad b. 'Ali, was assassinated in 1702. The chief conspirator in the assassination of Murad was the *agha* of the *spahis* (the cavalry), Ibrahim al-Sharif who emerged as ruler, with the titles of bey and dey combined in him. He ruled until 1705, when the dey of Algiers 'Ashshi Mustafa, perhaps seeking territorial aggrandizement, invaded Tunisia

---

[1] Ahmad Ibn Abi al-Diaf, *Ithaf ahl al-zaman bi akhbar muluk Tunis wa 'Ahd al-Aman*, II (Tunis, 1963), pp. 37ff.

and, having defeated him, took him captive to Algiers. The Husainid dynasty, which was to rule Tunisia until 1957, came into being in the process of repulsing the Algerian invasion.

The founder of the new dynasty, Husain b. 'Ali, an Ottoman of Greek extraction, was until 1705 the *agha* of the *spahis* in Baja (Beja). He took a leading part in driving back the Algerians in 1705, and in this way earned enough authority to make a bid to succeed Ibrahim al-Sharif. But being a *spahi*, and therefore an outsider to the infantry Janissary troops, the latter nominated to rule the country in his place one of their officers, called al-Asfar Dey, as soon as the Algerian threat receded. In the ensuing conflict with the al-Asfar party Husain followed the policy of the Muradists by seeking support from the local inhabitants. In this way, though an Ottoman, he identified himself with native opposition to the rule of the Turkish soldiery. After he recaptured power with the support of the Tunisian tribes in January 1706 he even chose a Malikite *qadi* to officiate in the Bardo. In the matter of the juridical rite he thus opted to associate himself with the Tunisians, though he as a Turk was a Hanafite. He also showed determination in curbing the power of the Turkish officers. Henceforth the deys could no longer order the execution of criminals, and the death penalty could be pronounced by a *shari'a* council subject to review only by the bey. Husain b. 'Ali also paid attention to reviving agriculture, particularly the planting of olives, and to building mosques and schools. In this way he styled himself as a popular Muslim ruler, justifying his exercise of power in terms of upholding the religious law and serving the economic interests of his people. That he was accepted as such, and for this reason the Tunisians preferred him to Ottoman functionaries ruling with the help of the Turkish troops, was clearly confirmed ten years later. In 1715 the kapudan-pasha of the Ottoman fleet, Ghanim, arrived in Tunis, bringing with him a Tunisian notable called Muhammad b. Mustafa seeking to instal him as governor of Tunisia. Husain b. 'Ali felt confident enough to summon a council comprising *'ulama*, the members of the *diwan*, and the army chiefs to discuss the order of the sultan which the kapudan-pasha claimed he was sent to carry out. The council decided to oppose the change, even if that meant resisting it by force, and Ghanim Pasha withdrew without pressing the matter further.

For about fifty years after 1705 Tunisia continued to be threatened by the expansionist ambitions of the rulers of Algiers. There is no evidence to suggest that the action of the Algerians was inspired by the wishes of Istanbul. Rather it seems to have arisen from the ambitions of Algeria's rulers and was occasioned by political conflict first between Husain b. 'Ali and his nephew and then between the latter and Husain's sons. Since until 1709 Husain b. 'Ali had no heir, he groomed his nephew 'Ali to succeed him. In this year he had his first son Muhammad, and when the boy became fifteen he appointed him heir-apparent and entrusted him with the important function of heading the *mahalla* (military column) sent twice a year to collect the taxes. To reconcile his nephew to this change of fortune in 1725 he procured from Istanbul his appointment as pasha. It is not known whether Tunisia had a pasha between 1705 and 1725, but in any case the rank could hardly have been any but a ceremonial one. 'Ali, who had grown used to the exercise of authority and had established a standing in the country, rebelled in 1728 in the neighbourhood of Qairawan. After four years of tribal strife which failed to enable 'Ali Pasha to capture power, he fled to Algiers, returning in 1735 with an Algerian army.

In September 1735 Husain b. 'Ali was defeated near al-Kaf, but he held out in Qairawan until in May 1740 'Ali Pasha's son Yunis captured the town. Husain b. 'Ali was killed in the battle of Qairawan, and his two sons Muhammad and 'Ali fled to Algeria. In the period of conflict between 'Ali Pasha and his uncle, the Tunisian tribes became divided into Pashiyya (supporting 'Ali Pasha) and Husainiyya (supporting his uncle Husain). This tribal division remained significant well into the nineteenth century, and determined the alignment of the tribes into two *suffs*[1] between whom cooperation was considered inconceivable.

'Ali Pasha ruled Tunisia until 1756. He was a distinguished ruler, able to keep the tribes in check and to assert the regency's strength in his dealings with the European powers, particularly France. The *'ulama* at first had some misgivings about the ruthlessness with which he suppressed his uncle's partisans, but they were gradually won over by his numerous favours. Conscious of the danger of a bid by Husain b. 'Ali's children to regain control of Tunisia with Algerian help, he tried to raise members of his family as an aristocratic class and to accustom the Tunisian people to regard them as the rulers of the land. He required his sons and immediate relatives to wear distinguishing clothes, and forbade them from engaging in commerce and agriculture, while he himself alone could wear cashmere and furs. He further added to his retinue a bodyguard of black slaves, thus adopting a mark of royalty dating back to the Hafsid period. At the same time he seems to have retained some relations with Istanbul, since he was able to recruit new troops from Asia Minor.

The anticipated attempt by Husain b. 'Ali's sons to conquer Tunisia with Algerian help occurred in 1746, but 'Ali Pasha was able to thwart it, defeating the Algerians near al-Kaf. His quarrel immediately afterwards with his eldest son Yunis, who had been his right-hand man in fighting Husain b. 'Ali and subduing the tribes, contributed towards weakening his regime and encouraged the exiled Husainid princes to renew the attempt.

[1] A corruption of the Arabic *saff* (class, line of troops, etc.), *suff* was used throughout the Maghrib to mean a party in a tribal conflict.

After a protracted civil war, in which Yunis was able to oust his father from the capital in 1752, 'Ali Pasha forced his son to flee to Constantine. Yunis too tried to win Algerian support, but in the end the Husainids, possibly offering the larger booty to the Algerians, were reinstated in 1756. Among other things Husain b. 'Ali's sons seem to have agreed to allow the Algerians to sack the Bardo palace in return for their help.

After their restoration the Husainids tried to rule Tunisia along the lines which the dynasty's founder had laid down. Grateful for the support they received from the population of the country, and conscious that their ability to resist Algerian expansion depended on the continuation of this support, the two great Husainid rulers of the eighteenth century, 'Ali (1759–77) and Hammuda (1777–1813) built their position on three foundations: prosperity through agriculture and commerce, the support of the religious leaders, and a disciplined Turkish army.

The first urgent task to which Husain b. 'Ali's two sons, Muhammad and 'Ali, had to address themselves in 1756 was to persuade the Algerians to evacuate Tunisia. The Algerian army which conquered Tunis from 'Ali Pasha was led by the bey of Constantine Hasan, who seems to have cherished the ambition of annexing Tunisia to the government of Algiers, which would in fact have meant annexing it to his own beylik. Though the Algerians were well rewarded by the booty they took, Hasan delayed the departure from Tunis. Keeping the deposed 'Ali Pasha in his custody, he sent messengers to Algiers trying to persuade Barmaq Saz Dey to annex Tunisia, or at least impose a tribute on the two brothers. While Tunisia's fate was thus held in the balance, the two brothers sought to rally the countryside to their help. Muhammad, the elder brother and the titular head of the Husainid family, remained in the capital to assert his family's rights; his brother 'Ali left Tunis on the pretext of collecting taxes, and toured the south. He visited Hammamat, Susa, Munastir, Sfax, and Qairawan, collecting from the inhabitants contributions in money and inciting them to join him and his brother in a bid to drive out the Algerians. Conflict between the Husainid princes and Hasan Bey was eventually averted when the dey of Algiers ordered his subordinate to put 'Ali Pasha to death and evacuate Tunisia. The nineteenth century historian Ibn Abi al-Diaf, writing from the viewpoint of the political controversy in his time about Tunisia's links with the Ottoman empire, states that the dey of Algiers abstained from demanding tribute from the Husainids on the grounds that Tunisia, like Algeria, was Ottoman territory and in both tribute could be paid only to the sultan. The Algerians evacuated Tunisia in September 1756. In addition to the prizes they carried by land, there were three ships filled with booty which was lost when the ships were wrecked shortly after leaving Tunis.

The international political context within which the question of

Tunisia's links with the Ottoman empire was raised in the nineteenth century did not exist at the middle of the eighteenth. The Husainids acted after their restoration as independent sovereigns, concluding treaties with foreign powers and declaring wars without seeking the opinion of the Ottoman government. But they also strove to retain some links with the empire. 'Ali prevailed upon his brother Muhammad Bey, in the short period the latter held authority (September 1756 to February 1759), to seek investiture as pasha of Tunisia from the Ottoman sultan. The insignia of investiture arrived after Muhammad's death and 'Ali assumed them himself. But investiture seems to have been viewed more as a papal consecration of a monarch's succession in medieval Europe than as a recognition of Ottoman sovereignty. Henceforth the beys applied for investiture after securing the throne, and sent gifts to the sultan on this occasion. They did not pay regular tribute. The Ottoman government demanded the payment of an annual tribute for the first time only upon the accession of Mustafa Bey to the throne in 1835; he was able to refuse to comply although he had to give the poverty of the country as the excuse for his refusal. Tunisian ships were sent to take part in Ottoman wars in the east, but that was clearly done in the name of Muslim solidarity and not as a requirement of vassalage.

To the Tunisians the question of their rulers' relations with the Ottoman sultan was not considered to be of any political consequence before the middle of the nineteenth century. They looked upon the Husainids as their sovereigns to whose absolute power only one limitation could be legitimately envisaged, namely that of the Muslim law. Muhammad Bey showed much deference to the Majlis al-Shar'i, a council in which the leading religious scholars and experts in the Muslim law were represented. It was an advisory council, specifically concerned with judging whether the decrees of the bey and his viziers accorded with the prescriptions of the religious law. Muhammad made the members of this council his consorts, invited them regularly to his Manuba residence where he spent most of his time, and established the custom that the beys could not smoke in the presence of the Majlis members. His brother 'Ali Bey and the latter's son Hammuda Bey also favoured the *'Ulama* and relied on the Majlis for counsel. 'Ali spent the entire state income from the *jizya* on religious learning, allocating from it fixed stipends to teachers and students. He also entrusted the *'ulama* with the investigation of charges of corruption made against the provincial governors. Also in the administration of justice, particularly with regard to the death penalty, 'Ali is reported to have been scrupulous in following the provisions of the Muslim law.

Both 'Ali and Hammuda Beys took a direct interest in developing agriculture and correcting government abuses which had hampered its growth. 'Ali began his reign by abolishing the system, called *al-mushtara,* of compulsory sale of crops to the state. Under this system the state bought the crops from the peasants before harvest at low prices, so that in years of bad harvest they often had to sell their cattle and equipment to repay the state. In order to give the peasants an incentive to extend the lands under cultivation, 'Ali Bey, besides abolishing *al-mushtara*, reduced the amount of crops collected under the tithe, a tax authorized by the law. He also removed an injustice connected with state lands. In the past state lands were leased to peasants for fixed payments in cash, and tenants were not permitted to surrender their leases until others made higher bids for them. This system meant that the tenants had to meet their obligations to the state even if the lands they cultivated no longer yielded enough crops to pay the value of the lease. 'Ali Bey replaced it by one of fixed periods of tenancy upon whose expiry the peasants could freely choose to retain or surrender the lands. And to encourage trade in Tunisian products he lent state money to Tunisian merchants without demanding interest.

Under Hammuda Bey Tunisia once more emerged as a Mediterranean power, able to deal with the Algerians on terms of equality, to defy the wishes of the Ottoman government with regard to Tripolitania, and to curtail the ability of the European states to dictate their own terms during periods of conflict. Taking over from his father at a time when Tunisia was prosperous, he increased its prosperity by the careful management of state revenue. We are told that he was so careful not to burden the public treasury with his personal expenditure, that he was often described by the vainglorious Tunisians as having a miserly disposition. He set an example to his ministers and government officials by wearing only locally produced garments; and in order to encourage them to take interest in agriculture he rode every week to his estate to supervise work in person. He discouraged the widely practised custom of giving charity to the poor, and urged its seekers to go and work. While delegating to the *'ulama* the tasks of administering justice, he looked personally into complaints about the conduct of government agents. The bey from the beginning of the Ottoman period in Tunisia was responsible for leading the *mahalla* (column of troops) that toured the country for the purpose of collecting the taxes. This function remained attached to the position of bey even after its holders became the rulers of the country. Hammuda began the practice of entrusting the command of the *mahalla* to the heir-apparent, who thus came to know the country well and acquired some authority before acceding to the throne. But at the same time he established direct personal contacts with the chiefs of the tribes and consulted them in the affairs of their people, and in this way gave them enough prestige to counterbalance the authority of the *qa'ids*. Although he treated his subordinates strictly, particularly the provincial governors, he encouraged them to express their opinions about state matters freely even when critical of his actions. This tended to bring to the fore the best men in the land, and it is no accident that the first great Tunisian statesman in the Husainid period, Yusuf Sahib al-Taba', was Hammuda's vizier for the greater part of his reign.

The sense of balance with which Hammuda exercised political authority also characterized his organization of the armed forces. He increased the number of Turkish soldiers in the regency, and established comradely relations with their leaders. At the same time he tried to reduce their contacts with the Tunisian population to the minimum. Although Arabic, not Turkish, was his first language, he spoke with the Turkish soldiers only in Turkish and prevented them from speaking Arabic. He made sure they were strictly disciplined, but also appealed to their national sentiment by having all inscriptions on their barracks and the gateways of the forts written in Turkish. From 1806, when preparing for war with the Algerians, he also began the practice of giving the Turkish troops free rations which previously they had to buy from their salaries. But he also created a counterbalance to the Turks by recruiting tribal warriors as auxiliaries, mostly from the Zawawa Berber tribe. In 1811, after a rebellion of the Turkish troops, he increased the Zawawa soldiery and made them a part of the regular army.

It appears that Hammuda's assiduous attention to the affairs of the army was inspired by his determination to stop the economic exploitation of Tunisia by Algeria. Hammuda's father 'Ali had vowed when exiled in Algeria to send olive oil to the shrines of Algiers should his family regain its authority in Tunisia. He sent the oil as long as he lived, although it was common knowledge that the large amounts of oil sent from Tunisia were mostly appropriated by the rulers of Algiers. The deys of Algiers and the beys of Constantine also developed the practice during 'Ali's reign of sending cattle they bought in Algeria for sale in Tunis at prices which they fixed, and the Tunisian government was required to prevent the sale of Tunisian livestock until the Algerians had sold their own. Furthermore, Algerian messengers regardless of rank acquired the right in 'Ali's reign to stay in the official guest house at the Bardo, where superintendents often complained of their abusive conduct. This was a situation which a proud monarch like Hammuda could not tolerate. In 1806 he gave the first instance of his intention to defy the rulers of Algiers by granting refuge in Tunisia to the dismissed bey of Constantine, Mustafa Ingliz, and promising to help him regain his position. The reply of the dey of Algiers to this action was to send cows for sale in Tunis and a letter to Hammuda drafted in commanding language, bidding him arrange for their sale and indicating the price he demanded. Hammuda had the cows offered for sale at market price, and sent to the dey of Algiers the money they had fetched with the message that henceforth the dey's agents would have to superintend his commercial transactions. At the same time he prepared his army for invading Constantine. The Tunisian army besieged Constantine in January 1807 and was driven back in May. But the Algerians were defeated on 13 July in Tunisian territory at a place called Salata, after which the Tunisian tribes looted the deserted Algerian camp. In June 1808 the Algerians again invaded Tunisia but were repulsed. A third Algerian attempt to invade Tunisia was made by sea in 1811. The Tunisian *ra'is* conspired to have their unpopular captain Muhammad al-Murali captured by the Algerians, but otherwise they were able to prevent them from attacking Tunisian ports. In 1812 the Algerians seized a few Tunisian merchant ships from Gouletta, but they failed to establish any control over Tunisia.

Hammuda's death in 1813 was a turning-point in the international standing of Tunisia and its internal development. After his death, particularly after 1815, a more determined and united European action to suppress piracy in the Mediterranean and the slave trade in the Maghriban countries deprived Tunisia of a large source of income. In internal affairs, after Hammuda the beys gradually lost touch with conditions in the country and, isolating themselves in their palace, came into contact with the public only when they dispensed justice at the court of Tunis. Conflict between members of the beylical family, averted by 'Ali's and Hammuda's dexterity, became an important aspect of Tunisia's political life for two decades after Hammuda's death. At the same time the ineptness of the beys enabled opportunistic statesmen to gain authority by satisfying the beys' love of show. The first instance of the departure from Hammuda's resolute political style occurred during the reign of his brother 'Uthman (1813–14) when Yusuf Sahib al-Taba' was relegated to the secondary position of treasury superintendent. Yusuf was able, honest, and loyal; but too blunt in his criticism to please the weakly and despotic nature of 'Uthman. This bey was assassinated on 21 December 1814 by his cousin Mahmud (Muhammad Bey's son), who had twice lost the opportunity of becoming bey and had been informed that 'Uthman intended to appoint his own son as successor. The crime was committed with the active support of the minister Muhammad Zarruq, who during Mahmud's first seven years as bey became the all-powerful vizier of the realm. Zarruq, together with Mahmud Bey's sons, undertook on 29 January 1815 the assassination of Yusuf Sahib al-Taba'. This venerable political figure was feared on account of his standing in the country and his persistence in urging the bey to curb his sons' whims and Zarruq's abuse of authority. Zarruq himself was killed on 29 October 1822. The bey's sons Husain and Mustafa had grown to look upon him as an obstacle to their greater exercise of power, and accused him of inciting the Turkish troops to rebel.

During Mahmud's reign the state reverted to the practice of augmenting revenues by increasing taxes and monopolizing the sale of produce. This was especially harmful to oil production in the Sahil. During the reign of 'Uthman a tax called *qanun* was introduced, under which the peasants paid a fixed annual levy on olive trees. It was protested that the *qanun* was an illegitimate tax under the Muslim law, and it was replaced in 1819 by the tithe on oil. The change was resented by the producers since the tithe was a larger tax and was accompanied by the establishment of state monopoly on the sale of oil. The producers were required to sell their oil to a special government agency which sold it to exporters, most of whom were French. The system was disliked by oil-producers and merchants alike, for it forced the former to sell their oil at fixed low prices and the latter had to pay more for it than in the free market since to its price were added taxes, profit to the state, and gratuities to officials. Furthermore, the merchants had to pay in advance, without being certain that the oil agency would later be able to provide all the oil promised or to reimburse them. In 1829 the oil gathered from the producers fell so much short of expectation that a crisis arose between the French merchants and the bey's government. The money already paid had been spent, and although Vizier Husain b. Khuja could claim that it went mostly to meet the expenditure of the bey's household, he was dismissed. He was replaced by Shakir Sahib al-Taba', who had to impose economies on the bey and collect contributions from Tunisian citizens to reimburse the merchants.

The deterioration in the standards of government which this incident illustrates was accompanied with the inability of the bey to resist European interference. Husain Bey (1824–35) was prevailed upon by the French consul Mathieu de Lesseps to sign a treaty on 17 August 1830 by which he undertook to abolish state monopoly on the sale of produce, suppress all acts of piracy by Tunisians, and enforce in Tunisia the capitulation treaties between the European countries and the Ottoman empire. The long-term implications of the last mentioned clause will be discussed in the next chapter. In the context of Franco-Tunisian relations in 1830, the treaty was important in determining the bey's attitude towards the French war in Algeria. In June an Ottoman functionary called Tahir Pasha had arrived in Tunis with the intention of reaching Algiers by land, since by then the French had blockaded Algeria's ports. It seems that Tahir Pasha was charged with persuading the dey of Algiers to undertake steps to reconcile the French and avert a conflict which the Ottoman government feared would lead to the loss of Algeria. The bey refused to allow him to land in Tunis; Tunisians were also permitted to sell cattle to the French army, and steps were taken to prevent the traffic in gunpowder between Tabarqa in Tunisia and Constantine. The bey's cooperation prompted General Clauzel, the French commander in Algeria, to offer to Tunisian princes the government of Constantine before the French conquered it, and Oran after they took it on 4 January 1831. On 21 November 1830 a

Tunisian delegation travelled on a French ship to Algiers. In Tunisia it was understood that the delegation was sent to affirm the bey's neutrality in the war, in spite of the anti-French ferment among the Tunisian tribes.[1] But on 18 December an agreement was reached between Clauzel and the Tunisians, providing for French recognition of Husain Bey's brother Mustafa as ruler of Constantine under French sovereignty. At about the same time emissaries were sent from Tunis to make contact with tribal chiefs in the province of Constantine, urging them to give up the futile war against the French, saying that Ahmad Bey of Constantine was not strong enough to drive the French out, and inviting them in the interests of Muslim solidarity to submit to the rule of Tunis. Nothing seems to have come out of these contacts. Nevertheless, as soon as the French captured Oran they offered its government to Mustafa's son Ahmad. On 19 January 1831 General Khair al-Din[2] was sent to Oran with 300 Tunisian soldiers to prepare for Ahmad's arrival. Khair al-Din remained in Oran until September, when he was recalled. It was impossible for him to impose any authority over the tribes surrounding Oran with such few soldiers, and to Khair al-Din's requests for reinforcements the Tunisian government replied by demanding the dispatch of money from the taxes which he was expected, but was unable, to collect.

While Khair al-Din was in Oran the bey sent a delegation to Istanbul trying to assuage the anger of the Ottoman authorities over his Algerian policy. This occurred amidst rumours that an Ottoman expedition was being prepared to be sent to Tunisia. The historian Ibn Abi al-Diaf, a member of the delegation, sought to justify Tunisia's action in terms of a provision in the Muslim law to the effect that, when faced with two evils, a Muslim was to choose the lesser one. The bey was thus represented as trying to avoid endangering the safety of Tunisia through choosing the lesser evil of cooperation with the French. The delegation also asked the permission of the Porte to adopt in Tunisia the uniform of the new Ottoman (*nizami*) army. The bey had already begun the reorganization of his army along new lines: in January 1831 he gathered the elite of his troops in new barracks in Muhammadiyya where they were trained by French officers. The adoption of the new Ottoman uniform was, therefore, more a gesture of attachment to Ottoman forms than a commitment to follow the lead of Istanbul.

The Ottoman government could not undertake military action against Tunisia without risking war with France. They tried, therefore, to use their religious links with the country to increase Ottoman control. The feeble arguments which Ibn Abi al-Diaf presented in Istanbul in 1831 to justify Tunisia's conduct were accepted at their face value, and in response

---

[1] Ibn Abi al-Diaf, *Ithaf ahl al-zaman*, III, 175.
[2] The future reformer. Cf. pp. 265 ff. below.

to the bey's request that he adopt the new Ottoman army uniform he was presented with a uniform to wear on special occasions. Husain Bey's death on 20 May 1835 occurred a week before the removal of the Qaramanlis from the government of Tripolitania and the imposition of direct Ottoman rule in it. Thus the Ottoman authorities felt strong enough to ask the Tunisian vizier Shakir, who in July went to Istanbul to apply for the documents of investiture to Husain's brother Mustafa Bey (1835–7), to convey their desire that Tunisia should pay a regular tribute. The bey could see what this demand meant, and rejected it.

The Ottoman fleet sent to Tripoli in 1836, commanded by Tahir Pasha, called on Tunis and demanded the dispatch of Tunisian troops to take part in the operations against dissident tribes. It arrived at a time when some reprisal for Tunisia's refusal to pay tribute was expected. In the past the Tunisian warships had taken part with the Ottoman fleet when fighting Christians, an action that could be represented as indicative of Muslim solidarity but not the acceptance of Ottoman authority. To take part with the Ottoman fleet in action against Muslim tribes in Tripolitania was an implied recognition of the authority of the Ottoman government. But the bey could not refuse to comply, and on 29 July 1836 nine Tunisian merchant ships carried Tunisian troops to Tripoli. It was feared in Tunis that Tahir Pasha would return there after accomplishing his task in Tripolitania. Mustafa Bey, alarmed by the activities of the Ottoman fleet, wanted to recognize Ottoman sovereignty, but his son and heir-apparent Ahmad restrained him, and the arrival of French warships to Gouletta ruled out Ottoman military action in Tunisia. Thus Tunisia remained a sovereign country, while recognizing the religious authority of the sultan as caliph. Tunisia's rulers after Mustafa were left with the difficult task of maintaining a balance between Ottoman and French interests in their country. In 1837, the year of Mustafa Bey's death, the French occupied Constantine and the French troops thus reached Tunisia's western frontiers. Five years later the Ottomans became firmly entrenched in Tripolitania, and the more the Tunisian people felt threatened by French expansion, the more they cherished their links with the Ottoman empire. Consequently the objective of preserving Tunisia's independence of Istanbul was gradually sacrificed to the purpose of staving off French ambitions. Tunisia was formally recognized a part of the Ottoman empire in 1871, but this did not prevent the country from falling under French rule ten years later.

The first Ottoman period in Libya

The area forming present-day Libya begins to have its own historical existence after the Arab conquest only with the establishment of Ottoman rule in it at the middle of the sixteenth century. Between the seventh and the fifteenth centuries it was a passageway for conquerors, merchants, and pilgrims, but little besides that. The Arab tribal invasions of the eleventh century contributed towards its Arabization, but also destroyed its agriculture. Tribalism and the inhospitable desert expanses that separated the few urban centres in the territory made the establishment of regular government in it beyond the means of either the eastern or western Muslim rulers, particularly since at this time they were preoccupied with the threat of Christian expansion in the form of the Spanish Reconquista, the crusades, and then piracy. The Mamluk sultans had to send their armies from time to time to drive the tribes of Cyrenaica from Egyptian territory, and two of them tried to bring these tribes to recognize their authority. Baibars (1260–77) entered into an alliance with the Arabian tribal chief 'Ata' Allah, head of the 'Azzaz clan of the Banu Sulaim tribe, in 1263 or 1264 (A.H. 662). The alliance meant that in return for the added dignity which the chief acquired through association with the Mamluks, he was to collect for them the tithe on agricultural produce and livestock. The tribes that could be made to accept indirect Mamluk control were further required to dig wells on certain routes where the Mamluk army might need to pass.[1] Although a later Mamluk sultan, al-Mansur Qalawun (1279–90), was to style himself in treaties with European states as "Sultan Tarablus al-Sahil 'ila Tarablus al-Gharb" (the sultan of the Tripolitanian hinterland as far as Tripoli of the west),[2] it appears that the Mamluks were unable to develop any connection with Cyrenaica beyond ephemeral alliances with specific tribal chiefs. In Cyrenaica, as in Tripolitania, the tribes remained in control of their respective districts, and when they yielded to authority it was to a tribe stronger than themselves. For the greater part of the four centuries from the eleventh to the end of the fifteenth the Hib tribe exercised control over the other tribes in Cyrenaica, both Berber and Arab, and over the Jews living in such places as Tulmaitha and Darna. In Tripolitania during the same period the Dabbab tribe was the leading power as far as the vicinity of Gabis in Tunisia.

Tripolitania was more in the political orbit of the Muslim rulers of the west than of the east. The desert land between Tripoli and Egypt contributed towards this, together with the tradition of Tripoli's dependence on Ifriqya (Tunisia) in the Roman and early Arab periods. But here too distance and tribal influence precluded any permanent or stable attachment to Marrakish in the times of the Almohads or to Tunis during the Hafsid period. In 1146 the Normans occupied Tripoli. Since their interest in it was purely commercial, they left a garrison to protect the Sicilian merchants who settled in it, and entrusted its governance to the local chief

---

[1] Ihsan 'Abbas, *Tarikh Libya mundhu 'l-Fath al-'Arabi hatta matla' al-qarn tasi' al-hijiri* (Beirut, 1967), p. 162.
[2] *Ibid.* p. 164.

Yahya b. Matruh under terms of vassalage. The Muslims of the town could thus lead their traditional life under the control of a council of ten *shaikhs* presided over by Ibn Matruh. Indirect Norman control of Tripoli ended in 1158. At this time the Almohads were preparing the land and naval expedition which in the following year was sent to Tunisia. Seriously alarmed by these military preparations, which were clearly directed against their positions in Tunisia, the Normans committed the political blunder of requiring the *imams* of mosques in Tripoli to denounce the Almohad movement. This sparked off a rebellion, initially led by the religious leaders of the town, but with which Ibn Matruh was able to identify himself. The small Norman garrison surrendered and was massacred. When in January 1160 the Normans surrendered Mahdiyya to the Almohads, Ibn Matruh led a delegation from Tripoli which made submission to 'Abdul-Mu'min.

Although the Almohads tried to associate the Tripolitanian tribes with their wars of religion in Spain, and lessened the value of the tithe exacted by one-third in order to induce them to submit to their rule, Almohad control of Tripolitania remained largely nominal. The urban population of Tripoli sought a close link with the Almohads and later with the Hafsids as a means of ensuring protection against the tribes and foreign invaders, but the rulers of neither Marrakish nor Tunis were able to ensure the safety of the town all the time. In the Hafsid period, consequently, Tripoli had its own *mufti* to supervise the administration of the Muslim law, and warriors for its defence, recruited from the Majris clan of the Huwwara and paid by the town's merchant families. The nominal attachment of Tripolitania to the Almohads and the Hafsids, without either being able to control it, made it the territory of the Maghrib towards which adventurers gravitated, and the springboard for rebels against the authority of Tunis.

As mentioned above,[1] al-Lihiani used Tripoli as a base for his political activities. When he left the town in 1311 to claim the Hafsid sultanate with Tripolitanian tribal support, his relative Ibn Abu 'Umran governed it on his behalf. The period of al-Lihiani and his deputy (*c.* 1307–21) witnessed the revival of the authority of Tripoli, during which some of the tribes of Cyrenaica agreed to pay tribute. When Ibn Abu 'Umran left Tripoli to give support to the Zayanids against the restored Hafsid sultanate, the town gradually relapsed into political insignificance. In the course of the thirteenth century several tribes established themselves in Tripoli and seized the position of ascendancy from the traditional urban families. In 1324 the Jawari tribe's chiefly clan, the Banu Thabit, became Tripoli's ruling dynasty. The Banu Thabit also controlled Gharian and Zanzur at a time when the Makki family controlled Gabis and the Jabal Nafusa, so that the Hafsids could do nothing to dislodge them. In 1354 the Genoese attacked Tripoli, sacked it, and handed it over to the Banu Makki against the payment of a large ransom, but the town reverted to the Banu Thabit in 1370 and remained in their hands until it was recovered from them by the Hafsids in 1401, in the period of their revival under Sultan Abu Faris. Hafsid control of Tripoli lasted until 1460, when a local chief called Mansur rebelled and captured power. Shaikh Mansur and his three successors ruled the town until it was conquered by Pedro Navarro in July 1510.

In Tripoli Navarro built a fortified *presidio* inhabited predominantly by Christians. He expelled its indigenous population, had its private houses and public buildings destroyed, and the materials obtained from them used for the construction of fortifications. Using Tripoli as a base, Navarro tried to occupy the two large islands off the southern coast of Tunisia. He attacked Jirba two weeks after his occupation of Tripoli. As he found it well-defended, he returned to Tripoli, where he received reinforcements from Sicily, and on 30 August attacked it again. This time he landed 1,500 of his men, many of whom were trapped near a watering-place and massacred. Although it is fairly certain that 'Aruj was by then active in organizing the resistance of the Jirbians, these undertook most of the fighting under the leadership of their Shaikh Yahya al-Samumni. Navarro evacuated Jirba on 31 August. On the way to Tripoli he landed 400 men to take possession of the island of Qarqanna, but these were massacred in the course of the year. Thus Tripoli remained a Spanish oasis in a Maghriban desert land with hostile tribes surrounding it on three sides, and no hope of speedy aid from the sea in times of grave danger. From 1511 the town was placed under the control of the viceroy of Sicily who appointed a deputy to rule over it. But as the government of Sicily had to provide Tripoli with an annual subsidy amounting to 12,000 ducats without any commensurate political or commercial advantage in return, the Spaniards gradually lost interest in it beyond ensuring that it did not fall again into the hands of the Muslims. Hence the idea of handing Tripoli over to the Knights of St John. This order had been founded in 1113 with the aim of defending Jerusalem, which the crusaders had occupied in 1099, against the Muslims. When the Muslims reconquered the town in 1187 the knights, whose ideal remained the recapture of Jerusalem, established headquarters in Acre, then in Cyprus, and then in Rhodes where they remained until this island was captured by the Turks in 1522. Henceforth they had no permanent base, but were settled in Viterbo and Nice as the guests of the Pope and the Duke of Savoy respectively. From the thirteenth century the order had become a naval force, and in these two centres its activities were limited. Nevertheless they were not enthusiastic about the offer which Charles V made to them that they should garrison Malta and Tripoli. Between 1523 and 1530, when negotiations between the order and the emperor were afoot, members of the order visited Tripoli and drew a detailed account of conditions in it. Eventually they accepted the offer only because they had no better home.

The position of the knights in Tripoli was very vulnerable. They were separated from Malta by 350 km of sea and could not hope to receive reinforcements from there if attacked. The financial resources of the order did not enable it to maintain large garrisons in both Malta and Tripoli, and the Ottoman fleet which Khair al-Din Barbarossa had recently reorganized formed a constant threat. In the town itself there remained some 500 Muslims who benefited from the presence of the knights and who could be relied upon to act as spies and to procure provisions, but the country around them was hostile. Furthermore, since 1531 the Turks had had a base in Tajura' (Taguira), 20 km to the east of Tripoli. Khair al-Din occupied this town to be used for operations against the Christians in Tripoli. He also established the Hafsid prince Rashid there who, after rebelling against his brother Ahmad, had sought the help of the Turks in Algiers. Tajura' became the centre on which militant tribesmen and political refugees from Hafsid territory converged with the intention of fighting under Turkish command the Hafsids and the Christians. In 1536 Qaraman, the Turkish officer commanding Tajura', attempted to capture Tripoli. He built a fort near it and prepared to blockade the knights inside the walls until surrender, but plague forced him to lift the siege. The order tried unsuccessfully in the 1530s and 1540s to obtain financial help from Charles V and the Pope to increase its fighting capacity. Nor would the emperor approve the order's suggestion that they evacuate Tripoli after blowing up the castle which they had rebuilt and blocking the harbour by sinking in it barges full of stone; the emperor merely promised that he would come to the order's rescue when necessary. Eventually in 1548 a general chapter of the order decided to concentrate all its force in Tripoli and to send fifty knights annually from Malta to Tripoli until eventually this island was vacated. Before this plan was implemented the Ottoman fleet captured Tripoli from the knights in August 1551, but the good offices of the French ambassador in Istanbul, Gabriel d'Aramont, who hurried to Tripoli on a brigantine belonging to the order when the siege began, enabled the knights to withdraw to Malta unmolested.

The kapudan-pasha Sinan who led the attack on Tripoli entrusted its government to Murad, the elderly Turkish officer who had governed Tajura' since 1539. Dragut, the corsair captain who had recently entered Ottoman service and had accompanied the fleet to Tripoli, was by-passed. But two years later he obtained the governorship of Tripoli from Sultan Sulaiman and became engaged in naval and land operations which made Tripoli an important privateering base and the capital of an Ottoman province. Among several other audacious acts of piracy, in 1558 he sacked

7 AHO

the Italian town of Reggio on the Straits of Messina and carried away most of its inhabitants to become slaves in Tripoli. This attack provoked the dispatch of a Spanish expedition in 1560 which was intended to capture Tripoli, but it was destroyed in Jirba and never reached its destination.

In the twelve years during which Dragut held the governorship of Tripoli, the tribes of Tripolitania and the inhabitants of Jirba were brought under Ottoman authority. The tribes at first ignored his demand for submission, but after the rifles and cannons of the Turkish troops were put to use against the primitive arms of the settled Berbers of Gharian, and the hardy people of Tarhuna to the south-east of Tripoli, the other tribes became compliant. Neither at this stage, nor at a later date in the Ottoman period, was the attempt made to interfere with the customary life of the tribes. As long as they paid tribute and abstained from hostile action against Ottoman functionaries and other tribes, they were left on their own. Dragut used tribal warriors in the occupation of Jirba in 1558, but it appears that these warriors came from a few tribes that were willing to cooperate – mostly the Berber Zawawa and the Awlad Siba' and Awlad Shibl clans of the Arabian Dabbab tribe – and therefore their recruitment was voluntary. In Jirba Dragut tried to avoid burdening himself with the responsibilities of direct government. When he entered the town in 1558 and formally annexed it to Tripoli, he left it under the control of Shaikh Mas'ud al-Samumni. Only in the following year, when the Jirbians sent messengers to Tunis seeking to counterbalance Ottoman influence by that of the Hafsids, did he appoint a Turkish officer to govern it. In Tripoli itself Dragut employed the wealth and slaves obtained from piracy in works of construction which gave the Ottoman administration a visible presence. He constructed a fort on the hill dominating Tripoli from the north, and on the site of Tripoli's Grand Mosque which Pedro Navarro had destroyed in 1510 he built a residential block which became known as Sarai Dragut. On the site of a chapel which the knights had constructed he built a mosque, in which he was later buried. Dragut died in 1565 in Malta when taking part with the Turkish troops of Algiers and the Ottoman fleet in an attack on the Knights of St John.

After Dragut, and until 1711, Tripoli was governed by pashas appointed by Istanbul. Tripoli had also a *diwan* whose function was to assist the pashas in the government of the regency which included notables from the country, and was presided over by an officer called the dey. The *diwan* seems to have had some authority, but the most powerful official was the bey, who in Tripolitania was the commander of the Janissaries: he was in a position to compete with the power of the pasha. The pashas held the office for short terms, forty-one of them governed Tripoli between 1565 and 1711. Much depended on the authority which the pasha could bring into his office through his own personal abilities. A few of them were able soldiers and were capable of controlling the Turkish troops and through them the tribes. But many were weak and sometimes their primary pre-occupation was self-enrichment. Under these conditions the tur-bulence of the Janissary troops could not be checked, and the latent hostility of the tribal population to centralized authority came to the fore in the form of rebellions. The most notable of these uprisings was that of Yahya al-Suwaidi who during the governorship of Ja'far Pasha (1586–1631) took control of Misurata and Tajura' and besieged Tripoli itself. Al-Suwaidi's rebellion was defeated with the cooperation of the Mhamid tribe, which consequently was given special concessions with regard to the territories it controlled.

In the Hafsid period Fazzan was nominally under the rule of Tunis, but actually it was controlled by the Khattab tribal dynasty. During the twenty years when the Knights of St John held Tripoli a Moroccan *sharif* called Muntasir b. Muhammad took control of Fazzan. From Murzuq, which he made his capital, he and his descendants ruled the province as far as Sukna in the north and controlled the caravan trade with the western Sudan. The pasha of Tripoli Muhammad al-Turki (1578–86) was able to bring the Banu Muhammad to recognize Ottoman sovereignty over Fazzan, but he left them to run the affairs of Fazzan themselves.

In Cyrenaica the nominal authority of the Mamluks was replaced by the nominal sovereignty of the Ottomans after the latter conquered Egypt in 1517. For over a century-and-a-half afterwards nothing is known about the political structure of this province, except that it remained the domain of tribalism. Two energetic pashas of Tripoli of the Saqizli family, Muhammad (1631–49) and 'Uthman (1649–72), made the Cyrenaican tribes aware of Ottoman power and recognize the sovereignty of the sultan but without imposing Ottoman control on them. Muhammad Saqizli sent an expedition which defeated a local chief who from his base in Jabal al-Akhdar controlled Barqa and had several of the tribes in the neighbour-hood recognize him as ruler. The ruthlessness with which this movement was crushed impressed upon the tribes their inability to defy the Turks. Thus with the Saqizli governors Libya began to emerge as one political entity, although neither Fazzan nor Cyrenaica were at this stage fully incorporated in the Ottoman administrative system.

At the beginning of the eighteenth century the Turkish regency of Tripolitania underwent a political development similar to that which Tunisia had recently experienced, and by which it might have been inspired. A *kouloughli* chief of the cavalry in Tripoli called Ahmad (or Hamid) Qaramanli usurped power in 1711 when the Turkish governor Muhammad Khalil Amis was on a visit to Istanbul. He forestalled opposi-tion by ruthlessly massacring 300 of the leading Turkish officers whom he summoned to a conference on the future of the regency. A Turkish expedition was sent against him a year later, by which time he had consolidated his hold on the territory and was able to repulse the attack. Through rich presents to Ottoman officials and expressions of loyalty he subsequently had himself formally appointed pasha of Tripoli by Sultan Ahmad III. Except for one year (1793–4) when Tripoli was governed by an adventurer from Algiers called 'Ali Burghul, the dynasty which Ahmad Qaramanli founded remained in power until 1835. Piracy had become in the period of the Saqizli governors a thriving activity in Tripoli. The Qaramanlis, by sponsoring the activities of the corsairs, earned prestige and international importance out of proportion to the power of their state, and prosperity which lasted as long as piracy in the Mediterranean remained unchecked.

The Qaramanli dynasty had its golden age during the reign of 'Ali Qaramanli (1754–93). The regency achieved prosperity through the pasha's pursuance of two contradictory attitudes towards Europe. He encouraged piracy and shared with the pirates the yields of their activities. In his reign the corsair captains became something of national heroes, honoured by cannon salutes when returning with a prize. 'Ali Qaramanli at the same time encouraged Christian and Jewish merchants to settle in Tripoli. The Jews handled the trade with Leghorn, and the pasha's goodwill towards them was ensured by the influence of Lady Esther, a Jewish lady who enjoyed his favour until he was forced to relinquish power in 1793. European Christians were mainly engaged in the trade with Malta, and were on the whole well treated. They were given protection against fanatical outbursts, and their consuls did not need to undergo any humiliating ceremonials when calling upon the pasha. Trade and piracy enabled Tripoli to flourish economically in spite of the ravages of famine, the disastrous epidemics of the plague in 1774 and 1785 and the civil disturbances which occurred at the end of 'Ali Qaramanli's reign.

'Ali Qaramanli's economic dependence on the corsairs made him unable to restrain them. Crimes multiplied in Tripoli, and in their despair the Tripolitanians started clamouring for direct Ottoman rule. In the late 1780s Tripoli was continually being threatened by the activities of the Ottoman fleet, whose admiral Hasan Pasha was given the task by 'Abdul-Hamid I to try and subjugate the independent principalities that had arisen in Ottoman territories on the Mediterranean: Jazzar Pasha's in Acre, the Mamluks' in Egypt, the Husainids' in Tunisia and the Qaramanlis' in Tripolitania. The Ottoman threat, at a time when 'Ali Pasha was unable to check lawlessness at home, led his son Yusuf to fear the loss of the dynasty's power. Supported by Shaikh Khalifa b. Mahmud, a Berber chief from Jabal Nafusa, Yusuf rebelled against his father and in April 1790 besieged Tripoli. Sultan 'Abdul-Hamid had died in 1789, and the struggle for power in Istanbul had the effect that the Ottoman fleet could not directly interfere to benefit from the conflict in Tripolitania. The adventurer Burghul, however, used it to try his fortunes in the regency.

'Ali Burghul had amassed a considerable fortune in Algiers where he was general superintendent of the navy. Having been expelled from Algiers he went to live in Istanbul, from where he followed developments in the Maghrib. Through rich bribes and the admiral's help he secured the Porte's approval for his invasion of Tripoli without any help from the empire with the understanding that he would rule it in the name of the sultan. On 29 July 1793 he arrived in Tripoli with 300 mercenaries, mostly Turkish, Greek, and Spanish, carried on nine merchant ships. His position in the Ottoman administration was uncertain, yet he claimed that he had been duly appointed pasha of Tripoli and on the day following his arrival he had the text of an apocryphal *firman* to this effect published in the town. Old and harassed by his son's besieging forces, 'Ali Qaramanli broke down. On 30 July he unceremoniously left Tripoli for Tunis, where he took refuge with Hammuda Bey. Tripoli remained under 'Ali Burghul's oppressive rule for seventeen months. Realizing that his government would not last long, Burghul extorted whatever money was to be found in the town. From the Jewish community he obtained 240,000 francs by the threat of a general massacre; and he put several wealthy Muslims to death under diverse pretexts and confiscated their property.

'Ali Qaramanli was well received in Tunis. The parallel between the political position of the Qaramanlis and the Husainids, as well as the fear that tribal disturbance might spread from Tripolitania into Tunisia, made Hammuda Bey want to help the Qaramanlis recover control of Tripoli. But as Burghul claimed that he acted upon the sultan's authority, Hammuda feared the consequences of acting against him. On 30 September 1794, however, a contingent of Burghul's men landed in Jirba and drove out its governor. This attack made the Tunisians fear that some operation against Tunisia too might be under way, and provided them with a pretext which they later used in justifying the dispatch of their army to Tripoli. It appears that Burghul needed Jirba to obtain basic provisions, since Tripoli was besieged by the tribes led by Yusuf Qaramanli. While the Tunisian army was advancing towards Tripoli, accompanied by 'Ali Qaramanli's eldest son Ahmad, Tunisian ships landed 4,000 soldiers on 8 November who took Burghul's men in Jirba captive. The land forces, with the help of the Tripolitanian tribes, entered Tripoli on 19 January 1795, after Burghul had evacuated it taking with him his captured treasures. The Porte acquiesced in the *fait accompli*, although Hammuda had to send a delegation in 1795 to justify the expedition in terms of Burghul's attack on Tunisian territory and assuage the anger of Ottoman officials by gifts.

The Tunisians installed Ahmad Qaramanli as pasha of Tripoli. His brother Yusuf was given a position similar to that held in the seventeenth

century by the bey in Tunisia, entitling him to command the *mahalla* sent
for the collection of taxes and to have jurisdiction over the tribes. This
position Yusuf used a few months later to usurp power from his brother.
With tribal support he proclaimed himself pasha while Ahmad was on a
visit to Tajura'. Unable to challenge this usurpation Ahmad accepted the
position of bey of Darna, but soon afterwards left the country to Malta
and eventually went to Egypt.

With Yusuf Qaramanli's accession to power the regency of Tripoli
revived, thanks to the authority which he was able to exercise over the
tribes and favourable international conditions at the beginning of his reign
of forty years. Like Hammuda Pasha he benefited from Europe's pre-
occupation with the Napoleonic wars to build a formidable fleet and use it
in piracy. Until the end of these wars most European states had to pay him
fixed annual sums to secure the safety of their ships in the Mediterranean.
Complications arose when a major state refused to pay. In the course of
1801 the Tripolitanian corsairs seized several American ships. As negotiations for their release failed, an American expedition was mounted against
the regency in 1803. In the course of the ensuing action before Tripoli,
the Tripolitanian corsairs lured the large American frigate *Philadelphia*
into a narrow passage (Bughas Aghraba) where it was wrecked and her crew
of 307 men captured. When Yusuf subsequently demanded a ransom of
three million dollars, the Americans brought his brother Ahmad from
Egypt, installed him in Darna, and encouraged him to claim the throne of
Tripoli. Yusuf thus was forced to retreat, accepting a ransom of 60,000
dollars and undertaking not to interfere with the passage of American
ships in the Mediterranean. Another incident in 1813 and the prompt
American action which followed made the pasha release all the Christian
captives he had and confirm the undertaking not to interfere with the
passage of American ships. The British consul Warrington in 1814 had a
Tripolitanian captain hanged from the mast of the British ship he had
captured; the smaller European states, unable to exercise a similar
pressure on the pasha, continued to pay the annual tribute. Sardinia had
to pay for the liberation of her captured ships in 1824 and Naples in 1828.

By and large, after the end of the Napoleonic wars piracy ceased to be a
profitable enterprise for the pasha of Tripoli. By this time another source
of revenue had opened up in the revival of the trans-Saharan trade. From
the end of the sixteenth century the caravan trade across the Sahara had
declined as a result of conflicts in the Sudan itself and insecurity along the
routes. But it revived after Yusuf Qaramanli conquered Fazzan in 1811
and his governor in Murzuq established law and order in the province.
Having occupied Fazzan, Yusuf Qaramanli controlled the caravan route
between Tripoli and Bornu and established relations with the *mai* of Bornu
and the sultan of Sokoto. Warrington, the enterprising British consul in

Tripoli, also exploited the pasha's control of the Tripoli–Bornu route to promote the exploration of the interior of Africa. From 1817 there was a British vice-consul in Murzuq, and when the explorer Ritchie went there in 1819 there was also an "English house" in which he was accommodated. The pasha's protection was a determining factor in the success of the mission led by Oudney, Denham, and Clapperton which left Tripoli in 1822 and explored Ghat and the Chad areas. The pasha was generously paid for protecting the explorers, but the outcry they raised over the slave trade proved troublesome.

From the increasing influence of the European powers in the regency after 1815 there arose rivalries which had a far-reaching effect on Yusuf Qaramanli's position and eventually led to the downfall of his dynasty. Having opened his career in the regency with strong measures against the Tripolitanian corsairs that attacked British ships, Warrington soon established a predominant position. He made wide contacts with the tribes and the settled people, gave advice on agriculture and health, and in 1816 introduced vaccination in Tripoli. But in the early 1820s French competition with Warrington became acute, reaching a climax in the conflict over the responsibility for the death near Timbuktu in 1826 of the English explorer Major Laing. Warrington had by then come to believe that the pasha and his foreign minister Hassuna D'Ghies were subservient to the wishes of the French consul Rousseau. Shortly after the news of Laing's assassination reached Tripoli the French traveller Caillie returned from Timbuktu. Warrington claimed, without any substantiated evidence, that Laing's assassination had been plotted by the pasha and D'Ghies, that D'Ghies had given Laing's papers to the French consul in return for a forty per cent reduction on a debt which he owed the consul, and that Caillie had never set foot in Timbuktu and the diary he had published under his name was compiled from Laing's papers. The pasha's denial that he or his foreign minister had anything to do with Laing's death, and Rousseau's exoneration by a French commission of inquiry, were to no avail in abating Warrington's or the British government's hostility to the pasha. What made things worse was that in August 1830 the pasha was prevailed upon, under the threat of a French squadron commanded by Admiral de Rosamel, to sign a treaty with France in which he undertook to abstain from taking part in the hostilities arising from the French occupation of Algiers, to suppress piracy, and to limit the size of the Tripolitanian fleet. In the text of the treaty he also denied Warrington's charges with regard to Rousseau's involvement in the Laing affair. From this date Warrington seems to have decided that British interests could best be served by Yusuf Qaramanli's removal.

The pasha's internal authority had by 1830 also declined. The prestige he had had as the master of valiant captains attacking Christian ships was replaced by the indignity of being tossed around by rival European consuls able to back their representations with the cannons of their countries' ships. Furthermore, instead of affluence the pasha faced increasing financial difficulties after the suppression of piracy, which made him debase the currency seven times between 1829 and 1832 and confiscate in 1830 any property for which no written deed of ownership could be produced. Rapaciousness and loss of prestige led to rebellion. In 1831 'Abdul-Jalil Saif al-Nasr, the shaikh of the Awlad Sulaiman tribe living between Fazzan and Sirta, initiated the uprising against Yusuf Qaramanli and took possession of Fazzan. Yusuf Qaramanli had savagely repressed these tribesmen in 1817, and their rebellion might have been a revenge for their past suffering; but Warrington's later conduct suggests that he may have given 'Abdul-Jalil the encouragement he needed for taking up arms against the pasha. Warrington's subsequent actions also caused the rebellion to spread. Upon his request an English naval squadron arrived in Tripoli in May 1832 to make the pasha pay his debts to his English creditors. The pasha did not have enough money and on 18 July offered to pay half the value of these debts, but the commander insisted on immediate payment in full. The pasha was thus forced to levy a special impost on the tribes of the Tripolitanian Sahil which had so far been exempted from taxation. On 26 July these tribes rebelled and from their base in Manshia they proclaimed Muhammad Qaramanli, the son of Yusuf's exiled brother Ahmad, as their pasha. Trying to save the situation, Yusuf Qaramanli abdicated on 12 August in favour of his son 'Ali, but Warrington would not be satisfied by this arrangement. In two dispatches to his government on 1 and 11 August he said that Yusuf Qaramanli and D'Ghies received French support, and stressed that only the success of Muhammad Qaramanli and 'Abdul-Jalil could re-establish British influence in the regency. Warrington had gone on board one of the English ships on 6 August. Upon Yusuf Qaramanli's abdication he returned to Tripoli and declared his support for the rebels. The French consul supported 'Ali Qaramanli and, as negotiations in 1833 between the British and the French governments upon French initiative failed to bring them to adopt a common stand with regard to Tripoli, a state of stalemate ensued. The stalemate was broken only by Ottoman intervention, an eventuality which Warrington might have considered an adequate alternative to Muhammad Qaramanli's installation as pasha.

With the British and French governments supporting the two rival parties in Tripolitania, the Ottoman government had to act with circumspection. In June 1832 an Ottoman emissary arrived in Tripoli on the pretext of supporting the financial claims of Albanian creditors of the pasha. He returned to Istanbul with a letter from Yusuf Qaramanli requesting the recognition of his son as pasha. In August and September

1833 another Ottoman emissary, Shakir Affendi, was in Tripolitania trying to persuade the rebels to recognize 'Ali Qaramanli, apparently with the intention of bringing the crisis to an end before further British or French intervention occurred. He failed in this mission, but nevertheless returned to Tripoli with a *firman* of investiture for 'Ali Qaramanli, then sailed to Tunis to try to persuade the bey to send military help to the new pasha of Tripoli. The Tunisian government had by this time begun to hope that the conflict in Tripolitania might lead to its annexation to Tunisia. The bey had ignored Yusuf Qaramanli's request for help at the beginning of the rebellion. In June 1834 he sent an emissary to Manshia to secure the release of a boat belonging to a merchant from Jirba which the rebels had captured. It seems that this emissary gave the rebels the impression that the bey favoured their cause, since in October 1834, when Shakir Affendi was in Tunis, they sent a letter asking the bey to convey to the sultan their determination of not accepting 'Ali Qaramanli as pasha and to inform him of the dire effects of the Tripolitanian civil war. Since in Tunisia the supreme religious council (al-Majlis al-Shar'i) represented the interests of the Muslim community against the transient ambitions of rulers of whom it was in theory independent, the bey brought the council into the matter of this attempt to have the sultan authorize him to take over the government of Tripolitania. The Majlis was made to verify the authenticity of the documents sent from Manshia, and append to them a statement on the evils of dissension in the Muslim community. The Tunisian historian Ibn Abi al-Diaf acted as liaison between the Tunisian vizier Shakir and the Majlis, and he records that Shakir expected the Porte's reaction to the documents to be in line with the bey's ambitions. This naive hope was soon disappointed. The Ottoman government seems to have wanted until then to retain the Qaramanlis as rulers of Tripolitania in preference to assuming direct responsiblity for this remote province, but they would not have it ruled by the Husainids, whose ambivalent policy with regard to the French occupation of Algeria was too recent to be forgotten. Thus on 20 May 1835 Shakir Affendi again came to Tripoli and announced that an Ottoman fleet was on the way to give help to the pasha, and asked that arrangements be made for the accommodation of the troops in the capital. The Ottoman ships were commanded by Tahir Pasha, but Najib Pasha came with it as commander-in-chief of the troops. 'Ali Qaramanli was arrested as he went on Najib Pasha's ship in order to escort him to his appointed residence on 28 May. The artillery force had been landed and settled in the fort the day before, so that the pasha's forces saw resistance was futile and submitted. The Qaramanli dynasty thus came to an end, and its remaining members in the country were taken to Istanbul. When the rebels of Manshia submitted to Najib Pasha on the 28th and were disarmed on the 29th, their pasha Muhammad Qaramanli fled and on the way to Misurata committed suicide.

8

Morocco consolidates her national identity, 1510–1822

The Sa'dians, 1510–1603

The Moroccan tribal system of government had exhausted itself by the fifteenth century. The major Berber groupings – Sanhaja, Masmuda and Zanata – had all taken their turn in founding states which followed Ibn Khaldun's cyclical pattern of rise and decline. The tribal system had showed its shortcomings by the failure to prevent Christian encroachment on Moroccan territory since the Portuguese occupation of Ceuta in 1415. It had demonstrated its inability to face a national challenge when in 1471 the Wattasid claimant to the Marinid throne, Muhammad al-Shaikh, who was a product of this system, made peace with the Portuguese and surrendered Asila and Larashe to them so that he could take Fez from the *sharifs*.

The sharifian cult had its first flowering in Morocco in the Idrisid period. It went into abeyance when the Almoravids, Almohads, and early Marinids gave Morocco an effective political and religious leadership; then it revived under the last Marinids. By this time the Sufi orders had become an important socio-political force in the country. In the twelfth century two scholars, Abu Midian al-Ghawth (d. 1198) and 'Abdul-Salam b. Mashish (d. 1228), had gained a reputation in Morocco as Sufi teachers. Since then Sufism made steady, if inconspicuous, progress. In the fifteenth century Sufi *shaikhs* and *sharifs* came to the fore as the symbols of disenchantment with tribal leadership and of the determination to resist the foreign enemies of the country and the faith.

These religious men still needed tribal support to succeed as political leaders, but no leader was able from this time to establish dynastic rule in Morocco on the basis of the exclusive domination of one tribal element as the Almoravids and the Almohads had done. The reason for this shift was not that Moroccans had become more religious; the reason is to be found in the growth of cities since the eleventh century and of the emergence of a large urban class of merchants and artisans. This class came to exercise a greater influence in political life during the period of Marinid rule, and viewed with suspicion any system which tended to aggravate tribal tensions and contribute towards instability. The two dynasties which have ruled Morocco since the sixteenth century both came from rural areas. But both were raised to power by settled communities with entrenched interest in stability and order and both were fitted by their sharifian descent to be symbols around which unity could be achieved. Neither dynasty started with a permanent tribal affiliation, although each had to harness some tribal support in the interest of its cause.

The urban character of the sharifian cult and its revival were demonstrated in the rebellion of Fez against the Marinid sultan ʿAbdul-Haqq in 1465. During ʿAbdul-Haqq's reign an influential and popular religious movement also grew up around the saintly personality of Shaikh Muhammad al-Jazuli. This Sufi teacher belonged to the Jazula Berber tribe of Sus, but spent several years in Fez, where he wrote a widely read manual of Sufi teachings.[1] Al-Jazuli was only a religious teacher, but his disciple al-Sayyaf transformed his followers into a political group. For twenty years following al-Jazuli's death in about 1465 al-Sayyaf was in rebellion against the Marinids, whom he accused of poisoning his master, then against the Wattasids. He carried al-Jazuli's remains as he went about his petty raids in the south, so that the master went to his resting place in Afughal in the Haha district only when al-Sayyaf himself died about 1485. Since then the Jazuliyya became an important religious cult, and the Saʿdians found it useful to identify themselves with it when they rebelled against the Wattasids.

The Wattasid state of Fez was a continuation of the tribal structure established by the Marinids. Its founder, Muhammad al-Shaikh, was the son of Abu Zakariyya, the Wattasid chief who acted from 1420 to 1448 as vizier-regent during Sultan ʿAbdul-Haqq's reign. He escaped death when ʿAbdul-Haqq assassinated other members of the family in 1457, and soon afterwards took possession of Asila. He was able to capture Fez in 1472 with the help of the officials and notables who had served under the Marinids and lost their authority during the rule of the *sharifs*. Muhammad al-Shaikh could not grow to the stature of a national ruler. The spirit of the time was against his kind of leadership, and the tribes of northern Morocco could not be made to pay him allegiance as long as he remained the ally of the Portuguese. During his reign (1472–1505) the Portuguese expansion in Morocco reached its height, and the ineffective Moroccan resistance was led by local chiefs and not by the Wattasids. The Portuguese took Tangier in August 1471, Larashe in 1473, and Azammur in 1486. From the beginning of 1489 they were also engaged in an attempt to penetrate into the interior of northern Morocco by establishing themselves on Wadi Lukkus. In August 1489 Muhammad al-Shaikh forced them to abandon the site of a fortress they were constructing on this river, but

[1] *Dalaʾil al-Khairat*, which is still studied assiduously by Sufis.

immediately afterwards he further compromised himself in the eyes of the Moroccan Muslims by renewing the peace treaty which he had signed with the Portuguese for ten years beyond its date of expiry in 1491. From about this date the Portuguese gave up expansion into the interior of northern Morocco. In the south, however, they established contact with the tribes through Agadir which João Lopes de Sequeira occupied in 1505. Near it Sequeira built the fortress of Santa Cruz, where a market frequented by tribesmen from the neighbourhood was held every Wednesday. Portuguese and other European merchants also traded with the people of Massa, a locality some 50 km south of Agadir.

A mixture of religious zeal and commercial enterprise lay behind the foundation of the Portuguese *presidios* on the Atlantic seaboard of Morocco. While wanting to fight a holy war against the Muslims, the Portuguese also counted on obtaining in Morocco commodities, such as horses and a cloth called *hambel*, which the negroes of West Africa were accustomed to receive from North African traders in exchange for gold and slaves. By the middle of the sixteenth century the Portuguese had reached the point of claiming a monopoly of trade in Morocco, and in the 1550s and 1560s they unsuccessfully tried to have Queen Elizabeth of England recognize this country as their political and commercial preserve. The Moroccans on the whole viewed the Portuguese occupation as an affront to their religion and national dignity for which the commercial advantages accruing from it could not atone.

From the Portuguese threat and internal conflicts there arose in Morocco a call for unity which was both a religious exhortation and political slogan. This call continued to be reiterated in the sixteenth and seventeenth centuries by every religious leader who aspired towards political leadership and found the divisions in the country sufficiently accentuated to give force to this appeal. The *sharifs* were considered the symbols of the ideal of Moroccan unity. But as the Sufi cult was also becoming important, the two sharifian families which came forward to lead the Moroccan Muslims against the Portuguese – the *sharifs* of Jabal 'Alam in the north and the Sa'dians in the south – both had Sufi affiliations.

The *sharifs* of Jabal 'Alam claimed descent from the Idrisid dynasty of the ninth century and the Sufi teacher Ibn Mashish of the twelfth. Soon after the Portuguese occupation of Asila they founded the town of Shafshawin (Xauen) which they intended to use as a base for attacks on the Portuguese in Ceuta and Asila. From the first decade of the sixteenth century there is evidence to indicate that the *sharif*-rulers of Shafshawin also controlled Tatuan. Nevertheless they could not become the leaders of a political movement extending its influence beyond the north-west of Morocco because they lived in the shadow of both the Wattasids in Fez and the Portuguese on the coast. By the beginning of the sixteenth century the principality of Shafshawin seems to have been viewed by the Portuguese on the coast and by the Wattasids in Fez as a convenient buffer. The conduct of the Shafshawin ruler in the 1520s and 1530s, Mawlay Ibrahim, clearly reflected this situation. Portuguese sources[1] describe him as a half-Spaniard (his mother was a Castilian), who made regular raids on Asila in order to justify his reputation as a holy warrior, but kept the conflict with the Portuguese within the limits of chivalric combat. He is said to have announced in advance his attacks on Asila in 1523 and 1528 to its Portuguese commander, and on both occasions to have offered to send him a horse. In 1530 he was treated for an illness by the Portuguese surgeon in Asila, and in 1532 had the same surgeon go to Fez to attend his sick wife. With the Wattasids Mawlay Ibrahim secured good relations by marrying Sultan Muhammad al-Burtughali's daughter. Upon this king's death in 1526 he helped his son Ahmad attain the throne which his uncle Abu Hassun occupied for a short time after the king's death. Thus unable to fulfil the original aims of Shafshawin's founders of driving the Portuguese from Morocco, its rulers were able to survive only through coexistence with them and the Wattasids.

In the south, where Portuguese military power was insignificant and Wattasid authority did not in reality exist, the Saʿdian *sharifs* were able to organize a religio-political movement which eventually unified Morocco and checked the Christian penetration. The Saʿdians had been living in the village of Tagmadart in the valley of Draʿa before they were brought into the limelight through the religious circles of Sus. It appears that the factors which led to their elevation were, in the first place, that their claim to be *sharifs*, which was questioned after the founding of the dynasty,[2] was at the time accepted as true; and, secondly, that the tribes of Sus, divided amongst themselves and unable to choose a leader from their midst to represent them in their dealings with the Europeans, were prepared to accept a *sharif* as their head.

Sus had attracted the interest of European merchants, especially Genoese and Spaniards, from about the same time as the Portuguese occupied Agadir in 1505. The presence of Genoese merchants in the region is noted as early as 1507. They operated in the Massa territory which was under Portuguese control, and the small port of Tarkuku in the Haha to the north of Agadir, buying the gold which reached Sus from the western Sudan, and such local products as wax, hides, gum-lac, and indigo. The Spaniards in the south acted independently of the Portuguese,

---

[1] Cf. Robert Ricard, *Etudes sur l'histoire des Portugais au Maroc* (Coimbra, 1955), pp. 261–80.

[2] The name "Saʿdian" was given to the dynasty by those who questioned the claim of its members to be *sharifs*. According to these detractors, the genealogy of the Saʿdians links them not to the Prophet but to the Arabian tribe of Banu Saʿd Hawazin.

channelled most of their trade through Tarkuku, and were interested in the same commodities as the Genoese. Unable to prevent other European merchants from penetrating a region whose trade they wished to monopolize, the Portuguese viewed their activities with much hostility, especially after the beginning of the Sa'dian movement.

The presence of the Portuguese prompted the people of Sus to organize themselves politically. The traditional account which Muslim historians give of the origins of the Sa'dian leadership has it that it was built upon the desire of the tribes of Sus to have a leader to organize them in their war against the Christians. A tradition recorded by al-Yafrani suggests that the impulse for the establishment of a central political authority in Sus came from the Portuguese themselves. Having taken some tribal warriors captive, the Portuguese in Agadir refused to repatriate them until the tribes chose a ruler with whom they could discuss terms. The man who, according to this tradition, conducted the negotiations with the Portuguese over the liberation of captives was the same saintly personage accredited with the choice of the head of the Sa'dian house, Abu 'Abdulla Muhammad al-Qa'im, as the leader of the holy war. This was Sidi Barakat, a Sufi master who had an important *zawiya* at 'Agga.

Al-Qa'im's formal installation as chief of Sus occurred in 1510 in the town of Tidsi near Tarudant. Both these towns are known to have been active in the trans-Saharan trade. For the following three years Tidsi remained al-Qa'im's base. In 1513 he moved to Afughal in the Haha, upon the invitation of the Shayazima tribe. His presence in Afughal identified his leadership with the Jazuliyya order and al-Sayyaf's rebellion against the Wattasids, since al-Jazuli was buried there and the Shayazima was al-Sayyaf's tribe. It also placed him in a better position to profit from European trade. The Genoese and Spanish merchants in the port of Tarkuku were willing to barter the goods they obtained from the local inhabitants for war materials including arms, copper, iron, sulphur, and even saltpetre.[1] The Portuguese in Agadir knew of the existence of this contraband trade as early as 1514, when they seized a Spanish ship transporting goods between Cadiz and Tarkuku. In 1517 they led an expedition against Tarkuku, pillaged it, and took as prisoners the Genoese and Spanish merchants they found there. This trade seems to have continued into the 1530s, for in 1532 it was the object of representations made by John III of Portugal to Charles V. In spite of these attacks on Tarkuku and the professed aims of al-Qa'im and his son al-'A'raj of driving the Portuguese out, the tribes in Sus continued to trade with the European merchants in

---

[1] Although Sus imported saltpetre at the time, it appears that it had an abundance of this mineral, but the local population were unable to exploit it. In the second half of the sixteenth century, English merchants supervised the production of saltpetre in Sus and exported it from Morocco.

Massa territory. Al-Qa'im's second son Muhammad al-Shaikh was left in Sus when the main base of the movement was transferred to Afughal, and controlled the trans-Saharan caravans which went from 'Agga and Tidsi to the western Sudan. He also encouraged the production of sugar which soon became the most important item in the exports of Sus. It was probably because of this profitable trade between Sus and the Europeans operating under Portuguese protection in Agadir that al-'A'raj between 1517, when he became head of the movement, and 1524, when he conquered Marrakish, directed his raids against Safi and Azammur instead of Agadir.

Preoccupied with their political problems in the north, the Wattasids could do nothing to check the growth of the Sa'dian movement. After al-'A'raj occupied Marrakish in 1524, they made several attempts to regain it. Having failed, they accepted the good offices of the leading religious scholars of Fez, and came to terms with al-'A'raj by recognizing him as ruler of Morocco south of Tadla. This compromise was reached in 1536 after the Wattasid army was routed by the Sa'dians at Wadi al-'Abid.

Until 1536 Muhammad al-Shaikh was content with acting as governor of Sus. But the agreement of this year with the Wattasids aroused his jealousy; and as by this time the basis of al-'A'raj's leadership had been broadened, the tribes of Sus also looked upon his successes as detrimental to their supremacy in the Sa'dian movement. From about 1536 relations between the two brothers worsened, culminating in an armed conflict in which Muhammad al-Shaikh used his Sus army to capture power from al-'A'raj in 1539 or 1540 (A.H. 946).

Muhammad al-Shaikh's bid henceforth to become the ruler of the entire country was aided by his success in the capture of Agadir in 1541 and the consequent disintegration of the Portuguese colonial system in Morocco. The construction work which Muhammad al-Shaikh undertook in the port of Agadir after its capture showed that he intended it to remain the commercial outlet of Sus. Its fall, coupled with financial difficulties at home, made the Portuguese withdraw from most of their other *presidios* on the Atlantic coastline of Morocco. Safi and Azammur were both evacuated in 1541. Qsar al-Saghir, on the Moroccan side of the Straits of Gibraltar, and Asila were evacuated in the summer of 1550, when Fez had fallen to the Sa'dians and a plan which John III of Portugal envisaged of handing Safi to the Wattasid prince Abu Hassun proved impracticable. Occurring at a time when the Wattasid sultan Ahmad (1526–48) was pursuing a policy of coexistence with the Portuguese in the north, the Portuguese withdrawal from Agadir, Safi, and Azammur gave the Sa'dians an advantage which neutralized the effect of the avowed hostility to them of the religious leaders of Fez and the growing influence of the Turks in the Wattasid state.

The penetration of the Wattasid state by the Turks occurred during the reign of Sultan Ahmad. Turkish troops fought with him in 1545, when Muhammad al-Shaikh captured the fortress of Fishtala on the route between Fez and Marrakish, and then defeated the Wattasid sultan at Wadi al-'Abid and took him captive. Ottoman pressure on Muhammad al-Shaikh to liberate the Wattasid sultan and Muhammad al-Shaikh's offer of an alliance with the Spaniards against the Turks have been discussed above.[1] In the period when the Wattasids were becoming prepared to accept some Ottoman control in return for military help, they won the support of the bulk of the religious leaders of Fez. Only the Shadhiliyya Sufi order, of which the Jazuliyya was an offshoot, inclined towards the Sa'dians. But the Qadiriyya order, and the religious scholars of Fez led by 'Abdul-Wahid al-Wanshirisi, rallied to the support of the Wattasids. The support of these groups seems to have been unconnected with that of the Turks, and it may have been due to the dislike which the urban and proud Muslims of Fez had for the uncouth Sa'dians. Al-Wanshirisi continued to oppose the Sa'dians even when Muhammad al-Shaikh's army was besieging Fez. The latter's agents, unable to prevail upon this influential religious leader to summon the Muslims of Fez to submit to their master, assassinated him at the gate of the Qarawiyyin mosque in January 1549, shortly before Muhammad al-Shaikh's entry to the town.

The Sa'dian leaders had from the start to balance considerations of expediency with their claim to be the revivors of Islam in Morocco. This was evident when al-'A'raj was leading his warriors against Safi and Azammur while sparing Agadir in order to retain it as the commercial outlet of Sus. After the conquest of Fez, when the dynasty had developed enough confidence, expediency outweighed the religious claims. Muhammad al-Shaikh, seeing in the popular religious groups, even those which contributed to his rise to power, potential sources of opposition, came down upon their leaders. The Sufi *shaikhs* of Fez were made to surrender precious articles which they obtained from looting the possessions of the Marinids. In Marrakish the sultan had the *zawiya* of the influential Sufi *shaikh* 'Abdulla al-Kush closed and his disciples dispersed. Considerations of expediency also led Muhammad al-Shaikh to undertake the step, unpopular on religious grounds, of entering into an alliance with the Spaniards for the purpose of driving the Turks from Algeria.

The supreme test in the Muslim state of whether the ruler would be prepared to allow reasons of state to come before religious considerations was the policy of taxation he followed. Muhammad al-Shaikh's father al-Qa'im had accustomed the people of Sus to the payment of taxes by having each fireplace at first contribute an egg. This contribution, which was later increased, was presumably levied for the purpose of financing

[1] Pp. 170–2.

the war against the Christians. With Muhammad al-Shaikh it became a regular tax which all had to pay, including the Sufi *shaikhs* and the *sharifs*. The populace called this tax *al-na'iba* (the affliction), but the apologists of the dynasty described it as *kharaj*. From the earliest Muslim period a distinction existed between the land-tax and the poll-tax. In the later Umayyad period and particularly under the 'Abbasids, "kharaj" became specifically applied to the land-tax, and "jizya" to the poll-tax which was restricted to non-Muslims. But in the earlier periods the two terms were interchangeable, referring to the taxes collected from the non-Muslims living in the Muslim state, at a time when the Arab ruling class mostly owned no lands in the conquered territories and paid no taxes. In Morocco the term "kharaj" retained its original confusion with "jizya", and seems to have meant predominantly the poll-tax. The Almohads began the practice of collecting *kharaj* in Morocco on the grounds that in the period of Muslim expansion the country was taken by conquest and not by the peaceful submission of its inhabitants to the Muslim armies. The Marinids exempted the inhabitants of the mountainous regions from the *kharaj* on the basis that they, unlike the peoples of the plains, were not conquered but capitulated at a later date. Muhammad al-Shaikh caused a *fatwa* to be issued, stating that no evidence existed to show that the mountainous regions of Morocco had capitulated and, therefore, they were subject to *kharaj*. The *na'iba* or *kharaj* of the Sa'dians was collected mainly in kind, but it was a poll-tax levied on the basis of a fixed sum for each family. At a time when the Muslim law had clearly taken the stand that the poll-tax was to be collected only from non-Muslims, the *na'iba* was an imposition without religious justification. The people of Sus, having been accustomed to its payment, continued to pay even when it was increased. But other communities resented it and rebelled. When Muhammad al-Shaikh's son al-Harran was engaged in his ill-fated expedition into the Shaliff region of Algeria in 1551,[1] his father was leading an expedition to Dra'a whose people refused to pay the tax, and he was unable to send him aid when the Turks made their counter-attack on Tlemsen. Muhammad al-Shaikh himself was killed while on an expedition into the High Atlas, trying to force its chiefs to pay the *kharaj* which had not been paid since 1547.

Muhammad al-Shaikh was killed on 23 October 1557 by a group of Turkish soldiers. He had enlisted in his army the Turkish soldiers who had served under the Wattasids. But his murderers, led by an officer called Salih Kahiya, are said to have been sent for this purpose from Algiers and pretended to be deserters. They were incorporated in the Turkish regiment which Muhammad al-Shaikh took with him in the campaign against the hardy mountaineers of the High Atlas. Some of the conspirators were

[1] See above, p. 171.

overtaken as they fled in the direction of Sijilmasa, but the rest were able to reach Algiers with his severed head.

After the failure of Muhammad al-Shaikh's grandiose ambition of driving the Turks out from Algeria with Spanish help,[1] his successors felt that their way to the east was closed by the Turkish presence. This feeling was confirmed by the failure of an expedition which Muhammad al-Ghalib (1557–74) sent in 1560 (or 1561) to take Tlemsen. In fact the fear of Turkish expansion remained a determining factor of Sa'dian policy for the rest of the sixteenth century. Because of it the sultans resided in Marrakish which was less accessible from Algeria and the tribes in its neighbourhood were more loyal. Fez was henceforth treated as the second capital. It was governed by the heir-apparent, and the troops which the Sa'dians kept in the north were garrisoned there. Also because of this fear Muhammad al-Shaikh's successors continued the policy of informal alliance with the Spaniards. The Turkish presence in Algeria led Morocco to develop its political identity independently from the rest of the Maghrib. Economically Morocco was forced to compensate for this isolation by greater interest in the wealth of the western Sudan and commercial relations with Europe.

The Turks almost realized their ambition of dominating Morocco politically when the Sa'dian prince 'Abdul-Malik usurped the throne from Muhammad al-Mutawakkil (1574–6). For two years (1576–8) Morocco was a political satellite of Algiers whose troops 'Abdul-Malik used in defeating his nephew. 'Abdul-Malik had prayers said in the name of the Ottoman sultan, dressed himself like a Turk, and followed the example of Algiers by sponsoring the pirates who operated from Larashe and Sala. His army was also controlled by the Turks. It included Turkish, Andalusian, and Zawawa mercenaries in addition to the Arabian warriors, but its officers were Turks. This situation was a threat to the remaining Portuguese *presidios* at Tangier, Mazagan, and Ceuta. It was to Portugal, therefore, that the deposed Sultan al-Mutawakkil went for help after taking refuge in Tangier.

In the summer of 1578 a Portuguese army led by King Sebastian (1557–78), and accompanied by al-Mutawakkil, invaded northern Morocco. At Wadi al-Makhazin, a tributary of Wadi Lukkus, this army was routed by 'Abdul-Malik's on 4 August 1578. Moroccan sources, inclined to exaggerate the importance of this Muslim victory, give the number of soldiers Sebastian brought with him as 125,000. It seems certain that the Portuguese army was about one-fifth this size. Nevertheless the Muslim victory had far-reaching consequences for Morocco. The three kings who took part in the battle were all killed, hence the name "The Battle of the Three Kings" usually given to it. This enabled al-Mutawakkil's brother Ahmad to become sultan and steer Morocco away from

---

[1] See above, p. 172.

political dependence on either the Turks or the Christians. Furthermore, as King Sebastian had no heir, Portugal was annexed to Spain in 1580. Consequently the Portuguese *presidios* in Morocco passed under the control of a country which was more committed to the preservation of the *status quo* than Portugal. The international standing of Morocco was also enhanced as a result of this victory against a European country. Ahmad, who called himself al-Mansur (the victorious), drew considerable political and economic advantage from his country's improved international standing. But as it also led him to pursue a policy of grandeur, the economic resources of the country were drained and the tensions this created came into the open upon his death.

Ahmad al-Mansur seems to have attributed the Moroccan victory at the Battle of the Three Kings to the salutary influence which the Turkish troops and officers who served under ʿAbdul-Malik had on the discipline and methods of warfare of the rest of the army. Consequently he embarked upon the apparently paradoxical step of giving the Turkish elements predominance in the army which he built mainly in order to protect Morocco against the Turks. But in fact this policy is less paradoxical than it seems, since many of those so-called Turks were soldiers of fortune, often of non-Turkish and non-Muslim extraction, who adopted the habits and religion of the Turkish ruling class in Algeria for the sake of advancement. The "Turks" were employed by Ahmad al-Mansur as instructors. Some of them were placed in charge of the royal arsenals, and others manned the artillery division. The widespread use of firearms by the Moroccans in the second half of the sixteenth century, which facilitated their conquest of Songhay territory in the 1590s, is credited to Turkish influence. Al-Yafrani's description of Ahmad al-Mansur's army indicates that the military titles and names used were Turkish: "beylerbey" for the commander of the two elite regiments, "pasha" for high-ranking officers, and "spahis" for the mounted troops. The army which al-Mansur built was of motley composition. Of the local regiments al-Yafrani mentions only those of Sus, which suggests that al-Mansur continued his predecessors' policy of reliance on the Sus tribal elements to the exclusion of other Moroccan tribes. The foreigners included "Turks", who possibly constituted the largest of the foreign groups, Zawawa, Andalusians (who were lancers), and renegades. The last two groups, probably being considered more loyal than the "Turks", were given the distinction of guarding the sultan when he led a campaign in person, and on pay-day received their remuneration before all the other regiments.

If the main impulse behind the creation of such a large professional army was to protect Morocco from the Turks, its existence was also instrumental in the unification of Morocco under the absolute authority of the sultan. The sultanate in al-Mansur's hands became a dominant institution dedicated to grandeur, oppressive but also efficient. Only five months after acceding to the throne he began the construction of a sumptuous residence in Marrakish to which he gave the name of al-Badiʿ (the splendid), thus relinquishing the *qasba* in which his predecessors had resided. For fifteen years artisans from various countries worked on this palace for which no expense was spared. Marble was brought from Italy, for which the sultan paid its equivalent weight in sugar. In this palace al-Mansur led a life of seclusion and pleasure, more like that of the ʿAbbasid caliphs in Baghdad at the zenith of their power than anything Morocco had known before. When he gave audiences he kept himself concealed from his guests behind a curtain, a practice which outraged the Timbuktu scholar exiled in Morocco, Ahmad Baba, and prompted him to tell the sultan that he imitated God by speaking from behind a veil. Al-Mansur also introduced the custom that the sultans of Morocco when riding out should have a parasol held over their heads to shade them from the sun. In order to underline the religious character of the dynasty and give it splendour al-Mansur held large official ceremonies on the feast of the Prophet's birthday and the ʿId al-Fitr. The official celebrations on these occasions included recitation of poetry in praise of the Prophet and of the sultan, Sufi *dhikr*,[1] and distribution of gifts. The sultan regularly distributed largesse to poets, musicians, and religious scholars, in this way displaying royal magnificence and making the religious leaders a prop to his regime. To meet his prodigious expenses the sultan levied heavy taxes on the Moroccans. We do not possess figures relating to the amount of taxes collected in al-Mansur's period, but al-Yafrani records that some religious scholars complained to the sultan about the misery to which the people of Morocco were reduced by excessive taxation. Al-Yafrani also quotes the reply which the sultan gave to one of these representations, thus summing up his view of government. He is recorded as having replied: "The people of Morocco are lunatics, and their madhouse consists of oppression." Al-Mansur's despotism was not tempered with inefficiency. In spite of his seclusion he took a personal interest in the everyday affairs of the government. He read all reports from the provinces, answered letters from the governors promptly, and required his secretaries to keep fixed hours of work so that no delay in correspondence should occur. His ministers and high government functionaries assembled in the *diwan* every Wednesday to discuss important aspects of policy in the sultan's presence.

Al-Mansur's only major military undertaking outside Morocco was the expedition to the western Sudan. As this expedition is well documented in Moroccan and West African sources we know enough about its aims and

[1] Litanies whose central theme is 'remembrance' (*dhikr*) of the Prophet: hence the name.

its results in West Africa, but much less about its consequences for Morocco. This expedition was the climax of the interest which the Sa'dians took in the riches of the western Sudan since the inception of their movement. In 1526 a Sa'dian force occupied Tuat. Al-'A'raj followed this shortly before he was deposed by demanding of the king of Songhay Askia Ishaq I (1539–49) that he place the salt mines of Taghaza under Sa'dian control. By controlling the chief source of salt in the western Sudan the Sa'dians would have become the main importers of its gold, since in exchange for gold no commodity was more valued than salt. As shortly afterwards al-'A'raj lost power, and his immediate successors were preoccupied with expansion northwards and consolidation, interest in this venue of economic expansion lapsed, and with it the political control of Tuat. Al-Mansur conquered the oases of Gurara and Tuat in 1583. In the previous year he had revived the question of the Taghaza salt mines by asking Askia Dawud (1549–82) to pay him the value of a year's taxes levied on the mines. Early in 1590 he asked Askia Ishaq II to pay him one *mithqal*[1] of gold on every load of salt extracted from the mines, a request which implied that the sultan considered himself the owner of these mines although the king of Songhay in fact controlled them. Upon receiving an abusive reply which Ishaq II sent to this request, al-Mansur began to prepare the expedition which he sent in the following year.

Al-Yafrani's account of the expedition shows that although it was motivated by greed, al-Mansur tried to give a religious justification to it. The request for a *mithqal* of gold on each load of salt he explained as a contribution by the Muslim kings of Songhay towards the war effort against the Christians. But when Askia Ishaq II's reply came, the sultan explained to his counsellors that the aim of the expedition was to unite the Muslims in the western Sudan with those of Morocco, and remove the Askias, who were not legitimate Muslim princes. It is also clear from al-Yafrani's account that in the invasion of the Sudan the sultan was seeking an outlet for his expansionist ambitions which were frustrated by the presence of the Turks in Algeria, and by the lack of interest with which the English met his proposals of 1589 for a joint action against the Spaniards which he hoped would result in the annexation of southern Spain to Morocco.

The outcome to the western Sudan of the Moroccan invasion of 1591 falls outside the scope of this book. It may be noted, however, that it caused the disintegration of the Songhay state, and the emergence of a distinct social group in Timbuktu which continued to rule this town and its dependencies until its conquest by the French in 1893. The expedition did not lead to the permanent political annexation of the former Songhay territory to the Sa'dian state. Timbuktu, which became the centre of the

---

[1] Equivalent to about three grams.

Moroccan administration, greeted the Muslim invaders with a revolt in October 1591. The Moroccan governors were able to establish some measure of control over the town after 1594, when they took into exile in Morocco the leading members of the scholarly Aqit family, to which Ahmad Baba belonged. However, after 1618 the governors of Timbuktu were no longer appointed from Marrakish, but chosen by the Moroccan troops and their descendants from amongst their midst. The supply of gold and slaves to Morocco in the last decade of the sixteenth century became abundant. Elephants also were brought from the Sudan for the first time in 1592, and their Negro drivers brought with them the habit of smoking tobacco, thus arousing a religious controversy as to whether smoking was permitted under the provisions of the Muslim law.

The policy of friendliness towards Spain, made necessary by the Turkish threat to Morocco, was an embarrassment to the Sa'dians. For the Spaniards were after all Christian, had a longer history of fighting the Moroccans than the hated Portuguese, and were colonizers of North African lands. The English endeavours after 1580 to obtain Moroccan support for the Portuguese claimant Don Antonio suggested to Ahmad al-Mansur the possibility of an alliance with England that would replace reliance on Spain. By this date commercial relations on a large scale between England and Morocco had been in existence for thirty years. English merchants had traded with Morocco in spite of protests from the Portuguese since the early 1550s that this country fell within Portugal's political and commercial spheres of influence and that the English merchants were supplying the Moroccans with war materials. The staple commodities in this trade were English cloth and Moroccan sugar. However, when in 1572 some London merchants learned that they could obtain saltpetre in Morocco, and asked Sultan al-Mutawakkil for a licence to buy it, he insisted that this commodity could be exported only in exchange for cannon-balls. From this date the English merchants trading in Morocco provided the sultan with some of the war materials he needed.

Trade and politics were closely interwined in Anglo-Moroccan relations after 1572. John Williams, the first Englishman to buy saltpetre in Morocco, tried to take with him in 1576 English craftsmen to cast cannon-balls for the sultan, but they were not allowed to sail from England. In the saltpetre trade Williams was acting on behalf of Edmund Hogan whom the queen sent as ambassador to Morocco in 1577. Hogan was instructed to state to the sultan that the exportation of arms to Morocco could not be allowed by the queen for fear of resentment from other Christian rulers. But since he had his own personal interests in Morocco to advance, it is known that he took with him some arms in secret. The annexation of Portugal to Spain in 1580 and the Anglo-Spanish wars led the English queen to attach special importance to Anglo-Moroccan cooperation. In

1581 the queen authorized the export of English naval timber to Morocco in return for saltpetre. The licence to export the timber was given to a certain John Symcot, an agent in the service of the Earl of Leicester, who in 1585 obtained a royal charter for the foundation of the Barbary Company for the express purpose of controlling the activities of all English merchants in Morocco. The first agent of this company in Morocco, Henry Roberts, was also the queen's ambassador. Though paid by the company, Roberts' main task while in Morocco (1585–8) was to secure Ahmad al-Mansur's aid in support of Don Antonio.

In his dealings with Roberts al-Mansur was evasive, but in January 1589 his ambassador to the queen spelled out clearly his terms for giving assistance to the Portuguese claimant. He wanted oars, carpenters, and shipwrights to be sent to Morocco. He offered to contribute 150,000 ducats towards the cost of an Anglo-Moroccan expedition against Spain but would want his own troops to be carried in English ships to take part in it. Furthermore, the sultan wanted a treaty that would enable him to hire English ships and marines when engaged in war with one of his non-Christian neighbours. As the queen would not consent to the embarkation of Moroccan troops and the sultan's demands for armament could be met only partially, al-Mansur met with evasion the further English representations on behalf of Don Antonio which continued to be made until his death in 1595. As these exchanges were kept secret, the sultan was able to avoid a rupture in his relations with Spain. Spanish merchants continued to trade in Morocco, and some of them together with a Spanish consul lived in Marrakish. When in 1586, during Roberts' stay in Morocco, the crew of an English vessel, the *Dolphin*, captured a Spanish caravel off the coast near Safi, the sultan ordered the confiscation of all goods discharged from the *Dolphin*.

Although the Anglo-Moroccan alliance proved difficult to establish, English trade in Morocco was substantial throughout the second half of the sixteenth century. In the first half of the century the foreign commerce of Morocco was in the hands of Portuguese, Spaniards, and Genoese. The Genoese, besides controlling a substantial part of the export-import trade, acted as financiers and factors for such merchants as the Portuguese whose presence in the interior would not be tolerated. In the second half of the century English merchants replaced the Genoese and the Spaniards. English factors resided in Safi, Agadir, and Marrakish, and between 1586 and 1589 there was an English factor in Tarudant supervising the production of saltpetre. The role of the Genoese as local agents was taken over by the Jews. This was made possible by the fact that the production of sugar and saltpetre was a state monopoly in Morocco, and the Jews were given concessions by the sultan for the production and export of these materials. As at the same time English cloth was exchanged mostly with these commodities, since the exportation of gold was prohibited by the sultan, the Jews came to have a monopoly of the sale of English cloth in Morocco.

Morocco dismembered, 1603–68

Ahmad al-Mansur's death in 1603 was a turning-point in the fate of the Sa'dian dynasty. Conflict for power amongst his three sons brought about its disintegration, and the religious chiefs once more came forward as the champions of suppressed groups and the advocates of unity which the Sa'dians were now held responsible for undermining. These dynastic conflicts had resulted by 1613 in the division of the country into two parts, one ruled from Marrakish by al-Mansur's son Zaidan, and the other by his grandson 'Abdulla from Fez. 'Abdulla's father, Muhammad al-Shaikh, further compromised the dynasty by handing Larashe over to Spain. Having been defeated in the struggle for power, he fled to Spain, returning in 1610 with a Spanish force to Badis. From there he summoned the *'ulama* of Fez. Those who went to meet him – and many chose to flee instead – were intimidated upon their arrival by the guns of the Spanish ships and were made to recognize him as their ruler. Subsequently he sent a force which facilitated the Spanish occupation of Larashe. Muhammad al-Shaikh was assassinated in 1613, and his son 'Abdulla, who ruled the kingdom of Fez until 1627, continued to bear the stigma of his father's betrayal. The leaders of Old Fez refused to accept his rule and closed the gates of their town to him. With the help of his Sharaqa[1] Arabian warriors he was occasionally able to force his way into the old city and loot it, but its people remained adamant in rejecting his authority. From 1619 Meknes and Tatuan were also in rebellion against him.

'Abdulla's uncle Zaidan in the south did not fare much better. Having taken control of Marrakish in 1609 he was driven out some three years later by a religious leader of Messianic pretensions called Abu Mahalli. This man was a religious scholar from Sijilmasa who in 1610 exploited the outrage caused by giving Larashe to the Spaniards to lead a rebellion against the Sa'dians, claiming to be the Mahdi. He succeeded in taking Marrakish from Zaidan and, marrying the latter's mother, settled down to establish his own rule in the south. Zaidan in desperation fled to Safi, and from there planned to travel to Spain. He was spared the need of asking for Christian help when the religious chief of mount Daran in the High Atlas, Yahya b. 'Abdulla al-Hahi offered him aid. The al-Hahi religious family had started to establish itself in mount Daran by the middle of the

---

[1] "Sharaqa" (eastern) is a collective name given to the Arabian tribes who penetrated north-eastern Morocco in the sixteenth century, coming from the region of Tlemsen to the east.

sixteenth century. During the reign of al-Ghalib (1557–74) their *zawiya* at Rada'a became an important religious centre from which the al-Hahis exercised religio-feudal rights over the peasants in the region. Zaidan was restored with the help of the al-Hahis, but he remained for the rest of his reign (1613–27) subservient to the wishes of his benefactor.

In the period of political upheaval following al-Mansur's death, civil strife in Morocco and external factors combined to bring about economic decline. The European merchants were hampered by the instability of public life, and found that most of the goods for which they came to Morocco were becoming scarce. The fall of Songhay and Morocco's inability to create a centralized political order in the western Sudan made the journey to Timbuktu by traders seeking gold too dangerous to be undertaken without vast preparation and expense. Instead of the annual caravans sent by al-Mansur for bringing to Morocco the gold levied in taxes and obtained commercially, after his death a caravan was sent every three years. The diminution of the supply of gold is reflected in its rate of exchange in Morocco with silver: one to four during al-Mansur's reign, and nearly one to twenty some twenty years later. In this century the eastern trans-Saharan routes took a larger volume of the trade to Algeria and Tunisia, and the Europeans on the West African coast dealt a severe blow to the activities of the trans-Saharan traders in general. A large part of the trade which had passed through Morocco was channelled from the 1640s to the French in Senegal and to the Dutch, who in 1638 replaced the Portuguese at Arguin. There was also since the beginning of the seventeenth century a decline in Morocco's production of sugar. By 1610 many of the sugar mills in the south were no longer functioning, and cultivation of sugar-cane declined except in such areas as the vicinity of Tarudant. Of importance to the political fortunes of the Sa'dians was the fact that the reduced trade which reached Morocco from the Sudan was no longer controlled by them, but by their political opponents in Sus.

By the late 1620s three important centres of opposition to the Sa'dians had emerged. The leaders of all three had religious pretensions which embodied and disguised political ambitions. In order of importance these opponents were the Dala'iyya in the Middle Atlas, Abu Hassun al-Samlali in Sus, and in the Gharb[1] the Andalusians organized in the republic of Bu Ragrag and the Arabian tribesmen led by the religious warrior al-'Ayyashi. Of these only the Dala'iyya chiefs made a bid for replacing the Sa'dians as the ruling dynasty of Morocco. Indeed between 1640 and 1660 they must have seemed to the Moroccans destined to become their rulers. But the uncertainties of Moroccan political alliances belied these expectations and

---

[1] The Gharb, literally "the west", is a geographical name for the part of the Atlantic littoral through which the Sibu river runs, including the towns of Meknes, Sala, and Wazzan.

favoured another family of *sharifs*, the 'Alawites, in uniting the country under their rule.

The republic of Bu Ragrag, on the river of this name which divides Rabat and Sala, was founded by Andalusian Muslims expelled from Spain between 1609 and 1614. These refugees were uncompromising in their hatred of the Christians, but they could not identify themselves with the country where they settled. When they arrived on the western coast of Morocco, other Andalusian refugees had already established a piratical principality in Tatuan, which was ruled by the Naqsis family. Like the Tatuanians, the Andalusian refugees who settled on the mouth of the Bu Ragrag soon became engaged in piracy against the Christians, especially the Spaniards. They founded two settlements, one on the northern bank of the river at Sala, and the other to its south around the Wadaya castle built by the Almohads at Rabat. The Andalusians on the Bu Ragrag formed a self-governing community, ruled by an elected governor who held office for a year with the assistance of a *diwan* of elders. Soon Sala, which in contemporary usage included the settlement at Rabat, became the most important base for piracy on the Atlantic Ocean. The activities of its corsairs were exceedingly profitable, since from their base they could intercept shipping between the New World and Europe. Sala pirates often went out to a distance of about 800 km, and on some occasions reached the English Channel and even Ireland. But the usual theatre of their activities was the Atlantic between the Straits of Gibraltar and the Azores, Madeira, and the Canaries.

In the late 1620s the Andalusians in Sala found themselves drawn willy-nilly into an alliance with Muhammad al-'Ayyashi, a rebel against the Sa'dians who made a career of attacking Spanish positions on the coast. Belonging to the Arab tribe of Banu Malik which had roamed the banks of the Sibu river, al-'Ayyashi represented the political ambitions of the Arabian tribes in the Gharb. He began his political career by acting as governor of Azammur for the Sa'dian sultan Zaidan. From this position he attacked the Spaniards at Mazagan. As he soon gathered around him a large number of warriors, the Spaniards could persuade Sultan Zaidan that al-'Ayyashi was as much of a threat to his own authority as to Mazagan. An army was sent from Marrakish to remove al-'Ayyashi from Azammur, whereupon he decided to move with his warriors northwards. The Spaniards in 1614 had built a fortress at al-Ma'mura (Mamora) on the Sibu river to the north-east of Sala, thereby threatening the piratical community on the Bu Ragrag. Playing on the fears of the Andalusians, al-'Ayyashi was able in 1615 to draw them into an alliance which deprived them of their freedom of action. For a quarter-of-a-century he led the life of a *mujahid* (holy warrior). He attacked al-Ma'mura, Larashe, and Tangier, scoring minor victories without being able to dislodge the Spaniards from any of these places. The Andalusians in the meantime had come to fear him more than they feared the Spaniards, and sometimes refused him needed help. In 1631, in the course of an attack on al-Ma'mura, they denied him a possible victory by not providing him with the scaling ladders he required them to make. In the face of this recalcitrance al-'Ayyashi resorted to repression, forcing more and more of the Andalusians to leave Sala. He was defeated and killed in April 1641 by the Dala'iyya army acting in cooperation with the Andalusians.

When in the early 1630s al-'Ayyashi completely eliminated Sa'dian authority in the Gharb, Sus had already fallen under the political control of 'Ali Abu Hassun al-Samlali of Iligh. Abu Hassun's grandfather was a saintly personage who achieved distinction in the early period of the Sa'dian state. Following Abu Mahalli's defeat in 1614 Abu Hassun organized the Berbers of Sus, especially the Berbers of the Jazula tribe, against the enfeebled Sultan Zaidan. On more than one occasion he fought with Yahya al-Hahi of mount Daran, the protector of Sultan Zaidan, who moved his base after 1614 to Tarudant and contested with Abu Hassun the mastery of Sus. With Yahya's death in 1626 and the consequent disintegration of the al-Hahi principality, Iligh became the capital of Sus and Abu Hassun its undisputed ruler. Within a few years he extended his authority over Dra'a and in 1631 into the oasis of Tafilalt. Abu Hassun's control of the trade with the Sudan made his state economically viable and enabled him to obtain arms from the Europeans in Sus.

The Dala'iyya group were Sanhaja Berbers belonging to the Majat tribe. They take their name from the *zawiya* of Dala' founded in the 1560s by their ancestor Abu Bakr near Khanifra in the Middle Atlas. But even before the foundation of the *zawiya* Abu Bakr's family were sufficiently important in the region as religious teachers for the Sa'dian Muhammad al-Shaikh to exempt them from the payment of taxes. The Sa'dian sultan viewed the activities of the family with favour, since they were the propagators of the Jazuliyya doctrine in the Middle Atlas. The Sa'dians, as previously mentioned, identified themselves in this period with the Jazuliyya movement. Furthermore, as the Jazuliyya, like the Shadhiliyya order of which it was an offshoot, taught an orthodox form of Sufism whose central theme was the exaltation of the Prophet, the Sa'dians – as descendants of the Prophet – considered the activities of the Dala'iyya *shaikhs* politically useful.

A recent study of the Dala'iyya[1] shows that its *shaikhs* owed their popularity and political power to the social services which they performed in the Middle Atlas. Abu Bakr founded his *zawiya* upon the suggestion of his Sufi teacher al-Qastali of Marrakish for the purposes of propagating the Shadhiliyya-Jazuliyya doctrine and feeding the poor. Abu Bakr used

[1] Muhammad Hijji, *Al-Zawiya al-Dala'iyya* (Rabat, 1964).

the contributions he received to tap the waters of springs for agriculture and to build near his *zawiya* hostels for students and the poor. His son Muhammad, the head of the community from 1612 to 1636, constructed a new *zawiya* some 12 km from the old one with its own houses and facilities for scholars to live and study. He is said to have been able to feed in this *zawiya* 7,000 people a day, and to have had 500 mules continually carrying provisions to it. In addition the two Dala'iyya *zawiyas* became important centres of learning where distinguished scholars taught or studied. Among the scholars who studied under the Dala'iyya *shaikhs* was Abul-Hasan al-Yusi, the greatest Moroccan scholar in the seventeenth century and a close associate of the first 'Alawite sultan Rashid.

In the period of chaos which followed Ahmad al-Mansur's death Muhammad b. Abu Bakr came to assume more and more the functions of political leader of the Middle Atlas. The Berber tribes looked to him for political leadership, and accepted his arbitration in their conflicts. The third chief of the Dala'iyya *zawiya*, Muhammad al-Hajj (1636–68), consciously sought political power. He began to construct a fortified capital not far from the original *zawiya* of the family immediately upon succeeding his father, and instead of the loose coalition of warriors his father had used in the Sijilmasa expedition of 1632,[1] Muhammad al-Hajj organized a regular army of Berber warriors. The policy of the Dala'iyya towards the Sa'dians and Muhammad al-'Ayyashi also reflected the change in the character of the movement.

The Sa'dian sultan of Marrakish Muhammad al-Shaikh was able to discern the shift in the nature of the Dala'iyya chief's authority but still hoped to be able to keep a rein on his ambitions. In 1636 he dispatched artisans who constructed a mausoleum for Muhammad al-Hajj's father, and sent his *qadi* to urge the new Dala'iyya chief to follow in his father's footsteps in recognizing the authority of the Prophet's descendant reigning in Marrakish. In a lengthy letter sent after the failure of the *qadi*'s mission, Muhammad al-Shaikh offered to make over to the Dala'iyya chief a part of the tribute of the Middle Atlas for the upkeep of the *zawiya* if he agreed to submit. But he also threatened him with the use of force if he refused. Muhammad al-Hajj replied[2] in 1637 in the form of address proper to a *sharif*, but stated in unambiguous language that the Sa'dians, in spite of their lofty descent, had lost their right to rule on account of their inability to give the country the benefits of effective government. The test of arms occurred in 1638, when an army sent from Marrakish to the Middle Atlas was completely routed. But Muhammad al-Hajj did not consider it in his political interests to follow the war against a descendant

---

[1] See below, p. 225.
[2] Muhammad al-Shaikh's letter and the Dala'iyya chief's reply are both quoted by al-Yafrani.

of the Prophet to the end, especially since he also considered his more profitable direction of territorial expansion to be towards the ocean.

With al-'Ayyashi Muhammad al-Hajj's father had maintained the proper relations between a Muslim man of religion and a holy warrior. He gave him financial help, and on more than one occasion used his religious influence to have some of the tribes of the Gharb, such as the Sajbar tribe, recognize al-'Ayyashi's leadership in the interests of the holy war. Muhammad al-Hajj, on the other hand, saw in al-'Ayyashi an impediment in his gaining control of Sala, his natural outlet on the ocean. Al-'Ayyashi's persecution of the Andalusians was therefore used as the pretext for fighting him. In 1640 the Dala'iyya army occupied Meknes, which was within al-'Ayyashi's zone of influence. Then after a protracted conflict between al-'Ayyashi's predominantly Arabian army and the Dala'iyya Berbers, the outcome was decided in an engagement on the Sibu river in April 1641. Al-'Ayyashi was killed, and his followers were dispersed, some of them going to the Rif mountains from which they were to lead the rebellion which started the collapse of Dala'iyya power.

Al-'Ayyashi's defeat enabled the Dala'iyya to occupy Sala. Fez was attacked immediately afterwards and surrendered to the Dala'iyya after six months of siege. This was followed by the occupation of the rest of the important towns of northern Morocco including Tatuan. To the government of this town Muhammad al-Hajj restored the Naqsis family who had lost power in it as a result of its occupation in 1631 by one of al-'Ayyashi's commanders. In Tatuan, as in Sala for ten years after its occupation, the Dala'iyya chief (or sultan as he became called) preserved the Andalusians' autonomy. They knew better how to deal with Europeans, and indirect contacts with the Christians did not unduly compromise the chief's religious standing, while securing the merchandise he needed, especially arms.

In the ten years (1641–51) when the Andalusians controlled Sala under nominal Dala'iyya rule, European agents, sent mostly to deal with questions arising from piracy or connected with commerce, dealt directly with them. From 1643 there was a Dutch consul in Sala, and in 1648 the French government appointed a substantive consul to reside there, after having been satisfied since 1629 with having a merchant living in Marseilles act as consul while having an agent in Sala. In 1651 Muhammad al-Hajj appointed his son 'Abdulla as governor of Sala. As 'Abdulla also acted as the superintendent of the Dala'iyya state's foreign affairs, his appointment suggests that relations of the Dala'iyya with Europe had become sufficiently important for them to be entrusted to a member of the ruling family. But the Andalusians continued to influence the conduct of foreign relations by acting as interpreters and secretaries, drafting 'Abdulla's letters to foreign rulers and advising him on the treaties he negotiated with some of them.

The most intimate of the Dala'iyya foreign relations was with the Dutch.

Lengthy negotiations between 'Abdulla and the Dutch over the provisions of a treaty signed in 1651, and revised in 1655 and 1659, suggest that the Dutch conducted an active trade with Morocco in the 1650s. A recurring problem in these negotiations arose from the dual character of Sala as a centre of trade and a base for piracy. The Dutch were ready to recognize the right of the Sala corsairs to attack the ships of their common Christian enemies, the Spaniards, while obtaining the promise that their own ships would not be molested. At the same time they were opposed to the friendly relations which the Sala pirates and the Dala'iyya chiefs maintained with the rulers of Algiers. The Algerine pirates were given facilities in Sala, and were allowed to sell their captured goods in it. The attempt by the Dutch to include in their treaty a provision barring the Andalusians from co-operating with the Algerine pirates and trading with Algiers often led to a deadlock in the negotiations. It is a revealing indication of the volume of Dutch trade with Morocco in this period that the Dutch attitude mellowed whenever the governor of Sala threatened to raise the duties on exports and imports beyond the customary ten per cent.

The Dala'iyya sultanate was a Berber state. Its successes under Muhammad al-Hajj were due to the martial valour of the Berber tribes of the Middle Atlas and their political cohesion under his leadership, at a time when Morocco was divided into principalities fighting one another and divided amongst themselves. But the base of Dala'iyya authority remained militarily and morally too narrow for Muhammad al-Hajj to be able to found durable government. The identification of his authority with the dominance of the Berber tribes of the Middle Atlas left for the major Arabian tribes no place in the Dala'iyya political structure. The moral authority of the Dala'iyya chiefs continued to be recognized in the Middle Atlas. Outside it their educational and social services were recognized, but these were outweighed by the fact that they were not *sharifs*. Furthermore, by fighting and killing al-'Ayyashi they ran against the spirit of the holy war without being able to stifle it. Muhammad al-Hajj was aware of these shortcomings, and tried to mitigate their adverse effects. When he wrote in 1637 to the Sa'dian sultan Muhammad al-Shaikh rejecting his political authority he was careful to extol his merits as a descendant of the Prophet, and after his victory of 1638 he abstained from attacking Marrakish in order not to bear the stigma of persecuting the *sharifs*. For the same reason he had his governor in Fez, Abu Bakr al-Tamili, leave the palace in new Fez to the remaining members of the Sa'dian family to reside in it. He showed similar restraint in dealing with the 'Alawite sharifian family as long as their political activities did not constitute a major threat to his power.

With the Arabian tribes in the Gharb and the Habt[1] the Dala'iyya chief

---

[1] This is the north-western tip of Morocco which includes the four major towns of Larashe, Tangier, Ceuta, and Tatuan.

could not reach any agreement without risking alienating the Berbers of the Middle Atlas. It was from these tribes that the first decisive blow to Dala'iyya authority came. One of al-'Ayyashi's army chiefs, al-Khadr Ghailan, started a rebellion against the Dala'iyya in the Habt in 1653. In this year he captured Qsar al-Kabir and used it as a base for attacks on other localities under Dala'iyya control. He himself was an Arab from the Jarfat tribe living near Larashe, and he attracted to him the local tribes of the Habt region and the Arabian tribes driven from further south by the Dala'iyya invasion. His successes in the north and an uprising in Fez precipitated a rebellion against the Dala'iyya in Sala in February 1660. It appears that Dala'iyya control lay heavily on the Andalusian chiefs, and with the help of the tribes nearby they sought to regain their independence. The Andalusians and their tribal allies succeeded in besieging 'Abdulla in the castle of Sala, and a Dala'iyya army sent to relieve him was defeated in June 1660 by Ghailan. But 'Abdulla was able to hold out in the castle for sixteen months, about the end of which he received a shipload of provisions from the English who had just occupied Tangier. 'Abdulla is said to have proposed to the authorities in Tangier an alliance with the Dala'iyya which would enable them to take possession of Sala in return for help against his enemies in the Gharb. The dispatch of the provisions seems to have been intended as an expression of interest in the proposed alliance, without the English governor of Tangier Teviot being committed to a definite policy at a time when he was still feeling his way in the complex political situation of northern Morocco. Ghailan's unhostile attitude towards the English takeover in Tangier in 1661 seems to have persuaded the governor not to pursue further the proposed alliance with the Dala'iyya. When in June 1661 'Abdulla eventually withdrew from the castle, the Andalusians, now in control, followed an ambivalent policy towards Ghailan. They allowed a commander whom 'Abdulla had left behind to control the castle, thereby retaining nominal Dala'iyya authority to counterbalance Ghailan's increasing power. This arrangement came to an end in 1664 when the Andalusians of Sala formally recognized Ghailan's sovereignty over the town and agreed to remit to him the taxes levied on trade.

The shifts in the attitude of the Andalusians of Sala towards the Dala'iyya sultanate paralleled developments in relations between the Berber sultanate and Fez, and it is very likely that the Andalusians measured the power of the Dala'iyya chiefs by their ability to persuade Fez to accept their rule. Though Fez ceased to be the political capital of Morocco from the middle of the sixteenth century, it continued to constitute the country's political pulse. The proud people of Fez, many of whose leaders were Idrisid *sharifs*, still looked upon their city as the cultural and religious metropolis of the country and submitted to new rulers only after much resistance. It appears that to the Andalusians of Sala the victories of Ghailan up to 1661 did not determine the basic question of political authority in the north, whereas the attitude of Fez and its allies did. This estimate of the position of Fez in the political scrambles in the north is borne out by the persistence of the 'Alawite *sharifs* to try and win the cooperation of Fez as a prelude to their struggle with the Dala'iyya.

As has been stated above the Dala'iyya chiefs were able to enter Fez in 1641 only after a siege of six months. In spite of the good treatment the *sharifs* received from the Dala'iyya chiefs, they rebelled against their governor al-Tamili in June 1650 and tried to enter into an alliance with the 'Alawite Muhammad al-Sharif. But the Dala'iyya chief could still bring the town to submission by force and entrusted its government to his own sons Ahmad (1650–3) and Muhammad (1653–9). Muhammad was poisoned in December 1659 or January 1660 (Rabi II 1070 A.H.), and a rebellion in Fez immediately followed. Sala rebelled two months later against its Dala'iyya governor. By now the Dala'iyya chief was no longer so certain of his own power as to be generous in his treatment of the rebellious people in Fez, and he had 100 of their leaders brought to the Middle Atlas where he put them to death.

The Dala'iyya sultan was able to bring Fez to recognize his authority once more but he avoided causing fresh disturbances by appointing a Berber to govern it. New Fez was placed under the authority of Abu 'Abdulla al-Duraidi, chief of Duraid, an Arabian tribe belonging to the Sharaqa group. Old Fez had a special regime in which two local chiefs shared power, and the *qadi* acted as arbiter in political conflicts. By 1662 the two cities of Fez were again in rebellion, and 'Abdulla, the former governor of Sala, was in vain trying to enter the city with a Berber army. But in September 1663, when Old Fez felt the heavy-handedness of the Duraid tribe and the pillage of another Arabian tribe, the Huyayna, living in the neighbourhood, its leaders voluntarily sought the imposition of direct Dala'iyya rule. By then Muhammad al-Hajj could no longer control al-Duraidi who had become a brigand-ruler scourging the countryside around Fez and Meknes. So he left Old Fez to fend for itself against the Arabian tribes as best it could. Sala simultaneously broke its last links with the Dala'iyya, and about the same time the 'Alawite *sharifs* intensified their activities in north-eastern Morocco.

The 'Alawites, 1668–1822

The 'Alawite *sharifs*, whose descendants still rule Morocco, came to Sijilmasa in the thirteenth century. By the beginning of the fifteenth they had started to establish a name in the country. One of them, 'Ali al-Sharif, took part in the wars against the Portuguese in Ceuta and in 1437 near

Tangier, and was invited by the Nasrids of Granada to join them for the purpose of holy war against the Castilians. But until the seventeenth century they had no defined political status. This they achieved as a result of the incursion into the oasis of Tafilalt of the armies of the two Berber principalities adjoining it, Abu Hassun's and the Dala'iyya. When Abu Hassun established a garrison in the oasis at the fort of Tabu'samt in 1631 and the Dala'iyya sent an army in the following year to assert their interests there and reinstate their allies, the Banu Zubair, in the fort, the 'Alawite Mawlay[1] al-Sharif assumed the role of defending the oasis and was recognized sultan by its religious chiefs. The *sharif* attacked Tabu'samt in 1635 or 1636 (A.H. 1045), trying to dislodge Abu Hassun's garrison. He failed, and was taken into exile in Sus where he spent the greater part of his remaining years. Abu Hassun treated the *sharif* well in exile, giving him among other gifts a Negro slave girl who bore him two sons, one of whom was the great sultan Mawlay Isma'il.

Mawlay al-Sharif exercised no more political influence after his exile. His son Muhammad al-Sharif remained in the oasis, and led its people in rebellion against Abu Hassun in 1640–1 (A.H.1050). He was able to drive out Abu Hassun's hated agents and have himself proclaimed sultan in place of his father. But the authority of the 'Alawites in Tafilalt remained overshadowed by the Dala'iyya who were in the 1640s at the zenith of their power. In 1646 the Dala'iyya in fact invaded Sijilmasa a second time and, having defeated Muhammad al-Sharif, forced him to recognize the semi-arid expanses between Sijilmasa and Dra'a as falling under their authority. Henceforth Muhammad al-Sharif was a sultan without a sultanate, a situation which spurred him on to begin the north-eastern expansion which was eventually to lead to the confrontation with the Dala'iyya in north-eastern Morocco. He penetrated with his warriors into the regions of Laghwat (Laghouat in southern Algeria) and of Tlemsen, and having made contact with the tribes of Banu Ma'qil and Saquna in the plains of Angad, he established a base for himself in Wajda. The Turks were incited by his activities to take interest in these neglected regions of Algeria and sent a column of troops to hunt down the *sharif* and his allies, forcing him to retreat to Sijilmasa. The *sharif* had no interest in a conflict with the Turks and so gave his promise to a legation from Algiers sent to him to Sijilmasa not to cross the Tafna river again except on terms of peace. In spite of his retreat before the Turks, the *sharif* was able later on to pose as a rival of the Dala'iyya, and the contacts he made in western Algeria proved useful when in June 1650 Old Fez broke out in its first rebellion against the Dala'iyya and closed its gates. In agreement with the Arabian tribes in the neighbourhood the leaders of Fez in this year sent an appeal to Muhammad

---

[1] This was a title given to all *sharifs*; it became a normal honorific name for the 'Alawite sultans.

al-Sharif to join them against the Dala'iyya. He reached and entered Fez in the same year, but as soon as the Dala'iyya army arrived the leaders of Fez requested him to leave, having realized that he did not possess the power to defend them against the Berbers.

The death of Mawlay al-Sharif in 1659 initiated a conflict between Muhammad al-Sharif and his brother Rashid, in which the latter was successful and to him therefore fell the realization of the family's ambitions. How this conflict started is not known. When his father died Rashid left Sijilmasa, fearing for his life from his brother, and went to the Dala'iyya capital in the Middle Atlas. It is not known what proposals he had to make to the Dala'iyya chief, but it is reported that the latter treated him well. Rashid moved around in the territories of north-eastern Morocco, passed some time in Fez, and eventually settled in Angad where he entered into an alliance with the Banu Ma'qil Arabs who had supported his brother, and with the Banu Yaznasin Berbers. In 1663 he was recognized sultan by these tribes and was in a position to benefit from the discomfiture of the Dala'iyya. About the same time Muhammad al-Sharif established a base in Azru. By now armed conflict between the two brothers who were waiting for the same political opportunities was unavoidable. Some time at the end of 1663 or early in 1664 Muhammad al-Sharif went to Angad to reassert his authority over the tribes now obeying his brother, but was defeated and killed.

Mawlay Rashid founded the 'Alawite state within less than a decade after his victory over his brother. By 1664 Dala'iyya authority had shrunk back to the Middle Atlas. The rest of the territory in the north-east, west, and north-west fell under the domination of the Arabian tribes. Apart from the tribes of Angad, Rashid won over the Sharaqa Arabs living in the vicinity of Fez, whose rebelliousness was partly the result of their exclusion from authority in the Dala'iyya period. By offering these Arabs a career under his banners Rashid was able to control them, and thereby earned the gratitude of the settled communities, and the instrument to impose his will on them. By the beginning of 1666 he had already established a base in Taza. Fez at first rejected his advances. In August 1666 he besieged it but withdrew in face of its people's fierce resistance. He returned after a year of campaigning in the Rif and making new allies. The leaders of Fez had in the meantime changed their mind and opened their gates to him without fighting. They seem to have feared at first that accepting his authority would mean a return to Arabian tribal rule. He was able to reassure them on this question, and when his wars of conquest ended he settled the Sharaqa Arabs in the lands between the Wargha river and the Sibu, after he had stationed them in the Khamis castle of Fez. The Dala'iyya were able to offer surprisingly little resistance when Rashid invaded their territory in June 1668, destroyed their capital, and took their chiefs captive. Marrakish was captured in the following month from 'Abdul-Karim al-Shabbani, the maternal uncle of the last Sa'dian sultan 'Abbas, who had usurped power in 1658 or 1659 (A.H. 1069).

The major problem which Morocco's rulers had faced since the sixteenth century was finding a stable military base for their authority. The loyalty of the tribes that Mawlay Rashid used in capturing power could be relied on only so long as they were allowed to form an exclusive and privileged segment of the population. To rely on them exclusively would make the sultan the victim of their whims, besides alienating other powerful groups in the country. Mawlay Isma'il, Rashid's half-brother who succeeded him in 1673, sought to solve the problem by the creation of a Negro army from the descendants of the slaves brought to Morocco since the days of Ahmad al-Mansur. The Negroes who were still in slavery were bought from their owners and enlisted together with freeborn Negroes in special 'Abid (black) regiments. This policy, which was especially attractive to the sultan because he himself was half-Negro, was a success since it produced a stable and reliable military basis for Mawlay Isma'il's authority. These soldiers were provided with Negro women and encouraged to have children so that at the end of his long reign Mawlay Isma'il had a black army estimated at 150,000 men. Negro boys were given special training from the age of ten, spending three years learning such crafts as carpentry, house-building, etc. and five more years receiving instruction in riding and the military arts. At the age of eighteen they would be formally enlisted in the fighting forces, at which time they were each given a wife from amongst Negro girls who had been trained in the domestic arts in the royal palaces.

During the first ten years of his reign Mawlay Isma'il, while building his army, constructed relatively formidable fortifications along the eastern borders of Morocco and the slopes of the Middle Atlas. Azru, Safru, Taza, Tawrirt, and Wajda became important military bases, supported by a chain of smaller forts extending from the Middle Atlas to the Mulawiyya. The advanced positions of Wajda and its supporting forts were garrisoned by Arabian warriors. 'Abid troops were stationed nearer home in Azru, Safru, Taza, and their supporting forts, while about half the effective force of the blacks, or about 70,000 men, were held in reserve in special barracks in or near the capital Meknes. These military arrangements clearly showed that the sultan feared encroachments from Algeria and the resurgence of some rival leadership amongst the Sanhajas of the Middle Atlas.

The dangers which prompted Mawlay Isma'il to undertake these military preparations were in fact real. Al-Khadr Ghailan, who fled to Algiers when Mawlay Rashid invaded northern Morocco, was brought by the Turks to Tatuan when Rashid died. He led a rebellion in the north in which the Naqsis leaders and Old Fez joined. The rebels recognized the authority of Ahmad b. Mahriz, Mawlay Isma'il's nephew, who had just occupied Marrakish and was recognized sultan by the tribes of Sus. This dangerous situation was brought under control when Mawlay Isma'il defeated and killed Ghailan in September 1673, and in the following month forced Fez to submit. Henceforth the Turks turned to stirring up trouble in the Middle Atlas through the Dala'iyya chiefs whom Mawlay Rashid had deported to Tlemsen. In 1677 Ahmad al-Dala'i, the grandson of the last Dala'iyya chief Muhammad al-Hajj, returned to the Middle Atlas with Turkish encouragement and possibly support too. In the course of the year his Sanhaja warriors drove out the sultan's troops from Tadla and defeated an expeditionary force sent against them. Ahmad was defeated in April 1678 on Wadi al-'Abid, where he brought the bulk of his warriors, hoping there and then to decide the political future of Morocco. But he remained at large moving freely in the Middle Atlas until his mysterious death at the beginning of 1680.

The pacification of Morocco reached its maximum limit with the defeat and death of Ahmad b. Mahriz near Tarudant in 1686. The Naqsis chiefs of Tatuan, who had taken refuge with the Spaniards in Ceuta since 1673 and hoped for Ahmad b. Mahriz' victory, hurried to Marrakish offering their submission to Mawlay Isma'il when the death of the rebel became known. Mawlay Isma'il had them taken to Tatuan and there put to death. From this date the only parts of the country remaining dissident were the higher parts of the High Atlas, but the dissidence of these regions did not constitute a political threat or disturb life in the cities or the greater part of the countryside.

Law and order were established in Morocco by brutal means. The sultan had criminals killed in the most cruel ways, and no mercy was shown to a vanquished rebel or political opponent. But in Morocco at the time and for more than a century later the possession of the means of suppression by a reigning sultan was the only alternative to anarchy and civil strife. Mawlay Isma'il's cruelty was denounced by both European and Moroccan historians, but the latter could also appreciate its advantages. The nineteenth century historian al-Nasiri could thus give credit to Mawlay Isma'il for the security of the roads which enabled a woman or a Jew to travel alone across the country without being molested. He noted that there was general prosperity during Mawlay Isma'il's reign, an abundance of cheap food, and an active internal trade. But he added that "the people of Morocco became like the fellahs of Egypt, toiling and paying [taxes] every week, month, and year. And any one of them who reared a horse hoping to ride it had to give it to the governor [of his province] together with ten *mithqals* [of gold] for the price of its saddle."[1]

[1] Al-Nasiri, Ahmad b. Khalid, *Kitab al-Istiqsa' li akhbar duwal al-Maghrib al-aqsa*, VII (Casablanca, 1956), 97.

Prosperity and stability apart, what made the harshness of Mawlay Isma'il's rule more palatable to Moroccan than to European writers was the fact that he used the country's military power against hated outsiders. The xenophobia of the Moroccans, nurtured by years of Turkish and Christian threats, received an outlet in the sultan's foreign policies. He replied to Turkish encroachment by sending his forces into Algerian territory on three occasions: in 1679, 1682, and 1695 or 1696 (A.H. 1107). These expeditions were not designed to conquer Algerian territory, but to deter further Turkish interference in Moroccan affairs. They all ended in the renewal of peace on the condition that existing frontiers be preserved.

Relations with Europe were more complex because of the religious nature of the confrontation combined with the fact that the sultan could not do without dealings with Europeans. Christians to Mawlay Isma'il, more than to any Moroccan sultan since the days of the Almoravids, were the enemies of the country and the faith. But since he needed European manufactured goods he had to allow Christian merchants to trade in Morocco. And since he could not recover the remaining positions still held in the country by Spain (Ceuta, Malila, Peñon de Velez, and Alhucemas), England (Tangier), and Portugal (Mazagan), without the help of other European countries, he went so far as to seek a military alliance with France. A draft treaty providing for a secret military alliance was in fact drawn up in 1681 at al-Ma'mura, but it came to nothing because of Louis XIV's unwillingness to ratify it. However, in 1682 Louis XIV allowed a treaty to be concluded with the sultan's ambassador in Paris, Muhammad Tamim, dealing with questions of commerce and piracy. But the value of such a treaty was small in view of the sultan's encouragment of piracy.

Up to a point piracy and commerce were not mutually exclusive in this period. In Sala and Tatuan, where the pirates had their bases, the European merchants had their more important houses. But the uncertainties of commercial activities remained great, especially after piracy became a state enterprise towards the end of the seventeenth century, with the sultan himself owning half the vessels operating from Moroccan ports. Together with the taxes levied on the profits of pirates working on their own, this meant that about sixty per cent of the pirates' gains went to the sultan's coffers. Consequently European commercial activities, which were resumed in the late 1660s after the short interval caused by the conflicts of Sala with the Dala'iyya, started again to decline from the beginning of the eighteenth century.

Nor were the continuous attacks of the sultan's warriors on the Christian positions in Morocco conducive to the development of commercial relations. These attacks were pursued more systematically than the attacks led by al-'Ayyashi. Tangier was besieged continually from 1678. The difficulties this caused to its garrison, and the mounting cost of developing its port, led the English to evacuate it in 1684 after blowing up its un-finished mole and the principal buildings. Larashe was conquered from the Spaniards in 1689 after a siege of three months, but the Spanish positions on the Mediterranean were able to resist the continuous attacks on them.

Meknes, the town Mawlay Isma'il governed during his brother's reign, became the capital of the 'Alawite state when he acceded to the throne. He liked its fresh air and pure water, but his decision to make it the capital seems to have been inspired by considerations of political stability and security as well. As has been suggested earlier Mawlay Isma'il avoided dependence on any tribal grouping by making the 'Abid army the mainstay of his power. To settle in either Fez or Marrakish would have identified the sultanate with the interests of one group of the country's established elite and their tribal allies to the exclusion of the other. In making Meknes the capital and, therefore, the main centre of military concentration, its geographical location was also an important factor. It was more central than either Fez or Marrakish, more removed than Fez from the main line of access to Morocco from Algeria, and better situated than the latter for directing operations against the Sanhaja and for guarding the main route leading to the south via Tadla. Mawlay Isma'il transformed Meknes by his large palace and four new major mosques into a regal and religious city. The Jews living in it were moved to a suburb outside it, and their houses were given to the people who had migrated with Mawlay Rashid from Sijilmasa and been settled in Fez.

The isolation from the Maghrib and the rest of the Muslim world since the sixteenth century resulted in the emergence of a characteristically Moroccan social and political outlook. Political authority was wielded in the absence of a caliph by a *sharif* whose exercise of power was rendered legitimate not so much by safeguarding the Muslim law, as Muslim political theory required, but by the mysterious spiritual gifts which his descent from the Prophet was supposed to give him. While the sultan was the centre of the cult of the mysterious in the country's social and political life, other *sharifs* and the Sufi *shaikhs* formed the focus of this cult on the local level. *Sharifs* and Sufi *shaikhs* led public opinion, moulded the intellectual outlook, and formed social habits. The spokesmen of the Moroccan Muslim community were thus no more the *'ulama*, whose train-ing in the law and the principles of its interpretation and application rendered them relatively rational and intellectually responsible. This shift in the nature of leadership was reflected in intellectual life in the emphasis in the teaching curricula on imitation and the blind obedience to authority characteristic of the Sufi method. On a political level this meant that the authority of the sultan could not be challenged by a powerful class of *'ulama* conscious of its duty before God to uphold the Muslim law against the whims of an unjust ruler. The *sharifs* as sultans demanded obedience to their persons, and the lesser *sharifs* and Sufi *shaikhs* taught the masses to obey and trust them even when they acted in apparent contradiction of the law.

Mawlay Isma'il was an effective ruler because his outlook tallied with that of his people, and because he was able to develop the military instrument to substantiate his demand for obedience. In so doing, and through holding power for so long, he confirmed the existing social and political pattern. When he died Morocco had no stable bureaucracy or recognized representative bodies that could ensure continuity in the government of the country. This negative political legacy implied that the existence of effective government depended on a new sultan's ability to develop the military means of having his authority obeyed. Most of Mawlay Isma'il's successors to the end of the nineteenth century were unable to achieve this. Consequently the discordant tribal constitution of the society and the strong local particularisms plunged the country into continuous political strife and led sometimes to chaos. Like Mawlay Isma'il his successors were in theory absolute rulers, but most of them were in fact unable to rule more than a part of Morocco. Hence a uniquely Moroccan political concept came into circulation: *blad al-siba* (the lands of no authority) to refer to those parts of Morocco which the sultan could not control, as distinct from *blad al-makhzan* (the government lands).

In the century which followed Mawlay Isma'il's death in 1727 the central question in Moroccan history was, therefore, how much authority could a reigning sultan bring to bear upon the task of ruling the country. All other questions, economic, intellectual, and social, seemed to depend on it. On one thing the Moroccans seemed agreed in this period, namely that they had no more eligible rulers than the 'Alawite *sharifs*, in whose gift of *baraka* (blessing) they put much trust to guide the rulers and bring blessings upon the country. But as Mawlay Isma'il left about 500 male children all endowed with *baraka*, and therefore fit to rule, this belief did not contribute to stability. On the contrary it accentuated conflicts, since many *sharifs* were available to claim power, and most of them could find tribal or religious groups prepared to back their ambitions for the sake of political aggrandizement.

Fez remained in this century an important centre of Morocco's political life since its attitudes reflected the interests of the urban and settled population in the north. But it was in Meknes, where the 'Abid troops were concentrated, that most of the changes of sultans were initiated in the first thirty years which followed Mawlay Isma'il's death. The 'Abid, after being the bulwark of stability, became the source of much of the disorder in this period. Their leaders were the chief viziers, and as they controlled the only relatively disciplined and well-trained force in the country, they became also the king-makers. They appointed as sultans and deposed seven of Mawlay Isma'il's sons between 1727 and 1757, keeping a new sultan only as long as he was able to meet their financial demands. But as their control of the sultanate left it no authority outside the area of Meknes, the taxes could not be collected, and the demands of the troops could not be satisfied. These consequently resorted to looting any person of wealth within their reach. During the reign of Mawlay Muhammad (August 1737–May 1738) the ravages of the 'Abid and the economic chaos which ensued are said to have caused the death from starvation of over 80,000 people in one month. The figure seems too high, but it nevertheless points to the great plight which afflicted the country in this period of disorder.

The disintegration of public life was arrested temporarily by Mawlay 'Abdulla, who was first appointed sultan by the 'Abid with the concurrence of Fez in April 1729. After this date he was effectively deposed three times by the 'Abid, who each time appointed one of his brothers in his place. Unlike other deposed sultans in this period Mawlay 'Abdulla was able to start an effective movement of opposition to the black troops through the loyal support of the Wadaya Arabs. At this time the Wadaya controlled New Fez, but as they were constantly at loggerheads with Old Fez, their support at the beginning did not enable Mawlay 'Abdulla to consolidate his authority, although it kept him a viable contender for the sultanate. In this period of chaos the leaders of Old Fez could ensure some relative security for their town from the Wadaya and the 'Abid through an alliance with the Sanhaja Berbers of the Middle Atlas, especially the tribes of Ait Idrasin. Mawlay 'Abdulla could create a substantial base for his authority only when he could bring Old Fez and Ait Idrasin together with the Wadaya under his leadership. This became possible as a consequence of the intrusion on the regions of Meknes and Fez of tribal forces from the north led by Ahmad b. 'Ali al-Rifi.

The chieftaincy led by Ahmad b. 'Ali until 1743 emerged as the dominant force in the north under his father 'Ali during Mawlay Isma'il's reign. From the relatively important position of governor of Tatuan, 'Ali augmented his power as a result of taking an active part in the siege of Tangier and being allowed to annex this town to his authority when it was evacuated by the English in 1684. Tangier was henceforth the capital of this chieftaincy, which under Ahmad became virtually independent. Ahmad prospered through foreign trade and monopolizing the supply of provisions to the English at Gibraltar, through whom he also obtained the arms and ammunition which made his forces unrivalled in the region. In 1727 the sultan Mawlay Ahmad tried to break Ahmad b. 'Ali's monopoly of contacts with the English by appointing a governor of Tatuan directly responsible to himself. But this arrangement did not work for long, since Ahmad b. 'Ali was able to occupy the town and even force this sultan to allow him to choose the ambassadors he sent abroad. After holding aloof from the political conflicts which centred around the appointment and removal of sultans in Meknes, Ahmad b. 'Ali became entangled in the affairs of Mawlay al-Mustadi' whom the 'Abid installed as sultan in May 1738. Al-Mustadi' secured Ahmad b. 'Ali's cooperation by giving formal sanction to his authority in the north including Tatuan. When the 'Abid deposed al-Mustadi' in January 1740 in order to reappoint Mawlay 'Abdulla, Ahmad began to work for his reinstatement. Having prevailed in 1741 upon the 'Abid to depose Mawlay 'Abdulla for the third time, he invaded the territory of Fez, where Mawlay 'Abdulla was under the protection of the Wadaya, for the purpose of crushing opposition to his protégé.

The grand alliance which Mawlay 'Abdulla was able to form comprising the Wadaya, Old Fez, and Ait Idrasin to counter this invasion achieved the purpose of destroying the northern chieftaincy. Ahmad b. 'Ali was twice defeated in 1743, and in the second encounter which occurred on Wadi Lukkus he himself was killed. Mawlay 'Abdulla used his victorious allies to put down other recalcitrant tribes in the western plains and make his authority accepted in the coastal towns. His son Muhammad used the enhanced prestige of his father to establish himself in Marrakish as viceroy, and even the 'Abid army in Meknes was brought to heel. But from 1749, when Mawlay 'Abdulla could no longer reconcile the ambitions of the Berbers with those of the Wadaya, he once more became a helpless spectator of another spate of disorder. From this date until his death in 1757 he lived under the protection of the Wadaya in Dar al-Dubaibigh near Fez, and only the refusal of his son Muhammad to accept the nomination of the 'Abid enabled him to retain the title of sultan.

The sultans who followed Mawlay 'Abdulla – his sons Mawlay Muhammad (1757–90) and Mawlay Yazid (1790–2), his grandson Mawlay Sulaiman (1792–1822) and the latter's nephew Mawlay 'Abdul-Rahman (1822–59) – had all to reconquer Morocco before they could rule it. With the exception of Mawlay Yazid they all achieved relative success in this reconquest, and gave the country a period of stability which lasted until the tribal groupings recovered from the political exhaustion resulting from the conflicts which ushered in the new reign. Consequently the last years of every reign were nearly as bloody as the opening ones. The 'Abid ceased to be able to play a decisive political role from about the middle of the eighteenth century. The resources they obtained from looting were insufficient for maintaining their large numbers, and consequently they dispersed. In the Middle Atlas the 'Abid troops were driven out from the forts they had garrisoned by the Berbers, who enslaved many of them with their families. Both Mawlay Muhammad b. 'Abdulla and Mawlay Sulaiman built up 'Abid armies, but their effective force was prudently kept small. The weakening of the central authority created a durable threat to the 'Alawite sultans in the presence of the Sanhaja Berber tribes near their main towns. With the removal of the restraining power of the 'Abid troops from the Middle Atlas the Sanhajas advanced westward: Ait Idrasin dominated the region of Fez and Azammur, and Gharwan reached the region of Azru and then advanced at the beginning of the nineteenth century to the Atlantic plains to the north of al-Ma'mura. Further south the Z'ayyin Berbers came to dominate the area between Khanifra and the ocean. These migrations accentuated the tribal character of political conflicts and rendered the task of maintaining order even in the plains dependent on ephemeral tribal submission to the reigning sultan.

The cultural and political patterns of the Moroccan society altered little in the century following Mawlay Isma'il's death. Mawlay Muhammad b. 'Abdulla and Mawlay Sulaiman attempted to revive the influence of the *'ulama* and counter the fatalistic character of the Sufi tradition, but achieved little success. Muhammad b. 'Abdulla's scholarly interest in the law and the classification of the Prophetic traditions left no noticeable impact on the state of learning in the country, and Sulaiman's attacks on the Sufi orders succeeded only in suppressing some of the more blatant aberrations in the conduct of their festivities but could not alter the attitude of mind from which the popularity of the Sufi way of life sprang. Both these sultans were aware that unity and stability could not be achieved in Morocco without reviving the regulative function of the Muslim law. Their failure, which was possibly inevitable, meant that no accepted system for settling political problems other than force could be evolved. And in the absence of such a system the centripetal forces remained inadequate to cope with local and group particularism.

The renewed European scramble for influence in the area which followed the French conquest of Algeria extended to Morocco. It came when the country was ill-prepared to face it. Technologically backward, its central government was furthermore unable to control the reaction of the various centres of power in the country to foreign encroachment when it occurred. The result was that European agents could always find a group ready to serve their interests or by its conduct undermine any aspect of foreign policy the sultan might consider advantageous. How this affected Morocco's future will be discussed in detail in the next chapter.

9

The Maghrib in the age of aggressive European colonialism, 1830–1914

The French attack on Algiers in 1830 had limited and ambiguous aims. Yet it set into motion forces which its initiators could not control, and which within twenty years made the French rulers of the whole of Algeria. The French installation in this country in turn had far-reaching effects on the development of French colonial ambitions in the rest of the Maghrib. It also, more than any other single factor, spurred on and coloured the major socio-political transformations which occurred in the region during the nineteenth century.

After 1830 the character of relations between the rulers of Tunisia, Morocco, and Tripolitania and the European powers underwent a change. The consuls of these powers emerged as centres of authority, using the weakness of the local rulers or their need for protection in order to advance the economic interests of their nationals at the expense of others, and by their ability to interfere in the functioning of the local administrations they fought with one another for prestige. The rulers of the Maghrib relied on compromise, concessions, and the rivalries between the powers to escape from being totally dominated by one of them. As long as the three European countries interested in the region, Britain, France, and Italy, were unable to agree on their respective zones of influence, France could not expand outside Algeria. But after 1878, when Britain gave up her policy of safeguarding the territorial integrity of the Ottoman empire, and by her occupation of Cyprus started the bargaining with France and Italy over the colonial prizes each was to obtain in North Africa, the Maghriban countries were no longer able to benefit from Europe's quarrels to remain independent.

Internally the increased European encroachment on the life of the Muslims was met in ways determined by inbred cultural and political reflexes. The Moroccan tribes met it in their usual way of rebelling against the authority of their 'Alawite sultans when they proved incapable of checking the Europeans. The Tunisians, who had a longer tradition of dealing with Europe and were simultaneously threatened by the Ottomans, tried through borrowing ideas from the west to reform the social and political structure of their society to render it more resilient to foreign pressures. The Tripolitanians for the first time accepted the harsh rule of the Ottomans as the only remaining means of warding off the Christians, and the Cyrenaican tribes to the east sought refuge in their desert lands and the mystical teachings of the Sanusiyya. In the end both negative and positive responses proved equally useless in preventing foreign rule. But since European rule failed to stamp out the Muslim character of the Maghriban society, and since by their exploitation, exclusiveness, and sometimes racism the European settlers caused the Muslims to rise above their traditional divisions, the foreign rulers generated the forces that were in the twentieth century to lead the Maghrib into political liberation.

The emergence of French Algeria

On 29 April 1827 the dey of Algiers, Husain, struck the French consul Pierre Deval on the face with a fly-swatter. This insult to the representative of France in the regency started a crisis in relations between the two countries as a result of which the French government stumbled upon one of its most important colonial ventures.

The background of the insult meted out to Deval might perhaps have justified the action. Husain Dey inherited when he came to power in 1818 a financial problem in the relations between the regency of Algiers and France dating back to the Napoleonic era. Between 1793 and 1798 Algerian wheat was bought for the French army through two Algerian Jewish merchant families, Bakri and Bushnaq. The arrears in the payment for this wheat amounted in 1798 to about eight million francs. The dey became entangled in this affair because the Jewish merchants were in debt to the Algerian government and claimed inability to repay their debts until reimbursed by the French. Deval, appointed consul in Algiers in 1815, did not seem capable of or interested in bringing the diplomatic wrangle over the debts to a speedy and amicable conclusion, especially since the dey suspected him of collaborating with Jacob Bakri to the detriment of his interests. The dey's suspicions were confirmed when no provision was made for his debts in a settlement adopted by the French government in 1820, although he made formal claims on the money owing to Jacob Bakri. The dey's hostility to Deval was confirmed as a result of the activities of the latter's nephew Alexandre Deval, the French vice-consul in Bona since 1825. Contrary to the agreements under which the French merchants operated in the regency, Alexandre Deval had the French factories in Bona and La Calle fortified and provided with cannons. The discussion between the dey and Pierre Deval on 29 April 1827 was thus the culmination of a long period of friction. On that occasion the dey was especially angered by the consul's statement that his government would not deign to reply to his letters dealing with the debts.

The French government at first resorted to traditional methods of handling a crisis, methods which were not unusual in the dealings of European consuls with the Maghriban rulers. The dey was asked to make reparations for the insult by a gun salute to the French flag when hoisted at the Qasba of Algiers. When the dey refused to comply, possibly with the encouragement of the British consul, the French government ordered a blockade of Algerian ports on 16 June. As the blockade did not prevent Algerian corsairs from their freedom of action even against French merchant ships, it failed to bring the dey to submission. At the same time the merchants of Marseilles clamoured for the ending of a blockade from which they themselves were suffering most. The French government tried to find a face-saving device for ending the senseless crisis by having the commander of the squadron blockading Algiers ask the dey in August 1829 to send a plenipotentiary to Paris to conclude an armistice. As the dey's reply was to have a few cannon-shots fired at the commander's flagship, the French government felt compelled to act.

A French military attack on Algiers was still ruled out even after the incident of August 1829. In its place the prime minister Polignac started to work towards having the Maghriban regencies annexed to Muhammad 'Ali's Egypt. Polignac envisaged a plan of creating a strong Arab state ruled by France's ally Muhammad 'Ali, thereby ensuring French dominance over the southern shores of the Mediterranean and accelerating the disintegration of the Ottoman empire, which the British were working to preserve, without France assuming the burdens of governing Algeria. But by 1829 internal pressure on the French government to send a French expedition to Algiers was becoming sufficiently strong to make Polignac modify the plan soon after it was accepted by Muhammad 'Ali in October. In November he proposed to Muhammad 'Ali that his troops should conquer the regencies of Tripolitania and Tunisia only, leaving the conquest of Algeria to the French. This modified plan Muhammad 'Ali rejected outright, on the grounds that it would undermine his political standing in the Muslim world by making him the recognized instrument of French expansion into Muslim lands.

Pressure on the French government to undertake the conquest of Algiers came from two directions. In the first place there were the ardent monarchists, represented in the cabinet by the minister of war Bourmont, who were seeking glory for the royal army. Secondly there were the commercial circles, especially in Marseilles, whose trade was made stagnant by the blockade of the Algerian ports and the Graeco-Ottoman War, and who looked upon the conquest of Algiers as a means of revitalizing trade. The deputy of Marseilles in the Chamber of Deputies, Roux, had begun in May 1828 a campaign in favour of the conquest of Algiers, and since 1829 he was supported by Thomas, Marseilles' second deputy. To these influences was added the political conflict between the king and the opposition in the Chamber of Deputies over the limits of the royal prerogative. The opposition were predominantly hostile to the invasion of Algiers which they thought would be an economic liability to France. Nevertheless the more the king felt unable to curb the tide of liberalism the more attractive the idea of a distracting military venture seemed. Charles X announced the decision to invade Algiers on 2 March 1830 when opening the new session of the Chamber of Deputies which he later dissolved. Henceforth a quick victory in Algiers, as Bourmont who led the expedition announced in May 1830 in Toulon, was considered the means for ensuring the victory of the royal party in the elections which were to take place in July.

In military and financial terms the expedition produced quick results, but it failed to achieve its political purpose. On 5 July Husain Dey capitulated. Having signed a convention with Bourmont giving France sovereignty over the whole of the Ottoman pashalik of Algeria, he left the country and settled in Naples. He was able to take with him only 30,000 golden sequins, a small part of his immense personal wealth. It is estimated that one hundred million francs reached France from Algiers in 1830, obtained from the dey's captured treasures and looting of private property. Only about half this sum reached the treasury, roughly equivalent to the cost of the expedition. The rest was pocketed by officers and other personnel who took part in the invasion. Politically the attack on Algiers failed: the elections returned a Chamber of Deputies with a two-thirds majority for the opposition, and the demonstrations in Paris on the 27–29 July eventually forced Charles X to abdicate on 2 August. Bourmont, whose forces had already occupied Bona and Oran, hastened to withdraw the troops from both towns when he learned on 11 August of Charles X's downfall. He planned to lead his men back to France to restore his monarch. Having found, however, that the lower ranks in the army were not willing to cooperate in this venture, he left his command and went into voluntary exile in Spain.

The Polignac government had decided in July 1830 to retain Algiers when conquered, contrary to assurances given to the other powers when the decision to attack it was taken in March that the aim of the expedition was merely to suppress piracy and slavery in the regency, and that they would be consulted about the country's future. Beyond this decision the French command in Algiers received little guidance from Paris as to the arrangements that were to be made for the rest of the country. Clauzel, who took up the command vacated by Bourmont in 1830, could thus use the absence of specific directions to evolve his own policy. He carried out negotiations with the bey of Tunis to establish Tunisian princes as rulers of Constantine and Oran under French sovereignty, and initiated a policy of colonization in the region of Algiers. Official circles in France became much concerned about the negotiations with the bey because they involved a conflict of jurisdiction between the army and the ministry for foreign affairs; but the policy of colonization he initiated, which had a more durable effect on the Algerian situation, went scarcely noticed at the time.

In the absence of a civil authority in Algiers to check the power of the army, Clauzel pursued his policy of colonization without restraint. He acquired three plots of land on his own account on which he intended to settle colonists, and he encouraged the foundation of a joint-stock company called "Ferme expérimental d'Afrique" to exploit 1,000 hectares of land near Maison-Carrée leased at a nominal annual rate of one franc per hectare. The speculative practices initiated by Clauzel, which his successor Berthezène tried unsuccessfully to stop, resulted in the following ten years in large-scale European colonization in the hinterland of Algiers and the Mitidja plain. The French historian C.-A. Julien believes that it was the influence of these early settlers, more than military debacles, that caused Berthezène's removal from his command in December 1831.[1] His successor Rovigo was given a civil superintendent named Pichon to lay the foundations of a civil administration of Algiers and to check the abuses of the military. This worthy civil servant found himself harassed by the settlers and his directions ignored by the commander. When after much friction with the army command and the settlers Pichon was recalled in May 1832, his successor was placed under the authority of the commander-in-chief. Rovigo was thus given a free hand. He converted the Fisheries mosque into a cathedral, and he destroyed two Muslim cemeteries for the purpose of building a road. Both acts clearly ran against the solemn undertakings Bourmont had given in August 1830 to respect the Muslim religion, and they could be carried out only by the use of force.

In the 1830s and 40s political circles in France were engaged in a lively public debate as to whether the colonization of Algeria was desirable and what shape it should take. The central issues discussed were the advantages which France would derive from ruling Algeria, the price she would have to pay in terms of money and endangering her security in Europe by committing large forces to the Algerian enterprise, and the fate of the indigenous population. The debate reflected the main currents of French thought at the time, but they are of no great significance to the history of Algeria because they hardly influenced French policy there. This policy was shaped predominantly and from the earliest period in the Algerian enterprise by two important factors: first, by the settlement of Frenchmen in Algeria who were eager to possess land and, as suggested earlier, were able to exert pressure on the French government; secondly, the assessment by

[1] Julien, *Histoire de l'Algérie contemporaine*, p. 87.

the military commanders (who until 1847 were able to evolve their own policies and defy the wishes of the French government) of the course of action best suited to serve French interests in Algeria.

Until 1840 the official French policy in Algeria was described as *occupation restreinte* (limited occupation). This meant that the French would occupy the main towns of the Algerian hinterland, and exercise sovereignty over the rest of the country through native or Turkish rulers. This policy took concrete shape in 1834 when the position of governor-general for Algeria was created (22 July), the first French agreement with Amir 'Abdul-Qadir concluded (26 February), and when the French were trying to bring the last remaining representative of Turkish rule in Algeria, Ahmad Bey of Constantine, to accept French sovereignty. The policy of limited occupation failed because it was incompatible with two dynamic elements in the Algerian situation: the implacable hostility of Algerian Muslims to Christian rule, and the uncontrollable ambitions aroused in a technically advanced community having political control over a less advanced society.

The creation of the position of governor-general for Algeria reflected the growing colonial entrenchment on the coast. The Tunisian regime initiated by Clauzel in Oran ended in failure in September 1831, and the French had to assume direct control of this town and defend it in face of the Moroccan penetration of the western region and the emergence of a centre of resistance around Amir 'Abdul-Qadir. Bona and Bougie, which had been evacuated by Bourmont in August 1830, were reoccupied in March 1832 and September 1833 respectively. In the region of Algiers itself the colonization of the Mitidja plain progressed rapidly in the period of Voirol's command (March 1833 to September 1834) and French control was strengthened by the creation of a military base at Blida in which 6,000 troops were stationed. In these coastal regions under French control the governor-general was to exercise the powers of military commander and head of the civil administration. A decree of 1 September 1834 gave him the power to draw up a budget for the colony, supervise public works and instruction, and administer justice. This decree also provided for separate judicial systems for the Muslims and Jews. But the irreversible character of French rule was affirmed by the stipulation that only those indigenous institutions compatible with French domination would be preserved.

The first reaction of the Algerian Muslims when faced with the Christian French invasion was to seek the help of their traditional Muslim protectors. While in the region of Constantine Ahmad Bey held out and became the symbol of Muslim defiance to the French in the name of the Ottoman sultan, the Muslim leaders of Tlemsen turned towards Morocco for help. Mawlay 'Abdul-Rahman was wary of involvement in a conflict with the French, but internal popular pressure left him no choice. From the end of 1830 he had a *khalifa* (deputy) in Tlemsen who made contacts with the tribes and with the help of those Sufi orders who had opposed the Turks, the Tijaniyya and Tayyibiyya, roused the Algerians to resist the new invaders. He established an administrative base at Mascara (Mu'askar), his agents were able to operate in Midia and Miliana, and from October 1831 his forces also made attacks on Oran. However, French pressure on Mawlay 'Abdul-Rahman led him to agree in March 1832 to withdraw his agents and troops from Algeria. The Algerian tribes, left to fend for themselves, had no agency of cohesion and coordination other than the Sufi orders. Immediately after the Moroccan withdrawal Muhyi al-Din of the Hashim tribe and *shaikh* of the Qadiriyya, the most influential Sufi order in the country, was recognized leader of the tribal *jihad* against the French. From May 1832 he was leading attacks on Oran. But as he was old and weak, his son 'Abdul-Qadir led the tribal warriors who obeyed him. Later in the year 'Abdul-Qadir was recognized sultan by the tribes of Hashim, Banu 'Amir, and the Gharaba branch of Awlad Sidi al-Shaikh.

The appearance of Amir 'Abdul-Qadir as a leader of the resistance marks the extension of the conflict with the French to involve the tribal pastoral communities after it had been limited mainly to the urban centres. When drawn into conflict with the people of the interior the French could not avoid extending their involvement, especially since the religious character of the amir's leadership excluded permanent co-existence with them. The amir's letters to the *mufti* of Fez 'Ali b. 'Abdul-Rahman al-Tasuli revived the juridical argument that Muslims who cooperated with non-Muslims engaged in war with a Muslim prince lapsed from the faith, and when defeated by Muslims they could be treated as infidels. This meant that their property could be confiscated, their men put to death, and their women and children enslaved. This position was dictated more by the amir's understanding of the nature of the Algerian tribal society than by unanimity amongst Muslim jurists over this controversial question. Their sustained support depended on the amir's ability to use force against the recalcitrant amongst the tribes and to justify its use by arguments which they could understand. The support of the Qadiriyya order gave the amir a good start. His command of the loyalty of the Algerian tribes depended on his successes against the French and his ability to chastize his tribal opponents.

It was because of this psychological factor in the amir's dealings with the tribes that his first agreement with the French was also important. The amir followed the fluctuations of French policies and public opinion over the Algerian question through French newspapers and his own agents and informants, some of whom were French, in the French occupied towns of Algeria and in France itself. He understood the dilemma which the French faced regarding the future of Algeria, and seems to have seen in it his opportunity for the consolidation of his hold over the province of

Oran. An agreement with the French would have the dual benefit of affording him respite from hostilities and enabling him to pose *vis-à-vis* the Algerian tribes in the role of a sovereign recognized by the French. On 26 February 1834 the commander of the French forces in Oran, General Desmichels, concluded with him an agreement which recognized his authority over the territory in the district of Oran outside the towns controlled by the French, namely Oran, Arzu (Arzew), and Mustaghanim. Desmichels acted in the spirit of the policy of limited occupation, but apparently without instructions from his government. It was later discovered that in order to have the French government accept the *fait accompli* with which he presented them, he deliberately had the concessions he had made to the amir glossed over in the French text of the agreement. The Arabic text stated that the amir could appoint consuls in the towns held by the French (the French text spoke of representatives), which implied a recognition of the amir's sovereignty. Of importance too was that Desmichels, interested in establishing law and order in the Oranian hinterland, provided the amir with arms and ammunition to be used in subduing the tribes that refused to accept his authority.

Although the French government accepted the Desmichels agreement, and the official French policy for Algeria remained that of limited occupation, Marshal Clauzel, governor-general between July 1835 and February 1837, tried to undermine both by his attacks on the amir and Constantine. He was irritated by the amir's enterprising plans of establishing a monopoly of commercial relations with European countries without channelling this trade through Oran, although the amir's right to do so was recognized by the Desmichels agreement. On 6 December 1835 Clauzel attacked Mascara, the amir's capital. 'Abdul-Qadir had evacuated it the day before, and so Clauzel withdrew from it two days later after setting fire to it. On 13 January 1836 he led a similar expedition to Tlemsen, on the pretext that the *kouloughlis* in it sought French help against the Arabs. He occupied the town and established a garrison in it, but the extortionist methods he used for levying the cost of the expedition from the *kouloughlis* caused much consternation in political circles in France. The change of government in Paris in 1836 saved Clauzel, who by this time had announced his intention to invade Constantine which was still held by Ahmad Bey. Thiers' cabinet, considering it politically imprudent to prevent the expedition to Constantine, nevertheless did not send Clauzel the reinforcements for which he asked. Clauzel in anger went ahead with the expedition. The army was dispatched on 13 November 1836, and suffered such hardships on the way, including having to march in snow-storms, that many soldiers cut short their suffering by committing suicide. On 21 November 8,700 exhausted and badly provisioned troops arrived before Constantine. After two attempts to take the town by storm failed, the troops retreated, abandoning their baggage and wounded, on the 23rd. They were pursued by Muslim warriors until they reached Bona a week later. The French lost in this expedition about a thousand men.

Although the French government remained inclined towards a policy of indirect rule in the interior of Algeria, it announced its decision to avenge the debacle of Constantine. The new governor-general Damremont was instructed to prepare a second expedition against the town, while entering into negotiations with Ahmad Bey with a view to securing his recognition of French sovereignty. At the same time General Bugeaud, who in the previous year had led a column of troops bringing provisions to the garrison in Tlemsen and defeated Amir 'Abdul-Qadir in an encounter at Sikkak on his way back, was directed to negotiate a peace treaty with him. On 20 May 1837 the French and the amir signed the Treaty of Tafna which redefined the boundaries between the territory held by the amir and the localities under French control. With Ahmad Bey the French found it more difficult to come to terms: the bey, who was used to the remote control of the Ottoman sultan, did not find the prospect of the stricter and politically compromising authority of the French attractive. In July 1837 he nearly signed a treaty which the French proposed to him, but when he was informed that the Ottoman fleet was approaching he changed his mind. In fact the Ottoman fleet was prevented from going west of Tripoli by a French naval squadron. On 13 October 1837 the French captured Constantine, but went on trying to persuade Ahmad Bey to accept French sovereignty in return for restitution. As the bey understood this to mean that the French were going to abandon the town in any case, he counted on regaining control of it without submitting to French control. In the meantime Valée, who became governor-general immediately after the fall of Constantine (Damremont was killed in the assault), established a degree of indirect control in the province. The French troops were maintained in isolated camps and instructed not to interfere unnecessarily in the life of the people in whose midst they lived. But as more troops were sent into Algeria, and money was invested in building barracks, roads, and hospitals for the army, the French commitment in it increased, without any alteration in the official policy of limited occupation.

Amir 'Abdul-Qadir used the two-and-a-half years which followed the signature of the Treaty of Tafna to penetrate the province of Constantine and enforce his authority over the tribes in the west and south of Algeria who still rejected it. In the second half of 1837 he campaigned in the region of Tittari, and in the summer of 1838 started to besiege 'Ain Madi, the main centre of the Tijaniyya order. The leaders of this order had a quarrel with 'Abdul-Qadir's tribe dating back to 1827. As the amir also identified his authority with a rival Sufi order, and the Tijani leaders had their own political ambitions, they refused to recognize him as ruler. In fact French reports spoke of them from 1833 as potential substitutes for the amir as native rulers of the distict of Oran. The amir took 'Ain Madi after a siege of five months, but the Tijanis still opposed his authority. Instead they entered in 1839 into an alliance with the French, and from 1841 led a group of Muslim dignitaries who called upon the Algerian Muslims to accept French rule. Nevertheless the peace of Tafna enabled the amir to consolidate his rule in the greater part of the districts of Oran and Tittari and to establish his government in them.

The amir's system of government was well suited to the tribal structure of the society. He himself held supreme authority over a federal-like structure of tribes. His *khalifas* (deputies) governed the major districts under his control, but the immediate control of the tribes was left to their chiefs who received from the amir the title of *agha*. Each *agha*, however, was provided with a supervisor from amongst the amir's trusted men, who directed the military activities of the tribal warriors and collected the canonical taxes. The amir's revenue came predominantly from the taxes and his monopoly of trade in the territories he controlled. His army and his central government were both mobile. After Clauzel's attack on Mascara the amir did not have any permanent political base. He had an economic capital at Tagdempt, an emporium of trade between the hinterland and the south, where he struck his coins and kept his stores of provisions and ammunition. Politically the capital was his camp which he moved about as the political and military exigencies demanded. His standing army was small, never exceeding 10,000 men, but it was reinforced by tribal auxiliaries usually drawn from the region where he was engaged in battle. Both auxiliaries and regulars were shock troops in the traditional tribal fashion, whose temperament and tactics were better suited for surprise attacks than for sustained fighting.

The firm authority which the amir could exercise in his state, and his reputation in France for probity and the fair treatment of captives, inclined a large segment of politically informed circles in France to view him as an able ruler worthy of being France's ally. The amir himself consciously cultivated this point of view. After signing the Treaty of Tafna he sent one of his *khalifas*, Mawlud b. 'Arrash, to Paris with a gift to Louis Philippe. The *khalifa* discussed the problems of Algeria with French politicians, and argued that the amir's control of the interior was the solution most favourable to French interests, since he alone could ensure stability. In spite of the hostility of the settlers to any agreement with 'Abdul-Qadir, Valée in Algiers accepted this viewpoint and supplied the amir with arms. But the fall of Constantine, and the French attempts to establish a land route between this town and Algiers, led to a conflict which ended the co-existence between the amir and the French.

In the year following the Treaty of Tafna the amir's authority was felt in eastern Algeria for the first time. He established a base at Hamza in the middle of the territory which Valée wished to control in order to ensure communications with Constantine, was able to win over the tribes living in the mountainous regions around Bougie and Dellys, and occupied the oasis of Biskra from which he forced the former ruler of Constantine Ahmad Bey to flee in May 1838. Valée had tried since 1837 to persuade the amir to revise the Treaty of Tafna, especially with regard to the limit of French territory east of Algiers, defined in the treaty as being Wadi Kaddara (40 km east of Algiers) or beyond. Bugeaud thought that by inserting "or beyond" in the text of the treaty, he reserved to the French the right of further expansion eastwards. The amir argued that the term was meaningless in a context where a definite boundary was specified. The conflict showed how inadequate the French policy of limited occupation had become after the conquest of Constantine. It also reflected the basic contradiction in the amir's position of continuing to advocate the holy war while coming to terms with the French. In a gesture of open defiance to 'Abdul-Qadir on 28 October 1839, Valée crossed the Biban pass on the route between Constantine and Algiers with the king of France's son, the duc d'Orleans, at the head of a military column. The amir responded by giving notice to Valée on 3 November that the state of war was resumed. He invaded the Mitidja plain on 20 November, killing on the 21st alone 108 European settlers. Within a few days his cavalry reached the suburbs of Algiers, thus creating a state of general panic. The French government, worried over the mounting cost of the Algerian war and the prospects of a conflict with Britain over Muhammad 'Ali's occupation of Syria, was not inclined to abandon the policy of limited occupation. But the amir's attack made evacuation the only alternative to the total occupation of Algeria, an alternative which very few in France were prepared to consider in 1840. Consequently in December 1840 Valée was recalled and replaced by General (later Marshal) Bugeaud who was to execute a policy of total occupation.

The Bugeaud period in Algeria (February 1841–June 1847) was a decisive one in Algerian history and not only because of the destruction of Amir 'Abdul-Qadir's authority. Two major and lasting problems of Algerian history under the French rule crystallized as a result of Bugeaud's military successes and indigenous policy. These were the conflict over land between the settlers and the Muslim population, and the demands of the French community in Algeria for the absorption of the country into the political and administrative structure of France.

The war took on a cruel character after Bugeaud's arrival. The tribal method of *razzia* (Ar. *ghazia* or *ghazuw*) with which La Moricière, the commander in Oran since 1840, had experimented, was henceforth employed by the French army as a basic instrument of war. Muslim encampments and villages were destroyed, the cattle was taken away, harvests were burnt, and trees hewed down. This method of fighting is not foreign to the Maghriban tribal community, but it was made especially brutal by the efficiency and cold-blooded planning with which the French army command employed it. There are also records of four incidents occurring between 1844 and 1847 in which French officers ordered the burning of defeated groups of Muslims in caves even after they offered to surrender. The morality of war apart, the method proved effective in demoralizing the Algerian Muslims, and continued to be used by the French army until the conquest of Algeria was completed with the subjugation of Kabylia in 1857.

The war against 'Abdul-Qadir was carried out with method and determination. In May 1841 the French army occupied Mascara and Tagdempt, and in February 1842 Tlemsen was reoccupied. While three commanders based in Mascara, Tlemsen, and Mustaghanim gave the chase to the amir between Tlemsen and the littoral, Bugeaud established in 1842 a base at al-Asnam, which he renamed Orleansville, to restrict the amir's movements in the Dahra mountainous regions. By the end of 1843 the amir was a beaten man, and was forced in November to seek asylum in Morocco. He was hailed as a hero by the Moroccan population, but the decisive military defeat of the Moroccan army by the French at Isly near Wajda on 14 August 1844 and the bombardment of Tangier and Mogador by a French naval squadron, forced the Moroccan government henceforth to withhold help from the amir. By the Franco-Moroccan Treaty of Tangier (10 September 1844) the Moroccan government agreed to treat the amir as an outlaw. A rebellion of the tribes in the Dahra against the French in 1845, led by a young religious chief claiming to be the Mahdi, called Bu Ma'za, enabled the amir to penetrate into the Tafna valley in 1846. There he scored two victories against the French which helped him to recover some of his lost prestige with the tribes, but were insufficient to alter the basic facts of the military situation. Soon afterwards he was again a refugee in Morocco. Bu Ma'za's surrender in April 1847, together with the strengthening of the French position on the frontier, made the amir's return to Algeria very difficult.

Bugeaud resigned the post of governor-general in June 1847 on account of the expedition he mounted during May and June of this year into Grand Kabylia. His troops penetrated the Banu 'Abbas mountains in the course of the expedition, destroyed all the villages they entered, looted large amounts of carpets and jewellery, and forced some sixty tribal chiefs to make their submission. The French Chamber of Deputies had denounced the proposed expedition in April, and the minister of war opposed it. Yet with characteristic defiance Bugeaud carried it out, took full responsibility for his disobedience, and in the face of censure resigned. The amir in the meantime was in the Rif where he received the cooperation of the tribes, but was viewed by the Moroccan government as an outlaw. Rumours circulating in Morocco that he intended to carve out a state for himself in the Rif and to usurp the sultanate from the 'Alawites were used to justify the Moroccan authorities' cooperation with the French in hunting him down. After some victories in 1847 against the Moroccan army the amir was defeated and forced to move to the left bank of the Mulawiyya. There he found himself pursued by the Moroccan troops, and the forces of La Moricière awaiting him on the right bank of the river. Realizing the futility of further fighting, the amir surrendered to the French on 23 December 1847 after receiving the pledge of the duc d'Aumale, the king's son and Bugeaud's successor as governor-general, that he would be given a safe passage either to Alexandria or Acre in Palestine. But the pressure of public opinion made the French government keep him in confinement in France until 1852, when Napoleon III had him released. He later settled in Damascus where some of his descendents still live.

From the beginning of the conquest, the regions of Algeria where Europeans settled in large numbers were governed separately from those where few Europeans lived and those which remained exclusively Muslim. Until 1832 the attempt was made to govern the Muslims through an indigenous chief with the title of *agha*. When the last holder of this post, Muhyi al-Din Mubarak of Kolea, resigned in 1832 having found that his functions only brought him into disrepute with his coreligionists, French officials specializing in Muslim affairs were organized into a *bureau arabe* to act as interpreters and liaison officers with the tribes. Valée dissolved the *bureau arabe* in 1839 upon the resignation of its director Pellisier de Reynaud, the author of the monumental *Annales algériennes*, over Valée's sending back to the amir a Negress and her son who had sought asylum with the French. Bugeaud reconstituted the institution of the *bureau arabe* in 1841, created branches in the provinces, and made the Algiers branch a central office of control and coordination. In the Bugeaud period the officers of the *bureaux arabes* came to perform the dual function of providing information to the government and governing the Muslim population. These officers considered the Muslims primitive and hypocritical and applied tyrannical methods in governing them. At the same time they saw themselves as their tutors, and attempted to teach them modern methods of hygiene and agriculture and to prepare them for gradual adjustment to living under French rule. Some of them developed a sense of mission in performing their functions and defended the Arab land rights against the civilian settlers.

The Europeans in Algeria, numbering 109,380 in 1847, of whom only one-seventh lived outside the big towns, were generally hostile to Bugeaud. Predominantly middle class, they resented his conservative monarchical convictions and his belief that only the army could effectively govern

Algeria. Because of his dislike of the press and all political ideologies, which made him impose on the settlers restrictions depriving them of many of their civil rights, he earned from them the appellation of *régime du sabre* for his system of government. The basic issue in the conflict between Bugeaud and the civilian settlers was colonization. The officers of the *bureaux arabes*, assuming a paternalistic role in their government of the Muslims, hindered the appropriation by the settlers of lands they coveted; and Bugeaud envisaged the colonization of Algeria by ex-servicemen who as farmers would remain under the control of the army. He prepared three projects for founding military colonies which were all rejected by the government, and three small settlements he set up on his own responsibility between 1841 and 1844 were a total failure. Nevertheless he did not relent in his opposition to civilian colonization which he considered unprofitable to the country and, bearing in mind the massacre of the settlers in the Mitidja plain in 1839, also dangerous. In opposition to Bugeaud's programme, the civilian settlers believed in assimilation, which to them meant the removal of the barriers set up by the *bureaux arabes* that deprived them of access to new lands. They also wanted to be freed from the control of the army in order to have French political and administrative institutions extended into Algeria.

The problem of land came to a head in the Bugeaud period because the state lands of the Turkish administration, and the lands confiscated from the amir's supporters after 1839, had all been distributed. There remained in 1840 three main categories of land: *habus* lands, being those constituted as pious trusts, privately owned lands existing mostly in the mountainous regions, and collective tribal lands. In 1843 the *habus* lands were placed under the control of the Domaine (land department) and a decree of 1 October 1844 brought to an end their unalienable character, thus making it possible for the settlers to take possession of them. Henceforth the settlers' ambitions were directed towards the extensive tribal lands which the tribesmen could use but whose ownership was not transferable. The settlers contended that the French had acquired the right to the lands of the Algerians by conquest, and a pseudo-legal justification of this contention was provided by a theory based on Muslim law propounded in 1844. The theory revived the argument in Muslim law that lands taken in the period of Muslim conquest by force were state lands on which the *kharaj* could be levied.[1] It further asserts that although only parts of Algeria were treated under the Turks as such, the whole of the country was *kharaj* land, that it was all *de jure* owned by the Turkish state, and that this ownership was transferred to the French state after 1830. The main defect of this theory is that, even if the whole of Algeria was *kharaj* land – something which had not previously been acknowledged – the Muslim law does not

[1] See above, p. 209 for the problem of *kharaj* lands in the Moroccan context.

permit the acquisition of *kharaj* lands by private owners, which is what the settlers wanted to justify by this theory. The theory did not receive formal official confirmation, but from the mid-1840s encroachment on tribal lands became systematic. A decree of 21 July 1846 which defined lands not in use as vacant, and grazing lands as being not in use, enabled the Domaine to acquire before the end of the Bugeaud period 200,000 more hectares of land of which only 32,000 went to Algerian Muslims. During the governorship of Randon (December 1851–June 1858) the acquisition of tribal lands was carried out within the framework of the policy of cantonment. This policy meant that the lands which in the governor's judgement were not needed for the use of a tribe, usually the most fertile, were taken away for the purposes of colonization. The tribes were thus left with only a small fraction of what they previously had for grazing, and in many cases, especially in the regions of the Shaliff valley and Oran, they faced financial ruin. In the period of Randon large companies and entrepreneurs benefited from the new lands acquired by the Domaine through cantonment. Between 1853 and 1863 some fifty-one concessionaries received about 50,000 hectares of land and state subsidies for the purpose of establishing agricultural villages for European settlers. Most of them did not fulfil their obligations, and instead had the lands they received cultivated on their account by Muslim farmers.

By the end of the Bugeaud period the settlers had come to look upon the assimilation of Algeria into metropolitan France as the only means of realizing their economic ambitions and guaranteeing their civil rights. As they also identified the *régime du sabre* with monarchy, they evinced strong republican convictions which made them vote in large numbers in the two plebiscites of December 1851 and November 1852 against the installation of Napoleon III as president and emperor respectively. The settlers' assimilationist aspirations had been encouraged by the statute of 15 April 1845 which reorganized the administration of Algeria. The statute gave formal recognition to the existence in Algeria of distinct civil territories which, on account of the large European communities living in them, merited the establishment of public services and the exercise of French civil rights. The mixed territories, where only few Europeans lived, could potentially be absorbed into the civil territories with the extension of colonization. These aspirations became a political issue in the French capital when the settlers' lobbyists in Paris, calling themselves the Algerian delegation, published in March 1847 a *Mémoire au Roi et aux chambres* which demanded the absorption of the whole of Algeria into the administrative structure of France. With the declaration of the second republic in 1848, an event which the settlers welcomed as a deliverance from military rule, some of their demands were satisfied. Decrees published in April and August 1848 gave them the right to elect their representatives to the Chamber of Deputies and placed the Algerian administrative offices under the direct control of the ministries in Paris. The constitution of November 1848 further declared Algeria, unlike other colonies, a French territory. As the administrative changes instituted in 1848 meant that the governor and the military governed only the Muslim population, since they were given no jurisdiction over the civil authorities, an administrative duality emerged which led to grave conflicts between civilian and military administrators. These conflicts gained public notoriety in Oran in 1850 when the military commander accused the civil authorities of a plot against the security of the state, with the result that the mayor was disqualified and several civilian leaders were tried and given prison sentences.

The Algerian settlers' path to victory, 1848–1914

The result of the constitutional and administrative arrangements of 1848 was to divide the inhabitants of Algeria into a privileged European and a suppressed Muslim community. Differences in political and civil rights, social outlook and organization, and economic opportunities separated them. This polarization was slightly blurred by the existence of a Jewish community sharing the traditional outlook of the Muslim society without being part of it, and a non-French European community not enjoying all the powers of the French. But the gulf between them was so real and great that a fusion could have been achieved only partially and over a long stretch of time. The alternative to fusion was to create the circumstances for meaningful coexistence within the framework of French sovereignty. This was what Napoleon III attempted to do after 1863.

For a decade after the establishment of his authority, Napoleon III's Algerian policy was shaped by his dislike of the republican settler community. This made him favour the allocation of Algerian lands to companies and entrepreneurs connected with the court, strengthen the hand of the military in governing Algeria, and in February 1852 suppress the right of the Algerian settlers to elect representatives to the Chamber of Deputies. The settler community resented what they considered an oppressive imperial regime. But as their domination in the economic life of Algeria was not much affected by the imperial policy, and their investments of the previous two decades began to bear fruit, they were prepared to wait for a change in the political climate. In addition to agriculture, the mining industry was beginning in the 1850s, when Algeria was already exporting iron, lead, and copper, to raise great expectations amongst the settlers. The interests of the settlers were also advanced by a law of 21 September 1851 exempting Algerian products from duty on being imported into France, at a time when non-French goods needed for development could be brought into Algeria duty-free.

The Muslim population hardly figured in Napoleon III's policy before 1863. Starting to feel the burden of French taxation and resenting the loss of their lands, the Muslims carried out sporadic but ineffective uprisings from 1848 onwards. The inhabitants of the Za'atsha oasis to the south-west of Biskra rebelled in 1848 because of the haphazard way the tax on their palms was assessed. Led by a religious leader called Bu Zian, they fought the French troops until in November 1849 the entire population of the oasis was wiped out. The invasion of Grand Kabylia in 1851 brought to light another religious chief called Bu Baghla. Claiming to be a *sharif*, he was able to keep the spirit of resistance amongst the tribes alive until his death in 1854, in spite of the systematic destruction of villages by the French troops. In the south another rebellion broke out in 1852 in the region of Laghwat against the *agha* appointed by the French. The leader, Muhammad b. 'Abdulla from the Awlad Sidi al-Shaikh tribe, also claimed to be a *sharif*. Defeated in December 1852, he fled to Tuggurt where he remained until this oasis was occupied by the French in December 1854 and opposition in the whole region of Suf was crushed. These rebellions reflect the latent hostility to the French which the Algerian muslims continued to nurse and which came into the open whenever political or economic grievances provided the spark, and the French military control seemed in doubt.

Napoleon III's Algerian policy crystallized between September 1860, when he made a three-day visit to Algeria, and 6 February 1863 when in a letter to the governor Pélissier (1860–4) he gave the first indications of what it was to be. The visit convinced him that the Muslim society was worthy of preservation, and henceforth he listened with attention to defenders of the policy of the *bureaux arabes*. Apart from these, Napoleon III discussed the Algerian question with Ismail Urbain, the natural son of a Marseilles merchant and a quadroon. Converted to Islam in Egypt, Urbain attacked in his writings the policy of despoiling the Algerian Muslims of their lands, and the policy of cantonment to which Pélissier was at the time trying to give a legal character. In the letter to Pélissier Napoleon described Algeria as being not a colony in the proper sense of the term but "un royaume arabe", an expression which henceforth was used to describe the emperor's Algerian policy. He also attacked the policy of cantonment and added that the Arabs as well as the settlers were entitled to his protection. The *senatus consult* of 22 April 1863 went further in amplifying the imperial policy by recognizing the tribal usufruct of land as equivalent to ownership, thereby rejecting the theory of state ownership of all Algeria's lands. It also required the authorities in Algeria to survey tribal lands, and subdivide them into *diwars* (groups of tents) each having its tribal chief with whom the administration could have dealings.

It was easier to formulate a new Algerian policy than to have it effectively implemented. In the survey to delimit tribal lands the interests of the settlers and their ability to put pressure on the local administration were reflected in the extension of lands classified as privately owned, which the settlers could therefore purchase, at the expense of tribal lands. The difficulty of altering the French administrators' attitude to the Muslims became clear when the rebellion of the Sharaqa (eastern) branch of the Awlad Sidi al-Shaikh tribe occurred in March 1864. This branch of the tribe had accepted French rule, and its chief at the time of the rebellion, Sulaiman b. Hamza, had been appointed by the French shortly before the rebellion. The arbitrary method of levying taxes made the tribesmen restive, but it was the high-handedness of the *bureaux arabes* which sparked off the uprising. Sulaiman b. Hamza himself led his tribesmen into rebellion when his *khuja* (chief assistant) was beaten up in public by officers of the *bureau arabe* of Geryville. In April 1864 the rebels defeated a column of French troops near Jabal 'Amur (Amour), killing the commanding officer and all but three of his men. Subsequently the rebellion spread into Flitta territory, the Dahra, and eastern Kabylia. By the end of the year it had been brought under control, but groups of the Sharaqa tribesmen remained unsubdued and continued, when pursued by the French, to take refuge with the Gharaba (western) branch of the tribe, which under the 1845 Franco-Moroccan agreement over the frontier had been placed in Moroccan territory.

The rebellion of 1864 formed the background for new measures undertaken by Napoleon III with a view to controlling the refractory Algerian administration and reconciling the Algerian Muslims to French rule. In July 1864 the position of director of civil affairs for Algeria was abolished and replaced by the post of secretary-general responsible to the governor and inferior in rank to the army generals commanding provincial divisions. The emperor then made a second visit to Algeria (3 May to 7 June 1865), in which he assured the settlers that he understood their problems and appreciated their achievements. Five weeks after returning from Algeria, where he inspected settler farms and other projects and had hardly any contact with the Muslim population, a new *senatus consult* on Algeria was published. This document pronounced the Algerian Jews and Muslims to be French subjects, entitled to enter the French civil service and enlist in the army. They could also obtain French citizenship upon agreeing to be governed by the French civil law instead of their religious laws. The provision for recognizing Algerians as French but not citizens until they agreed to be governed by the French civil law vitiated the effects of this reform, since until 1870 only 194 Algerian Muslims and 398 Jews chose to become citizens.

The *senatus consult* of 1865 increased the settlers' fears that with time they would be absorbed into Algerian society as a minority group without the power to control policy and safeguard their dominant economic interests. In this period of anxiety for the settlers, when their dislike for the Muslim society increased in proportion to their fears, the fanaticism of Monseigneur (later Cardinal) Lavigerie, who became archbishop of Algiers in 1867, seemed to them a meaningful attitude, agnostic though many of them were. Relying on his protected position as a cleric, Lavigerie gave expression to the views which the settlers did not dare utter in public. He asserted that conversion to Christianity was the only way the Muslims could be converted from barbarism, and was therefore the only humane policy the French government could follow in Algeria. He also attacked the military regime which he held responsible for preventing the assimilation and conversion of the Muslims. Lavigerie arrived when Algeria was hit by cholera and drought, which took their heaviest toll in 1868 when an estimated 300,000 people and about half the cattle of the Algerian Muslims perished. The settler community suffered less from these calamities because they had greater economic reserves than the Muslims and their lands were better irrigated. This period of distress divided the two communities in Algeria further, and Lavigerie contributed his share in arousing the hostility and suspicions of the Muslims by gathering together 1753 Muslim orphans in charitable foundations with the express purpose of converting them, and by rejecting all demands to hand them over to their relatives.

The inglorious end of the imperial regime of Napoleon III through defeat in the Franco-Prussian war had an aftermath in Algeria which brought about the total victory of the settler community. The patriotism of the settlers during the war and after it took the form of their reviling the army which was held responsible for the defeat. And as the imperial regime collapsed, they organized committees of defence in most Algerian cities which together with the municipal councils were prepared to resist by force the restoration of the military regime in Algeria. In October 1870 the agitation of the republicans of Algiers forced General Walsin-Esterhazy, appointed deputy governor until the new civilian governor Didier arrived, to quit his office within three days. The republican leaders in Algiers then attempted through decisions taken in the Algerian committee of defence and the municipal council, and through pressure on the French provisional government in Tours, to have the mayor of Algiers Vuillermoz recognized civil commissioner for the whole country. The French government were able to avert rebellion in Algeria only through concessions which gave the settlers most of their demands. A decree of 4 October 1870 gave them the right to elect six deputies to the Chamber. Two other decrees of 24 October confirmed the formal annexation of Algeria to France and abolished the centralized hierarchy of the *bureaux arabes*, making their officers mere agents of liaison with the Muslims and placing them under the authority of the civil administrators in their districts. A decree of 30 December further provided for the appointment of a civil inspector for each of Algeria's three departments, to be chosen by the minister of the interior. The economic triumph of the settlers was to come as a result of the Muslim uprising of 1871.

The Muslim uprising had its roots in the years of famine and epidemics preceding the Franco-Prussian war, the circumstances of the war, and the governmental changes which followed it. The Algerian Muslims looked upon the French defeat as the moment of liberation, and rumours circulated in the country about an imminent Turkish invasion and the return of Amir 'Abdul-Qadir's son Muhyi al-Din to lead resistance to the French. Some of the Sufi orders were active in rousing the Muslims, and the Muslim pupils refused to go to school in October 1870 in expectation of a change in the existing order. France was defeated, the army in Algeria was seen to be humiliated through the action of the civilian Frenchmen, and the Muslims expressed hostile sentiments. All this did not lead to an armed rebellion. The restiveness of the Algerian Muslims and their agitation might have petered out except for the action of Muhammad Mukrani, an Algerian Muslim leader working for the French, who hoped to achieve personal aims by starting a limited uprising but sparked off a general rebellion instead.

The Mukrani family had built its political fortunes since the 1830s by alliance with the French. Muhammad's father, upon accepting cooperation against Amir 'Abdul-Qadir, was appointed by Valée in 1838 *khalifa* over the territory between Farjuna in the east to Tittari in the west, which constituted the greater part of Grand Kabylia. When the father died in 1853 the French had already begun expanding their control into the region. His son Muhammad was given the title of *bash-agha*, which amounted to an administrative demotion. Furthermore, Muhammad's authority was eroded by the control of the French officials, and his resources diminished by the confiscation of his family's lands, the abolition of the traditional corvée enjoyed by the Kabylia chiefs, and the imposition of taxes on his tribe. In 1870 he found himself threatened with financial ruin as a result of guaranteeing debts amounting to a million francs contracted by his tribesmen in the period of famine (1867–8) from French and Jewish creditors. The governor-general Mac-Mahon had promised that in case of a failure to repay, the debts would be settled through additional municipal fees which the military authorities would institute especially for the purpose. By the end of 1870, with the civilians taking control of the administration, the military authorities in the region could no longer impose special levies, especially because from 7 December a civil commissioner was in residence at Burj (Bordj), the administrative centre of the district. Mukrani rebelled partly out of desperation when left in the lurch by the military authorities, and possibly in the hope that a show of force might enable him to regain some of his administrative authority.

The tribal rebellion of Muhammad Mukrani, which began in February 1871, triggered off a wider popular uprising for which the Rahmaniyya Sufi order had prepared the way. The rebellion quickly spread over an area about 300 km long from the suburbs of Algiers to the heights of Collo and southwards as a far as the desert, involving about one-third of the Muslim population of Algeria. The rebels devastated farms, and destroyed and pillaged villages. Finding that the rebellion was growing out of his control, Mukrani offered to lay down arms if the French gave him favourable terms of surrender. The governor, General Gueydon, being entirely under the influence of the settlers, told him that the only terms he would offer were that he should answer for his crimes before the Algiers assize court. Mukrani was eventually killed in action on 5 May 1871. The surrender at the end of June of the aged Rahmaniyya chief Shaikh Haddad and his son and war-chief 'Aziz, opened the way for the subjugation of Kabylia. Bu Mazrag, who led the southern branch of the rebellion, was captured in June 1872. In the course of suppressing the rebellion the French lost 2,686 men. The loss of Muslim lives was much greater. Economically the Muslims were ruined.

The settlers insisted that the rebels should be tried as criminals before the French courts whose juries were entirely French, and that the economic repression should ensure that the Muslims would no longer have the means to rebel again. A war indemnity of 36.5 million francs was imposed on the region of Kabylia, amounting to ten times the annual tribute. In addition all the lands of the tribes who had taken part in the rebellion were sequestrated by a decree of 31 March 1871 in accordance with the principle of tribal collective responsibility. As not all the lands obtained through sequestration could be used by the settlers, Gueydon allowed the Muslims to repurchase some of them. Alsatian and Lorrainian emigrants were settled on 100,000 hectares of sequestrated lands in the Summam valley and the regions of Sitif and Constantine. It is estimated that seventy per cent of the total capital of the peoples involved in the rebellion was levied from them in the form of war indemnity or for freeing their lands from sequestration. Less than one-third of the sixty-three million francs paid by the Muslims in repurchasing their lands went to the French victims of the rebellion; the rest was spent on expanding colonization.

From 1871 to the First World War the Muslims in Algeria had no alternative but to attempt to live in a society whose political and economic structures were geared to serve the interests of the settler community, and whose educational system was designed to submerge the Arab-Muslim identity. The instruments of this policy were the expansion of the civil territories through settling new French emigrants in the rural districts, levying higher direct taxes on the Arabs and using their revenue for colonization, keeping the Arabs subdued through a special penal system, weakening the Muslim educational system without giving the Muslim children access to French schools, and replacing the Muslim system of justice by the French. The custodians of the system and its protectors against the meddling of liberal circles in France were the settlers themselves who in this period developed a consciousness of their separate identity from that of the metropolitan French.

In 1871 the rural settlers numbered 119,000, about one-quarter of the total number of Europeans in Algeria. Through official facilities, subsidies, and the distribution of lands to settlers intending to work in agriculture, it was hoped to enlarge the European rural community. The settling of the refugees from Alsace and Lorraine did not prove successful. Most of these refugees had been factory workers and found it difficult to adjust to peasant life in Algeria. Consequently out of 1,183 families taken to Algeria, only 387 remained on the land. But in the 1870s the settling of peasants from south-eastern France proved more successful. Between 1871 and 1882 4,000 French peasant families were settled on lands in Algeria. Between 1871 and 1898 the French rural community rose from 119,000 to 200,000. But in the same period more Algerian land was bought by French businessmen and wealthy farmers than was acquired by the French peasants through official colonization. Consequently, in addition to the small French farmers working in the Algerian countryside, there emerged the large estates owned by a capitalist class of landowners who viewed agriculture as a business enterprise, and relied on Spanish, Maltese, and Muslim labour for the cultivation of their lands. It was these large landowners who expanded the cultivation of vines, particularly in the Tall regions, and employed the dry farming method to extend the cultivation of cereals into the south.

The cohesion of the settler community at the end of the century was strengthened by two factors. A law of 1889 gave French nationality to the children of Europeans born in Algeria who did not explicitly reject it. This created greater harmony between French and non-French Europeans in the country, and nearly doubled the number of French citizens by 1901, when the statistics were 364,000 French citizens as against 189,000 non-French Europeans. The second factor was the growth of a new generation of Frenchmen born and reared in Algeria, sharing the outlook, ambitions, and prejudices of the long-established settlers. From 1896, when the number of Europeans born in the country exceeded for the first time that of the immigrants, one can speak of the appearance of a new people. The French in Algeria came to distinguish themselves from the French of France through their emphasis on the non-French origins of many of them and the experiences they obtained through life and work in the midst of the Muslim society. As a group, calling themselves the *pieds noirs*, they developed a racist outlook, which determined their attitude towards non-Europeans. This made most of them oppose the naturalization of the Algerian Jews in 1870 and led to a violent anti-Jewish campaign in 1898. Emphasizing their role as the custodians of European civilization in Algeria, the settlers were suspicious of any liberal tendencies in France which tried to ameliorate the lot of the Muslims and usually opposed them.

The Muslims of Algeria numbered 3.5 million in 1891. The events of 1871 had impoverished them, and henceforth they were held down by force exercised under special powers granted by the Code de l'indigénat. This code, the outline of which was prepared by the governor Gueydon (1871–3), was held suspended during the period of his successor Chazy (1873–9), but was formally promulgated in 1881. Under this code civil administrators could impose severe penalties on the Muslims for any of forty-one specified offences without any legal procedure. Civil administrators could detain Muslims without trial, place them under surveillance, and order collective penalties and the sequestration of property. Muslims, furthermore, could no longer leave their districts without obtaining a special permission from the authorities. The code gave the administrators these powers for seven years in the first instance, but they were extended periodically until 1927.

The traditional Algerian Muslim leaders had been crushed by 1871. In their place the French attempted to form a class of loyalist *'ulama*, chosen and paid salaries by the administration, who could be relied on not to cause any disturbances. At the same time Sufi orders with whom the French had established relations in the early period of conquest, such as the Tijaniyya, were given official encouragement. In this period, the influence of the religious leaders generally was on the decline, either because they compromised themselves through cooperation with the French, or because of the measures taken by the administration to weaken Muslim education and replace the Muslim system of justice by the French. The settlers felt that the only instruction that could be given to the Muslims without creating a threat to French control was in the crafts and agriculture. Thus not only did the administration neglect the Muslim schools, but they failed to extend French education to the Muslims. Out of thirty-six Franco-Arab primary schools operating in Algeria in 1870, only sixteen remained in 1882 to give instruction to Muslim children. Contacts of the Algerian Muslims with other Muslim countries were also made difficult through restrictions on travel, and obstacles placed in the way of the pilgrimage to Mecca. In 1884 Louis Rinn, director of the department of native affairs, went to the extent of proposing that the Tijaniyya order should be made something of a national church for Algeria, and its head appointed Shaikh al-Islam of the country in order to counter the religious

9   A H O

propaganda of the Ottoman Shaikh al-Islam. In the field of justice French justices of the peace began to operate in place of the *qadis* in Kabylia from 1874, and the number of Muslim courts elsewhere in the country was reduced from 184 in 1870 to 61 in 1890. All litigation involving immovable property was removed from the jurisdiction of the *qadis*, and criminal cases, even when the two parties in them were Muslim, were judged by juries made up of Frenchmen.

Statistics collected by C.-R. Ageron[1] show that the Muslim society was impoverished after 1871 not only by contrast with the French but also in absolute terms. The Muslims paid until 1919 special direct taxes called *impots arabes* from which the administration obtained about nineteen million francs, as part of the average forty-one million per annum the Muslims paid in the 1880s. A large part of the income from the *impots arabes* went to augment the budgets of the municipal councils in which the Muslims had no representation. The Muslims were further impoverished by the reduction of their lands which meant that they raised less cattle and sheep than before and produced less cereals. While the Muslim population increased, their holdings of sheep and cattle in 1900 were three-quarters what they had been in 1865. The decline in the production of cereals by the Muslims accounts for the partial famines from which they suffered in 1893 and 1897. In the period following 1871 many Muslim farmers became share-croppers (*khammas*), cultivating lands owned by the Europeans for a fifth of the produce. Others became agricultural labourers. The average holding of the remaining Muslim landowners was considerably reduced. Thus by the end of the century, when there were eight times as many Muslims in Algeria as Europeans, they owned, according to official estimates, only thirty-seven per cent of the country's wealth. Nor was the decline in native agriculture compensated for by new opportunities in the cities. In 1886 only 6.9 per cent of the Muslims lived in urban centres, a percentage which was to rise to only 7.6 in 1906. The large-scale migration of the Algerian Muslims to the cities was to occur only in the post-First World War period.

Thus in the four decades preceding the First World War the triumphant settler community was confidently building l'Algérie française. In the process it confirmed the polarization of the society, and made any meaningful fusion impossible. The period of the war was important for the settlers and the Muslims. It created new economic opportunities for the former, and new hopes for the latter. From the frustration of the Muslim hopes at a time when the settlers enjoyed all the advantages of prosperity, there arose new forces that shaped the history of Algeria in the twentieth century.

---

[1] Charles-Robert Ageron, *Histoire de l'Algérie contemporaine* (Paris, 1966), pp. 67 ff.

Tunisia: beys, consuls, and financiers, 1837–78

Tunisia's attitude towards the French occupation of Algeria strained her relations with the Ottoman empire at a time when her rulers had lost the weapon of piracy which they had effectively wielded against the European countries in the eighteenth century. A turning-point in the relationship between Tunisia and Europe was the arrival on 21 September 1819 of a joint Franco-British squadron commanded by Jurien and Freemantle to notify the bey of the protocol adopted by the great powers on 18 November 1818 at Aix-la-Chapelle concerning the Barbary pirates, and he was made to state in writing that he would never again arm corsair ships. The treaty of 1830 with France marked another retreat before European power. In it the bey agreed to enforce the capitulation treaties between the European countries and the Ottoman empire which enabled the European consuls to act as judges in all cases involving European nationals. What the capitulation treaties did not provide for, but which the consuls practised in Tunisia as a customary right, was to try as well cases in which the defendant was a European national. The enforcement of the capitulation treaties in Tunisia enabled the consuls to establish around them circles of dependents by placing under their protection members of European communities not represented in Tunisia, Jews, and Arabic-speaking Christians. With the aid of these, and by threatening to employ the superior military power of their countries against the bey, the European consuls could meddle in purely Tunisian matters and, within the limits they placed on one another's influence, advance the interests of their nationals and protégés.

Simultaneously with the increased power of the European consuls, the Husainids found themselves faced with greater Ottoman activity, primarily intended to counter the French expansion, but which they feared might bring about their own downfall. The fear of Ottoman occupation became especially acute after the removal of the Qaramanlis in 1835. As indicated above[1] Mustafa Bey, alarmed by the activities of the Ottoman fleet in 1836, agreed to send Tunisian soldiers to participate with the Ottoman army in the suppression of the Tripolitanian tribes and considered recognition of Ottoman sovereignty in order to avoid being deposed. During the relatively long reign of his son Ahmad Bey (1837–55) Ottoman pressure was applied on Tunisia at regular intervals that the country accept some form of Ottoman sovereignty. A French warning to the Porte in 1836 that they would themselves resist any attempt to alter the *status quo* in Tunisia prevented the Ottoman government from using force against the bey. But they had other means of exerting pressure on him. When Ahmad Bey asked for the customary letter of investiture as pasha of

[1] P. 189.

Tunisia in 1837, the Porte sent an emissary urging him to pay an annual tribute as confirmation of the religious ties between Tunisia and the sultan-caliph. In 1840, the *firman* instituting the Ottoman reforms (*tanzimat*) of 1839 was communicated to the bey with the request that it be promulgated in the regency. Henceforth Tunisian officials visiting Istanbul were continuously reminded of their religious responsibilities towards the caliph, and were urged to advise the bey to comply with the two demands for tribute and enforcing the *tanzimat*. The Khedive Isma'il of Egypt after a recent visit to Istanbul also joined in 1849 in putting pressure on the bey, asking him to comply with the sultan's wishes and urging him to pay a visit to Istanbul.

Until the end of his reign Ahmad Bey rejected all forms of Ottoman sovereignty, while attempting to maintain the religious side of the bond with the empire. During his visit to Paris in 1846 the French government received him with all the honours normally extended to an independent sovereign, and while there he cancelled an intended visit to London when he learnt that the Ottoman ambassador was to introduce him to Queen Victoria. At the same time he was very generous in the gifts he sent to the Ottoman sultan and officials. When in 1838 he refused the demand for tribute, he sent the renowned scholar of the regency Ibrahim al-Riyahi to Istanbul to emphasize the bey's sentiments of loyalty to the sultan and plead the poverty of the regency, while bringing with him rich gifts. And when Ahmad Bey learnt of the Porte's misgivings over his refusal to adopt the *tanzimat*, he sent a military vessel fully equipped as a gift to the sultan and a delegation to plead his case. In 1854, when Tunisia's economy was already in disarray, Ahmad Bey sent 4,000 Tunisian troops to fight on the side of the Ottomans in the Crimean War, although he had to sell the jewellery of his house to equip this force. Two factors in particular determined the bey's desire to preserve the religious ties with the sultanate: the popular attachment in Tunisia to the caliphate, and his fear of European encroachment on the sovereignty he was not prepared to surrender to the sultan. The French in particular, while supporting his assertion of independence from the Porte, also aroused his apprehension. He had occasion immediately after his accession to the throne, and the French occupation of Constantine two weeks later, to use the ties with the empire in defending Tunisian territory against French demands. At the end of 1837 the French asked the bey to surrender to them a strip of land along the northern part of the frontier with Algeria inhabited by the Nahd tribe, on the grounds that a branch of the tribe lived in Algerian territory and the authorities in Algeria wanted to unite the tribe to avoid frontier incidents. The bey rejected the French demand, claiming that he could not dispose of any part of the territory under his control without the sultan's permission. But in general the more persistent the Porte became in demanding formal recognition of Ottoman sovereignty, the more alluring Ahmad Bey found the French support of his independence.

The allurement of independence and grandeur seems also to have been responsible for Ahmad Bey's expenditure on his army and palaces. His secretary Ibn Abi al-Diaf indicates that his obsession with the army arose from his fear of Ottoman occupation. In 1840 he founded a military school at the Bardo to train the officers of his army. Its first director, Luigi Calligaris, was Italian, but from 1842 French officers were appointed as instructors, and in 1852 it came to have a French director. The young cadets, recruited mostly from the traditional Turkish military class, were given instruction in mathematics, history, geography, French, and Italian in addition to Arabic. The army was considerably expanded, so that the bey came to have about 26,000 men in his standing army. The state revenue was not sufficient to maintain such a large force, but Ahmad Bey refused to reduce its size even when in the 1850s the state exhausted its means of extortion and was about to contract its first loan. The bey also spent a great deal on building three palaces: the main beylical residence at Bardo, a winter palace at Gouletta, and a summer palace at Muhammadiya which he intended to be a Tunisian Versailles. The burden of the additional expenditure fell on the Tunisian peasants in the form of new taxes on olives and palm trees, and excises on the sale of all agricultural produce, sheep, and cattle in the markets. The state came to demand as levy one-quarter the price of all sheep and cattle sold, and to monopolize the production and sale of soap, and the sale of tobacco, salt, and leather. All the tobacco and hides produced in the regency had to be sold to government contractors who resold these goods locally or exported them. The state also owned the only tanneries and olive presses operating in the country. This oppressive economic policy and the corruption of the officials who executed it caused the decline of agriculture. One sign of this was that the *rabita*, the office responsible for collecting the tithe on cereals, could no longer meet the needs of the army and distribution to the poor, and the bey had to import wheat and barley from Egypt.

Nevertheless the bey's position in the country as absolute ruler remained unchallenged. In addition to the army his authority had a prop in the religious leaders and other Tunisian leaders whose goodwill he cultivated. The religious leaders he won over through donations to religious institutions and by creating new teaching posts at the Zaituna mosque and positions of *qadis* for the army. He placed some tribal chiefs in positions of authority, and was the first Husainid bey to give a woman of his family in marriage to a native (non-Turkish) chief. The policy of identifying native Tunisian leaders with the beylical authority had served his predecessors in the eighteenth century well in resisting Ottoman control, and it seems to have been designed by him to the same end. In his hands this policy also became the instrument by which agitation against his financial policies was stifled. With the *'ulama* and tribal chiefs won over, only the feeble representations of his officials remained to restrain the bey. How feeble this restraint was can be seen from the fact that Khair al-Din Pasha, the reformist and the most courageous of the bey's ministers, was able to prevent him from obtaining the money, which he himself was sent to Paris in 1852 to borrow, only by procrastinating in contracting a loan until the bey died.

Ahmad Bey's successors inherited an authority which was in theory absolute, but which in practice was eroded by the powers of the consuls and the deterioration of the economy. Muhammad Bey (1855–9) attempted the impossible by asserting the traditional beylical authority to the extent of defying the consuls and viewing any reliance on the support of the local Tunisian leaders as humiliating and irrelevant to the exercise of his power. At the same time, as a conservative Muslim he expected that if the country returned to a policy of taxation more in conformity with the religious law, the economy would revive and his claim to absolute authority would be respected. By rescinding some of the most oppressive taxes on crops he contributed towards the extension of agriculture. That was not sufficient to revive an economy whose mainstay, piracy, had been permanently lost, and which the extravagances of Ahmad Bey had placed at the mercy of the European merchants living in the country. In 1858, when Muhammad Bey had had a trial of strength with the consuls and failed, the weakness of the economy came to light with the disappearance of gold and silver coins from circulation. Improvement in agriculture did not cause a sufficiently large increase in the exportation of cereals and olive oil to balance the imports, and the fact that from Ahmad Bey's days European merchants had received payment for their goods in the gold and silver coinage of the regency meant that the country was drained of her precious metals. The foreign merchants refused to accept the copper coins struck in large amounts by the government to keep enough money in circulation, and the foreign consuls threatened the government with reprisals if their nationals' interests were not protected. The bey thus had no alternative but to force the Tunisian people to provide a loan. In 1858 he had new copper coins struck worth half the value of the old ones, issued members of the public surrendering the old coins with only half the value of their money in the new coinage, and gave them treasury bills for the other half redeemable in four years. The only beneficiaries from this operation were the foreign merchants who exploited the fear of the Tunisians that their government might not redeem the bills, and bought them at reduced prices trusting that their consuls would ensure their repayment.

While dispensing with the support of those local notables that had achieved a position under his predecessor, Muhammad Bey defied the consuls over the question of slavery in the regency and the administration of justice. Ahmad Bey in 1841 and 1842 respectively had banned the sale of slaves in the markets of Tunisia and pronounced free the children of slaves born in the country. In 1846 he issued, in response to British pressure, a complete manumission decree which made all ownership of slaves illegal. Muhammad Bey could not accept the abolition of the institution of slavery which had become a traditional aspect of Muslim society. Having also learnt that some tribal chiefs in southern Tunisia still owned slaves, he arranged for slaves from Bornu to be bought for his own benefit. As this consignment did not arrive until after his death, it caused no repercussions during his reign.

Muhammad Bey since his accession to the throne had taken to the habit of administering justice in person. His judgements were arbitrary, and Ibn Abi al-Diaf records instances of the death sentence being passed on dubious evidence. One of the bey's verdicts, more justifiable in terms of the Muslim law than many others he passed, had grave consequences because he sought through it to defy the French consul. A Jew called Samuel Sfez, having quarrelled with a Muslim, cursed him and the Muslim faith. The bey saw in the case when it was brought before him a means of avenging a grievance he held against Sfez's employer, the Jewish *qa'id* and tax collector Nasim Shammama who, being under French protection, was personally out of his reach. Instead of trying Sfez in the beylical court which followed the Hanafite rite, one lenient in these cases, he referred this case to al-Majlis al-Shar'i (the religious judicial council) to be tried according to the Malikite rite. Under this rite the offence could be punished by death, and the bey made it known that he wanted the death sentence pronounced. It was passed on 24 July 1857, and the bey ordered the execution of Sfez on the same day.

At the time of the Sfez incident Britain and France were represented by two men of long experience in Arab affairs. The British consul Richard Wood had spent most of his working life in the Middle East before going to Tunisia in 1856. He was an able linguist and a scheming diplomat, besides being well versed in Arabic and the customs and traditions of Muslims. Since arriving in Tunisia he worked towards fostering closer links between Tunis and Istanbul in order to enable the bey to profit from the provisions of the Treaty of Paris of 1856 guaranteeing the territorial integrity of the Ottoman empire. The French consul Léon Roches had had a chequered career in Algeria in the course of which he acted as Amir 'Abdul-Qadir's secretary during the period of peace following the Treaty of Tafna. On arrival in Tunisia in 1855 he inherited the influence which the French consuls had built in the country since 1830, and the policy of steering the bey away from recognizing Ottoman sovereignty.

Though rivals and pursuing divergent policies over Tunisia's relations with the Ottoman empire, the British and French consuls exploited the Sfez affair towards the same end of having the bey promulgate reforms whose declared purpose was to ensure the security of Tunisians and foreigners in the country against arbitrary acts of government. A French naval squadron in Gouletta backed Roches' representations. The British consul argued that the reforms the bey was asked to adopt were justified on religious and legal grounds since they constituted compliance with the sultan's wish to enforce the *tanzimat* in Tunisia. He supported his representations by the threat of summoning the British fleet, then moored at Malta, and the possible arrival of Ottoman ships. On 10 September 1857 Muhammad Bey issued a fundamental law (*qanun asasi*) entitled 'Ahd al-Aman (the Pledge of Security) embodying principles which the bey pledged himself to apply in the treatment of his subjects and others living in Tunisia. This document was based on a text which Roches prepared, but which the bey's secretary Ibn Abi al-Diaf wrote in a form acceptable to the Muslim community. The law affirmed the inviolability of persons and property, and the equality of Muslims and non-Muslims before the law. It also granted foreigners the right to acquire property in Tunisia.

By granting non-Tunisians the right to own property, 'Ahd al-Aman opened Tunisia more than before to European economic penetration, and exposed the bey to rival pressures from the consuls for concessions. It also encouraged a group of Tunisian leaders led by Khair al-Din Pasha, at the time the bey's minister of marine, to press for structural changes in the Tunisian system of government designed to curb the corruption which the tyrannical nature of the bey's government made possible. The pressure of this group, enforced by threats from the consuls that they would use force against the bey if he did not put the provisions of 'Ahd al-Aman into effect, caused Muhammad Bey to appoint a commission to draft a constitution based on the principles outlined in the 'Ahd. The same dual pressure caused Muhammad al-Sadiq Bey, who succeeded Muhammad Bey in 1859, to accept the allegiance of his people on the basis of upholding 'Ahd al-Aman, and to reconvene the constitutional commission. Thus in the period between 1857 and the promulgation of the constitution in 1860, the Tunisian reformists found themselves relying on the consuls' coercive ability to have the bey undertake measures which they viewed as being partly designed to strengthen the Tunisian government, thus rendering it more able to curb the consuls' powers. But after the constitution came into force the Tunisian reformers, who came to dominate the supreme council formed under its provisions, found themselves in conflict with the consuls over the application of the reforms.

The constitution of 1860 converted Tunisia in theory into a limited monarchy. It recognized the bey as head of state and the succession as hereditary in his family. But the ministers were made responsible to a supreme council of sixty members, and not to the bey. The members of the council were chosen in the first instance by the bey, and the constitution provided that one-third of them were to be government officials. Every five years the older fifty members were to be replaced. In doing this the bey could appoint the representatives of the government, and three-quarters of the rest; the others would be chosen by cooption. The council was empowered to initiate legislation, and to control taxation, state expenditure, the size of the army, and the appointment and dismissal of high government officials. As the bey chose the supreme council's members it could not be a representative assembly. But since the leading reformers were members, and their leader Khair al-Din was its first president, the council was a useful forum for discussing government policy. Nevertheless the prime minister Mustafa Khaznadar carried on as before the constitution, and by tolerating the discussion of policy in the council he obtained the advantage of justifying some of his misdeeds as emanating from decisions of the council. Khair al-Din was infuriated and, when he found himself unable to make the ministers truly responsible to the council, he resigned its presidency.

The constitutional experiment failed in practice, and the constitution was suspended four years after its promulgation. The Tunisian reformers were few, and without consular support they had no means of getting the bey or his prime minister to comply with the decisions of the supreme council. Khaznadar had been in office as vizier for twenty-five years when the constitution was brought into force. He had become accustomed to exercising authority in the name of an absolute ruler, and to an extortionist method of collecting the taxes from which he and the *qa'ids* (provincial governors) made fortunes. The threat of the supreme council's censure was not sufficiently powerful to persuade him to surrender these advantages. The leading members of the *'ulama* class disapproved of the constitutional innovation which deprived them of their traditional right to advise the bey on legislation in the light of the Muslim law. They had expressed their disapproval by withdrawing from the commission which drafted the constitution, and since then they held aloof. To the Tunisian masses the experiment was irrelevant, since their life was not affected by it. In addition there were two decisive factors ensuring the failure of the constitutional experiment: the opposition of the French government, and the financial crisis in which the country was plunged in the 1860s.

In two respects the French government found the sequel to the 'Ahd al-Aman contrary to French interests. The 1860s were the period of rapid expansion of European economic interests in Tunisia, particularly those of France and Italy. The existence of the supreme council hindered the consuls from obtaining concessions from the bey through the traditional methods of bribing high officials and threatening the bey with the use of force. There was also opposition from the European consuls, particularly the French, to the placing of their nationals under the jurisdiction of Tunisian courts. The bey, having granted the Europeans equality with Tunisians in every respect, including the right to acquire property, expected them to submit to Tunisian justice. In this respect he was supported by the supreme council. In June 1861 he set up a special tribunal in the Bardo to try cases in which one of the litigants (plaintiff or defendant) was a European. The French consul Léon Roches objected, and with his government's support insisted on following the customary practice of having a case in which a European was the defendant tried by his consul. The bey had been received in September 1860 in Algiers by Napoleon III who congratulated him on issuing the constitution, and he also received decorations from Belgium and Sweden for the same action. He was consequently surprised that the French opposed a measure that seemed to him and his advisors to follow from the reforms he had introduced. The only means the bey had for coercing the European countries to accept the jurisdiction of Tunisian courts was to make the right to acquire property dependent on this acceptance. Britain agreed in 1863 to place her subjects in Tunisia, who were mostly Maltese, under the jurisdiction of Tunisian courts in return for the confirmation of their right to own land, thus enabling them to acquire lands in the Sahil and to move out from the Tunis slums in which they lived. The Austrian government accepted the jurisdiction of Tunisian courts in 1866, the Italian in 1868, and the French government finally in 1871. The acceptance of the jurisdiction of Tunisian courts by these governments was limited to litigation involving landed property. Those of a civil, criminal, or commercial nature remained subject to the customary arrangement.

From 1860 the application of the constitution gave Tunisia the semblance of a budget, and from 1861 the budget was examined by the supreme council. However, the prime minister Mustafa Khaznadar, through allies in embezzlement whom he placed in control of the treasury, made the effective supervision of state income and expenditure by the supreme council impossible. Nor could the council prevent the bey from spending money on reorganizing the army and on public projects from which the prime minister, who concluded all state contracts, made considerable profits at the expense of the state. These projects had no relevance to the financial resources of the state. Khaznadar was well aware of this and prepared to make up the deficit through contracting state loans on which he obtained a commission. Among the projects on which Khaznadar spent state money were the building of residences for the consuls of England and France and repairing the aqueduct of Carthage.

By 1862 the Tunisian state had borrowed twenty-eight million francs locally. In this year the bey began to look abroad for loans because it was represented to him that he could obtain credit outside Tunisia on better terms. The negotiation of the first loan, contracted in May 1863 with the Parisian Erlanger banking house, was carried out by a Lebanese adventurer, Rushaid al-Dahdah, who was the protégé and ally of the prime minister. The terms of the loan were very stringent: out of a nominal value of 65,100,000 francs repayable in five years the bey received after various deductions only 37,772,160 francs. In addition, fraudulent transactions carried out by Erlanger with Khaznadar's concurrence included the imaginary sale of the loan bonds and their imaginery repurchase for the Tunisian government by Erlanger at a lower price. The result was the reduction of the loan's real value by a quarter in one year. Henceforth the bey had not only to abandon the public works he in the first instance could not afford, but also to borrow locally and abroad to meet the obligations of the first debt. In December 1863 the Tunisian government also decided to increase the revenue by doubling the poll-tax to become seventy-two *riyals* per head. The decision was opposed by members of the supreme council, especially Khair al-Din who argued that the Tunisian government, in order to collect the tax at the new rate, would have to equip an army costing more than the additional income accruing to the state from it.

In the spring of 1864 a tribal rebellion broke out in Tunisia whose immediate cause was increasing the poll-tax. From the tribes the rebellion spread amongst the urban population whom the bey had alienated by his decision in 1863 to levy the poll-tax on the inhabitants of towns usually exempted from it: the capital, Susa, Munastir, Sfax, and the religious capital of the country Qairawan. Categories of people previously exempted from taxation were now taxed, including the *'ulama* and the soldiers. The collapse of security resulting from the rebellion caused Britain, France, and Italy to send squadrons to protect their subjects and interests in the country in April 1864. While the presence of the three squadrons prevented any one of the three European countries or the Ottoman government from interfering militarily, the bey sought to control the situation by promises designed to appeal to the leading groups in the rebellion: the reduction of taxes, the appointment of local chiefs as governors in place of the Turkish officers, and the abolition of the secular tribunals which the *'ulama* resented. By the end of the year several of the tribes that took part in the rebellion had been induced to give up arms. Beauval, the French consul since September 1863, used the occasion of the rebellion to force the bey to abolish the constitution. Jean Ganiage[1] has shown that the consul got in contact with 'Ali b. Ghadhahim, the rebel ringleader, assuring him

[1] *Les origines du protectorat français en Tunisie, 1861–1881* (Paris, 1959), pp. 246–51.

of French support, and used his position as mediator between him and the bey to dictate his own terms to the latter.

Thus by the beginning of 1865 the government of Tunisia had reverted to its former ways, and its financial position was worse than ever. The prime minister Khaznadar, who emerged victorious with the suspension of the constitution, was no longer subject to any restraint and within three years he had led the country into a state of financial ruin. The rebellion and its sequel of suppression caused many lands usually under cultivation to remain fallow, and natural calamities, drought, a cholera epidemic in 1867, and a typhus epidemic in 1868, reduced the country to a state of misery and impoverishment it had not known for over a century. To add to this, Khaznadar went on borrowing money locally and abroad, partly because the state could not meet the obligations of the 1863 debt, but primarily because he and his agents obtained rich commission on every loan contracted. Locally he borrowed from French, Italian (mainly Genoese), and Jewish merchants, the latter being mainly British subjects or protégés. He also placed the state in debt by receiving advance payment from locally established foreign merchants on olive oil and cereals accruing to the state from the tithe, which went beyond what the state could expect from these sources. By the end of 1866 the local debts of the state had reached about fifty million francs. In addition Khaznadar borrowed heavily from French bankers, always at exorbitant rates of interest, with high commissions and dividends shared between the bankers themselves, Khaznadar, and a horde of adventurers who acted as agents. Khaznadar's agents who enriched themselves from these operations were a motley group: the Lebanese al-Dahdah, the Copt Elias Musalli who enjoyed French protection and sometimes acted as the bey's superintendent of foreign affairs, a Tunisian Jew Chloumou Shammama, and a number of Frenchmen. Al-Dahdah, who was a Tunisian government official on a salary of 600 francs a month, amassed eight million francs in the three years between 1863 and 1866.

By 1866 the Tunisian financial situation had reached crisis point. The government could not repay any part of the debt of 1863 and two others contracted in 1864 and 1865 from Erlanger and Oppenheimer, nor even the interest on the loans. The bey struck more copper coins in 1866 to increase the currency in circulation which, however, neither the foreign merchants nor the local producers of cereals would accept. The latter started smuggling their crops for sale in Algeria. With the general decline in agriculture, this caused a shortage of food provisions which reached famine level in 1867. In 1866 Khaznadar tried to buy time by obtaining a loan from the Rothschild banking house in Paris for 115 million francs that would enable him to repay all foreign debts and have twenty million francs for current expenditure. But the project fell through. Another loan of four million francs obtained from Erlanger in 1867, for which he placed the tithe on cereals as a guarantee, helped the Tunisians only very little. And as the bankers who secured the loans acted merely as agents who floated the debts in the form of bonds, the general public in France became involved. In 1867 a committee was formed in Paris to represent 30,000 French holders of Tunisian government bonds. This committee made representation to the bankers and the Tunisian government to obtain the reimbursement of the small creditors; meeting with no success, they put pressure on the French government to intervene.

With the Tunisian economy approaching total collapse and a large number of small French creditors clamouring for repayment, the moment seemed opportune for a French military intervention in the country. A project for the occupation of some Tunisian ports and the establishment of a French administration under the bey's nominal authority was adopted by a French council of ministers under the presidency of Napoleon III on 17 October 1867. The professed aim of the French intervention was to stop the exploitation of Tunisia by financial adventurers and reimburse the bey's European creditors. The political situation in Italy, particularly the occupation of Rome by Garibaldi's forces which led the French government to intervene there, caused the abandonment of this project momentarily. In its place the French government persuaded the bey in April 1868 to set up an international financial commission to control the Tunisian government revenue and expenditure and organize the repayment of the debts. The French were to have predominance in the commission: four members out of eight were to be French, together with two Tunisian officials and two representatives of the creditors. The British and the Italians opposed this scheme in the form the bey accepted it in April 1868. After lengthy negotiations the three powers agreed in 1869 on a different organization of the commission which gave the French controlling power only of its executive committee. This committee was composed of two Tunisian officials and a French financial inspector. It was responsible for drawing up a budget for the Tunisian state and controlling all state expenditure. In addition a committee of control was set up to supervise the executive committee and represent the interests of the creditors. Its membership of six was divided equally among Italy, France, and Britain.

Tunisia lost its economic independence with the formation of the International Financial Commission. Nevertheless, and in spite of the insistence of the financiers on the committee of control to obtain their money at any cost to the country, there was a redeeming aspect of this situation. The French inspector Victor Villet, who acted as vice-president of the executive committee, was a man of great competence and integrity, and set to carry out the organization and control of Tunisian finances with unswerving tenacity. Fortunately for him, the prime minister Khaznadar chose Khair al-Din Pasha as the president of this committee. Khaznadar had anticipated the formation of the commission in sending troops in the summer of 1869 to collect the poll-tax for two years in advance. He made enough money and sufficiently compromised himself through this operation to want to conciliate the foreign consuls by the appointment of Khair al-Din. Villet and Khair al-Din worked in harmony and respected each other.

The executive committee managed to consolidate the Tunisian debt at 125 million francs, after being faced with claims totalling 275 millions. The consolidated debt was then converted into 250,000 treasury bills bearing an interest of five per cent, and for their gradual redemption the executive committee reserved 6.5 million francs, or about half the revenue of the Tunisian state as obtained in 1870. The bey was persuaded to effect some economies, which included reducing the size of the army to 8,000 men and closing the military academy. But the obstacles before the executive committee remained immense. To revive the economy the poll-tax and taxes on agriculture had to be lowered, thus reducing the revenue, and the establishment of a uniform system of taxation was opposed by the prime minister, who seemed bent on using his authority and prestige in the administration to hamper the committee's work. When in 1871 the revenue of the state fell below the one expected by the committee, Khaznadar proposed a new debt to meet the cost of the treasury bills due for purchase in that year, and the committee of control supported him. Villet and Khair al-Din were thus faced with this formidable dual pressure, and were able to resist it only through an appeal to the consuls. The prime minister then created a new problem for the executive committee by having the supervisor of the Tunisian mint strike in 1871 coins of debased alloy, a transaction from which he profited.

Through controlling the executive committee the French were able to extend their influence widely in the country. Villet became in fact, if not in form, the Tunisian minister of finance. His control of the budget also enabled him to interfere in the running of other government departments. But when in 1870 France's international standing was shaken by her defeat in the war with Prussia, Italy immediately stepped in to capture her ascendant position in Tunisia. Italian migration to Tunisia had increased rapidly in the 1860s. By 1870 there were more Italians in Tunisia than British subjects (they were mainly Maltese) who until the early 1860s formed the largest of the European communities in the country. With about 7,000 Italians in Tunisia, and a large number of Jews originally from Leghorn and other Italian cities who recovered their Italian nationality, the Italian government had the human resources for economic expansion. In the 1860s a large part of the Tunisian produce was transported to Europe on Italian ships, and the southern ports of Tunisia were served entirely by Italian ships. Although the French community was small, less than 1,000 in 1870, the French were the main economic competitors to the Italians. The export trade was shared equally between France and Italy, the imports from France were double those from Italy, and in shipping services the French were not far behind the Italians.

From 1870 the Italian consul Pinna put pressure on the bey and threatened him with the use of force in order to obtain far-reaching concessions. In 1870 the Italian director of an estate called al-Jadida in the Majirda valley leased from the prime minister Khaznadar, provoked a conflict with the *qa'id* of the region. The consul used the supposed encroachment of the *qa'id* on the director's home to demand, *inter alia*, that Italians in Tunisia be permitted to plant and export tobacco (though the exportation of tobacco was a government monopoly) and that Tunisian subjects employed by Italians be placed under Italian consular jurisdiction. To back these demands an Italian naval squadron arrived in Tunis in February 1871. The bey gave in, and a treaty signed in Florence by a Tunisian envoy formalized the conclusion of the al-Jadida conflict and the concessions made to the Italians.

During the period when the Italians were trying to replace the French influence in Tunisia by their own they were willing to affirm, in reply to Ottoman protests over the conclusion of an international agreement directly with the bey, that he was an independent sovereign. But the bey was alarmed by the unrelenting Italian pressure. The British consul Wood had advised Muhammad al-Sadiq Bey ever since his accession to the throne to recognize Ottoman sovereignty. Fearing French action, the Bey had accepted this advice and sent Khair al-Din twice to Istanbul, in 1859 and 1864, to have the regency's relations with the Ottoman empire formally defined. On both occasions French pressure on the Porte prevented the publication of a *firman* to that effect. In 1871 Khair al-Din was sent on the same mission, and this time the French were too weak to influence the Porte, even with the support of Italian representations. The *firman* was published in Istanbul on 24 October and in Tunis on 18 November. It was addressed to the "governor" (*wali*) of Tunisia, the "vizier" Muhammad al-Sadiq Pasha. While confirming him in the government of Tunisia and recognizing it to be hereditary in his family, the *firman* also contained the stipulations that an annual tribute was to be paid regularly, and prayers said and the coins struck in the sultan's name. Tunisia was also to provide the empire with troops when she was in a state of war with other countries.

The *firman* of 1871 strengthened the hand of Richard Wood. In the course of the following two years he obtained various concessions for English businessmen: to establish a railway line connecting Tunis with the Bardo and Gouletta and later its extension along the southern shore of the

Lake of Tunis; to build a gasworks to provide gas to the capital; and to form a bank, the London Bank of Tunis, which was opened in October 1873. In obtaining these concessions Wood was able to rely on the help of the prime minister Khaznadar, with whom he had established close relations soon after his arrival in Tunis. Wood's relations with Khair al-Din were never very close, although the two men cooperated on the question of the Ottoman *firman*. The consul considered the reformer pro-French, a belief which on the surface was confirmed by Khair al-Din's friendship with Villet and the admiration for the French which he expressed in a book he published in 1867, called *Aqwam al-Masalik*, containing his ideas on social and political reorganization of Muslim states.

The English success in Tunisia of 1871–3 was ephemeral. The projects established by Englishmen were unprofitable, Wood's ally, the prime minister Khaznadar, had compromised himself to such an extent in the question of the debts that a campaign could be effectively launched against him by Villet, and by 1873 the French had sufficiently recovered from their defeat to resume their diplomatic activities with vigour. Khaznadar's swindling operations could not be easily documented, but Villet could prove in 1873 that he personally owned one-fifth of the treasury bills of the unified debt, with a value of about twenty-four million francs. As the largest single owner of treasury bills, he made large profits from manipulating their price in the market and undertaking speculative purchase and resale operations. Villet's revelations were made at a time when the bey had a new favourite, Mustafa b. Isma'il. Khaznadar had denied Mustafa a ministerial post, and so the ambitious young man readily agreed to use his influence with the bey against the prime minister. Khaznadar was dismissed in October 1873, after acting as vizier for thirty-six years. His successor was Khair al-Din.

It is an irony of the Tunisian situation that Khair al-Din became prime minister through French intrigue. He admired the French, could speak French adequately, and his stay in Paris from 1852 to 1856 was important in the formation of his reformist tendencies. But he was also, more than most other Tunisian leaders, conscious of and concerned over European, particularly French, ambitions in the country. He also shared with other nineteenth century Muslim reformers the naive conviction that cultural borrowing could be restricted to specific areas, so that the Muslim society would be rejuvenated while retaining its religious beliefs and values. Khair al-Din's experiences in the previous fifteen years had made him doubt the utility of adopting foreign political institutions which had no roots in the country. Consequently as prime minister he did not restore the constitution of 1860, and proceeded cautiously but persistently to revive the authority of government through surveillance of the *qa'ids* and state expenditure. He carried out a general reduction in taxation and, while allowing the tax-collectors to retain as salaries one-tenth of the taxes they gathered, he required them to submit annual accounts of their work. While thus curbing the abuses of the tax-collectors, he tried to stimulate agriculture and the crafts through the positive intervention of the state. In the region of Sfax he gave state lands to peasants willing to plant olives on them, and tried, but failed because of consular opposition, to impose heavy tariffs on imported goods to protect the interests of the local craftsmen. Under Khair al-Din the capital had its first cleaning department financed from municipal taxes imposed on house owners. And in 1875 the prime minister founded the Sadiqiyya College, the first Tunisian school to have a modern curriculum. For financing the college Khair al-Din instituted a *habus* consisting of the property obtained from the former prime minister Khaznadar in partial reimbursement of his debts to the state. At first put at fifty-three million francs, these debts were later reduced through a legal settlement and the bey's intervention to twenty million. The college was not an ambitious intellectual institution. Its curriculum, which included instruction in French, Italian, mathematics, and the sciences, was best suited for training civil servants. For Tunisia in the 1870s, however, this was a revolutionary curriculum, and the college was to serve during the French period as the model for the Franco-Arab system of schools.

The experiences of the previous fifteen years also taught Khair al-Din to be cautious in the execution of projects which encroached on the privileges of the European consuls. He inherited the chronic problem of consular jurisdiction. In 1871 he had introduced a project with the consent of Khaznadar for the creation of a mixed tribunal to try all cases between Tunisians and Europeans. This court was to have a majority of European members and a Tunisian president, and was to apply a special code based on Ottoman legislation. At the time England accepted the project, France did not oppose it, and Italy after much hesitation agreed to it in principle. When in 1874 Khair al-Din proceeded to form the court, Italy opposed it and was later joined by France. Khair al-Din set up in this year a provisional tribunal, and the consuls were prepared to accept its jurisdiction in financial disputes involving not more than 1,000 Tunisian piastres (about 500 francs). Unable to go further, Khair al-Din let the mixed tribunal operate on this small scale hoping for future enlargement of its jurisdiction.

On the economic level Khair al-Din was successful through a mixture of good luck and sound policy. In his first three years as prime minister, when the tax-collectors could no longer swindle the treasury with the concurrence of the officials in Tunis, the country also hadod go harvests. This enabled Khair al-Din to redeem all the treasury bills that fell due, and to have some reserves. The Tunisian economy was unusually buoyant at this time, and in April 1875 the capital witnessed the extraordinary spectacle of Europeans organizing a popular demonstration to express their gratitude to a Tunisian prime minister. The members of the Financial Commission were satisfied, and on the international money markets the value of the Tunisian treasury bills improved.

The rivalry among the powers and the scrambling among the consuls for concessions were, however, matters that Khair al-Din could not do much about. He attempted to preserve a balance between the interests of the three European countries most involved in Tunisia, and succeeded only in depriving himself of French support without winning that of the Italians or the British. Richard Wood was resentful because the English enterprises he had initiated between 1871 and 1873 all collapsed in the first three years of Khair al-Din's term as prime minister, and the British government was not prepared to back unprofitable economic ventures that had no great political value for the general British policy in the Mediterranean. The London Bank of Tunis closed in July 1876 and the gas company was in a state of insolvency in 1875 when its works of construction were not even complete; the railway lines were losing money and their administrators refused to construct the line to Baja. The Italians, anxious to consolidate their political influence in the regency, came forward to take over some of the concessions vacated by the English.

From 1874 the Italians attempted to take over the Tunis–Baja railway for which the English had also obtained a concession but in which they were no longer interested. They also began exploiting a lead mine at Jabal al-Rasas for which they had obtained the concession during Khaznadar's period. To maintain a balance between the Italians and the French, Khair al-Din gave the concession for the Baja line to a French company in 1876, but he rejected the French consul Roustan's request that a concession be granted to the Frenchman Oscar Gay to build the port of Carthage, and turned down another French project for forming an artificial lake in the depressions of the Algero-Tunisian *shutts* by cutting the isthmus of Gabis. The French company which obtained the concession for the Tunis–Baja line also founded in Algeria the Bona–Gulma line in 1877. Enjoying a guarantee from the French government of six per cent interest on its construction capital, the company attempted through Roustan to obtain Khair al-Din's permission to connect its Algerian line with the Tunisian. This project clearly had a political purpose, as it could be used in a French invasion from Algeria. Once more Khair al-Din had to refuse the French consul's demands. Roustan, who had seen in Khair al-Din an instrument for French infiltration, never forgave him his failure to execute projects which were politically important to France, and in which he had a personal interest.

Khair al-Din's uncompromising spirit and haughty character had earned him many enemies in Tunisia. The bey resented the reduction of his civil list, and Mustafa b. Isma'il, the bey's favourite and a friend of the French, was willing to use his influence against Khair al-Din. In 1877 Khaznadar still had two more years to live, and he had many friends in the regency who welcomed an opportunity to avenge the disgrace they suffered at the hands of the reformer. The British and Italian consuls had never liked Khair al-Din, and so he had no support from them. In 1876 Roustan initiated a strong and carefully calculated campaign against Khair al-Din. Because of the bad harvests that year, the Tunisian government had difficulty in meeting its obligations to the Financial Commission. Roustan bought space in French and Maltese newspapers to write articles which spread panic about the conditions of the Tunisian finances, thus causing a drop in the value of the Tunisian treasury bills. To his own government Roustan exaggerated the political consequences of Khair al-Din's gesture of sponsoring a subscription from the public to aid the Ottoman war effort against Russia. Roustan could argue that the Tunisian prime minister was a fanatical Muslim who had in the past worked towards bringing Tunisia under Ottoman sovereignty, and was still prepared to sacrifice his country's independence and the interests of the European nations in Tunisia for the sake of his religious convictions. Aided by Roustan's representations with the bey and his public campaign against Khair al-Din, Mustafa b. Isma'il prevailed upon the bey to demand his prime minister's resignation in July 1877. The reformer still had a brief career as minister of justice and then as grand vizier in Istanbul during 1878. In Tunisia Mustafa b. Isma'il became prime minister in August 1878, after a period during which this office was held by Muhammad Khaznadar (not to be confused with Mustafa Khaznadar, the former prime minister), who had served with Khair al-Din as Tunisian member of the executive committee of the Financial Commission.

With Mustafa b. Isma'il's accession to power, Tunisia reverted to her past tyranny and extortion with the authority of the prime minister. While the tax-collectors enriched themselves, and the prime minister built a palace for himself in Tunis, bought scores of villas, and acquired large estates, the country's economy was ruined. By the end of 1878 the government was once more unable to meet its obligations to the Financial Commission. The ambitious intriguer Mustafa was grateful to Roustan and was prepared to cooperate with him. This cooperation was rewarded by the extension to him of French protection in June 1879. But shortly afterwards he broke with Roustan over Khair al-Din's property in the country which Mustafa wanted to appropriate even though his predecessor had sold it to a French company.

Tunisia: the establishment of the French protectorate

The Congress of Berlin of 1878 gave a new turn to the Tunisian question by assuring France of Germany's and Britain's acceptance of an eventual French occupation of Tunisia. Bismarck unambiguously encouraged the French to occupy Tunisia so as to divert their attention from the loss of Alsace-Lorraine. In Britain the traditional policy of preserving the Ottoman empire was ending, and the prospects of an eventual partition of Ottoman territories between the powers were viewed with cheerful equanimity. While the congress was in session Britain signed with the Porte on 4 June a treaty enabling her to occupy Cyprus. In order to persuade the French not to cause difficulties over Cyprus, Lord Salisbury, the British foreign secretary, assured the French foreign minister Wadding-ton during the congress of Britain's acceptance of the French occupation of Tunisia, and confirmed this acceptance in writing on 7 August. The Italians were simultaneously given assurances by the British and the French that they could take possession of Tripolitania, but they remained unhappy. Tripolitania was not the fat prize that Tunisia was, and the assurances made about its future occupation by Italy were not sufficiently precise to quieten excited Italian public opinion. But Italian anger was a minor obstacle. The French government was more hampered in the occupation of Tunisia by the hostility of the French public to new colonial ventures, which were considered more expensive than useful, and the prevalent view that Bismarck was out to weaken France in Europe by encouraging the Tunisian enterprise. The French government tried, how-ever, to achieve control of Tunisia through a negotiated treaty with the bey. Roustan, assisted by Mustafa b. Isma'il, proposed to the bey in August 1879 an agreement providing for a French protectorate and involving French occupation of strategic points in the regency, and the organization by the French of the Tunisian police force. The bey refused the proposed agreement. But within two years the increasing activities of the Italians in Tunisia and their open rivalry with the French sufficiently aroused passions in France to enable the government to act without regard to repercussions at home.

From 1878 an Italian deputy, Giovanni Mussi, was placed in charge of the Italian consulate in Tunis, and he mounted an open campaign against French interests. He increased the demands for concessions to Italians, including a demand for allowing an Italian company to take charge of the port of Bizerta. In his four months in Tunis Mussi created much com-motion but produced no results, and was replaced in December 1878 by a veteran Italian diplomat, Licurco Maccio, who had served in the Middle East and had been consul in Cairo and Beirut at the same time as Roustan. As the British government in response to French pressure forced the veteran Richard Wood to retire in February 1879, and his successor Thomas Reade did not have his ability or the support of his government to enter the cold war among the consuls, the foreign communities in the capital became polarized around Roustan and Maccio. Each had his agents in the Bardo, his local protégés, his instruments of propaganda, and means of attracting capital from his country to use in concessions obtained from the bey.

After his failure to persuade the bey to accept a French protectorate peacefully, Roustan looked for incidents to justify the sending of an expedition. In 1878 he turned into an issue of French national honour a case involving a Frenchman called de Sancy expelled from the stud-farm of Sidi Thabit on the Majirda for which the bey had granted him a concession in 1866. De Sancy had defaulted on his obligations under the concession, and it was generally agreed that he was an adventurer seeking to use his government connections in Paris to exploit the Tunisian government. In December 1878 a Tunisian commission which included the Tunisian director of foreign affairs and the French vice-president of the executive committee Queillé was sent to expel de Sancy from the estate. Roustan, after having Queillé recalled, presented the bey with an ultimatum demanding reparations for de Sancy and the dismissal of two Tunisian officials who took part in expelling him and whom he considered hostile to French interests. The ultimatum was delivered to the bey on 8 January 1878, a day after Roustan was notified that a French expeditionary force was ready at Toulon to sail for Tunis if the bey obliged by refusing the ultimatum. The manoeuvre was foiled by the bey's compliance with all the demands. Mustafa b. Isma'il went in person to the French consulate to make an official apology on the 10th and the two officials lost their posts. De Sancy, restored to the estate, leased it to the Société Marseillaise de Credit which had founded a branch in Tunis earlier that year.

In the economic rivalry with Italy the French received a severe setback when the English concession for the Tunis–Gouletta–Marsa railway was bought by an Italian company. On 22 March 1880 the Italian company Rubattino, enjoying Italian government backing, signed a preliminary agreement for the purchase of the line for £90,000 sterling. The French Bona–Gulma company, also enjoying government backing, then prevailed on the English company, Tunis Railways Co., to sign a definite contract of sale on 14 April for £105,000 sterling, twice the value of the line. The Italians instituted legal action in London to stop the sale on the basis that the English company was bound by a previous offer of sale to them. Eventually the line was sold by auction on 7 July to the Rubattino company for £165,500 sterling. Almost simultaneously Mustafa b. Isma'il started to create difficulties for the French over their purchase of Khair al-Din's property. The former prime minister, having despaired of finding a Tunisian buyer for his property, and knowing that as long as Mustafa b. Isma'il was in power and waiting for an opportune moment to lay his hands on it no Tunisian would dare buy it, sold the property to the Société Marseillaise in July 1880. Khair al-Din's property consisted of three palaces in Tunis and its suburbs, olive groves, and a vast estate called Enfida consisting of 100,000 hectares of land. Bin Isma'il delayed the transfer of ownership to the French company while trying to persuade Khair al-Din to sell the land to some of his protégés. When Khair al-Din refused, the prime minister had the land registered in the name of the French company, but resorted to a legal device provided for by Muslim law to annul the sale. He had a Tunisian Jew of British nationality called Joseph Levy acquire a piece of land adjoining the Enfida estate, and had him secure it by pre-emption: the Muslim law entitles a person with a land contiguous to a property offered for sale priority in its acquisition if he is prepared to pay the price offered by other purchasers. By December 1880 Levy had formally purchased the land in this way, and immediately occupied a house in it without, however, making any payment, a fact which the Tunisian authorities were willing to overlook.

While involving the British in the conflict with the French through choosing Levy as the instrument of his manoeuvre, Mustafa b. Isma'il tried to make a deal with the Ottoman government. In November 1880 his agents were in Istanbul trying to exploit Ottoman fears of French designs which he could then claim to be able to oppose, to obtain from the sultan the title of *mushir*, which the Husainid beys had borne since it was bestowed on Ahmad Bey, and a promise of being permitted to succeed Muhammad al-Sadiq. At the same time he improved his relations with the Italian consul. The British consul Reade supported Levy's claims and Broadley, the correspondent of the London *Times* in Tunis, launched a campaign to win British official and public support for Levy. The combination of forces which Mustafa b. Isma'il unleashed, prevented the French company from entering into possession of the estate, although it had paid its price to Khair al-Din.

In the midst of the excitement in French business circles over Rubattino's purchase of the railway line and the Enfida affair, the French government decided to send an expedition to Tunisia. The decision was taken in March 1881. On the 30th of this month an excuse for the French invasion was provided by a raid into Algerian territory of the Khrumir tribe living in the region of al-Kaf. A list of previous raids by the tribe was immediately presented to the bey. He readily offered compensation and to punish the marauding tribesmen, but the French insisted on bringing them to account themselves. However, when a French cavalry detachment crossed the Tunisian frontier from Algeria on 9 April, it made for the capital instead of the Khrumir territory. A few days later a sea-borne force occupied Bizerta. The French forces arrived in Tunis without facing any resistance on 25 April, and on 12 May Muhammad al-Sadiq Bey signed at the Bardo palace the treaty presented to him by Roustan. The only request he made before signing, so that his prestige should not be destroyed, was that French troops should not be stationed in the capital. The French readily obliged.

In order to minimize hostility to the occupation in France, Italy, and Tunisia itself, no reference to a protectorate was made in the Treaty of Bardo. The military occupation was stated to be temporary and was to end whenever the Tunisian administration became able to re-establish order in the country and ensure the security of the frontiers. The bey remained the head of state, and France pledged herself to protect his person and family. In addition the treaty provided that existing agreements between Tunisia and other countries were to be upheld, but in future the bey might not conclude any international agreements without France's consent. France's control over Tunisia's foreign relations was made complete with the bey's appointment of the French resident-minister in the country on 9 June as Tunisia's minister for foreign affairs. But although the Treaty of Bardo deprived the bey of his independence, it did not give enough powers to the French resident to carry out the reorganization of the state and establish the firm control over its various branches necessary for reaping fully the economic fruits of the military occupation.

Paul Cambon, who was appointed resident-minister in Tunisia in February 1882, realized the need for a new treaty that would establish a protectorate *de jure*. Soon after his arrival he also started to negotiate with the consuls of Italy and Britain to obtain the dissolution of the International Financial Commission, whose existence prevented the French from taking direct control of Tunisia's finances, and the renunciation of the powers enjoyed by the consuls under the capitulation treaties which prevented the extension into Tunisia of the French legal system and caused numerous administrative problems. Cambon persuaded Muhammad al-Sadiq Bey to accept a supplementary treaty with France along the lines he wanted. When this bey died in October 1882 his successor 'Ali Bey was prevailed upon to sign the al-Marsa Convention on 8 June 1883 establishing a protectorate. Cambon concluded the convention although he was aware that the French Chamber of Deputies was hostile to the instituting of a definite protectorate because this would make France responsible for Tunisia's debts. Cambon made several trips to Paris to defend his policy and finally succeeded in having the Chamber ratify the al-Marsa Convention in April 1884. The convention provided for a French government guarantee of a loan to the bey of 125 million francs, a sum which enabled him to repay the debts and dissolve the International Financial Com-

mission. In order to aid the negotiations with the powers over the renunciation of the capitulation rights, Cambon also had the Chamber of Deputies
pass a law on 27 March 1883 creating a tribunal of first instance in Tunis
annexed to the jurisdiction of the Court of Algiers, and authorizing the
appointment of French justices of the peace in the major Tunisian cities.
This law further provided that the bey could by edict extend the authority
of the French judges over all the foreign residents in Tunisia. The implicit
threat that the bey would deprive the consuls of their special powers if
they did not relinquish them had quick results. England and Italy
renounced their capitulation rights in Tunisia in January 1884, and all the
other major powers, except the U.S.A., followed suit.

The protectorate system which emerged from the al-Marsa Convention
and Paul Cambon's policy preserved a semblance of beylical authority
while enabling the resident-minister (who was called resident-general
from 1885) to become the real ruler of the country. The bey continued to
have a cabinet consisting of a prime minister and a minister of the pen;
and all decrees and central government orders were issued respectively by
the bey and the prime minister. But the convention gave the resident the
right to introduce all administrative, judicial, and financial reforms he
deemed necessary and a French presidential proclamation of 1884 empowered him to approve all the bey's decrees, thereby giving them the
force of French law. The residents-general used their powers to remove
all important government departments from the control of the bey's
cabinet. The resident himself acted as foreign minister, the commander of
the French forces of occupation acted as the minister of war, and the
former vice-president of the executive committee of the Financial Commission, M. Depienne, became the director-general of finance. In addition
the French secretary-general of the government, whose post was created
before Cambon's arrival, replaced the prime minister in the functions of
coordinating and controlling the work of the various government departments. In the provincial administration the French kept the traditional
hierarchy of *qa'ids* (provincial governors), *khalifas* (deputy governors),
and *shaikhs* (administrators of tribal clans). But from 1884 *contrôleurs civils*
(civil controllers) were appointed to supervise these functionaries. In their
districts the *contrôleurs civils* supervised the collection of taxes by the
qa'ids, advised the administration on public works, and watched for
smuggled arms and the political activities of the local leaders. In the field
of justice the protectorate arrangement was to have French courts try
cases involving Europeans; *qadi* courts were to try those between two
Muslim parties, and a rabbinical court in Tunis was to try the cases
involving Jews only. The French courts had jurisdiction in all cases
involving a European party and a Tunisian, and the beylical court in Tunis
passed judgement in cases of criminal or penal nature involving Muslims.

While preserving the beylical court the French altered it so that it studied the cases referred to it and recommended appropriate verdicts to the bey, thus making it difficult for the bey to pass summary and arbitrary judgement.

The protectorate opened Tunisia for French colonization by creating a suitable political and legal framework for the acquisition of lands by the settlers. But the settlers had to buy their lands. Most of the lands they acquired came from either the public domain or *habus* property. Making only these two categories of land available to the settlers was as much a matter of political choice as dictated by the distribution of land-ownership in the country. As in Algeria there existed in Tunisia four categories of land-ownership: privately owned lands, collectively owned tribal lands, public domain, and *habus*. Unlike Algeria, the tribal lands formed only a small fraction of the cultivable land, whereas *habus* property constituted about one-third, including most of the fertile Majirda valley. The *habus* lands, though fertile, were generally neglected, and their administrators had no great interest either in developing them or preserving their *habus* character. The protectorate officials could thus avoid arousing the great indignation which appropriating the privately owned and tribal lands for the use of the settlers would have caused, and still make enough lands available to the settlers from the public and *habus* lands. Large plots of public lands in the south suitable for the cultivation of olives were sold to the settlers at the nominal price of ten francs per hectare. With regard to *habus* lands, two legal methods based on the Muslim law were devised to enable the settlers to acquire them. One was renting in perpetuity, a procedure permitted by the Malikite rite, and the other was based on a provision in the Hanafite rite permitting the exchange of *habus* lands with others. In 1898 a beylical decree permitted "exchanging" *habus* lands for money, on the understanding that the money so obtained would be used to buy other lands.

Because Frenchmen in Tunisia had to buy their lands, the country was colonized by persons with capital, or by ex-officials who chose to remain in the country. Colonization through official aid involving the free distribution of lands was avoided by the protectorate authorities. In consequence, the size of the French community in Tunisia remained small. As late as 1901, when there were 71,000 Italians in Tunisia, only about 24,000 Frenchmen lived there. In order to increase the number of French citizens in the country, a decree of 1887 gave the right of French nationality to any European living in Tunisia who had been there or had lived in Algeria or France for three years. Under the provisions of this decree only about 150 persons were naturalized in five years. The need to create a large French community in Tunisia led the protectorate authorities in 1897 to take more interest in encouraging colonization than in the past. A colonization fund was established in this year to buy lands for settlers, and in the following year a special institute for training prospective farmer-settlers in Tunisia was set up. Nevertheless the growth of the French community remained slow, and not until 1930 were there more French in Tunisia than Italians. The French on the other hand owned ten times as much land as the Italians and controlled most of Tunisia's industrial sector. Consequently they had to rely on Italian skilled labour, and the need for harmonious relations between the two European communities was felt strongly. The Catholic Church created a bond between them, and by a Franco-Italian agreement of 1896 the goodwill of the Italians was cultivated by giving them the right to sit on juries, enter the professions including law, and maintain their own schools, and Italian children born in Tunisia were allowed to retain their Italian nationality.

On the whole the urban and settled parts of the Tunisian population did not evince great hostility to the French protectorate in the pre-First World War period. But the tribes in the south, encouraged by the Ottoman authorities in Tripolitania, resisted the French forces in the second half of 1881 when they were engaged in the military occupation of the south. Many of the tribesmen who fought the French migrated to Tripolitania. As no defined boundary existed between Tripolitania and Tunisia, the French could not start building a system of posts to control movements of people to and from Tripolitania. All they could do was to halt the advance of their troops in May 1882 at Wadi al-Fasi, this being a geographical landmark whose Tunisian character was not in doubt, and start persuading the Ottomans to agree to the delimitation of the frontier. The Ottomans were not interested in making the French task of controlling Tunisia an easy one, and agreed to establishing a definite boundary only in 1910. In the meantime they conducted an active anti-French propaganda programme amongst the Tunisians. With Ottoman assistance, Hamza Zafir, a *shaikh* of the Madaniyya Sufi order, which had an important following in Tunisia, was engaged from about 1882 in making contact with Muslim groups in Tunisia from his headquarters in Tripoli. On the whole Ottoman propaganda was ineffective. More than half the Tunisian émigrés into Tripolitania, numbering about 120,000, had been repatriated by the end of 1882 at the expense of the French government and through the agency of the French consulate in Tripoli.

The relatively unhostile attitude of the majority of the Tunisians to the French protectorate was due to the flexible pragmatic policy followed by the French. In theory, at least, the Tunisian Muslims continued to be ruled by a Muslim, and in most litigation suits they did not need to submit to French justice. As the Tunisian Muslims did not experience any real form of representative government before 1881, they were not disturbed by the paternalistic nature of the protectorate system. The French in Tunisia wanted representative institutions. Their pressure led to the formation in 1891 of the Consultative Conference in which the settlers' Chamber of Commerce and Chamber of Agriculture met jointly every two years as a deliberative council to discuss public problems in the presence of the heads of the government departments. In 1896 a third college of the Conference was formed to represent Frenchmen not represented in the two chambers. Tunisians were not represented in the Conference until the First World War; but this does not seem to have caused any serious misgivings on their part. Nor was the hostility of the pious inflamed by a campaign of conversion to Christianity. In 1881 Monseigneur Lavigerie took control of the European Catholic community in the country. When in 1882 he became cardinal, he persuaded the Pope to restore the see of Carthage and he was granted the title of archbishop of Carthage and Algiers. Through his ecclesiastical control of the Italians, he was in a position to be of use to the protectorate authorities. But as his ardour for conversion, which he had shown in Algeria, had been softened by the experience of working amongst the Muslims, he concentrated his activities on philanthropic work through the twin societies of the White Fathers and the White Sisters which he founded. On some occasions, as when he intervened in 1882 to revoke the indemnity imposed on the people of Sfax because of their resistance to the French troops, he also seemed to act in the interest of the Muslims.

There was still another important factor which helped in averting conflicts between the Tunisian Muslims and the French rulers. Most of the politically conscious leaders of the capital were the disciples of Khair al-Din. Like him they were interested in reform, and they tended to tolerate French rule since they saw in it an instrument of modernization. This group, led by a former follower of Khair al-Din called Bashir Sfar, founded in 1888 an Arabic newspaper called *al-Hadira* (the Capital) whose aim was to spread modern ideas amongst the Tunisians without attacking the French. The group tried to have the French authorities appoint Tunisians educated in the Sadiqiyya College founded by Khair al-Din to the administration. In their newspaper they advocated the education of women, and attacked the Sufi orders which they held responsible for the spread of religious superstition. This group also founded the Khalduniyya school in 1896 intended to give instruction in modern subjects to the graduates of the traditional Zaituna university-mosque. At the beginning of the twentieth century some of these reforming intellectuals, calling themselves the Young Tunisians, came into the open in favour of creating a modern liberal Tunisian state through cooperation with France. The group was even willing to accept French colonization as long as it helped to introduce modern methods of farming and the Tunisians were not deprived of their best lands. Through a French-language newspaper, *Le Tunisien*, which the Young Tunisians founded in 1907, they tried to attract French public opinion to their programme.

While the energies of the Young Tunisians were spent on conducting propaganda for their idealistic programme, two events in 1911 and 1912 indicated its irrelevancy to the problems of life under the protectorate. In 1911 the passions of the Muslims in Tunis were aroused when the protectorate authorities tried to encroach on the boundaries of the Jallaz cemetery near the capital for the purpose of expanding a stone quarry. In the ensuing incidents between Muslims and the security forces, nine Europeans were killed and twenty injured. The number of Tunisian Muslim casualties is not known, but is believed to have been much larger. The incident showed how fragile was any programme of amity between Muslims and Europeans. In 1912, when the Young Tunisians took part in a labour dispute that led to a direct clash with the administration, they were disbanded. In this year, a Muslim child was run over by a tram operated by an Italian. The Muslims employed in the tramway system used the incident to demand the dismissal of the Italian employees in it, and to have their own conditions of service improved to match those of the Europeans. The Young Tunisians supported the Muslim employees' demands and the strike they called. The resident-general Alapetite struck hard. Two of the leaders of the Young Tunisians, 'Ali Bash Hanba and 'Abdul-Aziz al-Tha'alibi were deported, and others were imprisoned. Later in the year martial law was imposed and was not lifted until 1921, thus putting an end to all political activity. Until this happened, the moderate attitude of the Young Tunisians gave the protectorate a moral sanction which enabled it to avoid major political conflicts. Their disappearance from the scene was possibly inevitable, and the incidents of 1911 and 1912 served as a foretaste of a new pattern of confrontation between French and Muslims that was to emerge after the war.

Morocco: the end of isolation, 1830–60

Morocco entered the nineteenth century with the political system it developed since the sixteenth century little altered. The acceptance of sharifian authority as a symbol of unity, and the submission to it by the tribes only to the extent that the sultans possessed the means of coercion, remained the basic features of the system. But some stability had been achieved about the time of Mawlay Sulaiman's death in 1822. The *blad al-makhzan* became consolidated roughly to comprise the regions of Fez and Marrakish and the land between them to the Atlantic. The *blad al-siba* included most of the Rif, the Middle and High Atlas regions, and the Southern oases. This consolidation was due more to the fact that the strong tribes which had descended to the plains after the death of Mawlay Isma'il were able to prevent others from doing the same, than to the restraining power of the central government.

It would be wrong to understand from what has just been said that a formal and permanent division of the country into two parts existed in Morocco, with the parts always at loggerheads with one another. Economic and cultural interaction between the two parts continued. And although the tribes in *blad al-siba* refused to pay the taxes, they showed no signs of rejecting the spiritual authority of the *sharif*-sultans as long as they were allowed to enjoy autonomy. When in 1819 Mawlay Sulaiman was defeated and taken captive by the Berbers of Ait Umalu in the course of an expedition to Fazzaz in the Middle Atlas, he was given the traditional hospitality for three days and escorted to Meknes amidst signs of deference. After Mawlay Sulaiman the sultans recognized their inability to bring the inhabitants of *blad al-siba* under central authority, and gave tacit recognition to the authority of their local chiefs. This tended to confirm the authority of these chiefs and make them act as links between their peoples and the government. Consequently in the course of the nineteenth century several feudal principalities appeared in *blad al-siba*, the more important being the High Atlas chieftaincies, and in the north the principality of the Idrisid *sharifs* of Wazzan.

The relative stability in *blad al-makhzan* resulting from the compromise between the central government and the insubordinate tribes led to the revival of agriculture. During Mawlay Sulaiman's reign Morocco was able to export wheat to France and to Tunisia when this country was struck by famine in 1803. The country still had some trade with the western Sudan in slaves, and gold dust in small amounts coming from the Sudan was being sought in Morocco by European merchants in the 1860s. But the country's products had few outlets abroad. Until the European merchants expanded their activities in Morocco in the late 1840s, the economy remained undeveloped but stable, and the government's income sufficient for its primitive structure. The viziers and the high officials were not paid salaries, as they were expected to receive gratuities in the exercise of their functions, and little money was spent on the army. In the 1820s the country still had some regular black troops, but they were so much neglected that when Mawlay 'Abdul-Rahman ordered those in Meknes to accompany him on his tour of the country when he acceded to the throne in 1822, he found them armed with sticks. The rest of the armed forces consisted of tribal contingents provided by the Wadaya, Sharaqa, and Awlad Jami' tribes, and these were paid only when called to battle. As ruling the country thus cost the sultan little expense, his income from taxes was sufficient for his needs. His income came from the canonical taxes; *al-na'iba* which was considered a war contribution, as in the Sa'dian period, and became a permanent levy; and the *hadiyya*, which was a gift to the sultan expected from the urban population and the tribes on the occasions of the religious feasts, a visit by the sultan, or an important royal family event. To these were added indirect taxes on markets and ports, and in the form of customs duty.

In the first three decades of the nineteenth century Morocco remained closed to the outside world. Mawlay Sulaiman had no interest in Europe or in European trade. Even when in 1816 he liberated Christian captives taken by the pirates, and in 1817 banned piracy, he did this more in order to avoid conflicts with Europeans than to foster closer relations with them. The Moroccans objected on religious grounds to exporting the products of their country to Europeans, and whenever exports were allowed some religious justification had to be found, such as obtaining arms and ammunition in return. While exports were formally banned, Mawlay Sulaiman discouraged imports by imposing a fifty per cent duty on them. This attitude towards foreign trade, and Moroccan hostility to the movement of Europeans in the country, restricted the activities of the few Europeans in Morocco (numbering 248 in 1832) to the ports of Tangier, Rabat, Tatuan, and Mogador. The consuls of the European powers all resided in Tangier. They were out of touch with events in the interior, and were debarred from making direct representation to the sultan or his viziers, having instead to channel all their communications through the governor of Tangier. In addition to these obstacles European trade with Morocco was hampered by Mawlay 'Abdul-Rahman's revival of piracy after 1825.

After the French occupation of Algiers the Moroccans could no longer maintain the attitude that the hated Europeans should better be shunned and that their activities were of no interest to the sharifian government. The weakening of the Turkish state in Algeria had led in the eighteenth century to the renewal of the political and cultural relations between western Algeria and Morocco which had existed until the end of the Marinid state. The town of Wajda, on the northern part of the Algero-Moroccan frontier, which had fallen into the hands of the Turks after Mawlay Isma'il's death, was reoccupied by the Moroccans in 1796 or 1797 (A.H. 1211). Mawlay Sulaiman for political reasons also cultivated good relations with the Sufi orders in western Algeria, most of whom were on bad terms with the Turks, although in Morocco itself he was known for his hostility to the Sufi religious practices. He welcomed to Fez Ahmad al-Tijani, the founder of the Tijaniyya order, when he fled from Algeria in 1789 on account of Turkish persecution. And when in 1805 the people of Tlemsen led by the *shaikhs* of the Darqawiyya Sufi order rejected the authority of the Turks, they offered to recognize Mawlay Sulaiman as their sultan. Unwilling to go to war with the Turks, the sultan prevailed upon both parties in the conflict to reconcile their differences. These relations and popular pressure at home caused Mawlay 'Abdul-Rahman to send his troops to western Algeria in 1830. French threats and British advice made the sultan withdraw his troops and agents from the regions of Tlemsen and Oran in 1832. He could do so without much loss of face, as the withdrawal was officially explained by the misconduct of the Moroccan troops, especially the Wadaya who looted Tlemsen. Later Moroccan intervention could not be avoided or withdrawn with the same ease and without loss of dignity. The enthusiasm aroused in Morocco by Amir 'Abdul-Qadir's early exploits made it difficult for Mawlay 'Abdul-Rahman not to give him support. Also the sultan's inability to control the northern part of the frontier with Algeria enabled the amir to obtain arms through the Rif from Gibraltar.

The Algerian conflict drew Morocco out of her isolation from international power politics. Moroccan involvement in the Algerian war resulted in French reprisals, which in turn made Morocco dependent on British protection. In the 1830s and 1840s the British obtained guarantees from the French that even if a conflict with Morocco could not be avoided, no part of Moroccan territory would be occupied. In return for these guarantees the British used their influence with the Moroccans against greater involvement in the Algerian conflict. Two basic factors determined British policy in this period and for the rest of the century. By helping the Moroccan sultan preserve the independence of his country, the British prevented any other European government, particularly France or Spain, from threatening British control of the Straits of Gibraltar which were vital for the British position in the Middle East and the communications by land and sea which had recently been established with India. Secondly, the influence which British diplomacy gained with the sultan could be used for safeguarding the small but potentially expandable British commercial interests in Morocco. English merchants based in Gibraltar controlled about seventy-five per cent of Morocco's foreign trade in the 1830s. Her major imports of sugar, tea, and Manchester cotton were also in the hands of English merchants. Gibraltar was active too in the export of Moroccan wool and cereals, although these commodities were bought by other European countries besides England.

Internal political pressure on the Moroccan government and a misguided belief in unlimited British support brought the Moroccans into their first major battle with a European army since the sixteenth century. At the end of 1843 Amir 'Abdul-Qadir was a refugee in northern Morocco, and the sultan could not have forced him to leave the country even if he had wished to do so. The Moroccans sent their army to Wajda early in 1844 for the purpose of preventing the French from pursuing the amir into Morocco. Bugeaud, apparently without instruction from Paris, attacked the Moroccans in the plain of Isly near Wajda. The crushing defeat at Isly on 14 August 1844 and the bombardment of Moroccan ports by the squadron commanded by the Prince de Joinville destroyed the illusions, which the isolation of the Moroccans had led them to cherish, about their superiority to Europeans.

The results of this defeat were grave both for the sultan's internal authority and for his relations with Europe. The tribes, even when not obeying the sultan, expected him to defend the country against the Christians. His failure to do so caused them to rebel. The less the sultan could succeed in controlling the tribes in their reactions to European dealings with Morocco, the more they were able to undermine the advantages gained by diplomacy. The defeat of Isly sparked off tribal rebellions in various parts of Morocco. The Dukkala tribesmen in the region between Safi and Mazagan massacred government officials and looted Mazagan. Mogador, one of the ports bombarded by the French, was pillaged by the tribes when its inhabitants deserted it. Rebellious tribes threatened Marrakish, and in September 1845 Rabat rebelled and its leaders chose a local notable to replace the governor appointed by the sultan. The sultan's international standing was also weakened as a result of this defeat. The Scandinavian countries immediately ceased to make him the customary annual gift to retain commercial relations with Morocco. And the sultan, aware that much harm to the country could be avoided through speedy communications with the European consuls, appointed in 1845 a *na'ib* (deputy) to conduct relations with them on behalf of the sultan. Though the *na'ib* resided in, and often held the post of governor of, Tangier, he became in fact if not in title a minister of foreign affairs.

The French considerably expanded their activities in Morocco after the battle of Isly. French representatives in Morocco, since the dispatch there in 1845 of the veteran Léon Roches, were no longer consuls but chargés d'affaires. Between 1846 and 1849 the French financier F. A. Seillière established a network of agencies for the purchase of Moroccan wool, operating not only in the usual ports of European trade but also in Casablanca, Safi, and Mazagan. Two mining concessions in the Rif were issued in 1846, one to an Algerian and the other to a Moroccan, both associates of French firms, and through them French engineers were brought into Morocco. And from 1846 French ships provided a regular monthly service between Tangier and Oran. The British countered the expansion of French consular and economic activities by reinforcing their consular personnel and promoting their consul in Tangier John D. Hay to the position of chargé d'affaires. And when the Paris revolution of 1848 temporarily weakened French diplomacy, Hay encouraged the sultan in acts of defiance against the French. Hence Mawlay 'Abdul-Rahman's refusal in 1849 to make reparations for the beating up of a French consular agent by a Moroccan, and in 1851 to grant compensation to the owners of two French ships which had been sacked when wrecked near Sala.

The expansion of European trade contributed to the rise of a small number of wealthy Moroccan merchants who favoured its continuation, but popular hostility to dealings with the Europeans remained strong. The sultan himself, while drawing extra revenue from customs duty, also feared the political and social consequences of European penetration. Nor could he ignore the popular tendency of blaming all Morocco's economic difficulties, such as the famine of 1847, on European trade. The sultan since 1846 had started to establish government monopolies on certain items of trade which were handled in his name by local, usually Jewish, merchants. From 1848 he exploited the agitation caused by the famine of 1847, and the fact that British and French influences in the country neutralized one another, to establish total governmental control on foreign trade by establishing a large number of monopolies. Between 1848 and 1850 local merchants trading in the sultan's name controlled all the major imports (sugar, coffee, tea, metals, gunpowder, and tobacco), and such vital exports as cereals. The tanning and sale of leather also became a government monopoly, and in 1852 the free exportation of wool and oil was banned.

The British consul John D. Hay tried, until 1856 unsuccessfully, to have the sultan abandon the policy of monopolies, which caused considerable harm to the Gibraltar mercantile community and especially to the English merchants trading in Morocco. Hay's efforts at first failed because in the late 1840s the French were trying to divert Moroccan trade to Algeria, and were consequently not interested in encouraging the freedom of trade in Moroccan ports. But in 1854 they were compelled to reverse their attitude by the great demand in France for cereals and woollen clothing for the army in the Crimean War. The French merchants buying Moroccan wheat raised its price. In consequence the Moroccan peasants were encouraged to increase cultivation, and the sultan obtained an increased revenue from the tithe on crops and the duty on exportation. He became less hostile to the freedom of trade, and the French were prevailed upon to join the other powers in putting pressure on the sultan in favour of free trade in Morocco. In January 1856 a conference of all European representatives in Tangier could thus be held in the house of the *na'ib* upon Hay's initiative to discuss the need for removing restrictions on trade. This broke the sultan's final resistance, and Hay obtained a new Anglo-Moroccan commercial treaty in December 1856.

The treaty of December 1856 was geared to serve specifically British interests. While abolishing all monopolies, except those on arms, ammunition, and tobacco, it set the duty on all imports, which were handled mostly by English merchants, at ten per cent, which meant a reduction ranging from ten to twenty per cent, without reducing the duty on exports. The treaty also enabled British subjects to own property in Morocco, and

10 AHO

gave the British consular court the power to try cases in which a British subject was the defendant. The other European powers were invited to adhere to this treaty on the same terms. All European countries represented in Morocco, with the exception of France and Spain, gave their agreement. France resented the high duty on exports and, still believing in the possibility of diverting the bulk of Morocco's trade to Algeria, started organizing customs points on the frontier and reduced tariffs on goods entering Algeria by land.

Spain had her own objections to the British successes in Morocco. In 1848, when French influence in the country momentarily ebbed, the Spaniards had added the three small islands of Zaffarin to the remaining Spanish positions on the Moroccan mainland, namely Alhucemas, Ceuta, Malila, and Peñon de Velez. Neither the islands nor the other positions were commercially very valuable, but the Spaniards were willing to bear the expense of maintaining them for the purpose of expanding their influence in the Rif. With the British fleet frequently in the straits, and John Hay making wide contacts with the Rifian tribes, the treaty of 1856 seemed to the Spaniards to complete a British design to dominate the country to the exclusion of all other European powers. From 1857 they started to talk about the need to assert their presence militarily in the Rif. Hay advised the sultan to be conciliatory, and succeeded in having him offer the Spaniards in August 1859 land around Malila. This morsel did not satisfy the Spaniards and shortly afterwards the 'Anjara tribesmen provided them with an excuse for military action by attacking and demolishing newly constructed fortifications in Ceuta. A Spanish ultimatum was delivered to the sultan demanding the surrender of twelve of the 'Anjara leaders to the Spanish authorities in Tangier for trial. Even if the sultan had been prepared to end the crisis in this humiliating way, he was prevented from doing so by the popular unrest which the Spanish demand had already caused, and its denunciation by the *sharif* of Wazzan, the spiritual leader of the north. With the British not prepared to go to war with Spain as long as Tangier was not attacked, and the French supporting the Spanish demands in order to demonstrate to the Moroccans the inefficacy of British protection, the Spaniards were able to send an army into Morocco without fear of international complications. The Spanish forces landed in Ceuta, moved southwards and defeated the 'Anjara warriors, and occupied Tatuan on 6 February 1860. The sultan sent two columns commanded by his brothers who reached the region of Tatuan after it was occupied, and took no part in this short war.

Mawlay 'Abdul-Rahman had died at the end of August 1859, and was succeeded by his son Muhammad (1859–73). As usual in Morocco defeat at the hands of the Christians caused internal rebellions. The Rahamna tribesmen rebelled in the suburbs (*hawz*) of Marrakish, pillaged markets, attacked travellers, and while besieging the city harvested its crops. In spite of the great distress this caused to the capital of the south, the new sultan could not come immediately to its rescue because of another rebellion in the north, also connected with the defeat of 1860. The rebellion in the north occurred in the mountainous region of Kurt south of Wazzan. Its leader al-Jilani al-Rugi (the pretender) had no social position of any distinction. Such was the popular disaffection with the government, however, that his claim to religious sanctity and miraculous powers which could be used to attain the throne gathered around him an important tribal following. After al-Jilani's initial successes in Kurt against the governor in the second half of 1861, the rebellion spread northwards and Tangier was for some time threatened. The rebellion collapsed in February 1862 when the sultan's army dispersed the main concentration of the rebels, and al-Jilani himself was assassinated in the shrine of Mawlay Idris on mount Zarhun. The Rahamna were dispersed later in the same year.

To the tribal insurrections were added the problems which the terms of the peace with Spain created. The peace treaty, signed in May 1860, provided for the occupation of Tatuan by Spain until the payment by Morocco of a war indemnity of twenty million duoros; enlarging the Ceuta and Malila enclaves and the stationing of Moroccan troops near their borders to prevent the tribes from attacking them; surrendering a port on the Atlantic coast of Morocco to Spain; and the negotiation of a separate Spanish-Moroccan commercial treaty which should include permission to instal Spanish missionaries and a consul in Fez. The commercial treaty was signed on 20 November 1861. It contained the same guarantees as had the treaty of 1856 with England, and additional clauses granting Spaniards the rights of anchorage in various Moroccan ports and fishing off the coasts. The promise to surrender a port on the Atlantic was viewed by Spain as a guarantee for the future, and was fulfilled only in 1934 by the granting of Ifni to Spain. The clause which the Moroccan government found most burdensome was the one linking the evacuation of Tatuan with the payment of the indemnity.

Being the first part of Morocco to be occupied by Europeans for two hundred years, Tatuan became a symbol of the new wave of the Christian threat which the Moroccans had started to feel since 1830. The pressure on the sultan to ensure its speedy evacuation was great. Furthermore, as a corollary to the indemnity clauses the Moroccan government had to permit Spanish commissioners to control a part of the customs revenues, with the result that Spanish functionaries operated in an official capacity in the ports and could meddle in the conduct of Moroccan government business. In 1860 the Moroccan treasury could not provide more than five per cent of the value of the indemnity. Taxes had to be increased, but the additional income was needed to compensate for the loss to the state from the customs revenue. The British consul Hay tried in 1860 to obtain a loan for the sultan through an English merchant in Gibraltar called Richard Glover, but he failed because the British government refused to guarantee it. The sultan, disappointed that the British did not interfere to prevent the Spanish occupation of Tatuan, and angered by the failure to obtain the loan, decided that his friendship with Britain paid little dividends. He dismissed his *na'ib* in Tangier, Muhammad Khatib, who was noted for his friendship with the English, and replaced him by one called Barghash known for his French connections. The British influence in Morocco seemed at the time to depend on a settlement of the question of Tatuan. British pressure on Spain and the realization by the Spaniards that the right to appoint commissioners to control customs revenue was more useful politically than the continued occupation of Tatuan, which more-over was financially costly, led to a settlement. On 30 October 1861 a new agreement was signed between Spain and Morocco, providing for the evacuation of Tatuan upon the payment of only three million duoros, and levying the rest of the indemnity from customs. Tatuan was evacuated on 2 May 1862. The sultan was able to pay the sum specified in the agreement of October 1861 only by contracting a loan for two million duoros which was floated in London by Lewis Forde, an English merchant trading in Moroccan grain. The British government guaranteed this loan when the sultan agreed to set aside a part of the customs revenue for its servicing and gradual repayment.

Morocco at the crossroads, 1860–1912

If the Battle of Isly demonstrated Morocco's military weakness *vis-à-vis* Europe, the war with Spain in 1860 and its aftermath showed that Morocco's independence could be preserved only as long as the European powers were prepared to check one another's ambitions. Internally by this time the sultan's sovereignty had already been compromised by the independent action of local leaders. Of particular importance was the *sharif*-ruler of Wazzan, who was also the chief of the Tayyibiyya Sufi order, who emerged in this period as the head of a theocratic principality and in practice independent of the sultan. The sultan had to recognize his authority in order to retain some control, albeit indirectly, over the unsubdued tribes in the sensitive regions around Tangier and Ceuta. From 1843 communications were established between Wazzan and the French authorities in Tangier, and in 1884 the *sharif* was placed under French protection. The sultan's sovereignty was also eroded by the activities of the Spanish tax commissioners operating in Morocco's ports, and by the agents of public services established by Europeans to cater for needs arising from the expansion of their commercial activities. From 1846

European merchants in Morocco established a private postal service to ensure speedy communication between the various Moroccan ports. Not willing to leave this service in the hands of private individuals at a time when their need for it was increasing, the consulates organized official postal systems. In 1857 an English post office was founded in Tangier, and in the following year the British consulate organized a postal service between Mogador and Tangier. In 1860 a French post office was also founded in Tangier as a branch of the postal service of Oran, and in 1861 the Spaniards established their own post office. While providing a useful service to European and Moroccan merchants, the existence of the foreign post offices constituted an enlargement of the normal extra-territorial rights and an encroachment upon Moroccan government functions. A similar encroachment, also arising from the deficiency of the Moroccan government services, occurred in the field of sanitation. The Europeans living in the ports were concerned about health conditions, particularly about the spread of contagious diseases. As no regular sanitary service was provided by the Moroccan government, the consular sanitary council of Tangier was authorized in 1846 to appoint officials to supervise health conditions in the Moroccan ports. A representative of this council was also authorized to go on board ships calling at Moroccan ports and grant or withhold clearance for entry, even when Moroccan subjects were on them.

From 1860 Morocco was opened once and for all to European economic penetration. The size and the activities of the European community expanded as a result of the concessions obtained from the sultan. In 1867 about 1,500 Europeans were settled in Morocco, a sixfold increase on their number in 1832. The Europeans in Morocco were no longer bachelors coming for brief periods: they were now establishing families through local marriages, usually with Spanish women, and building residences. Commerce was no longer the only activity they engaged in. Many in the 1860s invested money in raising cattle and sheep in partnership with local farmers. It has been estimated that in 1866 members of the French community alone owned about half a million sheep. As the activities and powers of the Europeans in Morocco expanded, the number of Moroccan citizens enjoying consular protection increased. In 1863 the sultan tried with the help of Béclard, the French chargé d'affaires, to obtain the total abolition of the system of protection. Béclard would not agree to its total abolition, but in August 1863 he signed an agreement with the sultan limiting the number of protected agents the French could have in each port to two. The British and Spaniards gave their support to the agreement, but in practice like the French they ignored it.

Morocco seemed on the way to revival during the reign of Mawlay Hasan (1873–94). This sultan understood the causes of his government's loss of authority at home and abroad and embarked on a programme of reforms designed to remedy them. After the Battle of Isly the Moroccans had the plan of creating a modern army to replace the tribal contingents, and some ineffective measures were taken to that effect. Mawlay Hasan imposed a fixed levy of recruits on each of the major cities, and enlisted them in new regiments. For their training he recruited instructors from Belgium, England, France, Germany, and Spain; and he bought their weapons abroad – rifles from Belgium, coastal batteries from England and Germany, and field-guns from France. To strengthen the central government the sultan redivided the country into 330 small administrative units each with its own *qa'id*, to replace the eighteen large provinces in existence. And in order to induce foreigners to pay taxes, he devised a uniform system of taxation to which Christians and formerly exempted religious leaders would be subject. He delegated some of his powers to the grand vizier, and led expeditions in person to remote parts of the country to make his authority felt. He led a campaign against the Rahamna in the south in 1875, made a military demonstration in the Rif and the region of Tangier in 1889, and crossed the High Atlas in 1893; he died in 1894 on the way back while near Tadla in the Middle Atlas. In the economic sphere he tried to stabilize the value of the Moroccan currency artificially by setting a fixed rate of exchange in 1869. In 1881 he also struck new silver *riyals* designed as prescribed by the Muslim law in terms of weight and material used.

Mawlay Hasan's ambitious plans and untiring activity aroused great hopes in Morocco. Like other weak Muslim rulers in the nineteenth century he hoped to check European penetration by a rapid adoption of European ways and technical skills. As these reforms came too late, and the structure of the society could not be adjusted quickly enough to profit from them, they weakened the structure and became themselves the means of greater European penetration. Reorganizing the army proved more expensive than the treasury could afford, without it producing a reliable military force. Discipline of the new troops was bad, and there were many desertions. Moreover, the foreign instructors who accompanied the sultan wherever he went were more useful to their own countries, on account of the information they gleaned, than to the sultan. When the sultan sent young Moroccans to Spain to study medicine, engineering, and other sciences, these students were unable to profit from their studies because of insufficient previous education and they returned unable to adjust to the traditional structure of their society. The sultan's economic reforms were also abortive. The fixed rate of currency exchange was ignored by the European countries and the sultan had no means of enforcing it; and when the new *riyals* were minted the foreign merchants smuggled them out and in this way further weakened the currency by draining the country of its precious metals.

European penetration of Morocco after 1860 was so great that whatever good the sultan's ability and sound policies could have produced was annulled by the influence and rivalries of the European powers. Mawlay Hasan hoped to check these rivalries by not relying exclusively or even principally on any one power, and distributing concessions amongst all the powers who had recognized interests in Morocco. The failure of this policy became apparent at the Conference of Madrid of 1880. The sultan had tried through negotiations with the diplomatic corps in Tangier to end the system of consular protection, and he called the Conference when he had failed to achieve his end by these means. Britain was willing to support the sultan on the question of consular protection in order to thwart further French penetration; and Spain, not feeling strong enough to profit from the competition with France over Morocco, also supported the sultan's initiative. All the other powers joined the French in wrecking it. The sultan obtained the agreement of the powers in principle to having their subjects pay taxes under the uniform scheme he had promulgated; but he failed to get the system of protection abolished, and by raising it at the conference he inadvertently gave it international recognition.

Mawlay Hasan's death in 1894 was a turning-point in Morocco's history more because of his successor's failures than because of the successes of his own policy. Mawlay 'Abdul-'Aziz (1894–1908) was a boy of fourteen when he attained the throne. Mawlay Hasan's chamberlain Ba Ahmad proclaimed the boy sultan without consulting the *'ulama*, a step which caused dissension and was exploited by a party supporting Mawlay Hasan's elder son Mawlay Muhammad. Muhammad's party included Mawlay Hasan's grand vizier al-Jamma' and his followers, and was supported by the Sanhajas of the Tadla region and the Rahamna in the south. Ba Ahmad, acting both as regent and grand vizier, was able to consolidate 'Abdul-'Aziz's authority. However, when 'Abdul-'Aziz found himself alone exercising authority upon the death of Ba Ahmad in about 1900, a new and distinctive era of Moroccan chaos set in.

Mawlay 'Abdul-'Aziz meant well and was interested in reform. He was also too young, inexperienced, and impetuous to cope with the pressures and influences operating on him. Surrounded by strong opposing forces, he was unable to pursue any consistent policy. After Declassé became foreign minister in 1898, the French followed a more aggressive policy of penetration. In executing this policy they worked to prevent the reformation of the Moroccan government while at the same time drawing it towards greater recognition of France's special interests in Morocco by continually raising problems connected with incidents on the frontier with Algeria. The English urged the sultan to reform the administration and the system of taxation, but they were not prepared to give him material assistance; while the conservatives amongst the Moroccans, represented by the grand vizier Faddul Gharnit, regarded change as a means whereby the Europeans would extend their influence and the traditional values of the society would be undermined. In addition a group of European adventurers, many of whom had found their way into Morocco through Mawlay Hasan's zeal for European technical skills, catered for the young sultan's passion for modern gadgets in a way which made a mockery of his authority and squandered state revenues.

In his reorganization of the tax system, Mawlay Hasan had amalgamated the *'ushr* (the tithe on produce) with the *zakat* (in Morocco a tax on animals, the level being 2.5 per cent) into one tax called *tartib*, and abolished all the exemptions from which *sharifs*, Sufi *shaikhs*, tribal chiefs acting as *qa'ids*, and the nationals of the Christian countries benefited. As the Conference of Madrid admitted the principle of having Europeans in Morocco pay Moroccan taxes, the consuls agreed in 1881 to have their nationals pay the taxes on condition that the other groups who had been exempt also paid them. As the consuls no doubt expected, the *sharifs* and Sufi *shaikhs* refused to pay, and the *qa'ids*, who themselves were to collect the taxes, worked to obstruct the new system under which they themselves had to pay for the first time. Consequently the old tax system remained in force until 1901, when under Mawlay 'Abdul-'Aziz a new scheme of uniform taxation was adopted. This scheme abolished the *'ushr* and *zakat*, imposed a fixed tax on all cultivated lands, beasts of burden, and fruit trees, instituted a special tax of five per cent on sheep and cattle, and made all taxes payable only in cash. The new scheme was approved by the consuls in 1903. This reform also failed because the big landowners, the *qa'ids*, and the not inconsiderable number of well-to-do men of religion refused to pay. By their example and by denouncing the new scheme as being uncanonical, these leaders encouraged others not to pay. Consequently for a few years hardly any income was forthcoming from taxes.

Conservative Muslim groups could further justify their refusal to pay taxes on the grounds that the sultan was squandering state revenue on his European toys and Christian playmates. Europeans at the court suggested articles for the sultan's entertainment and provided them at exorbitant prices. The sultan bought hansom-cabs, automobiles, fireworks, wild animals in cages, theatrical costumes, etc. He ordered a state coach from London for which he had no suitable roads, and obtained a crown from Paris when told that a king should have one and shown pictures of Edward VII's coronation. While these objects, neglected by the sultan soon after their arrival, littered the gardens of the imperial palace in Fez, his European companions irritated the conservative Muslim population by their presence and obvious bad influence on the sultan. As the sultan thus compromised his religious standing, and his weakness was demonstrated in the failure to collect the new taxes, his authority was challenged from many sides. The Sanhajas of the Middle Atlas and the Jbala tribes near Wazzan were restive and raided the settled communities around Safru and Meknes. In the midst of this anarchy a *rugi* appeared in 1903 in the person of Jilali b. Idris al-Zarhuni, commonly called Bu Himara, who pretended to be a *sharif* and at first passed himself off as the sultan's disgraced elder brother Muhammad. Taking his base at Wajda, Jilali roused the entire eastern frontier and the Middle Atlas against the sultan. As chaos set in, and neither the sultan nor Jilali was able to attain complete victory, France could justify intervention in Morocco on the grounds that the deterioration of public order could, if not checked, threaten the interests of all Europeans in that country and cause serious problems to the authorities in Algeria.

France had refused since 1845 to delineate the southern frontier between Algeria and Morocco, in spite of the recurrence of frontier incidents and the incursion of Moroccan tribes into Algerian territory. During 1899 and 1900 the French occupied the oases of Gurara, Tidikelt, and Tuat. The last, having been occupied by the Sa'dians in the sixteenth century, was still considered Moroccan by the sultan. The occupation of these oases was part of a general scheme of French expansion into the western Sahara, including the peaceful penetration of Mauritania which Coppolani started to carry out in 1902. The Moroccan government was alarmed by the occupation of Tuat, and asked the British government to obtain guarantees from the French about the territorial integrity of Morocco. Britain, with problems pending with France arising from the British occupation of Egypt in 1882, would not assist the sultan. A Moroccan ambassador Bin Sliman was consequently sent to Paris to conclude an agreement over a definite boundary between Morocco and Algeria. The agreement Bin Sliman signed in July 1901 left the boundary undefined but provided for the establishment of frontier posts by both the French and the Moroccans for the collection of customs and defensive purposes each on territory unquestionably belonging to themselves. The tribes living between these posts could choose to submit to either side as they preferred, and France had the right to intervene militarily to make the sultan's authority obeyed on the Moroccan side of the frontier. The legal instrument for French military intervention in Morocco was thus provided by this final clause.

From the late 1890s the French foreign minister Declassé tried to obtain from the powers a recognition of what was termed in diplomatic language as France's special interests in Morocco. Italy, having no ambitions in this part of North Africa, gave her blessing in 1900 in return for a reciprocal recognition by France of her interests in Tripolitania and Cyrenaica. Negotiations with Spain over Morocco failed in 1902 because of disagreement over the limits of the future Spanish zone and the insistence of the French on reserving to themselves the right of intervention in it. The British had been interested since the turn of the century in coming to terms with France over Morocco in return for a free hand in Egypt. After protracted bargaining involving colonial interests elsewhere, a Franco-British agreement was reached on 8 April 1904, involving the relinquishment by France of her rights and interests in Egypt to Britain in return for British acceptance of a future French take-over in Morocco. The Franco-British agreement specified the zone to be entrusted to Spain when it became necessary for France to occupy Morocco, and subsequent British pressure on Spain was instrumental in having this country accept France's terms for an agreement on Morocco. The Franco-Spanish agreement, signed on 3 October 1904, defined Spain's sphere of influence to be, in the north, from the Mulawiyya to Larashe and, in the south, from the Spanish territory of Rio de Oro, which the Spaniards had occupied in 1884, to the Sus valley. French supremacy in this arrangement was affirmed by Spain's agreement not to undertake any action within her sphere of influence in the following fifteen years without France's consent, and to allow France to intervene militarily in the Spanish zone merely upon notifying the Spanish government. Both the treaties of April and October 1904 affirmed in their public clauses the desire of the three European countries concerned to preserve Morocco's "political status" and the freedom of trade in it.

The sultan was provided by the French with an Arabic translation of the public clauses of the Franco-British agreement, which contained a reference to the need for progressive reforms in Morocco and France's special role in carrying them out. The sultan, who did not understand the significance of the agreement, was easily soothed. Simultaneously with the notification to the sultan of the glossed text, the French government offered him help in obtaining a loan. Mawlay 'Abdul-'Aziz had obtained three loans from French, Spanish, and English sources in 1902 and 1903. His need for money was so great that he was still looking for new sources of credit. Through the agency of the French government the sultan obtained a loan in 1904 from a consortium of eleven French banks headed by the Banque de Paris et des Pays-Bas. The nominal value of the loan was 62.5 million francs. After deductions for commission and services the sultan received only fifty million francs bearing an interest of five per cent. For servicing and redeeming the loan the Moroccan government agreed to reserve sixty per cent of the customs duties collected in the ports and to have this part of the revenue collected by French officials. Two clauses in the loan agreement had a special political significance: the amortization of the loan, which was to be completed within thirty-six years, could not be accelerated in the first fifteen years (this being the period when Spain could not undertake action in Morocco without France's consent); and the banks providing the loan were given preference in any new loans the sultan might wish to obtain, in coining Moroccan money, and in buying and selling gold and silver in Morocco.

Internally political fragmentation increased from the beginning of Jilali's rebellion. Jilali expanded his influence from Wajda northwards, rallying to his support the tribes in the neighbourhood of Malila, and set up a new base at Salwan (Selouan). Further west the *sharif* Ahmad al-Raisuni acted as brigand chief in the Jbala region south of Tangier, and his activities took a religious character by being directed mostly against the Christians. In May 1904 his men carried away from their home in Tangier a wealthy Greek-American, Ion Perdicaris, and his English son-in-law. Raisuni demanded as the price of their release a large ransom and his appointment by the sultan as governor of the district. He obtained what he wished, but soon afterwards the sultan yielded to the pressure of the foreign communities in Tangier by dismissing him. Remaining at large, Raisuni continued his brigandage and harassment of Europeans until the Spanish conquest. Among his notable captives was the Scot Sir Harry MacLean, the sultan's military advisor, for whose release he obtained £20,000.

In the second half of the nineteenth century the High Atlas was dominated by three Berber chieftaincies: the Mtuga occupying the southernmost parts, the Gundafa to the north-east, and the Glawa controlling the northern parts of the range to the east of Marrakish. The wealthiest of the three was the Glawa chieftaincy, whose control of a salt mine at Talwat (Telouat) attracted trans-Saharan traders to it. The three chieftaincies remained isolated from the mainstream of Moroccan politics until the end of the century. Their chiefs were recognized *qa'ids* by the sultan, but they did not pay taxes. When in 1893 Mawlay Hasan passed through the Glawa territory on his way back from Tafilalt, the *qa'id* Madani al-Glawi gave the sultan and his army much needed hospitality which enabled them to survive their hazardous journey across the snow-covered passes. The Glawis subsequently established closer relations with the government. Shortly after the outbreak of Jilali's rebellion, Madani and his brother Thami took part at the head of their warriors together with the sultan's army in an engagement with the rebel's forces. The sultan's troops were defeated, and Madani received several wounds. He expected some reward for having taken part in a war which did not directly concern him; but when he went to Fez hoping for a position in the central government, he found himself ignored by the sultan and indifferently received by the grand vizier 'Umar al-Tazi. From this time (about 1905) the Glawis turned against 'Abdul-'Aziz.

The south was in a state of commotion following the conclusion of the Franco-British agreement in 1904. 'Abdul-'Aziz's brother 'Abdul-Hafiz, the governor of Marrakish, denounced his brother's readiness to allow himself to be dominated by foreigners. In a sense he had no choice in taking this attitude, because the people of Marrakish, having had less contact with Europeans than the people of the north, misjudged Moroccan ability to resist them and were outraged by 'Abdul-'Aziz's subservience. 'Abdul-Hafiz had to court the populace, and could not ignore the Rahamna Arabs, who had twice rebelled in 1844 and 1860 when the Moroccan army was defeated by Europeans, and were able to threaten Marrakish. 'Abdul-Hafiz could in fact establish some order in the capital and its suburbs only through a *modus vivendi* with the Rahamna chief, the *qa'id* al-'Ayyadi.

The part played by the Germans in inciting Moroccan resistance to the French is still insufficiently understood. Germany had been one of Mawlay Hasan's suppliers of arms. During Mawlay 'Abdul-'Aziz's reign German agents are said to have operated in Marrakish and to have encouraged 'Abdul-Hafiz to rebel against his brother. It is also said that the assassination on 19 March 1907 of the French doctor and philanthropist Mauchamp in Marrakish was incited by German anti-French propaganda. Their diplomatic role in the Moroccan crisis is better understood. They tried to subvert the Franco-British entente by thwarting the implementation of the two countries agreement on Morocco, for reasons connected with the emerging system of alliance in Europe and not for any specific aims they had in Morocco itself. At the time of the negotiations between Spain and France in 1902 and 1904 the Germans encouraged Spain to insist on being allowed to police Tangier, whose future international character was a central issue already accepted by the French and the British. Since 1904 they directed their efforts towards the internationalization of the Moroccan question. With this intention Kaiser William II made his famous visit to Tangier on 31 March 1905, and stated while there that he regarded the sultan as an independent ruler, warned against hasty reforms (a reference to France's mandate in the 1904 agreement with Britain to "reform" the Moroccan structure), and warned that Germany's interests in Morocco would be protected. The Kaiser's visit was followed by the German demand that an international conference on Morocco be convened. The French, anxious to avoid conflict with Germany, and relying on the diplomatic support of Britain, Spain, and Italy, agreed to the demand in July. The Moroccan conference, attended by the representatives of thirteen countries, was opened in Algeciras on 16 January 1906. Its objectives, as stated in the opening session by its president, the duke of Almodovar, were to prepare a programme of reform for Morocco that would preserve the sultan's sovereignty and Morocco's territorial integrity, and maintain the policy of the open door in commercial activity. As the principal consideration in the minds of the delegates was the balance of power in Europe, it proved difficult to agree on the share that each of the powers represented was to have in carrying out the so-called reforms. After nearly three months of diplomatic wrangling the powers adopted the Act of Algeciras on 7 April which provided for "reforms" amounting to a joint Franco-Spanish control of Morocco's police and finances. The policing of the major Moroccan ports was entrusted to France and Spain, with Spaniards in charge of Tatuan and Larashe, the French of Safi, Rabat, Mazagan, and Mogador, and both French and Spanish policemen in Casablanca and Tangier. A Swiss officer stationed in Tangier was to act as inspector of the foreign police forces and to report to the sultan and the diplomatic corps in Tangier. The Act also provided for the creation of a Moroccan state bank financed by the powers, with France controlling it by virtue of providing a third of the capital.

The sultan, realizing that Britain had relinquished her role as protector of the Moroccan *makhzan* and seeing Germany unable to restrain France, accepted the Act of Algeciras. But the Moroccan tribes were provoked by the increasing activities of Europeans in the country. In their attacks on Europeans they provided France and Spain with the excuse for military intervention. The assassination of Mauchamp led to the occupation of Wajda in 1907 by French forces stationed on the frontier. In the west the French Compagnie marocaine began works in May 1907 in the port of Casablanca. Neighbouring Shawiyya tribesmen and Muslims from Casablanca attacked the European workmen, killing nine of them. Casablanca was soon afterwards bombarded by a French warship, and in August 3,000 French and 500 Spanish troops were landed in it. The dispatch of the Spanish troops was a formality intended to give to the intervention the character of a police operation in accordance with the joint Franco-Spanish mandate to police the town under the Act of Algeciras. While the Spanish troops took no part in fighting, the French forces under General Drude, and then under General d'Amade, during 1907 and 1908 proceeded to subjugate the Shawiyya region around Casablanca. In the meantime Lyautey took over the command in Wajda from his subordinate Catroux and began to form a "band of security" around the town the western limit of which was the Mulawiyya river.

In August 1907, when the French designs in Morocco and Sultan 'Abdul-'Aziz's total incapacity to prevent their realization became clear, 'Abdul-Hafiz rebelled against his brother with the active support of the Rahamna and the Glawis. 'Abdul-'Aziz, fearing for his life even in Fez, fled to Rabat and placed himself under French protection. The French had since April 1907 expanded southwards from Casablanca and established posts at Sittat, Bin Ahmad, Bushirun (Bousheroun), and Azammur. The occupation of Azammur on the mouth of Wadi Umm al-Rabi' brought about the submission of the Dukkala living south of the river. Nevertheless the French decided for the moment not to station troops beyond the river in order to preserve the appearance of neutrality in the conflict between the two brothers. Hoping for help from the Mtugis, whose rivalry with the Glawis placed them in the opposing camp to 'Abdul-Hafiz, Mawlay 'Abdul-'Aziz advanced southwards in July 1908 with a small army and some French advisors. As soon as his column passed the southernmost French post at Sittat and the hostile tribesmen began their attacks, his regular troops started to desert him. He was rescued by the French, and immediately afterwards relinquished the sultanate and went to live in Tangier.

With 'Abdul-Hafiz now the only sultan, the question of his recognition by the powers gave rise to another diplomatic wrangle. France was prepared to recognize him on condition that he accepted the Act of Algeciras. Germany wanted him recognized without conditions, thus in effect trying to bring the Moroccan question back to its pre-Algeciras situation. With French troops occupying Wajda, Casablanca, and the Shawiyya region, this was too much to hope for. Eventually on 5 January 1909 'Abdul-Hafiz was recognized on the French terms. A Franco-German friendship seemed in the offing at the beginning of 1909, heralded by Germany's recognition on 9 February of France's special responsiblity for maintaining law and order in Morocco. Nevertheless the Germans sent the gunboat *Panther* to Agadir on 1 July 1911, thus provoking a crisis similar to that caused by the Kaiser's visit to Tangier. The German government was by then prepared to pull out from Morocco altogether, and the *Panther* episode seemed designed to have France offer a compensation to quiet German public opinion. The French obliged, and ceded to Germany two strips of territory in the French Congo giving her access to the Congo river.

Mawlay 'Abdul-Hafiz cut a much poorer figure before his people as a sultan than as a rebel. He achieved one success by defeating the rebel Jilali and taking him captive in 1909, but in the vital issue of opposing European expansion he proved as ineffective as his brother. In 1909 the Spaniards began the conquest of northern Morocco. They expanded their territory around Malila, and the forces commanded by General Marina occupied Nador and Salwan. The Spaniards immediately afterwards started to work on building roads linking Malila with Salwan and Ceuta with Tatuan. In December 1910 the king of Spain made a visit to Malila, then inspected construction works in the Zaffarin islands, and reviewed troops in Salwan. While the Spaniards were taking control of northern Morocco piecemeal the French were expanding the area under their control. Early in 1910 Tawrirt was occupied by the French forces in eastern Morocco, and Zair by the forces in the west. The sultan was totally helpless. The French and the Spaniards told him that their military action was made necessary by the attacks of the tribes on their nationals. He accepted this unlikely explanation, and agreed to sign agreements with France and Spain in March and November 1910 respectively making the evacuation of the territories recently occupied dependent on the formation of Moroccan forces trained and commanded by the Spaniards in the north and the French elsewhere. These agreements legalized the occupation and, had circumstances permitted them to take effect, they would have enabled the two powers eventually to conquer the rest of the country with Moroccan troops. The tribes did not permit the smooth and systematic transfer of power to the two European countries. Early in 1910 the Shrarda and Banu Mtir tribes, to the north and south of Meknes respectively, became alarmed by the French expansion in their direction from the west and east and rose in rebellion. Simultaneously, a new member of the 'Alawite house, Mawlay al-Zain, was proclaimed sultan in Meknes. As the tribes advanced on Fez, the French were able to intervene on the pretext of defending the sultan and the Europeans in the capital. A French column under General Moinier in 1911 repulsed the tribes and occupied Meknes after taking Mawlay al-Zain captive. On 30 March 1912 Mawlay 'Abdul-Hafiz signed the treaty establishing a French protectorate over Morocco. Within a year after this the French removed 'Abdul-Hafiz, who became obsessed with fear for his life and whom the French found difficult to deal with.

In this country where people took escape from the hard realities of life in the Sufi way of life, it was customary for sultans to tell functionaries whom they wished to disgrace to go and find a Sufi *zawiya* to pray in. 'Abdul-Hafiz was at first a critic of the Sufi tradition. After his abdication, and while living in Tangier on a French pension, he joined the Tijaniyya Sufi order and wrote a volume of verse extolling the Sufis. While the disgraced sultan was seeking solace in mysticism, the French and Spaniards were creating new realities in Morocco.

Libya: an advance Ottoman post, 1835–1912

From the sixteenth century the Ottomans were motivated towards intervention in the Maghrib only when the Christian powers of the western Mediterranean threatened any part of it. The Maghrib, consciously or not, was to the Porte a buffer between the major Christian countries in the western Mediterranean and the heart of the empire in the Near East. This attitude survived into the nineteenth century and seems to go a long way towards explaining the Porte's policies in Tunisia and Tripolitania after the French attack on Algiers. In the case of the former, the Ottomans attempted to obtain from the beys a recognition of Ottoman sovereignty. In Tripolitania they removed the Qaramanlis from power and assumed direct control when they felt that internal strife might enable the French to occupy it. Henceforth Tripolitania became a base for preventing French expansion eastwards from Algeria.

After taking Tripoli in 1835 the Turks had to reconquer Tripolitania and Fazzan from the leaders that had opposed the Qaramanlis. 'Abdul-Jalil remained the master of Fazzan and Sirta, and Ghuma and Mrayyid held the mountainous regions of Gharian and Tarhuna respectively. All three leaders had been suppressed in 1842, and in 1843 the Ottoman administration of what was to become the state of Libya took shape. Because of the attitude described above, and the vast predominantly desert expanses of the country, the Turkish presence in it took the form of dispersed military posts which were also administrative centres. Cyrenaica, with an administrative capital at Banghazi, was made a *mutasarrifiyya*. Its governor, the *mutasarrif*, was directly responsible to Istanbul, but in military matters, justice, and customs Cyrenaica was attached to the second province, the *wilaya* of Tripolitania. This second province, which included the rest of present-day Libya, was divided into three *sanjaqs* (districts): Khums, comprising this town together with Misurata, Zlitan, and Sirta; the western or Jabal Nafusa district which had its administrative centre at Yafran; and Fazzan with its administrative centre at Murzuq. The two provincial capitals (Tripoli and Banghazi), and the three administrative centres of the districts were all garrison towns. In addition Ottoman troops were stationed after 1835 in Tajura' and Zawiya on the Tripolitanian coast, and after 1842 in Ghadamis.

Generally the Ottoman governors in Tripolitania and Cyrenaica did not take any direct interest in developing the resources of these provinces. A notable exception was 'Ali Rida Pasha, the governor of Tripolitania from 1867 to 1870. Having spent seven years in France undergoing military training, he spoke French well. Through French technical assistance he dug artesian wells, started work on dredging the port of Banghazi, and tried to develop Tubruq into an important port. But as he granted concessions to French nationals allowing them to settle in Tubruq, his activities aroused British suspicions and caused his recall. The Ottoman administrators usually interfered with the life of the tribes only to settle conflicts and ensure the payment of taxes. Under 'Ali Rida Pasha the Ottoman judicial system was introduced into the coastal towns, but in the countryside the traditional methods of justice based on a mixture of elements of Muslim law with tribal customary practices remained in force.

In one aspect of Tripolitania's economic life the Ottoman administration became involved, namely the trans-Saharan trade. This interest had both political and economic motives. The Tripolitanian route of Bornu–Fazzan–Tripoli had lost much of its importance at the time of the Ottoman occupation of Murzuq and Ghadamis, and a large part of the trade reaching the Maghrib from Bornu was being diverted after the middle of the century towards Cyrenaica. Very little gold dust was in any case reaching North Africa from south of the Sahara in the nineteenth century, and the only major commodity the Turks were interested in was the slaves, for whom there was much demand in Asia Minor. When slavery was abolished in Tunisia in 1846 and in Algeria in 1848, the Tripolitanian route enlarged its share of this trade. In 1847 the pressure of the British Anti-Slavery Society on the British government made the latter force the sultan to order the governor of Tripoli to ensure that some of the blatant atrocities of the slave trade were avoided. In 1848 the Ottoman officials were told they should not take part in the trade. Nevertheless the volume of this trade increased, so that whereas 1,474 slaves reached the Levant via Tripoli in 1849, 2,733 went in the same direction from Tripoli in 1850. A firman issued in 1857 finally abolished slavery in Tripolitania. Yet slaves continued to reach other parts of the Ottoman empire from Tripoli, even after the abolition of slavery in Turkey itself in 1889.

When the French reached the oasis of Tuggurt from Algeria in 1854 their interest became directed towards the trans-Saharan trade. Together with the purpose of preventing the further expansion of Ottoman influence southwards, interest in trade led the French consuls in Tripoli to advocate after 1857 the occupation of Ghat and through it the establishment of relations with the Azjar Tuaregs. Practical difficulties stood in the way of occupying Ghat, but in 1859 the French explorer Henri Duveyrier made contact with the Azjar chief Ikhenoukhen. This was followed up by a French mission commanded by Mircher who travelled from Tripoli to Ghadamis in 1862 and there met two delegates sent by Ikhenoukhen and concluded with them a treaty providing that this chief would protect French travellers and Algerian merchants in Azjar territory in return for the payment of tolls. Alarmed by French activities, the Turks henceforth cultivated closer relations with the Azjar through their posts at Ghadamis and Murzuq. In 1875 they exploited a conflict within the Azjar confederacy between Ikhenoukhen and an opposing faction to interfere on the side of the latter, and in the process occupied Ghat.

For the greater part of the second Turkish period in Libya (1835–1911), Cyrenaica had a distinct history of its own. Administratively separated from the rest of the country, its social and political life came to bear the stamp of the Sanusiyya, a Sufi order which had less influence in Tripolitania and Fazzan. This order was founded in Mecca in 1837 by an Algerian holy man, Sidi Muhammad b. 'Ali al-Sanusi (1787–1857). In 1841 he travelled back to the Maghrib, intending to return to Algeria; but when he reached Gabis in Tunisia and learnt of the progress of the French occupation of his home country, he went to Tripoli and two months later settled in Banghazi. In 1843 he founded the mother lodge of the order, al-Zawiya al-Baida on Jabal al-Akhdar. Between 1846 and 1853 he was again in Mecca, and after his return he moved his headquarters further away from the centre of Turkish government in Banghazi to the oasis of Jaghbub. After Sidi Muhammad al-Sanusi's death, the headship of the order went to his son Sayyid al-Mahdi. Under him the order became a force in the Sahara. To be nearer to the peoples the Sanusis influenced, Sayyid al-Mahdi moved his headquarters in 1895 to Kufra and four years later to Qiru between Borku and Tibesti.

The bedouins of Cyrenaica were dominated by the Jibarna and Harabi tribes, both derived from the Banu Sulaim Arab invaders of the eleventh century and forming a homogeneous tribal community. Their allegiance to Islam was strong, but they were ignorant of its doctrines, hardly practised its rites, and were generally given to a life of lawlessness. They were, however, great believers in saints and in the grace channelled through them. Muhammad b. 'Ali al-Sanusi was a man of learning and a religious and social reformer, but to the Cyrenaican bedouins he was first and foremost a saint. Through the belief in his sainthood and his ability to adapt himself to the tribes' way of life, he spread his influence over the entire Cyrenaican bedouin community. In Jaghbub he trained religious scholars (*ikhwan*, brethren) whom he sent to found *zawiyas* among the various tribal groups. In the *zawiyas* the *ikhwan* administered justice, provided religious instruction to the children, and arbitrated in conflicts. Because they were so useful, the tribes contributed lands and labour to build the *zawiyas*, and donated cultivable lands for their upkeep.

The influence of the Sanusiyya order outside Cyrenaica was also considerable. In 1900, out of its 143 *zawiyas*, 45 were in Cyrenaica, 25 in Fazzan, and 15 were distributed among Waday, Kanem, Zinder, and Timbuktu. While contributing through its southern *zawiyas* towards the revival of Islam in the desert and remote parts of Africa, the order was able to control the trans-Saharan trade along the Waday–Kufra–Banghazi route. The *zawiyas* of the order along this route profited from tolls they received from the traders, and their *shaikhs* often traded to their own account. This route continued to flourish under Sanusi auspices until its activity was disrupted by the French occupation of Waday, Tibesti, and Borku between 1906 and 1914 and the Italian invasion of Libya in 1911.

The Sanusiyya and the Turks accepted one another, though grudgingly. The founder of the order considered that the Turks were usurpers of the caliphate; but as the Sanusis fought French influence in the Sahara and were extremely hostile to the French occupation of Algeria, their leaders were compelled to recognize the advantages of the Turkish presence as a check to further French expansion. The Turks understood the Sanusis' sentiments, were realistic enough to overlook their attitude on the caliphate, and took steps to cultivate their goodwill. In a charter issued in 1856 Sultan 'Abdul-Majid I exempted the property of the Sanusiyya order from taxation and recognized the right of its leaders to collect the tithe from their followers. A later charter also recognized the right of sanctuary in Sanusi *zawiyas*. After 1879, when the *mutasarrifiyya* of Cyrenaica was completely separated administratively from the *wilaya* of Tripolitania, the Sanusis helped the Turkish officials in the collection of taxes and the maintenance of law and order. The result was that "the administration of Cyrenaica might be called at this period [1879–1911] a Turco-Sanusi condominium".[1]

Upon the occupation of Tunisia by the French in 1881 the first impulse of the Ottoman government was to use Tripolitania as a base for a campaign of religious propaganda directed towards encouraging the Tunisian tribes to resist the French. The migration of Tunisians from the southern towns to Tripoli and of some of the tribes, including the entire Hamama, was considered by the Ottomans an indication of the success of their activities, and was viewed with apprehension by the French because of the implied rejection of their authority and the difficulties it caused in controlling the frontiers. The French were compelled, however, to act with restraint in dealing with both the question of Tunisian refugees in Tripolitania and the movement of tribesmen in the no-man's-land between Wadi al-Fasi, where the French stopped in May 1882, and the indisputedly Tripolitanian territory. While the French consular agents in Tripolitania tried to induce the refugees to return by offering to defray their expenses in travelling back to their homes, the French military authorities abstained from further expansion beyond Wadi al-Fasi and waited for the Ottoman authorities to agree to the delimitation of the frontier, which they did only in 1910. In the meantime the military authorities established posts at Zarzis, Matamur, and Tatawin, and recruited tribal auxiliaries to control the movements of the tribes. Although Ottoman and French officials in the region of the frontier faced each other with hostility, and friction between them continued to occur, the Ottoman authorities in Tripoli became conciliatory to the French after 1885. Between 1882, when the members of the Flatters' mission were assassinated in the eastern Sahara, and 1890, when the occupation of Segu on the Niger opened the way to the conquest of Timbuktu and aroused interest in establishing a conjunction between the French possessions in North Africa and the Niger region, the French did not pursue their efforts to penetrate Azjar territory. The assurance this gave the Ottomans, coupled with increasing Italian aggressiveness in Tripolitania, changed the Ottoman attitude towards the French in Tunisia. The Ottomans would not conclude an agreement on the question of the Tunisian–Tripolitanian frontier because this would constitute an overt recognition of French control in Tunisia. Nevertheless after 1889 they agreed to the formation of a Turco-French delegation to look into frontier

[1] E. E. Evans-Pritchard, *The Sanusi of Cyrenaica* (Oxford, 1954), p. 98.

clashes. In 1885, when the Ottomans were expecting an imminent Italian attack on Tripolitania and were reinforcing their garrisons there, they made their first conciliatory gesture to the French by giving the Tunisian refugees in Tripolitania the choice between settling in Sirta, which was hardly an inducement for them to stay, and returning to Tunisia.

The Italian ambitions in Libya, which were encouraged by the French and British hints at the Congress of Berlin in 1878, became a matter of national honour when the French occupied Tunisia in 1881. From this time onwards the Italians in Tripolitania adopted the tone of future rulers. Incidents between them and Ottoman officials multiplied after 1882. In 1883 the Italian government threatened to use force to protect Italian nationals in Tripolitania, and succeeded in having the governor whom they held responsible for the incidents recalled. But without the other powers' clear acquiescence the Italians could not proceed to encroach upon Ottoman sovereignty. In the 1880s neither the French in Tunisia nor the British in Egypt were sufficiently secure in their control of these countries to want to see Italy, who had become a partner with Germany and Austria-Hungary in the Triple Alliance, in occupation of Libya. Germany, on the occasion of the renewal of the Triple Alliance in 1888, signed a treaty with Italy recognizing her interests in Libya. In 1902 when France and Britain were approaching an agreement amongst themselves on Morocco and Egypt, both gave Italy a free hand in Libya. Austria followed suit in the same year on the occasion of the second renewal of the Triple Alliance. But these developments in favour of Italy's action in Libya were marred by the friendliness of her two partners in the Triple Alliance, particularly Germany, with the Ottoman government. As long as Germany acted as protector of the decrepit empire against the designs of France and Britain, she felt compelled to restrain Italy as well. As the Italians waited for the opportune moment to send troops to Libya, they pursued a programme of systematic economic penetration. After 1902 an Italian post office and medical services were established in Tripolitania. The Banco di Roma started to sponsor Italian economic enterprises in Libya, which included the foundation of an esparto grass mill in Tripoli, a flour mill in Banghazi, and the purchase of lands for agricultural schemes.

The Young Turk revolution of 1908 had its impact on the Libyan situation in two ways. In the first place it widened the gulf between the Sanusiyya and the Porte, and led the Italians to believe that the Sanusis would not interfere in the war on the side of Turkey. Secondly, the new rulers of Turkey, by their determination to resist Italian economic expansion, made the Italians feel that immediate military action was the only alternative to withdrawal. In October 1910 a new governor, Ibrahim Pasha, arrived in Tripoli with instructions to enforce a law prohibiting foreign corporations from owning lands in both Tripolitania and Cyrenaica, and in November a Turkish commission visited Libya and recommended specifically the cessation of purchase of land by Italians. The registration of lands purchased by Italians immediately stopped, and it was resumed only when Austria intervened. By this time Italy had grown to suspect German collusion with the Ottoman government in preventing her occupation of Libya. In June 1911 Germans bought tracts of land in Tripolitania, and a German banking agency was actively competing with the Banco di Roma. With her friendliness towards the Porte, and the *Panther* episode in Morocco pointing to a German colonial drive, Germany seemed bent on sharing the control of North Africa with Britain and France.

Early in September 1911 the Italian military preparations for the attack on Libya were completed and the powers informed of the impending campaign. None raised any objections, On the 23rd Italy protested to the Porte about the activities of the Tripoli branch of the Committee of Union and Progress which, she claimed, endangered the lives of Italians living in Tripolitania, and warned against the dispatch of weapons. The Ottoman government tried to placate the Italians through German channels by offering to grant them all the economic concessions they wanted in Libya provided that these did not constitute total monopoly. At the same time 12,000 rifles and ammunition were sent on the *Darna* to Tripoli. On the day this vessel reached Tripoli, the Porte replied to the Italian protest, denying the existence of any anti-Italian activities in Libya. The dispatch of the *Darna* gave Italy her *casus belli*. On the 28th an Italian ultimatum was delivered to the Porte stating that in order to protect Italian nationals the Italian government intended to occupy Tripolitania and Cyrenaica, and demanding an answer indicating the Porte's consent within twenty-four hours. In reply the Porte offered Italy all the guarantees required for the safety of Italians short of surrendering sovereignty over the Libyan provinces. Italy's answer was the declaration of war on the Ottoman empire on 29 September.

During the month of October 1911 the Italians occupied five important ports on the Libyan coast: Tubruq, Tripoli, Darna, Banghazi, and Khums (Homs). Two proclamations by the Italian command promised the inhabitants equality with Italians, non-intervention by Italian authorities in the religious life of the Muslims, and great material benefits. The proclamations also spoke of the Turks as foreign oppressors. But as the Muslims of the country still preferred them to the Italians, the Turks did not have to fight the war alone. Until the signing of the Treaty of Lausanne in October 1912 between Italy and the Ottoman empire, the Italian forces were contained in the five coastal towns they had occupied a year earlier. The extent of the local support for the Turks can be gauged by the fact that the Ottoman forces in Tripolitania and Cyrenaica did not exceed

7,000 men at the time, whereas the Italian expeditionary troops numbered about 60,000.

The Sanusis had received the attempts of the ruling Committee of Union and Progress in Turkey to spread its ideas in Libya with misgivings, and resented in particular the foundation of a branch of the committee in Banghazi. However, the threat of Italian expansion from the north, and of French penetration of the Sahara, caused them to cooperate with the Turks more than they had done in the past. In 1910 the head of the order, Sayyid Ahmad al-Sharif, allowed a Turkish *qa'imaqam* (district governor) to reside in Kufra, then the headquarters of the order, and the Ottoman flag to be flown there. This policy was as much the result of prudent considerations as of Muslim sentiment, since the recognition of Ottoman sovereignty entitled the Sanusis to benefit from the international guarantees of the territorial integrity of the empire.

When the Turks withdrew from the posts occupied by the Italians, Sanusis and non-Sanusis alike enlisted under Turkish command to fight the invaders. One of the first Muslim leaders to rally to the support of the Turks was the Berber chief Shaikh Sulaiman al-Baruni from Fassatu in Jabal Nafusa. Al-Baruni had been imprisoned by the Turks before 1908 for his political agitation, but after the Young Turk revolution he became a deputy in the Ottoman parliament. In October 1911 he joined Nash'at Pasha, the commander of the Turkish troops withdrawn from Tripoli, at his new base at Gharian, and recruited 1,000 volunteers from the Jabal. As other volunteers joined the Turks, three training camps were set up: one at Gharian, another near Banghazi, where 'Aziz 'Ali al-Misri was in command, and a third near Darna where the commander was Enver Pasha assisted by the future Ataturk, Mustafa Kamal. In addition to the training given locally, Enver Pasha in June 1912 sent 365 sons of *shaikhs* to be trained as officers in Istanbul; however, only thirty of those who received their commission before the outbreak of the First World War returned to Libya and joined the head of the Sanusiyya, Sayyid Ahmad Sharif.

It had become clear early in the Libyan war that local resistance would prolong the fighting and make it costly to the Italians. Heavy fighting outside Tripoli from 23 to 26 October 1911 between the Italian forces and the retreating Turks supported by local warriors, received wide coverage in the European press, and thereafter stories of Italian atrocities were widespread. Italian public opinion, aroused by these stories, was further outraged by the inability of the Italian forces to advance into the interior, and by reports about the heavy casualties of the war. In the year of fighting, in which the Italians could claim little military success, 3,380 soldiers died, over 4,000 men were wounded, and about fifty million lire spent in the prosecution of the war. As the clamouring of the Italian public for a speedy and successful conclusion of the war mounted, the

Italian government made changes in the high command in Libya in September 1912 in preparation for a new offensive. Simultaneously, the Italian government threatened to open a new front in the Aegean Sea if the Ottoman government did not agree to negotiate for peace. This threat, and the pressure of the powers on the Porte, led to the opening of negotiations at Ouchy (Lausanne). Anxious to bring the war to an end quickly, the Italian government made a number of concessions which the Ottomans considered necessary to allay Muslim sentiments at home. The result was the conclusion of peace on ambiguous terms which enabled the Ottoman government to continue to exercise an indirect influence in Libya. In a secret treaty concluded on 15 October 1912 it was agreed that the Ottoman sultan would issue a *firman* granting autonomy to Libya, and three days later would make a declaration containing a reference to Italian sovereignty over this country, which an Italian royal decree had proclaimed in November 1911. This declaration would, however, also affirm that the sultan remained, in his capacity of caliph, the spiritual head of the Libyan Muslims. The sultan would henceforth be represented in his religious capacity by someone residing in the country, and he would be able to appoint the chief *qadi* of Tripoli. The public treaty signed on 17 October brought hostilities to an end, and provided for the withdrawal of Ottoman officials and troops from Libya.

Turkey's defection left the Libyans to fight the war on their own. 'Aziz 'Ali al-Misri remained in Cyrenaica with a few other Turkish officers directing Sanusi operations until the end of 1913 when he was withdrawn. From Egypt no assistance was forthcoming except for the paltry aid obtained from voluntary contributions through charitable organizations such as the Society of the Red Crescent. The khedive was prevented from giving military assistance by British officials, and the contraband movement of ammunition across the Egyptian-Cyrenaican boundary was checked by the British officers placed in command of the Egyptian frontier posts after 1913.

From the end of 1912 the Sanusis posed as the legitimate rulers of the whole of Libya. Sayyid Ahmad al-Sharif, the head of the order, moved his base about this time from Kufra to Jaghbub to be near the scene of the fighting, and in May 1913 he was in the camp of Sidi 'Aziz near Darna when the Italians attacked and failed to take it. Sanusi political authority in Cyrenaica rested on religious grounds. Their claim to authority in the rest of Libya is based on a message from the sultan said to have been conveyed verbally to Sayyid Ahmad al-Sharif in November 1912 by Enver Pasha, the commander of the Turkish forces near Darna. In it the sultan is said to have entrusted the leadership of the whole of Libya to the head of the Sanusiyya, and told him that by granting independence to this country he intended that its people should become responsible for defending it.[1] From the end of 1912 the Sanusis spoke of their authority as an amirate, and their correspondence bore the stamp of the "Sanusi government". To the west of Cyrenaica the Sanusis had an important *zawiya* in Sirta at Nawfaliyya through which they exercised influence on the Awlad Sulaiman tribe. But further west their religious influence was minimal, and their claim to political authority was consequently ignored. While the Italians controlled Tripoli and Khums, local chiefs exercised in other places of Tripolitania the authority vacated by the Turks. The more important of these were Ramadan al-Suwaihili (also known as al-Shtiwi) in Misurata, Ahmad al-Mrayyid in Tarhuna, the Ku'bar family in Gharian, and Sulaiman al-Baruni in Jabal Nafusa. When in 1912 the Turks declared Libya independent, al-Baruni announced the formation of a Tripolitanian government under his leadership. In this way he tacitly rejected Sanusi authority, without being able to obtain the cooperation of the other Tripolitanian leaders.

As the Turkish troops were withdrawn and few Ottoman officers remained to organize and lead the tribesmen in battle, the Italians found the task of expansion from their five main positions much easier. By the end of 1913 they had occupied all the important coastal towns in Cyrenaica and Tripolitania, occupied Ghadamis, penetrated across Jabal Nafusa to the Tunisian frontier, and occupied key positions in Fazzan including Murzuq. In Cyrenaica they surrounded the main concentration of Sanusi forces in Jabal al-Akhdar by occupying Tulmaitha, Barqa (al-Marj), and Abiar in April, Martuba in May, and al-Zawiya al-Baida in September 1913. With the occupation of Nawfaliyya in March 1914 they had all the main positions on the Libyan coastline. But in 1914 it became clear that they were far from controlling the population in the interior. Sulaiman al-Baruni tried, after the Italians occupied Jabal Nafusa, to obtain from them a recognition of Tripolitania's autonomy under his leadership in return for his acceptance of Italian sovereignty. He was spurned and subsequently left for Istanbul. But in Fazzan resistance from the tribes directed by a delegate of the head of the Sanusiyya called Muhammad al-Ashhab forced Colonel Miani to withdraw the Italian forces in the course of 1914 from Murzuq, Ubari, and Sabha. By December the Italian forces had evacuated Bu Njaim as well, so that the whole of Fazzan and most of the Sirta escaped Italian control. The Sanusi forces in Jabal al-Akhdar and the Cyrenaican plateau were in great difficulties because of shortages of food and ammunition, but their will to resist remained great. Thus when the First World War broke out, the interior of Libya was still to be conquered by the Italians. The arrival during the war of Ottoman and German military advisors and material assistance for the Sanusis and Tripolitanians prolonged the conflict and gave it a new political direction.

[1] Cf. Muhammad Fu'ad Shukri, *Al-Sanusiyya din wa dawla* (Cairo, 1948), p. 146.

10

The Maghrib, 1919 to independence

After periods of varying length under European rule, the four territorial
entities of Libya, Tunisia, Algeria, and Morocco emerged as independent
and relatively integrated nation-states. Of them only Tunisia had had the
potential for nationhood because of her homogeneous population, and a
tradition of effective and centralized administration under the Husainids
since the middle of the eighteenth century. In Tunisia, as in the other
three countries, foreign rule acted as the catalyst in nation-building.
Through the bringing of the disparate parts of the colonized country
under the authority of the colonizing power and the weakening of the
organization of the tribes, as well as through the advances in communication and transportation achieved in the colonial period, the various
groups came to have a greater sense of belonging to the same community.

The heterogeneous native groups were further brought together by the
realization that regardless of their locality, social background, or
educational attainment, they were all treated as different from and
inferior to the class of foreign colonizers. As racial differentiation on the
basis of colour was not always possible, and some of the Maghriban
Muslims adopted the customs and ways of the Europeans, the distinction
between colonizer and colonized came to be based on religion. The term
"Muslim" in Algeria, for example, became a generic one for all the
indigenous people. As a counterpart to "colon" or "French Algerian" it
signified backwardness, unprivileged political status, and generally being
economically dispossessed. The Muslim faith had inspired opposition to
Christian expansion into the Maghrib since the fourteenth century. Under
the French and the Italians it became something of a national label. This
partly explains not only why in the programme of the religiously motivated
leaders, such as the Salafis, Islamic revival and the rejection of colonial
rule were identified with each other, but also that the thoroughly Frenchi-
fied nationalist leaders, even those who had Marxist leanings, affirmed their
attachment to Islam. Hence the great agitation over the Berber *dahir* in
Morocco, the simultaneous insistence of the Algerian *évolués* on retaining
their Muslim personal status and being treated as fully qualified French
citizens, and the agitation of the Neo-Destour leaders in Tunisia over the

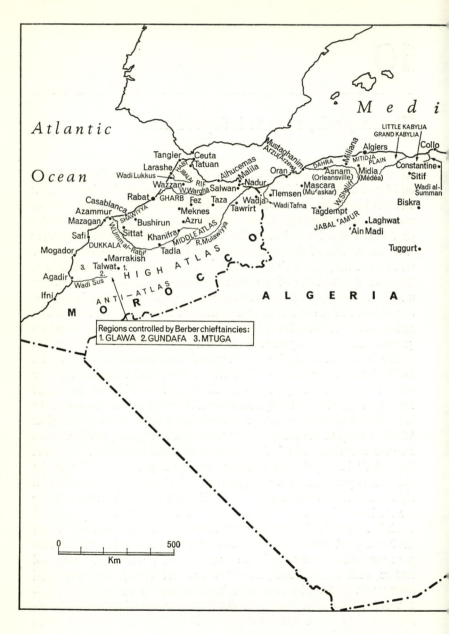

Regions controlled by Berber chieftaincies:
1. GLAWA 2. GUNDAFA 3. MTUGA

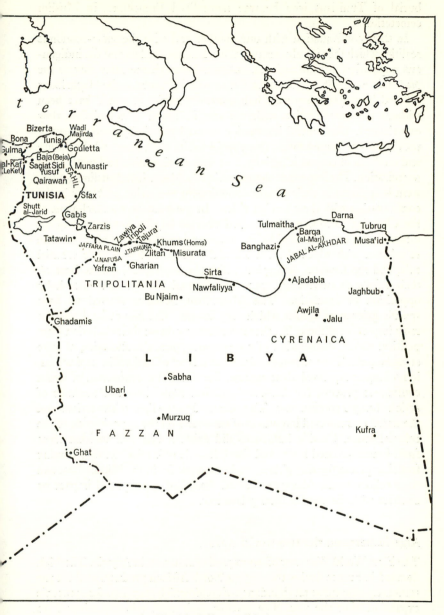

6   The Maghrib: a political map

burial of Tunisians who became naturalized Frenchmen in Muslim
cemeteries.

In their confrontation with one another and with the socio-economic
realities which they jointly created, the colonizing settlers and the indigenous population transformed one another. In much the same way as the
pieds noirs were different from the Frenchmen in France, so the Maghribans
differed from what they were half a century earlier or would have been
without the confrontation with the specific brand of colonialism they
experienced. This mutual interaction covered practically every aspect of
the life of both communities, from social habits and values and the nature
and methods of economic activity, to political orientation and methods of
organization. The important change which the Maghriban Muslims underwent is apparent in their greater commitment to specific problems in the
confrontation with their foreign rulers. In the past the encroachment of
the Christian European was resisted because he was foreign (*rumi*), an
infidel, or because his social habits were considered distasteful. The sense
of mission with which the French and Italians endowed their colonial
rule, and the fanatical dedication which the settlers brought to bear on
their efforts to survive and prosper, changed the Muslim outlook by
opposition or emulation. The Maghriban Muslims started to have
specific grievances against which they fought. The loss of land was the
most important of these, but there were many others: their exclusion from
political power, distribution of government posts, the allocation of state
subsidies, etc. Thus although Islam was a label of nationalist aspirations,
it no longer expressed their nature. But since the confrontation was a
continuous process, the Muslims' political aspirations and methods of
action changed continuously. They changed in the light of the actions and
the stated or suspected intentions of the others on the opposite side of the
colonial fence. Outside influences did exist: liberal and socialist ideas
from France aroused hopes and fears. Islamic reformist concepts coming
from Egypt and the rise of Arab nationalist parties in the Middle East had
their echoes in the Maghrib. But all these had a peripheral impact by
contrast with the specific local grievances.

Algeria between the two world wars

The First World War created an explosive situation in Algeria. The high
demand in France during the war for North African products enabled the
settlers to accumulate an abundance of credit which they used for economic
expansion after the war. The greater their economic commitment to
Algeria became, the more determined the settlers were to keep intact the
political structure through which they controlled the country. But the
Algerian Muslims emerged from the war with awakened political hopes.

They served France loyally during the war and expected political rewards. Some 173,000 Algerian Muslims served in the French army, 87,000 of them were engaged in combat, and about 25,000 lost their lives. A grateful French government intended to reward the Muslims, but the settlers forced Paris to retreat. Frustrated hopes revived the Muslim Algerians' old grievances and brought new ones into the open.

In the years immediately before the war the Algerian Muslim consciousness had had a fillip in the controversy over conscription in the French army. The controversy also served to consolidate the division in the Muslim ranks between the conservatives or "Old Turbans" (Vieux Turbans), as they were called, and the French-educated progressives. The reaction of the conservatives to conscription was traditionally negative. Upon the call of the *mufti* of Tlemsen, some 800 Algerian Muslims migrated in 1911 to Syria, about 600 from Tlemsen itself. The progressives, organized since 1912 in a group calling itself the Party of Young Algeria, stated openly their objective of assimilation into the French community, but on terms of equality. This demand, which appears today to most Algerians as a national betrayal, was then revolutionary. Had the settlers accepted it, they would have been gradually absorbed into a Muslim-French Algeria as a religious minority.

After the war bitter political battles were fought over whether the Young Algerians, or the *évolués* as the French called them, were to be given the full rights of French citizens. In the concessions of 1919 designed to reward the Algerian Muslims for their loyalty, the French government moved cautiously in that direction. In addition to the suppression from the Indigénat Code of the provisions for administrative internment and the abolition of the *impôts arabes*, the number of Muslim members in the general councils[1] was increased from six to nine or a quarter of the total, and the qualified Muslim electorate for these councils and the *délégations financières*[2] was increased to 100,000. The settlers reacted, as they had done in 1870, by threatening to take over the Algerian administration. They dismissed the 1919 legislation on Algeria as invalid because it was enacted by incompetent bodies and demanded the formation of an Algerian assembly to rule and legislate for Algeria. The French government once again yielded to the Algerian settlers' threat. By 1924 the Indigénat Code

[1] Each of the three prefectures of Algiers, Oran, and Constantine had one of these general councils to assist the prefect in his conduct of the general local administration.

[2] The *délégations financières*, created in 1898, were three elected bodies functioning on a communal basis. Two of these "delegations", each of twenty-four members, were entirely French, one representing the agricultural and the other the non-agricultural settlers, such as traders, industrialists, etc. The third was a native delegation consisting of twenty-one members, seven of whom, forming a special section, came from Kabylia. Each delegation deliberated separately, but the governor-general could authorize a plenary session to discuss specific questions of common interest.

had been restored to its full vigour, and loans of 1,600 million francs were made available to the Algerian administration to spend on public works, which were to include the irrigation of the colonized lands and the modernization of the railway system. In 1924 also Amir Khalid, Amir 'Abdul-Qadir's grandson, was exiled from Algeria. The amir was a graduate of Saint-Cyr, and had served in the French army for twenty-seven years, attaining the rank of captain in it. The settlers considered him undesirable because he outlined a programme of equality in assimilation similar to that of the Young Algerians.

The leaders of the Young Algerians, such as Ben Djelloul (Bin Jallul) and Farhat 'Abbas, continued to harp on the theme of assimilation on terms of equality until the beginning of the Second World War and to create new variations of it. In 1931 'Abbas published a volume of articles written by *évolué* leaders under the title *De la colonie vers la province: le ieune Algérien*. As the title indicates, the aim of these intellectuals was to have Algeria develop into a full province of France with the Algerian Muslims treated not as a colonized people but as French citizens. The contributors were anxious to demonstrate the greatness of Muslim civilization in order to give grounds for the demand that Muslims should be given the full rights of French citizenship without surrendering their personal status as Muslims. These leaders were not thinking in Algerian nationalist terms, and 'Abbas made this amply clear in 1936 by an article in *Entente*, a periodical he published, in which he denied that an Algerian nation had ever existed. French liberals were impressed by the reasonable demands made by the Young Algerians and the courteous tone in which they were expressed, and urged the nation not to allow them to be driven by the short-sightedness of the settlers to turn from friends into enemies of France. This was the warning which Maurice Viollette gave in his book *L'Algérie vivra-t-elle?*, published in 1931. While governor of Algeria between 1925 and 1927, Viollette made friendly gestures to the *évolués* which led to the settlers' hostility and his recall. The upshot of the argument in his book was that if this elite was not satisfied, Algeria would be lost to France within twenty years.

Viollette's prophetic warning is less significant in understanding later political events in Algeria than it seems. The *évolués* were not the leaders of Muslim Algeria that French liberals wished to see in them, nor was their problem the most important one in Algerian history after the end of the First World War. They were intelligent and articulate, but their social background and French education prevented them from identifying themselves with, or speaking for the majority of, the Algerian Muslims. Until 1939 the more significant developments in the Algerian society should be sought instead in two other directions: the socio-economic problems of the dispossessed, and the Muslim revival.

By 1930 Algeria was experiencing a migration from the countryside similar to that which occurred at the same time in Tunisia and Morocco. The natural increase in the population contributed towards this trend, but the impact of colonization and French administrative practice were more important contributing factors. The Algerian Muslim population was more than doubled in the half-century between 1872 (2,125,000) and 1931 (5,588,000), and thereafter it continued to increase at the rapid annual rate of 2.85 per cent, reaching 8,450,000 in 1954. French colonization of the countryside resulted in the reduction of the land available to Muslim cultivation. As the lands owned by the settlers continued to increase until 1954, those in the hands of the Muslims continued to decrease, and were divided into smaller holdings. With the growth of population the land was insufficient to support a large section of the Muslims. The subdivision of the tribes into *dimars* and the encroachment of French administrators on the authority of the chiefs also weakened the bonds of the clans, thus leading more and more of the young Algerian Muslims to seek their livelihood outside their traditional setting. The superfluous Muslim labour could not be absorbed by the French agricultural enterprises because of the expansion of mechanization. Unemployed young men from the countryside flocked to the cities, and during the First World War large numbers of them found employment in France. The number of Muslim workers in France from the three North African countries continued to increase in the post-war years, reaching 92,000 in 1923. The Algerian settlers resented the migration of Algerian workmen. Their prosperity depended on using cheap Muslim labour and selling their produce at French metropolitan prices. The exodus of workmen to France increased wages in Algeria, and the large-scale contact of Algerians with France had its political dangers too. In order to curtail this migration, after 1924 the Algerian administration required Algerian workmen to hold a work contract before they were allowed to leave for France.

The Algerians in France experienced all the hardships common to poorly paid workmen in industrial countries, in addition to living in a foreign society, without any family life and having to deprive themselves of basic comforts in order to make regular remittances to their dependents at home. It was in their midst that the first organized Algerian movement in the twentieth century to advocate the total rejection of Algeria's association with France was born. This was the Étoile Nord-Africain (the North-African Star), a movement founded in 1926 to coordinate the political activities of the North African workers in France. The movement had Marxist inspiration and connections, and its leader, Messali al-Hajj, was a member of the Communist Party when he founded it. But he was also an Algerian and, as Mostefa Lacheraf has pointed out,[1] his ideology

---

[1] Mostefa Lacheraf, *L'Algérie: nation et société* (Paris, 1965), p. 195.

from the start was a hybrid, combining a nostalgic and sentimental attachment to Algeria with Muslim loyalties under a Marxist façade. In 1933 Messali was imprisoned for two years for his activities with the Étoile. Released in 1935, he took up residence in Switzerland to avoid fresh arrests. There he met the Lebanese publicist Shakib Arslan who had published *La Nation arabe* in Geneva since 1930. *La Nation arabe* was a periodical dedicated to the defence of the Arab cause against colonialism. The meeting confirmed Messali in his nationalist, as distinct from Marxist, tendencies. Allowed by the government of the Popular Front in 1936 to return to Algeria, Messali soon became the head of an important mass-nationalist movement. This movement crystallized into the Parti du Peuple Algérien (P.P.A.) which he launched in 1937.

The Islamic revivalist activities which gained momentum in Algeria from the late 1920s arose under the impact of the local Algerian situation, but received inspiration from the Salafiyya movement which at this time was becoming influential in Morocco and to a lesser extent in Tunisia. The original Salafiyya ideology propagated in Egypt at the end of the nineteenth century by Muhammad 'Abduh argued that the Islam of the early forefathers (*salaf*) was a religion of progress, that the backwardness and superstition of Muslims was due to the corruption of Islam, and consequently the faith in its pristine purity was compatible with the adoption of modern (European) technology and methods of political organization. The movement was a Muslim response to the challenge of European superiority, a response that made it possible for the Salafis to advocate the learning from the west, while affirming the moral superiority of Muslims. In Algeria, as in the other North African countries under French rule, Muslims became more committed socially than in the past since they were challenged by the French over land and their Muslim identity. The Salafiyya doctrine seemed fitted to express the Muslims' involvement in the fate of the country, and affirm their attachment to their Arab-Muslim heritage, without bringing them into a frontal clash with the administration.

The leading advocate of the Salafiyya in Algeria in the 1930s was 'Abdul-Hamid b. Babis who had met 'Abduh during a brief visit which the Egyptian reformer made to Algiers and Constantine in 1903. Ibn Badis came from a well-to-do pro-French family from Constantine, and the group of religious scholars that formed around him, such as Shaikhs Tayyib al-'Uqbi from Algiers and Bashir al-Ibrahimi from Tlemsen, came like him from comfortable urban surroundings. Through the periodicals they founded, *al-Muntaqid* (the Critic) in 1925 and later *al-Shihab* (the Meteor), they advocated the recognition of Arabic as Algeria's official language, demanded the restoration of the *habus* lands acquired by the settlers to their former status, and attacked the Sufi orders. The Sufi *shaikhs* had compromised themselves by their political cooperation with the French. They were denounced for this, but were more bitterly attacked as the embodiment of Islamic doctrinal corruption.

In 1931 Ibn Badis founded with al-'Uqbi, al-Ibrahimi, and others the Association of the 'Ulama, which worked until 1954 to reform Islam and revive interest in Arabic language and culture, mostly through the foundation of schools. By 1954 the association had about 200 schools in operation using modern methods in teaching a curriculum in which much stress was put on Arabic. Politically the Association of the 'Ulama remained cautious. Their attack on the Sufi *shaikhs* was an indirect attack on the French administration, the emphasis on the Arab-Muslim character of Algeria was an implied rejection of assimilation, and Ibn Badis publicly attacked 'Abbas for his statement in 1936 that an Algerian nation did not exist. But the 'Ulama were not prepared to undertake or support positive action hostile to French sovereignty before the outbreak of the revolution in 1954. In 1936 and 1937 they took a stand similar to that of the *évolués* with regard to the gradual amelioration of the Algerian Muslims' life within French sovereignty.

The years 1930 to 1939 are decisive ones in the crystallization of the nationalist movement in Algeria, as well as in Tunisia and Morocco. The centenary of the French landing in Algiers was a great occasion for French North Africa. Triumphant colonialism congratulated itself on its achievements through the holding of congresses on such subjects as malaria, water resources, rural settlement, and so on. The celebrations included a ceremony at Sidi Farrush where the French troops first landed, and the inauguration at Bufarik of a monument in honour of the unknown colonist. The Moroccan and Tunisian administrations, not to be outdone by their Algerian counterpart in asserting their triumph over Muslim North Africa, promulgated the Berber *dahir* in the same year in Morocco and organized a Eucharistic Congress in Carthage. In Algeria the French affirmed that the country was assimilated economically and culturally. The French in Tunisia and Morocco, unable to boast of as much, invoked images of a glorious Christian past for Tunisia and in Morocco gave recognition to pre-Islamic Berber institutions which Islam failed to stamp out. Occurring at a time of religious revival amongst the Muslims of the Maghrib and of widespread socialist propaganda, the exhibition of the naked colonial image served as a catalyst in the crystallization of Muslim opposition.

Of special importance for Algeria were also the hopes aroused by Léon Blum's Popular Front government in France, and their unfulfilment because of the settlers' pressure. These hopes sprang from the general liberal disposition of the government towards the colonies and the fact that Maurice Viollette participated in it as a minister without portfolio. The victory of the Popular Front was the occasion for convening an Islamic Congress in Algiers (June 1936) which was dominated by the *évolués* and the 'Ulama. The resolutions of the congress demanded the suppression of all special legal restrictions on the Muslims, total administrative assimilation of Algeria into France including the abolition of the position of governor for Algeria and the dissolution of the *délégations financières*, preserving for the Muslims their personal status under the Muslim law, and universal suffrage. Ibn Badis associated himself with the loyalist attitude of the *évolués*, and in his address he said "when French liberty was sleeping, we kept silence. Liberty has revived in France, and we intend to follow it."[1] Messali dissented, however, from this loyalist note and reiterated his party's demand for independence in a meeting held on 2 August to welcome upon its return the delegation sent to Paris to affirm the confidence of the Algerian Muslims in the government of Léon Blum.

In December 1936 the French government submitted to the Chamber of Deputies the so-called Blum-Viollette Bill which provided for the extension of full citizenship rights to certain categories of Algerian Muslims, namely former officers of the French army, holders of university degrees, high government officials and so on. If it had been passed, the bill would have given full rights of French citizenship to about 20,000 Muslims in the first instance. The opposition of the settlers and their allies in Paris, and the public campaign that was launched against the bill, ensured that it was never brought before the Chamber for debate. It was examined by the Chamber's Committee on Universal Suffrage, but a negative vote in the Senate in 1938 eventually caused it to be dropped. In Algeria the *évolués* and the communists openly welcomed the Blum-Viollette Bill, the 'Ulama accepted it as a step to further improvements, and the Messalists rejected it. Its failure to become law was a decisive blow to the trust which most of Algeria's leaders still placed in metropolitan France as distinct from the France of the Algerian settlers. Even 'Abbas underwent a change of heart. He parted company with the extreme pro-French group amongst the *évolués*, such as Ben Djelloul and R. Zénati, and founded in 1938 a new political party, the Union Populaire Algérienne (U.P.A.). Henceforth the slogan of assimilation with equality no longer figured in his political pronouncements. He spoke in 1938 of *rattachement* between France and an Algeria that had "her own physiognomy, her language, her customs, her traditions..."

Algeria: the nationalism of the *évolués*

The importance to the growth of Algerian nationalism of France's defeat in the Second World War, and of the hopes aroused by the activities of Robert Murphy, President Roosevelt's special representative in the country

[1] Quoted in Jacques Berque, *French North Africa, The Maghrib between the two world wars* (London, 1967), p. 276.

after the American landing at Sidi Farrush in 1942, has been greatly overestimated. Generally the Algerian Muslims followed 'Abbas' lead of remaining loyal to France even after her defeat, on the hope of being rewarded politically. The Vichy regime found its most ardent sympathizers in Algeria between 1940 and 1942 not among the Muslims but among the settlers whose anti-semitic and Fascist tendencies could then be brought to the open without restraint. 'Abbas became the spokesmen of Algerian nationalism during the war by default. The 'Ulama had been in eclipse since 1938, and Messali was in prison or under house arrest until 1946. 'Abbas' moderation and repeated tactical retreats enabled him to remain politically active for most of the war period. In a letter to Marshal Pétain in 1941 he demanded equality before the law for all in Algeria. Murphy's reiteration of the American professed anti-colonial aim of entering the war led 'Abbas to address himself to the American envoy, telling him that the Algerian people wanted to become free in an "Algerian fatherland". 'Abbas followed up the contacts with the Americans by drawing up in February 1943, together with fifty-five other *évolués*, the Manifesto of the Algerian People on the basis of which he intended to negotiate with the French Committee of National Liberation. The manifesto demanded equality, agricultural reform, and free compulsory education. In a supplement the leaders also demanded an Algerian state. Catroux, the governor of Algeria appointed by de Gaulle, summoned 'Abbas to discuss with him counter-proposals, which amounted to the revival of the Blum-Viollette project of extending full French citizenship to the *évolués*. When he refused to discuss these proposals, 'Abbas was arrested but was released shortly afterwards upon reaffirming his loyalty to France.

The French Committee of National Liberation hoped that the demand for the Algerian state would be forgotten once the *évolués* were satisfied. On 12 December 1943 de Gaulle announced in a speech delivered in Constantine the decision to grant the rights of French citizens to the Algerian elite. Some of the *évolués* were grateful. But 'Abbas had gone too far to be able to retreat, and he knew that Messali's consent was necessary for any lasting agreement with France. Messali had been released from prison in April 1943, but remained under house arrest in Shallala (Chellala). 'Abbas, who was allowed to see him, records[1] Messali's scepticism about success in creating an Algerian state, even one associated with France, through negotiation. 'Abbas launched a new organization on 17 March 1944 in his home town of Sitif, the Amis du Manifeste de la Liberté (A.M.L.) whose ultimate aim was to create an Algerian republic federated with France. Ten days earlier a decree had given the force of law to de Gaulle's promises of the previous December, and so 'Abbas could

[1] Ferhat Abbas, *La nuit coloniale* (Paris, 1962), p. 151.

act in relative freedom. He published a new French-language newspaper called *Egalité* through which he tried to generate sympathy in France for the aims of the A.M.L.

The error of ascribing much importance to the impact of France's defeat and American intervention on the growth of Algerian nationalism is connected with another error, namely accepting 'Abbas as the embodiment of Algerian nationalism in the war period. The Free French exaggerated the importance of American influence because in this way they had an alibi for their failure to satisfy 'Abbas and his followers by the concessions of March 1944: concessions which they believed were generous and the settlers considered outrageous. 'Abbas had definitely turned his back on assimilation in 1938, and his new political position was not, therefore, the result of France's defeat. The circumstances of the war, by removing the extremist Algerian leaders from the scene, enabled him to pose in his new political garb as the embodiment of Algerian Muslim aspirations. Furthermore, the demand for an Algerian state was not made to the Vichy government which embodied the defeat of France but to the Free French who seemed likely to redeem it. In any case, whatever connection there existed between 'Abbas' modified political stance and France's defeat, in two important respects he did not represent the majority of Algeria's Muslim population: in his acceptance of the idea of a federation with France, and in his readiness to distinguish between a metropolitan France which could be trusted eventually to do what is right and fitting, and the settlers who were to him the enemies of both France and the Algerian Muslims. By their virulent campaign against 'Abbas, the settlers enhanced his political stature. But how little he represented Muslim Algeria the events of 1945 were to make clear beyond question.

The P.P.A. activists operated clandestinely throughout the war, spreading their influence amongst the masses in the cities. The strength of this party and its leaders' rejection of 'Abbas' political programme were revealed in the A.M.L. Congress, held in Algiers from 2 to 4 March 1945. Messali was still under house arrest, but his followers dominated the congress. They defeated a motion by 'Abbas calling for an autonomous Algerian republic federated with France, and had the congress pass two motions they put to it, one calling for the release of Messali, "the undeniable leader of the Algerian people", and another for the formation of an Algerian parliament and government without any commitment as to future ties with France. The French authorities became aware of the extent of Muslim agitation and its direction immediately afterwards: leaflets distributed in the streets and inscriptions on walls called for death to the French and the constitution of a Muslim authority in Algeria; and on 24 April the prefect of Constantine reported the occurrence of acts of sabotage, attacks on property, and demonstrations in the streets. The extent of P.P.A. responsibility for these acts is not clear. However, it seems doubtful that a plot against the state and an organized Muslim insurrectionary movement existed in 1945, as the settlers and some of their defenders such as Michael Clark[1] have claimed. Nevertheless clashes between Muslim demonstrators and the police on 8 May in Sitif created a spontaneous and ill-coordinated insurrectionary situation.

Much controversy has arisen over who was responsible for the initial clashes and the justifiability, morally and politically, of the subsequent brutal suppression. 'Abbas has claimed that the prefect of Sitif, acting upon the promptings of settler leaders, authorized a Muslim demonstration on VE Day, knowing that it would lead to clashes, for the purpose of justifying the repression of the nationalists, i.e. himself and his colleagues in the A.M.L.[2] Whatever the aim of the authorities was in granting permission to the Muslims to demonstrate, it seems clear the masses that took to the streets were not 'Abbas' men. They were led by the P.P.A. activists, they waved the flag of Amir 'Abdul-Qadir (white and green) which had become the symbol of Algerian nationalism, and shouted slogans for Messali and a free, independent Algeria. The police intervened causing the masses to disperse. Police brutality was answered by the Muslims' attacks on the unarmed French in the town. In the afternoon the trouble spread to Bona and Gulma, then to other parts of the region of Constantine and even to some parts of the Oran region.

The prefect of Constantine had indicated in his report of April 1945 that Algeria was threatened with famine and warned of a political upheaval that would accompany it. The outburst of the Muslims in May in the form of murder, arson, rape, etc. directed against the French was one of anger against those they held responsible for their misery and who, because of their superior resources, did not endure the privations experienced by the Muslims during the war. The Messalists represented the rejection of the colonial structure which perpetuated this misery, and characteristically it was they who sparked off the outburst. The number of Muslims the French forces killed in the process of restoring order has also been the object of much controversy. The figures cited range from 1,500, which official sources give, to the extravagant estimate of 80,000 given by Algerian nationalists. Whatever the truth may be, it is clear that the repression was brutal, no effort was made to distinguish between guilty and innocent Muslims in the areas involved, and the Algerian administration used the occasion to intimidate the Muslims into political submission. 'Abbas was arrested together with 4,560 others, the A.M.L. was banned, and in the trial which followed ninety-nine were sentenced to death and sixty-four to life imprisonment. Whether the brutality of the suppression

[1] Michael Clark, *Algeria in turmoil* (London, 1960), pp. 29ff.
[2] Cf. Abbas, *La nuit coloniale*, pp. 153 ff.

was justified by the attacks of the Muslims on innocent French men, women, or children is not a problem for the historian to determine. The Algerians behaved as if they considered the most innocent French settler in Algeria responsible for the colonial system which humiliated and deprived them of the means of decent livelihood. Repression could not eradicate this belief, and it taught the new generation of Algerian Muslims the lesson that violence was the only effective means of achieving political ends.

After the repressions of 1945 the settlers demanded the nullification of the decree of March 1944. The French government, fearing another outburst, acted differently. Projects to aid the Muslim peasants, such as services for the preservation and fertilization of the soil, were set up, new municipal centres were established in Muslim areas, and in August 1945 Algerian Muslims were given the right to elect the same number (thirteen) of representatives to the French Constituent Assembly as the French citizens in Algeria. In this way it was hoped that the Muslim political organizations would be induced to operate within the colonial system instead of outside and against it. 'Abbas, released in March 1946, justified this hope. He immediately set out to organize a new group, the Union Démocratique du Manifeste Algérien (U.D.M.A.) He claimed that the programme of the new organization was the same as that of the A.M.L., but his tone had become subdued since the Sitif riots. On 7 May he published in *Le Courier algérien* an "Appeal to the Algerian youth, French and Muslim" in which he described his political aspirations as being neither assimilation nor separatism. He appealed to the French youth to overcome their "colonial complex" and to the Muslim youth to rise above "anachronistic Muslim nationalism". A project which he submitted to the French Constituent Assembly in August demanded the establishment of an Algerian republic federated to France in such a way as to enable Frenchmen in Algeria to be Algerian citizens, and Algerians in France to be French citizens. In the absence of leaders committed to a more extreme form of independence, 'Abbas' party achieved a clear victory in June 1946 in the election of the second college (i.e. Muslim) candidates to the French Constituent Assembly. His party obtained seventy-one per cent of the 50,000 Muslim votes cast and eleven out of the thirteen seats. His only opponents, the communists and the socialists, obtained no seats and two seats respectively, a result which shows that the greater the commitment of the contending group to internationalism the less successful it was in the election.

Messali was released only after the elections of June 1946 and was permitted to resume his political activity from a suburb of Algiers. There he launched a new party, the Mouvement pour le Triomphe des Libertés Démocratiques (M.T.L.D.), whose principal demands were the convening of an Algerian constituent assembly and the evacuation of the French troops from Algeria. Messali continued to have a charismatic appeal for the poor Muslims in the cities. But, although his programme went beyond what the French would willingly grant, he too became the head of a party working within the colonial system and his continued political activity became dependent on its tolerance. In fact by 1946 he had become more a symbol embodying the will of the amorphous Muslim Algerian masses to defy alien rule than a leader undertaking political action. There is no ground for believing Clark's claim that Messali "retained the outlawed Algerian People's party (P.P.A.) as the clandestine nucleus of a future underground resistance movement".[1] It is true that the first Algerians dedicated to organized armed resistance came from amongst the Messalists. But they acted independently of the veteran leader and were convinced that his type of leadership was not likely to lead Algeria to independence.

On 20 September 1947 the first National Assembly of the Fourth Republic passed the "Algerian statute", which was based on a project submitted by the French government. 'Abbas' proposals and six others were brushed aside. The statute recognized for Algeria a civil personality and fiscal autonomy, but in fact altered nothing in the uneven distribution of political power and economic capacities between the country's two communities. It provided for the election of an Algerian assembly of 120 members divided into two colleges of equal numbers. But the first college was elected by the French citizens, constituting an electorate of only 60,000, and the second college was elected by the Muslim voters numbering about 1,300,000. The assembly's main function was to ratify the Algerian budget after it had been approved by the French ministers of the interior and finances. Should it refuse to do so, the assembly could be dissolved by decree. The Algerian administration remained under the control of the governor-general, who was responsible to the French minister of the interior and not to the Algerian assembly.

The Algerian revolution and independence

By 1947 the reconstituted Algerian Muslim parties had exhausted their political potential. Before the promulgation of the Algerian statute their leaders were feverishly active, trying to have some form of Algerian independence recognized by the French legislature. The statute was clearly a defeat, and it could hardly be argued that it was likely to lead gradually to independence. Furthermore, the rigging of the 1948 elections for the Algerian assembly shattered whatever faith Muslims still had in democratic procedure. With the terror of May 1945 still not forgotten, the

[1] Clark, *Algeria in turmoil*, p. 43.

failure of the recognized parties to achieve any political success made armed resistance seem the only way of salvation still open to Algerians.

The first organization dedicated to the use of violent means for attaining Algeria's independence, the Organisation Secrète, emerged in 1948. Its leaders were all young men in their twenties, neither crippled by 'Abbas' intellectual hesitations nor enamoured by Messali's almost Messianic charisma. Unlike the majority of the *évolués* they came from humble origins, and unlike other supporters of Messali they did not believe in disorganized mass agitation. They were practical men who saw in the recourse to arms the only means of destroying the myth of French Algeria. The O.S. had a collective leadership of former M.T.L.D. members, amongst whom Ahmad Ben Bella was the dominant personality. From the beginning O.S. leaders devoted themselves wholly to the task of building up a force of resistance fighters, and were prepared to wait until they could start action in an effective way. The first important strike undertaken by the group was the attack in 1949, led by Ben Bella personally, on the central post office in Oran in which they got away with three million francs. The Oran attack did not suggest a political plot, and so the authorities were not unduly alarmed. The administration's complacency was also not shaken when a plot for a strike in Bona was discovered, Ben Bella was jailed, and the other leaders of the O.S., including Muhammad Khider, a member of the French National Assembly, fled from the country. Ben Bella escaped from his prison at Blida in 1952 and went to Cairo. The plot was dismissed as the work of a handful of agitators who ceased to be dangerous when they left the country. The complacency of the authorities enabled the members of the O.S. to reorganize and take the whole country by surprise on 1 November 1954. In 1953 four of the leaders of the O.S. who remained in Algeria, hiding either in Algiers or the Auras region, formed the Comité Révolutionnaire pour l'Unité et l'Action (C.R.U.A.) with the aim of galvanizing the M.T.L.D. and directing it towards revolutionary action. This group, who had contacts with Khider, Ben Bella, and other leaders exiled in Switzerland or Cairo, plotted the revolution and organized the ranks of its warriors. Twenty-two leaders meeting on 22 July 1954 at Clos Salembier in Algiers drew up the plans for the revolution. In a second meeting in an Algiers suburb in October the date of the revolution was agreed upon, and the name "Front de Libération Nationale" (F.L.N.) was adopted.

The Algerian revolution did not start as a mass uprising. The M.T.L.D., the only Muslim mass political party, became divided over whether or not to support the F.L.N. Messali himself denounced the revolution in 1955 and grouped those who remained loyal to him in the Mouvement National Algérien (M.N.A.) which opposed the F.L.N. and remained active, particularly amongst the Algerian workers in France, until independence.

Nor does it appear that the F.L.N. leaders made any effort towards mass political mobilization before 1956. The early 1950s, particularly 1954, were bad years for French morale: both in Morocco and Tunisia nationalist opposition was taking a militant turn, and there was also the defeat of Dien Bien Phu in Indo-China. The F.L.N. seems to have hoped that the shock of several synchronized attacks (there were seventy of them on the night of 1 November) would quickly bring the demoralized France to concede what political pressure had failed to achieve. This explains the exclusive emphasis on military preparations: the F.L.N's Armée de Liberation Nationale (A.L.N.) numbered about 3,000 fighters in 1954. It also explains the tone of the leaflets distributed on 1 November in most of Algeria's towns in which the F.L.N. called on the Algerian Muslims to volunteer for the armed conflict, and invited the French government to negotiate a peace agreement with the F.L.N. on the conditions of recognizing Algerian independence and having the settlers remain in the country as Algerian citizens. The F.L.N. was to rely widely on the political support of the masses after 1956, when the exiled leaders, the so-called *délégation extérieure*, were supplementing the military action of the "internals" (those in Algeria) by international diplomatic work. But the F.L.N. was right to begin by relying on military action, although its army was never to achieve a total victory. The French army did not have an Algerian Dien Bien Phu, but the guerrilla warfare of the A.L.N. made the French position in Algeria untenable. As the French army and police became indiscriminate in arresting Muslims and destroying villages, the Algerian masses became involved in the rebellion. As the settlers felt threatened by A.L.N. action and the hostility of the masses they had taught to submit, they carried out their own reprisals and further alienated the Muslims. And as the metropolitan French felt the increasing cost of the war in terms of lives and economic resources, they became aware of the dangers to France herself of the settlers' intransigence and the army's increasing political involvement.

France was taken by surprise in November 1954 but not cowed. The French government's first response was to send more troops to reinforce the 50,000 soldiers in Algeria, and have some 160 Messalist and M.T.L.D. activists arrested. When it became clear by the end of the year that a fullfledged revolution was afoot, new tactics were adopted. On 26 January 1955 Jacques Soustelle arrived in Algeria as the new governor, bringing with him a programme of "integration". As this meant the integration of the Muslims in the French community and the gradual extension of political rights to them, the settlers were at first suspicious and generally hostile to the new governor. Much effort was directed during the year in which Soustelle held office towards isolating the rural Muslim population from the upheaval taking place around them. Soustelle organized the

Sections Administratives Spécialisées (S.A.S.) to resettle villagers away from the regions affected by the fighting and to give leadership and technical assistance to the Muslim rural communities. The S.A.S. officers, like the officers of the *bureaux arabes* in the nineteenth century, directed public works in the villages, instructed the villagers in agriculture and health matters, and administered justice, while at the same time supervising their political activities. A similar organization, the Sections Administratives Urbaines (S.A.U.), was also created to operate amongst the Muslims in the urban areas.

The paternalistic system of the S.A.S. and S.A.U. achieved little success on the whole: in the middle of the twentieth century, with the mass media penetrating the remotest parts of Algeria, it was not possible to impose a political *cordon sanitaire* on the Algerian Muslim masses. Algerian Muslims followed the events of the fighting through newspapers and the radio. From Cairo the Voice of the Arabs mounted an anti-French propaganda and enabled the exiled Algerian leaders to keep the Algerian Muslims informed about their activities. Furthermore, by 1955 the F.L.N. could no longer be dismissed easily by French publicists in Algeria as a group of insignificant rebels. In April F.L.N. representatives were allowed to attend the Bandung Conference, though without enjoying a delegate status, and later in the year the U.N. General Assembly adopted an Afro-Asian resolution declaring that the French government was preventing the Algerians from exercising their right of self-determination. The fact that the A.L.N., though suffering heavy casualties, continued to fight against the 120,000 French troops assembled in Algeria in 1955, left a deep impression on the Algerian masses. Indiscriminate repression also helped to galvanize the non-committed Muslims. In August the settlers carried out indiscriminate attacks on Muslims in the region of Constantine in reprisal for the death of seventy-one Europeans at the hands of the A.L.N. acting in cooperation with the local population. These reprisals formed the immediate cause for the publication of the *Manifeste des 61* signed by sixty-one Algerian Muslim deputies, senators, and others associated with the French administration, affirming their faith in the "Algerian national idea". 'Abbas in January 1956 also aligned himself with the F.L.N. In an interview with the Tunisian newspaper *L'Action* he stated that he and his party (U.D.M.A.) supported the cause for which the F.L.N. worked and that henceforth he would not undertake any political action without being authorized by the F.L.N. leaders.

It was at the moment when the F.L.N. was winning the support of the more vocal Muslims that the European settlers destroyed a gesture of reconciliation which the newly installed socialist premier Guy Mollet initiated. In his address of 31 January 1956 Mollet defined the main objectives of his Algerian policy as being to re-establish peace, to ensure the coexistence of the two communities, while respecting the "Algerian personality" to establish an indissoluble union between Algeria and France, to hold free elections for an Algerian assembly in a single college, and to promote social and economic progress. General Catroux, who had been designated the new governor of Algeria, made it clear about the same time that the new Algerian programme would not mean the foundation of an Algerian national state nor negotiations with the F.L.N. It is doubtful whether any important Muslim leader would, in 1956, have stepped forward to deal with the French on the basis of the Mollet programme. But to the settlers the programme was a surrender to the Muslims, and the choice of Catroux, who only a few months before had gone to Madagascar to see Muhammad V and prepare for his return to Morocco, was considered an affront. The settlers' chagrin over the new government's Algerian policy and Catroux' appointment led them to withdraw their former hostility to Soustelle. On his departure Soustelle was hailed as a hero, and when Mollet came to Algiers on 6 February he was treated like a traitor. He was pelted with tomatoes and cabbages as he was laying a wreath at the war memorial. Mollet succumbed to mob pressure. On the same day Catroux, who was still in Paris, resigned and on the 9th Robert Lacoste, the minister of economic affairs, was appointed in his place. Mollet's pronouncements after the 6th dwelt more on the indissoluble link of Algeria with France than on the Algerian personality.

Until de Gaulle's coming to power in 1958 the authority of the French government, weak in France itself, was negligible in Algeria. Lacoste survived in Algeria only by surrendering much of his power to the army, whose command henceforth dealt not only with the military aspects of the conflict but also with political propaganda. From March 1956, when two F.L.N. men were executed, the F.L.N. resorted to terrorism against French civilians, and settlers' terrorist organizations operated against Muslims. By the end of the year terrorism reached a high pitch of violence, as trained Muslim terrorists operated from the Qasba of Algiers with the cooperation of its inhabitants. In January 1957 Lacoste handed over all security measures in the capital to General Massu and his tenth parachute division, thus making the army command take responsibility for the torture, destruction of houses, and other acts of brutality to which the Muslims were subjected. In this way also the French army in Algeria became involved in the cause of the French settlers, an involvement which prepared the way for the mutiny of 13 May 1958. Muslim terrorism was largely the responsiblity of Ramdane Abbane, a Kabylia Berber and an original founder of the F.L.N. who emerged in 1956 as the leading figure amongst the "internal" F.L.N. leaders.

With the growing scope of the revolution the F.L.N. leaders in Algeria felt the need for greater coordination of their activities. With this aim in mind, the Summam Conference was held in August 1956 (in the Summam valley in Algeria) and was attended by 250 F.L.N. "internal" leaders. The members of the *délégation extérieure* in Cairo, who had come to handle the problems of finances, arms supplies, and diplomacy, could not attend. The most important decisions of the conference were the creation of the Conseil National de la Révolution Algérienne (C.N.R.A.) as a sovereign parliament, and a committee of execution and coordination (C.C.E.) controlled by the "internals". The Summam Conference decided that the *délégation extérieure* was henceforth to be responsible to the C.N.R.A. It also endorsed Abbane's policy of urban terrorism. A conflict between the "internals" and the "externals" might have come into the open, except for the kidnapping of Ben Bella and other "external' leaders by the French on 22 October 1956, Abbane's death in the spring of 1958 as he was trying to cross over to Tunisia, and the fact that other C.C.E. members were forced to flee Algeria sometime in 1957.

In 1956, when both Morocco and Tunisia had become independent, a Tunisio-Moroccan project for ending the Algerian war was discreetly proposed to the exiled Algerian leaders and the French. It seems that the moving spirit behind the project was President Bourguiba who was growing concerned over the effects which the continuation of the conflict might have on his country. Most of the A.N.L. arms were channelled through Tunisia, A.N.L. recruits received their training either in Morocco or Tunisia, and refugees crossed over to Tunisia from eastern Algeria in large numbers. Both Morocco and Tunisia, particularly the latter, were interested in promoting a new form of cooperation with France. But both were committed to supporting the F.L.N., and Bourguiba feared the reactions of the Algerian fighters on Tunisian soil to an entente with France. Thus the creation of a Franco-Maghriban community was conceived as a means of settling the Algerian problem and forging new links with France. The good offices of the Moroccan and Tunisian governments were directed towards persuading the F.L.N. to accept in the first instance the autonomy of Algeria within the proposed community with the understanding that Algeria would attain full independence gradually. The French government was informed of the Tunisian and Moroccan overtures. But on 22 October 1956 an Air Atlas aeroplane carrying Ben Bella, Ait Ahmad, Muhammad Boudiaf, and Muhammad Khider, the most important leaders of the *délégation extérieure*, from Rabat, where they had conferred over the proposed community with Muhammad V, to Tunis, was forced to land in Algiers, and the four leaders were taken captive. It is not yet certain whether the organizers of this plot knew of the peace project and by their act of piracy sought to prevent it from being pursued further. It is certain, however, that the kidnapping was not authorized by Lacoste, but he and the Mollet government took responsibility for it. The inability of the French government to control the army in Algeria was further illustrated by the bombardment of the Tunisian village of Saqiat Sidi Yusuf (Sakiet Sidi Youssef) on 8 February 1958, in which 69 civilians were killed and 130 wounded. The Gaillard government had authorized the army to pursue retreating A.L.N. units into Tunisia but banned air attacks on Tunisian territory. The order for the attack on Saqiat seems to have come from a colonel in the Bona air base, but when it occurred the French government found itself compelled to accept responsibility for it.

By the end of 1957 the settlers and the French army in Algeria felt that the end of the rebellion was at hand. The so-called "Battle of Algiers" came to an end with the capture by Massu's paratroops of the last surviving leaders of the F.L.N. terrorist cells operating from the Qasba. At the end of the year Algiers was quiet and its Muslim population subdued by the combined pressure of the paratroops and the S.A.U. officers. The completion of the electrified Morice Line along the Tunisian frontier seriously hampered the flow of supplies to the A.L.N. units and the movement of fighters to and from Tunisia. To add to the assurance of the French leaders in Algiers that the authority of the F.L.N. had been sapped, Messali's M.N.A., which had so far operated mostly in France, appeared in Algeria as a rival force to the F.L.N. and having its own armed units. The M.N.A. still demanded the total independence of Algeria, but it was an organization which the French felt they could control. Indeed in November 1957 one of the M.N.A. commanders, Bellounis, agreed to coordinate his activities against the F.L.N. with the French army, and with the blessing of the French he set up a base for himself at Jalfa (Djelfa). He soon afterwards fell out with the French army and was hunted down and killed in July 1958.

By the end of 1957 the French government too felt confident about the future and set about creating a new political structure designed to keep Algeria divided amongst its various distinctive units and permanently annexed to France. The French National Assembly passed on 5 February 1958 a *loi-cadre* which affirmed that Algeria was an integral part of the French republic, and provided for its division into five distinct territories: Oran, Shaliff, Algiers, Kabylia, and Constantine. Each territory was to have a one-college assembly elected jointly by the Muslims and French citizens and a government responsible to it. In addition it was to have a council in which French citizens and Muslims were to be equally represented, and whose function was to supervise the actions of the territorial assembly and government and ensure their conformity with the provisions of the *loi-cadre*, particularly with respect to the limitations placed on their powers. Two years after the election of the territorial assemblies a federal organ could be constituted if the various assemblies so wished. In the *loi-cadre* the French government reserved responsibility for Algeria's

external affairs, defence, general security, the administration of justice,
fiscal policy, mines, and sources of energy to itself. A resident minister was
to exercise the responsibilities reserved for the French government in
Algeria and was to have representatives in each of the five territories. Both
the F.L.N. and the M.N.A. denounced the *loi-cadre*; before the new law
had time to prove whether it was at all workable, General de Gaulle came
to power and changed the direction of France's Algerian policy.

The settlers and the French army's conviction that the A.L.N. was
beaten was over-optimistic. It is true that the Morice Line was a serious
handicap and A.L.N. units breaking through it in 1958 suffered very
heavy casualties. But arms in limited amounts and trained recruits continued to reach the A.L.N. from Tunisia in addition to what came from
Morocco. So that its units could have the maximum impact, after June
1958 the A.L.N. command abandoned the practice of using battalion-
sized formations in engagements with the French army, and reverted
to the guerrilla tactics of the first year of the revolution. The battalions
were broken up into companies using hit-and-run tactics and avoiding
positional battles. This meant that the A.L.N. no longer aimed at a
military Dien Bien Phu, but at providing the foundations of a political
victory by the threat of an indefinite continuation of the fighting. And it
was such a political victory which the settler leaders and the army in
Algeria came to fear most in the first months of 1958. When shortly after
the Summam Conference most of the C.C.E. in Algeria had either died or
escaped to Tunisia it became possible to concentrate the political leadership of the F.L.N. outside Algeria. The C.N.R.A. met in Cairo in August
1957, enlarged its membership from thirty-two to fifty-four, and reorganized a new C.C.E. of nine members, each having specific responsibilities. 'Abbas had joined the F.L.N. in 1956, and was elected member of
the C.N.R.A., thus enabling the F.L.N. to make use of his great political
experience and wide international contacts, although most F.L.N. leaders
were out of sympathy with his past political career. One of the most
important political successes of the F.L.N. in the first months of 1958 was
the Tangier Conference, held from 27 to 30 April and attended by representatives of the F.L.N., the Istiqlal, and the Neo-Destour parties. The
Tunisian and Moroccan parties affirmed their full support to the F.L.N.,
and recommended the creation of an Algerian government after consultation with the Tunisian and Moroccan governments. This committed
Tunisia and Morocco publicly to the immediate independence of Algeria,
and created a new political atmosphere which neither the French government nor the French leaders in Algeria could ignore.

The bizarre events of 13 to 16 May 1958 in Algiers, which led to
General de Gaulle's return to power, had their roots in both the conviction
of the settlers and the French army that the A.L.N.'s strength was sapped,

and the fear that outside political manoeuvres threatened to rob them of the fruits of their military success. After the attack on Saqiat Sidi Yusuf, the Tunisian government complained to the U.N. Security Council, and the embarrassed French government found itself unable to turn down an Anglo-American offer of mediation. Robert Murphy of the U.S.A. and Harold Beeley of Great Britain formed a mediation mission, which succeeded in improving the atmosphere between Tunisia and France and in bringing about a new agreement over the lease of the Bizerta naval base to France. What disturbed the Algerian settlers and the French army was that the two-man mission did not limit itself to the Saqiat incident, but sought to find a political settlement to the Algerian conflict. The French army, angered over the American attitude in the Suez crisis, now found itself confronted with American intervention in the Algerian problem which many of its senior officers had come to consider their own responsibility. Edward Behr, who was then in Algiers, records[1] how concerned the settler leaders and army officers were over the consequences of American intervention, and their extravagant anti-American sentiments. They believed that the Americans were after the oil of the Sahara and that they were determined to humiliate the French army. Massu even told Behr that before starting to defend the rights of the Algerian Muslims, the Americans should concern themselves with helping the American Negroes, whose lot he and many others in Algiers believed was much worse. Furthermore, the French in Algeria believed that the Anglo-American mediation only hardened the position of the F.L.N., as shown in the Tangier Conference, and they became determined to prevent it from going any further. In Paris the Gaillard government fell on 16 April when the new agreement with Tunisia, which resulted from the Murphy-Beeley mission, was rejected by the French National Assembly. Georges Bidault gave up an attempt to form a new government on 22 April, and a government formed by René Pleven failed to gain a vote of confidence on 8 May because it included as defence minister André Morice, the man responsible for the Morice Line, whose presence seemed to the National Assembly to preclude any liberalization of the French policy in Algeria. A new government was formed by Pierre Pflimlin excluding Morice, and when on 13 May it was due to submit its programme to the National Assembly, the settlers in Algiers struck.

The settler leaders were convinced that the Pflimlin government would yield to Anglo-American pressure to find a political settlement of the Algerian conflict, and therefore were determined to prevent its investiture by the National Assembly. The F.L.N. provided a rallying point for the settlers when on 9 May, the day after Morice was dropped from the government, it announced the execution of three French soldiers as a

[1] Edward Behr, *The Algerian problem* (London, Penguin edition, 1961), pp. 124-5.

reprisal for the execution of A.L.N. fighters by the French. Settler leaders started to talk of action and their committees of public safety posed as official public organs. Noting that a political storm was coming, Lacoste went on leave on 10 May. On the 13th the settlers occupied the building of the government-general in Algiers. Massu, who as commander of the Algiers area was responsible for security, placed a cordon of paratroops around the building without interfering in the activities of the dissidents within. Muslim demonstrators, mobilized by S.A.U. officers, were then brought from the Qasba of Algiers in army trucks to join the rioters at the Forum and give the semblance of a common Franco-Muslim front against concessions to the F.L.N. Massu and General Salan, the commander-in-chief in Algeria, soon joined the Algiers Committee of Public Safety, thus indicating that the army would not intervene to suppress the insurrection. Soustelle, who had become a hero to the settlers shortly before leaving Algeria, arrived on 17 May to give them his support. In a statement on 15 May de Gaulle said that "in face of the trials that again are mounting towards her [France], she should know that I am ready to assume the powers of the republic". De Gaulle's return to power became the principal demand of the demonstrators of Algiers the following day. To the officers it was a means of extricating themselves from the dilemma which they faced of either putting down by force the insurrection with which many of them sympathized or coming out in open mutiny. The Europeans and Muslims seem to have pinned opposite hopes on de Gaulle's return: the former believing that he would end the rebellion and keep Algeria French, the latter that he would negotiate a settlement with the F.L.N. The French National Assembly, having realized that only de Gaulle's return could control the uprising in Algiers and avert conflicts in France itself, invested him as premier on 1 June.

General de Gaulle's Algerian policy which was gradually unfolded between 4 June, when he visited Algeria, and the end of the year, consisted of by-passing the F.L.N., checking the extremists amongst the settlers and the army officers (about a thousand of the latter were transferred within two years), and through massive economic aid induce moderate but representative Algerian Muslim leaders to negotiate a viable solution. During his visit in June he declared that a settlement would be negotiated with representatives of Algeria to be elected in a single electoral college. A referendum in Algeria on 26, 27, and 28 September seemed to herald the victory of this policy: eighty per cent of the electorate voted, and ninety-seven per cent of these favoured de Gaulle's policy. On 3 October de Gaulle announced in Constantine a plan of massive industrialization that would create 400,000 new jobs and under which 250,000 hectares of arable land would be distributed to Muslims. Then in a speech on the 23rd he proposed to the F.L.N. the "peace of the brave", offering the F.L.N.

leaders a safe conduct to France to discuss means of arriving at a solution after laying down their arms. The condition of ending hostilities before starting talks, and de Gaulle's insistence that a solution could be negotiated only with elected representatives, did not encourage the F.L.N. to respond. About the same time Salan was replaced as commander-in-chief in Algeria by the younger General Challe, who immediately set about organizing small mobile units that penetrated into the remotest districts held by the A.L.N. One of de Gaulle's trusted men, Paul Delouvrier, was also sent at the end of the year as his delegate-general with special responsibility for executing the Constantine Plan.

The F.L.N. reacted to de Gaulle's programme by intensifying the A.L.N.'s guerrilla action, organizing terrorist raids in France, and announcing the formation in Tunis of the Gouvernement Provisoire de la République Algérienne (Provisional Government of the Algerian Republic – G.P.R.A.) on 19 September. The government included members of the Association of the 'Ulama and the U.D.M.A. in addition to F.L.N. leaders, and its presidency was given to 'Abbas, thus emphasizing its broad representative character. The F.L.N. then demonstrated its influence in Algeria by calling upon the Muslims to boycott the elections due to take place on 30 November and dissuaded Muslims of standing from taking part in them. As the M.N.A. also boycotted the elections, all the forty-eight Muslim deputies elected (out of seventy-one) were partisans of total integration with France, and were elected with the support, and in some cases the votes, of the settlers. These men were not the representative leaders with whom de Gaulle might be able to arrive at a viable solution and so he ignored them, hoping that time and the Constantine Plan would produce the desired third force standing between them and the G.P.R.A. In an address delivered on 16 September 1959, intended to avert the appearance of the Algerian problem for the fourth year in succession on the agenda of the U.N. General Assembly, he indicated his reliance on time. He promised the Algerians that, not later than four years after the restoration of peace in Algeria, they would be able to choose one of three possible solutions to the problem: secession which would bring with it the cessation of French aid, complete union with France under terms of equality, and federation with France in which case Algeria would be united with France in its economy, educational policy, defence, and foreign affairs. The G.P.R.A. offered on 28 September to discuss the terms of a cease-fire and the guarantees of self-determination on condition that the national unity of Algeria, including the Sahara, was recognized. The offer was not taken up.

Whatever chances of success de Gaulle's endeavours to produce the desired third force in Algeria had were frittered away by the settlers' and the army's violent opposition to his policy of self-determination. After the events of 13 May 1958 the European activists reorganized their ranks. Numerous organizations were formed, the most powerful being the Front National Français (F.N.F.) led by a café-owner called Joseph Ortiz. In the army the settlers still had a prop in Massu, who was kept in his position because of his devoted Gaullist past, and Jean Gardes, the director of the army's *cinquième bureau*, whose obsessive fear of communism led him to consider the success of the settlers' cause the only alternative to the victory of communism in the form of the F.L.N. Already agitated by de Gaulle's self-determination speech, the settlers were provoked to insurrection by Massu's recall, following the publication on 18 January 1960 in the West German *Süddeutsche Zeitung* of an interview in which he criticized de Gaulle's Algerian policy and hinted that most of the army officers in Algeria would not obey him. Barricades were immediately raised in Algiers, and a "camp retranché" was thus formed, manned by the armed followers of Ortiz and the student leader Lagaillarde. The aim of the insurgents was once more to involve the army and bring it to take a public stand against de Gaulle, thereby causing his downfall. The insurrection was a total failure. The Muslims would not be drawn into the venture and the bulk of the army did not take the hoped-for stand against de Gaulle. The men of Massu's tenth parachute division had mounted guard around the insurgents' "camp" to give them moral support. They agreed to be transferred when Delouvrier, accompanied by the commander-in-chief Challe, set up headquarters at the Raghaya air base, thus threatening to bring the air-force in. De Gaulle, in a broadcast on 29 January, firmly stated that he would not be forced by the insurrection to change his Algerian policy.

But still de Gaulle was not prepared to recognize the competence of the G.P.R.A. to negotiate on behalf of the Algerian Muslims. In a speech on 14 June 1960 he described his policy as one leading to an "Algerian Algeria linked with France". The G.P.R.A. offered immediately afterwards to negotiate, and a conference was held from 25 to 29 June between French and G.P.R.A. representatives at Melun. When the G.P.R.A. representatives soon discovered that they were expected to lay down their arms before substantive negotiations could begin, they broke off the talks. De Gaulle made his position towards the G.P.R.A. clear when in a speech on 4 November he stated that whereas his Algerian policy implied the eventual transfer of authority to Algerians, that did not mean recognizing the "rebels" solely as the representatives of the Algerian Muslims. The extremism of the settlers, however, led soon afterwards to the affirmation of the Algerian Muslims' support for the F.L.N., and made de Gaulle realize that if a solution was to be reached, it had to come through negotiations with the G.P.R.A. Early in December he went to Algiers to gauge the extent of the army's and the settlers' opposition to his Algerian policy and his popularity with the Muslims. While he was there, settler terrorists opened fire on Muslims in Belcourt, a suburb of Algiers. The Muslims countered by demonstrating for several days, carrying the F.L.N. flags and exclaiming "Abbas au pouvoir". In these few days 120 Muslims were killed either by settler terrorists or by the paratroops sent to disperse the demonstrations. The shift in de Gaulle's Algerian policy which these events occasioned was heralded by another referendum that took place on 8 January 1961, in which the question put to the electorate was whether or not they approved the offer of self-determination to the Algerians. The returns gave him the mandate he wanted: in France 75.26 per cent were in favour. In Algeria, where the G.P.R.A. boycotted the referendum and most of the settlers voted against, sixty per cent were in favour. Immediately after the results were published contact with the G.P.R.A. was resumed, but before the formal talks opened the "Generals' insurrection" occurred in Algiers, creating a temporary diversion.

The "Generals' insurrection" was an all-army attempt to force General de Gaulle to step down. It was launched on 22 April by four generals who had served in Algeria: Salan, Zeller, Jouhaud, and Challe. The last, who was the chief organizer, had resigned his post as commander-in-chief in Algeria in November 1959 in disagreement with de Gaulle's Algerian policy. This policy was resented by the high-ranking officers mostly because it constituted a humiliation to the army and was interpreted by some, such as Challe who after leaving Algeria served with N.A.T.O., as a surrender to international communism. The insurrection fizzled out in four days, although on 23 April it was feared that the rebels might be able to send paratroops to occupy Paris. It failed because the navy refused to cooperate, most of the air-force pilots disobeyed their commander who had joined the rebellion and flew their aircraft to France, the Algerian police did not commit themselves, the conscripted troops refused to obey those of their officers who joined the rebellion, and metropolitan France expressed its support for de Gaulle by a one-hour strike on the 24th in which an estimated ten million people took part. The failure of the insurrection demonstrated to the settlers that France was no longer prepared to pay dearly with the lives of its young men and money to protect their interests, and consequently they had recourse to terrorism as a last and desperate means to prevent a settlement with the F.L.N. The rebelling generals refused to involve the settler leaders in their action and disdainfully ignored Ortiz, who declared himself the head of an Algerian provisional government when the insurrection broke out. But the leaders of the insurrection distributed a large amount of weapons to the settlers, and only a part of these arms was subsequently recovered by the police. These weapons augmented the armoury of the newly founded Organisation de l'Armée Secrète (O.A.S.) in which all the extremist settler groups were

united from April 1961. The O.A.S. continued its terrorist acts until June
1962. Its members attacked French government officials at first. Later on,
particularly from March 1962, they came to act on a large scale against the
Muslims, trying thereby to provoke A.L.N. reprisals against the French
that would lead to the intervention of the French army and the resumption
of hostilities. The O.A.S. did much damage, especially in May 1962 when
it followed a scorched earth policy with the aim of leaving little of value to
the independent Algerian government. But the greatest damage it did was
to the settlers themselves, since it prevented them from being able to
adjust to life in independent Algeria. When eventually the O.A.S. leaders
realized that their struggle had become hopeless and ordered their men to
cease fire on 26 June 1962, some 300,000 Europeans had already left
Algeria.

The negotiations between the French government and the G.P.R.A.,
which opened at Evian on 20 May 1961, faced two major problems: the
position of the settlers for whom the French government demanded a
special status, and sovereignty in the Algerian Sahara, which the French
wanted to consider separately. On 29 June de Gaulle even hinted at the
idea of grouping the Europeans around Oran and Algiers, where they
would form a separate entity from the rest of Algeria. The importance of
the Sahara arose from the major oil discoveries made in 1956 at Hassi
Mas'ud (Messaoud) and Ajila (Edjeleh) which opened up before the
French the prospects of saving the 300 million dollars spent annually on
oil imports. The G.P.R.A. held firmly to their position of refusing to give
the settlers a special status and treating the Algerian Sahara as an integral
part of Algeria. This caused the interruption of the talks from 28 July to
2 October. Eventually the French government yielded on both questions,
and an agreement was reached on 18 March 1962 by which France
recognized Algeria's independence.

The question whether an Algerian nation existed before the French
occupation became irrelevant when in the referendum of 1 July 1962 in
Algeria, out of a ninety-one per cent poll (including the Europeans),
ninety-seven per cent voted in favour of independence. In fact the question
had become an academic one after 1956, when the Algerian Muslim
masses felt that the F.L.N. aim of independence was their own. The fact
that the foreign European community formed an exploiting class of landowners and entrepreneurs and that the F.L.N. received diplomatic and
military assistance from communist countries, gave to the Algerian
conflict something of the character of a doctrinal confrontation between
Marxism and capitalism. The leftist leanings of some of the leaders of
independent Algeria confirmed this impression. Nevertheless the dominant aim of the struggle was one of national liberation. To the Algerian
Muslims the distinction between themselves and the settlers was not one

to be defined in terms of economic resources, but in terms of identity. Little sympathy existed between the Muslims and the European poor in Algeria, and the well-to-do *évolués* insisted throughout on retaining their Muslim personal status. As David Gordon points out,[1] to most F.L.N. leaders Algerian socialism involved Arabization. And when the Algerian "Code of Nationality" was passed at the end of 1962, a native-born Algerian was defined as one of "Muslim status" whose father and grand-father had been born in Algeria. As they were fighting a war of liberation against France, even the French-educated Algerians came to consider Arabic and the Muslim status as the symbols of their identity. The two symbols are interdependent because of the close identification of Arabic culture with Islam. This, however, did not mean a rejection of the west, for under its impact they not only attained a new consciousness of their identity but also learned to reject the traditional Arab east.

Tunisia: from anti-colonialism to nationalism, 1919–34

Like Algeria, Tunisia experienced in the post-First World War period the tensions arising from the clash of interests between a settler community which benefited from the circumstances of the war and was bent on economic expansion, and a Muslim community expecting rewards for services rendered to France during the war. About 63,000 Tunisians served during the war in the French army, and of these 10,500 were either killed or listed missing. Like Algeria also, Tunisia was to experience in the 1920s and 30s the migration of unemployed peasants and tribesmen from the countryside to the cities, and the spread of political consciousness to the lower strata of the society. In the person of Shaikh 'Abdul-'Aziz al-Tha'alibi, she also knew a diluted brand of Salafi reforming tendencies. Nevertheless, the socio-political framework of post-war Tunisian society was different from the Algerian, and the country's transformation into an independent nation-state bore the mark of this difference.

As the French in Tunisia ruled in the name of a king who was, *de jure* if not *de facto*, sovereign, Tunisia retained her political personality. Furthermore, the size of the French settler community remained small, and the Italian community was large and unwilling to be absorbed into the French by naturalization. The problem of a French settler community determining the stance of the protectorate authority did not, therefore, arise in the same magnitude as in Algeria. And as the French authorities preserved the pre-protectorate administrative hierarchy of *qa'ids*, *khalifas*, and tribal *shaikhs*, and won over the "clerical" Muslim class of Sufi *shaikhs* and *'ulama*, the leadership of the Muslim community remained conservative and traditionalist. In Algeria the traditional "clerical"

[1] David Gordon, *The passing of French Algeria* (London, 1966), p. 161.

Muslim leaders had by the 1920s lost their standing in the society and were being challenged by a new generation of men of religion who were reared in the Salafi doctrine and committed to social reform. In Tunisia social reform was initiated in the nineteenth century by the non-"clerical" Muslim leaders. The "clerics", who generally turned their back on the reforming movement, welcomed the opportunity provided by the protectorate to regain some of their lost power, and resigned the role of defending social Muslim issues to others, particularly those with political implications. Another important difference between Tunisia and Algeria was that in the former the advocates of total assimilation in the French community had exhausted their potential as leaders before the First World War. Consequently when mass political forces appeared in Tunisia in the 1920s and 30s, they were not distracted from facing clearly nationalist issues by an assimilationist programme of the Algerian *évolués'* brand. Tunisian nationalism which crystallized in the 1930s in the Neo-Destour party thus combined in a unitary movement the grievances of the lower classes with the defence of the Muslim identity and the political skills of the *évolué* leaders.

The decade of the 1920s was one of awakening anti-colonialist, as different from nationalist, sentiments. This was the period when the Destour (Constitution) party, founded in 1920, acted as the spokesmen of Tunisia's politically conscious groups. The impulse which led to its foundation was the direct result of the hopes aroused by the Wilsonian doctrine of self-determination and the Arab aspirations for independence and unity which emerged during the war. The party's leader, al-Tha'alibi, was a product of the traditional Zaituna education, but he had had contacts with 'Abduh and his disciples in Egypt at the turn of the century and before the war was associated with the Young Tunisians. Since July 1919 he was in Paris with other Tunisian leaders trying to persuade the Peace Conference to take account of their demand for Tunisia's independence. The failure of this self-appointed mission led Tha'alibi in 1920 to publish, with another future Destourian leader called Ahmad Saqqa, a book entitled *La Tunisie martyre: ses revendications*. The main argument of this book is that before the protectorate Tunisia was a developing country, progressing within its proper Islamic framework. The French, instead of continuing this programme along the sound lines already charted, introduced educational and judicial systems foreign to the country and, by usurping all powers, destroyed the country's constitutional heritage. The programme of recovery which the book advocated included the restoration of the 1860 constitution, the modernization of the judicial system while preserving the supremacy of the *shari'a*, making Arabic the main language of instruction, developing health and social services, and redirecting the economy towards serving the needs of the entire population and not only the foreign settlers. The book also speaks of a liberal future for Tunisia, but this liberalism is only an echo of Khair al-Din's emphasis on the curtailment of governmental tyranny through upholding the rule of law.

The Destour party started its activities in 1920 with the radical demand for independence, but soon afterwards it settled down to a programme of reform, relying for advancing it on a legalistic debate with the French and on diplomatic manoeuvres. At times its leaders provoked demonstrations, but reliance on mass support was not characteristic of their methods even after the party came to have branches in most of Tunisia's towns and big villages. More typical of its methods was to have in 1920 two professors of the Paris Faculty of Law pronounce an opinion that granting a constitution was not incompatible with the protectorate regime, and in 1922 to prevail upon al-Nasir Bey through the influence of his relatives to express sympathy with the Destour. The Destourian leaders' lack of interest in mass support and their methods of action reflect their social background: al-Tha'alibi was the grandson of an Algerian *qadi* who migrated to Tunis in the 1840s, where the family then lived in ease and enjoyed governmental patronage; Ahmad Saqqa's family produced many *qa'ids*; Farhat b. 'Ayyad was the scion of a once famous family; and Muhammad al-Riyahi came from a family with a tradition of religious learning long associated with high government service. As L. C. Brown has suggested,[1] the formalistic legalism characteristic of the Destourian leaders' political manoeuvres was inspired by their contacts with the west, but was "supported by the attitudes of the traditional society". This legalism enabled them to undertake political action on behalf of the Tunisian society without totally committing themselves either to the society or to the action itself. They were not and could not be revolutionary either socially or politically, and they tended to ignore the political importance of the new intelligentsia and social groups that appeared through the educational and economic impact of the protectorate. Without mass organization, and as its leaders remained isolated in their exclusive social milieu, the Destour party lacked the resilience necessary for withstanding political repression. Thus since the imposition in January 1926 of restrictions on the press and political activity, the Destour party languished in passivity.

Tunisia did not experience the settlement of large numbers of political refugees and farmers from France under a policy of official colonization, as Algeria did. In spite of the foundation of a colonial fund in 1897 to encourage Frenchmen to settle on the land in Tunisia, the size of the French community remained small, numbering 108,000 in 1936, of which the agricultural population constituted roughly ten per cent. By 1914 land in the hands of the French in Tunisia amounted to nearly 770,000 hectares

[1] See Brown's contribution to Charles A. Micauld, *Tunisia, the politics of modernisation* (London, 1964), pp. 38–45.

(about one-fifth of the arable land of the country), and increased very little thereafter. From the beginning French agriculture in Tunisia was predominantly a capitalist enterprise. Out of 443,000 hectares of land owned by the French in 1892, 416,000 belonged to sixteen owners. On the eve of the Second World War twenty-three per cent of the lands owned by the French belonged to four companies, and the average French holding was 286 hectares, against 29 hectares for Italians. The same French companies often invested in agriculture, in mining industry, and transportation. Frenchmen and Italians provided much of the skilled labour required by French agricultural and industrial firms, and Tunisian Muslims the bulk of the unskilled and only a very small proportion of the skilled labour. By 1956, about 160,000 Tunisian Muslims were employed in the modern sector of the economy: mining, mechanized agriculture, transportation, and construction and public works. The result of the French economic activity was therefore to create a modern proletariat. It also resulted in the movement of population from the south to the north, where the French farms and industrial works were concentrated. The Sahil, where French economic penetration remained limited but which had always been more populous than other parts of the country, and the north (together constituting one-fifth the area of Tunisia) came to accommodate between 1936 and 1946 seventy per cent of the population. In this same period about 100,000 people moved to Tunis and its suburbs from the countryside including the south. This labour force, unemployed or employed in menial jobs, was an important political force.

In conformity with their conservative attitudes, and in compliance with the wishes of the settlers, the protectorate authorities as a matter of conscious policy did not attempt to extend French education to the Tunisians. They preserved the traditional Islamic schools, the *kuttab*, to which in the early period of the protectorate the conservative Muslim parents still preferred to send their children. The Young Tunisians, however, from the beginning of the century advocated the extension of modern education to the Tunisians. One of them, Khairalla b. Mustafa, set up in 1906 a "reformed *kuttab*", but the general trend of the Young Tunisians was towards making Tunisian children have a thorough French education, maintaining that only through this education could Tunisians compete and justify their demand for equality with the French. Their arguments, and the realization that to succeed one needed modern education, gradually broke Muslim hesitations. Moreover, the desire of the Muslims to give their children education in Arabic in addition to French, and the existence of a tradition in the Sadiqiyya College of an Arabic modern education, led to the appearance of the so-called Franco-Arab system of schools. The system emerged from the introduction of French and modern subjects to the *kuttab* and giving more weight to

Arabic in government primary schools having a predominantly Tunisian student body. To supplement the shortage of places in government schools and avoid the difficulties involved in admission to them, local initiative resulted in the creation of private Franco-Arab institutions. The Sadiqiyya College was recognized in 1911 as a diploma-granting institution, and in 1930 its curriculum was reorganized along the Lycée pattern. Several other secondary schools modelled on the Sadiqiyya appeared in the 1940s, but the Sadiqiyya remained at the apex of the French-Arab system, providing secondary education to select graduates of the primary schools operating within the system.

Whereas the children of the capital's old families went to French schools, the Franco-Arab schools educated a new Tunisian elite[1] drawn mostly from the middle and lower classes of the villages and towns of the Sahil. It was in this region of Tunisia that the Franco-Arab schools abounded: seventy out of the ninety private Franco-Arab schools in existence in 1950 operated in the Sahil, and they provided education to about one-quarter of the school-going Muslim children. Out of eighty new students admitted to the Sadiqiyya College in 1939, forty came from the Sahil. By the 1930s, the sons of humble families were competing with the scions of the old Tunis families in the prestige professions and for appointment to the high administrative jobs open to Muslims. The Neo-Destour party was the political expression of the new elite. It embodied the spirit of a new generation which was both progressive and Tunisian Muslim, ambitious and mobile but retaining its roots in the home village or town, of humble social background but determined to succeed in the face of a system that still favoured the established aristocracy. It was predominantly a Sahilian movement. Most of its leaders came from the Sahil, including Bourguiba, and when in 1934 these leaders rebelled against the leaders of the Destour, they symbolically did so at the party congress held in the Sahil at Qsar Hilal (Ksar Hellal).

It was not until 1946 that a viable Tunisian labour union came into being with the foundation of the Union Générale Tunisienne du Travail (U.G.T.T.). Because the capitalist class was predominantly French, labour grievances tended to be transformed into anti-colonial sentiments and to find expression in nationalist agitation. This was apparent in the strike of the tramway employees in 1912 which turned into an anti-French and anti-Italian agitation. In the 1920s those Tunisians who developed a labour class-consciousness joined the French C.G.T. (Confédération Générale des Travailleurs) and had the satisfaction of hearing French socialist activists attack capitalist French and feudal Tunisian institutions and situations. The genuine sympathy which French socialist leaders in

---

[1] A detailed analysis of the rise of the new Tunisian elite is to be found in Clement H. Moore, *Tunisia since independence: the dynamics of one-party government* (Berkeley, 1965).

Tunisia showed for Tunisians, and the dedicated social work of some of them, temporarily gave an international direction to labour agitation. But the latent nationalist content of labour grievances could not remain submerged. In 1924 it came into the open in an abortive attempt at constituting a separate Tunisian labour union. In this year Muhammad 'Ali, a Tunisian and former chauffeur who managed to obtain a German degree in political economy, returned to Tunis. He was shocked to observe the apathy of the Muslim workers, and his activities amongst them soon resulted in a number of strikes including one by the dockers of Tunis in August 1924. Under his inspiration the Confédération Générale des Travailleurs Tunisiens (C.G.T.T.) was launched in December. Muhammad 'Ali's ideology, in the words of Jacques Berque, was "a specific mixture of Marxist criticism, nationalism, and Arab taste".[1] He and his biographer Tahir Haddad were modernist in the sense that they directed their attention to modern social problems, such as the standard of living and the social position of Tunisian women. But both also blamed the most important of their country's social problems on the French, and called on the Tunisian workers to rely on themselves in fighting their economic and social battles. Muhammad 'Ali was arrested soon after the foundation of the C.G.T.T. on the charge of conspiracy against the state, and both the C.G.T.T. and the Tunisian branch of the C.G.T. were dissolved. In the absence of a national trade unionist movement, the Neo-Destour party could attract into its ranks those Tunisians who might have expressed their labour grievances through the C.G.T.T. And when in 1946 the U.G.T.T. was founded, it became until independence the political ally of the Neo-Destour.

The Neo-Destour came into being as a result of the dissatisfaction of the new Tunisian elite with the Destour political leadership. Its leaders introduced into Tunisian politics not so much a new political aim (for the aim of independence was implied if not always explicit in the Destourian position), but a new style of action, a greater sense of mission and commitment, and the will not only to achieve independence but also to create a new society. Habib Bourguiba represented this orientation and led the Neo-Destour from the start, although a fellow-founder of the party, Dr Mahmud Materi, was its president from 1934 to 1938. Bourguiba's background is typical of the new elite. Born in Munastir in the Sahil, he studied at the primary section of the Sadiqiyya, then at the college itself. After passing through the Lycée Carnot, he went to Paris where he obtained a degree in law. He returned in 1927 to practise law in Tunis, where he found himself neither admitted into the traditional society nor treated as an equal by the French. He had joined the Destour party in 1922, but after his return from France he was out of sympathy with its orientation.

[1] Berque, *French North Africa*, p. 101.

Tunisia: the Neo-Destour and independence

The convening of the Eucharistic Congress in Carthage in May 1930 was an important landmark in the crystallization of a mass nationalist movement in Tunisia. The congress was the work of Monseigneur Lemaître, the archbishop of Carthage, who was also responsible for the erection of a statue of Cardinal Lavigerie facing the Muslim sector (Madina) of Tunis. The Shaikh al-Islam, the highest "clerical" Muslim authority in Tunisia, and the bey attended the opening session of the congress, but there was much popular agitation against what was viewed as a crusading policy. Bourguiba dates the beginning of his nationalist commitment from the period of the congress. Later in the year he joined the editorial staff of an independent nationalist newspaper called *Le Voix du Tunisien*. In 1932 he launched with other Tunisian university graduates – Mahmud Materi, Tahir Sfar, and Bahri Guiga – the newspaper *L'Action Tunisienne*. These men were still members of the Destour, but in the columns of *L'Action* they introduced a new approach to politics.

From the beginning the *L'Action* group confronted the dual task of remoulding the Tunisian society while preserving its Islamic features. Their education made them feel the need for social progress. But they also could not turn their back on Islamic traditions in which they were themselves more or less rooted and which to the Muslim masses were symbols of national identity. In the first two years of their activity, the *L'Action* group, still trying to establish a link with the submerged Tunisians, made effective use of the Islamic symbols. At one occasion in his early political career, Bourguiba defended the custom of veiling women. At the end of 1932 the *L'Action* group was provided with an opportunity to demonstrate its attachment to the Muslim law. This occurred when a controversy arose over the burial of Tunisian Muslims who were naturalized French under the provisions of a law passed in 1923.

In a *fatwa* issued in December 1932 the *mufti* of Bizerta advanced the view that naturalized Tunisians, by ceasing to be under the jurisdiction of the Muslim law, had lapsed from the faith. Consequently they were not entitled to burial in Muslim cemeteries. The Hanafi jurists in Tunis, anxious to avoid a clash with the protectorate authorities, dissented, and the distinguished Malikite jurist Tahir b. 'Ashur gave an opinion stating that a naturalized Muslim could be buried in Muslim cemeteries if he repented his lapse before his death. *L'Action* used the controversy to affirm the Islamic identity of Tunisia and defeat the pro-French "clerics" on their own ground. Taking the position of the *mufti* of Bizerta, it affirmed that the Muslim law was clear on the question, and condemned the loyalist *'ulama* for their failure to clarify to the Muslims the religious implications of accepting French nationality. After several incidents in which the graves of naturalized Muslims were dug out and their remains removed from Muslim cemeteries, the protectorate authorities gave way in 1933 and assigned separate cemeteries to the naturalized. At the same time *L'Action* was banned.

The attitude of the *L'Action* group on the cemeteries' issue was the beginning of an open split with the Destour leadership. The split became formal and final at the Destour Party Congress at Qsar Hilal in March 1934. Bourguiba resigned from the party when censured by its executive committee over supporting a demonstration in his home town of Munastir against the burial of a naturalized child. The other *L'Action* leaders followed him to form the Neo-Destour party.

The Neo-Destour developed its organs and spread its influence under the continuous threat of suppression. The party was formally banned six months after its foundation and remained illegal for the following twenty years. Bourguiba was arrested in 1934 as a result of the disturbances which occurred between the Neo-Destour and the Old Destour and remained at Bordj Le Boeuf on the Tunisian edge of the Sahara until 1936 when he was released by the French Popular Front government. Between 1936 and 1938, when Bourguiba was at liberty, the structure[1] of the party was organized. It was both a democratic and centralized structure. The local branches had each an elected executive committee, and several branches were united in a "federation" having an executive committee elected by the branch delegates. The highest authority in the party was the National Congress comprising all branch delegates. The central executive organ of the party was the Political Bureau elected by the National Congress. Between the meetings of the Congress the work of the Political Bureau was supervised by a National Council, half of whose members were elected by the National Congress and the other half composed of one delegate representing each federation. The mass character of the party is evident from its membership of about 100,000 in 1937 organized in 400 branches. The membership remained steady: in 1954 it was estimated at 106,000. From the beginning the leaders of the Neo-Destour aimed at giving it the character of a party that cut across social distinctions and educational backgrounds. The new bourgeoisie of the Sahil found a place in it side by side with the dockers of Tunis, and tribesmen of the interior. Although the top leaders were all the products of the Franco-Arab system of education and many received a French professional education, graduates of the Zaituna formed a large part of its cadres, especially as activists at local level. The party's efficient organization and broad basis enabled it to survive French administrative persecution and the stresses of the Second World War period. Bourguiba acted as its secretary-general until 1938,

---

[1] On the organization of the Neo-Destour, see Moore, *Tunisia since independence*, pp. 105 ff.

when Dr Materi, its first president, withdrew from the party in protest over the campaign of violence conducted with Bourguiba's sanction against the Old Destour. Bourguiba henceforth assumed full command. The party's organization and cohesion was such that although he was either in prison or in exile for most of the period between 1938 and 1955, the party still carried on the struggle.

In 1937-8 the Neo-Destour scored a public victory against the Old Destour. Tha'alibi was allowed to return to Tunisia in 1937 after fifteen years of exile. His tour of the country in a bid to revive the Old Destour was a failure: harassed by the Neo-Destourians, he had to rely on the colonial police for protection. His final political downfall came in the following year when a complaint he had made to the police against Bourguiba was published by the Neo-Destour. But police repression which followed prevented the Neo-Destour from completing its victory over the Old Destour. The C.G.T.T. was reorganized at the end of 1937 and, together with the Neo-Destour, was responsible for the riots which broke out in January 1938 in Bizerta over the dismissal of an Algerian workman. On 9 April riots in Tunis led to the arrest of 'Ali al-Balhawan (Bel-haouane), a Neo-Destour activist. Next day when he was being taken to court, demonstrators attempted to release him. The police fired, killing 112 and wounding 62. In the same day Bourguiba was arrested and later in the year was taken to France, together with other political prisoners.

The extreme repression of 1938 quietened nationalist agitation. As at the same time Fascist agents became very active amongst the Italians in Tunisia, thus reviving the Tunisians' fears of Italian colonial ambitions in the country, the French presence started to appear, at least momentarily, an advantage. The relative lull in political activity continued even after the fall of France and the arrival of a new resident-general, Admiral Esteva, representing the Vichy government. Until the beginning of November 1942, when Allied troops landed in Morocco and Algeria, and soon afterwards Tunisia became the theatre of major military operations, mass nationalist activities remained curtailed because of the tight restrictions imposed.

Munsif Bey, who acceded to the throne in June 1942, was not subject to the same restrictions as his people. To the surprise of all concerned, not least the Tunisians themselves, the bey posed as the symbol of nationalist aspirations and sought to renew the bond between the throne and the people. He received nationalist leaders, Destourians and Neo-Destourians alike, in the palace, abolished the traditional hand-kissing ceremonial to which Tunisians were subjected in their audiences with the bey, and in his outings he made a point of mixing with the masses. He personally interfered to hasten the execution of public works, and told a meeting of *qa'ids* that they could rely on his support in resisting the restrictions of the

French *contrôleurs civils*. In August 1942 he also sent a demand to the Pétain government for changes in the protectorate regime that should include the creation of a consultative assembly with a Tunisian majority, and reorganizing the administration to place it under Tunisian control. From November 1942, when German troops arrived in the country and Admiral Esteva was divided between his sympathy for the Free French and his personal loyalty to Pétain, the bey's ability to act independently was greatly increased. In the end he dismissed the existing government, and had a new one formed by Muhammad Shanniq, a sympathizer of the Neo-Destour. The government also included Dr Materi and Salah Farhat, the latter being the secretary-general of the Old Destour. Within six months Munsif Bey's standing overshadowed that of any political leader in the country. Even Bourguiba's political future might have been different had the bey remained in power. But he was deposed on 14 May 1943 by the Free French authorities a week after the Allied forces entered Tunis. He was accused of collaboration with the Axis, but the more likely reason for his removal from the throne was his attempt to shake off French control.

In 1938 the Neo-Destour had set up a clandestine Political Bureau organized by Dr Thamir and Tayyib Slim. In the lower ranks of the party there was a strong current of sympathy for Nazism, but the upper leadership remained generally uncommitted to either side in the war. Bourguiba from his prison in Marseilles took a definite stand against collaboration with the Axis. In a message he smuggled from his prison in August 1942 he urged the Neo-Destour Political Bureau to enter into relations, and coordinate their political action, with the Free French, leaving until after the war the question of Tunisia's independence. Bourguiba was sent to Rome by the Germans at the beginning of 1943, where the Italian government tried to obtain a statement in favour of the Axis from him. He refused. Nevertheless he was released to arrive in Tunisia in time to attend the anniversary of his arrest which the Neo-Destour was organizing on 8 April 1943. The Italians hoped that his activities would be hostile to France and the Allies, but they were wrong. In May he issued a proclamation denouncing Fascism and Mussolini's expansionist designs, affirming his loyalty to France, and calling on Tunisians to form a bloc with the French against the Fascists. He added that "the whole of France, once liberated from the Nazi yoke, would not forget... her true friends, those who stood by her side in the days of trial".

The end of the war did not herald any change that was likely to bring Tunisia nearer to independence. In order to solicit international support for Tunisia, Bourguiba left the country secretly in March 1945, went first to Egypt, where he hoped to obtain help from the newly founded Arab League, then spent two years touring Asia, Europe, and the United States. In Tunisia, where the U.G.T.T. was founded in 1946, there was a tendency towards coordinating the action of the various anti-colonial groups in a National Tunisian Front. A congress was held on 23 August 1946 in which the Destour, Neo-Destour, and U.G.T.T. took part. The police broke in to disrupt the meeting as Salah b. Yusuf (Youssef), then the secretary-general of the Neo-Destour, was delivering his address. Before the gathering dispersed, the leaders present had time to pledge themselves to work for Tunisia's independence. In the face of the demonstrations, strikes, and other forms of agitation which followed, the French made minor concessions accompanied by police repression. In July 1947 a new Tunisian government was formed, with Mustafa Ka'ak as prime minister, in which the number of Tunisian ministers was made equal to the French. This did not seem to make any significant difference since real authority remained in the hands of the resident-general.

In theory the protectorate treaty did not abrogate the bey's sovereignty, and for this reason protectorate officials acted in the bey's name. In practice, however, the French settlers in the country were made to share in the bey's sovereignty by being given the opportunity to form the Consultative Conference.[1] A decisive step in the direction of Franco-Tunisian co-sovereignty was taken in 1922 with the creation of the Grand Council which replaced the Consultative Conference. The Council had two sections, one French consisting of fifty members and another indigenous of twenty-six members, one of whom had to be a Jew. On the face of it, this reform was a liberal act in that it allowed representatives of the Tunisian people to participate in controlling the acts of government. In fact it constituted an encroachment on Tunisian sovereignty without granting Tunisians any real power: the Tunisian candidates for election to the council were chosen by the administration from amongst the loyalist wealthy families, their section of the council was presided over by an official chosen by the resident, and in plenary sessions of the council the Tunisians were outnumbered by the French. Unlike the Consultative Conference, the council furthermore was no longer merely an advisory body but had power to scrutinize the budget. The same trend towards co-sovereignty was evident in the constitution of the local councils. By another decree of 1922 each of Tunisia's five provinces (*qiadat*) was endowed with a *qiadat* council in which eighty-six seats were reserved for the French and sixty-nine for indigenous representatives, and whose president was a *contrôleur civil* appointed by the resident.

From 1950 the question of co-sovereignty became the major bone of contention between the French and Tunisian nationalists. In August Muhammad Shanniq was made to form a new government of nine Tunisians and three French. The formation of the government was understood to herald political changes of significance, and so the Neo-

[1] See above, p. 283.

Destour agreed to take part in it. Salah b. Yusuf, the party's secretary-general, became the minister of justice. The French reforms which were announced soon afterwards involved upgrading the prime minister by having his orders countersigned not by the French secretary-general of the government but by the resident. The Grand Council was henceforth to have equal French and Tunisian membership. The settler organization Rassemblement Français de Tunisie had for some time insisted that only a joint Franco-Tunisian sovereignty would be compatible with the dominant interests the French had in the country, and the French government upheld this viewpoint. Prime Minister Shanniq and three other Tunisian Ministers went to Paris in October 1951 to demand Tunisian independence and the recognition of total Tunisian sovereignty, while retaining close cultural, economic, and military relations with France. The French government's reply given on 15 December was that a fruitful Franco-Tunisian association required French participation in Tunisia's governmental institutions.

Riots which broke out in Tunisia when on 15 January 1952 the resident Hautecloque demanded that the bey dismiss the Shanniq government, led to Bourguiba's arrest on 18 January together with other Neo-Destour leaders. Shanniq and three other Tunisian ministers were arrested on 25 March, the day al-Amin Bey once more refused to dismiss him. Shanniq's imprisonment was as much a warning to the bey as it was a means of installing a more cooperative government. The frightened bey without demur appointed the two successive governments headed by the loyalist prime ministers chosen by the French: Salah al-Din Bakkush (Baccouche) on 28 March 1952 and Muhammad Salah Mzali in March 1954. The formation of each of these two governments was accompanied by reforms which failed to lead to an agreement with the nationalists because on both occasions the concept of co-sovereignty was upheld. The reforms of June 1952 enabled the Tunisian prime minister to issue his orders without their being countersigned by the resident, and provided for the creation of two assemblies having purely consultative functions: an all-Tunisian legislative council of thirty members appointed by the bey, and a financial council in which the French had equal representation with the Tunisians. They also provided for the creation of an administrative tribunal headed by a Frenchman against whose decisions an appeal could be lodged to a special commission in Paris. When Mzali was installed premier in March 1954 a new reform was published increasing the members of the Tunisian legislature to forty-five, and providing for its election by the vote of adult males. But the legislature still had no control over budgetary matters. These were placed under the jurisdiction of a special council comprising members of the Tunisian legislature and an equal number of Frenchmen.

The atmosphere in Tunisia after January 1952 was not conducive to compromise or to the acceptance of the partial solutions the French were proposing. Police repression was countered by demonstrations and strikes. The U.G.T.T. and the Neo-Destour formed a united front for the following three years, and Farhat Hashshad (Hached), the founder of the U.G.T.T., served on the clandestine Political Bureau of the Neo-Destour from 1952. Whereas most of Neo-Destourian leaders were in prison, Hashshad was kept free because of his international connections through the U.G.T.T. membership in the International Confederation of Free Trade Unions. From 1952 Tunisian guerrillas (*fellaga*) also operated from mountain bases against French settlers. By the end of 1954 they had an estimated force of 3,000 men. The settlers countered by forming their own terrorist organization, the Red Hand, which attacked Tunisian political leaders still at liberty. Its most important victim was Farhat Hashshad who was assassinated on 4 December 1954.

Violence eventually led the French government to give in. On 30 July 1954 the Mendès-France government adopted a project of granting autonomy to Tunisia. On the 31st Mendès-France went to Tunis to explain the new policy and to ask the bey to choose a new government to negotiate the form of Tunisian independence. The composition of the government which was formed on 8 August suggests that with the consent of the bey the French were trying to outflank the Neo-Destour. At its head was an independent, Tahir b. 'Ammar, and its other three members were Old Destourian leaders. The negotiations made slow progress and were interrupted when the government of Mendès-France fell on 5 February 1955. When they were resumed on 15 March Bourguiba was allowed to take part in them, and soon acted as the leader of the Tunisian side. The *fellaga* had intensified their action in the second half of 1954, and it appears that the continuation of terrorism was a decisive factor in leading the French government to allow Bourguiba join in the negotiations. An agreement on granting autonomy to Tunisia was concluded with Bourguiba on 22 April 1955, and the conventions embodying it were published on 3 June.

Bourguiba accepted autonomy as a basis for pressing on for complete independence. The militants in the Neo-Destour led by Salah b. Yusuf denounced this agreement, but the Party congress of 17 November 1955 gave Bourguiba full support. As the French accepted the principle of Morocco's independence on 6 November, Bourguiba had a basis for demanding independence for Tunisia. Negotiations were opened on 29 February 1956 and led to the protocol of 20 March in which France recognized Tunisia's independence.

When Tunisia attained her independence the Husainid dynasty had exhausted whatever *raison d'être* it once had. Since the passing of 'Ahd al-Aman in 1857 the beys had fought for survival in power against many threats: European penetration, Ottoman intervention, and the reforming tendencies of their subjects. The French protectorate enabled the dynasty to survive, but with its political authority and prestige sapped. Except during Munsif Bey's reign and the years 1950 to 1952 in al-Amin Bey's reign, the Husainids seemed to perform only one function, namely to justify the exercise of power by the French. This function they could perform because the absolute authority of the bey remained in theory recognized. Could the beylical institution with its 250 years of traditions and associations with absolute rule be transformed overnight into a constitutional monarchy? The question is possibly irrelevant because the seventy-six-year-old al-Amin Bey was too old to adjust to new ways and ideas, and Bourguiba's background and temperament precluded any workable arrangement with the monarchy. He had risen on the crest of a mass movement, and to him the people were the source of authority, particularly so because their political consciousness was awakened in Tunisia by his party. Furthermore, he and his party represented progress, whereas the bey was the symbol of tradition and therefore backwardness. Thus the logical outcome of the Neo-Destour victory was the abolition of the monarchy. In the elections to the Tunisian constituent assembly of March 1956 the Neo-Destour presented the electorate with a list of candidates representing what the party called national unity. There was no opposition, but the high poll of eighty per cent indicated popular support. The constituent assembly then started to strip members of the Husainid house of their special privileges. Eventually on 25 July 1957 it abolished the monarchy by a unanimous vote, pronounced the foundation of a republic, and invested Bourguiba as head of state exercising also the powers of prime minister.

Morocco: the French and Spanish protectorates

Morocco was still a traditional Muslim monarchy when the French protectorate was established in 1912. European penetration since the 1840s had compromised the sultan's already weak authority, but the country was not thereby opened up to Europe's cultural influence in a way that could lead to the appearance of a reforming movement similar to that led by Khair al-Din in Tunisia, aiming at remoulding the country's political, social, and educational institutions. Mawlay Hasan's reforms were limited in scope and, as they were hastily conceived and executed, they only led to Mawlay 'Abdul-'Aziz's expensively playful "modernism". Moroccans upholding Salafi doctrine had also advocated reform since the reign of Mawlay Hasan. But their efforts before the First World War were restricted to introducing changes in the curriculum of the Qarawiyin mosque-university. In the late 1870s 'Abdulla b. Idris al-Sanusi, having imbibed Salafi ideas in Egypt, attacked the system of *ta'wil* (allegorical interpretation of the sacred texts) which the Salafis believed was responsible for the aberrations which crept into traditional Islam, especially in Sufi beliefs and practices. The hostility with which he was met from the learned circles forced him to travel into the Middle East, returning in 1910 to settle in Tangier where he remained until his death in 1931. During the reign of Mawlay 'Abdul-Hafiz another Salafi leader succeeded in reintroducing *tafsir* (philological exegesis which the Salafis considered the only valid means of expounding the sacred texts) into the Qarawiyin curriculum, but there was no time for the Salafi orientation to have a bearing on wider social and intellectual issues before the protectorate was instituted.

Thus when the French took charge of Morocco its traditional outlook, characterized by intellectual passivity and the irrational cults of Sufi *shaikhs* and *sharifs*, was still dominant. Lyautey (1912–25), the resident-general in the formative period of the protectorate, was by temperament and social convictions indisposed to interfere in the country's traditional life beyond what was necessary for the proper functioning of the protectorate. In 1912 the French also inherited the division of Morocco into *blad al-makhzan* and *blad al-siba*. Lyautey was quick to realize that the *blad al-makhzan* was, in his expression, the Maroc utile, the part containing the fertile lands and the mineral resources which the future settlers and the entrepreneurs would want to exploit. Priority was consequently given in the extension of French control to the former *blad al-makhzan*, comprising the coastal plains and the regions of Fez, Meknes, and Wajda. But since *blad al-siba* was inhabited mostly by Berber mountaineers, Lyautey's conservatism, as well as political expediency, led him to keep the Berbers isolated from the predominantly Arabized lowlands. The outcome of Lyautey's policy was to create two distinct reservations, a Berber one mostly in the mountainous regions, and a traditional Islamic one in the cities of the Maroc utile, existing side by side with a dynamic European community undertaking the rapid development of the country's resources to its own advantage.

In 1912 the French were already in control of the regions of Wajda and the Shawiyya, in addition to Casablanca. Lyautey was appointed in May to replace Regnault, who had negotiated the Treaty of Fez with Mawlay 'Abdul-Hafiz, because the situation in the region of Fez required prompt military action following an uprising in the capital on 17 April in which the Muslim population massacred unprotected Frenchmen. Lyautey was able to disperse the tribesmen surrounding Fez, control agitation in the city itself, and start the conquest of the remaining parts of the Maroc utile. In the following two years French troops occupied the coastal towns in the French zone and Marrakish and its suburbs. The capture of Taza in May

1914 enabled the French to establish contact between their forces in eastern Morocco and those in the west.

In the south the situation was complicated by the intrusion of the Mauritanian leader al-Hiba. Al-Hiba's father, Ma' al-'Ainain, had in the first years of the century recognized the Moroccan sultan's sovereignty over the north-western parts of Mauritania which he controlled, and with Moroccan help prepared the Adrar tribes for resisting French penetration of Mauritania. After the Algeciras conference, the French could prevail upon Mawlay 'Abdul-'Aziz to sever his links with the Mauritanian leader. Ma' al-'Ainain then supported 'Abdul-Hafiz. But as this sultan too proved unable to stand in the face of the French, Ma' al-'Ainain rejected his authority and declared himself sultan early in 1910, proclaiming that it was his duty to free the Muslims from Christian control. He led his warriors into Morocco in the spring of 1910, reaching the region of Tadla. Defeated there by the French forces under General Moinier, he withdrew to the south and died in October at Tiznit. Al-Hiba's intervention in 1912 took place in the same spirit of recognizing the unity of Morocco and Mauritania under the authority of one Muslim prince and, in view of the 'Alawites' failure to resist the "infidel", posing as the defender of the faith. Having proclaimed himself sultan at Tiznit in May 1912, about a month after the signature of the Treaty of Fez, al-Hiba set out on the way to Marrakish.

In the region of Marrakish the Glawis had by now emerged as the dominant chieftaincy. Madani al-Glawi had been rewarded for his cooperation with 'Abdul-Hafiz by being made war minister and briefly grand vizier. In the three years during which Madani was in the sultan's favour, he consolidated his authority in the south: he made his brother Thami the pasha (governor) of Marrakish, appointed his son-in-law Hammu as *qa'id* of Talwat, Tinaghir (Tinerhir), Wazarzat (Ouazrzat), and Zagura (Zagora) in the High Atlas, and placed other relatives and protégés in less important chiefly positions. An Arab-Berber confederacy seemed to be making its appearance in Morocco, and the sultan found it convenient to secure the bond by exchanging daughters in marriage with the lord of the south. But in 1911 'Abdul-Hafiz suddenly dismissed Madani with the help of Mtugi, who benefited from the sultan's coup by being allowed to appoint one of his own men, Idris Mannu, as pasha of Marrakish. Madani's dismissal from his official posts was not sufficient to deprive him of his power in the south, based as it was on the family's feudal authority in the High Atlas.

When al-Hiba arrived in the south the local chiefs did not dare oppose him openly. His entry to Marrakish on 15 August was not resisted by the Mtugis, who were officially responsible for defending it, and Madani surrendered to him five of six Frenchmen whom Lyautey had ordered to remain in Marrakish to organize resistance to al-Hiba even after all other

Europeans had left. Madani kept the sixth of the Frenchmen in his custody to testify to his loyalty to the French. Both the Mtugis and the Glawis entered into contact with the French column commanded by Colonel Mangin advancing towards Marrakish, and when the French approached the city, Idris Mannu stormed the prison where the five Frenchmen were kept, thus saving their lives.

It became clear soon after Mangin defeated al-Hiba and his forces occupied Marrakish in September 1912, that the French policy was to be favourable to the local chiefs. The Mtugi and the Glawi, together with the Gundafi and al-'Ayyadi of the Rahamna were confirmed in their positions as *qa'ids*, and were offered arms to conquer the southernmost parts of *blad al-siba* and govern them under French authority. Madani al-Glawi had entered into relations with the French while in Fez, and being the head of the largest chieftaincy, was treated as the supreme chief. Thami was reappointed pasha of Marrakish, and together with the Gundafi he led a campaign against al-Hiba in Sus, and forced him to evacuate his new base at Tarudant in May 1913. When Madani died in 1918, Thami inherited his feudal position and wealth, becoming soon afterwards the undisputed lord of the south. All the other local chiefs were eclipsed by his power. Madani's son-in-law Hammu remained the master of his mountainous *qiadat* and refused to accept French authority until his death in 1934. Thereafter this area too passed under Thami's, and French, control.

Lyautey's reliance on the grand Berber chiefs in governing the south in the name of France has its justification not so much in his professed respect for traditional institutions, but in the political advantages it held. In 1912 it freed him from the need to commit large forces to the south at a time when the conquest of the Maroc utile had not been accomplished. On the eve of the First World War, when Lyautey had to send most of the troops under his command for the war in Europe, his trust in Madani's loyalty enabled him to hold on to the interior of Morocco, contrary to the wishes of the French government. This policy also became in 1914 a way of using the Berber bloc of peoples as a counterbalance to the Arabized or Arab Muslims in the plains and the major cities. This aspect of Lyautey's policy is clear from the Berber *dahir* (royal decree) published on 11 September 1914.

The *dahir* of 1914 was inspired by the experiences of the French both in the south and during their penetration of the Middle Atlas region in the course of 1913–14, when they occupied Tadla, Azru, and Khanifra. The Sanhaja Berbers of the Middle Atlas, unlike the southern Berbers, resisted the French ferociously. Lyautey ascribed this to the Sanhajas' fear of being made to submit to the authority of the Muslim-Arab dynasty which they had resisted since the seventeenth century, and of having their customary life altered by the *qadis* and the *makhzan* administrators. To assure them that acceptance of French rule would not lead to what Lyautey thought the Sanhajas feared, the *dahir* of 1914 recognized the *jamaʿas* (village councils) as governing councils. From 1915 these councils were also empowered to administer justice according to customary law. Giving the *jamaʿas* judicial powers was a novelty in Berber areas. So was the recognition of customary practices as a system of law both independent of and incompatible with the Muslim law. The Berbers, particularly the Sanhajas of the Middle Atlas, were enthusiastic if ignorant Muslims. They were no more conscious of being anti-Islamic in their customary practices than any other professing Muslim group living in isolation from the centres of Islamic learning and government.

The Berber policy which evolved after the First World War was aimed not so much at the conservation of the traditional Berber identity, as at forging a new one under direct French influence. The fact that forty per cent of Morocco's population spoke Berber dialects either solely or together with Arabic was held to be evidence of the existence of a distinct Berber identity. But since the Berber dialects could not be used for instruction, preserving the Berber identity came to mean replacing Arabic as the language of culture for the Berbers by the French. In 1923 five Franco–Berber schools were founded in which the curriculum was entirely French. In the following eight years thirteen others of these schools were established, and in 1927 a Franco–Berber *école normale* was founded in Azru. On the legal level the culmination of the Berber policy was the publication of a second Berber *dahir* on 16 May 1930. The first *dahir* had detached Berber customary law from the Muslim system of justice, the second incorporated it in the French judicial machinery. The *jamaʿas'* judicial powers were transferred to special Berber customary tribunals having competence in cases of civil and commercial natures, and in property disputes. These customary courts could also try criminal cases involving imprisonment of not more than two years, but appellate jurisdiction and prison sentences of longer than two years were reserved to the French courts.

The protectorate arrangement preserved the sultan as the ruler of Morocco while forcing him to share his legislative and executive powers with the French resident-general. *Dahirs* (being the only instruments of legislation) were issued by the sultan, but the initiative in them could come only from the resident. To the sultan was reserved the right to withhold his approval, thereby annulling decrees or delaying their publication. This was a right which in practice he could not exercise without great risks, as the events of 1951 and 1953 were to prove. The sultan had a cabinet consisting of a grand vizier, a minister of justice, and a minister of *habus*, which, except in religious matters, had no real power. The same loyalist grand vizier, Muhammad al-Muqri, who had been in office before the protectorate, held the post for the entire French period of forty-four years, dying shortly after independence at the age of 105 years. The minister of justice was directly responsible only for Muslim justice, and had no control over the Jewish, Berber, or French courts. Even in Muslim justice his decisions were subject to the approval of the directorate of sharifian (i.e. government) affairs. On the local level the *qadis*' judgements were scrutinized by the *contrôleurs civils* or the officers of Affaires Indigènes.

The resident-general was the real ruler of Morocco since he was the representative of the occupying power, initiated all royal decrees, and nominated all high functionaries. A secretary-general directly under him coordinated the work of the nine departments responsible for the economic development of the country, the most important being the departments of finances, agriculture, and public works. Political control remained the direct responsibility of the resident, and was carried out through the directorates of the interior, public security, and of sharifian affairs. Pashas and *qa'ids* continued to govern the towns and tribes respectively and to be appointed by the sultan. But they were nominated to their posts by the residency, and in the execution of their functions were subject to the supervision of the *contrôleurs civils* in civil and the officers of the Affaires Indigènes in military territories, the latter comprising the regions of Fez, Meknes, Taza, Agadir, and parts of the region of Marrakish.

The exploitation of Morocco's resources under the protectorate remained predominantly a capitalist venture, not one carried out by large numbers of settlers brought to the country under a programme of official colonization. Much of the colonization capital came from the banks which developed interests in Morocco through the loan contracted by Mawlay 'Abdul-'Aziz in 1904. These banks, led by the Banque de Paris et des Pays-Bas, financed the major public and private works of constructions, and themselves exploited mineral concessions. Either directly or through its control of the Compagnie Générale du Maroc and the Omnium Nord-Africain, the Banque de Paris participated in the exploitation of the lead deposits at Awli (Aouli) and Mibladen, manganese at Tiwin (Tiouine), and cobalt at Bu Azzar (Bou Azzer). The protectorate authorities assisted French investment by keeping the taxes low, and by providing a protective barrier against foreign competition. The Act of Algeciras provided for the freedom of economic activity in Morocco, and when a statute regulating the terms of mining concessions came into force in 1914 the principle of free competition was upheld. However, later arrangements ensured French domination of the mining industry. In 1920 the mining of phosphate was placed under state control, and in 1928 the Bureau de Recherches et de Participations Minières was set up. At first its functions were limited to the exploitation of coal and oil, but they were expanded in 1938 to include all other minerals except phosphate. Consequently the Moroccan mining industry remained, with a few exceptions, in French hands.

The Moroccan mining industry was almost entirely limited to the actual extraction of the minerals. Except for oil, coal, and in the early 1950s about 100,000 tons of phosphate (a quarter of the output) consumed locally, the minerals were exported in their raw state to European countries, particularly Great Britain, West Germany, and Spain. Thus the mining industry contributed little to the industrial development of Morocco. A few processing industries were established during the Second World War, but political unrest, eventually leading to independence, did not encourage their expansion.

The process of land acquisition for colonization in Morocco reflected the experiences of the French authorities in both Tunisia and Algeria. In 1913 a Land Registration Act was introduced, followed in 1914 by a *dahir* dividing Moroccan lands into alienable and inalienable. The first included privately owned lands (*mulk*) and public domain. Early colonization depended on these two categories, but in 1919 a cantonment policy similar to that practised in Algeria in the 1850s was put into effect to enable Frenchmen to acquire the tribal collective lands pronounced inalienable by the *dahir* of 1914. An office was set up headed by the director of the Affaires Indigènes to determine the tribes' needs of their lands. Lands considered not needed by a tribe, usually the more fertile and better irrigated, were sold to Europeans. The American economist Charles Stewart[1] has ascertained that this office operated on the principle that between 12 and 20 hectares of land, depending on fertility, was sufficient for a tribal tent, whereas 400 hectares was an adequate land holding for the large, and between 100 and 150 hectares for the medium-sized French farmer. Stewart also estimates that the price paid for the seized lands was equivalent to no more than a year's income from them. From 1919 the French acquisition of lands in Morocco increased rapidly, reaching 675,000 hectares in 1932 and one million hectares in 1953, in addition to large tracts rented in perpetuity. Of the lands owned by the French in 1953, sixty per cent were distributed amongst 900 holdings. These lands were concentrated in the fertile and well-irrigated plains: 210,000 hectares in the plains of the Fez-Meknes region, 200,000 in the plains of the Gharb (north-western coastal region), 130,000 in the Shawiyya plains, and the others distributed between the regions of Wajda, Sus, and the Hawz of Marrakish.

The size of the European community quadrupled in the thirty years following the First World War, reaching 325,000 in 1951. Within it there were great variations in wealth. Whereas some four to five thousand people,

[1] Charles E. Stewart, *The economy of Morocco, 1912–1962* (Cambridge, Mass., 1964), p. 73.

mostly French, owned large fortunes and enjoyed political influence, about 80,000 people consisting of Spaniards, Portuguese, Italians, and Greeks had a standard of living not much higher than the average for the Moroccans. Between these two extremes lay the bulk of the French community earning their livings in various walks of life. In spite of the wide income differentials within the European community, it generally enjoyed a much higher standard of living than the Moroccan: in 1953 fifty per cent of the revenue receipts in the French zone was in the hands of Europeans, and their average income per capita was twenty times as large as that of the Moroccans.

Protecting and advancing the French community's economic interests was a primary preoccupation of the protectorate authorities. This was as much due to their understanding of what the real aims of the protectorate were, as to the collective pressure which the settlers were able to bring to bear on them. This pressure was exerted through lobbying in Paris, through the Council of Government, or through agitation. The Council of Government grew out of the French administrators' need to consult the leaders of the French business community on economic planning. In 1919 it took a definitive shape when it came to comprise the elected representatives of the French chambers of commerce, agriculture, and industry together with representatives of those Frenchmen having no vote in the chambers' elections. A few select Moroccans were appointed to this council, but it was not until 1947 that the Moroccan chamber of agriculture and the chamber of commerce and industry were made elective, and were enabled to choose the Muslim members of the council. But whereas in the election of the French chambers and the independent French members of the council the principle of universal vote was upheld, the right of vote for the Muslim chambers granted in 1947 was restricted to the *évolués*, numbering about 11,000 electors in all. The Muslim and French sections met separately, and the Muslim section was able to start its deliberations only when the French had completed its own. Through pressure in the council and lobbying in Paris the French in Morocco were able to steer the economic policy along lines especially favourable to their interests. And when formal pressure proved ineffective the French resorted to other means. In 1934 when the chamber of agriculture failed to persuade the resident Ponsot to concede its demands for the suspension of tax collection for three years, and for more generous subsidies to agricultural colonization, and restrictions on the importation of wine and cattle, the French farmers led demonstrations against the resident and sent telegrams to Paris. On this occasion the settlers did not achieve much, but on others they succeeded in having a recalcitrant resident-general recalled. An example of the preferential treatment given to the French is the rebate on *tartib*, the tax on land revenue instituted by Sultan 'Abdul-'Aziz. From

1923 a fifty per cent rebate was granted to farmers employing "European methods". The justification of such an arrangement was to encourage the Moroccans to employ modern agricultural techniques. But since this depended on skills, credit, and large enough lands, all unavailable to the average Moroccan farmer, the French farmers were the ones who profited most from the rebate. Thus in 1951–2, whereas Moroccans contributed more than eighty per cent of the tax income, they received only twenty per cent of the money refunded under the rebate system.

One of the protectorate's greatest achievements was the development of Morocco's economic infrastructure. Between 1911, when a narrow gauge railway link between Casablanca and Rabat was completed, and independence the French built 1,600 km of railway track mostly of standard gauge. The French also built a road network of over 48,000 km of which about a third consisted of tarred all-weather highways. Moroccan ports were extensively developed to meet the need of the increased economic activity particularly in the mining industry. Special efforts were made to develop the port of Casablanca where Frenchmen had been established since 1907, although it was a poor natural harbour. Casablanca became the principal port of Morocco, handling at the end of the protectorate period seventy-five per cent in terms of weight, of all imports and exports. The port of Safi was also developed to handle phosphate from Yusufiyya (Youssefiah), and Qanitra (Kenitra) to cater for the needs of the Gharb region. Important hydraulic works were undertaken with the capacity to irrigate half a million hectares of land. In 1954 the production of electric power reached 850 million kWh. Although this development was designed for the needs of the Europeans, it was an important legacy of great value to independent Morocco's programme of development. However, the emphasis on the Europeans' needs in development planning was of the greatest importance in the rise of Moroccan nationalism. It could be seen that the railway system was planned to follow French agricultural colonization and the development of the mining industry. The Moroccan taxpayer contributed the greater part of the cost of building modern roads from which he was unable to profit: of 91,000 cars plying the roads in 1953, 78,000 were owned by Frenchmen. From the irrigation schemes the French farmers profited more than the Moroccans, and of the electrical energy produced in 1953 seventy-three per cent was consumed by the European factories, mines, and the railway system. Even in lighting, to which twenty-three per cent of electrical energy went, the share of Moroccans was disproportionate to their numbers since the countryside and about half the towns remained without electricity.

In contrast to the French zone, the Spanish zone did not undergo any radical economic transformation. Having an area of 22,000 square km, it was about one-twentieth the size of the French zone. Its population, including Spaniards and other foreigners, was about one million in 1955, or nearly ten per cent of the total population of the country. Its economic resources were meagre. The nineteenth century belief, which survived into the 1920s, in the existence of rich mineral deposits in the Rif was proved unfounded. Except for iron ore at Kalata near Malila, the mineral deposits of the north were found to be poor. Thus agriculture, particularly the cultivation of cereals, remained the basis of the economy. The industries remained few and were geared to local consumption: cement, tile, and canning factories, tanneries, and four foundries. Colonization by Spanish farmers was not encouraged, and except for 15,000 hectares cultivated in the valley of Wadi Lukkus by the Lukkus Agricultural Company, little interest existed in the commercial exploitation of agricultural lands. Only about 1,000 km of roads had been paved by 1956, only half of these were surfaced, and the Spanish efforts to improve and maintain ports were half-hearted. Economically the northern zone was thus a liability rather than an advantage to Spain, and was retained mainly for the sake of prestige.

Under the terms of the special Franco-Spanish treaty signed in November 1912, the northern zone was governed jointly by a *khalifa* representing the sultan and chosen by him from two candidates nominated by the Spanish government, and a Spanish high commissioner. The executive functions were carried out by a council of ministers consisting of three Moroccans: the premier, and the ministers of justice and *habus*. The high commissioner controlled directly the parts of the administration dealing with modern services through special departments attached to the high commission and indirectly the rest of the administration through the *khalifa*. The local administration was in the hands of *qa'ids* governing the sixty-nine tribal areas into which the zone was divided. But these were placed under the very close control of district officers (*interventores*) whose work was coordinated by the native affairs office in the high commission.

Tangier had a special regime for the greater part of the protectorate period. Through the services organized by the consuls in the nineteenth century the city acquired a special status, a situation which was recognized in the Franco-Spanish agreement of 1904, in the Act of Algeciras, and in the Treaty of Fez of 1912. Negotiations between Britain, France, and Spain after the First World War resulted in the Statute of Tangier in December 1923. The statute provided for a form of international protectorate. The sultan was represented by a *mandub* (delegate) who was also responsible for the administration of the 120,000 Moroccans in the zone. Legislative powers were vested in a special assembly composed of seventeen Europeans, and six Muslim and three Jewish Moroccans; a committee of control composed of European consuls supervised the administration. A European administrator, until 1940 a Frenchman, was the chief executive officer in the European sector of the administration. In June 1940 Spain realized the long-standing wish to annex Tangier to her zone. In 1945 the international regime was re-established with some modifications which, among other things, prevented the French from controlling it by having each national group choose one representative in the assembly instead of the former arrangement allowing France a predominance through her own four members and the nine Moroccans who were amenable to French influence. The administrator had henceforth to be either Belgian, Dutch, Portuguese, or Swedish. The French could still exercise a special influence through the *mandub* whose choice depended on them, but the international character of the regime was preserved. This proved useful to the nationalists who were able to make contacts through the international zone, and in the period of terrorism after 1953 they were also able to obtain arms through it.

In the Spanish zone proper the extension of Spanish control was rendered slow by the mountainous terrain and the opposition of the tribes both in the Jbala region and the Rif in the east. In the Jbala region Raisuni was still strong, and he hoped upon the signature of the protectorate treaty that the Spaniards would be content with a system of indirect rule and appoint him as the sultan's *khalifa* for the entire zone. As the Spaniards were not prepared to give the troublesome *sharif* so much authority, he became a rebel. After three years of intermittent warfare, Raisuni was recognized in 1915 as governor of the region he in fact controlled. This was only a *modus vivendi* the Spaniards considered necessary for the period of the war. In 1919 they resumed operations against him, forcing him in 1920 to retire to a base at Tazirut (Tazerout) where he remained unbeaten but also unable to play any significant political part.

'Abdul-Karim's uprising in the Rif was a more serious threat to Spanish control, not so much because it had a different character from Raisuni's but because it brought together the strong Rifian group of Berber tribes under effective leadership. Muhammad 'Abdul-Karim, the father of the Rif uprising's leader, was a man of religious learning and chief of the Uriaghil Rifian tribe. As a tribal chief he cooperated with the sultan's army in suppressing the rebel Jilali in 1909. As a scholar he served in the protectorate administration as chief judge (*qadi al-qudat*) of Malila. Immediately after the First World War he fell out with the Spaniards as a result of the policy of direct military rule which they were introducing into the Rif with the help of some loyalist chiefs. What he and his son 'Abdul-Karim stood for at this period was a system of indirect rule that would preserve the traditional leadership and customary practices of the tribes similar to the system applied by Lyautey in southern Morocco. When in 1921 'Abdul-Karim launched his rebellion his authority was tribal. On

1 February 1922 he declared the foundation of an Islamic republic, he himself assumed the title of president, and divided his government into specialized departments. But beneath the façade of modernity it presented, his state was a confederacy of Rifian tribes, not one embodying a national identity associated with a fixed territorial unit. Working within the traditional Moroccan system, he also expressed his political aspirations in religious terms: he claimed descent from the Prophet and declared the aim of his war against the Spaniards and, in 1925, against the French as a war of religious liberation.

'Abdul-Karim's republic survived until 1926. Having scored a decisive victory against the Spanish forces commanded by General Silvestre at Anual in July 1921, he occupied the important towns of Salwan and Nadur (Nador) in August 1921. After this victory he seems to have been able to obtain arms and to recruit European instructors for his army through the help of businessmen interested in the mineral resources of the Rif. It is believed[1] that an English group of financiers acting jointly with a German businessman called Hacklander obtained a mining concession in June 1923 from 'Abdul-Karim and that this group helped in the recruitment of European instructors for his army, and arranged for the shipment of armaments to the Rif. In May 1924 'Abdul-Karim was able to put 120,000 well-trained and well-equipped soldiers in the attack on Spanish positions in Wadi Lau west of Tatuan and in the east. General Primo de Rivera, who had a year earlier assumed dictatorial powers in Spain, was compelled by the magnitude of the attacks to withdraw the Spanish forces into easily defendable positions. Spanish withdrawal enabled 'Abdul-Karim to penetrate into Jbala territory, occupy Shafshawin, and in January 1925 take Raisuni's stronghold at Tazirut.

By 1925 'Abdul-Karim felt confident enough to attack the French forces whom Lyautey had stationed north of the Wargha river to protect the approaches of Fez and Taza. Within a few weeks of commencing the attack his forces were only 25 km away from Fez. This was the beginning of the end for 'Abdul-Karim's republic. Lyautey was blamed for allowing the Rifians the opportunity to penetrate so deep into the French zone. He was relieved of his functions as commander-in-chief of the forces in Morocco, and later in the year he resigned as resident. Marshal Pétain, who took over the army command, coordinated operations with the Spaniards and brought in reinforcements. By May 1926 'Abdul-Karim had been defeated and forced to surrender. Lyautey's departure and 'Abdul-Karim's defeat mark the end of an era in the history of the protectorate. Lyautey's successors lacked his refined touch and respect for traditions and consequently tended to rule directly, instead of acting

[1] See Pierre Fontaine, *Abd-el-Krim, origine de la rébellion nord-africaine* (Paris, 1958), pp. 56–83. Fontaine, a French journalist, visited the Spanish zone during the Rif War.

through the traditional structure. 'Abdul-Karim's defeat initiated his myth as a hero fighting for faith and country. The myth gave a nationalist direction to a movement in the French zone which until 1925 had remained one of political and social protest.

Morocco: traditional elite and new aspirations

The Salafiyya doctrine, having been introduced into the intellectual circles of Fez before the First World War, had its time of gestation during the war. When it reappeared in the 1920s it had become the basis of a wider movement of social and religious reform. The acknowledged leader of the Salafiyya circle in this period, Mawlay al-'Arabi al-'Alawi, attributed this metamorphosis to the study of Salafi literature which reached Fez during the war. Nevertheless, the social commitment of the new generation of Salafis can be better explained in terms of the emerging shape of the protectorate and the changing situation of Fez.

The traditional ruler of Morocco, the 'Alawite sultan, became the captive of the French administration after 1912. In the past the 'Alawite sultans had been found wanting in their religious leadership, and condemned for this reason. 'Abdul-'Aziz had been denounced for his frivolous European company and 'Abdul-Hafiz for signing the protectorate treaty. Nevertheless the 'Alawite sultanate remained the symbol of Morocco's Islamic identity. To use the sultanate as the instrument of French control, instead of reconciling the Muslim leaders of Morocco to the protectorate, was considered a religious outrage and the sultan was viewed as a victim of French policy rather than a collaborator. On the other hand the Sufi leaders, to whose teachings the Salafis took exception, were obvious collaborators. The *sharifs* of Wazzan, who were also the leaders of the Tayyibiyya Sufi order, had been allies of the French since the nineteenth century. The members of the Tijaniyya order in Fez opposed the French, but a *shaikh* from the mother *zawiya* of the order at 'Ain Madi in Algeria toured southern Morocco in 1912 calling on Muslims to submit to French rule, and was decorated with the order of the Legion of Honour. Thami al-Glawi's membership of the Tijaniyya highlighted this order's collaboration with the French. From the 1920s, furthermore, the French had an ally in 'Abdul-Hayy al-Kittani, the head of the Kittaniyya Sufi order. The Salafis, therefore, could assert that a close connection existed between what they considered to be the doctrinal corruption of the Sufis and their collaboration with the French. Religious reform to the Salafis, in addition to being an end in itself, consequently becomes a means of political revival.

Fez became the centre of Salafi agitation in the early 1920s because it was Morocco's foremost centre of religious learning. As the former capital of independent Morocco and the bastion of its traditional bourgeois society, its fortunes were altered by the protectorate regime more than other

Moroccan cities. The full consequences to Fez of the economic and political structures established by the French were not to become fully apparent
until the 1930s, but stresses were already being felt in the early 1920s.
From the economic investments of the protectorate Fez benefited much
less than other areas, and as the country's leading centre of commerce
Casablanca supplanted it. The modern banking facilities deprived the
money-lenders of Fez from much of their financial business, and the
mass-produced goods were starting to cause hardships for its artisans. And
by 1925 when the officers of the Affaires Indigènes had already severed
the city's traditional links with the tribes around it, French settlers in its
vicinity were diverting to their lands some of the waters of Wadi Fez.
Thus in Fez the religious grievances and the economic ones buttressed one
another, and the Salafiyya movement, many of whose leaders came from
the city's most respected families, combined political protest with the
aims of Islamic rejuvenation.

Until 1925 the most important activity of the Salafi group was the
foundation of modern Islamic schools, the so-called free schools. The first
of these was opened in 1921. In the following four years four other schools
were founded in Fez, and four in Rabat. By 1937 the free schools were
providing primary education for about 5,000 pupils. In Fez, where
twenty of these schools were operating at the time, enrolment was about
1,500. The free schools reflected the limitations as well as the positive
achievements of the Moroccan urban upper middle class society in which
the Salafiyya movement was rooted. The protectorate administration
founded French schools exclusively for the settlers' children: as late as
1938–9 only 450 Moroccan children attended the French schools out of an
enrolment of 30,648. On Muslim education the protectorate spent very
little: in 1931, for example, out of 41.8 million francs allotted to education,
only 14.8 million went to the Muslim schools. In addition to the schools
founded under the Franco-Berber system, the government established
special schools for the children of the aristocratic families traditionally
associated with government service. These schools, called the *écoles des
fils de notables*, offered a curriculum, taught mostly in French, designed to
prepare the children of the traditional political elite for government
service. The scope of these schools was limited. Six primary schools and
three Lycée-type "colleges" formed the entire system at its highest point
of expansion in 1936, providing instruction in 1930–1 to 1,600 pupils
when all the primary schools and two of the "colleges" in the system were
already in operation. For ordinary Muslim children an insufficient number
of primary and technical schools was founded, so that as late as 1950 only
about fifteen per cent of Muslim children of school-going age received
regular instruction of any kind. In the context of the protectorate educational policy the founding of the free schools does not, therefore, reflect a

concern over the general scholastic needs of the country or the belief that French education had a religiously harmful effect on Muslim children. It reflected the need of a social class which the policy of the "reservation" made the protectorate virtually ignore. The foundation of the free schools was therefore a programme of self-help. To the Salafis who filled most of the teaching posts in them, these schools were a symbol of defiance and of affirming that a substitute to French education did exist. To teach in a free school was also an outlet for a didactic predilection characteristic of the Salafi movement, and a substitute for political action.

In the second half of 1925, when 'Abdul-Karim's warriors were still near Fez, two Muslim secret societies were founded in the French zone. One was established in Fez by the Salafi group, and included amongst its prominent members Muhammad Ghazi, 'Allal al-Fasi, Mukhtar al-Susi, Ibrahim al-Kittani, and several others connected with the free schools. The other appeared in Rabat, and its leaders were from amongst the few who could obtain a French education: Ahmad Balafrej, Muhammad Hasan al-Wazzani, 'Umar 'Abdul-Jalil, Muhammad Lyazidi and others. In a book published in 1926 by a member of the Rabat group, Muhammad al-Nasiri, the two societies of Fez and Rabat were referred to as Hizb al-Islah (the Reform party). They in fact did not constitute anything like a political party, but were two allied groups of nationalist intellectuals who met in the houses of members to discuss Morocco's problems, and occasionally shared their views with a similar society founded in Tatuan in 1926. Neither group attempted to create a political organization or seemed interested in arousing the political consciousness of the traditional masses or the new labour class that started to emerge in the cities. The Salafi group in Fez, being the more religiously committed, took the initiative in political agitation expressed in a religious form. An example is the *fatwa* issued in February 1925 by the Qarawiyin Council of Learning, of which many of the Fez groups were members, condemning the Tijani writer Muhammad al-Nazifi for blasphemy. The act of blasphemy was a statement in al-Nazifi's book *al-Tib al-Fa'ih* to the effect that the Tijani litany Salat al-Fatih was a part of God's eternal speech. This Tijani belief was known to Moroccans since the arrival of the founder of the Tijaniyya in Fez in 1789; and, furthermore, al-Nazifi's book had been in circulation for a number of years. To the Salafis, therefore, the condemnation of al-Nazifi was a way of publicizing their thesis that only the morally corrupt Muslim would cooperate with the foreign rulers. It was also a means of embarrassing the sultan's cabinet or leading its members to a clash with the French, since the *fatwa* called on the minister of justice to reprimand al-Nazifi and order his book to be burnt. The agitation which followed the publication of the Berber *dahir* in May 1930 was incited by the same method of manipulating inbred religious attitudes and beliefs for the purposes of political protest. The Salafi leaders organized on this occasion special prayers in mosques, ending with a supplication usually reserved for times of great calamity to the Muslim community in which God is addressed as the Latif (the Kind One). Members of the Fez group travelled to other towns to organize these prayers, so that before the end of September all the cities and major towns had had their share of them.

The anti-*dahir* campaign united the two societies of Fez and Rabat into an organization calling itself the National Group (al-Jama'a al-Wataniyya). The campaign demonstrated the need for organization and secrecy, since the police had to interfere to break up demonstrations and some of the leaders were briefly detained for questioning. In spite of the wide agitation it aroused, it did not lead the leaders to widen the scope of their organization to become a mass political movement. By the end of 1930 a caucus within the Jama'a comprising about twenty-five of the top leaders calling themselves the Zawiya, controlled the movement without being known except to a small number of their supporters. The name "Zawiya" was a camouflage, since the police expected no trouble from the Sufi *zawiyas*. It also reflects the withdrawn and paternalistic disposition of these leaders. While the members of the Zawiya moved in their isolated orbit, their followers were enrolled in one of two concentric circles with the more trusted ones forming the inner one and constituting the link between the Zawiya and the outer ring. The whole organization received the name Kutlat al-'Amal al-Watani (the National Action Bloc), a name which by 1932 had replaced the "Jama'a". The membership of the organization remained small and was to reach several thousands only after December 1936 when a new policy of recruitment was adopted.

Between 1930 and 1936 the activities of the Zawiya were reminiscent of the Tunisian Old Destour party between 1920 and 1925. Efforts were made to draw the sultan, Mawlay Muhammad b. Yusuf (Muhammad V), out of his political isolation. The sultan had been chosen by the French to succeed his deceased father in 1927 because of his retiring temperament. But in August 1930, in spite of French disapproval, he agreed to receive a delegation organized by the Zawiya leaders to protest to him over the Berber *dahir*. Although he was non-committal, the fact that he received the delegation was an encouragement to its organizers. Gradually a rapport between the throne and the Zawiya developed, although direct contacts had to be avoided in order to avert conflicts with the residency. From 1933 the Zawiya organized celebrations on the anniversary of Muhammad V's accession to the throne (18 November), and when he visited Fez in May 1934 the Zawiya encouraged demonstrations of loyalty to him which led the French authorities to curtail his visit. Simultaneously the Zawiya directed its efforts to influence French public opinion in favour of reforming the structure of the protectorate. Through the patronage of distinguished French sympathizers the Zawiya published in Paris from 1932 to 1934 the French-language periodical *Maghreb* in whose columns attention was drawn to Morocco's major problems. And in 1934 a detailed Plan of Reform was drawn up, of which copies were presented to the French government, the sultan, and the residency. The document analysed the administrative, economic, and judicial abuses of the protectorate and its educational failures, and urged the introduction of reforms reflecting Salafi ideas and French practice in the field of law, French instruction in agriculture,[1] and an admiration for French labour legislation and the French party system. The Plan of Reform did not attack the protectorate treaty but demanded its faithful application. Ponsot, the resident-general, ridiculed the plan's academic tone, saying that it would make an excellent doctorate thesis, and he and the French government ignored it.

The Plan of Reform reflects the growing importance of the French-educated leaders in the Kutlat. J. P. Halstead[2] has identified the plan's principal authors as being Muhammad Lyazidi, 'Umar 'Abdul-Jalil, Makki al-Nasiri, Muhammad Hasan al-Wazzani, and Hasan Bu 'Ayyad. Of these only the last had received an entirely Islamic education, and three of them, Lyazidi, 'Abdul-Jalil, and Wazzani, had been regular contributors to *Maghreb*. The growing influence of these leaders explains the greater attention now given by the nationalists to the particular social and economic grievances. It also prompted some of the original Salafi leaders, such as 'Allal al-Fasi, to make an impressive effort to acquire a basic knowledge of European social and political thought. But the average Muslim-educated members of the Zawiya were at a disadvantage in their political confrontation with the French, and resented being replaced in positions of leadership by the French-educated. A clash between the two groups occurred in October 1936 on the occasion of the elections of the Kutlat's executive officers. Al-Wazzani, elected secretary-general, resented 'Allal al-Fasi's election to the presidency to which he considered himself better suited. He withdrew from the Kutlat and in the following year founded his own separate political group. Nevertheless, the Salafi and the French-educated leaders in the Kutlat continued to complement one another in abilities and style of action. In the position of secretary-general al-Wazzani was replaced by another French-educated member of the Zawiya, Ahmad Balafrej.

By the mid-1930s the growth of Morocco's population, the administrative practices of the protectorate, and the modern sector of the economy, had combined to produce a proletariat, both urban and rural. Morocco's population grew rapidly under the protectorate: in the French

---

[1] The part on agricultural reform was written by 'Umar 'Abdul-Jalil, a graduate of the École nationale supérieure agronomique of Montpellier.

[2] John P. Halstead, *Rebirth of a nation: the origins and rise of Moroccan nationalism, 1912–1944* (Cambridge, Mass., 1967), p. 214.

zone it rose from 3.37 million in 1921 to 6 million in 1936, reaching 8.2 million in 1952. The administrative divisions introduced by the French and the direct interference of French officials disrupted the solidarity of the tribes, thus encouraging greater individual mobility; and the progress of European colonization left the Moroccans with less lands to cultivate. French peasants and tribesmen, unable to obtain a livelihood from cultivating their lands or rearing their sheep and cattle, turned into sharecroppers or farm workers for Europeans, or migrated into the cities seeking work. Before the Second World War about 60,000 Moroccans were employed on the settlers' farms. A much larger number moved to the cities where, because they were generally unskilled, they formed a floating labour force without a specific or permanent employment. Figures available for Casablanca, the largest city in Morocco, indicate that in the years immediately after the Second World War the Muslim labour force was about 400,000, of which only three per cent had any skill or trade and about twenty per cent were partially or wholly unemployed. The newcomers to the cities were crowded either in the *medinas* or in tin huts forming small towns (*bidonvilles*, from *bidon*, French for tin) in the suburbs.

Until 1936 the nationalist leaders neglected to draw the masses into their confrontation with the protectorate. As a result of labour disputes in June and November, Muslim workers took part with the French in demonstrations which occurred in most of the major cities. In December the new resident-general Noguès decided to permit the formation of trade unions in order to avert further labour unrest, but the Moroccans were banned from participation in them. By this act the resident made the Muslim workers' leaders realize that the improvement of their conditions was dependent on national liberation, and the Zawiya leaders conscious that the discontented working classes could be harnessed to the nationalist cause. In the same month the Zawiya decided to extend recruitment into the Kutlat. By February 1937 emissaries were already active creating local cells, and issuing membership cards and administering oaths of loyalty to peasants in the countryside and workers in the cities. On this popular level the religious component of the nationalist movement was a great asset, as the Kutlat activists could project 'Allal al-Fasi as the spokesman of a religious revivalist and liberating movement hailing from the religious metropolis of the country. By the time the Kutlat was banned by a prime minister's decree on 18 March 1937, its membership had increased several-fold to 6,500. But since the ban was not accompanied by repression, the nationalists were able to reorganize themselves in a new party named the National Party for Realizing the Reforms (al-Hizb al-Watani li tahqiq al-matalib). The party's programme professed to be merely reformist, but as its leaders could no longer cut themselves off from mass agitation the political struggle with the administration became its principal *raison d'être*. In such a struggle, as the events of October–November 1937 were to demonstrate, a reformist programme had little or no relevance to action.

The harvests of 1937 were exceedingly bad, and in June the residency forecast that about 1.4 million, or about twenty per cent of the Moroccan Muslims, would be threatened by starvation before the next harvest. No part of the country escaped distress, but the spark which led to an explosion came from Meknes. In the neighbourhood of this town two important tribes, Gharwan and Ait Yusi, had been deprived of their best lands and reduced to a state of destitution. As the shadow of starvation hovered over the dispossessed Muslims, Meknes awoke to the fact that by insisting on their full quota from the waters of the Bu Fakran river to irrigate their farms in the dry period of the year, the settlers did not leave enough for the mosques and the public baths. Water, the symbol of life, also became the symbol of the misery under which the Moroccans lived. A demonstration starting from a mosque in Meknes on 2 September led to a clash with the police and the death of many. The National Party could not ignore such an important grievance and through its cells organized demonstrations which broke out on 6 September in Casablanca, Fez, Rabat, Wajda, Marrakish, and Meknes itself. Before the agitation occasioned by the water crisis had died down, an announcement was made in October that a Catholic pilgrimage was to take place to the Church of St Theresa in Khammissat (Khemmisset). The pilgrimage was a provocation because Khammissat was in the neighbourhood of Meknes, and because the church, built in 1932 in the midst of the Ait Zammur Berbers, was a reminder of the policy of detaching the Berbers from the Muslim community of Morocco. Starting from a Fez mosque a demonstration of protest on 22 October led to fresh clashes with the police. Noguès, a relatively liberal resident and representing the Popular Front government, felt compelled to resort to decisive repression. Before the end of the month 'Allal al-Fasi and most of the other leaders of the National Party had been arrested, together with Muhammad Hasan al-Wazzani. 'Allal was taken soon afterwards into exile in Gabon where he spent the next nine years. Balafrej, who was at the time in Paris, remained outside the French zone until 1943, in the meantime visiting Tatuan and Tangier to make contacts with the party cadres still active in Morocco.

In the year from December 1936 to November 1937 nationalism came of age, as it came to embody national aspirations instead of being the channel of the grievances of a single social class. The role of popular leadership was thrust on the normally withdrawn Zawiya by the labour unrest of 1936 and the agitation of the hungry masses over the supply of water. Henceforth, although the nationalist leaders did not publicly relinquish their reformist programme, the only path of action that opened before them was the struggle for power with the protectorate administration. The resident-general Noguès tried to quieten agitation after the wave of repression of November 1937 by concessions to the Muslim population. These included reducing the salaries of French officials, appointing two Muslim advisors in the residency, and launching programmes aimed at building new schools for Muslim children, reviving the native crafts, and creating new irrigation facilities from which the Muslim farmers would benefit. With most of the nationalist leaders either in prison or outside the country, these conciliatory measures and the outbreak of the Second World War resulted in a political lull. They, however, did not alter the nature of the confrontation from the situation reached in 1937. Consequently when political activity was resumed on a large scale in 1943, the nationalists started to work not for reform but for independence.

One encounters in the context of Moroccan, as with Algerian, nationalism the generally held belief that the defeat of France, and the anticolonial stance of the Americans during the war, had a decisive influence on the consolidation of the nationalist outlook. As with Algerian nationalism this belief seems to rest on the fact that it was only after France's defeat and the American landing in Morocco and Algeria in November 1942 that the nationalists demanded independence. In fact it seems that the only important contribution France's defeat and the American presence had on the Moroccan nationalist movement was to enable it to reorganize. The National Party was revived in 1940, and had since 1941 a *conseil supérieur* organized by Ahmad Maqwar and Muhammad Lyazidi who had been allowed to return to Morocco in 1940 and 1941 respectively. Following the American landing in November, the French authorities permitted Ahmad Balafrej, the former secretary-general of the party, to return to Morocco. Soon after his return in January 1943 the party expanded its political activities. The American officials had made statements about the rights of peoples to self-determination since their arrival, and in January 1943 President Roosevelt spoke along the same lines in the course of his meeting with Mawlay Muhammad V in Casablanca. In December Balafrej reconstituted the National Party into the Istiqlal (Independence) Party and in January 1944 a manifesto demanding independence was issued. Apart from the fact that the American presence and the consequent loss of French authority enabled the nationalists to reorganize, there is no evidence to support the contention that the demand for independence was encouraged or even inspired by American promises. Halstead has shown that after the flirtations of the nationalists in the northern zone with the Germans and the Spaniards, and after the Americans made their vague promises in the southern zone, by mid-1943 the nationalists in both zones "had come to realize the futility of outside leverage, and clinging to their determination to abolish the protectorate, they now took matters into their own hands".[1] Whatever hopes the Moroccan nationalists might have had of receiving American help were dashed by an official American statement made in July 1943 to the effect that the attainment of independence by a colonial people had to be dependent on their ability to govern themselves.

From the beginning the Istiqlal was a national party aiming at winning a nationwide support for its goal and working to educate its members politically. 'Allal al-Fasi, who was brought back to Morocco in 1946 upon the appointment of a liberal, Labonne, as resident, assumed the supreme leadership of the party. His appeal as a religio-nationalist leader, enhanced by his exile, enabled the party to expand its ranks (by 1947 it already had 15,000 members), and consequently to pose as the spokesman of the nation's political aspirations. The nationalists' good relations with the sultan were confirmed from 1946, and by 1947 the sultan was already emerging, so far as the restrictions of the protectorate permitted, as the embodiment of the nation's will to regain her independence. From 1947 onwards he cautiously but firmly worked towards this end. On 10 April 1947 he delivered a speech in Tangier in which he spoke of Morocco's Arab ties and omitted from his speech a complimentary reference to the French which the residency had inserted. About the same time he insisted that the budget should be examined by a special Moroccan commission before he would approve it.

In view of the sultan's growing recalcitrance the French government in May 1947 appointed a soldier, General Juin, to deal with the Moroccan situation. His remedy was a show of force accompanied by concessions leading to some Moroccan participation in the government. He introduced the practice of convening a council comprising the Moroccan ministers and the French heads of departments to discuss important policy decisions after these were taken in the residency. The Council of Government which debated the budget was to include elected Moroccans and Frenchmen, and in the municipal councils elected Moroccan members were to sit with Frenchmen. These measures seemed an improvement in a structure where the French had held all powers. Some of them were accepted as such and, in spite of the small electorate allowed to vote for the Moroccan members of the Council of Government, those elected included Istiqlal members such as Muhammad Lyazidi, Muhammad Laghzawi and others. These men used their membership of the council to attack the protectorate's economic policy. Nevertheless these measures were also viewed as a way of giving legality to extra-legal practices implying a Franco-Moroccan co-sovereignty. The *dahir* dealing with the municipal elections seemed in particular to imply co-sovereignty, and Muhammad V refused to ratify it even after signing other objectionable decrees. The French government tried to mollify the sultan by inviting him to Paris in 1950 and

[1] Cf. Halstead, *Rebirth of a nation*, p. 261.

giving him a lavish reception. He remained adamant and the French, realizing the strength of his position both legally and in popular esteem, had to exercise patience. However, a crisis occurred at the end of 1950 when Moroccan members of the Council of Government attacked the budget for 1951 prepared by the residency on the grounds that it was geared to the settlers' interests. When the resident expelled one of them, Muhammad Laghzawi, from the meeting, the other Istiqlal members followed him and immediately were received by the sultan.

What General Juin's reforms especially achieved was to bring the Istiqlal and the sultan even closer by providing members of the party with an opportunity to execute a nationalist programme whose defender and symbol, if not the author, he had become. There remained for the French only the Berber bloc and the Sufi *shaikhs* as allies, and when Juin decided that the time had come for the use of force he turned to them in order to create the occasion and the excuse. In January, before Juin left on a trip to the U.S.A., he gave the sultan an ultimatum: he must either disavow the Istiqlal or vacate the throne. Upon his return he repeated the ultimatum on 12 February, and at the same time Thami al-Glawi's warriors started to descend into Rabat and Fez. Al-Glawi had prepared the ground for Juin's first ultimatum by telling Muhammad V that he was the sultan of the Istiqlal, not of Morocco. The presence of the Berber warriors in Rabat and Fez, apart from being a show of force, was intended to demonstrate that Morocco was not all with the Istiqlal, and that the sultan's nationalist policy was a partisan one which would lead to civil conflicts. The sultan yielded to the combined Franco-Berber pressure on 25 February. He authorized the grand vizier to condemn the methods of a "certain party" which were founded on intimidation, paralysed just institutions, and aggravated divisions amongst Moroccans. The sultan also signed some of the controversial *dahirs*, though not the one dealing with municipal elections.

The Istiqlal seemed to be losing its *raison d'être* from 1947, when the sultan took the initiative in leading the nationalist movement, and the battle with the French was being fought within the political organs of the protectorate. 'Allal al-Fasi left for Cairo in May 1947 to solicit the help of other Arab countries for the cause of Morocco's independence, thus removing himself from direct contact with the party. By this time the sultan's leadership had come to overshadow that of any other's in Morocco. All that 'Allal al-Fasi and other Istiqlal leaders could do was to be the unofficial defenders and publicists for political goals which, even though formulated by them, gained more popular acceptance because the sultan supported them. After 1951, when the sultan himself became threatened, the Istiqlal found a new purpose for its activities, namely to give support to the sultan. It was this new role which explains the growth of the party's popularity with the Moroccan peasants and working classes after 1951, to whom the sultan was the head of the Moroccan Muslim community and the symbol of its identity. The anti-French mass sentiment which the threat to the sultan aroused found expression in the demonstrations on 7/8 December 1952 on the occasion of the assassination of Farhat Hash-shad, the Tunisian trade unionist leader.

A nationalist sultan was not what the French had expected to have when they placed Muhammad V on the throne. After his retreat of February 1951 the sultan took time to regain self-confidence, and resumed the battle only in March 1952 by writing a letter to the president of the French Republic demanding total sovereignty. The reply, delivered six months later, was a rebuff. It not only insisted on maintaining the mixed character of the Moroccan administration but also reminded the sultan of the *dahir* on municipal elections which was still pending. From about this time various plans for his replacement were being considered. According to Le Tourneau[1] some residency officials even considered changing the dynasty altogether by appointing 'Abdul-Hayy al-Kittani, who could claim sharifian descent, to the sultanate. The public campaign against the sultan was led by the Sufi orders and the Berber chiefs obeying al-Glawi. In April 1953 'Abdul-Hayy al-Kittani, although no longer regarded as the future sultan, summoned a conference of Sufi *shaikhs* in Fez which condemned the sultan's religious politics. Al-Glawi toured the country about the same time gathering signatures to a document demanding the removal of the sultan. He and al-Kittani had in the meantime found a candidate for the sultanate in the person of a retiring member of the 'Alawite family living in Fez called Muhammad b. 'Arafa. In order to indicate that al-Glawi was prepared to use force to instal him on the sharifian throne, Berber warriors started again to descend on Rabat and Fez. In the middle of August Muhammad V once more made a tactical retreat. He signed all the *dahirs* he had kept pending, and agreed to a French demand to delegate his legislative power henceforth to a mixed council consisting of the Moroccan viziers and the French heads of government departments. The aims of co-sovereignty seemed thus fulfilled. However, by August 1953 al-Glawi, al-Kittani, and several high French officials had gone too far to be able to retreat. Al-Glawi gave an ultimatum on 18 August in which he said: "If, contrary to our expectation, it [the French government] does not show the firmness which the Moroccan people expect of it, France will lose her place in Morocco." This was a threat which the French government could not ignore, coming from a man who had served French interests loyally for forty years and was still very strong.

Muhammad V's defeat once more turned into a victory, and within two

[1] Roger Le Tourneau, *Évolution politique de l'Afrique du Nord musulmane, 1920–1961* (Paris, 1962), p. 234.

years of the beginning of his period of exile in Madagascar the French government was compelled to restore him to power. The decisive factor was that the Moroccan people were prepared to fight for his return, in a spontaneous and disorganized manner but also relentlessly. Several attempts were made on the life of Muhammad b. 'Arafa, and terrorists attacked other Moroccans working with the police and *imams* who agreed to say the Friday prayer in the name of Ibn 'Arafa. Because the terrorist attacks were not coordinated by a central agency, and the crowds were always ready to protect the terrorists, preventing these acts was extremely difficult. The arms for terrorism were bought in Tangier, and were moved across the Spanish zone with the connivance, it seems, of the Spanish authorities. The terrorist campaign reached a high pitch in June 1955 when a new resident, Grandval, was appointed. From this moment the French government began to retreat. On 1 October the abdication of Muhammad b. 'Arafa was announced. It had been understood by then that a council of regents was to be formed upon his abdication, and the nationalists were prepared to counter it with force. On 2 October armed bands trained in the Spanish zone and calling themselves the Liberation Army attacked French posts in the region of Taza. As organized armed resistance in the Algerian pattern was not something the most fanatical of French colonial officials could view with equanimity when the Algerian revolution was causing much concern, a sudden reversal of French policy was immediately effected. After Muhammad V was brought to France, a communiqué on his talks with the French foreign minister Pinay made a reference to Morocco's independence, which was formally recognized on 2 March 1956.

Thus Morocco's independence was achieved under the leadership of the country's traditional ruler. The share of the Istiqlal in this victory is difficult to assess. Evidently it was not as great as the Neo-Destours' in achieving Tunisia's independence. The Istiqlal and its precursors, particularly the National Party, helped in fostering the political conscious- ness of the Moroccan middle and, to a lesser extent, working classes. But at the decisive moment in the struggle the Istiqlal became an element, possibly a significant one, in a much wider resistance movement. This helped to ensure political continuity under 'Alawite rule, though not returning, even in government, to the methods of 1912.

Libya: three entities in one nation, 1915–51

Libya did not possess even at the end of the Second World War any of the essential prerequisites of an independent nation-state. It had a predomi- nantly nomadic population, local and tribal particularisms were very strong, and, except for the period between 1932 and 1939, it did not have the experience of living under a political authority which effectively united the whole country. Nevertheless it was the first Maghriban country to become independent. In the other three the attainment of independence was connected with the growth of an important nationalist movement deriving strength from economic and social conditions which came into being during the colonial period. In Libya the nationalist movement was weak and, indeed, the form which the independent Libyan state took points to the unusual fact that independence became possible only when the nationalists compromised on some of their most cherished aspirations. The following account of Libya's history between 1915 and 1951 highlights the unique aspects of its development in order to explain the unusual way, in the Maghriban context, by which the Libyan state was formed and independence was achieved.

When Italy joined the First World War in 1915, her forces had evacuated the interior of Libya and held only the coastal regions. During the war the Turks tried to organize the local forces in Cyrenaica and Tripolitania so that they could exert pressure on the Italian positions and attack the British in Egypt. Since 1912 Sayyid Ahmad al-Sharif, the head of the Sanusiyya order, had claimed to be the leader of the whole of Libya on account of the authority he is said to have received from the Ottoman sultan. He could not, therefore, ignore the sultan's declaration of the *jihad* against the Allies in November 1914. From the beginning of 1915 the Sayyid had his headquarters at Musa'id not far from the Eygptian port of Sallum. He was joined there by a few Turkish officers who started organizing a regular army of Sanusi warriors. As the Allies' naval blockade prevented the Turks and Germans from bringing enough arms into Cyrenaica, the Turkish officers could not raise as large a force as they had hoped for. Nevertheless on Istanbul's orders, Nuri Bey (brother of Enver Pasha who had served in Cyrenaica until 1912) led the Sanusi army of about 3,000 men into Egyptian territory in November 1915. Sallum was taken and the Sanusis penetrated as far as Marsa Matruh.

The attack on the British in Egypt was a turning-point in Sanusi history. The British counter-attacked with large forces, which inflicted heavy losses on the Sanusis and by March 1916 they had driven them back into Cyrenaican territory. Sayyid Ahmad, having allowed the Turkish officers to draw the Sanusis into this disastrous war, was forced immediately afterwards to vacate his position as head of the Sanusi administration. After a brief stay in the Siwa oasis he went to Tripolitania, and from there was taken by submarine to Turkey. Until his death in the Hijaz in 1933 he remained the nominal head of the Sanusiyya. In his absence the headship of the order was filled by his cousin Sayyid Muhammad Idris who was prepared to come to terms with the British and steer the order away from further involvement in the world conflict.

Having dispersed the Sanusi army and brought about a change in Sanusi leadership, the British authorities in Egypt established amicable relations with Sayyid Idris on the hope that they would not need to make another military diversion westwards. They made concessions to the order so as to strengthen Sayyid Idris' hand against the pro-Ottoman party in Cyrenaica, and acted as mediators between the Sanusis and the Italians. The port of Sallum was opened to free trade, thereby enabling the Cyrenaican nomads to sell their produce and obtain the foreign commodities they needed. The *zawiyas* of the order in Egypt were closed, but the Sanusi *shaikhs* living in the country were permitted to collect contributions from their followers. And Jaghbub, though Egyptian territory, was left to the Sanusis to administer. Through the good offices of the British negotiations began between the Sanusis and the Italians, and the mediation of a British officer, Colonel Talbot, helped in bringing about the agreement of 'Akrama, signed in April 1917 after nine months of uneasy talks. This agreement was of the nature of a *modus vivendi*, as it left important questions of substance unresolved. But it served the Anglo-Italian aim of neutralizing the Sanusiyya order and thereby forcing the Turkish and German officers operating in Cyrenaica to leave. Without making any reference to Italian sovereignty, the 'Akrama agreement recognized Sayyid Idris' jurisdiction over the parts of Cyrenaica outside the coastal towns held by the Italians. It also provided that in the parts under Italian rule, the Muslims' personal status would be governed by the Muslim law, and the property of the Sanusiyya order would remain exempt from taxation, as in Ottoman times. In this agreement, the Sayyid consented to disband Sanusi warriors and to help in disarming the tribes. But the Italians did not, for the rest of the war period, insist on the execution of this part of the agreement. Realizing that by coming to terms with them the Sayyid made his position vulnerable at a time when Turkish officers were active in Tripolitania, the Italians even provided him with rifles and ammunition to enable the Sanusis to protect themselves against hostile tribes.

In Tripolitania Nuri Bey and 'Abdul-Rahman 'Azzam (an Egyptian Arab nationalist and the future first secretary-general of the Arab League) had been trying to create a centralized authority since 1916. As they were unable to achieve much militarily, these self-appointed advisors hoped that at least by the end of the war Italy would be confronted with a local Tripolitanian administration obeying the Ottoman sultan with which she had to deal. They tried first to have Tripolitania's leaders unite under the leadership of Sayyid Ahmad al-Sharif. When they failed the Ottoman prince 'Uthman Fu'ad was brought from Istanbul to act as the sultan's representative in Tripolitania. The continuous rivalry between the chiefs, particularly between the al-Mrayyid and al-Suwaihili families, defeated all efforts at achieving unity. When in November 1918 Turkey surrendered and 'Uthman Fu'ad left, 'Azzam renewed his attempts to create a united Tripolitanian front. His efforts led the leaders to meet at al-Qasabat on 18 November and proclaim the foundation of a Tripolitanian republic.

That this so-called republic was not a viable organism must have been clear to 'Azzam and the leaders who proclaimed it. It was in fact a coalition of notables rather than a state. Its only organs were: a supreme council comprising the four most influential chiefs, Ramadan al-Suwaihili, Ahmad al-Mrayyid, Sulaiman al-Baruni, and 'Abdul-Nabi Ba 'l-Khair; a consultative council consisting of twenty-four less important chiefs; and a judicial council consisting of members of the *'ulama*. In the deliberations which preceded the declaration of the republic, the suggestion was made to invite Sayyid Idris to become the amir of the whole of Libya. The proclamation of the republic meant the defeat, temporarily at least, of this idea. In any case it appears that neither the proposal of having the Sayyid recognized amir of Tripolitania, nor the declaration of the republic, was intended as a constructive plan. Both seem to have been viewed as tactical measures designed to wring political concessions from the Italians. This is evident from the fact that the Tripolitanian notables sent to meet Garioni, the Italian commander in Tripoli, made him understand that they would be prepared to drop their demand for independence if they were granted internal autonomy and Italian nationality with all the rights appertaining to it. The Italian government responded to this political manoeuvre by promulgating the Fundamental Law of Tripolitania on 1 June 1919, granting the native population of the province Italian nationality and civil and political equality with Italians. The law further provided that Tripolitania would be governed by an Italian governor, acting on the advice of an elected local parliament and a council of government consisting of ten members, eight of whom should be chosen by the parliament. The Tripolitanian leaders accepted this arrangement and dissolved the republic in August. But as the Italians did not seem in a hurry to implement the law, a National Reform Party was formed in September with the professed aim of exerting pressure on the Italians to put the law into effect. The active leaders of the party were 'Azzam and such urban personalities as Khalid al-Qarqanni and 'Uthman al-Ghariani, the editor of *al-Liwa' al-Tarabulsi* (the Tripoli Standard).

Having obtained the dissolution of the republic, the Italians were able to manipulate traditional local rivalries to prevent the formation of a united front against them. The organizers of the National Reform Party tried to associate al-Suwaihili and al-Mrayyid with their political activities by recognizing them respectively as honorary and active presidents of the party. This does not seem to have brought the two leaders any nearer to a reconciliation. Al-Mrayyid was bent on weakening al-Suwaihili, and was prepared to help the Italians in having al-Suwaihilis and their people in Misurata disarmed. When it proved impossible to bring about unity from within, 'Azzam and al-Qarqanni revived the project of recognizing Sayyid Idris' leadership. From the end of 1919 they worked towards holding a national congress which would adopt a resolution to this effect. Since September 1920 the active leaders of the National Reform Party were joined by Bashir al-Sa'dawi, a notable from Khums who had emigrated from Libya upon the signing of the Treaty of Lausanne in 1912 and had since held important administrative positions in the Arab parts of the Ottoman empire. Thanks to his constant appeals and mediation between the chiefs the congress was held in Gharian in November 1921.

Like the proclamation of the republic, inviting Sayyid Idris to become the amir of Tripolitania seems to have been more a tactical device designed to make the Italians carry out their political promises than a programme of action on which the Tripolitanians were agreed. The resolution adopted by the congress stated only that the Tripolitanian leaders considered the foundation of an amirate necessary for the welfare of Tripolitania, without any reference to Sayyid Idris being made in it. It was also decided at the congress to send a delegation to Rome to make a final attempt at persuading the Italian government to enforce the Fundamental Law. It was only after the delegation returned in failure that the National Reform Party started to campaign openly in favour of recognizing the Sayyid as amir in Tripolitania. Al-Suwaihili associated himself with this plan, but not al-Mrayyid and his party. After a meeting between representatives of the National Reform Party and some Sanusi leaders in Sirta during the months of December 1921 and January 1922, a delegation was sent to meet the Sayyid in Ajadabia and formally offer him the amirate. The Sayyid did not take part in the Sirta meeting, but was undoubtedly informed of the discussions that took place. When he was eventually invited to become amir of Tripolitania, he needed much prodding before he gave his consent. And as soon as he formally announced his acceptance in November 1922 he put it about that he was ill and asked the Italians to authorize him to travel to Egypt for treatment; when they refused, he travelled clandestinely by land in December. He was not to take up residence again in Cyrenaica until 1947, and visited the country for the first time since his departure only in 1944.

Since the end of the war Sayyid Idris had had to make political compromises in order to survive in the face of renewed Italian strength. He seems to have realized that the end of the war made it impracticable for the 'Akrama agreement to remain in force and was prepared to accept the diminution of his political power in order to retain his religious leadership more or less intact. In October 1919 the Italian government enacted the Fundamental Law of Cyrenaica which granted the Cyrenaicans rights, and outlined a system of government, similar to those provided for in the Tripolitanian Law. Although Sayyid Idris could see that the law implied the recognition of Italian sovereignty, he accepted it and in October 1920 signed the al-Rajma agreement which redefined his position. By this agreement the Sanusi amirate was recognized hereditary. The amir, apart from his religious position as head of the Sanusiyya order, was given the power to administer the oases of Jaghbub, Jalu, Awjila, and Kufra. He could have his own flag and an official seat of administration at Ajadabia, and on state occasions he was entitled to a position of honour next to the governor of Cyrenaica. In addition the Italian government agreed to subsidize the Sanusi administration and provide stipends to members of the Sanusi family and the *shaikhs* of the Sanusi *zawiyas*. On the other hand Sayyid Idris pledged himself to uphold the Fundamental Law and liquidate the military camps and Sanusi political organizations outside the area placed under his administration. In a later agreement signed in August 1921 the amir also consented to remove all *shaikhs* of Sanusi *zawiyas* whose activities the Italian authorities considered harmful to good relations between the people and the government.

By signing al-Rajma agreement Sayyid Idris relinquished his political authority over more than eighty-five per cent of Cyrenaica's population. In 1923, out of Cyrenaica's population of 185,000, about 160,000 lived in the area recognized under direct Italian control. In fact from 1920 the Sayyid seemed content with becoming an honoured religious chief with limited administrative functions. Cyrenaica's tribes, however, would not permit him to relinquish his political leadership altogether. Since the middle of the nineteenth century the tribes knew no political authority other than that of the Sanusis, and their leaders could not accept Italian rule with equanimity because it involved the loss of their traditional powers and much of their people's grazing lands. The tribes, therefore, expected Sayyid Idris to lead them in fighting the Italians and not in submitting to their rule. After al-Rajma agreement the Italians complained to the Sayyid that the Sanusi military camps in the north had not been disbanded as provided for in the agreement. He argued, most probably rightly, that he could not order the army chiefs responsible for them to disband their forces. The Italians proved understanding of the difficult position in which the Sayyid found himself, and accepted a compromise. They agreed at the end of 1921 to retain the military camps, and to have the five most important camps held jointly by Italian and Sanusi forces. The question of the military camps illustrates the ambivalence of the Sayyid's position. He could not overtly renounce his political leadership, nor could he exercise it in the way his people expected of him. All he could do was to bide his time until the tribes accustomed themselves to Italian rule. The offer of the Tripolitanian amirate to him destroyed this negative strategy.

The Italians warned him against interfering in Tripolitania's affairs, and he knew that there was no great unanimity in Tripolitania behind the offer. Nevertheless he could not refuse it without bearing the stigma of religious and national betrayal. Hence the acceptance and the voluntary exile.

Before leaving for Egypt Sayyid Idris delegated his authority as amir of Tripolitania and the powers that he had exercised in Cyrenaica before the al-Rajma agreement. He chose his cousin Sayyid Safiy al-Din to be his deputy in Tripolitania. In Cyrenaica his brother Muhammad al-Rida was to represent him in religious matters, and as commander of Sanusi forces he delegated his authority to 'Umar al-Mukhtar, a tribal leader and a dedicated member of the Sanusiyya. These appointments do not seem to have made any difference in the conduct of the war against the Italians, apart from the fact that in Cyrenaica it was fought in Sayyid Idris' name. By the time Sayyid Safiy al-Din set out for Tripolitania with Bashir al-Sa'dawi in March 1923, the Italians had already driven the al-Suwaihilis, the main supporters in Tripolitania of the Sanusi amirate, from their base in Misurata. After April the Tripolitanian tribal warriors had a camp in Wadi Nafadh, but they were hampered by divisions amongst the chiefs from carrying out coordinated military action. The Awlad Saif al-Nasr leaders resented the fact that their authority in Fazzan had been taken away from them by Sanusi *shaikhs*. They demanded as the price of fighting the Italians on the side of al-Suwaihilis that the latter use their influence with the Sanusis to have the government of Fazzan restored to them. When al-Suwaihilis, who acted as the leaders of the camp, refused to recognize the claim of Awlad Saif al-Nasr to Fazzan, the latter withdrew their forces and the al-Mrayyids followed suit. Sayyid Safiy al-Din, finding his authority recognized by none of the chiefs, retired to Jaghbub in September. The remaining forces in the camp were attacked from the air and in December they dispersed. By 1924 opposition in Tripolitania had practically ended, and Bashir al-Sa'dawi left the country.

In Cyrenaica the Italians had to fight an exasperating war for eight years before tribal resistance to them collapsed. They started the fighting when they took possession of the mixed Italo-Sanusi camps on 6 March 1923. Six weeks later an Italian mechanized unit occupied Ajadabia, the Sanusi administrative centre, and on 1 May the governor of Cyrenaica, General Bongiovanni, pronounced all agreements with the Sanusiyya null and void. The war was thus declared against the Sanusiyya on the assumption that the tribes would not continue their resistance if not instigated by the *shaikhs* of the order. The members of the Sanusi family who remained in Cyrenaica in fact did not play any important part in the war, and by 1928 they had either made private deals with the Italians or left the country. The tribes did fight the war in the name of the Sanusiyya, and many of the tribal army chiefs were adherents of the order. Having been so long associated with the life of the tribes, the Sanusiyya became its symbol, the outer emblem of the Cyrenaican tribal society. As such it evoked emotions which kept the tribes united, and enabled them to forgive the members of the Sanusi house their defection. Nevertheless the tribesmen endured the ravages of eight years of war not for the sake of a doctrine, but to defend their lands and their customary life.

It was easy enough for the Italians to occupy the Sanusi camps and take Ajadabia; forcing a united tribal society fighting for its lands and freedom into submission was a different matter. By the middle of 1923 Italian air-raids and mechanized units had driven the tribesmen behind the line al-Buraiqa-Zawiyat Masus, where they were less exposed. There they reorganized for guerrilla warfare. 'Umar al-Mukhtar, using his position as tribal chief and representative of Sayyid Idris, assumed the supreme command and organized a central administration. The main functions of this administration were to collect the tithe from the tribes, and organize the caravans which brought supplies from Egypt. The military organization was simple but effective. Each tribe formed its own guerrilla band, complete with a commander, officers, and a *qadi*. 'Umar al-Mukhtar commanded his own tribal band (Minifa) and coordinated the general strategy. The bands engaged the enemy often and in as many different places at the same time as practicable, while not permitting the Italian forces an opportunity to engage large concentrations of their men. As the bands remained parts of their respective tribes, and when not in battle and their rifles hidden they led the ordinary life of tribesmen, it was not possible for the Italians to distinguish between warrior and non-warrior. Nor could they trust the loyalty of the tribes that submitted to them. For through them the bands of warriors obtained much of their arms and information about army movements. Consequently the only way the Italians could end resistance was by crushing the whole community. Genera Graziani realized this and after 1930 designed the strategy accordingly. Most of the Cyrenaican auxiliary units serving in the Italian army were disbanded, and 80,000 of Cyrenaica's tribal population moved together with their animals to Sirta where they were crowded in camps under strict surveillance. Graziani's plans also included the construction of a barbed-wire barrier over a distance of about 300 km between Jaghbub, which the Italians had occupied in 1926, and the sea. With the observation posts and the mobile units placed to protect it, this barrier cut the flow of supplies from Egypt. Without supplies and the supporting population, the bands could not operate effectively. By the end of 1931, when the barbed-wire barrier had been completed, resistance started to collapse. 'Umar al-Mukhtar was captured on 11 September 1931 and hanged five days later before recovering from wounds he sustained in his last battle. Marshal

Badoglio was able to announce in January 1932 that the war had been brought to a successful conclusion.

Until 1921 Italian colonization of Libya had barely started. The Italians took possession of the public domains previously owned by the Turkish administration, amounting to 9,313 hectares of which only 3,613 had been allocated to settlers by 1921. Under Count Volpi, governor of Tripolitania between 1921 and 1925, the Italian administration for the first time took an interest in encouraging colonization. Tribal collective lands were made available for this purpose by a decree of 18 July 1922, which pronounced uncultivated lands to be state property. Another decree of 10 February 1923 defined the terms under which these lands could be sold or leased out to Italians. Most of the lands obtained during Volpi's term of office were in the semi-arid Jaffara, where a few nomadic groups grazed their cattle. For political reasons expanding colonization into the populous oases and Jabal Nafusa was avoided. Volpi viewed colonization as an economic enterprise, in which cheap native labour could be exploited by Italians with capital. Generous concessions were made to encourage investment in Tripolitanian agriculture: the prices demanded for lands were low (on average 50 lires per hectare, about 55 pence or eleven old shillings at those days' rate of exchange), and exemption from taxation for twenty-five years. Nevertheless the progress of colonization remained limited. During Volpi's term of office only 31,538 out of the 58,087 hectares acquired by the state were allocated.

From 1925 onwards the Fascist leaders of Italy started to take an interest in Libya's colonization. Volpi was replaced by a Fascist of high standing, General de Bono, and Mussolini visited the country in 1926. De Bono drew up a programme of demographic colonization to be carried out through state aid. This programme began to be executed in 1928 when Cyrenaican tribal resistance started to weaken and Cyrenaica and Tripolitania were united administratively under the governorship of Marshal Badoglio. The Fascists henceforth spoke of Libya as Italian land, the peninsula's "fourth shore". They also spoke of building a great Italian nation worthy of being the heir of ancient Rome. For Libya this implied not only that Italian farmers were to revive the tradition of Roman agriculture, but also that the character of its native inhabitants was to be remoulded to make them suitable fellow-citizens to the Italians.

Since 1928 Italian peasants were encouraged by state subsidies to move to Libya. A law brought into force in June provided that public lands in Libya suitable for agriculture could be allocated only to Italians. The raising of livestock would be left to the nomadic tribes, and the local peasants were to be employed as farm labourers or given public lands to cultivate on annual leases. In Tripolitania the areas specifically chosen for the settlement of Italians were the plains of Tajura', the hills of Khums, the Tarhuna mountains, and the central Jaffara plains. After the end of the war in Cyrenaica in 1932 the Sanusi estates were taken over for the purpose of colonization. More lands were obtained by the pseudo-legal device of renunciation. Tribal lands considered suitable for colonization were indicated in an official proclamation. If those using the lands did not object, they were presumed to have renounced them to the state and compensations were paid to them. Lands were often taken from tribesmen who did not know of these proclamations or did not understand their significance. By the method of renunciation about half a million hectares of lands in Cyrenaica were made available for colonization. The state defrayed the expenses of founding the rural centres where the Italian peasants settled, and a large part of the cost of developing the lands and settling the peasants on them. In 1928 it was estimated that the state paid in direct subsidy twenty-five per cent of the cost of colonization, and fifty per cent was provided in loans from state-sponsored banks. In later years, as greater political importance was attached to colonization, the share of the state in the cost of colonization was further increased. In addition to granting subsidies, the Italian government mounted a campaign to induce Italians to volunteer as colonists. In 1938 the embarkation for Libya of 20,000 Italians was a public occasion in Genoa, and Venice witnessed a similar show in the following year when 10,000 more peasants left for Libya. In 1939 44,000 and 40,000 Italians lived in Tripolitania and Cyrenaica respectively. The exact size of the indigenous population of the two provinces is not known. A census for Tripolitania carried out in 1931 put the indigenous population at 523,000. For Cyrenaica the census of 1923 gave the native population as 185,000. Taking into account the ravages of the Second Italo–Sanusi War and natural increase, it can be assumed that at the outbreak of the Second World War nearly one-tenth as many Italians as native Libyans lived in these two provinces.

Remoulding the Libyan Muslim community involved the destruction of the tribal structure, combating the Sanusiyya, and the establishment of Italian schools for the Libyans. Although the Cyrenaican tribesmen taken to Sirta in 1930 were permitted to return to their regions in 1932, they lived under very close surveillance and could not move from their camps without an official permit. As most of the lands of the Cyrenaican plateau were taken over for the purposes of colonization, only its northern and southern fringes were left for the tribes to graze their herds there. The *shaikhs* of the tribes were chosen by the administration, and military officers deprived them of their ability to interpose between their people and the higher authorities by governing the tribes directly. The *shaikhs* of the Sanusiyya were sent into exile after 1932, and the Sanusi *zawiyas* were either destroyed or converted into military posts. But the Italians were also careful to uphold the general Islamic customs and institutions. No attempt at converting Muslims to Christianity was allowed, the personal status of Muslims remained governed by the Muslim law, and mosques and shrines were built or repaired. The pilgrimage to Mecca was facilitated through arrangements made by the authorities, and in 1937 Governor Balbo prohibited the sale of alcoholic drinks during Ramadan, the month of Muslim fasting. Special schools were built for the Muslim population in which the curriculum was Italian, but Islamic religious instruction was also given in Arabic.

Libya was the only country in the Maghrib where the circumstances of the Second World War were of decisive political importance. The war came before Italy had time to reshape the character of the Libyan society in the substantial way that would make the reversal of Italian rule impracticable. Her defeat in the war also internationalized the Libyan question, and rendered the restoration of Italy's rule in Libya dependent on the arrangements to be made by the victorious powers for the disposal of the Italian colonies. The occupation of Cyrenaica and Tripolitania by the British and Fazzan by the French, when neither of these European countries had important economic interests in Libya, meant that the demand for independence would not be strongly opposed by the controlling powers. This occupation also meant that Italy's claims to Libya had to be balanced against those of France and Britain. The restoration of Italian rule in Libya had, therefore, to depend on the acceptance by the international community of a package-deal satisfactory to all three European powers. Thus when the United Nations General Assembly in 1949 refused Italy's demand for Tripolitania, it had also to reject Britain's and France's claims on Cyrenaica and Fazzan respectively.

Of decisive importance to Libya's independence was the fact that the Libyan refugees who had lived in other Arab countries since the beginning of the Second Italo-Sanusi War had not had the time to settle and establish roots in the host countries. In addition to the refugees of the 1911–23 period, some 20,000 people left Cyrenaica between 1923 and 1932. A few were persuaded by the Italian consular officials to return, but the Libyan community abroad, especially in Egypt, remained large. These refugees, Tripolitanians and Cyrenaicans alike, saw in the outbreak of the war a political opportunity which should be exploited. In October 1939 their leaders in Cairo decided that Sayyid Idris should explore means of action with the help of a committee representing both communities. The first problem encountered was to decide with what side in the war the leaders were to align themselves. Whereas Sayyid Idris held fast to his ties with the British, the Tripolitanians, like many other Arabs at the time, believed in the victory of the Axis powers. Sayyid Idris forced the issue by agreeing in June 1940 to the organization of a Sanusi force to fight under British command in Cyrenaica. Henceforth the rift between Cyrenaicans and Tripolitanians started to widen. Ahmad al-Suwaihili, Tahir al-Mrayyid, and other Tripolitanian leaders in Egypt set up the Tripolitanian Committee to safeguard their interests. In August they offered the British authorities their help in the recruitment of a Tripolitanian force. But as they made their cooperation conditional on a commitment by Britain that Tripolitania would be granted independence after the war, their offer was ignored. The Sayyid, for his part, was content with informal assurances given by the British officials in Egypt about Cyrenaica's independence under his leadership. And throughout the war the British government would not go beyond a statement made by Sir Anthony Eden in the House of Commons on 8 January 1942 that "at the end of the war the Sanusis in Cyrenaica will in no circumstances again fall under Italian domination".

Between the time General Graziani led the Italian army in Libya into Egypt in September 1940 and the destruction of the German army in Africa (Afrikakorps) commanded by Rommel at 'Alamain in Egypt on 23 October 1942, Cyrenaica witnessed some of the important battles of the war. After October 1942 the British forces under Montgomery encountered little resistance as they pursued the retreating Axis forces, with the result that by February 1943 the British had taken complete control of both Cyrenaica and Tripolitania. Two separate military administrations were set up in the two provinces. The British occupation authorities emphasized the need for the preservation of law and order, the restoration of disrupted facilities, and the avoidance of all discussion of the country's political future until the end of the war. The Free French forces occupied Fazzan and Ghadamis in the course of 1942 and set up in them a military administration similar to that of the southern Algerian regions. In the administration of Fazzan the French relied on the cooperation of the Awlad Saif al-Nasr family, and proceeded to create a tribal structure of government which functioned independently of the other two Libyan provinces. Consequently as a result of the different military administrations that appeared during the war the local particularisms were enforced, and in Cyrenaica and Fazzan traditional patriarchal leaderships re-established themselves.

Although during the war the military administrations banned political activity, some measure of political association was tolerated. Sayyid Idris continued to live in Egypt. He made several visits to Cyrenaica after 1944 but refused until 1947 to reside there, explaining this refusal by the need to have his position clearly defined before resuming his functions as political leader. As almost all the Italians had left Cyrenaica before 1943, going either to Italy or Tripolitania, the political life in Cyrenaica was polarized between the traditional patriarchal leadership and the younger generation in the towns whose political outlook was formed by the Arab nationalist influences of Egypt. There was a general unanimity in

Cyrenaica over the goals of independence and the recognition of Sayyid Idris' leadership. However, from 1943 a group calling itself the 'Umar al-Mukhtar society, at first recognized by the administration as a sports society, interested itself in wider political questions such as relations with the Arab world and unity with Tripolitania. From 1945 older leaders, such as 'Umar Mansur al-Kikhia, agitated for the proclamation of Sayyid Idris without further delay as the amir of Cyrenaica. This demand was espoused in 1946 by the National Front (al-Jabha al-Wataniyya) which was dominated by Cyrenaica's veteran leaders and tribal chiefs. Henceforth, the main political issue dividing this organization from the 'Umar al-Mukhtar society was unity with Tripolitania. The Jabha leaders thought primarily in terms of Cyrenaica's independence through British help. They were prepared to envisage a future unity with Tripolitania, but wanted this question separated from that of Cyrenaica's independence which to them had to come first in time and importance. The leaders of the Jabha feared that by linking the question of Cyrenaica's independence with that of unity, they would be dominated politically by the more numerous and sophisticated Tripolitanians before they had time to consolidate their positions. The more idealistic 'Umar al-Mukhtar group had no such fears, and believed that the Cyrenaicans should use the promises made by the British to Sayyid Idris as a lever, from the results of which both Tripolitania and Cyrenaica would benefit. The Sayyid was persuaded to reside in Cyrenaica in 1947 after a British Working Party which visited Libya in 1946 recommended that Cyrenaica should gradually become independent under his authority, and that the unification of Cyrenaica and Tripolitania be carried out in stages. After his return Sayyid Idris ordered the two Cyrenaican political organizations to unite in a National Congress. This amounted, in effect, to placing the 'Umar al-Mukhtar group under the leadership of the Jabha and thereby stifling their wider nationalist aspirations. In spite of the Sayyid's injunction, the two groups remained separate and in the first elections for the Cyrenaican parliament held in April 1950 the 'Umar al-Mukhtar society contested the elections as an independent party. The allocation of seats to constituencies which preceded the elections is believed to have been weighted against the urban communities where the 'Umar al-Mukhtar group had most of their supporters. Consequently it is probable that the ten seats out of sixty which they won do not reflect their real strength. In parliament the gulf separating these idealistic young nationalists from the National Congress group became more pronounced. The 'Umar al-Mukhtar parliamentary group led their attack on the Saqizli government by forcing a discussion of the government's project of entering into a commercial agreement with Israel. The government was defeated, but instead of resigning the parliament was prorogued in 1951.

In Tripolitania Arab nationalist consciousness was more widely spread, but the nationalist circles were hampered from pressing on for their political goals by the fear that if they offended the Sanusis and the British too much they might again be placed under Italian rule. The British government had made no commitments to them, and the Italian community in Tripolitania was still large and politically active. The Italian government led by Signor Bonomi, which had been formed upon Mussolini's fall in 1943, was trying to salvage some of Italy's colonies by stressing that it was the Fascists who had brought Italy into the war, and their removal from power made Italy friendly to the Allies. The Italian government accepted the British pledge that the Sanusis would not be placed under Italian rule and renounced any interest in Cyrenaica, but they demanded to be given back Tripolitania. Britain, France, the U.S.A., and the Latin American countries supported Italy's claim to Tripolitania. In 1949 the British foreign secretary Bevin and the Italian foreign affairs minister Sforza proposed to the United Nations a plan to establish a United Nations trusteeship over the Libyan provinces with Britain holding the trusteeship over Cyrenaica, Italy over Tripolitania, and France over Fazzan. The fear of the restoration of Italian control made some of the more realistic of Tripolitania's political leaders accept Sayyid Idris' authority. This attitude was dictated by the desire of these leaders to benefit from the British guarantees to him and make it difficult for the powers to justify the continuation of foreign control by the difficulty of creating a unified viable state out of the three disparate Libyan provinces.

About ten different nationalist groups operated in Tripolitania after 1945. They were all agreed over the demands for immediate independence and the unity of the three Libyan provinces. Otherwise they differed on a number of vital issues. Whereas the United National Front (al-Jabha al-Wataniyya al-Muttahida) led by Salim al-Muntasir was in favour of accepting Sanusi authority at least for reasons of expediency, others wanted a united Libya without the Sayyid's leadership or preferred unity under the Egyptian crown. These differences made the Cyrenaicans even more wary of immediate unity with Tripolitania. In March 1947 the Libyan Liberation Committee was formed in Cairo by the veteran Tripolitanian leader Bashir al-Sa'dawi. The committee started by standing in favour of unity under Sanusi authority, and al-Sa'dawi was able to rely on his advocacy of offering the Tripolitanian amirate in the 1920s to Sayyid Idris to enable him to bring the Tripolitanians and Cyrenaicans together. However, he was forced by the attitude of other Tripolitanians and the circumstances of having to operate from Egypt to put more emphasis on unity than on Sanusi leadership, an attitude which was resented by Cyrenaicans. But the announcement of the Bevin-Sforza plan in 1949 forced the Tripolitanians to tone down their hostility to the Sayyid, and made their relations with the Cyrenaicans more congenial.

At the United Nations the defeat of the Bevin-Sforza plan on 17 May 1949 by a vote in the General Assembly meant that this body had no choice but to recognize the independence of a united Libya. A resolution providing for Libya's independence was adopted on 21 November. In order to influence the shape that the united Libya was to take, Britain recognized Cyrenaica's independence in June 1949, i.e. immediately after the Bevin-Sforza plan was defeated. The French started, for the same purpose, to set up a separate administration in Fazzan upon the adoption of the resolution providing for Libya's independence. In February 1950 elections were held in Fazzan, and a representative assembly of fifty-eight members was formed. The assembly then chose Ahmad Saif al-Nasr, the French ally, as chief of the province. Some sort of a protectorate arrangement came into being, with Ahmad Saif al-Nasr holding the titular headship, and a French resident exercising the executive powers in his name.

The United Nations General Assembly resolution of 21 November 1949 set the deadline of 1 January 1952 for the transfer of authority in Libya from the foreign military administrations to the local government. It also provided for the appointment of a United Nations Commissioner for the purpose of helping the Libyans frame their constitution and set up a national government, and the appointment of a council of interested parties to advise him. The council had ten members, one representing each of the three Libyan provinces, one the minorities (i.e. Jews) in the whole of Libya, and one representative of each of the following countries: Britain, Egypt, France, Italy, Pakistan, and U.S.A. The commissioner, Adrian Pelt, was Dutch. The central problem in the framing of the Libyan constitution was whether the state was to be a unitary or a federal one. The Tripolitanian leaders favoured a unitary government and received the support of the Egyptian and Pakistani representatives on the advisory council. Egypt had advocated since 1945 the unity of Libya and Egypt under the Egyptian crown; failing that, she demanded a trusteeship by Egypt or by the Arab League. A unitary government would have given the Tripolitanians predominance in the united Libya and would have ensured close ties between it and the countries of the Arab League. However, the local administrations already set up by the British and the French in Cyrenaica and Fazzan stood in the way. The method of choosing the National Assembly which drafted the constitution also favoured the federalists who wanted the preservation of local particularisms. Its sixty members were divided equally between the three provinces, notwithstanding the fact that the population of Tripolitania equalled that of the two other provinces combined. Furthermore, instead of having these members elected, they were appointed by the local administrations for Cyrenaica and Fazzan and by the Mufti of Tripoli for Tripolitania. When on 16 November 1950 the first annual report of the United Nations Commissioner in Libya was debated in the General Assembly, the Egyptian representative attacked the way by which the members of the National Assembly were chosen and demanded their replacement by an elected body. The Arab League took the same stand, and its council decided on 17 March 1951 not to recognize the regime that would emerge from the work of the National Assembly.

The united Libya that became independent at the end of 1951 was a federal monarchical state. Sayyid Idris was recognized king of Libya on 2 December 1950 by a resolution of the National Assembly, and at a later date both Tripoli and Banghazi were recognized as national capitals. In the period after 1945 when the Libyan leaders searched for a solution to their national problem, patriarchal conservative leadership fought for its position against a modern nationalist concept. The solution that was adopted was not a compromise, as Adrian Pelt put it to the General Assembly debate on 16 November 1950, but the victory of the patriarchal leadership. However, because of the popular nationalist forces within, the regime that emerged in 1951 could not insulate itself against the influence of the other Arab countries, particularly that of Egypt. Its overthrow by the military coup of 1969 represents the turning of the tables on the forces which international circumstances had favoured in 1951.

Bibliography

Works in European languages

Abbas, Ferhat. *La nuit coloniale*. Paris, 1962.

Africanus, Leo. *Description de l'Afrique*. Translated from the Italian by A. Épaulard. Paris, 1956. 2 vols.

Ageron, Charles-Robert. *Histoire de l'Algérie contemporaine*. Paris, 1966.

Albertini, Eugène. *L'Afrique romaine*. Algiers, 1949.

Albertini, E., G. Marçais and G. Yver. *L'Afrique du Nord française dans l'histoire*. Lyons, 1937.

Anderson, E. N. *The first Moroccan crisis, 1904–1906*. Hamden, Connecticut, 1966.

Ashford, D. E. *Political change in Morocco*. Princeton, 1961.

Askew, William C. *Europe and Italy's acquisition of Libya, 1911–1912*. Durham, U.S.A., 1942.

Ayache, Albert. *Le Maroc, bilan d'une colonisation*. Paris, 1956.

Barbour, Nevill. *Morocco*. London, 1965.

(ed.) *A survey of North West Africa*. London, 1959.

Basset, Henri and Henri Terrasse. *Sanctuaries et forteresses Almohades*. Paris, 1932.

Behr, Edward. *The Algerian problem*. London, 1961.

Bel, Alfred. *Les Benou Ghânya, derniers représentants de l'empire Almoravide et leur lutte contre l'empire Almohade*. Paris, 1903.

Berque, Jacques. *French North Africa, the Maghrib between two world wars*. Translated by Jean Stewart. London, 1967.

Structure sociale du Haut-Atlas. Paris, 1955.

Beylie, Général L. de. *La Kalla des Beni-Hammad, une capitale Berbère de l'Afrique du Nord au XIᵉ siècle*. Paris, 1909.

Boahen, A. Adu. *Britain, the Sahara, and the Western Sudan*. Oxford, 1964.

Boardman, John. *The Greeks overseas*. Penguin, 1964.

Bourdieu, Pierre. *The Algerians*. Translated by Alan Ross. Boston, 1962.

Bourrilly, Joseph. *Élément d'ethnographie marocaine*. Paris, 1932.

Brignon, Jean *et al. Histoire du Maroc*. Paris, 1967.

Brown, P. "Christianity and local culture in late Roman Africa", *Journal of Roman Studies*, Vol. LVIII, 1968, parts 1 and 2, p. 85.

Caillé, Jacques. *Une ambassade autrichienne au Maroc en 1805*. Paris, 1957.

Cambon, Henri. *Histoire de la régence de Tunis*. Paris, 1948.

Carcopino, Jérôme. *Le Maroc antique*. Paris, 1943.

Catroux, General. *Lyautey le Marocain*. Paris, 1952.

Cerych, Ladislav. *Européens et Marocains, 1930–1956: sociologie d'une décolonisation.* Bruges, 1964.

Charles-Picard, Gilbert. *Carthage.* Translated by Kochan. London, 1964.

La civilisation de l'Afrique romaine. Paris, 1959.

and Colette. *La vie quotidienne à Carthage au temps d'Hannibal.* Paris, 1958.

Clark, Michael K. *Algeria in turmoil.* London, 1960.

Cour, Auguste. *L'établissement des dynasties des chérifs au Maroc et leur rivalité avec les Turcs de la Régence d'Alger, 1509–1830.* Paris, 1904.

Courtois, Christian. *Les Vandales et l'Afrique.* Paris, 1955.

Despois, Jean. *L'Afrique du Nord.* Paris, 1958.

La colonisation italienne en Libye. Paris, 1935.

Diehl, Charles. *L'Afrique byzantine, histoire de la domination byzantine en Afrique (533–709).* Paris, 1896. 2 vols.

Doutté, E. and E. E. Gautier. *Enquête sur la dispersion de la langue Berbère en Algérie.* Algiers, 1913.

Drague, Georges. *Esquisse d'histoire réligieuse du Maroc.* Paris, 1951.

Dufourcq, Charles Emmanuel. *L'Espagne Catalane et le Maghrib aux XIIIᵉ et XIVᵉ siècles.* Paris, 1966.

Dunbabin, T. J. *The western Greeks.* Oxford, 1948.

Evans-Pritchard, E. E. *The Sanusi of Cyrenaica.* Oxford, 1954.

Féraud, L. C. *Annales Tripolitaines.* Tunis, 1927.

Fisher, Godfrey. *Barbary Legend.* Oxford, 1957.

Fontaine, Pierre. *Abd-el-Krim, origine de la rébellion nord-africaine.* Paris, 1958.

Frend, W. H. C. *The Donatist Church, a movement of protest in Roman North Africa.* Oxford, 1952.

Ganiage, Jean. *Les origines du protectorat français en Tunisie, 1861–1881.* Paris, 1959.

Gautier, E. F. *L'Islamisation de l'Afrique du Nord: les siècles obscurs du Maghreb.* Paris, 1927.

Goldziher, I. "Muhammad Ibn Toumert et la théologie de l'Islam dans le Maghreb au XIᵉ siècle": the introduction to Luciani (ed.), *Le livre de Mohammed Ibn Toumert.* Algiers, 1903.

Gordon, David C. *The passing of French Algeria.* London, 1966.

Gouroud, General. *Au Maroc 1911–1914, souvenirs d'un Africain,* Paris, 1949.

Guen, Moncef. *La Tunisie indépendante face à son économie.* Tunis, 1961.

Halstead, John P. *Rebirth of a nation: the origins and rise of Moroccan nationalism, 1912–1944.* Cambridge, Mass., 1967.

Harden, Donald. *The Phoenicians.* London, 1962.

Harris, W. B. *Journey to Tafilet.* London, 1895.

Hau checorne, François. *Chrétiens et Musulmans au Maghrib.* Paris, 1963

Haynes, D. E. L. *Ancient Tripolitania*. Tripoli, 1953.

Hourani, Albert. *Arabic thought in the liberal age*. London, 1962.

Hunwick, J. O. "Ahmad Baba and the Moroccan invasion of the Sudan", *Journal of the Historical Society of Nigeria*, vol. II, no. 3, December 1962, pp. 311–28.

Julien, Charles-André. *L'Afrique du Nord en marche*. Paris, 1952.
Histoire de l'Afrique du Nord. Paris, 1956. 2 vols.
Histoire de l'Algérie contemporaine. Paris, 1964.

Khadduri, Majid. *Modern Libya*. Baltimore, 1963.

Lacheraf, Mostefa. *L'Algérie: nation et société*. Paris, 1965.

Le Tourneau, Roger. *Évolution politique de l'Afrique du Nord musulmane, 1920–1961*. Paris, 1962.
Fez in the age of the Marinides. Translated by B. A. Clement. Norman, Okla., 1961.

Ling, Dwight L. *Tunisia from protectorate to republic*. Indiana, 1967.

Mahon, Lord. *The life of Belisarius*. London, 1848.

Marçais, Georges. *La Berbérie musulmane et l'Orient au Moyen Age*. Paris, 1946.

Martel, André. *Les confins Saharo-Tripolitains de la Tunisie, 1881–1911*, Paris, 1965. 2 vols.

Maxwell, Gavin. *The Lords of the Atlas*. London, 1966.

McBurney, C. B. M. *The Stone Age of Northern Africa*. Pelican, 1960.

Medina, Gabriel. "Les Karamanlis de la Tripolitaine, et l'occupation temporaire par Ali Boulgour", *Revue Tunisienne*, vol. XIV, 1907.

Mellor, F. H. *Morocco awakes*. London, 1939.

Mercier, Ernest. *Histoire de l'Afrique Septentrionale (Berbérie) depuis les temps les plus reculés jusqu'à la conquête française (1830)*. Paris, 1888. 2 vols.

Micaud, Charles A. with L. C. Brown and C. H. Moore. *Tunisia, the politics of modernisation*. London, 1964.

Miège, Jean-Louis. *Le Maroc et l'Europe (1830–1894)*. Paris, 1961.

Mikesell, M. W. *Northern Morocco, a cultural geography*. Berkeley, 1961.

Montagne, Robert. *Les Berbères et le Makhzen dans le sud du Maroc*. Paris, 1930.

Moore, Clement H. *Tunisia since independence: the dynamics of one-party government*. Berkeley, 1965.

Mountjoy, A. B. and C. Embleton. *Africa, a geographical study*. London, 1965.

O'Balance, Edgar. *The Algerian insurrection, 1954–1962*. London, 1967.

Oppermann, Thomas. *Le problème algérien*. Paris, 1961.

Ricard, Robert. *Études sur l'histoire des Portugais au Maroc*. Coimbra, 1955.

Roy, B. "Documents sur l'expédition de Tripoli", *Revue Tunisienne*, vol. XII, 1906.

Ruff, Paul. *La domination espagnole à Oran sous le gouvernement du Comte d'Alcaudete, 1534–1558*. Paris, 1900.

Serres, Jean. *La politique turque en Afrique du Nord sous la monarchie du juillet*. Paris, 1925.

Slousch, N. "La Tripolitaine sous la domination des Karamanlis", *Revue du Monde Musulman*, vol. VI, 1908.

Les sources inédites de l'histoire du Maroc. Particularly vol. I, Paris, 1934, edited by Pierre de Cenival and vol. III, Paris, 1948, edited by Robert Ricard.

Stewart, Charles E. *The economy of Morocco, 1912–1962*. Cambridge, Mass., 1964.

Stuart, Graham H. *The international city of Tangier*. Stanford, 1955, second edition.

Terrasse, Henri. *Histoire du Maroc*. Paris, 1949. 2 vols.

Tully, Richard, *Narrative of a ten years' residence at Tripoli in Africa*. London, 1816.

Vaughan, Dorothy M. *Europe and the Turks, a pattern of alliances 1350–1700*. Liverpool, 1954.

Villard, H. S. *Libya, the new Arab kingdom of North Africa*. Ithaca, N.Y., 1956.

Warmington, B. H. *Carthage*. New York, 1960.

The North African provinces from Diocletian to the Vandal conquest. Cambridge, 1954.

Willan, T. S. *Studies in Elizabethan foreign trade*. Manchester, 1959.

Wulsin, F. R. *The prehistoric archaeology of north-west Africa*. Cambridge, Mass., 1941.

Works in Arabic

'Abbas,' Ihsan. *Tarikh Libya mundhu 'l-Fath al-'Arabi hatta matla' al-qarn tasi' al-hijri*. Beirut, 1967.

al-'Ayyashi, 'Abdulla b. Muhammad b. Abi Bakr. *Rihlat al-Shaikh al-'Ayyashi*. Fez, n.d. 2 vols.

Bairam, Muhammad. *Safwat al-'i'tibar bi mustawda' al-amsar wa al-aqtar*. Cairo, A.H. 1302, Vols. I and II.

Ba'iyyu, Mustafa. *Al-Mujmal fi tarikh Lubya*. Alexandria, 1947.

al-Bakri, 'Abdulla b. 'Abdul-'Aziz. *Kitab al-Mughrib fi dhikr bilad Ifriqya wa 'l-Maghrib*. Paris, 1965.

al-Baruni, 'Umar. *Al-Isban wa fursan al-Qiddis Yuhanna fi Tarablus*. Tripoli, 1952.

al-Fasi, 'Allal. *'Aqida wa jihad*. Rabat, n.d.

Al-Harakat al-Istiqlaliyya fi 'l-Maghrib al-'Arabi. Cairo, 1948.

Ghirrit, Muhammad. *Fawasil al-juman fi anba' wuzara' wa Kuttab al-zaman*. Fez, A.H. 1346.

Hasan, Hasan Ibrahim. *Tarikh al-dawla al-Fatimiyya*. Cairo, 1958.

Hijji, Muhammad. *Al-Zawiya al-Dala'iyya*. Rabat, 1964.

Ibn Abi al-Diaf, Ahmad. *Ithaf ahl al-zaman bi akhbar muluk Tunis wa 'Ahd al-Aman*. Tunis, 1963-6. 8 vols.

Ibn Abi Dinar. *Al-Mu'nis fi akhbar ifriqya wa Tunis*. Tunis, A.H. 1350.

Ibn al-Khatib, Lisan al-Din. *Kitab 'A'mal al-'A'lam*, part III published under the title *Tarikh al-Maghrib al-'Arabi fi 'l-'asr al-wasit*. Casablanca, 1964.

Ibn al-Qattan. *Nazm al-juman*. Rabat, n.d.

Ibn Ghalbun, Muhammad b. Khalil. *Tarikh Tarablus al-Gharb*. Cairo, A.H. 1349.

Ibn 'Idhara. *Al-Bayan al-Mughrib fi ikhtisar akhbar muluk al-Andalus wa 'l-Maghrib*. Tatuan, 1963.

Ibn Khaldun, 'Abdul-Rahman. *Kitab al-'ibar wa diwan al-mubtada' wa 'l-khabar fi ayyam al-'Arab wa 'l-'Ajam wa'l-Barbar*. Beirut, 1956-60, 7 vols.

Ibn Khuja. *Al-Dhail li basha'ir 'ahl al-'iman fi futuhat 'al 'Uthman*. Tunis, 1908.

Ibn Mariam. *Al-Bustan fi dhikr al-awliya' wa 'l-'ulama' bi Talamsan*. Algiers, 1908.

al-Idrisi. *Sifat al-Maghrib wa 'ard al-Sudan wa Misr wa al-Andalus*. Amsterdam, 1969.

Mahmud, Hasan Sulaiman. *Libya baina al-madi wa 'l-hadir*. Cairo, 1962.

al-Maqri, Ahmad. *Rawdat al-'as al-'atirat al-anfas fi dhikr man laqiytahu min' a'lam al-hadratain Marrakish wa Fas*. Rabat, 1964.

al-Maqrizi, Taqiyyudin. *Itti'az al-hunafa' bi akhbar al-'a'imma al-Fatimiyyin al-hunafa'*. Cairo, 1948.

al-Marrakishi, 'Abdul-Wahid. *Al-Mu'jib fi talkhis akhbar al-Maghrib*. Cairo, 1949.

Mu'nis, Husain. *Fath al-'Arab li 'l-Maghrib*. Cairo, 1947.

al-Na'ib, Ahmad Husain. *Al-Manhal al-'adhb fi tarikh Tarablus al-Gharb*. Istanbul, A.H. 1317.

al-Naifar, Muhammad. *'Unwan al-'arib 'amma nasha'a bi 'l-Mamlaka al-Tunisiyya min 'alim adib*. Tunis, A.H. 1351. 2 vols.

al-Nasiri, Ahmad b. Khalid. *Kitab al-istiqsa' li akhbar duwal al-Maghrib al-'aqsa*. Casablanca, 1954-6. 9 vols.

al-Sanusi, Muhammad. *Musamarat al-zarif bi husn al-ta'rif*. Tunis, A.H. 1298.

Shukri, Muhammad Fu'ad. *Al-Sanusiyya din wa dawla*. Cairo, 1948.

al-Tijani, Abdulla b. Muhammad. *Rihlat al-Tijani*. Tunis, 1958.

al-Yafrani, Muhammad al-Saghir. *Nuzhat al-hadi bi akhbar muluk al-qarn al-hadi*. Paris, 1888.

al-Zayani, Abu 'l-Qasim. *Al-Khabar 'an awwal dawlat min duwal al-ashraf al-'Alawiyyin*. Paris, 1886, being a part of *al-Turjuman al-Mu-'rib 'an duwal al-mashriq wa 'l-maghrib*.

Index